Handbook The Global History of Work

Handbook The Global History of Work

Edited by
Karin Hofmeester and Marcel van der Linden

DE GRUYTER
OLDENBOURG

ISBN 978-3-11-064662-7
e-ISBN (PDF) 978-3-11-042458-4
e-ISBN (EPUB) 978-3-11-042470-6

Library of Congress Cataloging-in-Publication Data
A CIP catalog record for this book has been applied for at the Library of Congress.

Bibliographic information published by the Deutsche Nationalbibliothek
The Deutsche Nationalbibliothek lists this publication in the Deutsche Nationalbibliografie;
detailed bibliographic data are available on the Internet at http://dnb.dnb.de.

© 2019 Walter de Gruyter GmbH, Berlin/Boston
This volume is text- and page-identical with the hardback published in 2018.
Cover image: Reciprocal labour: Winnowing rice grains, China c. 1700. Source: Keng-tschi t'u, Ackerbau und Seidengewinnung in China; ein kaiserliches Lehr- und Mahnbuch. Transl. and ed. by Otto Franke (Hamburg, 1913), plate 49, ill. 1.20 Chinese woodblock edition, 1696 , © Walter de Gruyter GmbH.
Printing and binding: CPI books GmbH, Leck

♾ Printed on acid-free paper
Printed in Germany

www.degruyter.com

Contents

Karin Hofmeester and Marcel van der Linden
1. Introduction —— 1

2. Regions

Christine Moll-Murata
2.1. China —— 15

Rana P. Behal
2.2. South Asia —— 33

Bill Freund
2.3. Sub-saharan Africa —— 63

Rossana Barragán and David Mayer
2.4. Latin America and the Caribbean —— 83

Bryan D. Palmer
2.5. Canada and the United States —— 111

Susan Zimmermann
2.6. Eastern Europe —— 131

Andrea Komlosy
2.7. Western Europe —— 157

Touraj Atabaki
2.8. Iran (Persia) —— 181

Gavin D. Brockett and Özgür Balkılıç
2.9. The Ottoman Middle East and Modern Turkey —— 201

3. Types of Work

Eric Vanhaute
3.1. Agriculture —— 217

Ad Knotter
3.2. Mining —— 237

Prasannan Parthasarathi
3.3. Textile Industry —— 259

Peter Cole and Jennifer Hart
3.4. Trade, Transport, and Services —— 277

Therese Garstenauer
3.5. Administrative Staff —— 297

4. Labour Relations

Karin Hofmeester
4.1. Introductory Remarks —— 317

Eileen Boris
4.2. Subsistence and Household Labour —— 329

Christian G. De Vito
4.3. Convict Labour —— 345

Rosemarijn Hoefte
4.4. Indentured Labour —— 363

Patrick Manning
4.5. Slave Labour —— 377

Jan Lucassen
4.6. Wage Labour —— 395

Karin Hofmeester
5. Attitudes To Work —— 411

Marlou Schrover
6. Labour Migration —— 433

Marcel van der Linden
7. Work Incentives and Forms of Supervision —— 469

8. Organization and Resistance

Marcel van der Linden
8.1. Mutualism —— 491

Matthias van Rossum
8.2. Desertion —— 505

Sjaak van der Velden
8.3. Strikes, Lockouts, and Informal Resistance —— 521

Marcel van der Linden
8.4. Trade Unions —— 551

Acknowledgments —— 571

Notes on Contributors —— 573

Subject Index —— 579
Index of Names —— 597

Karin Hofmeester and Marcel van der Linden
1. Introduction

The realization that we all live in the same world and that distant regions are interconnected has become increasingly common in recent times. Communication satellites, the Internet, and mobile phones are daily reminders of this. But our supermarkets, too, are proof: coffee from Central America, Vietnam, Indonesia, East Africa; wine from Chile, California, Australia, South Africa, and Italy. But what we often fail to realize is that all these products are based on labour. Somewhere in the world, miners are extracting from the earth the copper, iridium, and coltan that are required to manufacture our mobile phones. Farmers and farm labourers are cultivating and producing the many types of food and drink we consume. Indeed, numerous consumer products involve the combination of disparate work processes. A simple pair of jeans, for example, is the result of a global division of labour: the soft cotton for the pockets might come from Benin, the harder cotton for the jeans themselves from Pakistan, zinc for the zipper from Australia, the blue dye from a German chemical plant, with the whole garment being finally assembled in a low-wage country – perhaps Tunisia.

The global economy is increasingly reliant on collaboration among workers who do not know each other and who are not even aware of each other's existence. Very occasionally we are given a glimpse of that interconnectedness, as in 2013 when the collapse of Rana Plaza in Bangladesh gave us a chilling reminder that much clothing is produced in appalling conditions by women and children – and men of course – in poor countries. Generally, however, we do not dwell on such global connections, but more and more historians nowadays want to understand them. What is the day-to-day reality for workers in various parts of the world, and how was it in the past? Under what conditions do they work today and how did they work in the past? What is their remuneration for their backbreaking labour? What did they receive in the past? How can we characterize past and present relationships between men, women, and children? Did workers ever protest? If so, how did they express their disaffection? These and many other questions comprise the field of the global history of work – a young discipline that we should like to introduce with this handbook.

Of course, a great deal of research has already been carried out into the history of work – the roots of labour history go back to the nineteenth century.[1] However, earlier studies usually had clear limitations using a very restricted definition of "work". For example, the cleaning and cooking carried out by housewives was generally not

---

[1] Jan Lucassen, "Writing Global Labour History c. 1800–1940: A Historiography of Concepts, Periods, and Geographical Scope", in: *idem* (ed.), *Global Labour History: A State of the Art* (Bern, 2006), pp. 39–89; Marcel van der Linden and Lex Heerma van Voss, "Introduction", in: Lex Heerma van Voss and Marcel van der Linden (eds), *Class and Other Identities: Gender, Religion and Ethnicity in the Writing of European Labour History* (New York and Oxford, 2002), pp. 1–39.

regarded as work, nor were "ignoble" activities such as prostitution. And even those studies that ventured beyond Europe tended to focus only on Europe's colonies or former settler colonies in the Americas, or perhaps Australia. There, too, was the same tendency to study only the "respectable" work of artisans and wage earners, as if the labour of the enslaved and other unfree labour did not count. But as George Orwell observed just before the Second World War: "All people who work with their hands are partly invisible, and the more important the work they do, the less visible they are. Still, a white skin is always very conspicuous. In northern Europe, when you see a labourer ploughing a field, you probably give him a second glance. In a hot country, anywhere south of Gibraltar or east of Suez, the chances are that you don't even see him. I have noticed this again and again."[2] Most historians and social scientists have been guilty of the same omission.

Only in recent decades has a slightly wider audience realized that the labour of housewives, domestic servants, slaves, and others is important and deserves attention, and that we should also look at the Global South. This growing awareness has multiple causes. One is the process of decolonization that began in the late 1940s. Often, African and Asian historians wanting to write the history of their own countries could not escape the realization that unfree labour had played a vital role in it. At the same time, they discovered that the "national" historiography that predominated in Europe and North America was impossible in former colonial territories since their history was inextricably linked with that of the colonial metropoles. A second key factor was the wave of feminism that spread across much of the world from the late 1960s and which demonstrated convincingly that housewives, too, worked, even if they received no pay in return. An extensive debate about the role of women ensued, and continued into the 1980s. A third factor has been the trend towards globalization, which has gained increasing momentum over the past thirty or forty years. Gradually and inevitably there emerged the realization that we live in one world, and that the vicissitudes of even the most varied individuals are interrelated. And all these insights have left their mark on the social and economic historiography of recent years.

Work and labour relations

Work is an essential element of any human society. But what is work? It can be difficult to see whether some particular activity as such constitutes "work". Let us suppose we observe a man leaving his house to chop wood. He might be collecting firewood in order to cook food. Or perhaps he wants to light a fire in his hearth. Or, it might be that something else is going on: perhaps he is angry about something

---

[2] "Marrakech" (1939), in: George Orwell, *Collected Essays* (London, 1968), pp. 24–30, at 27.

and is venting his frustration. Is he a boxer, say, getting fit for his next bout?[3] To make the correct interpretation of what we see, we must know not only the direct purpose of the act (here, the chopping of wood), but also the indirect purpose – *why* is the wood being chopped? A man venting his anger by going to chop wood is not working, but a man chopping firewood for the kitchen certainly is. Some indirect purposes result in work, but others do not.

A second difficulty is that work can take on myriad different forms, and it is not always easy to find a common denominator. There is heavy physical labour such as that performed by the rickshaw driver, miner, or navvy; there is the highly skilled work of the software engineer or nuclear physicist; there is the physically intimate work performed by nurses – and prostitutes. Then there is the stultifying work of the assembly line, or the symbolic work of the shaman or priest; there is paid work, and there is unpaid work. What all these activities have in common is that their purpose is to a great degree indirect: *the production of goods or services deemed useful by people, or at least by some people.* In that sense work is not play because a game has a purpose in itself; it is played for its own sake. On the other hand the purpose of work transcends the work itself. Its object is to produce goods or services that can be used by either the worker himself/herself or by someone else. Adam Smith put it like this: "Consumption is the sole end and object of all production."[4] Of course, not everyone will find all goods and services equally useful. Some find the manufacture of fur coats useful, others do not. Usefulness is therefore always subjective. But as soon as there are individuals who require a particular good or service, the production of that good or service will constitute work.

Work as a labour process comprises four elements: (i) the effort of workers in converting their physical and mental energies into productive activity; (ii) the means to do so (tools, machines, etc.); (iii) the objects they process (change, move); and (iv) the result of their efforts, the product. Coal miners, for example, drill, blast, and set props. To do so they need lamps, drills, dynamite, and pit props to enable them to mine the seams for the coal that is their product. However, in the service sector those four elements are not always clearly distinguishable. The product of the work of, say, a waitress or a janitor is largely what they do.

Ultimately, all human production of goods and services is based on just two resources: nature and human labour. The economist Alfred Marshall rightly noted that, "In a sense there are only two agents of production, nature and man. [...] If the character and powers of nature and of man be given, the growth of wealth and knowledge and organization follow from them as effect from cause."[5] All other so-called factors of production (capital, organization, etc.) are ultimately the product of inter-

---

[3] This example is taken from Heiner Ganßmann, "Ein Versuch über Arbeit", in: Frithjof Hager (ed.), *Geschichte denken. Ein Notizbuch für Leo Löwenthal* (Leipzig, 1992), pp. 254–293, at 259.
[4] Adam Smith, *The Wealth of Nations*, Books IV–V, edited by Andrew Skinner (Harmondsworth, 1999), p. 245.
[5] Alfred Marshall, *Principles of Economics*, 4th edn. (London, 1898), p. 214.

actions between human beings and their physical and biological environment. And humans, too, are, of course, physical and biological beings. All elements of the work process therefore comprise both a natural and a social aspect:

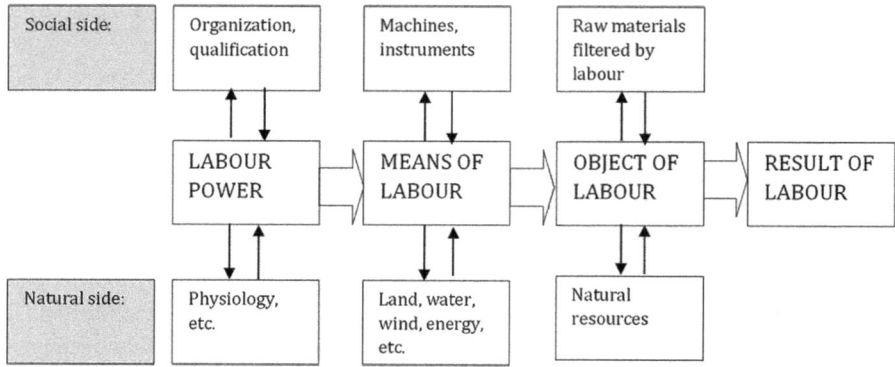

In this handbook, more attention is paid to the social aspect than to the natural aspect. Nonetheless, it is important to realize that work is both made possible and constrained by physiological, biological, and environmental factors.

In the past, all manner of unpaid activities were regarded as work. In Shakespeare's *Henry IV, Part 1* (c. 1597), the Prince of Wales says of the Earl of Northumberland: "he that kills me some six or seven dozen of Scots at a breakfast, washes his hands, and says to his wife, 'Fie upon this quiet life! I want work'".[6] The concept of "work" subsequently took on a narrower meaning.

> The specialization of *work* to paid employment is the result of capitalist productive relations. To be *in work* or *out of work* was to be in a definite relationship with some other who had control of the means of productive effort. *Work* then partly shifted from the productive effort itself to the predominant social relationship. It is only in this sense that a woman running a house and bringing up children can be said to be *not working*.[7]

The global history of work is therefore in effect a reversion to a broader interpretation of work, and looks at more than work done simply for payment.

The present handbook frequently refers to labour relations. Labour relations define for whom or with whom one works, and under what rules. Those rules, implicit or explicit, written or unwritten, determine the type of work, type and amount of remuneration, working hours, degrees of physical and psychological strain, and the degree of freedom and autonomy associated with the work.

---

6 Act II, Scene IV.
7 Raymond Williams, *Keywords. A Vocabulary of Culture and Society* (London, 1976), p. 282.

Global history

Work takes on thousands of different forms. Even the same type of work, for example, weaving cotton or loading a ship, might vary greatly from place to place and from time to time. Moreover, work is embedded in dozens of different labour relations, which in turn continuously change. Understanding the overwhelming range of variation and the historical logic underlying that change is a task far beyond the capacity of individual researchers. No single individual understands enough languages nor can read enough documents and secondary literature to be able to envisage everything of the subject. So teamwork is essential. There are many obstacles to developing a global approach, though some are simply practical. In Thailand, for instance, large quantities of archival material were destroyed when the capital, Ayutthaya, was razed to the ground by Burmese troops in 1767. Archives elsewhere might exist, but in poor condition because of atmospheric pollution, the destructive activities of insects, or adverse weather conditions.

More important, however, are probably the epistemological difficulties. The past twenty or thirty years have seen challenges to the two main weaknesses of traditional historiography, namely methodological nationalism and Eurocentrism.[8] *Methodological nationalism* – not to be confused with *political* nationalism – links society and state, and methodological nationalists are the victims of two important intellectual errors. First, they normalize the nation state. What we mean by that is that even though they recognize that nation states flourished only in the nineteenth and twentieth centuries they consider them to be the basic analytical unit of historical research. They then continue to interpret traditional history as the *prehistory* of the later nation state and consider cross-border or border-subverting processes as distractions from the "pure" model. So in fact we are dealing with a teleology. Secondly, they postulate a direct link between "societies" and "nation states". Societies are seen as co-extensive with national borders, in the sense that one may talk about a French, Japanese, or Nigerian society. It seems more logical, however, to proceed from the premise that all people who influence one another's social lives belong to the same society. "Society" then becomes a border-crossing entity in which, by reason of migration, commodity flows, wars, and so on, people in different regions are in contact with one another, although there do exist people who do not belong to the global society because their own society is isolated from it. In this vein the sociologist Michael Mann defined societies as "confederal, intersecting networks" of relatively dense and stable social interactions, "at the boundaries of which is a certain level of interaction cleavage between it and its environment".[9] Within such so-

---

[8] The following paragraphs are based on Marcel van der Linden, "Labour History: The Old, the New and the Global", *African Studies*, 66, 2–3 (2007), pp. 169–180.
[9] Michael Mann, *The Sources of Social Power* (Cambridge, 1986), vol. I, pp. 17, 13.

cieties individual nation states seek to incorporate the inhabitants of their own territories into their own particular systems.

Eurocentrism is the mental ordering of the world from the standpoint of the North Atlantic region, so that the "modern" period begins in Europe and North America and extends step by step to the rest of the world. The temporality of this "core region" therefore determines the periodization of developments in the rest of the world. Historians reconstructed the history of the working classes and workers' movements in France, Britain, and the United States as separate developments. Insofar as they paid any attention to the social classes and movements in Latin America, Africa, or Asia, those were all interpreted according to North Atlantic schemes. There are three variants of Eurocentrism which we should mention. The *first* is simply *neglect:* attention is paid to only one part of the world, and the authors assume that the history of "their piece of the world" may be written without considering the rest. That attitude is neatly expressed by the popular distinction between "the West" and "the Rest", mentioned by Samuel Huntington and others. The *second* variant is *prejudice:* the authors do consider global connections, but nevertheless believe that Greater Europe (including North America and Australasia) "shows the way". That variety of Eurocentrism is especially evident among modernization theorists. Robert Nisbet characterized their approach to development as follows:

> Mankind is likened to a vast procession, with all, or at least a very large number of peoples made into the members of the procession. [...] Naturally, Western Europe and its specific, historically acquired pattern of economic, political, moral, and religious values was regarded as being at the head, in the vanguard, of the procession. All other peoples, however rich in their own civilization, such as China and India, were regarded as, so to speak, "steps" in a procession that would some day bring them too into the fulfilment of development that was the sacred West.[10]

The *third* variant consists of *empirical beliefs*, and is the variant that is most difficult to recognize and combat. We are dealing there with academic viewpoints that have seemingly been confirmed time and again by research. Empirical Eurocentrists make assertions because they think that all of it is *fact*. They believe, for instance, that trade unions are always most effective if they concentrate on some form of collective bargaining. That, they think, has been proven repeatedly. Historians defending such a view would deny emphatically that they harbour any Eurocentric prejudices, and very few of them actually do hold such prejudices knowingly. Attacking the first two variants, neglect and prejudice, is relatively straightforward but the third variant presents a bigger obstacle. As the late Jim Blaut wrote: "Eurocentrism, [...] is a very complex thing. We can banish all the value meanings of the word, all the prejudices, and we still have Eurocentrism as a set of empirical beliefs."[11]

---

[10] Robert Nisbet, "Ethnocentrism and the Comparative Method", in: A.R. Desai (ed.), *Essays on Modernization of Underdeveloped Societies* (Bombay, 1971), vol. I, pp. 95–114, at 101.
[11] James Blaut, *The Colonizer's Model of the World* (New York, 1993), p. 9.

In looking for alternatives, a range of possibilities have been considered. Thus, for example, in France the concept of *histoire croisée* was invented. That amounted to a focusing on the reciprocal transfers between nations, civilizations, regions, and so on as well as emphasizing mutual influences and reception mechanisms.[12] In the English-speaking world the concept of *entangled history* has been introduced, which likewise looks at such interconnections. More frequently mentioned than those two terms is the idea of *transnational history*. However, that concept takes the nation state as the self-evident point of departure which needs to be transcended, and is also often used for an international comparative historiography that does not consider entanglements. Moreover, all three concepts are usually – but not always – applied to the historiography of contiguous regions, even if very-long-distance connections are involved. The concept of *world history* might offer a solution, except that much research published under its rubric (though certainly not all) is additive: at a certain point in time, X happened in Europe, Y in China, and Z in America. *Global history* overlaps significantly with world history but does not suffer from the same limitation, because the term refers to connections across the globe. But there is a disadvantage to that concept, too, because "global history" creates the impression that only "Big History" is included – the "great divergence" between China and Europe, for example, or the connection between world wars and hegemonies. Every term we choose therefore has its own drawbacks.

In this handbook we use the term "global history". However, we do not mean it to imply only large-scale history. It can include micro-history as well, for it is of course quite feasible to write a global history of a small village, a work site, or even a family. The important thing is to follow the tracks of what interests us, wherever they might lead, across political and geographical frontiers, timeframes, territories, and disciplinary boundaries. Migration patterns, mass media, world markets and corporations, religious hierarchies, climate changes, wars; all can be bridges to a wider world. Sometimes we will not need to travel far to discover the interconnections and explanations; but sometimes we will have to. Obviously, there have been groups of people who have lived in relative isolation from each other and who were connected to others at most through sporadic long-distance trade. Though global history is not a "history of everything", they, too, belong to the field of inquiry, inasmuch as the interactions and transfers that did *not* eventuate are also of interest. It is all about recognizing the big picture in small details and vice versa, to discover micro-realities in macro processes.[13] Global history is therefore in the first instance a question of mentality. Researchers should be bold in their inquiries, and dare to venture outside terrain that is familiar to them.

---

[12] Michael Werner and Bénédicte Zimmermann (eds), *De la comparaison à l'histoire croisée* (Paris, 2004).
[13] An interesting attempt to connect the micro and macro levels can be found in Timothy Brook's *Vermeer's Hat. The Seventeenth Century and the Dawn of the Global World* (London, 2008).

Global history of work

In principle there are no restrictions on the timeframe of the global history of work; work is after all as old as human society. Yet until now historical research has been largely restricted to the past four or five centuries, with an emphasis on the past one or two hundred years. That temporal limitation is reflected in many of the contributions to the present handbook, but it should not be considered a prerequisite.

In the historiography of work, workers, and their labour relations two approaches are of particular importance: comparison and connection. Comparison takes many forms. The simplest and most frequently used is contrasting comparison highlighting similarities and differences between two or more instances. Some believe that therein lies the most important role of comparison. The social scientist Hugh Stretton, for example, wrote that "[c]omparison is strongest as a choosing and provoking, not a proving device: a system for questioning, not for answering".[14] More difficult are the comparisons that attempt to explain similarities and differences, or even to make them the basis of comprehensive narratives.[15] In the field of the global history of work, many attempts have been made at global comparison, but the emphasis continues to be on contrasts, not explanations.

A useful tool that can be used to make global comparisons in the field of work and especially labour relations is the Global Collaboratory on the History of Labour Relations, 1500–2000, a project set up by the International Institute of Social History in Amsterdam.[16] Together with a large group of colleagues living and working in different parts of the world the project group is busy collecting data on labour relations across the world. A taxonomy of labour relations has been developed especially for the purpose, to cover all types of labour relations from slavery to free wage labour. Using the taxonomy an inventory has been drawn up of labour relations worldwide from 1500 to 2000. The inventory is designed primarily to identify shifts in labour relations, and secondly to explain the shifts. A detailed description of the taxonomy can be found in chapter 4.1 of this handbook.

The second approach focuses on connections. We have already noted that in various parts of the world work processes are often connected to each other, an obser-

---

[14] Hugh Stretton, *The Political Sciences. General Principles of Selection in Social Science and History* (London, 1969), p. 247.
[15] This is covered more extensively in Marcel van der Linden, *Transnational Labour History: Explorations* (Aldershot, 2003), ch. 11.
[16] This project would not have been possible without the financial support of the Gerda Henkel Stiftung in Düsseldorf. For further details, see https://collab.iisg.nl/web/LabourRelations/; Karin Hofmeester *et al.*, "The Global Collaboratory on the History of Labour Relations, 1500–2000: Background, Set-Up, Taxonomy, and Applications" (October 2015), available at http://hdl.handle.net/10622/4OGRAD. For the labour relations datasets, see https://datasets.socialhistory.org/dataverse/labourrelations.

vation dating back as far as Adam Smith.[17] The products of labour are the result of effort, means, and objects. But those means and objects are themselves generally the result of the efforts of others. So types of "product chain" exist, which take the form of tree-like sequences of production processes and exchanges by which a product for final consumption is produced. From this we may infer that even if the final consumer is blissfully unaware of it, *each commodity has its own individual history*; if we trace the histories of products they can tell us a great deal about *global interconnections*, or what are sometimes referred to as "teleconnections".[18]

However, there are also all kinds of other transcontinental connections, including cross-border political influence, as with the famous nineteenth-century British campaign for the abolition of the slave trade and later of slavery itself, which led to major changes in labour relations in Africa and South Asia and, somewhat later still, in South-east Asia too. Or the International Labour Organization, established in 1919, whose conventions changed global working conditions. Moreover, worker opposition is a transnational phenomenon. The 1956 Hungarian Uprising inspired major strikes in Shanghai the following year, and protests in France and Czechoslovakia in 1968 paralleled rebellions in Mexico, Argentina, and Senegal.

Up to now teleconnections have seldom been studied, and insofar as they have been considered the primary focus has been on the twentieth century. But teleconnections are considerably older, and they have already been the subject of a considerable amount of thought, especially by authors interested in the economy. That theoretical side, too, has been little investigated, although in some cases it foreshadowed subsequent developments. One example will serve as an illustration. In 1701 an anonymous pamphlet was published in London in which the author complained that ships built in the Netherlands were much cheaper than ships built in England. He therefore proposed the relocation of production to the Caribbean, to make use of local slave labour:

---

17 "The woollen coat, for example, which covers the day-labourer, as coarse and rough as it may appear, is the produce of the joint labour of a great multitude of workmen. The shepherd, the sorter of the wool, the wool-comber or carder, the dyer, the scribbler, the spinner, the weaver, the fuller, the dresser, with many others, must all join their different arts in order to complete even this homely production. How many merchants and carriers, besides, must have been employed in transporting the materials from some of those workmen to others who often live in a very distant part of the country! How much commerce and navigation in particular, how many ship-builders, sailors, sail-makers, rope-makers, must have been employed in order to bring together the different drugs made use of by the dyer, which often come from the remotest corners of the world! What a variety of labour, too, is necessary in order to produce the tools of the meanest of those workmen!" Adam Smith, *The Wealth of Nations, Books I–III*. Edited by Andrew Skinner (Harmondsworth, 1999), p. 116.
18 Studies that, at least partly, integrate labour in the context of product chains include Sidney Mintz, *Sweetness and Power. The Place of Sugar in Modern History* (New York, 1985), Ulbe Bosma, *The Sugar Plantation in India and Indonesia: Industrial Production, 1770–2010* (Cambridge, 2013), and Sven Beckert, *Empire of Cotton: A Global History* (New York, 2014).

> Materials for Building there are cheaper; that these may be wrought by cheaper Labour, the Work might be perform'd by Negroes. To single Parts of Ships, single Negroes might be assign'd, the Manufacture of Keels to one, to another Rudders, to another Masts; to several others, several other Parts of Ships. Of which, the variety wou'd still be less to puzle and confound the Artist's Skill, if he were not to vary from his Model, if the same Builders wou'd still confine themselves to the same Scantlings and Dimensions, never to diminish nor exceed their Patterns. [...] So that the same Negroes might be imploy'd in only single Parts of Ships of the same Scantlings and Dimensions, by which the Work of every one wou'd be render'd plain and easie. [...] The Wages of Negroes are not so great as of the *Dutch* Builders; the annual Service of a Negroe might be hir'd for half the Price that must be given to one of these.[19]

The relocation would have been accompanied by a division of labour, and thus deskilling. When, in the 1970s and 1980s, most shipbuilding, like a number of other industries, relocated from Europe and North America to lower-wage countries, the same principles were applied – though of course without recourse to slave labour. The global history of work is sometimes highly relevant to the present.

This volume

The past two decades have seen a vast amount of research carried out into the global history of work and the labour relations in which that work is embedded. The present handbook is intended as a survey of the findings of that research so far, and as inspiration for further research. We have been fortunate that some of the most renowned scholars in the field have been willing to share their expertise, and we have also been able to build on the excellent "state-of-the-art" work published by Jan Lucassen eleven years ago.[20] Drawing on this solid basis, we begin this handbook with an overview of regional developments, covering most of the world.

To transcend regional boundaries, the second group of articles looks at economic sectors and the various forms of labour characterizing them. A number of studies have been published looking at workers in various trades worldwide, including dockworkers, textile workers, soldiers, sex workers, and shipbuilders.[21] The chapters pre-

---

19 [Henry Martyn] *Considerations Upon the East-India Trade* (London, 1701), pp. 72–73. It was not until 1983 that the author's identity was proved. See Christine MacLeod, "Henry Martin and the Authorship of 'Considerations Upon the East India Trade'", *Historical Research*, 56, 134 (1983), pp. 222–229.
20 Lucassen, *Global Labour History*.
21 Sam Davies *et al.* (eds), *Dock Workers. International Explorations in Comparative Labour History, 1790–1970*. 2 vols (Aldershot, 2000); Lex Heerma van Voss, Els Hiemstra-Kuperus, and Elise van Nederveen Meerkerk (eds), *The Ashgate Companion to the History of Textile Workers, 1650–2000* (Farnham: Ashgate, 2010); Erik-Jan Zürcher (ed.), *Fighting for a Living. A Comparative Study of Military Labour 1500–2000* (Amsterdam, 2014); Magaly Rodríguez García, Elise van Nederveen Meerkerk, and Lex Heerma van Voss (eds), *Selling Sex in the City. Prostitution in World Cities, 1600 to the Present* (Leiden and Boston, 2017); Raquel Varela, Hugh Murphy, and Marcel van der Linden (eds), *Shipbuilding*

sented here on the various economic sectors aim to supplement that literature and to offer an even broader view, to make global comparisons possible. We hope they will inspire others to discover connections.

A third set of articles studies the various types of labour relations. How they might be inventoried, compared globally, and explained is described in chapter 4.1 on the Global Collaboratory on the History of Labour Relations. The various labour relations are then described using the taxonomy developed by the Collaboratory. How workers respond to political and socioeconomic changes, especially changes in work and labour relations, is explored in subsequent chapters which look at attitudes to work and workers, forms of migratory labour, work incentives, and managerial forms of supervision. Those chapters form the bridge to the final group of articles on the forms of organization and resistance employed by different types of workers. A list of "Suggested reading" is appended to each chapter, which we hope will help readers familiarize themselves quickly with the relevant literature.

Two final remarks. The authors of the contributions to this handbook are from various disciplines and intellectual cultures, reflected in the different ways in which they write about their subjects. We have not tried to standardize their diversity. On the contrary, we believe that pluriformity is an essential aspect of "global" projects, and that we can learn a great deal from it.

Because the global history of work is a new field of research, large parts of it have still been barely explored, if at all. We know much more about certain regions or themes than we do of other regions or themes. That, too, is reflected in this handbook, which remains afflicted with lacunae. But, as Francis Bacon acknowledged: "As the births of living creatures are at first ill-shapen, so are all innovations, which are the births of time."[22]

---

and Ship Repair Workers around the World: Case Studies 1950–2010 (Amsterdam: Amsterdam University Press, 2017).
22 Francis Bacon, "Of Innovations", *The Essays* (Harmondsworth, 1985), p. 132.

Suggested reading

Applebaum, Herbert (ed.). *Work in Market and Industrial Societies* (Albany, NY: State University of New York Press, 1984).
Applebaum, Herbert (ed.). *Work in Non-Market and Transitional Societies* (Albany, NY: State University of New York Press, 1984).
Davies, Sam *et al.* (eds). *Dock Workers. International Explorations in Comparative Labour History, 1790–1970*. 2 volumes (Abingdon: Routledge, 2000)
Eckert, Andreas (ed.). *Global Histories of Work* (Berlin: De Gruyter Oldenbourg, 2016).
Hiemstra-Kuperus, Els *et al.* (eds). *The Ashgate Companion to the History of Textile Workers, 1650–2000* (Farnham : Ashgate, 2010).
Lucassen, Jan (ed.). *Global Labour History. A State of the Art* (Bern: Peter Lang, 2006).
Ness, Immanuel. *Southern Insurgency. The Coming of the Global Working Class* (London: Pluto Press, 2016).
Pahl, R.E. (ed.). *On Work. Historical, Comparative and Theoretical Approaches* (Oxford: Blackwell, 1988).
Potts, Lydia. *The World Labour Market. A History of Migration* (London : Zed Books, 1990).
Rodriguez-García, Magaly *et al.* (eds). *Selling Sex in the City. Prostitution in World Cities, 1600 to the Present* (Leiden and Boston: Brill, 2017).
Salgado, Sebastião. *Workers: Archaeology of the Industrial Age* (London: Phaidon, 1993).
Schlager, Neil (ed.). *St. James Encyclopedia of Labor History Worldwide*. 2 volumes (Detroit, MI: St. James Press, 2004).
Silver, Beverly. *Forces of Labor. Workers' Movements and Globalization since 1870* (Cambridge: Cambridge University Press, 2003).
Thomas, Keith (ed.). *The Oxford Book of Work* (Oxford: Oxford University Press, 1999).
Van der Linden, Marcel. *Workers of the World. Essays toward a Global Labor History* (Leiden and Boston: Brill, 2008).
Varela, Raquel *et al.* (eds). *Shipbuilding and Ship Repair Workers around the World. Case Studies 1950–2010* (Amsterdam: Amsterdam University Press, 2017).
Wallman, Sandra (ed.). *Social Anthropology of Work* (London: Academic Press, 1979).
Zürcher, Erik-Jan (ed.). *Fighting for a Living. A Comparative Study of Military Labour 1500–2000* (Amsterdam: Amsterdam University Press, 2014).

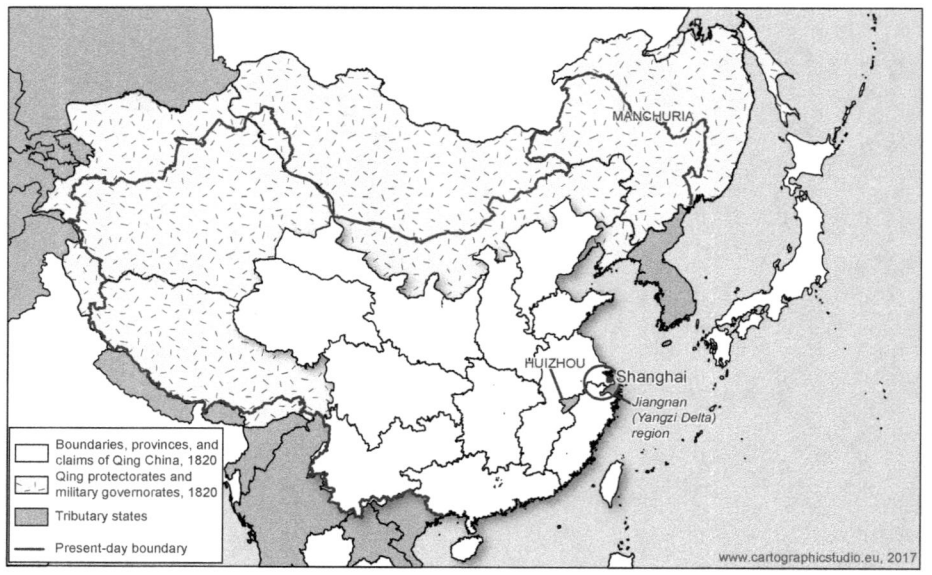

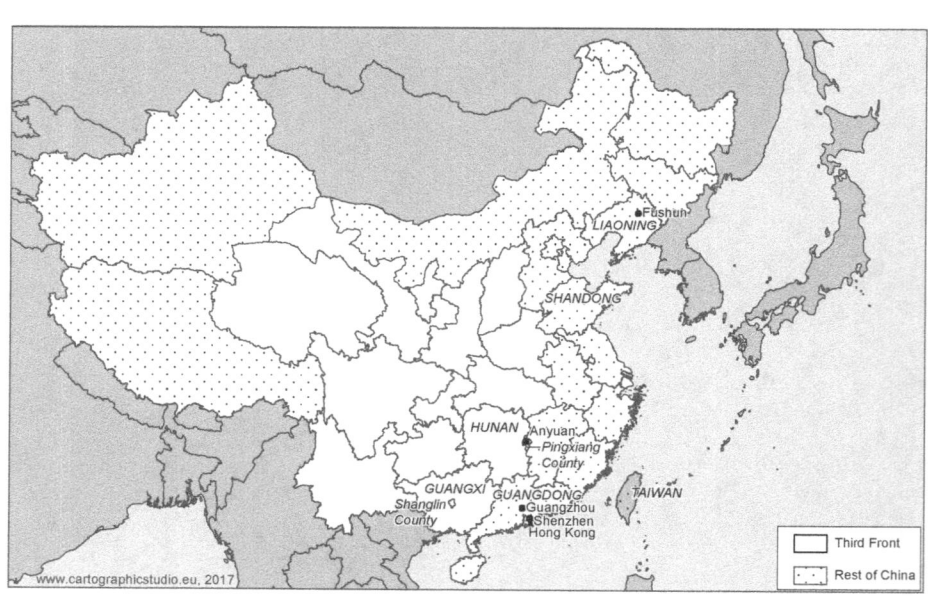

2. Regions

Christine Moll-Murata
2.1. China

This contribution focuses on the state of the field of research on work and labour relations in China from the rise of commercialization in the sixteenth century until today. This long span of time can be divided into the era when production consisted exclusively of handicrafts up until the mid-nineteenth century, the period of the rise of mechanization and early industrialization under the circumstances of imperialist encroachment upon Chinese sovereignty between 1840 and 1949, the period of the socialist planned economy until 1978, a transitional phase of economic reform, and the subsequent market liberalization after the entry into the World Trade Organization in 2001.

Work and labour in dynastic China: debates and topics

Until today, historical materialism still forms the theoretical framework for Chinese socioeconomic history written in mainland China. Consequently, the evolution of the socioeconomic stages of feudalism, capitalism, and socialism also constitute important paradigms for the perception of processes in labour history and concerning labour relations, even though criticism of the empirical value of these notions has become much more pronounced. An earlier discourse, which was developed from the 1950s onwards, exists regarding the ideas about the rising *sprouts of capitalism* in the period before mechanized production was adopted. For the study of work and labour relations, this implies the discussion of the existence and spread of wage labour, wage levels, and proto-industrial production in rural household-based settings. The criticism of this concept is quite pronounced nowadays.[1] It pinpoints the rigidity

---

1 Du Lihong, "Xin Zhongguo chengli hou guanyu jindai Zhongguo zibenzhuyi fazhan de taolun" (The discussion on the development of modern Chinese capitalism after the foundation of New China), *Lanzhou xuekan* (Lanzhou Academic Journal), 2016/02, pp. 65–75; Sun Jie and Sun Jinghao, "Jiangnanshi yanjiu yu wenti yishi: Zhongguo shehui jingjishi yanjiu lilun de jiantao" (Jiangnan History Study and Problem Awareness: A Reexamination of Theories on Chinese Socio-economic History), *Zhejiang daxue xuebao / Renwen shehui kexue xuebao* (Journal of Zhejiang University / Humanities and Social Sciences), 2016/02, pp. 1–13; Ye Xianming, "Guanyu Makesi wannian xiangguan sixiang yanjiu de wuqu – jianlun 'Zhongguo zibenzhuyi mengya' suo sheji de 'wuxing taolun' wenti" (About some misconceptions in the research on Marx's late thought – together with a discussion of the problem of the 'Debate on the Five Phases' addressed in the 'Sprouts of Capitalism in

of the expectation that European socioeconomic processes should occur in China and elsewhere in a similar manner. Nevertheless, for studies of the pre-nineteenth century the empirical research on China associated with this line of thought still provides a sound basis for further intellectual explorations. Yet comparative approaches need to take into consideration that the China of the Ming and Qing empires may have been comparable in size with other large empires but certainly not to individual European states. The results of this type of approach can be found in *Chinese Capitalism, 1522–1840*, edited by Xu Dixin and Wu Chengming—particularly in Shi Qi and Fang Zhuofen's contribution.[2]

Studies of Chinese socioeconomic history outside of China which focus on work and labour relations largely endorse the empirical findings of research on the beginnings of capitalism. However, they mostly set them in different—or varying—epistemological frameworks. These centre on global comparisons of living standards and issues regarding wage labour. Kenneth Pomeranz's work, *The Great Divergence*, inspired and provoked economic and social historians in Europe, Asia, and the United States to reflect on the differences in timing and the relative efficiency of pre-modern economies in comparison with each other. Besides attacking the idea of European exceptionalism, Pomeranz argues against Philip Huang's notion of *involution*. Labour, and its marginal product, stands at the core of this issue. Pomeranz, pointing to Kaoru Sugihara on the one hand and Esther Boserup on the other, is not convinced —at least for the pre-1800s—that a rising population would *per se* lead to immiseration; while Philip Huang insists that, even if impoverishment is not the immediate result, the marginal product of labour will necessarily decline and lead to impoverishment unless technological innovation can raise productivity. This seems to be the aporia of proto-industrialization—or will, in Ester Boserup's sense, an increased population find ways out of their predicament?

At the heart of this discussion is the scarce data used to calculate the exact differences between the standards of living in the East and the West. An attempt made by Robert Allen and his colleagues highlights the *small divergence* within Europe and concludes that even by 1800 the standards of living between the largest Asian and North-Western European countries diverged markedly.[3] Recently, Kent Deng and Patrick O'Brien have taken issue with what they consider a too small dataset

---

China') (*Makesi zhuyi yanjiu*) (Studies on Marxism), 2015/01, pp. 123–132. For a typical earlier critique, see Li Bozhong, *Jiangnan de zaoqi gongyehua* (Proto-Industrialization in the Yangzi Delta) (Beijing, 2000), pp. 524–527. The names of Chinese and Japanese authors of publications in Chinese and Japanese are rendered in the sequence of family name – personal name.

2 Wang Shixin, "Agriculture and the Changing Relations of Production" and Shi Qi and Fang Zhuofen, "Part II: Capitalism in Agriculture in the Early and Middle Qing Dynasty", in: Xu Dixin and Wu Chengming (eds), *Chinese Capitalism, 1522–1840* (Houndmills, 2000), pp. 23–45 and pp. 113–162.

3 Robert C. Allen, Jean-Pascal Bassino, Debin Ma, Christine Moll-Murata, Jan Luiten Van Zanden, "Wages, Prices, and Living Standards in China, 1738–1925: In Comparison with Europe, Japan, and India", *The Economic History Review*, Special Issue: *Asia in the Great Divergence*, 64, 1 (February 2011), pp. 8–38.

to come to definite conclusions about incomes. As earlier studies have found out, until the twentieth century people engaged in wage labour constituted only a small part of the population. However, as William Guanglin Liu has observed, the nominal wage data that *do* exist nevertheless allow us to model the outlines of real incomes necessary for survival or for raising families for the period preceding that under observation here.[4]

In a very interesting part of their book *Before and Beyond Divergence*, Rosenthal and Wong point to employment within the family as an alternative to a labour market. They spell out the differences between this type of self-sustaining households as opposed to labour relations which are more dependent upon the outside world.[5] This leads to the question regarding the relationship between gender and the household economy, an issue which is also at the core of Li Bozhong's research and the entire field of inquiry into protoindustrial labour.[6] In order to classify this development and the decisive role of female and child labour the eminent Japanese socioeconomic historian Hayami Akira coined the term *industrious revolution*. First used to examine the Japanese evidence, it has been adopted by Li Bozhong[7] and also by Sugihara Kaoru, as a paradigm for Chinese socioeconomic history.[8] It has been debated and defended in recent research, as is shown in the latest publication of collected essays on the *labour-intensive industrialization* that spans the pre-modern, modern, and contemporary periods and the large echo of reviews, appraisals, and critique it has evoked.[9]

The issue of a gendered division of labour in the pre-modern period is also analysed in depth from the perspectives of technical and social history.[10] The views on

---

[4] William Guanglin Liu, *The Chinese Market Economy, 1000–1500* (Albany, NY, 2015), p. 245.
[5] Jean-Laurent Rosenthal, and Roy Bin Wong, *Before and Beyond Divergence? The Politics of Economic Change in China and Europe* (Cambridge, MA, 2011), pp. 50–66.
[6] Li Bozhong, *Agricultural Development in Jiangnan, 1620–1850* (New York, 1998), especially the chapter "The Rise in Labour Productivity", and *idem*, *Jiangnan de zaoqi gongyehua* (Proto-Industrialization in the Yangzi Delta) (Beijing, 2000).
[7] Li Bozhong, " 'Zhongnian qindong': Kuazhang haishi xianshi? 19 shiji chu Songjiang diqu ge hangye congye renyuan nian gongzuori zhi kaocha" ("Working All the Year Round": Reality or Exaggeration? A Study of Working Days Per Year of Workers in Major Vocations in Songjiang of the Early Nineteenth Century), *Xueshu yuekan* (Academic Monthly) 2008/4, pp. 134–139, at 139; *idem*, "'Jiangnan jingji qiji' de lishi jichu: Xin shiye zhong de jindai zaoqi Jiangnan jingji" (The Historical Basis of the Jiangnan Economic Miracle: The Early Modern Economy of the Yangzi Delta in a New Perspective), *Qinghua daxue xuebao/Zhexue shehuikexue ban* (Journal of Tsinghua University/Philosophy and Social Sciences), 2011/02, pp. 68–80, at 78.
[8] Sugihara Kaoru, "The East Asian Path of Economic Development: a Long-term Perspective", in: Giovanni Arrighi, Mark Selden, and Hamashita Takeshi (eds), *The Resurgence of East Asia: 500-, 150- and 50-year Perspectives* (London, 2003), pp. 78–123, at 84–86.
[9] Gareth Austin and Sugihara Kaoru (eds), *Labour-Intensive Industrialization in Global History* (New York, 2013), especially Sugihara, "Labour-intensive industrialization in Global History: An interpretation of East Asian experiences", in: *ibid.*, pp. 20–64.
[10] Francesca Bray, *Technology and Gender. Fabrics of Power in Late Imperial China* (Berkeley, CA, 1997), pp. 173–272; Harriet Zurndorfer, "Cotton Textile Manufacture and Marketing in Late Impe-

the role of foot-binding differ. The argumentation regarding this topic centres on the questions of the causes, functions, and distribution of this custom. In their recent book, Lauren Bossen and Hill Gates refine an argument they made earlier about the predominantly economic rather than cultural function of foot-binding and insist upon its continued validity.[11] They maintain that a mother's incentive to bind her daughter's feet was based upon the desire and the economic necessity of patriarchal rural families to use the handicraft items (mostly textiles), which girls, that were usually between the ages of six and sixteen, could produce, either for family consumption or for sale. In this argumentation, forcing female children to become accustomed to sedentary manual labour (since walking had become painful) assisted the mothers, whose tasks were more complex and whose products could be sold at higher prices, with their work.[12] Rather than intending to please future husbands or enhancing respectabilities by confinement to the home, the practice served the purpose of ensuring the livelihoods of rural households and assisting busy mothers.

The cultural historian Dorothy Ko emphasizes the aesthetic appeal of the often lavishly embroidered shoes for bound feet.[13] However, from the perspective of the economic historians Bossen and Gates, this decoration rather indicated skill and craftsmanship.[14] While Dorothy Ko points to the many reasons for foot-binding, settings in which foot-binding took place, and the agency women maintained although their feet were bound,[15] Bossen and Gates point to the household economy, both in rural and urban settings, for which child labour generated an important form of additional income.[16] Bossen and Gates expand their earlier argumentation, which looks at the demise of foot-binding between the 1920s and 1940s, and observe significant connections between the rise of mechanized production, especially in the textile industry, and the disappearance of this custom. To a certain extent, this proves their hypothesis that foot-binding was linked to the economic value of girls' handicrafts at home.[17]

---

rial China and the 'Great Divergence'", *Journal of the Economic and Social History of the Orient*, 54/5, 2011, pp. 701–738, 710–720; Dagmar Schäfer, "Silken Strands: Making Technology Work in China", in: *idem* (ed.), *Cultures of Knowledge: Technology in Chinese History* (Leiden and Boston, 2011), pp. 45–73; Susan Mann, "Women, Families, and Gender Relations", in: Willard Peterson (ed.), *The Cambridge History of China*, Volume 9, Part One, *The Ch'ing Empire to 1800* (Cambridge, 2002), pp. 428–472, 448–471.
11 Laurel Bossen and Hill Gates, *Bound Feet, Young Hands. Tracking the Demise of Footbinding in Village China* (Stanford, CA, 2017).
12 *Ibid.*, pp. 139, 148.
13 Dorothy Ko, *Cinderella's Sisters. A Revisionist History of Footbinding* (Berkeley etc., 2005) and *idem*, *Every Step a Lotus: Shoes for Bound Feet* (Berkeley etc., 2001).
14 Bossen and Gates, *Bound Feet*, pp. 14, 175.
15 Ko, *Cinderella's Sisters*, p. 2.
16 Bossen and Gates, *Bound Feet*, p. 153.
17 *Ibid.*, p. 138.

It is a great merit of Bossen and Gates' approach that they studied urban and rural regions in both East China, where mechanization was further advanced, and in the interior provinces, where handicraft textile work remained in existence for much longer. Applying an econometric model, they came to the conclusion that the girls who were born between 1920 and 1940, who worked for gain, and/or who were engaged continuously rather than intermittently in handicraft production were more likely to have bound feet. Interestingly, they point to the regions under the control of the Chinese Communist Party (CCP) in the 1930s and 1940s, where due to warfare and economic blockades handicraft spinning and weaving were maintained. Yet foot-binding was not taken up again in these regions because the communists promoted work in cooperative workshops and generally women's work outside the home, and, as they formulate, "higher authorities would ensure the labor discipline."[18] Finally, this leaves one wondering whether cultural (including ideological) paradigms rather than sheer economic necessity first caused mothers to cripple their daughters' feet, with lifelong consequences, and then impeded them from continuing with this practice. After all, child labour was a worldwide phenomenon in the premodern era, and severe limitations to personal freedoms, including those of one's own kin, were far from unknown worldwide. However, foot-binding was specific to China. What emerges from this very valuable approach that explores the social institution of foot-binding and its demise is a clearer picture of women's work and women's agency in China. Bossen and Gates interpret their evidence in terms of an involutionary growth in the rural Chinese family economy between about 1850 and 1950, in which output increased and labour efforts intensified but returns diminished.[19]

While work for one's own household could thus be controlled by bodily confinement, up until the end of the dynastic era a legal distinction was made between *ordinary* and *debased* people. This had consequences for the level of personal freedom, the position as legal subjects, and also for the types of labour which people were expected to do. The most recent contribution to this field of inquiry is Claude Chevaleyre's study on unfree labour during the Ming dynasty, which starts out with the information that the status of unfree household slaves was legally abolished in 1910, but focuses on the Ming dynasty bond service in the rest of the text. [20] Despite the author's statement that the Ming bond service has so far not been studied *by itself*, it may be good to recall that previous scholars have in fact addressed the issue. For example, the different categories of bondservants, including both agricultural and household servants, are well explained in Harriet Zurndorfer's book on Huizhou,[21]

---

18 *Ibid.*, pp. 88 f.
19 *Ibid.*, p. 175.
20 Claude Chevaleyre, "Acting as Master and Bondservant: Considerations on Status Identities and the Nature of 'Bond-Servitude' in Late Ming China", in: Alessandro Stanziani (ed.), *Labour, Coercion, and Economic Growth in Eurasia, 17th-20th Centuries* (Leiden and Boston, 2013).
21 Harriet Zurndorfer, *Change and Continuity in Chinese Local History. The Development of Hui-chou Prefecture from 800 to 1800* (Leiden and Boston, 1989).

in an article by James Cole,[22] or in Anders Hansson's monograph on the debased classes,[23] to name just a few works. The bondservant rebellions in the Ming-Qing transition are the subject of a dissertation in German by Andreas Mixius,[24] and in the context of mining labour, Bernd Eberstein's study needs to be mentioned as well.[25] It is thus not a question of too little information on the events and the Chinese categorizations of the types of bondservants or slaves during the Ming dynasty. The field is evolving, and lately it also includes a special focus on prostitution during the Ming-Qing transition.[26] What makes Chevaleyre's contribution important is the impulse it gives to the contextualization of bond service in China within unfree labour worldwide, showing the differences and the parallels. Interestingly, the memorial requesting the abolition of bond service submitted to the Chinese emperor in 1906, which Chevalayre refers to, emphasized that the sale of human beings was no longer tolerated in Europa and America.[27]

Global contextualization also lies at the core of the research programs in the framework of Global Labour History, and it is of particular importance to the Global Collaboratory on the History of Labour Relations, which aims at explaining and quantifying labour relations and work ethics worldwide between 1500 and 2000, including labour relations in China. As for the work ethics in the Ming-Qing transition, they are the topic of one of the present author's contributions, which shows the varieties of the perceptions of labour during the Ming dynasty, the dynamics during a period of commercialization and commodification of labour, as well as the longer continuities in thought about work.[28]

---

[22] James H. Cole, "Social Discrimination in Traditional China: the To-Min of Shaohsing", *Journal of the Economic and Social History of the Orient*, 25, (1982), pp. 100–110.
[23] Anders Hansson, *Chinese Outcasts. Discrimination and Emancipation in Late Imperial China* (Leiden and Boston, 1996).
[24] Andreas W. Mixius, *"Nu-pien" und die "Nu-p'u" von Kiangnan. Aufstände Abhängiger und Unfreier in Südchina 1644/45* (Hamburg, 1980).
[25] Bernd Eberstein, *Bergbau und Bergarbeiter zur Ming-Zeit* (1368–1644) (Hamburg, 1974).
[26] Harriet Zurndorfer, "Prostitutes and Courtesans in the Confucian Moral Universe of Late Ming China (1550–1644)", *International Review of Social History*, 56 (2011), Special Issue 19, *The Joy and Pain of Work*, pp. 197–216; Hsieh Bao-hua, *Concubinage and Servitude in Late Imperial China* (Lanham, MD, 2014).
[27] E.T. Williams, "The Abolition of Slavery in the Chinese Empire", *The American Journal of International Law*, 4, 4 (1910), pp. 794–805, at 795, and "Report to the Throne of the Imperial Chinese Commission on Constitutional Government Recommending the Abolition of Slavery […]", *ibid.*, "Supplement: Official Documents", pp. 359–373, 360. For a detailed discussion of the abolition, see Johanna S. Ransmeier, *Sold People. Traffickers and Family Life in North China* (Cambridge, MA, 2017), p. 112.
[28] Christine Moll-Murata, "Work Ethics and Work Valuations in a Period of Commercialization: Ming China, 1500–1644", *International Review of Social History*, 56 (2011), Special Issue 19, pp. 165–195; idem, "Non-Western Perspectives: The Chinese Dimension" (Contribution to the Debate Issue on Catharina Lis and Hugo Soly, *Worthy Efforts. Attitudes to Work and Workers in Pre-industrial Europe*), *Tijdschrift voor Sociale en Economische Geschiedenis*, 11, 1 (2014), pp. 141–152.

Interpretations of the quantifications in the shifts of labour relations have been jointly published by members of the Collaboratory group, for instance on the impact which states have had upon labour relations. The volume *Conquerors, Employers, and Arbiters: States and Shifts in Labour Relations 1500–2000*[29] contains essays on work in the service of states and polities or regulated by state institutions. For its global comparative approach, it was inspired by Tilly's conceptual division between coercive and capital-driven modes of state building. From the perspective of labour, this implies a distinction between the coercion and remuneration of workers—especially of those serving states and polities. In seventeenth- and eighteenth-century China the soldiers, the largest group in the service of the state, were both coerced and remunerated. The Manchurian rulers of the Qing dynasty defined themselves as ethnically distinct from the large majority, comprized of the Han Chinese population.[30] Working for the dynastic state was an obligation from which especially Manchurians and their associates-in-arms, the so-called banner people, could not free themselves. Nevertheless, this type of service was prestigious and well remunerated, constituting a particular, costly type of labour relation of the tributary type that lasted for more than two hundred years, almost until the end of the dynasty. It was complemented by a commodified form of labour relations in the second army of the Qing, the Green Standards. In the last century of the Qing rule, especially after the hiatus of the Taiping rebellion (1852–1864), commodification of the labour relations in the armies was even more evident in the provincial armies, which were financed by regional commanders. These became the dominant forces that saved the dynasty from an earlier collapse. This long-term change in the largest single group of hired workers serving states and polities is analysed, using a global comparative approach, in the book *Fighting for A Living*.[31]

To sum up the state of the field of research on work and labour relations in the pre-mechanized period, there are few publications that are dedicated exclusively to labour issues. However, work and labour relations are part of a growing number of studies that perceive labour as an integral part of the entire economic system, consider the gender-specific division of labour, or concentrate on particular branches of the economy.

---

29 *International Review of Social History*, 61 (2016), Special Issue 24, *Conquerors, Employers, and Arbiters: States and Shifts in Labour Relations 1500–2000*, ed. by Karin Hofmeester, Gijs Kessler, and Christine Moll-Murata.
30 Christine Moll-Murata, "Tributary Labour Relations in China During the Ming-Qing Transition (Seventeenth to Eighteenth Centuries)", *International Review of Social History*, 61 (2016), Special Issue 24, pp. 27–48, at 34–40.
31 Christine Moll-Murata and Ulrich Theobald, "Military employment in Qing dynasty China", in: Erik Jan Zürcher (ed.), *Fighting for a Living: A Comparative Study of Military Labour 1500–2000* (Amsterdam, 2013), pp. 353–391.

Work and labour relations in the era of mechanized production and capitalist organization in the Republic of China[32]

Recent studies on the period of early industrialization and proletarianization after 1850 include those on the earliest shipyard for steamships, the Shanghai Arsenal,[33] and on the rise of mechanical printing in Shanghai.[34] As in the case of the pre-mechanized production, chapters or sections on work organization and processes as well as labour relations are included in publications that focus on particular branches of production or on the mining sector.[35] Research on labour during the period of the loss of sovereignty from the Opium Wars in the mid-nineteenth century until the foundation of the People's Republic of China and the installation of the Kuomintang government in Taiwan concentrates on the questions of the relative impact of Western and Japanese technology and the issues relating to the rise of labourers' consciousness, organization, and protest activities. Limin Teh, for instance, has studied the important issue of labour contracting and the bureaucratization and replacement of the previous more independent labour contractors in the Manchurian coal mine of Fushun, which was under Japanese management. Migrational patterns from the Chinese inland (Shandong province) thwarted efforts to build up a continuously employed workforce in order to raise productivity.[36]

Workers' agency and labour struggles constitute an issue of particular concern in Chinese studies concerning the pre-socialist period. For instance, an important works on this topic are the economic historian Zhu Cishou's set of three volumes on the industries of China (ancient, early modern, and modern), which has been praised as the first systematic and continuous presentation of industrialization, in a very broad sense of the term, and moreover his monograph on *industrial labour*,[37] which starts in the second millennium BC and ends in the late twentieth century.

---

[32] For the Republican and Socialist period, the present account discusses research published after or not included in Arif Dirlik's overview "Workers, Class, and the Socialist Revolution in China", in: Jan Lucassen (ed.), *Global Labour History: A State of the Art* (Bern, 2008), pp. 373–396.
[33] Christine Cornet, *Etat et entreprises en Chine, XIXe–XXe siècles: le chantier naval de Jiangnan, 1865–1937* (Paris, 1997).
[34] Christopher A. Reed, *Gutenberg in Shanghai. Chinese Print Capitalism, 1876–1937* (Vancouver, 2004); Rudolf G. Wagner, "*Gutenberg in Shanghai. Chinese Print Capitalism, 1876–1937.* By Christopher A. Reed", in: *MCLC Resource Center Publication,* January 2005. *Modern Chinese Literature and Culture,* website maintained by Ohio State University, http://mclc.osu.edu/rc/pubs/reviews/wagner.htm, and Reed's response on the same website, last accessed 17 March 2017.
[35] Tim Wright, *Coal Mining in China's Economy and Society, 1895–1937* (Cambridge, 1984).
[36] Limin Teh, "Labor Control and Mobility in Japanese-Controlled Fushun Coalmine (China), 1907–1932", *International Review of Social History,* 60, Special Issue *Migration and Ethnicity in Coalfield History: Global Perspectives*, pp. 95–119.
[37] Zhu Cishou, *Zhongguo gongye laodong shi* (History of Chinese industrial labour) (Shanghai, 1999).

These are voluminous compendia of factual knowledge, which are obviously compiled for didactic purposes and firmly grounded in the Chinese version of Marxist orthodoxy. The six-volume series *Zhongguo gongren yundong shi* [38] edited by the labour historian Liu Mingkui (1925–2004) and his colleagues, focuses on the Chinese labour movement in the period between 1840 and 1949. In thousands of pages it gives a comprehensive account of workers' actions all over China. Moreover, Liu and his colleagues edited a collection of relevant historical materials in a total of 14 volumes with the title *Zhongguo jindai gongren jieji he gongren yundong* (The modern Chinese working class and labour movement). Each volume comprises more than 800 pages. The edition was published by the publishing house of the Party School of the Central Committee of the Communist Party of China.[39]

The period between 1911 to 1949 falls into the formative phase of the Chinese Communist Party. In the discourse that mainly exists outside of China, dominant CCP narratives are being questioned or given different nuances.[40] A prominent example is Elizabeth Perry's book on the early CCP efforts to mobilize mining and railroad workers in the mining town of Anyuan in Hunan Province in late 1921, several months after the founding of the CCP. This involved establishing a night school for the workers and organizing a work stoppage in 1922, all the while gaining the acknowledgement of the local secret society (Red Gang) and struggling with the labour contractors who were deeply concerned about the strike. Mao Zedong is presented as the mastermind behind these strikes, but other party leaders, Li Lisan and Liu Shaoqi, actually resided in Anyuan and organized the workers on a daily basis. According to Perry, this early experience in worker mobilization thus came before the later Maoist perception of the peasants as the dominant revolutionary force. Moreover, Perry presents a much more complex picture of compliance and alliance with local groups, from the elites down to the outlaws, and shows that the strike, which was approved by Mao Zedong at that time, was non-violent and successful. These are multiple revisions of the legends built around Anyuan, first after the foundation of the People's Republic, when Liu Shaoqi tried to establish himself as the successful Anyuan leader, side-lining Li Lisan, then during the Cultural Revolution, when Mao was presented as the focal figure, and Liu Shaoqi was blamed for his non-militant approach during the outage.[41] Perry demonstrates what happened in Anyuan from (at least) two critical perspectives. Firstly, she shows that culture mattered: the young intellectual organizers who also embodied traditional learning and came to the miners as teachers wearing scholars' gowns were able to convince both the workers and the local elite of their educational agendas. Secondly, she demonstrates that the credibility

---

38 Liu Mingkui, Tang Yuliang, Liu Jingfang, Zhao Yongbo (eds), *Zhongguo gongren yundong shi* (History of the Chinese labour movement) (Guangzhou, 1998), 6 vols.
39 Liu Mingkui et al., *Zhongguo jindai gongren jieji he gongren yundong* (The modern Chinese working class and labour movement) (Beijing, 2002), 14 vols.
40 Elizabeth Perry, *Anyuan: Mining China's Revolutionary Tradition* (Berkeley, CA, 2012).
41 Ibid., p. 13 f.

of the CCP is an important issue in today's antagonism between workers and management. Back in the Republican era, CCP leaders were the first to take the illiterate miners seriously and advise them on how to struggle for their rights and recognition vis-à-vis the mining corporation. However, after decades of socialist rule, miners and workers at the same locations feel let down due to layoffs and welfare reductions that are taking place under the aegis of the CCP. For readers of Chinese, the field study that Yu Jianrong, the Chinese scholar who, as Perry explains in the introduction, called her attention to Anyuan, conducted in the first decade of the twenty-first century should be an interesting complement.[42]

Recent research in migration and diaspora studies evidently also relates to labour. Qin Yucheng explored the functions of the Chinese native-place associations in San Francisco, the so-called Six Companies, for labour recruitment among Guangdong natives. In the 1880s these immigrant institutions were accused of importing servile coolie labourers and faced with allegations of slave trade. Scholarly opinions are still divided as to their actual role.[43] Qin Yucheng comes to the conclusion that the Six Companies had beneficial rather than exploitative intentions; Lawrence Hansen concedes this, yet points to the partly illegal character of this aid, even though the Six Companies were not slave smugglers. A volume of collected essays on Chinese diasporas, *Chinatowns around the World: Gilded Ghetto, Ethnopolis, and Cultural Diaspora*, portrays Chinatowns in Vancouver, New York, Chicago, Sydney, Lima, Havana, Paris, Lisbon, and Tokyo. Among these, especially the contribution on Havana elaborates on indentured labour in the nineteenth century.[44] A monograph on the Chinese in Mauritius develops in greater detail the function of the Chinese labourers on the Mauritian sugar plantations in the nineteenth century and describes the activities of the subsequent immigrant groups until the present, discussing attempts to maintain identities and processes of taking root and uprooting in a multicultural surrounding.[45] Two recent studies on the Chinese in South Africa look at a shorter span of time. Andrew Macdonald has researched the British policies of disciplining the imported Chinese labour force, a total of over 60,000 people, for the gold mines in

---

[42] Yu Jianrong, *Zhongguo gongren jieji zhuangkuang: Anyuan shilu* (The Situation of China's Working Class: Annals of Anyuan) (New York, 2006).

[43] Qin Yucheng, "A Century-old 'Puzzle': The Six Companies' Role in Chinese Labor Importation in the Nineteenth Century", *Journal of American-East Asian Relations*, 12, 3 (2003), pp. 225–254, at 226 note 3; Lawrence Douglas Taylor Hansen, "The Chinese Six Companies of San Francisco and the Smuggling of Chinese Immigrants across the U.S.-Mexico Border, 1882–1930", pp. 37–61.

[44] Adrian H. Hearn, "Chinatown Havana: One Hundred and Sixty Years below the Surface", in: Bernard P. Wong and Tan Chee-Beng (eds), *Chinatowns around the World. Gilded Ghetto, Ethnopolis, and Cultural Diaspora* (Leiden and Boston, 2013), pp. 163–186, at 166–172, "From deception to deception".

[45] Marina Carter and James Ng Foong Kwong, *Abacus and Mah Jong. Sino-Mauritian Settlement and Economic Consolidation* (Leiden, 2009), esp. "Slaves, Convicts, Field Workers and Artisans: The Chinese in the Colonial Labour Diasporas", esp. pp. 29–48.

South Africa.⁴⁶ Rachel Bright's book on *Chinese Labour in South Africa* expands on the topic from the perspective of trans-colonial relationships, asking why the British employed Chinese rather than African or Indian labour for mining work in the Transvaal.⁴⁷ For an even shorter period of time, Chinese labourers in Europe were indispensable as paramilitary workers in the First World War. Their numbers are not quite clear, and estimates range from 85,000 to 150,000. The events, recruitment channels, ideological justifications, and gains and losses on all sides have been discussed at conferences, and publications regarding these topics are being created in the context of activities surrounding the centenary memorial of World War I.⁴⁸ The standard book length publication is Xu Guoqi's *Strangers on the Western Front*,⁴⁹ followed up by the monograph by James Gregory,⁵⁰ an excellent overview article by Alex Calvo and Bao Qiaoni,⁵¹ as well as a growing number of detailed investigations on Chinese paramilitary labourers in specific localities in France and Belgium, such as the volume of collected essays from the 2010 conference, edited by the French-based China scholar Ma Li.⁵² While the plight of the Chinese workers on the Western Front is currently more well known, the number of people who served in similar functions in Russia is just about to be discovered. It has been researched by historians such as Li Zhixue, Li Xiang, and Xie Qingming.⁵³

---

46 Andrew Macdonald, "In the Pink of Health or the Yellow of Condition? Chinese Workers, Colonial Medicine and the Journey to South Africa, 1904–1907", *Journal of Chinese Overseas*, 4, 1 (2008), pp. 23–50.
47 Rachel Bright, *Chinese Labour in South Africa: Race, Violence, and Global Spectacle* (Houndmills, 2013).
48 The largest thematic conference, "Chinese Workers in the First World War" was jointly held in Boulogne-sur-mer and Ypres, see the conference homepage and abstracts at http://www.iccwww1.org/Conference-2010/Home_files/Resumes-abstract.pdf, last accessed 15 March 2017.
49 Xu Guoqi, *Strangers on the Western Front. Chinese Workers in the Great War* (Cambridge, MA, 2011).
50 Gregory James, *The Chinese Labour Corps 1916–1920* (Hong Kong, 2013).
51 Calvo, Alex and Bao Qiaoni, "Forgotten Voices from the Great War: the Chinese Labor Corps", *The Asia-Pacific Journal*, 13, 1 (49) (2015), available at http://apjjf.org/-Alex-Calvo/4411, last accessed on 15 March 2017.
52 Ma Li (ed.), *Les travailleurs chinois en France dans la Première Guerre mondiale* (Paris, 2012); a Chinese version of the book was published in 2015.
53 Li Zhixue, " 'Yizhan' qijian Beiyang zhengfu zhi qiaowu zhengce ji bao qiao cuoshi" (The policy of assignment of Chinese workers in WW I by the North China Government and the protective measures for Chinese citizens), *Xuexi yu tantao* (Study and Exploration), 2012/11, pp. 151–156; Li Xiang and Xie Qingming, "Yizhan Eguo huagong de shuzi wenti" (The issue of the numbers of Chinese workers in Russia during WW I), *Lantai shijie* (Lantai World), 2013/04, pp. 38–39.

Labour under Socialism

For the period after 1949, a recent trend is the inquiry into the inclusion, not always by free volition, of rural women into the agricultural and industrial labour forces. This has been studied by Jacob Eyferth,[54] and scholarly articles in Chinese also increasingly address the issue. Currently, the positive effects of women's liberation from their confined roles in reproductive labour are being acknowledged and applauded in the mainstream Chinese discourse. Yet the policy, as Eyferth points out, resulted in a heavy dual burden of feeding and clothing the family in a non-mechanized setting, which implied not only sewing, but sometimes spinning, and often weaving the cloth, in addition to the eight to eleven hour work shifts in agricultural labour.[55]

The labour policies during the Cultural Revolution, especially those of the Third Front hinterland industrial development program, are another field of increased interest in China and abroad. Since the Third Front Program of the 1960s and 1970s implied, in Barry Naughton's terminology, the "defence industrialization in the Chinese interior", the plants were often hidden in the hinterland for strategic reasons. The secrecy of some of these projects compounds the difficulties in conducting on-site research. For this reason, although the scholarly interest is rising, the hindrances for investigation are also high. The concern for the policies regarding labour and the implementation of labour-related measures during the period of High Maoism can be attributed to the growing uneasiness and disappointment of the generation that witnessed the workers' relative empowerment up until the late 1970s. After the economic reforms of the 1980s up until today they have experienced an acute loss of agency and welfare benefits. This is the big theme that for instance Li Ju has researched.[56]

By far the largest number of scholarly studies on labour issues are being dedicated to the period of economic reform after 1978 and the gradual opening to the world market after 2001. Marxist views on class struggle and class consciousness, as those formulated by Chesneaux and outlined by Dirlik, seem to be becoming less prominent, although they are being published both in China, from the perspective of the New Left, and abroad, for instance by Elaine Sio-ieng Hui, who has been inspired

---

[54] Jacob Eyferth, "Women's Work and the Politics of Homespun in Socialist China, 1948–1980", *International Review of Social History* 57, 4 (2012), pp. 365–391.
[55] Ibid., 389.
[56] Li Ju, "How It Was/Is Told and How It Is Remembered: History and Memory of the Third Front Construction", *Journal of Historical Sociology*, 28, 3 (2015), pp. 314–341; idem, "From 'Master' to 'Loser': Changing Working-Class Cultural Identity in Contemporary China", *International Labor and Working-Class History* 88 (2015), pp. 190–208; idem, "Victory and Defeat: The Contentious Politics of One Generation of State Workers in China since the 1960s", *International Review of Social History*, 61, 2 (2016), pp. 197–222. See also Covell Meyskens, "Third Front Railroads and Industrial Modernity in Late Maoist China", *Twentieth Century China*, 40 (2015), pp. 238–260.

by the Gramscian concept of capitalist cultural hegemony.[57] Research is proliferating on issues related to migrants' rights on the job and to the social circumstances of the locations where they settle.[58] In an assessment of the state of the field of Chinese labour studies, the labour scholar Anita Chan recalls that over the last few decades the scholars outside of China engaging in Chinese labour studies have increased from a handful to a few dozen. She considers the concentration on the study of migrant labour and the labour protests in South China as disproportionate in view of other labour issues that are likewise of general interest.[59] Labour struggles concerning wages and working conditions, including housing and social security, are not only monitored on the Internet, such as on the websites of the Hong Kong based *China Labour Bulletin*[60] and Asia Monitor Resources Centre,[61] the U.S. based China Labor Watch,[62] or Forum Arbeitswelten in Germany,[63] but also analysed in a growing number of publications and periodicals in China and abroad.[64] Questions of worker representation in collective bargaining and labour struggles command the interest of sociologists, economists, and historians of contemporary China.[65] Most important in this respect

---

[57] For a study of labour in what the author conceives of as post-socialist China, see Elaine Sio-ieng Hui, "The Labour Law System, Capitalist Hegemony and Class Politics in China", *The China Quarterly* 226 (2016), pp. 431–455, and *idem*, "The Neglected Side of the Coin: Legal Hegemony, Class Consciousness, and Labour Politics in China", in: Ivan Franceschini, Kevin Lim, and Nicholas Loubère (eds), *Made in China Yearbook 2016* (Canberra, 2017), pp. 80–83.
[58] Chris King-Chi Chan and Pun Ngai, "The Making of a New Working Class? A Study of Collective Actions of Migrant Workers in South China", *The China Quarterly*, 198 (June 2009), pp. 287–303; *idem* and Jenny Chan, "The Role of the State, Labour Policy and Migrant Workers' Struggles in Globalized China", in: Paul Bowles and John Harriss (eds), *Globalization and Labour in China and India: Impacts and Responses* (Houndmills, 2009).
[59] "Interpreting Chinese Labour: Informalisation or Empowerment?" Group interview with Anita Chan, Kaxton Siu, and Sarah Swider, ed. by Ivan Franceschini and Kevin Lin, *Made in China Yearbook 2016*, pp. 33–39, at 39.
[60] *China Labour Bulletin*, available at http://www.clb.org.hk/, see also "Strike map", http://maps.clb.org.hk/strikes/en, last accessed 15 March 2017.
[61] Available at http://www.amrc.org.hk/, last accessed 19 March 2017.
[62] Available at http://chinalaborwatch.org/home.aspx, last accessed 19 March 2017.
[63] Peter Franke, "Forum Arbeitswelten – ein Konzept zu internationaler Basis-Zusammenarbeit", available at https://www.forumarbeitswelten.de/projekte/selbstdarstellungen/Forum%20Arbeitswelten%20Artikel%20Franke%202012-10.pdf/view. For links to further forums on labour in China, see the list at *Forum Arbeitswelten*, available at https://www.forumarbeitswelten.de/themenbereiche/linkliste, last accessed 19 March 2017.
[64] For instance, *Made in China: A Quarterly on Chinese Labour, Civil Society, and Rights (since 2016)*, edited by Ivan Franceschini and Kevin Lin.
[65] For state of the field overviews after Dirlik, see McQuaide and Zhang Xiaodan, and the interview "Interpreting Chinese Labour", *Made in China Yearbook 2016*, see note 60. Relevant publications include Lee Ching Kwan, *Against the Law. Labor Protests in China's Rustbelt and Sunbelt* (Berkeley, CA, 2007); Sarosh Kuruvilla, Lee Ching Kwan, and Mary E. Gallagher (eds), *From Iron Rice Bowl to Informalization. Markets, Workers, and the State in a Changing China* (Ithaca, NY, 2011); Christoph Scherrer (ed.), *China's Labour Question* (Munich, 2011); Nooman Majid, *The Great Employment Transformation in China* (Geneva, 2015); William Hurst, *The Chinese Worker after Socialism* (Cambridge, 2012); Jackie

are the activities of the official, pro-government All-China Federation of Trade Unions (ACFTU), the largest trade union in the world, with its regional and industrial branches[66], and of the large number of Non-Government Organizations concerned with labour issues.[67]

Moreover, gender equality in legislation and in the workplace since the economic reforms is being examined in China-related and comparative gender studies. Women's participation in labour is high in global comparison,[68] yet gender discrimination in terms of wages, retirement age, and access to highly qualified jobs and top networks exists.[69] An often argued position emphasizes that many working women experienced a backlash of patriarchy after the 1980s.[70] However, with the responsibilities of childcare, housekeeping, and productive work outside the home largely shouldered by women, the intended implementation of the egalitarian ideals from the 1950s until the late 1970s brought an additional pressure upon the female workforce.

On the reverse side of the economic boom, since the 1990s, urban unemployment constitutes a problem that increasingly attracts researchers' attention. [71] Among the manifold facets of the transition from a socialist planned economy to greater market orientation and liberalization, the question of the legalization of labour rights in the sense of codification and law enforcement is of particular concern.

Sheehan, "Labor Representation and Organization Under State Capitalism In China", in: Vincent Kelly Pollard (ed.), *State Capitalism, Contentious Politics and Large-Scale Social Change* (Leiden, 2011).
66 Rudolf Traub-Merz, *All China Federation of Trade Unions: Structure, Functions and the Challenge of Collective Bargaining* (Geneva, 2011); Tim Pringle, *Trade Unions in China: The Challenge of Labour Unrest* (London, 2011); Jenny Chan, Pun Ngai, and Mark Selden, "Chinese Labor Protest and Trade Unions", in: Richard Maxwell (ed.), *The Routledge Companion to Labor and Media* (New York, 2016), pp. 290–302.
67 See, for instance, the memoirs of the union leader and labour activist Han Dongfang, who established the *China Labour Bulletin* in Hong Kong: idem and Michaël Sztanke, *Mon combat pour les ouvriers chinois* (Paris, 2014).
68 Nancy E. Riley, *Gender, Work, and Family in a Chinese Economic Zone: Laboring in Paradise* (Dordrecht, 2013), p. 61, quotes a labour force participation rate of 73% as of 2013.
69 Qin Min *et al.*, "Gender Inequalities in Employment and Wage Earning Among Internal Labour Migrants in Chinese Cities", *Demographic Research*, 34 (2016), pp. 175–202, at 177 and 193–195, who point out that women accounted for over 50% of internal labour migrants in the last decade, and in the sample presented, male migrants' average wages were 26% higher than female wages (p. 176). There is research that assumes that discrimination barriers can be overcome, such as Jennifer Zeng and Michael Thorneman, "Advancing Gender Parity in China: Solutions to Help Women's Ambitions Overcome the Obstacles", *Bain Brief* (Beijing and Shanghai, 2014), pp. 11–15, available at http://www.bain.com/publications/articles/advancing-gender-parity-in-china.aspx, accessed 23 March 2017.
70 Esther Efron Pimentel, "Gender Ideology, Household Behavior, and Backlash in Urban China", *Journal of Family Issues*, 27, 3 (2006), pp. 341–365, at 344–346 outlines the main arguments of this debate.
71 Thomas Gold, William Hurst, Jaeyoun Won, Li Qiang, *Laid-Off Workers in a Workers' State: Unemployment with Chinese Characteristics* (Houndmills, 2010).

This has led to the contending views on the state and the workers' representation (ACFTU) that advance and foster labour rights versus the opinion that the hegemonial state should allow workers to criticize—but not fundamentally challenge—the current socioeconomic and political system.[72]

Studies on the global repercussions of the situation of Chinese labour have become a new field of enquiry. The focus is on Africa in particular, with examples from Zambia and Ghana. State owned Chinese companies have invested in Zambian copper mines since the privatization in the 1990s. From that time on, problematic safety standards, low wage payment, and even physical abuses of local workers have become issues.[73] In some gold mining regions of Ghana a short-lived rush attracted Chinese illegal small-scale miners from one particular county: Shanglin in the Guangxi province. They sometimes arrived as investing partners, and sometimes they were obviously hired workers, perhaps recruited by work contractors in China.[74] In Europe, Chinese sweatshops in Italy[75] and Chinese employment of the local workforce in Germany[76] are further examples of the globalization of labour that are being discussed in labour and migration studies.

Finally, the horizon of the future of labour in China is expanding. At its core remain the questions of worker representation, bargaining power, and ultimately political participation. The discourse consists of both optimistic and pessimistic views.[77] Pessimistic views concentrate on the large-scale restructuring, especially of state-operated enterprises, including enormous numbers of lay-offs,[78] the repression of independent group bargaining by NGOs, and especially the suppression of foreign NGO activities.[79] Conversely, optimism shows in William Hurst's hope for an innovative al-

---

[72] Hui, "The Neglected Side of the Coin", pp. 80–83.
[73] Mukete Beyongo Dynamic, "Fighting the Race to the Botton: Regulating Chinese Investment in Zambian Mines", *Made in China Yearbook 2016*, pp. 112–115, at 112.
[74] Nicholas Loubere and Gordon Crawford, "There and Back Again: Conceptualising the Chinese Gold Rush in Ghana", *Made in China Yearbook 2016*, pp. 116–121. The authors point out that to date some aspects of this rush, such as the labour relations between miners and employers of the so-called "Shanglin Gang", remain obscure.
[75] Antonella Ceccagno, "The Hidden Crisis: The Prato Industrial District and the Once Thriving Chinese Garment Industry", *Revue Européenne des migrations internationales*, 28, 4 (2012), pp. 43–65.
[76] Annette Schnoor, "Chinesische Investitionen in Deutschland – Besser als ihr Image", in: Stiftung Asienhaus *et al.* (eds), *Chinesische Arbeitswelten – in China und der Welt*, pp. 61–63.
[77] "Interpreting Chinese Labour", pp. 33–39.
[78] Kevin Lin, "Remoulding the State Sector: Back to the 1990s?", *Made in China Yearbook 2016*, pp. 20–23, 23.
[79] "A Civil Society Under Assault: A Debate among International Activists" (ed. by Ivan Franceschini and Kevin Lin), *Made in China Yearbook 2016*, pp. 69–72, as stated by Ellen Friedman (p. 69), Kevin Slaten, and May Wong (p. 70); Anita Chan, "The Resistance of Walmart Workers in China: A Missed Opportunity", *ibid*, pp. 50–55, at 54–55. Chan assumes that foreign funding of NGOs as well as the lack thereof can have a "corroding effect on labour solidarity", and that this effect will exacerbate over time.

ternative between traditional, European style trade unions and the hitherto common cycle of repression and accommodation of labour issues as seen in China. [80]

Conclusion

As shown above, work and labour relations constitute a rapidly growing field of studies regarding the events of the last two decades. In contrast, formulating a perspective on more than 500 years is a challenge not usually taken by labour historians. Nevertheless, the diachronic view reveals structures of interest. The transition from a predominantly household-based, modestly market-oriented, or what Hill Gates would refer to as a *petty capitalist* socioeconomic regime since the late Ming to proletarianized wage labour from the late nineteenth century onwards did not concern the largest part of the working population. At present, the apex of wage labour may already have passed, yet with the process of urbanization or de-ruralization still ongoing, two tendencies converge which hold both conflicts and opportunities. Women's labour has always played a critical role, and the ushering in of socialist ideals of equality in labour has reversed patriarchal convictions, yet at a slow pace. Opening up to the world market under different conditions than after the Opium Wars has led to situations where role changes of employers and employees can produce amazing results and coincidences, as the contrast in the position of mining labourers in the first decade of the twentieth century in South Africa and in the twenty-first century in Zambia and Ghana illustrates. Not only asking whether China could have changed to become like Europe, but also considering whether Europe (or any other world region) could have become like China was one of the fundamental lines of thought of the California School when developing the paradigm of the *Great Divergence*. In consideration of the state of the field of Chinese labour studies within and outside of China, when transposed to the present and the future, this approach seems less counterfactual now than it was twenty years ago.

---

[80] William Hurst, "The Chinese Working Class: Made, Unmade, in Itself, for Itself, or None of the Above?", *Made in China Yearbook 2016*, pp. 16–19, at 19.

Suggested Reading

Bossen, Laurel and Hill Gates. *Bound Feet, Young Hands. Tracking the Demise of Footbinding in Village China* (Stanford, CA: Stanford University Press, 2017).

Bowles, Paul and John Harriss (eds), *Globalization and Labour in China and India: Impacts and Responses* (Houndmills: Palgrave Macmillan, 2009).

Bray, Francesca. *Technology and Gender. Fabrics of Power in Late Imperial China* (Berkeley, CA: University of California Press, 1997).

Chan, Anita. *China's Workers Under Assault: The Exploitation of Labor in a Globalizing Economy* (Armonk, NY: M.E. Sharpe, 2001).

Chesneaux, Jean. *The Chinese Labor Movement, 1919–1927*. Trans. H.M. Wright (Stanford, CA: Stanford University Press, 1968).

Dirlik, Arif. "Workers, Class, and the Socialist Revolution in China", in: Jan Lucassen (ed.), *Global Labour History: A State of the Art* (Bern, 2008), pp. 373–396.

Eyferth, Jacob (ed.). *How China Works: Perspectives on the Twentieth-Century Industrial Workplace* (London, 2006).

Eyferth, Jacob. *Eating Rice from Bamboo Roots. The Social History of a Community of Handicraft Papermakers in Rural Sichuan, 1920–2000* (Cambridge, MA: Harvard University Press, 2009).

Gold, Thomas, William Hurst, Jaeyoun Won, Li Qiang. *Laid-Off Workers in a Workers' State: Unemployment with Chinese Characteristics* (Houndmills: Palgrave Macmillan, 2010).

Hansson, Anders. *Chinese Outcasts. Discrimination and Emancipation in Late Imperial China* (Leiden and Boston: Brill, 1996).

Hershatter, Gail. *The Workers of Tianjin, 1900–1949* (Stanford, CA: Stanford University Press, 1986)

Honig, Emily. *Sisters and Strangers. Women in the Shanghai Cotton Mills, 1919–1949* (Stanford, CA: Stanford University Press, 1986).

Hsieh Bao Hua. *Concubinage and Servitude in Late Imperial China* (Lanham, MD: Lexington Books, 2014).

Lee Ching Kwan, *Against the Law. Labor Protests in China's Rustbelt and Sunbelt* (Berkeley, CA: University of California Press, 2007).

Liu Mingwei and Chris Smith (eds). *China at Work: Labour Process Perspective on the Transformation of Work and Employment in China* (Houndmills, 2016).

McQuaide, Shiling. "Writing Chinese Labor History: Changes and Continuities in Labour Historiography", *Labour/Le Travail*, Vol. 61, Spring 2008, pp. 215–237.

Perry, Elizabeth. *Anyuan: Mining China's Revolutionary Tradition* (Berkeley, CA: University of California Press, 2012).

Perry, Elizabeth. *Shanghai on Strike. The Politics of Chinese Labor* (Stanford, CA: Stanford University Press, 1993).

Pringle, Tim. *Trade Unions in China: The Challenge of Labour Unrest* (London: Routledge, 2011).

Ransmeier, Johanna S. *Sold People. Traffickers and Family Life in North China* (Cambridge, MA: Harvard University Press, 2017).

Wright, Tim. *Coal Mining in China's Economy and Society, 1895–1937* (Cambridge: Cambridge University Press, 1984).

Xu Dixin and Wu Chengming (eds). *Chinese Capitalism, 1522–1840* (Houndmills etc., 2000).

Zhang Xiaodan. "Bringing Ideology Back In: Chinese Labor Studies in a Time of Transformation", *International Labor and Working Class History*, 82 (Fall 2012), pp. 144–155.

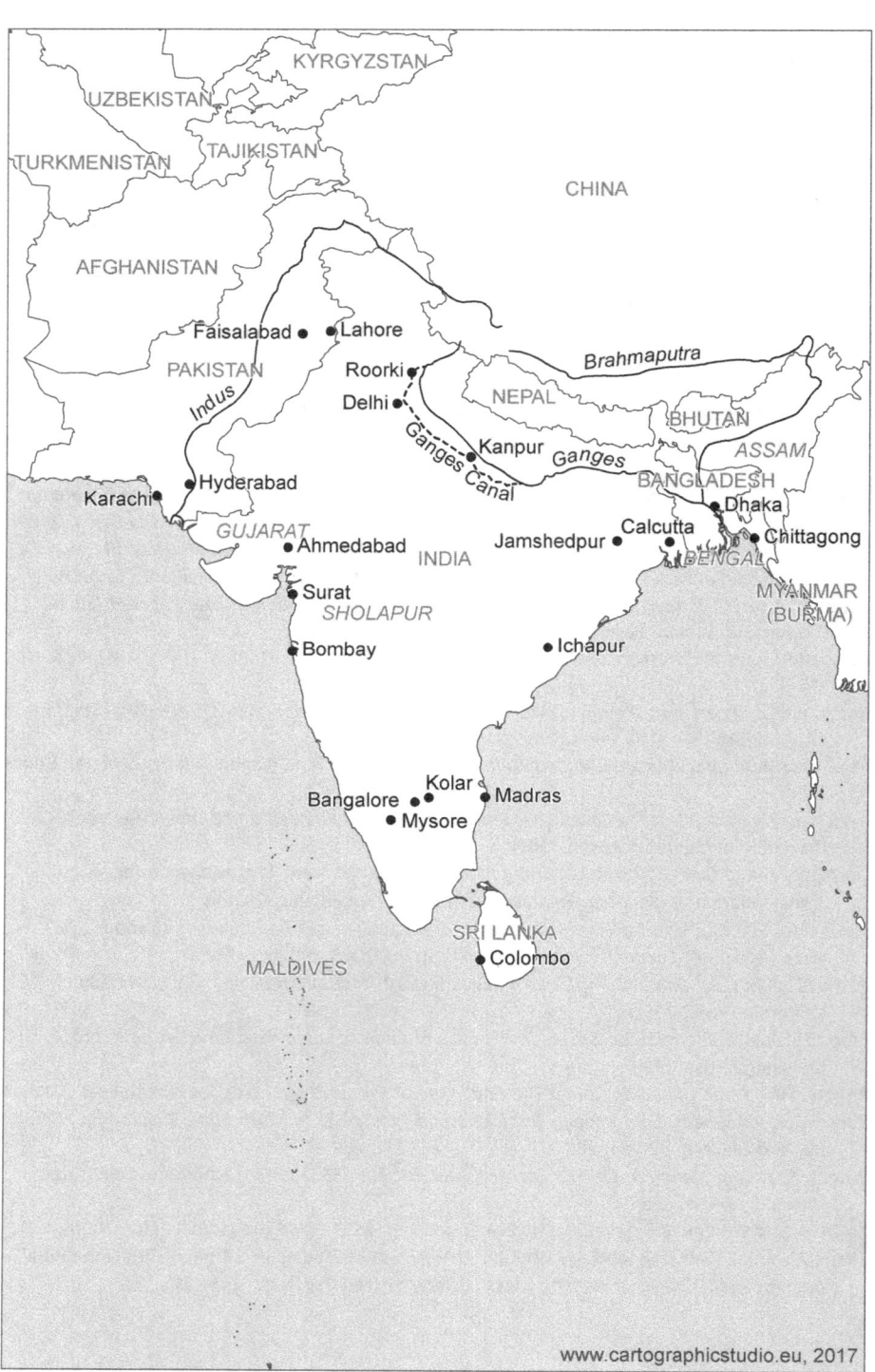

Rana P. Behal
2.2. South Asia*

The past twenty-five years or so have witnessed renewed scholarly interest in historical studies of labour in India and other parts of the world. This revival is distinctive both in terms of its location and its central concerns. It has emerged from the countries of the South and its preoccupations are not confined to the traditional working class alone. Earlier, the major emphasis of labour history was on the core countries, such as the USA, Canada, Western Europe, and Japan. Since then, there has been a shift of focus to nation states on the peripheries of world capitalism. The reversal of location and the broadening of the scope of labour history provide a basis for innovative global comparisons. As the dualities of free/unfree labour, wage-work/non-wage work, and formal/informal labour blur, labour historians have to take into account the multiplicity of relationships, locations, and temporalities that underpin labour forms and within which the individual worker is embedded.[1] These issues are being increasingly raised and discussed by historians in many parts of the world, including South Asia. In this essay I will attempt to relate the renewal of labour studies to the changing landscapes of labour in the South Asian countries of India, Pakistan, Sri Lanka, and Bangladesh.

India

Bringing labour into the public domain

We begin with a reflection on the changing traditions of Indian labour history writing.[2] Contrary to the long-held perception in the Indian labour historiography that Indian labour history began in the 1880s and 1890s, there has been a perceptible change concerning the periodization of labour history. Following in the tradition

---

* An earlier version of this essay was jointly authored by Chitra Joshi, Prabhu P. Mohapatra, and Rana P. Behal and published in: Joan Allen, Alan Campbell, and John McIlroy (eds), *Histories of Labour. National and International Perspectives* (Pontypool, 2010), pp. 290–314. The present essay owes much to their contributions.
1 Marcel van der Linden, *Workers of the World. Essays toward a Global Labor History* (Leiden, 2008).
2 For detailed, critical analyses of the Indian labour historiography, see Sabyasachi Bhattacharya, "Introduction", in: Rana P. Behal and Marcel van der Linden (eds), *India's Labouring Poor. Historical Studies c.1600–c.2000* (New Delhi, 2007), pp. 7–20; Chitra Joshi, "Histories of Indian Labour: Predicaments and Possibilities", *History Compass*, 6, 2 (2008), pp. 439–454; Prabhu P. Mohapatra, "Situating the Renewal: Reflections on Labour Studies in India", *Labour and Development*, 5 (1999), V.V. Giri National Labour Institute, pp. 1–30; Sanat Bose, "Indian Labour and its Historiography in Pre-Independence Period", *Social Scientist*, 13, 4 (1985), pp. 3–10.

DOI 10.1515/9783110424584-003

of European labour history and orthodox Marxism that privileged the Industrial Revolution as the harbinger of modern labour, Indian labour history was perceived as beginning with the arrival of modern industry during the 1880s and 1890s. The preceding period was perceived as "feudal" or "mercantile capitalism", and hence the "pre-history" of labour remained neglected. Jan Lucassen has questioned this binary of "modern labour" history and its perceived "pre-history" by presenting two empirically rich essays: on the Ichapur Gunpowder Factory, near Calcutta, in the 1790s, and on the Ganga Canal construction site in Roorki, in 1848–1849. In these essays he presents an analysis of the successful collective action of the labour force during the late eighteenth and mid-nineteenth centuries in India. Lucassen has demonstrated that the tradition of collective labour action existed before the building of India's railways.[3] Similarly, Ravi Ahuja's essays analyse labour relations in Madras, involving construction workers, artisan groups, transport workers, domestic workers, and watchmen/runners during the early period of colonial rule, between 1750 and 1800.[4] Prasannan Parthasarathi's essay offers a comparative analysis of prevailing wages in early colonial Madras city and British industry during the eighteenth century.[5] Michael Fisher's essay shows the employment of Indian maritime labourers on board the wooden, wind-powered European-owned vessels and with the advent and expansion of transoceanic shipping between India and Europe during the period 1600 to 1857.[6]

The bulk of writings on labour in the colonial context, however, appeared from the mid-nineteenth century onwards, with the development of modern industries such as textiles, jute, iron ore, gold and coal mining, tea, coffee and rubber plantations, and expanding infrastructural activities such as roads, railways, and irrigation systems. Two distinctly opposed approaches can be discerned in the official and nationalist writings on labour issues. The colonial state became actively involved with labour issues because of its concern with the supply of labour, beginning with the mobilization of labour for railways, plantations, and mining. The main objective of official policy was, on the one hand, to ensure a steady and adequate supply of suitable labour for the emerging industries and plantations, and, on the other, to "pro-

---

[3] Jan Lucassen, "Working at the Ichapur Gunpowder Factory in the 1790s" (Part I), *Indian Historical Review*, 39, 1 (2012), pp. 19–56, and *idem*, "Working at the Ichapur Gunpowder Factory in the 1790s" (Part II), *Indian Historical Review*, 39, 2 (2012), pp. 251–271; *idem*, "The Brickmakers' Strikes on the Ganges Canal in 1848–1849", in: Behal and van der Linden, *India's Labouring Poor*, pp. 47–84.
[4] Ravi Ahuja, "Labour Relations in an Early Colonial Context: Madras, c.1750–1800", *Modern Asian Studies*, 36, 4 (2002), pp. 793–826; *idem*, "The Origins of Colonial Labour Policy in Late Eighteenth-Century Madras", *International Review of Social History*, 44, 2 (1999), pp. 159–195; *idem*, "Labour Unsettled: Mobility and Protest in the Madras Region, 1750–1800", *Indian Economic and Social History Review*, 35, 4 (1998), pp. 381–404.
[5] Prasannan Parthasarathi, "Rethinking Wages and Competitiveness in the Eighteenth Century: Britain and South India", *Past and Present*, 158 (February 1998), pp. 79–109.
[6] Michael Fisher, "Working across the Seas: Indian Maritime Labourers in India, Britain, and in Between, 1600–1857", in: Behal and van der Linden, *India's Labouring Poor*, pp. 21–46.

tect" labour. Growing labour militancy and the growth of nationalist politics during the 1920s as well as the onset of the Depression in 1929 formed the backdrop to the appointment of a Royal Commission on Labour in India, which published a multi-volume report in 1930–1931. The main focus of the report remained on large industries and plantations, though there was a slight gesture towards seasonal and unregulated factories.

Complementing analysis at the state level, the second strand of writing on labour emerged during the reformist phase of Indian nationalism. Contemporary urban intelligentsia and foreign Christian missionaries articulated their concerns about labour. The British social reform tradition influenced some of the early Indian reformers, such as Sasipada Banerji in Bengal and Narayan Meghaji Lokhande in Bombay.[7] The nationalists adopted a more adversarial position, and Brahmo reformists such as Ram Kumar Vidyaratna and Dwarkanath Ganguly in Calcutta published *Coolie Kahani* and "Slave Trade in India" articles depicting the terrible work and living conditions of plantation labour in Assam in nationalist papers *Sanjibani* and *Bengalee* during 1880s.[8] The Rev. Charles Dowding, an English Christian missionary, published *Tea-Garden Coolies in Assam* in 1894, a very radical critique of the indentured regime.[9]

The post-World-War-I years in India, as elsewhere, constituted a period of intense upsurge in working-class activity: Bombay, Calcutta, Ahmedabad, Kanpur, Jamshedpur, Sholapur Assam, and other regions witnessed a series of strike actions. It was against the background of these events that the condition and history of labour emerged into the public domain and the realm of state policy. The establishment of the first organized federation of trade unions (All India Trade Union Congress) in 1920, legalization of trade unions in 1926, the appointment of the Royal Commission on Labour, and an official focus on the depression generated academic research publications in labour studies focusing for the first time on the condition of industrial and plantation workers and their standard of living and welfare.[10] Supporters

---

7 Dipesh Chakrabarty, "Sasipada Banerjee: A Study in the Nature of the First Contact of the Bengali Bhadralok with the Working Classes of Bengal", *Indian Historical Review*, 2 (1976), pp. 339–384; Rajnarayan Chandavarkar, *The Origin of Industrial Capitalism in India. Business Strategies and the Working Classes in Bombay, 1900–1940* (Cambridge, 1994), pp. 426–427.
8 Ram Kumar Vidyaratna's articles were translated and presented in book form to Lord Ripon, the Viceroy, as part of a memorandum to champion the cause of labour in Assam's tea gardens by the Indian Association. Dwarkanath Ganguly's articles were compiled and published as *Slavery in British Dominion* (Calcutta, 1972), p. vii; Bose, "Historiography", p. 8.
9 Rev. Charles Dowding, *Tea-Garden Coolies in Assam* (Calcutta, 1894).
10 Daniel H. Buchanan, *The Development of Capitalistic Enterprise in India* (New York, 1934); Margaret Read, *The Indian Peasant Uprooted* (London, 1931).

of workers' interests and trade unionists produced accounts of colonial labour policies and of the emergent labour and trade union movement.[11]

Two paradigms

Studies of labour in India became more prominent in the context of the strategies for planned economic development launched in the first decade after independence in the 1950s. To the nationalist leadership, industrialization was the preferred route for economic growth and modernization. Insofar as labour was recognized as a crucial "factor of production", its deployment, bargaining practices, and conflict behaviour became objects of methodical scrutiny. Since the 1950s two competing paradigms have dominated labour studies in India: one was defined by theories of modernization and the other by Marxism. Despite fundamental differences, the two paradigms shared certain similar assumptions. Both saw the formation of industrial factory labour and its action and behaviour through an optic of transition. In both these frameworks, the newly industrializing countries were perceived as being in a stage similar to the early stage of industrialization in advanced countries.[12] For modernization theorists, a major corollary of this transition in consciousness was the degree of commitment on the part of workers to the industrial way of life. The "labour commitment" thesis, as it came to be termed, posited that in the early stages of the industrialization process workers remained uncommitted to industrialism because of their rural and kinship connections. A mature industrialism required the full commitment of workers through an internalization of work norms and discipline and a complete severance of their ties with the land.[13] However, M.D. Morris's study of the emergence and deployment of the labour force in the Bombay textile mills struck a discordant note in the modernization thesis by suggesting that the standard arguments about the cultural unsuitability of Indian labour for industrial employment had no empirical basis in historical data.[14]

The Marxists explained the problems of modern industry by referring to colonial constraints. The craftsmen displaced by the process of deindustrialization were pushed back into agriculture instead of being absorbed into modern industry. This partial nature of industrialization had a profound effect on working-class formation. Thus,

---

11 Diwan Chaman Lall, *Coolie. The Story of Labour and Capital in India* (Lahore, 1932); Narayan Malhar Joshi, *The Trade Union Movement in India* (Bombay, 1927); B. Shiva Rao, *The Industrial Worker in India* (London, 1938).
12 Wilbert Ellis Moore and Arnold Feldman (eds), *Labor Commitment and Social Change in Developing Areas* (New York, 1960), p. 4.
13 Clark Kerr et al., *Industrialism and Industrial Man. The Problems of Labour and Management in Economic Growth* (London, 1962), pp. 170–174.
14 Morris David Morris, *The Emergence of an Industrial Labour Force in India. A Study of the Bombay Cotton Mills, 1854–1947* (Bombay, 1965).

M.N. Roy wrote: "The normal course of industrial development was obstructed in India. Industry did not grow through the successive phases of handicraft, manufacture, small factory, mechanofacture and then mass production. So the Indian worker has not been trained in industry. He lacks the proletarian tradition."[15] In 1940, the Marxist theoretician Rajani Palme Dutt examined the formation of the Indian working class in the crucible of colonial economic formation. He visualized the growth of working-class consciousness in the emerging anti-imperialist struggle, focusing mainly on the role of the Communist Party in imparting in the working class a revolutionary consciousness. The equation of working-class movement and consciousness with its institutions (trade unions and political party) and its leadership became the hallmark of subsequent detailed investigations into labour in India.[16]

A series of writings in the 1950s and 1960s by the left-wing trade union activists traced the growth of the labour movement and organization. Their focus was primarily on formal institutional history, on leaders and parties and not on the many conflicting currents and pressures from below that shaped the course of labour organization and politics.[17] In these accounts, the history of labour organization appears as the gradual unfolding of a politically conscious working class. It was difficult to grapple with the complexities of the historical context in India within the limits of such teleological frameworks.

Towards social history: beyond culturalist paradigms

A problem that Marxist histories had to continuously confront was the persistence of consciousness of caste, religion, and region among workers. In this situation, class-consciousness seemed a perpetually elusive goal. It was always "emergent", "elementary", "embryonic", or "incipient", gestating in a morass of primordialism. A second related problem was the continued existence of several forms of labour that were only partially proletarianized. Given such a scenario, a pure class-conscious working class seemed illusory.[18] However, the conventional framework of

---

15 M.N. Roy, *India in Transition* (Bombay, 1971), p. 113.
16 Rajani Palme Dutt, *India Today* (London, 1940), ch. XII.
17 Sanat Bose, *Capital and Labour in the Indian Tea Industry* (Bombay, 1954); Indrajit Gupta, *Capital and Labour in the Jute Industry* (Bombay, 1953); A.S. Mathur and Jagannath Swaroop Mathur, *Trade Union Movement in India* (Allahabad, 1957); Vasant B. Karnik, *Indian Trade Unions. A Survey* (Bombay, 1960); Giriraj K. Sharma, *Labour Movement in India: Its Past and Present* (Jullunder, 1963); Shiva Chandra Jha, *The Indian Trade Union Movement* (Calcutta, 1970); C. Revri, *The Indian Trade Union Movement, An Outline History, 1880–1947* (New Delhi, 1972); Sukomal Sen, *Working Class of India: History of Emergence and Movement, 1830–1970* (Calcutta, 1977).
18 Ranajit Dasgupta, "Material Conditions and Behavioural Aspects of Calcutta Working Class 1875–1899", Centre for Studies in Social Sciences, Occasional Paper No. 22 (Calcutta, 1979); Ira Mitra, "Growth of Trade Union Consciousness among Jute Mill Workers, 1920–40", *Economic and Political Weekly*, 16, 44/46 (1981), pp. 1839–1848; Dipesh Chakrabarty, "Class Consciousness and the Indian

Marxist labour history came to be vigorously debated even as the limits of alternative modernization models were becoming evident in the 1970s.

The present resurgence of interest in labour studies in India can be traced back to certain shifts since the late 1970s. The surge of interest in popular movements culminated on the one hand in the writings of what came to be known as the Subaltern Studies group in the early 1980s and, on the other, a series of independent publications on labour. With the exception of Dipesh Chakrabarty's work, the dominant concern of the historians of the Subaltern Studies group was with peasant movements. This was also a period when the influence of ideas drawn from E.P. Thompson's approach to social history became manifest. Two seemingly contradictory trends in writing emerged against this background. A series of writings since the late 1970s focused on the social origins of labour and tried to understand the transformative impact of modern industries. Others critiqued reductionist approaches that characterized modern industry as an agent of change: industrial culture in India in this framework was perceived as essentially premodern.

Historians writing social histories of labour probed into the social origins of workers and their caste and community background. Among the pioneering works was Ranajit Dasgupta's study of workers in the Calcutta jute mills, their experience of work, discipline, and protest. For Dasgupta, as for other Marxist writers of the 1970s and early 1980s, working-class culture was located within a model of transition, which assumed that pre-industrial forms of consciousness – ties of community and religion – would be gradually displaced by mature forms of class consciousness. Dasgupta's impassioned defence of class provided the context for a very lively debate with critics of his reductionist argument.[19]

A critique of reductionist frameworks was powerfully articulated by Dipesh Chakrabarty. Chakrabarty carried on a sharp polemic against the dominant assumptions in labour history in India. Most writings, he argued, even those more sensitive to issues of culture, tended, in the end, to reduce culture to certain economic variables.[20] Chakrabarty's radical culturalism disturbed the certainties of conventional Marxist approaches and presaged some of the later shifts in the historiography of labour. In opposition to Marxist writings that see working-class history in terms of a continuous unfolding of class identities, Chakrabarty's account valorizes certain fixed notions of caste and community identities. While Chakrabarty critiques frameworks, which reduce culture to economic determinants, he tends to reify culture by seeing identities in terms of fixed cultural meanings.

Working Class: Dilemmas of Marxist Historiography", *Journal of Asian and African Studies*, 23, 1–2 (1988), pp. 21–31.
19 See, for example, Dipesh Chakrabarty and Ranajit Das Gupta, "Some Aspects of Labour History in Bengal in the Nineteenth Century: Two Views", Centre for Studies in Social Sciences, Occasional Paper No. 40 (Calcutta, 1981).
20 Dipesh Chakrabarty, *Rethinking Working-Class History. Bengal 1890–1940* (Princeton, NJ, 1988).

A series of other writings since the1980s have developed a critique of the teleological assumptions underlining liberal and Marxist historiography; yet they do not identify with the culturalist logic of Chakrabarty's framework. A number of labour historians have engaged critically with issues of culture and community, but from a differing perspective. Notable among these are the outstanding contributions by Rajnarayan Chandavarkar and Chitra Joshi on the history of textile workers in Bombay and Kanpur respectively. Their writings have questioned the assumption that the persistence of primordial ties of community and religion, as well as the rural connection, acted as a hindrance to labour consciousness or militancy. Their work has shown that the cultural and community ties were continuously reworked in the neighbourhood, streets, living and leisure spaces of working-class areas and subject to changes and ruptures.[21]

Other studies over the past two decades have enriched and complicated notions of community and identity in the urban industrial context. Nandini Gooptu's work on the urban poor in North India demonstrates how particular patterns of exclusion and subordination of the "labouring poor" in the interwar years created the basis for new networks of solidarity in the 1920s and 1930s. But solidarities around these movements were often fragile and fractured.[22] New alignments in the cities also involved the creation of coalitions of lower-caste groups in their struggles against upper castes: in cities like Kanpur, castes considered ritually "impure" came together in opposition to Brahmanical norms of purity and pollution.[23] Yet these assertions of community involved processes of appropriation and contestation. Nair's work on the Kolar goldfields in South India, for instance, shows how the Adi Dravidas contested Brahmanical distinctions between "pure" and "impure"; yet in trying to acquire status and respectability they tended to reaffirm many of these distinctions.[24] These shifts and realignments illustrate how lines of difference between communities were drawn through conflicts and confrontations.

---

21 Rajnarayan Chandavarkar, "Workers' Politics and the Mill Districts in Bombay between the Wars", *Modern Asian Studies*, 15, 3 (1981), pp. 603–647; idem, "From Neighbourhood to Nation", in: Meena Menon and Neera Adarkar (eds), *One Hundred Years, One Hundred Voices. The Millworkers of Girangaon. An Oral History* (Calcutta, 2004), pp. 7–80; Chitra Joshi, "Bonds of Community, Ties of Religion: Kanpur Textile Workers in the Early Twentieth Century", *Indian Economic and Social History Review*, 22, 3 (1985), pp. 251–280; idem, *Lost Worlds. Indian Labour and its Forgotten Histories* (Delhi, 2003).
22 Nandini Gooptu, *The Politics of the Urban Poor in Early Twentieth-Century India* (Cambridge, 2001), pp. 185–243.
23 Joshi, *Lost Worlds*, pp. 245–256.
24 Janaki Nair, *Miners and Millhands. Work, Culture and Politics in Princely Mysore* (New Delhi, 1998), pp. 101–106.

Working-class politics: changing frames

The shifts in historiographical perspectives over the past few decades have raised important issues concerning the nature of working-class politics. The conventional Marxist view of working-class politics was exemplified in Sukomal Sen's 1977 work,[25] which narrated a linear growth of trade union organizations and leadership since the colonial period. The study of organization and leadership became synonymous with the study of working-class politics as a whole. This teleological frame was seriously questioned by Chakrabarty. He problematized the conventional equation of trade union leadership with the workers' movement and argued that both were embedded within the overarching "pre-bourgeois hierarchical culture". Chakrabarty's radical revisionism evoked strong debates within academic Marxist history writing.[26] Raj Chandavarkar's work on Bombay textile mills located working-class sectionalism and solidarities within the peculiarities of the labour market in the city. The remarkable fact that Bombay workers could sustain eight general strikes of long duration between 1919 and 1938 was attributed by Chandavarkar not so much to the communists and their ideologies as to the micro-politics and intersecting networks in the neighbourhoods where the colonial state, employers, and the communists competed for influence with each other and local *dadas*, jobbers, and money lenders. The solidarities displayed in general strikes were contingent upon particular political conjunctures rather than representing the results of the unfolding of workers' consciousness.[27]

Moments of upsurge in Ahmedabad, Bombay, or Kanpur were momentous times in workers' lives – times that shaped their collective memory and refigured the social space of the city. In workers' imaginations, Kanpur of the 1930s, for instance, became "Red Kanpur". In the present context, when former centres of industry are in decline and memories of collective solidarities and struggles like that of 1928–1929 in Bombay or 1938 in Kanpur have been virtually effaced, the recovery of such moments by labour historians has special significance. Recent work on Ahmedabad, Bombay, and Kanpur using oral accounts of workers provides some insights into what such events meant to workers, both in the past and in the transformed present.[28]

---

25 Sen, *Working Class of India*.
26 Ranajit Das Gupta, "Indian Working Class and Some Recent Historiographical Issues", *Economic and Political Weekly*, 31, 8 (1996), pp. 27–31; Parimal Ghosh, "Communalism and Colonial Labour: Experience of Calcutta Jute Mill Workers, 1880–1930", *Economic and Political Weekly*, 25, 30 (1990), pp. 61–72; Amiya Kumar Bagchi, "Working Class Consciousness", *Economic and Political Weekly*, 25, 30 (1990), pp. 54–60.
27 Rajnarayan Chandavarkar, *Imperial Power and Popular Politics. Class, Resistance and the State in India, c.1850–1950* (Cambridge, 1998), ch. 5.
28 Jan Breman, *The Making and Unmaking of an Industrial Working Class. Sliding Down the Labour Hierarchy in Ahmedabad, India* (Amsterdam, 2004), pp. 201–231; Menon and Adarkar, *One Hundred Years*; Joshi, *Lost Worlds*, chs 6 and 9.

While the social history of labour dominated these debates, the study of working-class politics did not disappear altogether from Indian labour history. Sabyasachi Bhattacharya's pioneering essay on the politics of Bombay strikes from 1928 to 1929 critically analysed colonial state action, mill owners' strategies, and the responses of workers and the communist trade unions within a finely nuanced theoretical framework that took into account the interplay of structural and ideological determinants.[29] Dilip Simeon's study of the labour movement in the coal and steel industries of eastern India analysed the institutional structures of the labour movement. But it broke new ground in shifting the explanation of the ebb and flow of the movement from leadership initiatives to rank-and-file pressure.[30] Subho Basu's work traversed the terrain of the labour movement in the jute mills of Calcutta, territory already made familiar in Chakrabarty's work, in order to uncover the complexity of conflicts between European-manager-dominated local government and often unruly workers' neighbourhoods. Workers' politics were scarcely confined to the flimsy structures of trade unions but were shaped by collective experience forged daily on shop floors and neighbourhoods.[31] Janaki Nair's study of workers' movements in the former princely state of Mysore, in Kolar goldmines, and Bangalore city similarly examines the contradictory pressures that went into the making of the labour politics of the 1920s and 1930s.[32] Shashi Bhushan Upadhyay's study of Bombay workers in the late-nineteenth and early decades of the twentieth century looks at the interface between the regional Maratha identity and trans- regional identities of religion, nation, and class.[33]

The shifts in historiographical perspectives have raised important issues concerning the place of the political in working-class lives. Beginning with Chandavarkar's 1981 essay on the working-class neighbourhood in Bombay in the 1920s and 1930s, other writings have looked outside the formal structures of organization in order to understand the political culture of the working class. Chandavarkar scrutinized the close inter-connections between the neighbourhood and the factory, arguing that spaces outside work, such as the gymnasium and the street, were crucial to the generalization of disputes that originated in the workplace. In the postwar context of the 1920s, when repressive measures by the state and mill owners restricted the activities of radical trade unionists, networks forged in the neighbourhood be-

---

29 Sabyasachi Bhattacharya, "Capital and Labour in Bombay City, 1928–29", *Economic and Political Weekly*, 16, 42/43 (1981), pp. 36–44.
30 Dilip Simeon, *The Politics of Labour under Late Colonialism. Workers, Unions and the State in Chota Nagpur, 1928–1939* (Delhi, 1995), ch. 2.
31 Subho Basu, *Does Class Matter? Colonial Capital and Workers' Resistance in Bengal, 1890–1937* (New Delhi, 2004).
32 Nair, *Miners and Millhands*.
33 Shashi Bhushan Upadhyay, *Existence, Identity and Mobilization. The Cotton Millworkers of Bombay 1890–1919* (New Delhi, 2004), pp. 209–211.

came crucial for mobilization by communists in Bombay.[34] These contestatory practices also tell us about the ways in which rules were created and actively redefined through worker practices. In recent times, with the decline of traditional large-scale industries and a proliferation of small workshops, such everyday forms of resistance possess greater significance. Studies of power-loom workers in South India and of diamond workers in Surat, for example, show how practices such as the giving of *baki* (advance pay) were often manipulated by workers to secure better terms for themselves.[35] Recent work on the labour history of indentured labour regimes in Assam tea plantations has focused on the politics of labour and labour laws. Rana Behal and Nitin Varma have analysed the nature of labour laws, labour relations, and resistance in the indentured plantation regimes in colonial Assam.[36]

Indian labour in the global arena

Yet another new area that has recently attracted the attention of labour historians is the history of India's global workers, its maritime labour force. Ravi Ahuja's two essays bring out the story of the lascars, the Indian seafarers employed by European-owned shipping companies, and their mobility across territorial frontiers and cultural spheres during the nineteenth and twentieth centuries. This South Asian seafaring labour force, he argues, was structured at the bottom of a rigidly racist hierarchy in the maritime labour market of that period.[37] Gopalan Balachandran's work delves deeper into the lives of Indian seafarers – their social and regional origins, experiences of living ashore in foreign ports, and their transformation into a global labour force during the course of their employment by European shipping companies.[38] Aaron Jaffer's work on Indian lascars covers the period from the late eighteenth century to the mid-nineteenth century, and Matthias van Rossum's essay highlights the

---

34 Chandavarkar, "Workers' Politics and the Mill Districts".
35 Geert De Neve, *The Everyday Politics of Labour. Working Lives in India's Informal Economy* (New Delhi, 2005), pp. 169–203; Miranda Engelshoven, "Diamonds and Patels: A Report on the Diamond Industry of Surat", in: Jonathan P. Parry, Jan Breman, and Karin Kapadia (eds), *The Worlds of Indian Industrial Labour* (New Delhi, 1999), pp. 353–378.
36 Rana P. Behal, *One Hundred Years of Servitude. Political Economy of Tea Plantations in Colonial Assam* (New Delhi, 2014), ch. 6; Nitin Varma, *Coolies of Capitalism. Assam Tea and the Making of Coolie Labour* (Berlin, 2016).
37 Ravi Ahuja, "Mobility and Containment: The Voyages of South Asian Seamen, c. 1900–1960", in: Behal and van der Linden, *India's Labouring Poor*, pp. 111–142; Ravi Ahuja, "The Age of the 'Lascar': South Asian Seafarers in the Times of Imperial Steam Shipping", in: Joya Chatterji and David Washbrook (eds), *Routledge Handbook of the South Asian Diaspora* (London, 2014), p. 110.
38 G. Balachandran, *Globalizing Labour? Indian Seafarers and World Shipping, c. 1870–1945* (New Delhi, 2012).

employment of Indian sailors on the Dutch East India Company's ships.[39] Jaffer focuses on the conditions of work and modes of resistance put up by Indian sailors to the punitive regimes and regulations on board the European merchant ships.

Gender and labour

Until quite recently there was no serious engagement with questions of gender and women's work in labour history writing in India. At one level this was because women remained invisible in the pages of history in general, while labour historians, for their part, did little to make them visible for posterity. At another level it was because, with few exceptions, labour history in India remained, till very recently, factory-centric.[40] An exclusive focus on the factory as the site of productive work and workers' activity meant a neglect of sites of work outside the factory, in rural areas, and within homes.

A key issue addressed in discussions on women and work in the European context was the issue of the displacement of women from factory industries by the late nineteenth century. This question triggered an animated debate around the emergence of the "male breadwinner" in working-class families.[41] In India the situation was different, yet many of the issues emerging from the "breadwinner" debate resonate in discussions on women and work. Samita Sen's study of women in the jute mills of Bengal in the colonial period brings two important issues into focus: the first is the significance of ideological issues in understanding the gendered composition of the labour force; the second is the connection between rural work and women's lives.[42] Sen brings out the shared assumptions underlining the masculinist discourse of mill managers and male-dominated unions that legitimized the exclusion of women by valorizing ideals of motherhood and domesticity.

---

39 Aaron Jaffer, *Lascars and Indian Ocean Seafaring, 1780–1860: Shipboard Life, Unrest and Mutiny* (Rochester, 2015); Matthias van Rossum, "Claiming their Rights? Indian Sailors under the Dutch East India Company (VOC)", in: Maria Fusaro et al. (eds), *Law, Labour and Empire. Comparative Perspectives on Seafarers, c. 1500–1800* (London, 2015), pp. 272–286.
40 Douglas Haynes, "Artisan Cloth-Producers and the Emergence of Powerloom Manufacture in Western India 1920–1950", *Past and Present*, 172 (2001), pp. 170–198; Tirthankar Roy, *Rethinking Economic Change in India: Labour and Livelihood* (London, 2005).
41 See, for instance, Colin Creighton, "The Rise of the Male Breadwinner Family: A Reappraisal", *Comparative Studies in Society and History*, 38, 2 (1996), pp. 310–337; Angélique Janssens, "The Rise and Decline of the Male Breadwinner Family? An Overview of the Debate", *International Review of Social History*, 42, Supplement (1997), pp. 1–23; Wally Seccombe, "Patriarchy Stabilized: The Construction of the Male Breadwinner Wage Norm in Nineteenth-Century Britain", *Social History*, 11, 1 (1986), pp. 53–76.
42 Samita Sen, *Women and Labour in Late Colonial India. The Bengal Jute Industry* (Cambridge, 1999), pp. 21–53, 89–141, and idem, "Gendered Exclusion: Domesticity and Dependence in Bengal", *International Review of Social History*, 42 (1997), pp. 65–86.

The rural ties of workers have usually been examined in terms of the masculinist assumptions that denote the urban as "main" and women's earnings as "supplementary". The obverse – the contribution of the family in the village, particularly of women, to the reproduction of labour – is rarely recognized. Their contribution was important in sowing, weeding, reaping, winnowing – almost all operations apart from ploughing. The contribution of women within the family was in fact often critical in providing the links connecting the working-class household in the city with the village. Overall, however, Sen's argument about the hegemonic power of ideas of seclusion is problematic. Within this logic, women marginalized from public employment retreat into the home and domesticity. The ways in which women may contest normative ideas or try to exercise their agency are not taken into account.[43]

The idea of a "male breadwinner", never quite an adequate category, is very dubious in today's context. In a scenario when traditional large industries are in decline and there is an expansion of "informal" work, women's waged work at home is the basis of subsistence for large numbers of urban working-class families. What we see today in fact points towards a "feminized" workforce, with women engaged in a range of activities in households and small industrial units.[44] What implications do these changes have for the production of gendered identities, male and female? Recent studies look at the ways in which the everyday culture of work in industrial establishments goes into the making of urban masculinities.[45] Recent writings argue that, with the decline of employment in traditional centres of industry and the erosion of spaces from which men derived their sense of masculinity in the past, there was a crisis of male identities.[46]

The informal sector and the labouring poor

But by far the most significant shift in focus in the recent historiography has been in the direction of embracing the concept of workers' history in the informal sector, for so long excluded from the purview of mainstream Marxist and liberal moderniza-

---

[43] For an interesting essay that looks at some of the ways in which women exercised their agency in their day-to-day lives, see Radha Kumar, "Sex and Punishment among Mill-Workers in Early-Twentieth-Century Bombay", in: Michael R. Anderson and Sumit Guha (eds), *Changing Concepts of Rights and Justice in South Asia* (New Delhi, 2000), pp. 179–197. See also Chitra Joshi, "Notes on the Breadwinner Debate: Gender and Household Strategies in Working-Class Families", *Studies in History*, 18, 2 (2002), pp. 261–274.
[44] These changes were grudgingly recognized in government policy. See, particularly, *Shramshakti. Report of the National Commission on Self-Employed Women and Women in the Informal Sector* (New Delhi, 1988).
[45] Shankar Ramaswami, "Masculinity, Respect, and the Tragic: Themes of Proletarian Humor in Contemporary Industrial Delhi", in: Behal and van der Linden, *India's Labouring Poor*, pp. 203–228.
[46] Chitra Joshi, "On 'De-industrialization' and the Crisis of Male Identities", *International Review of Social History*, 47 (2002), special issue, pp. 159–175.

tion accounts. The informal sector, initially identified with urban self-employment, was viewed as the solution to the growing crisis of employment generation through industrialization. The movement of labour from the "traditional" and agricultural sector to the "modern" industrial sector was now seen to have included a wayside stop in the urban informal sector. The dualism of a modern and a traditional sector was replaced by the dualism of a formal and an informal sector. The failure of the Bombay textile strike in 1982–1983, the massive restructuring of the textile mill industry, and the shift to power looms highlighted the accelerating process of informalization.[47]

The analytical division between "formal" and "informal" sectors found expression in Holmström's 1976 study, where the image of the walled-in citadel of the formal sector surrounded by a vast, unorganized sector was first utilized.[48] Yet the concept of an informal sector and its explicit dualism was simultaneously critiqued by Jan Breman, drawing on his longitudinal fieldwork in the Southern Gujarat region, which was then embarking on a path of rapid industrialization. Breman pointed out that the vast majority of informal workers were not labouring in urban locations but were to be found in the agrarian sector and in non-agrarian rural sites.[49]

Historians have increasingly focused attention on the linkage between informal and formal labour. Chandavarkar and Joshi had pointed to the intimate links between the two. Others, such as Sabyasachi Bhattacharya, have argued for the need for a different category – the labouring poor – to indicate the permanently transitional status of workers who moved across the porous boundaries between industrial waged employment, on the one hand, and non-waged homework and self-employment of various kinds on the other.[50] While the category of "labouring poor" has the merit of incorporating forms of labour usually excluded from standard Marxist descriptions of working class, its usefulness as an analytical category that can substitute for an ideal type "working class" is an issue historians are still grappling with. Studies of informal labour have highlighted two distinct processes of informalization: from above through a dismantling of the existing formal sector, and from below, through the circulation of seasonal migrant and casual, footloose labour.[51]

---

47 *Report on Conditions of Work and Promotion of Livelihoods in the Unorganised Sector* (New Delhi, 2007), p. 4.
48 Mark Holmström, *South Indian Factory Workers: Their Life and Their World* (Cambridge, 1976).
49 Jan Breman, "A Dualistic Labour System? A Critique of the 'Informal Sector' Concept", *Economic and Political Weekly*, 11, 48–50 (1976), pp. 1870–1876, 1905–1908, and 1939–1944.
50 Sabyasachi Bhattacharya, "The Labouring Poor and their Notion of Poverty: Late 19th and Early 20th Century Bengal", *Labour and Development*, 3 (1998), pp. 1–23, and *idem*, "Introduction", in: *idem* and Jan Lucassen (eds), *Workers in the Informal Sector. Studies in Labour History 1800–2000* (New Delhi, 2005), p. 4.
51 See Arjan de Haan, "The *Badli* System in Industrial Labour Recruitment: Managers' and Workers' Strategies in Calcutta's Jute Industry", in: Parry *et al.*, *Worlds of Indian Industrial Labour*, pp. 271–301; Douglas E. Haynes, "Just Like A Family? Recalling the Relations of Production in the Textile Industries of Surat and Bhiwandi, 1940–60", in: *ibid.*, pp. 141–169; Chitra Joshi, "Hope and Despair: Tex-

Recent studies by Barbara Harriss-White, Nandini Gooptu, and Rohini Hensman have made a significant contribution to understanding the role of the state, worker resistance, and organization in shaping the worlds of informal labour.[52]

Bondage and unfree labour: old and new

Labour history writing, focused as it was on urban, factory labour, had consistently marginalized rural labour relations. In the 1970s a vigorous controversy on the mode of production in agriculture inconclusively debated the extent to which capitalist relations had penetrated agriculture. The debate focused on key issues such as the "semi-feudal" in labour relations and the existence of "debt bondage" in labour in large parts of rural India.[53] Major contributors to this debate were Jan Breman, Utsa Patnaik, and Sudipto Mundle.[54]

These debates on contemporary forms of "unfree" labour have parallels in the new historical studies on forms of labour unfreedom. Gyan Prakash's provocative work viewed "debt bondage" as a construction of "colonial discourse".[55] His radical view, which denied the existence of "debt bondage" in the precolonial period and gave primacy in its construction to colonial discourse, has in turn been contested by several scholars.[56] The legal distinction between free and unfree labour has been at the heart of most writings on histories of servitude and freedom. However, recent research on colonial labour laws has problematized the conceptual divide between free and unfree labour. One area of investigation has been around the colonial laws of indenture in plantations inside India and in overseas colonies, which immobilized labour after transporting them over long distances.[57] Traditionally, labour

---

tile Workers in Kanpur in 1937–38 and the 1990s", in: *ibid.*, pp. 171–203; Dilip Simeon, "Work and Resistance in the Jharia Coalfield", in: *ibid.*, pp. 43–75.

52 Barbara Harriss-White and Nandini Gooptu, "Mapping India's World of Unorganized Labour", *Socialist Register 2001*, pp. 89–118; Rohini Hensman, "Organizing Against the Odds: Women in India's Informal Sector", in: *ibid.*, pp. 249–257. See also Barbara Harriss-White, *India Working. Essays on Society and Economy* (Cambridge, 2003).

53 The debate was carried on in the pages of *Economic and Political Weekly* and published later as Utsa Patnaik (ed.), *Agrarian Relations and Accumulation. The "Mode of Production" Debate in India* (Bombay, 1990).

54 Jan Breman, *Patronage and Exploitation. Changing Agrarian Relations in South Gujarat, India* (Berkeley, CA, 1974); Utsa Patnaik, "Introduction", in: Utsa Patnaik and Manjari Dingwaney (eds), *Chains of Servitude. Bondage and Slavery in India* (New Delhi, 1985), pp. 1–34; Sudipto Mundle, *Backwardness and Bondage. Agrarian Relations in a South Bihar District* (New Delhi, 1979).

55 Gyan Prakash, *Bonded Histories Genealogies of Labour Servitude in Colonial India* (Cambridge, 1990).

56 Neeladri Bhattacharya, *Labouring Histories. Agrarian Labour and Colonialism* (Noida, 2004); Jan Breman, *Labour Bondage in West India. From Past to Present* (New Delhi, 2007).

57 Rana P. Behal and Prabhu P. Mohapatra, "'Tea and Money versus Human Life': The Rise and Fall of the Indenture System in the Assam Tea Plantations 1840–1908", in: E. Valentine Daniel, Henry

history had seen labour law mainly as a post-World-War-II phenomena and colonial labour policy was construed as one of "laissez faire". In stark contrast, recent important studies of labour regulation have constructed a history of state intervention in the labour market from the early colonial period in the form of the master and servant laws.[58]

Emerging trends

The historiography of Indian labour has oscillated between conceptualizing the Indian experience as merely an instance of Eurocentric capitalist development and as uniquely indigenous. The renewal of labour history in recent decades has been marked by a definite movement away from this somewhat sterile conceptual straitjacket. The founding of the Association of Indian Labour Historians (AILH) in 1996 was, at least in part, a reflection of this renewal. Since its inception the AILH has sought with some success to provide a forum for intellectual interaction between labour historians from India and from developed and developing countries, as well as trade unionists and activists from other social movements. The last decade or so, in fact, has seen similar initiatives in many other countries of the south, marking what Marcel van der Linden has referred to as the "globalization of labour history".[59]

What is common to many of these associations is their attempt to break out of old Eurocentric frames and their search for other comparisons, other temporalities. The themes on which AILH conferences have focused include questions of "transition", marginality, mobility, skill and labour process, law, labour regimes and labour markets, informalization, and rural labour. The publication of essays presented at the conferences reflects the major paradigm shifts in the historiography of labour today: the turn towards a focus on the history of labour in the informal sector and the move towards a new comparative global history.[60]

Active interaction between scholars has been complemented with the creation and sharing of materials to promote labour studies. In Delhi, for instance, the

---

Bernstein, and Tom Brass (eds), *Plantations, Proletarians and Peasants in Colonial Asia* (London, 1992), pp. 142–172; Prabhu P. Mohapatra, "Assam and the West Indies, 1860–1920: Immobilizing Plantation Labour", in: Douglas Hay and Paul Craven (eds), *Masters, Servants, and Magistrates in Britain and the Empire, 1562–1955* (Chapel Hill, NC, 2004), pp. 455–480.

58 Prabhu P. Mohapatra, "Regulated Informality: Legal Constructions of Labour Relations in Colonial India 1814–1926", in: Bhattacharya and Lucassen, *Workers*, pp. 65–96; Michael Anderson, "India, 1858–1930: The Illusion of Free Labour", in: Hay and Craven, *Masters*, pp. 422–454.

59 Marcel van der Linden, "Labour History: An International Movement", *Labour History*, 89 (2005), pp. 225–233.

60 Behal and van der Linden, *India's Labouring Poor*; Marcel van der Linden and Prabhu P. Mohapatra (eds), *Labour Matters. Towards Global History* (New Delhi, 2009); Sabyasachi Bhattacharya (ed.), *Towards a New History of Work* (New Delhi, 2014); Sabyasachi Bhattacharya and Rana P. Behal (eds), *The Vernacularization of Labour Politics* (New Delhi, 2016).

AILH was instrumental in setting up a specialized digital repository of documentary, visual, and oral resources on labour.[61] These efforts have been important in energizing a new generation of scholars of labour and in creating a space for labour studies within academia.

Pakistan

India and Pakistan, the two newly emerging independent states in South Asia at the end of colonial rule in 1947, shared a common history of labour relations, labour laws, labour politics, and labour life during the colonial period. This equation was to change after the partition of the Indian subcontinent in 1947 into two independent nations. At independence, the majority of Pakistan's 75 million inhabitants were dependent upon agriculture for their livelihood. The country had inherited a small and fragile industrial base comprising only nine per cent of the total industry of the pre-partition period. The numerical strength of its working class in 1949 was estimated at 482,165, i.e. just 0.63% of Pakistan's population were wage earners employed in factories, mines, on the railways, or tea plantations. A third of these workers were organized into 150 trade unions, with a total membership of around 190,000, most of them working on the railways. Trade unions existed for the railways, post offices, seaports, textiles, airports, and to some extent cement factories. The majority of this labour was concentrated in urban centres such as Karachi, Faisalabad, and Hyderabad in West Pakistan. Karachi, the port city and the capital, had thirty-six unions with 15,000 workers. In East Bengal a sizeable number of workers (27,000) on the tea plantations were unionized.[62]

Aware of its meagre industrial assets and impoverished population, Pakistan's leaders, like their Indian counterparts, decided that industrialization was the route to economic growth. To encourage industrialization and foster a class of private entrepreneurs, in April 1948 Mohammad Ali Jinnah announced a policy of industrialization.[63] The state policy of promoting industrial development remained in vogue during 1950s and 1960s. Most of this industrial development was centred around Karachi and fostered the concentration of the newly generated wealth and industry in fewer hands.[64] The government took direct control of several industries: arms and munitions; hydroelectric power generation; and the manufacture of railway wagons,

---

[61] The archives are freely accessible at www.indialabourarchives.org.
[62] Nikki R. Keddie, "Labor Problems of Pakistan", *Journal of Asian Studies*, 16, 4 (1957), pp. 575–589; *History of Labour in South Asia-Pakistan*, www.nutufpak.org, p. 3.
[63] Zafar Shaheed, *The Labour Movement in Pakistan. Organization and Leadership in Karachi in the 1970s* (New York, 2007).
[64] *Ibid.*, p. 17.

telephones, telegraphs, and wireless apparatus. Postal and telegraph services were already owned by the state.[65]

The government's commitment to rapid industrialization in the 1950s coincided with a period of "political instability" in Pakistan's history. The inability of the civilian government of the Muslim League to hold on to power and an army coup led to the imposition of military rule under General Ayub Khan. During Ayub Khan's rule (1958–1969) bureaucrats and ex-army officers began directly running major industrial units and continued the policy of rapid industrialization. This was an era of unprecedented growth in the wealth and holdings of Pakistan's major industrial houses. They moved into banking and insurance, which supplied them with funds for further expansion.[66]

Among the earliest labour history writings in the independent state of Pakistan is an essay by Nikki R. Keddie, published in 1957, before the imposition of martial law. This essay focused on contemporary labour in Pakistan after independence, taking up wide-ranging issues of industrial expansion, employment, labour relations, wages, absenteeism, gender, child labour, strikes and work, state labour policy, labour movements, trade unions, and living conditions in urban industrial centres.[67] With the exception of Zafar Shaheed's work on Karachi's textile working class during the 1960s and 1970s, no subsequent scholarship has offered such an in-depth study of the labour history of the post-independence era.

Karachi working class

Zafar Shaheed's participatory-observation ethnographic study is an excellent social history of labour in the Karachi textile industry and remains the most nuanced and valuable contribution to the literature on labour in and the labour history of Pakistan in the post-independence era.[68] His work (which was not published until three decades after its completion) examines the nature of labour resistance and labour's diverse ethnicity at the workplace and in Karachi's working-class neighbourhoods during the 1960s and 1970s. This study covers one of most historic and crucial periods in Pakistan's history, one that witnessed emerging collaboration among students, left-leaning groups, the urban poor, and labour activists in the reorganization of trade unions. In the late 1960s this joint collaboration brought about a mass civil disobedience movement aimed at dislodging Ayub Khan's military regime. Shaheed's study is based on empirical material and fieldwork focusing on recruitment processes, middlemen such as jobbers, professional trade union leaders, and the emerging leader-

---

65 Ibid.
66 Kamran Asdar Ali, *Communism in Pakistan. Politics and Class Activism 1947–1972* (London, 2015), p. 172.
67 Keddie, "Labor Problems of Pakistan".
68 Shaheed, *Labour Movement in Pakistan*.

ship from among the ranks of the working class.[69] In 1972 the struggles reached a new highpoint when workers occupied a significant part of the city.[70]

Labour laws and trade unions

Among later writings on labour history, those by Ali Amjad and Christopher Candland analyse issues of legality and institutional reforms.[71] Ali's methodology is that of the comparative study of labour laws and labour organizations in Pakistan and India during colonial rule and its aftermath. Similarly, Candland focuses on a comparative study of industrialization policies, trade union movements, and labour legislation in Pakistan and India after independence. The changing nature of labour laws and their impact on labour relations and the status of trade unions in post-independent Pakistan are presented in detail. These authors have shown that from its inception the state of Pakistan, both during civilian and martial rule, was hostile towards working-class rights and welfare. Both authors have argued that state policies favoured private-sector and government-controlled industries while enacting legislation that constrained trade union organizations, working-class rights to protest, and collective bargaining.

The key moment in the militant upsurge in labour activities is studied by Christopher Candland in another essay, where he also addresses the question of the failure of working-class solidarity, despite the successful mass mobilization of workers against the military regime during the late 1960s and early 1970s. The fault lines are attributed to religion, ethnicity, language, and the hostile attitude of the Pakistan state. He argues that ethnic, linguistic, and religious identities overlapped class solidarity.[72]

The Communist Party of Pakistan

There is an emerging body of historical writing on left-wing politics in Pakistan which touches upon the questions of labour mobilization and trade union organizations. Essays by Kamran Asdar Ali, Ali Raza, and Anushay Malik are devoted to the history of the formative years of the Communist Party of Pakistan (CPP) and its tu-

---

69 Ibid., p. 3.
70 Kamran Asdar Ali, "The Strength of the Street Meets the Strength of the State: The 1972 Labor Struggle in Karachi", *International Journal of Middle East Studies*, 37, 1 (2005), pp. 83–107.
71 Ali Amjad, *Labour Legislation and Trade Unions in India and Pakistan* (Oxford, 2001); Christopher Candland, *Labor, Democratization and Development in India and Pakistan* (New York, 2007).
72 Christopher Candland, "Workers' Organizations in Pakistan: Why No Role in Formal Politics?", *Critical Asian Studies*, 39, 1 (2007), pp. 35–57.

multuous relationship with the Pakistan state.⁷³ They also provide glimpses of the left-wing mobilizations in the immediate post-independence years. The most significant contribution is the recent publication by Kamran Asdar Ali, which provides an intimate narrative of the dwindling fortunes of the Communist Party of Pakistan and of trade union organizations in the early decades of independence. It is an excellent social, cultural, and intellectual history of the Pakistan communist leadership, trade union movement, and left-wing mobilization. The book narrates the marginalization of the leftist intelligentsia and the Communist Party of Pakistan through state repression by the Muslim League government and, later, under military regimes.⁷⁴

While these writings provide detailed and in-depth analyses of the history of left-wing mobilization, trade union movements, and the Communist Party of Pakistan, "labour" and its politics are paid hardly any serious attention, and the labour movement essentially emerges from this narrative as an appendage of the party. The history of communist elite intellectuals is foregrounded at the expense of the perspective of worker militants and proletarian labour leaders. Indeed, there is scarcely any reference in these narratives to or a discussion of the role of the lower- or even middle-ranking leadership and workers. As in the case of orthodox Marxist narratives of Indian labour history, these studies, too, equate the working-class movement and working-class consciousness with the institutional history of trade unions and political parties.

Sri Lanka (Ceylon)

The British colonization of Sri Lanka (Ceylon) in the early nineteenth century created huge opportunities for British capital investment in this tropical island. British private capital opened up coffee plantations between the 1830s and 1880s, followed by tea and rubber from the 1880s and 1890s. These plantations produced tea, coffee, and rubber exclusively for the growing global market by employing large-scale migrant labour mobilized from agrarian South India. The colonial state actively supported the opening up and growth of plantation enterprise through land grants at extremely lucrative prices, building infrastructure and mobilizing large-scale cheap labour force from British South India.⁷⁵

In plantation-dominated colonial Ceylon the bulk of the historiography on labour history in the immediate aftermath of independence was devoted to plantations

---

73 Kamran Asdar Ali, "Progressives, Punjab and Pakistan: The Early Years", *South Asian History and Culture*, 4, 4 (2013), pp. 483–502; Ali Raza, "An Unfulfilled Dream: The Left in Pakistan ca. 1947–50"; ibid., pp. 503–519; Anushay Malik, "Alternative Politics and Dominant Narratives: Communists and the Pakistani State in the Early 1950s", *ibid.*, pp. 520–537.
74 Ali, *Communism in Pakistan*.
75 Roland Wenzlhuemer, *From Coffee to Tea Cultivation in Ceylon, 1880–1900. An Economic and Social History* (Leiden, 2008), pp. 57–60.

and labour migration from South India. Studies by Kondapi, Naguleswaran, Chattopadhyaya, Roberts, Jayaraman, and vanden Driesen analysed the process of labour mobilization and the nature of labour relations, work, and living conditions under the *kangani* system on Sri Lankan plantations during colonial rule.[76] Labour relations between capital and labour on the plantations were mediated through the evolving *kangani* system. Along with the work by Kondapi, later studies by Heidemann, Peebles, and Kurian and Jayawardena carried further the narrative on the origins, evolution, character, and politics of the *kangani* system.[77] Roland Wenzlhuemer situates the significance of the opening of plantations and the mobilization of migrant labour from South India at the centre of his broader history of colonial Ceylon in the late nineteenth century.[78]

In some labour history writing the push/pull factors for migration were explained by reference to the backwardness of the agrarian economy of South India and the incentive offered by better earnings on the Sri Lanka plantations. Another argument was the cyclical nature of labour migration to the coffee plantations, as determined by the seasonality of agricultural conditions in the catchment areas. The labour on the Ceylon plantations, unlike the indentured plantation regimes, was perceived to be "free" by the colonial state, planters, and their supporter because, it was argued, they were not subjected to contractual obligations. These perceptions were contested by later labour historians, who pointed to the growing incidence of indebtedness, coercion, and consequent bondage and immobility of the labour force under the *kangani* system. Equally significant was the fact of a series of punitive ordinances introduced by the colonial state confirming the master and servants laws that constrained labour mobility and perpetuated labour bondage to the employers and the *kanganis*.[79]

---

[76] Chenchal Kondapi, *Indians Overseas, 1838–1949* (New Delhi, 1951); P. Naguleswaran, "History of the Working Class Movement in Ceylon. II: The Problem of Indian Immigrant Labour in the Nineteenth Century", *Ceylon Historical Journal*, 1 (1951), pp. 230–241; Haraprasad Chattopadhyaya, *Indians in Sri Lanka. A Historical Study* (Calcutta, 1979); M.W. Roberts, "Indian Estate Labour in Ceylon during the Coffee Period, (1830–1880)", *Indian Economic and Social History Review*, 3, 1 (1966), pp. 1–52; R. Jayaraman, "Indian Emigration to Ceylon: Some Aspects of the Historical and Social Background of the Emigrants", *Indian Economic and Social History Review*, 4, 4 (1967), pp. 322–324; Ian vanden Driesen, "The Genesis of Indian Immigrant Labour in Sri Lanka, 1835–1849", *South Asia: Journal of South Asian Studies*, 21, Special Issue (1998), pp. 19–37; Ian vanden Driesen, *The Long Walk. Indian Plantation Labour in Sri Lanka in the Nineteenth Century* (New Delhi, 1998).
[77] Kondapi, *Indians Overseas*; Chattopadhyaya, *Indians in Sri Lanka*; Frank Heidemann, *Kanganies in Sri Lanka and Malaysia: Tamil Recruiter-cum-Foreman as a Sociological Category in the Nineteenth and Twentieth Century* (Munich, 1992); Patrick Peebles, *The Plantation Tamils of Ceylon* (London, 2001); Kumari Jayawardena and Rachel Kurian (eds), *Class, Patriarchy and Ethnicity on Sri Lankan Plantations: Two Centuries of Power and Protest* (Delhi, 2014).
[78] Wenzlhuemer, *From Coffee to Tea Cultivation*.
[79] Peebles, *Plantation Tamils*; Visakha Kumari Jayawardena, *The Rise of the Labour Movement in Ceylon* (Durham, NC, 1972); Jayawardena and Kurian, *Class, Patriarchy and Ethnicity*; Vijaya Samaraweera, "Masters and Servants in Sri Lanka Plantations: Labour Laws and Labour Control in an Emer-

Labour resistance

In early historical studies of labour, the theme of labour resistance on the plantations remained elusive. Visakha Kumari Jayawardena's pioneering work presented an in-depth analysis of individual and collective forms of labour resistance in Sri Lankan labour history.[80] The most significant feature of her work is that, apart from the plantation sector, it also covers the history of labour movements and trade unions in urban and other industrial sectors in colonial Ceylon. The narrative of labour resistance on the plantations forms an integral part of her study, and the later scholarship further developed and elaborated this important theme in labour history writing.[81] She adopts the conventional Marxian framework, which considers rural and primordial ties of workers constraining the growth of working-class consciousness and politics. As pointed out earlier, for both conventional Marxism and modernization theory the optic of transition from traditional rural to urban industrialization formed the basis of the formation of the proletariat. In the case of Ceylon, Jayawardena argues that the break with rural ties was an important factor in the emergence of the urban working-class movement, which coincided with the rise in Sinhalese nationalism.

James Duncan's excellent work traces the rise and fall of coffee production in highland Sri Lanka from the 1830s to the 1880s and shows how the plantation system was constituted through interpenetrating networks of "nature/science/governmentality/culture". He argues that the prevailing perceptions of race in the contemporary Western world shaped the attitude of British planters towards their labour force. European planters adopted coercive methods to manage, discipline, and regulate the everyday life of migrant labourers. Plantations in Ceylon, like plantations in other British colonies, adapted industrial methods and Western technologies of "rationalization, calculation and discipline" for the production of coffee. One important contribution of Duncan's work is the issue of labour resistance on Sri Lankan coffee plantations during the nineteenth century.[82]

The disconnect between Sinhalese nationalism and the migrant plantation working class and the lack of solidarity between the Sinhalese and the Indian working classes are explained in terms of growing ethnic animosity between the two, which was exacerbated by the economic downturn of the 1930s in Ceylon. Chattopadhyaya, Peebles, and Kurian and Jayawardena provide very detailed analyses of fractured relationships and ethnic hostilities between Sinhalese nationalism and

---

gent Export Economy", *Indian Economic and Social History Review*, 18, 2 (1981), pp. 123–158; James S. Duncan, *In the Shadows of the Tropics. Climate, Race and Biopower in Nineteenth Century Ceylon* (Aldershot, 2007); Dharmapriya Wesumperuma, *Indian Immigrant Plantation Workers in Sri Lanka. A Historical Perspective, 1880–1910* (Nugegoda, 1986).
80 Jayawardena, *Rise of the Labour Movement*.
81 Chattopadhyaya, *Indians in Sri Lanka*; Peebles, *Plantation Tamils*; Duncan, *In the Shadows*; Jayawardena and Kurian, *Class, Patriarchy and Ethnicity*.
82 Duncan, *In the Shadows*.

the migrant Tamil working class, both on the plantations and in urban areas. As George Jan Leski's study shows, during the late 1930s and early 1940s the Trotskyite political leadership was at the forefront of the opposition to chauvinistic bigotry that gripped the growing ethnic divide between Sinhalese nationalism and the Tamil working class. In particular, they stood firm in opposing any discrimination against the permanently domiciled plantation workers.[83]

Trade unions

In Ceylon, the emergent trade union politics of the 1920s and 1930s was dominated by middle-class intellectual activists, both Tamils and Sinhala, and the issue of "outsiders" in political mobilization and trade union movements came under scrutiny in writings on labour history. Given the authoritarian nature of the plantation regime operationalized through a hierarchy of planters and *kanganis*, which effectively curbed labour mobility and freedom of movement, the intervention of such "outsiders" in political mobilization finds special emphasis in the works of Jayawardena, Chattopadhyaya, Peebles, and Kurian and Jayawardena. These studies have underlined the important role of the middle-class Tamil intelligentsia in plantation labour politics and trade union organization.[84]

Gender, ethnicity, and labour

Issues of patriarchy and gender, race, caste, and ethnicity impacting labour relations on Sri Lanka plantations are the focus of recent work by Rachel Kurian and Visakha Kumari Jayawardena. It covers a long span in the history of labour on Sri Lanka plantations, in two parts: the colonial and the postcolonial. The first part considers the perspective of historians, focusing on the emergence of the plantation economy; the second presents the insights of social scientists into the nature of political activism in the postcolonial period. Drawing by analogy on the history of indenture on the Caribbean plantations, they argue that the *kangani* labour system on the Sri Lanka plantations was more akin to slavery than to a free labour regime. It is argued that the institutionalization of economic and extra economic coercion and the nature of social hierarchies on the Sri Lankan plantation regimes were a legacy of slavery. The most significant contribution of their work is to the subject of gender and labour

---

[83] George Jan Lerski, *Origins of Trotskyism in Ceylon. A Documentary History of the Lanka Sama Samaja Party, 1935–1942* (Stanford, CA, 1968).
[84] Jayawardena, *Rise of the Labour Movement*; Peebles, *Plantation Tamils*; Jayawardena and Kurian, *Class, Patriarchy and Ethnicity*.

on the plantations, a subject ignored by most other studies of the history of labour in Sri Lanka.[85]

Bangladesh

At independence in 1971 Bangladesh's Awami League government took over the industries and other establishments left behind by private capitalist owners from West Pakistan. Some of these industries, including jute, textiles, and sugar, were nationalized. Having inherited a predominantly poor agrarian society at independence, the newly formed Bangladesh state embarked upon a process of developing its economy through industrialization to eradicate poverty.[86] A set of state industrial policies were announced, aiming to encourage industrial development: these included the Industrial Policy of 1973, the New Industrial Policy of 1982, the revised Industrial Policy of 1986, the Industrial Policy of 1999, followed by a number of other policies, the latest being the Industrial Policy of 2010.[87]

The most important development in post-independence Bangladesh was the emergence of an export-oriented garment industry, encouraged and backed by a policy of liberalization enunciated in the New Industrial Policy of 1982. Actively supported by the state, the export-oriented ready-made garment industry grew spectacularly in urban centres such as Dhaka and Chittagong. Beginning with just a handful in the late 1970s, the number of factories grew to 3,500 by the mid-1990s.[88] The most remarkable characteristic of this industry was the dominance of female labour. From an estimated 50,000 in 1980, the number of women workers grew to 225,000 by 1989.[89] And out of a total of 3.6 million workers employed in Bangladesh's garment industry in 2012, 2.8 million were women, an exception among all South Asian countries.[90]

---

[85] Jayawardena and Kurian, *Class, Patriarchy and Ethnicity*.
[86] Mesbahuddin Ahmed, *Trade Union Movement in Bangladesh: Issues, Agenda and Legislation*, mimeograph, Jatiyo Sramik Jote, Bangladesh, no date, http://jatiyosramikjote.org/tubook.pdf, last accessed 22 February 2017.
[87] Mohammad Yunus and Tatsfumi Yamagata, "The Garment Industry in Bangladesh", in: Takahiro Fukunishi (ed.), *Dynamics of the Garment Industry in Low-Income Countries. Experience of Asia and Africa*, interim report, 2012, http://www.ide.go.jp/English/Publish/Download/Report/2011/2011_410.html.
[88] Naila Kabeer, "Cultural Dopes or Rational Fools? Women and Labour Supply in the Bangladesh Garment Industry", *European Journal of Development Research*, 3, 1 (1991), pp. 133–160; and *idem* and Simeen Mahmud, "Globalization, Gender and Poverty: Bangladeshi Women Workers in Export and Local Markets", *Journal of International Development*, 16, 1 (2004), pp. 93–109.
[89] Kabeer, "Cultural Dopes?", p. 134.
[90] Ferdous Ahamed, "Improving Social Compliance in Bangladesh's Ready-Made Garment Industry", *Journal of Labour and Management in Development*, 13 (2012), pp. 1–26, 2.

Trade unions and labour movements

Most studies on labour in post-independence Bangladesh are devoted to the issues of trade unions, gender, and labour relations in the export-oriented garment-manufacturing industry. There is a solitary contribution by Kamruddin Ahmad on the history of labour and trade union organizations in pre-independence Bangladesh (East Pakistan).[91] A union activist in the labour movement in East Pakistan during 1950s, he was the elected President of the East Pakistan Federation of Labour. Based on personal experiences, he provided an intimate narrative of labour movements and trade union organizations and their leadership in industries including jute, tea plantations, cotton textiles, and the railways. However, his references to labour resistance in the jute industry and on tea plantations offer only sketchy details. The main focus is on the leadership and organization of trade unions.

Labour movements and trade union histories in post-independence Bangladesh attracted both scholarly and journalistic attention, with essays by Mohammed Nuruzzaman and Mesbahuddin Ahmed presenting brief accounts. Their emphasis was on the nature of labour resistance to the pro-market reforms initiated by the state during 1980s and 1990s. With the working class playing an important role in the War of Independence in 1971, Nuruzzaman asserts that the newly formed Awami League government initially adopted measures to promote and protect working-class interests. But while nationalizing key industries, the government also adopted carrot-and-stick policies to curb trade union activities by banning strikes and lockouts in those industries. The overthrow of the socialist Awami League government by the military regime of Ziaur Rahman and the consequent shift to privatization, with disinvestment and the denationalization of state-owned enterprises, brought a change in the trade unions too.[92] According to Mesbahuddin, one immediate consequence of this was the contraction in the size of workforce in those industries, resulting in trade unions losing influence.

Nuruzzaman's work studied the upsurge in labour resistance in Bangladesh to the privatization of industries in 1982 dictated by pro-market reforms: street demonstrations and violent activities, including lockouts, disruptions to production, and the detention of management. He argues that the spate of resistance in the industrial sector during 1980s and 1990s had the potential to halt or roll back the reform programme, but that resistance did not lead to any broad-based social coalition of workers. Despite early successes, a host of factors, including ideological differences and the internal organizational weakness of trade unions, prevented working-class solid-

---

91 Kamruddin Ahmad, *Labour Movement in East Pakistan* (Dhaka, 1969).
92 Mohammed Nuruzzaman, "Labor Resistance to Pro-Market Economic Reforms in Bangladesh", *Journal of Asian and African Studies*, 41, 4 (2006), pp. 341–357; Ahmad, *Labour Movement in East Pakistan*.

arity. Moreover, the government discouraged the formation of trade unions in the newly emergent export-oriented garment industry.[93]

Mesbahuddin's study focuses on the changing nature of labour laws during Pakistan control and post-independence in Bangladesh. The independent state of Bangladesh amended the existing colonial labour legislation, which contained some protective provisions for workers, covering the working environment, working conditions, compensation for accident and disability, death, discharge, dismissal, termination, retrenchment, layoffs, lockouts, and maternity. These amendments to the existing legislation in 1992 were not appreciated by the trade unions, because they were aimed at restricting their activities.[94]

While these essays provide a detailed analysis of the changing political world of Bangladesh's trade unions and allude to workers' resistance to privatization and pro-market reforms, barely any information is given concerning that labour resistance itself – no study of any specific strike, demonstration, or movement. The activities of the trade unions are themselves assumed to constitute the labour resistance, without any specific details being provided. Edward Bearnot mentions the growing cost of living and continued low wages in Bangladesh's garment industry leading to resistance and protests. He reports the burning of buses and forced closure of factories in 2012, when rents in Dhaka increased fourfold, but he provides no details of these acts of resistance.[95]

An essay by Zia Rehman raises issues concerning the success or failure of trade union organizations in defending the rights of workers in the Bangladesh export-oriented garment industry. He argues that a combination of World Bank and local elites led to the emergence of an export-oriented ready-made garment industry as the main manufacturing sector in Bangladesh, employing large numbers of unskilled rural women. In this sector, he shows, the trade unions were unable to combat low wages, the deteriorating working and physical conditions in the factories, the lack of welfare facilities, and the physical and sexual coercion of workers. Historically, he argues, even those partially successful movements in which workers participated were the offshoots of various larger political movements opposing repressive colonial and military regimes. Therefore, though integrally related to the broad political movements, many historical peasant and worker movements lacked an independent working-class character.[96] Similar arguments are also put forward by Syeda Sharmin

---

93 Nuruzzaman, "Labor Resistance".
94 Mesbahuddin, *Trade Union Movement*, p. 6.
95 Edward Bearnot, "Bangladesh: A Labor Paradox", *World Policy Journal*, 30, 3 (2013), pp. 88–97, available at www.worldpolicy.org/journal/fall2013/Bangladesh-Labor-Paradox, last accessed 21 February 2017.
96 Zia Rahman, "Bangladesh: Failure of the Trade Unions to Defend Workers Rights", *South Asia Citizens Web*, 3 May 2009, available at http://www.sacw.net/article889.html, last accessed 21 February 2017.

Absar in her essay on wages in the ready-made garment manufacturing industry. She has argued that Bangladesh's trade union movement was weak and male-oriented.[97]

Gender

The significant scholarly attention given to gender issues is one the most significant features of the historiography on Bangladesh labour. This is obviously because of the predominance of female employment in the country's ready-made garment industry. Over the years, Naila Kabeer has produced an impressive body of writing on gender and patriarchy in the history of women workers in the export-oriented ready-made garment industry in post-independent Bangladesh.[98] Kabeer regards the growth of the export-oriented garment industry as a response to the pressure exerted by international donors and financial institutions such as the IMF and the World Bank. The newly initiated industrial policies of economic liberalization promoted private-sector participation and opened the economy up to international trade.[99]

Kabeer argues that the garment factories created a first-generation female industrial proletariat in a society where purdah was long believed to constitute an impenetrable barrier to female labour mobility and dramatically changed the profile of female labour-force participation in the country. In just a short span of time women workers became the single largest category of labour in Bangladesh.[100] Women's entry into factory employment represented a radical departure in the traditional female-seclusion society of Bangladesh. Kabeer attributes this to women's agency to decide on their participation in the labour market by renegotiating norms of purdah. She further argues that the decisions to participate in the labour market entailed a close interaction between economic incentives and cultural norms. Discussing pull and push factors, Kabeer and Absar have shown that while many women workers responded to the pull of new incentives in the labour market there were others who were pushed into factory employment by the failure of the "patriarchal bargain" and the loss of male guardians.[101]

---

[97] Syeda Sharmin Absar, "Problems Surrounding Wages: The Ready Made Garments Sector in Bangladesh", *Labour and Management in Development Journal*, 2, 7 (2001), pp. 1–17.
[98] Kabeer, "Cultural Dopes?"; idem, *The Power to Choose. Bangladeshi Women and Labour Market Decisions in London and Dhaka* (London, 2000); idem, "Globalization, Labor Standards, and Women's Rights: Dilemmas of Collective (In)action in an Interdependent World", *Feminist Economics*, 10, 1 (2004), pp. 3–35; idem and Mahmud, "Globalization, Gender and Poverty".
[99] Kabeer, "Cultural Dopes?".
[100] Ibid.
[101] Ibid.; Absar, "Problems Surrounding Wages".

Wage discrimination

Absar's study of wages in the garment industry shows that the work process in the garment industry was organized based on a gendered division of labour. Women accounted for over eighty-five per cent of production workers in factories, working mainly as helpers, machinists, and, less frequently, as line supervisors and quality controllers. A very small minority of men worked on the factory floor as machinists or in packing, pressing, cutting, and loading. But women workers suffered gender discrimination in relation to wages, receiving less than their male counterparts. Indeed, the employers' rationale in employing large numbers of women workers was to reduce labour costs and to have "pliable" workers who were far less likely to get involved in trade union activities and disrupt production. In a hugely competitive international garment industry, these factors were extremely important in Bangladesh.[102]

---

[102] Absar, "Problems Surrounding Wages".

Suggested reading

Ahmad, Kamruddin. *Labour Movement in East Pakistan* (Dhaka: Progoti Publishers, 1969).
Ahuja, Ravi. "Labour Relations in an Early Colonial Context: Madras, c.1750–1800", *Modern Asian Studies*, 36, 4 (2002), pp. 793–826.
Ahuja, Ravi. "The Origins of Colonial Labour Policy in Late Eighteenth-Century Madras", *International Review of Social History*, 44, 2 (1999), pp. 159–195.
Ali, Kamran Asdar. *Communism in Pakistan: Politics and Class Activism 1947–1972* (London: I.B. Tauris, 2015).
Ali, Kamran Asdar. "The Strength of the Street Meets the Strength of the State: The 1972 Labor Struggle in Karachi", *International Journal of Middle East Studies*, 37, 1 (2005), pp. 83–107.
Amjad, Ali. *Labour Legislation and Trade Unions in India and Pakistan* (Karachi: Oxford University Press, 2001).
Balachandran, Gopalan *Globalizing Labour? Indian Seafarers and World Shipping, c. 1870–1945* (New Delhi: Oxford University Press, 2012).
Behal, Rana P. *One Hundred Years of Servitude. Political Economy of Tea Plantations in Colonial Assam* (New Delhi: Tulika, 2014).
Behal, Rana P. and Marcel van der Linden (eds). *India's Labouring Poor: Historical Studies c.1600–c.2000* (New Delhi: Tulika, 2007).
Bhattacharya, Sabyasachi (ed.). *Towards a New History of Work* (New Delhi: Tulika, 2014).
Bhattacharya, Sabyasachi and Rana P. Behal (eds). *The Vernacularization of Labour Politics* (New Delhi: Tulika, 2016).
Breman, Jan. *Patronage and Exploitation: Changing Agrarian Relations in South Gujarat, India* (Berkeley, CA: University of California Press, 1974).
Buchanan, Daniel H. *The Development of Capitalistic Enterprise in India* (New York: Macmillan, 1934).
Candland, Christopher. *Labor, Democratization and Development in India and Pakistan* (London: Routledge, 2007).
Chakrabarty, Dipesh. *Rethinking Working-Class History. Bengal 1890–1940* (Princeton, NJ: Princeton University Press, 1988).
Chandavarkar, Rajnarayan. *The Origin of Industrial Capitalism in India. Business Strategies and the Working Classes in Bombay, 1900–1940* (Cambridge: Cambridge University Press, 1994).
De Neve, Geert. *The Everyday Politics of Labour. Working Lives in India's Informal Economy* (New York and Oxford: Berghahn, 2005).
Gooptu, Nandini. *The Politics of the Urban Poor in Early Twentieth-Century India* (Cambridge: Cambridge University Press, 2001).
Jayawardena, Visakha Kumari. *The Rise of the Labour Movement in Ceylon* (Durham, NC: Duke University Press, 1972).
Jayawardena, Kumari and Rachel Kurian (eds). *Class, Patriarchy and Ethnicity on Sri Lankan Plantations: Two Centuries of Power and Protest* (Delhi: Orient Blackswan, 2015).
Joshi, Chitra. *Lost Worlds: Indian Labour and its Forgotten Histories* (Delhi: Permanent Black, 2003).
Kabeer, Naila. *The Power to Choose. Bangladeshi Women and Labour Market Decisions in London and Dhaka* (London: Verso, 2000).
Linden, Marcel van der Linden and Prabhu P. Mohapatra (eds), *Labour Matters. Towards Global History* (New Delhi: Tulika, 2009).
Lucassen, Jan. "Working at the Ichapur Gunpowder Factory in the 1790s", *Indian Historical Review*, 39, 1 (2012), pp. 19–56, and 39, 2 (2012), pp. 251–271.

Morris, Morris David. *The Emergence of an Industrial Labour Force in India. A Study of the Bombay Cotton Mills, 1854–1947* (Berkeley, CA: University of California Press, 1965).

Nair, Janaki. *Miners and Millhands. Work, Culture and Politics in Princely Mysore* (New Delhi: SAGE, 1998).

Nuruzzaman, Mohammed. "Labor Resistance to Pro-Market Economic Reforms in Bangladesh", *Journal of Asian and African Studies*, 41, 4 (2006), pp. 341–357.

Peebles, Patrick. *The Plantation Tamils of Ceylon* (London: Leicester University Press, 2001).

Prakash, Gyan. *Bonded Histories. Genealogies of Labour Servitude in Colonial India* (Cambridge: Cambridge University Press, 1990).

Sen, Samita. *Women and Labour in Late Colonial India. The Bengal Jute Industry* (Cambridge: Cambridge University Press, 1999).

Shaheed, Zafar. *The Labour Movement in Pakistan: Organization and Leadership in Karachi in the 1970s* (Oxford: Oxford University Press, 2007).

Simeon, Dilip. *The Politics of Labour under Late Colonialism. Workers, Unions and the State in Chota Nagpur, 1928–1939* (Delhi: Manohar, 1995).

Wenzlhuemer, Roland. *From Coffee to Tea Cultivation in Ceylon, 1880–1900: An Economic and Social History* (Leiden and Boston: Brill, 2008).

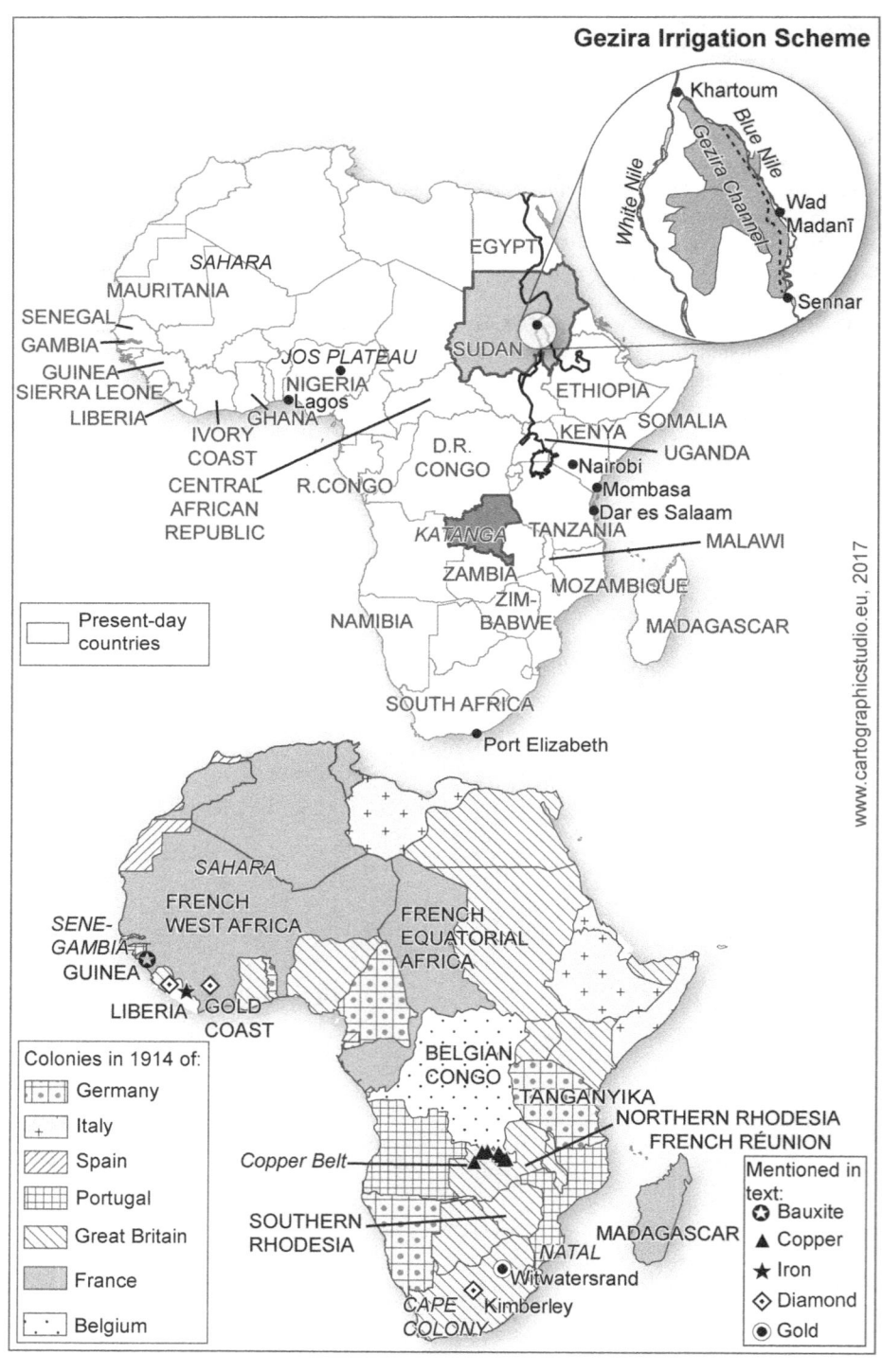

Bill Freund
2.3. Sub-saharan Africa

Before looking at labour systems in Africa south of the Sahara, it might be important to consider this proviso. Africa is a very large continent with considerable human variety, very different societies that have developed with some continuity of contact but with strong regional differences and sometimes markedly different economic systems based on environmental possibilities. As Valentin Mudimbe has written, the 'idea', or invention of Africa as he put it is itself a product of a Eurocentric imagination, still more one defined in racial terms. Sub-saharan Africa moreover has never been isolated from Eurasia. The Sahara is and was not a barrier to human movement and contact. If the Atlantic Ocean was difficult to navigate, monsoon winds opened up the East African coast to ancient contacts and the Red Sea is, of course, quite narrow. Both these factors need to be considered in generalizations about labour history in the very long and broad sense in Africa.

The literature considering the long-term evolution of African societies generally emphazises the gendered division of labour because this has often been a notably distinctive feature of many of them. Within the household, and most societies are ideally polygamous, men tended to define their work as hunting, defence and the care of livestock, above all cattle. Cattle were prized in areas where they could be raised in good health as the basis of wealth and exchange. Migrations, long and short-term, reflected the search for available pasture land. However, it is generally thought that the domestication of livestock, and especially cattle, preceded the development of agriculture and might have taken place in South Sudan. There are peoples in eastern Africa such as the Nuer and Dinka speakers of South Sudan, the Oromo of southern and central Ethiopia, most of the Somali and the Maasai of Tanzania and Kenya, who farmed very little and were almost entirely focussed on cattle keeping. In West Africa, Fulfulde speakers were specialized cattle keepers who traded systematically with the agriculturalists amongst whom they found themselves.[1]

In the southern half of Africa, however, a distinctive pattern developed that Ester Boserup called 'female farming'.[2] Here men were stock herders and women cultivated grains which were probably first grown systematically in West Africa, especially millet and sorghum. These grains were not farmed intensively except where permanent sources of water existed; they were very hardy and could survive long dry seasons. Millet especially could be the source of nourishing beer whose manufacture was also a female specialty. In Namibia and South Africa, this kind of livelihood system tended to marginalize more ancient pre-agricultural patterns where men hunted

---
[1] John Galaty, and Pierre Bonté (eds), *Herders, Warriors and Traders; Pastoralism in Africa* (Boulder CO, 1991); Andrew Smith, *Pastoralism in Africa. Origins and Development Ecology* (London, Johannesburg and Athens, OH, 1992).
[2] Ester Boserup, *Women's Role in Economic Development* (London, 1970).

and women gathered. Female farming systems could be associated with patriarchal social forms where households accumulated based on cattle wealth and exchanged women as wives. Such households agglomerated into lineage groups and so-called tribes.[3] In general, households were also hierarchical in terms of age. Age was linked to fitness to time of life but so long as formation of a household depended on exchange of goods and the agreement of elders, youths were essentially dependent and for the time being exploitable labour.

The other phenomenon which has attracted a very large literature on pre-colonial Africa is the prevalence in many societies, but notably in West Africa, of different categories of what can be translated into English as slavery. In some form or another, slaves were captives, foreigners, who had few (albeit increasingly some, as time went on) rights. The interest in slavery inevitably has to do with the transport of millions of Africans from broader and broader areas of the continent across the seas to the Americas where they were essentially put to work on plantations aimed at capitalist profits secured through international trade. Sugar was the key commodity of this trade but in the nineteenth century, cotton from North America was equally important. The largest number of slaves were brought to the Americas in the century beginning in 1750 having built up from the earliest contacts in the 15th century.

It is difficult to prove the prevalence of slavery before the establishment of the Atlantic slave trade. However, there is no question that such a trade had been significant for many centuries back into classical times and particularly from early in the Islamic era. In the 8th century, a revolt associated with black slaves on plantations is reported from irrigated land in southern modern-day Iraq, for instance.[4] It would be a mistake however to consign the slaves of West Africa into a systematically exploited class without further definition.[5] Islamic societies in the West African interior (and on the East African coast) featured slaves who were used on a large scale as soldiers, trusted eunuchs and household women whose children did not necessarily inherit this status.[6] In a typical successful household, slaves did not really do particular jobs apart from free members. The majority of slaves were women whose status was equally marked by their gender; indeed women slaves tended to have a higher market value than men.[7] If we take it to be a typical West African forest society, Asante (located in modern-day Ghana) was characterized by several categories of un-

---

[3] Jack Goody, *Technology, Tradition and the State in Africa* (London, 1971); J. Guy, "Analysing Pre-capitalist Societies in Southern Africa", *Journal of Southern African Studies*, 15 (1987), pp. 18–37; Claude Meillassoux, *Maidens, Meal and Money* (Cambridge, 1981).
[4] Ralph Austen, *Trans-Saharan Africa in World History* (New York, 2010).
[5] Frederick Cooper, "The Problem of Slavery in African Studies", *Journal of African History*, 19 (1979), pp. 103–25; Paul Lovejoy (ed.), *Ideologies of Slavery in Africa* (Beverly Hills and London, 1982); Claude Meillassoux (ed.), *The Anthropology of Slavery; The Womb of Iron and Gold* (London 1991).
[6] Frederick Cooper, *Plantation Slavery on the East Coast of Africa* (New Haven, 1977); Marion Johnson, "The Slaves of Salaga", *Journal of African History*, 27 (1987), pp. 341–62; Paul Lovejoy, *Transformations in Slavery* (Cambridge, 1983).
[7] Claire Robertson and Martin Klein (eds), *Women and Slavery in Africa* (Madison, WI, 1983).

free labour and generally speaking slaves born in the household were not considered chattel that could be sold.[8] An important category of unfree labour here and elsewhere are usually labelled as pawns. Pawns were placed into households to repay debts, very often for life but they were not considered as slaves to be bought and sold either and they were not generally forced out into the slave trade In some areas such as the Niger Delta, the lower Congo river and coastal Madagascar, the slave trade can be associated with rapid social mobility in which ex-slaves became leaders and small-scale rulers just as did elsewhere the children of European traders and African women.[9] West African societies reached a more complex division of labour than most other parts of the continent south of the Sahara. Certain groups of people, perhaps in terms of their relationship to authority, such as blacksmiths and praise-singers, formed the heart of what have been termed castes, largely endogenou.[10] Polygamous households which consisted of men, women and children, slaves and pawns, and which could be very large were typically involved as well in craft activity and participated in local and sometimes long-distance markets while men raided and went to war. Craft activity involved masters and apprentices. Participation in larger households offered security although smaller, less complex societies existed in environmentally more challenging areas—marshlands, plateau or broken hill country, etc.[11]

Male involvement in farming was also crucial in the Ethiopian highlands where agriculture was based on the use of cattle-harnessed ploughs, with relatively high population densities and a distinctive repertoire of unique crops first domesticated locally. The level of commercialization was low and towns were historically virtually non-existent but the highlands early on accepted Eastern Christianity and harboured a large monastic population. The church was a large landholder and extracted pro-

---

8 Gareth Austin, *Labour, Land, and Capital in Ghana: From Slavery to Free Labour in Asante 1907–1956* (Rochester, 2005).
9 Sandra Evers, *Constructing History, Culture and Inequality* (Leiden and Boston, 2002); Robert Harms, *River of Wealth, River of Sorrow: The Central Zaire (Basin in the Era of the Slave and Ivory Trade, 1500–1891* (New Haven, 1981); Philip Havik, "From Pariahs to Patriots; Women Slavers in 19th century 'Portuguese' Guinea", in: Gwyn Campbell, Suzanne Miers and Joseph Miller (eds), *Women and Slavery I* (Columbus, OH, 2007), pp. 308–333; Robin Horton, "From Fishing-Village to City-State: A Social History of New Calabar" in Mary Douglas and Phyllis Kaberry (eds), *Man in Africa* (London, 1969); Peter Mark, "The Evolution of Portuguese 'Identity'; Luso-Africans on the Upper Guinea Coast from the 16th century to the early 19th century", *Journal of African History*, 40 (1999) pp. 173–191.
10 Abdoulaye-Bara Diop, *La société Wolof* (Paris, 1981).
11 Nicholas David, "Patterns of Slavery, Prey-Predator Interfaces in and around the Mandara Mountains (Nigeria and Cameroun)", *Africa*, 84 (2014), pp. 371–397; Kristin Mann, *Slavery and the Birth of an African City, Lagos 1760–1900* (Bloomington and Indianapolis, 2007); Marcia Wright, "Women in Peril", *African Social Research*, 20 (1975), pp. 800–819.

duce from the peasantry as did the aristocracy.¹² Commerce and craft work was often carried on by Muslims who had no access to land. Inland Madagascar was another area where a ruling class from the late 18th century made large demands for troops and foodstuffs from the rice-growing peasantry of the central highlands while raiding for slaves elsewhere.¹³

By the nineteenth century, three tendencies should be stressed. The first is the impact of commodity trade. The African gold trade existed from at least the 8th or 9th century in West Africa and a couple of centuries later in south-central Africa, but the actual mining was not the product of a new distinctive working class. In what is today Zimbabwe, it is thought that most mining labour, including the sifting and separation of the ore, was performed by women in the dry season as an alternative to craft and other chores.¹⁴ In the nineteenth century, there is good evidence that gold mining in what is today Ghana and the Ivory Coast was also the result of activity, including migration, by households otherwise engaged in agriculture and essentially by individuals who were free. Profits accrued to the merchants with the state having some capacity to extract revenue.¹⁵

However, in the 19th century, commercial life intensified. This led to the establishment of massive caravan traffic that engaged tens of thousands of workers. The ivory of the East African interior or the tin of the Jos Plateau in Nigeria called into life these cities on the move. Rockel has demonstrated that the caravan, with a complex social order of its own, consisted of entrepreneurial free individuals as key figures in which slave participants were secondary.¹⁶

However, slaving itself expanded in many areas and incurred large-scale violence. So did the advent of guns. Caravan leaders were amongst those who created raw, new political units while older states such as the Merina principality in central Madagascar, the contested monarchy of Ethiopia, the gigantic domain of Muhammad Ali, the Albanian representative of the Ottomans in Egypt, and others began a partition of Africa. As the imperial era took off, Europeans depended on African recruits

---

12 Allan Hoben, *Land Tenure among the Amhara of Ethiopia. The Dynamics of Cognatic Descent* (Chicago, 1975); Donald Crummey, *Land and Society in the Christian Kingdom of Ethiopia from the 13th to the 20th Century* (Oxford, 2000).
13 Gwyn Campbell, *An Economic History of Imperial Madagascar, 1750–1895. The Rise and Fall of an Island Empire* (Cambridge, 2008).
14 David Beach, "The Shona Economy: Branches of Production", in: Neil Parsons and Robin Palmer (eds), *The Roots of Rural Poverty in Southern and Central Africa* (London, 1977),pp.37–66.
15 Raymond Dumett, *El Dorado in West Africa. The Gold-Mining Frontier, African Labour and Colonial Capitalism in the Gold Coast 1875–1900* (Oxford and Athens, OH, 1998); B. Marie Perinbam, "Political Organization of Traditional Gold Mining: The Western Loby c. 1850–c. 1910", *Journal of African History*, 29 (1988), pp. 437–462.
16 Bill Freund, *Capital and Labour in the Nigerian Tin Mines* (Harlow, 1981); Stephen Rockel, *Carriers of Culture. Labor on the Road in Nineteenth-Century East Africa* (Portsmouth, NH, 2006).

such as the West African Frontier Force and the *Tirailleurs sénégalais*.[17] Indeed, the French systematically developed an African army (which they would use in time in Europe itself) creating an important new class of workers. Slaves also were in some areas systematically put to work to produce cash crops such as palm oil in coastal West Africa or cloves in Zanzibar.

A third phenomenon was the emergence starting in the seventeenth century of a geographically extensive Dutch settler colony from the southern tip of Africa. Through the eighteenth century, thousands of slaves were imported here. In the Cape Colony slaves and landless indigenous people were the crucial workforce; they outnumbered the European minority in the population and, after the abolition of slavery, formed the basis of the Coloured population which basically was excluded from land ownership. Affluent whites tended to combine commercial and service activities at the Cape with the ownership of vineyards, grain farms and, in the deeper interior, cattle and sheep ranches.[18] By the later nineteenth century however, urban life was well-established with a variety of European colonial institutions of every sort and very economically diverse activities, albeit an unspecialised working population. Another slave-based colony of some importance was the French, then British, colony of Mauritius, where a plantation society based on sugar production emerged in the last quarter of the eighteenth century.[19]

In the age of abolition, Mauritius and Natal, the second British South African colony, both sugar producers, came to depend as did the other Mascarene island of French Réunion, on indentured labour organized from India. Indentured workers were paid and came under the protection of a government official, of the sort appointed in the later days of slavery but in fact under harsh conditions while slaves freed from ships at the Cape were put to work in the colony for a fixed period. However, notably in Natal, indentured workers found opportunities to farm small pieces of land and establish market gardens near the towns and sugar plantations. Most chose not to return to India when their time for indenture was over.

The eruption of colonial rule in the final quarter of the nineteenth century related to economic shifts that made huge new demands on African labour using both economic and non-economic means. The historical literature on colonial Africa contains a virtual library about labour. One aspect of this lay in the complexities of labour governance by business and especially by the state. Colonial legislation permitted forced labour and Africans were obliged to fulfil demands for taxes in colonial

---

17 Myron Echenberg, *Colonial Conscripts. The Tirailleurs Senegalais in French West Africa, 1857–1960* (Portsmouth NH, 1991); Edho Ekoko, "The West African Frontier Force Revisited", *Journal of the Historical Society of Nigeria*, 10 (1979), pp. 47–63.
18 Hermann Giliomee, *The Afrikaners. Biography of a People* (Charlottesville, VA, 2003); Nigel Worden, *Slavery in Dutch South Africa* (Cambridge, 1985).
19 Daniel North-Coombes, *Studies in the Political Economy of Mauritius* (Moka, 2000); Meghan Vaughan, *Creating the Creole Island. Slavery in Eighteenth Century Mauritius* (Durham and London, 2005).

currency. The most characteristic new form of labour use lay in mining and transport but agrarian systems also came to use massive amounts of dependent labour paid in cash or kind.[20]

After colonial conquest, labour demands on the African population increased and altered to feed the restructuring of economies so as to produce raw materials desired in Europe. The massive caravans gradually gave way to railway and then road traffic which freed up large numbers of workers for other activities. Railway construction, for instance the Congo-Océan railway in the forests of French Equatorial Africa, proceeded at considerable cost to human life[21]. However just as in Europe the railways created a distinctive working class with particular skills and expectations, often transferred far from home and settled in created neighbourhoods.[22] Port workers also grew as a workforce although here the role of migrants shifting between wage labour and other activities was more significant.[23] Sailors from certain communities, notably the Kru from coastal southern Liberia, crossed the seas and occasionally settled in other continents.

Slavery died a slow death. If enslavement ceased, no laws prevented the continued holding of slaves whose presence only diminished markedly as the cash economy expanded and allowed for alternatives.[24] Settlements such as the French *villages de liberté* allowed for considerable use of compulsory labour from ex-slaves, important especially where population densities were low.[25] In general, the first couple of generations of colonial rule saw extensive use of compulsory labour, often organized through the agency of chiefs and other traditional authorities, beneficiaries of colonialism who fitted the needs of a system that did not have sufficient subordinates. This compulsory labour ranged from the construction of colonial administrative buildings and roads to crop cultivation in order to meet the cash needs promoted by taxation. Compulsion and the imposition of chiefs were critical, for instance, in

---

20 Y.M. Ivanov, *Agrarian Reforms and Hired Labor in Africa* (Moscow, 1979).
21 Gilles Sautter, "Notes sur la construction du chemin de fer Congo-Océan", *Cahiers d'études africaines*, 26 (1967), pp. 220–299.
22 Ralph Grillo, *African Railwaymen* (Cambridge, 1973).
23 Frederick Cooper, *On the African Waterfront* (New Haven, 1987); David Hemson, "Dock Workers, Labour Circulation and Class Struggles in Durban 1945–1959", *Journal of Southern African Studies*, 4 (1977), pp. 88–124.
24 Carolyn Brown, "Testing the Boundaries of Marginality: Twentieth Century Slavery and Emancipation Struggles in Nkam, Northern Igboland 1920–29", *Journal of African History*, 37 (1995), pp. 51–80; Jan-Georg Deutsch, *Abolition Without Emancipation in German East Africa* (Columbus, OH, 2005) Suzanne Miers and Richard Roberts (eds), *The End of Slavery in Africa* (Madison, WI, 1988); Mohammed Bashir Salau, "The Role of Slave Labour in Groundnut Production in Early Colonial Kano", *Journal of African History*, 51 (2010), pp. 147–165; Timothy Weiskel," Labor in the Emergent Periphery: From Slavery to Migrant Labor among the Baule Peoples 1880–1925", in: Walter L. Goldfrank (ed.), *The World-System of Capitalism. Past and Present* (London and Beverly Hills, 1977), pp. 207–233.
25 Denise Bouche, *Les villages de liberté en Afrique Occidentale Française, 1887–1910* (The Hague, 1968).

the running of the government coal mining industry in eastern Nigeria.²⁶ This in turn was one important feature that fed the massive scale of labour migration in colonial Africa. This labour had antecedents but now took on massive proportions all over the continent.²⁷ One important aspect of these migrations, which often crossed territorial boundaries, was that they captured individuals' sense of adventure and potential opportunity. Workers would keep a crucial social platform in their own societies while accumulating cash or even new fields to cultivate far away.²⁸ Another was that instances of cruelty and hardship were balanced for some by calculations as to where it was possible to earn the most and organize a life on the most advantageous terms. In Senegal and the Gambia, the *navétanes* were workers in the peanut economy with antecedents being slaves brought from the interior in caravans; now they were free migrant workers.²⁹

Vail and White created a remarkable hierarchy for Mozambican and Malawian workers as to a pecking order of jobs within the poorly-paid local economies on plantations and in colonial towns, as workers on the Northern Rhodesian Copperbelt and the Southern Rhodesian farms and on the goldfields of South Africa where the best wages could be found. The tin mines of Northern Nigeria and the gold mines of the Gold Coast were largely worked by cash-poor peasants in the dry season: long-distance migrants, many from across the borders in French territory escaping the onerous tax system imposed from Paris.³⁰ In Southern Rhodesia, the initial system of semi-compulsory labour in mining gave way throughout the cash economy, even in towns, to dependence on men from across the borders while Rhodesian men preferred to earn money through the sale of cattle and crops nearer home.³¹

Mining was the biggest destination of European investment capital in colonial Africa by far and the most important mines of all were the gold mines of the Witwatersrand.³² Reconstruction after the Anglo-Boer War war had to proceed through the

---

26 Pierre Babassana, *Travail forcé en Afrique: expropriation et formation de salariat en Afrique noire* (Grenoble, 1978); Carolyn Brown, *"We Were All Slaves". African Miners, Culture and Resistance at the Enugu Government Colliery* (Portsmouth, NH, Oxford and Cape Town, 2003); Babacar Fall, *Le travail forcé en Afrique orientale française 1900–46* (Paris, 1993).
27 Samir Amin, *Modern Migrations in Western Africa* (London, 1974); Jean-Luc Amselle, *Migrations africaines* (Paris, 1976); Jonathan Crush, "Uneven Labour Migration in Southern Africa: Conceptions and Misconceptions", *South African Geographical Journal*, 66 (1984), pp. 115–131; Sharon Stichter, *Migrant Labor* (Cambridge, 1985); Landeg White, *Capital and Colonialism in Mozambique* (London, 1980).
28 Gareth Austin, *Labour, Land, and Capital in Ghana*; François Manchuelle, *Willing Migrants. Soninke Labor Diasporas* (Columbus, OH, and London, 1997).
29 Philippe David, *Les navétanes* (Dakar and Abidjan, 1980).
30 Bill Freund, *Capital and Labour*; Roger Thomas, "Forced Labour in British West Africa: The Case of the Northern Territories of Ghana 1906–27", *Journal of African History*, 14 (1973), pp. 79–103.
31 Charles van Onselen, *Chibaro. African Mine Labour in Southern Rhodesia* (Nottingham, 1976).
32 V. L. Allen, *The History of Black Mineworkers in South Africa* (Keighley, 2003); Frederick Johnstone, *Class, Race and Gold* (London, 1976); Dunbar Moodie with V. Ndatshe, *Going for Gold. Men, Mines and Migration* (Berkeley and London, 1994).

import of tens of thousands of Chinese workers.[33] The Chinese were sent home before the Union of South Africa was established in 1910. By then the labour force was approaching 200,000 in size; at the very peak in the 1980s, the gold mines would employ half a million miners.

Over time, and marked by important shifts in sources of labour, a system was worked out that resembled the organization of a huge army. This system derived in turn from the one that developed when DeBeers secured a monopoly by the 1880s in diamond mining at Kimberley, an industry that preceded the massive gold discoveries.[34] Before that already in the middle decades of the 19th century large numbers of African workers from what is today South Africa and surrounding countries were already slipping into Kimberley, the docks at Port Elizabeth and farms in order to earn cash to purchase guns, horses and livestock.

At peak, African workers confronted a superbly well-organized agency spread through rural areas that structured transport to the mines and oversaw contracts, albeit with the use of middlemen. Advances as well as deferred payments (held by the Portuguese authorities in Mozambique) were a key part of the system.[35] Younger men used the mines to get round the authority of fathers and to accumulate money to buy cattle in order to marry. Once on the mines, workers lived in compounds (although there were phases, for instance in the 1940s, where the open compound system allowed many to live outside) where health care and food together with grain beer and forms of entertainment were made available on a huge scale. This modern system co-existed with what appeared to be a traditional way of life to which miners had to return. The mines were increasingly deep and incurred not only many fatal accidents but also insidious dust prevalence that led to large-scale prevalence of tuberculosis and silicosis before watering systems reduced the danger after World War I. The basic welfare system of course did not extend to miners once they ceased taking contracts.

The mines also employed many thousands of whites. Originally these were typically immigrants, often with the experience of California or Canadian gold mining and sometimes with the radical syndicalist or anarchist politics that went with those labour forces. However, especially after the defeat of the first major strike of white miners in 1907, local whites, particularly Afrikaner farmers unable to survive on the land or made landless by the war, started to take their place. In the early decades, their death rate from accidents exceeded that of blacks and they also succum-

---

[33] Peter Richardson, *Chinese Mine Labour in the Transvaal* (London, 1982).
[34] R.V.Turrell, *Capital and Labour on the Kimberley Diamond Fields* (Cambridge, 1987); William Worger, *South Africa's City of Diamonds. Mine Workers and Monopoly Capitalism in Kimberley* (Johannesburg and Cape Town, 1987).
[35] William Beinart, *The Political Economy of Pondoland* (Cambridge 1982); Alan Jeeves, *Migrant Labour in South Africa's Mining Economy* (Montreal, 1985); Ruth First et al., *The Mozambican Miner. Proletarian and Peasant* (Brighton, 1983); Patrick Harries, *Work, Culture and Identity. Migrant Labour in Mozambique and South Africa c. 1860–1910* (Oxford, Johannesburg and Portsmouth, NH, 1994).

bed to lung diseases to a large extent. Some of these men were genuinely very skilled workers; others were really just overseers and individuals whose sense of mining, just as with black Africans, was tacit rather than learnt. A set of very large strikes culminating in the Rand Revolt of 1922 had a strong racial bias, no doubt overshadowed by the structural insecurity of the white miners who feared replacement by blacks.[36] After the arrival in power of the Pact government in 1924, a system was worked out which kept a restrained but still very significant white minority of workers who had the vote and were employed at a vastly higher rate of pay than the black migrants in supervisory or skilled roles.[37] On the contrary the strong unions whites set up (but not on the gold mines) in South Africa as their numbers expanded were focussed on organizing genuine skilled workers in the British tradition and were sometimes flexible in terms of the colour bar when it suited their purposes[38]. Black mineworkers also struck frequently in the early days although the stories about these strikes are almost hidden in the records.[39] Not much is known about the 1920 strike where 70,000 workers went out for almost a week, the largest example. In South Africa generally, a racially demarcated labour force grew extensively with oppressive conditions notable not merely on the mines but on farms which often had a somewhat feudal character.[40] Helen Bradford discussed the most notable resistance movement, the Industrial and Commercial Workers' Union, which had its main strength in the countryside. The ICU inspired many farm workers but never organized actual strikes or practical resistance.[41] At the same time, radical currents brought from white workers to the increasingly large black urban population, increasingly under the aegis of a small Communist Party, waxed and waned in this period.[42] The oppressive side of labour in underground gold mining has to be coupled with mention at least, as elsewhere in such situations in Africa, with some grasp of the way Africans bargained and turned elements of the system to their advantage

---

36 Jeremy Krikler, *White Rising. Insurrection and Racial Killing in South Africa* (Manchester, 2005).
37 Robert Davies, *Capital, State and White Labour in South Africa* (Brighton, 1979); David Yudelman, *The Emergence of Modern South Africa* (Westport, CT, 1983).
38 Jon Lewis, *Industrialisation and Trade Union Organisation in South Africa 1924–55* (Cambridge, 1984); Martin Nicol, "Riches from Rags: Bosses and Unions in the Cape Clothing Industry 1926–37", *Journal of Southern African Studies*, 9 (1983), pp. 239–257; Eddie Webster, *Cast in a Racial Mould* (Johannesburg, 1985).
39 Peter Limb, *The ANC's Early Years. Nation, Class and Place in South Africa Before 1940* (Pretoria, 2010).
40 T.Keegan, *Rural Transformations in Industrializing South Africa: The Southern Highveld to 1914* (Johannesburg, 1986); J. B. Loudon, *White Farmers and Black Labour-Tenants* (Cambridge and Leiden, 1970); Stanley Trapido, "Land and Labour in a Colonial Economy: The Transvaal 1880–1910", *Journal of Southern African Studies*, 5 (1978), pp. 26–56.
41 Helen Bradford, *A Taste of Freedom. The ICU in Rural South Africa 1924–30* (New Haven, CT, 1987).
42 H.J. Simons and R. Simons, *Class and Colour in South Africa* (Harmondsworth, 1969).

through informal relations with white miners and supervisors and internal interactions.[43]

The mine world for blacks was a male world. Women were not welcome on the compounds. Many men preferred to confine their sexual prowess to their own sex, with senior miners making use of newcomers, in good part as a means of saving money that could build homesteads at their point of origin rather than looking out for women in mining settlements.[44] Petty capitalist enterprise could emerge out of pilfering valuable materials.[45]

Perhaps two further aspects of the colonial labour scene deserve some mention. It would for instance be a mistake to see labour migration as being directed entirely to white employers. Very large numbers of Africans migrated to the cotton fields of the Gezira in the Sudan, to the peanut harvests of Senegambia, to the cocoa tree plantations of African planters in the Gold and Ivory Coasts and the cotton and coffee farms of Uganda.[46] Africa became, in Amin's schematic view, divided between labour-rich and cash producing feeder zones.[47] In favourable cases, notably amongst cocoa producers, where cocoa was par excellence Amin's example of a rich crop, the chances for migrants to establish their own farms with time were considerable.[48]

Moreover, Africans continued to work in diverse ways that reflected older patterns and often eluded government statistics. In Nigeria, craft production of cloth, household shelter and foodstuffs continued on a large scale, making use of the new forms of transport to reach wider markets.[49] Commerce expanded in these goods as well as in imports while the cash nexus developed or expanded.[50]

---

43 Robert Gordon, *Mines, Masters and Migrants* (Johannesburg, 1977) and, with reference to Nigeria, Carolyn Brown, *"We Were All Slaves"*; Enrique Martino Martin, *"Dash-Peonaje:* The Contradictions of Debt Bondage in the Colonial Plantations of Fernando Pó", *Africa*, forthcoming.
44 Moodie with Ndatshe, *Going for Gold.*
45 Ralph Callebert, "Cleaning the Wharves: Pilferage, Bribery, and Social Connections on the Durban Docks in the 1950s", *Canadian Journal of African Studies*, 46 (2012), pp. 23–38. Bill Freund, "Theft and Social Protest among the Tin Miners of Northern Nigeria", *Radical History Review*, 26 (1982), pp. 66–88.
46 Jean-P. Chrétien, "Des sédentaires devenus migrants: motif des départs des burundais et rwandais vers l'Uganda", *Cultures et développement*, 10 (1978), pp. 71–102; Jean Copans, *Les marabouts de l'arachide* (Paris, 1980); Polly Hill, *The Migrant Cocoa Farmers of Southern Ghana* (Cambridge, 1963); Jay O'Brien, "The Formation of the Agricultural Labour Force in Sudan", *Review of African Political Economy*, 26 (1983), pp. 15–34; A.F. Robertson, "Abusa: Structural History of an Economic Contract", *Journal of Development Studies*, 18 (1982), pp. 447–478; John Tosh, "The Cash Crop Revolution in Tropical Africa: An Agricultural Appraisal", *African Affairs*, 79 (1980), pp. 79–94.
47 Amin, *Modern Migrations.*
48 Austin, *Labour, Land, and Capital in Ghana.*
49 Judith Byfield, "Innovation and Conflict: Cloth Dyers and the Interwar Depression in Abeokuta, Nigeria", *Journal of African History*, 38 (1997), pp. 77–99; Mahir Saul, "Development of the Grain Market and Grain Merchants in Burkina Faso", *Journal of Modern African Studies*, 24 (1986), pp. 127–153.

Secondly, the workplace was not entirely filled by low-skilled men from rural areas. Colonial economies also required subaltern participation and leadership. Educational systems, at first largely created by missionaries, were developed so as to create opportunities for skilled and clerical workers, first and notably in West Africa. The best schools in Nyasaland, now Malawi, sent such workers all over the mining and commercial world of southern Africa. If whites were all too successful in closing out participation by others at desirable levels of work in South Africa, the situation was different in other areas. In Kenya there was considerable scope for Indian skilled workers. In the Katanga province of the Belgian Congo where militant South African white miners were replaced by more pliant and cheaper Belgians from the coal mines after 1920 and black labour was 'stabilized' with opportunities for miners, at least while in service, to bring their wives to settle and garden outside the provided housing, and to acquire skills.[51] The emerging educational system, the churches themselves, the police and the army, the health system, all were sites of growing numbers of employment hierarchies. The Katanga system was very different than the Rand (lung disease was not an issue in open-cast mining) but also highly articulated with one big corporation dominant.

Women were gradually becoming a feature of urban life too, as highlighted by Luise White in her path-breaking study of prostitutes and their many-faceted provision of 'the comforts of home' and their acquisition of urban property in East African towns.[52] Some women found employment in the intimate circumstances of the colonial household where they replaced men over time in many parts of Africa.[53] Not every worker went home from sites like Katanga when the Great Depression struck. The future, where a growing population of Africans not employed by Europeans, came into a new and often urban economy, began to unfold. This is what Furedi was to term an African 'crowd' in the case of Nairobi.[54]

The Second World War marked a significant new departure in the world of work. The post-war years saw a hunger for African agricultural goods and enabled the ideology of development to take off as a marker of late colonialism. This represented

---

50 Alain Morice, "Underpaid Child Labour and Social Reproduction: Apprenticeship in Kaolack, Senegal", *Development and Change*, 13 (1982), pp. 515–526; Kenneth Swindell, *Farm Labour* (Cambridge, 1985).
51 Michael Burawoy, *The Colour of Class on the Copperbelt* (Manchester, 1972); Bruce Fetter, "L'Union minière du Haut-Katanga 1920–40: la naissance d'une culture totalitaire", *Cahiers du CEDAF*, 6 (1973), pp. 1–40; Jane Parpart, *Capital and Labour on the African Copperbelt* (Philadelphia, 1983); Charles Perrings, *Black Mineworkers in Central Africa* (London, 1979).
52 Luise White, *The Comforts of Home. Prostitution in Colonial Nairobi* (Chicago, 1990); Claudine Vidal, "Guerre de sexe à Abidjan: masculin, feminine, CFA", *Cahiers d'études africaines*, 14 (1974), pp. 52–74.
53 Duncan Clarke, *Domestic Workers in Southern Rhodesia* (Gwelo, 1974); Jacklyn Cock, *Maids and Madams* (Johannesburg, 1980); Karen Hansen, "Domestic Service in Zambia", *Journal of Southern African Studies*, 13 (1986), pp. 57–81.
54 Frank Furedi, "The African Crowd in Nairobi", *Journal of African History*, 17 (1973), pp. 75–90.

an intensification of earlier trends to some extent. Roads and harbours were extended while mining now included base metal export operations such as the bauxite mines of Guinea, the iron ore of Liberia as well as the diamond industries of the Gold Coast and Sierra Leone. However, secondary industry created sometimes by resident European and Asian immigrants and sometimes directly by the state, also took off on a small scale in the countries with bigger markets.[55] On the one hand, colonial governments were more willing to provide worker housing and medical care, the beginnings of welfare. The British even imported labour union organizers to help structure orderly labour relations. On the other, the encouragement of new and larger waves of white settlement, for instance in the Portuguese colonies and the Belgian Congo, intensified racism at the workplace and elsewhere while development specialists created new kinds of pressure on African cultivators, often out of ignorance that pretended to be scientific wisdom such as with the notorious Groundnut Scheme in Tanganyika (the mainland of modern-day Tanzania). Fred Cooper has shown, both with regard to the dockers of Mombasa and the railway workers of French West Africa, however, that reforms aimed at creating some kind of industrial democracy with legal trade unions and social benefits typical of European conditions, were not necessarily desirable to Africans who had a foot in households with other economic rationales and activities. Workers were apt to resist being turned into proletarians of the classic sort.[56]

This, plus the politically opener climate which gingerly permitted the beginnings of African representation, intensified the potential for resistance. The labour historiography of this period, much of it written in the generation after independence, is dominated by political questions.[57] The 1940s saw big strikes in virtually every colony, notably the great railway strikes in Southern Rhodesia (modern-day Zimbabwe) and French West Africa, dock strikes in cities such as Mombasa and general strikes in Nigeria and the Gold Coast.[58] Trade unions now took on autonomous existence and

---

[55] Angela Cheater, *The Politics of Factory Organization. A Case Study in Independent Zimbabwe* (Gwelo,1986); Bruce Kapferer, *Strategy and Transaction in an African Factory* (Manchester, 1972); Paul Lubeck, *Early Industrialization and Social Class Formation among Factory Workers in Kano, Nigeria* (Evanston, IL, 1975); Adrian Peace, *Choice, Class and Conflict: A Study of Southern Nigerian Factory Workers* (London, 1979).

[56] Cooper, *On the African Waterfront*; Frederick Cooper, *Decolonisation and African Society. The Labour Question in French and British Africa* (Cambridge, 1996); Ian Henderson, "Early African Leadership: The Copperbelt Disturbances of 1935 and 1940", *Journal of Southern African Studies*, 2 (1973), pp. 83–97.

[57] Peter Gutkind, Robin Cohen and Jean Copans (eds), *African Labour History* (Beverly Hills and London, 1971); Richard Sandbrook and Robin Cohen (eds), *The Development of an African Working Class* (London, 1975). An even more committed and enthusiastic literature greeted the trade union insurgency in South Africa a generation later: Steven Friedman, *Building Tomorrow Today* (Johannesburg, 1987).

[58] Frederick Cooper (ed.), *The Struggle for the City* (London and Beverly Hills, 1984); Cooper, *On the African Waterfront*; Cooper, *Decolonisation;* Baruch Hirson, *Yours for the Union. Class and Community*

intense political salience; pressure from workers obliged colonial regimes to move farther and faster in political reform than was at first intended.[59] The rising nationalist movements made use of labour strife to build momentum and accede to power with some labour leaders rising themselves such as Sékou Touré in Guinea, Rashidi Kawawa in Tanzania and Tom Mboya in Kenya.

The hopes of workers that independence would improve their lives markedly proved largely vain. The new regimes felt threatened by independent unions which they tended to take over into state controlled structures with strikes repressed harshly. This was the history of organized labour in Nkrumah's Ghana, the model Pan-Africanist and nationalist state.[60] The Senegalese government under Senghor made it clear that industrious peasants were its first support base and workers making excessive demands could only cripple the economy, as did Nyerere in Tanzania.[61] Moreover, the economic demands on these governments were excessive; it was not possible for Nkrumah, as the typical Ghanaian package of exports–minerals and cocoa–stagnated in value after 1960, to give a better life to employed formal sector workers.

South Africa in the generation after World War Two, however, was remarkable for its level of industrialization. The state, particularly in the last Smuts government (1939–48) promoted investment in heavy industry, notably through the creation of parastatals. Steel, chemicals, shipbuilding took off and consumer goods industries also were hungry for workers. The big companies imitated the gold and other mines in the way large workforces were divided by race and administered at the workplace in almost military forms of control where workers had few rights. African industrial workers were typically described as 'semi-skilled'.[62] When the apartheid system took off, it precipitated segregated administrative and political systems, especially in the Bantustans but also in the big cities, that promoted black hierarchies via

---

Struggles in South Africa (London, New Jersey and Johannesburg, 1989); Bogumil Jewsiewicki, Kiloma Lema and Jean-Luc Vellut, "Documents pour servir à l'histoire sociale de Zaïre: grèves dans le Bas-Congo (Bas-Zaïre) en 1945", *Etudes d'histoire africaine*, 5 (1973), pp. 155–186; Robert Melson, "Nigerian Politics and the General Strike of 1964", in: Robert Rotberg and Ali Mazrui (eds), *Protest and Power in Black Africa* (New York, 1970), pp. 171–187; Dan O'Meara,"The 1946 African Miners' Strike and the Political Economy of South Africa", *Journal of Commonwealth and Comparative Politics*, 12 (1975), pp. 146–173; W. Oyemakinde, "The Nigerian General Strike of 1964", *Genève-Afrique*, 13 (1974), pp. 53–71; Timothy Scarnecchia, *The Urban Roots of Democracy and Political Violence in Zimbabwe: Harare and Highfield, 1940–1964* (Rochester, NY, 2008); Jim Silver, "Class Struggles in Ghana's Mining Industry", *Review of African Political Economy*, 12 (1978), pp. 67–86.

59 Robin Cohen, *Labour and Politics in Nigeria* (London, 1974); Ioan Davies, *African Trade Unions* (Harmondsworth, 1966).

60 Jeff Crisp, *The Story of an African Working Class: Ghanaian Miners' Struggles 1870–1980* (London, 1984); Richard Jeffries, *Class, Ideology and Power in Africa. The Railwaymen of Sekondi* (Cambridge, 1975); Silver, "Class Struggles".

61 Bill Freund, *The African Worker*; Issa Shivji, *Class Struggles in Tanzania* (London, 1976).

62 Owen Crankshaw, *Race, Class and the Changing Division of Labour under Apartheid* (London and New York, 1997); Doug Hindson, *Pass Controls and the Urban African Proletariat* (Johannesburg, 1987).

high schools and universities. The virtual absence of black skilled workers with recognized certification, were balanced by the rapid growth of white-collar workers in the social services, the police and the administration generally.[63] Apartheid also aimed at clearing out what remained of feudal type relationships on the land, removing farm workers to intensive settlements in the Bantustans and minimising the population in large stretches of countryside.[64] Work in industry and mining effectively now subsidised life in these supposed emerging independent states. By the 1980s, development efforts located there, as well as heavily subsidised industry in selected locations, were changing the economic basis of life in yet other parts of the country. The number of black women in towns almost equalled the number of men. Where before mid-century urban black women could really only find work in domestic service, as laundresses, or perhaps providing men with beer illegally, they began to be employed as well in factories.[65] Industrial activity was aimed, not at export, but at the local market and was supported by the seemingly limitless profits in natural resource exports with gold mining at the core.

After independence elsewhere and following the end of apartheid in South Africa, economic conditions tended to work against the retention of large unskilled labour forces under regulated conditions. Plans for industrialization were increasingly frustrated and a classic proletariat formation typical of the north-west European Industrial Revolution only existed in fragments. African society became substantially more urbanized but work conditions were dominated by precarity, enormous and expanding geographical mobility and the different activities grouped together as the "informal sector". In South Africa, the system of massive structured labour migration feeding mining, industry and agriculture gave way to equally massive rates of unemployment by the 1990s.

The economic history of independent Africa with its impact on political and social life can be divided into several distinct layers. In the first couple of decades after independence, some African produce prices held out (for instance for coffee) while aid poured in to Africa, in part as a Cold War stratagem. The new governments generally tried to extend the late colonial development efforts promoting social welfare in the form especially of class formative education and the beginnings of industrialization. However, they were increasingly indebted while Africa played a diminishing part in world commerce.

In the 1970s this trajectory halted. Debt crises were declared, aid was tied to narrow ends and ceased to increase while growth faltered or went into reverse. In some areas, such as the former Belgian Congo, the collapse of infrastructure and of the

---

[63] Crankshaw, *Race, Class and the Changing Division of Labour.*
[64] Michael de Klerk, "Seasons that will Never Return", *Journal of Southern African Studies*, 11 (1984), pp. 84–105; Cosmas Desmond, *The Discarded People* (Harmondsworth, 1971).
[65] Iris Berger, *Threads of Solidarity: Women in South African Industry, 1900–1980* (Bloomington, IN, 1992); Alex Lichtenstein, "Challenging *umthetho we femu* [the law of the firm]: Gender Relations and Shop Floor Battles for Union Recognition in Natal's Textile Industry, 1973–1985", *Africa*, forthcoming.

structuration of the colonial economy was spectacular as European-owned firms were 'indigenized' to the advantage of those with connections to the regime. Welfare started to become the province of so-called Non-Governmental Organizations, Western initiatives that teetered between charity and agencies of neo-liberal policy. NGO employment became an important resource for educated Africans who formed their own NGOs to liaise with the international outfits. In some areas such as Mozambique, central government control gave way to violent secession movements and cult-led insurgencies.

This phase, which I have elsewhere called the age of structural adjustment from the typical programmes pursued by the International Finance Institutions, could be said to have lasted to approximately the end of the twentieth century.[66] The best-off African economies such as those in Ghana, the Ivory Coast and Zambia were often the biggest debtors and here the most dramatic regressions occurred.[67]

In such countries as Nigeria, Sierra Leone and Zambia, mining, the ultimate prop of the African exchange economies, collapsed as a corporate enterprise giving way to so-called artisanal mining whereby large numbers of Africans tried their luck under very dangerous conditions to earn money individually with profits accruing to merchants, licensed and illicit.[68] The remarkable Murid Islamic order shifted its adepts from the peanut cultivation and export sector in Senegal to the import of industrial, notably electronic goods, and Murid traders spread throughout the major commercial nodes of the world—New York, Rome, Hong Kong and elsewhere.[69] Political disasters created African diasporas, for instance, of Somali speakers who also emigrated to most continents but retained commercially and socially significant network linkages.[70] Sahara oasis towns were amongst those that swelled up into small cities full of temporary residents who hoped to be on their way somewhere, most likely north.[71] The scale of urban growth, no longer accompanied by the availability of structured employment, was spectacular.

---

[66] Bill Freund, *The Making of Contemporary Africa*, 3rd edition (London and Boulder, CO, 2016).
[67] Jean-Pierre Dozon, *Les clefs de la crise ivoirienne* (Paris, 2011); James Ferguson, *Expectations of Modernity. Myths and Meanings of Urban Life on the Zambian Copperbelt* (Berkeley, CA, 1999); Johan Pottier, *Migrants No More, Migrants No More. Settlement and Survival in Mambwe Villages* (Manchester, 1988).
[68] Deborah Bryceson, *Mining and Social Transformation in Africa: Tracing Mineralizing and Democratizing Trends in Artisanal Production* (London, 2014); Filip de Boeck, "Garimpeiro Worlds: Digging, Dying and 'Hunting' for Diamonds in Angola", *Review of African Political Economy*, 90 (2001), pp. 548–562; Miles Larmer, *Mineworkers in Zambia; Labour and Political Change in Post-Colonial Africa* (London, 2007).
[69] Cheikh Guèye, "New Information and Communication Technology Use by Muslim Mourides in Senegal", *Review of African Political Economy*, 98 (2003), pp. 609–625.
[70] Jonny Steinberg, *A Man of Good Hope. A Refugee's Tale* (New York, 2015).
[71] James McDougall and Judith Scheele (eds), *Saharan Frontiers. Space and Mobility in Northwest Africa* (Bloomington and Indianapolis, 2012); Martin Verlet, *Grandir à Nima, Ghana, Les figures de travail dans un faubourg populaire d'Accra* (Paris, 2005).

However, as Potts has noted particularly, urbanization is not always one-way traffic.[72] It is more that Africans in a country such as Zimbabwe shift between the rural and urban just as they cross international boundaries or use the cities as platforms for further emigration.[73] This set of circumstances has created a conjuncture of internationalization, globalization of movement and of work in which borders have melted and requiring new ways of understanding human trajectories and endeavours.

The trend which dominates current literature was the so-called informal sector. By this was meant labour that the state did not regulate, register or control. This range of diverse activities already emerged, and possibly submerged, the early industrial workforce in growing African cities. For some writers, the informal sector seemed to offer new opportunities, divorced from the parasitical grasp of African states, especially for women who escaped from patriarchal structures imposed by the so-called traditional sector that typically dominated the countryside. However others have criticised this approach and noted that this 'sector' is very loosely defined and actually embraces large numbers of irregularly employed, poorly paid and very oppressed workers such as the bus drivers of Dar es Salaam or the large network of shoemakers in the lower Niger valley of eastern Nigeria.[74] In a poor society catering to a consumer population living hand to mouth, the scale of opportunities is small and mobility fairly rare. Perhaps a better way of understanding these trends than informality, with its echoes of state or corporate control as analytically decisive, is precarity. The precarity of modern African life and its implications are profound.

After 2000, with the swing, especially promoted by the economic rise of China, towards higher commodity prices and lower prices of industrial goods, Africa experienced a new wave of significant economic growth measurable in figures. This wave has promoted some return, notable in Zambia for instance, from artisanal to corporate mineral production.[75] It has allowed the coffers of the state to become less empty. Secondary industry for the local market has revived to a limited extent and the state has been able to sustain the renewed expansion of services especially in health and education with corresponding expansion of employment at all levels. Trade unions have re-emerged from state control or dominance, sometimes playing a key role in agitation for greater democratization.[76] They are gradually losing

---

[72] Deborah Potts, *Circular Migration in Zimbabwe and Sub-Saharan Africa* (Oxford, 2010).
[73] See also Helena Pérez Niño, "Migrant Workers into Contract Farmers: Processes of Labour Mobilisation in Colonial and Contemporary Mozambique", *Africa*, forthcoming.
[74] Kate Meagher, *Identity Politics; Social Networks and the Informal Economy in Nigeria* (Oxford, 2010); Matteo Rizzo, "'Life is War': Informal Transport Workers and Neoliberalism in Tanzania 1998–2009", *Development and Change*, 42 (2012), pp. 1179–1206.
[75] Larmer, *Mineworkers*.
[76] Bjørn Beckman, Sakhela Buhlungu and Lloyd Sachikonye (eds), *Trade Unions and Party Politics. Labour Movements in Africa* (Cape Town, 2010); Jon Kraus (ed.) *Trade Unions and the Coming of Democracy in Africa* (London, 2007).

their affiliation to the ruling– or any other–political party as well as any orientation to a clear alternative political agenda.

Where conflict zones persist or develop, as in the Congo, Somalia or the Central African Republic, international agency employs significant numbers of African soldiers usually under the rubric of the United Nations. For unskilled workers in South Africa and elsewhere, a huge growth area of employment has been in 'security', as much or more focussed on the private sector to defend the lives and property of the well-off against massive crime rates. Criminals themselves form a network of labour of sorts. In some countries such as Gambia, Senegal, South Africa and Kenya, a tourist economy focussed on beaches and game parks, has fed into a general expansion of services and the financial sector which typifies twenty first century capitalism more generally.

Also to be noted is the emergence of what can be called an entertainment sector. Musicians form a fascinating and important part of the urban economy in virtually every country.[77] The plastic arts and sculpture employ those who produce for tourists, visitors and the African middle class as well as a few individuals with international reputations for innovation and quality. In Nigeria, 'Nollywood' (e.g. Lagos) makes and exports throughout the continent videos reflecting African popular culture.[78] It is coupled with another area of employment and enterprise—charismatic religion equipped with the full range of contemporary communications technology. Sport, above all football but also, for instance distance running especially in Ethiopia and Kenya, is increasingly professionalised with an increasingly familiar international success hierarchy. Finally, one might mention one impact of urban growth— the unsteady but often spectacular expansion of physical plant and the construction industry which employs so many migrants and individuals greatly ranging in origins and skills.

Class becomes a clearer factor. If capitalist enterprise involving significant profits —new mines, big construction projects, agro-business, the organized tourist industry —largely seem to engage remaining, sometimes growing, white and Asian minorities or foreign interests, this is not to negate the gradual emergence of some very wealthy and dynamic African capitalists. The development baton, so laden with the hand of paternalistic European late colonialism, is off the ground again but more in the hands of local states and elites. The local is becoming marginalised or at least beginning to be tied to global patterns.

---

[77] Steven Feld, *Jazz Cosmopolitanism in Accra* (Durham and London, 2012); Mark Perullo, *Live from Dar es Salaam. Popular Music and Tanzania's Music Economy* (Bloomington and Indianapolis, 2011).
[78] Bruce Larkin, *Signal and Noise. Media Infrastructure and Urban Culture in Nigeria* (Durham and London, 2008); Okomo Onookome, *Global Nollywood. The Transnational Dimensions of an African Video Film Industry* (Bloomington and Indianapolis, 2013).

Suggested reading

Austin, Gareth. *Labour, Land, and Capital in Ghana: From Slavery to Free Labour in Asante 1907–1956* (Rochester: University of Rochester Press, 2005).
Brown. Carolyn. *"We Were All Slaves". African Miners, Culture and Resistance at the Enugu Government Colliery* (Portsmouth, NH, Oxford and Cape Town: Currey, 2003).
Cooper, Frederick. *Decolonisation and African Society. The Labour Question in French and British Africa* (Cambridge: Cambridge University Press, 1996).
Davies, Robert H. *Capital, State and White Labour in South Africa. An Historical Materialist Analysis of Class Formation and Class Relations* (Brighton: The Harvester Press, 1979).
Deutsch, Jan-Georg. *Abolition without Emancipation in German East Africa* (Columbus, OH: Ohio University Press, 2005).
Echenberg, Myron. *Colonial Conscripts: The Tirailleurs Sénégalais in French West Africa, 1857–1960* (Portsmouth, NH: Currey, 1991).
Freund, Bill. *The African Worker* (Cambridge: Cambridge University Press, 1988).
Galaty, John G. and Pierre Bonté (eds), *Herders, Warriors and Traders; Pastoralism in Africa* (Boulder, CO: Westview Press, 1991).
Grillo, Ralph D. *African Railwaymen. Solidarity and Opposition in an East African Labour Force* (Cambridge: Cambridge University Press, 1973).
Gutkind, Peter C.W., Robin Cohen and Jean Copans (eds). *African Labour History* (Beverly Hills and London: SAGE, 1971).
Harms, Robert W. *River of Wealth, River of Sorrow: The Central Zaire Basin in the Era of the Slave and Ivory Trade, 1500–1891* (New Haven, CT: Yale University Press, 1981).
Harries, Patrick. *Work, Culture and Identity. Migrant Labour in Mozambique and South Africa c. 1860–1910* (Oxford, Johannesburg and Portsmouth, NH, 1994).
Hart, Keith. "'Informal Income Opportunities and Urban Employment in Ghana", *Journal of Modern African Studies*, 11 (1973), pp. 141–169.
Hill, Polly. *The Migrant Cocoa Farmers of Southern Ghana. A Study in Rural Capitalism* (Cambridge: Cambridge University Press, 1963; reprint 1977).
Jeffries, Richard. *Class, Ideology and Power in Africa. The Railwaymen of Sekondi* (Cambridge: Cambridge University Press, 1978).
Kraus, Jon (ed.) *Trade Unions and the Coming of Democracy in Africa* (Basingstoke: Palgrave Macmillan, 2007).
Larmer, Miles. *Mineworkers in Zambia. Labour and Political Change in Post-Colonial Africa* (London [etc.]: Tauris Academic Studies, 2007).
Lewis, Jon. *Industrialisation and Trade Union Organisation in South Africa 1924–55. The Rise and Fall of the South African Trades and Labour Council* (Cambridge: Cambridge University Press, 1984).
Lovejoy, Paul E. *Transformations in Slavery. A History of Slavery in Africa* (Cambridge: Cambridge University Press, 1983; second edition 2000).
Miers, Suzanne and Richard Roberts (eds). *The End of Slavery in Africa* (Madison WI, University of Wisconsin Press, 1988).
Moodie, T. Dunbar with V. Ndatshe. *Going for Gold. Men, Mines and Migration* (Berkeley and London: University of California Press, 1994)
Parpart, Jane L. *Capital and Labour on the African Copperbelt* (Philadelphia: Temple University Press, 1983).
Peace, Adrian. *Choice, Class and Conflict: A Study of Southern Nigerian Factory Workers* (Brighton: The Harvester Press, 1979).

Rockel, Stephen. *Carriers of Culture. Labor on the Road in Nineteenth-Century East Africa* (Portsmouth NH: Currey, 2006).

Sandbrook, Richard and Robin Cohen (eds), *The Development of an African Working Class. Studies in Class Formation and Action* (London: Longman, 1975).

Shivji, Issa. *Class Struggles in Tanzania* (London, Heinemann, 1976).

Stichter, Sharon. *Migrant Labour* (Cambridge: Cambridge University Press, 1985).

Swindell, Kenneth. *Farm Labour* (Cambridge: Cambridge University Press, 1985).

Van Onselen, Charles. *Chibaro. African Mine Labour in Southern Rhodesia, 1900–1933* (London: Pluto Press, 1976).

White, Luise. *The Comforts of Home. Prostitution in Colonial Nairobi* (Chicago: Chicago University Press, 1990).

Worger, William H. *South Africa's City of Diamonds. Mine Workers and Monopoly Capitalism in Kimberley* (New Haven, CT: Yale University Press, 1987).

Rossana Barragán and David Mayer
2.4. Latin America and the Caribbean

One of the main aspirations of Global Labour History is to include all groups of workers into the historical analysis. Going beyond the classical domain of labour historiography up until the 1990s–(mostly male) industrial factory workers–it has set out to include the history of slaves and other unfree labourers, as well as of self-employed, informal, precarious, unpaid, or subsistence workers, all both male and female. In this regard, research from and about Latin America has played a peculiar 'double role'. On the one hand, it has been a pivotal reference point for the emergence of the field of Global Labour History and for formulating some of its central ideas: the combination of the history of slavery with the study of industrial workers in order to create a reformed *labour history* was experimented with in Brazil much earlier than in other parts of the world and was institutionalized in 2000 with the foundation of *mundos do trabalho*,[1] giving way to one of the most versatile labour historiographies. For a much longer period, researchers from and about Latin America have debated the idea that a commercially oriented production of export goods for the world market–from bullion to crops–can be combined with all kinds of labour relations on the spot: from slavery, *corvée*, and other forms of coerced labour to debt peonage, share cropping, and free wage labour; this assessment was indeed a central issue in the heated controversies around *dependency* which arose in the 1960s.

On the other hand, and as against this role of a vanguard and reference point, labour history from and about Latin America in many cases still functions in very conventional ways, featuring a number of limitations. Firstly, most of the literature still reduces the history of labour to that of industrial workers. Such self-restraint has recently been expressly affirmed by a major proponent in the field.[2] This, however, would mean treating slavery and the multiple other forms of unfree work as the area of specialists and not necessarily labour historians. In addition, it indirectly implies that from a certain moment on, free wage-labour became the only or major form of labour, thus excluding a series of other groups that constitute a substantial part of the active population in Latin America today. Secondly, historical labour research in

---

[1] *Mundos do trabalho* constituted itself as working group of the Brazilian History Association (Associação Nacional de História, ANPUH). Apart from regular academic gatherings and congresses, since 2009 it publishes an academic journal with the same name.

[2] James P. Brennan, "Latin American Labour History", in: Jose C. Moya (ed.), *The Oxford Handbook of Latin American History* (Oxford, 2011), pp. 342–366, at 359–360. Brennan's (by no means unfounded) reservation is that the specific raison d'être of labour history gets diluted if too many other fields (such as rural history, urban history, etc.) are included; in that, he critically replies to an earlier cue by John French who in 2006 explicitly called for a broader temporal and conceptual scope of Latin American labour history: John D. French, "The Labouring and Middle-Class Peoples of Latin America and the Caribbean: Historical Trajectories and New Research Directions", in: Jan Lucassen (ed.), *Global Labour History. A State of the Art* (Bern, 2006), pp. 289–333, at 322–331.

and about Latin America is still mostly national. Again, recently, this has not quite been vindicated, though it has certainly been presented as something that little can be done about.[3] Meanwhile, the lack of comparative studies or transnational approaches is reflected in the relative isolation of researchers vis-à-vis their continental peers: exchanges are often more intense between Latin America and the North Atlantic than among Latin Americans themselves. Similarly compartmentalized along the lines of given polities and their spaces is the lack of comparisons between the different colonial empires (Spanish, Portuguese, Dutch, and British).

In this chapter, we will suggest widening the temporal scope of Latin American labour history (beginning with the subcontinent's colonization in the fifteenth and sixteenth centuries) and including all groups of workers. In the given space, only a general outline can be presented. Several other fields of historical research are involved–such as colonial history, rural history, the history of slavery, economic history, etc.–all with their respective concerns and accumulated, often immense literature. For labour history alone (based on its conventional meaning as the *history of urban industrial workers and their organizations*) a number of bibliographical overviews and interpretative surveys exist on which the following considerations build.[4] While such an approach must necessarily entail a series of gaps and neglect the considerable variations among regions in Latin America for almost any labour relation, our aim is, firstly, to illustrate the wide variety of forms of labour prevalent since colonial times and, secondly, to outline the demarcations and debates of a broadened field of historical labour studies in Latin America.

From the sixteenth to the nineteenth century

Labour systems in colonial Latin America[5] saw a marked geographical and chronological differentiation. Indigenous labour was predominant in the two mainland regions of the Spanish empire, the Mesoamerican region (chiefly what later became Mexico and Guatemala) and the Andean Region (largely today's Ecuador, Peru, and Bolivia). Meanwhile, African slavery was key in Brazil and in the mainland and Caribbean territories seized by the Dutch, the British, and the French.

---

[3] Peter Winn, "Global Labour History: The Future of the Field?", *International Labor and Working-Class History*, 82 (2012), pp. 85–91, at 86–88.

[4] Wide-angled vantage points of the 'biblioscape' are offered, for instance, by: Brennan, "Latin American Labour History"; French, "Laboring and Middle-Class Peoples of Latin America"; John D. French, "The Latin American Labor Studies Boom", *International Review of Social History*, 45 (2000), pp. 279–308.

[5] The notion of *Latin America* was introduced only in the 1840s. It was coined in France among a transnational cosmopolitan elite born in Panama, Chile, and Argentina, and living in Paris. The term 'Latin' emphasized their shared history of colonialism, Catholicism, and opposition to Anglo-Saxon North America. See: Michel Gobat, "The Invention of Latin America: A Transnational History of Anti-Imperialism, Democracy and Race", *American Historical Review*, 118, 5 (2013), pp. 1345–1375.

Indigenous Labour

In 1492, the native population of the American Continent is estimated to have been between fifty and sixty million. At least six million people were living in the Aztec Empire, five to ten million in the Mayan states, and eleven million in the Inca Empire. The estimates for Brazil speak of three million people in 1500. This population then served as the main component of the labour regimes established after the Spanish and, to a lesser degree, Portuguese conquests.

These regimes were characterized by comprehensive, albeit varying, mechanisms of coercion. Indigenous forced labour in this early period sometimes took the form of slavery (in Central America and the Caribbean region).[6] Almost simultaneously, the institution of the *encomienda* became the main modality to access the indigenous labour force. The *encomienda* (from *encomendar*, to commission) was awarded to Spanish conquerors and first generation settlers by the Spanish Crown. It delegated a series of duties to these *encomenderos* (christianization of the indigenous population, maintaining order, etc.) and conferred them fundamental privileges, the most important being the labour service of these people (or a tribute in kind). The *encomenderos* depended on the traditional indigenous authorities (*caciques*) to guarantee tribute payments and to channel labour to different economic activities. Although in its early conception the encomienda was relatively short-lived, it nevertheless established some fundamental and recurring mechanisms of labour provision through coercion for the colonial period and beyond, including the intermediating role of indigenous dignitaries and leaders.

The violence of the conquest and the dramatic decline of the population (ninety to ninety-five percent of the population vanished, although the rates varied among the different regions) led the Dominican Friar Bartolomé de las Casas to famously plea for the abolition of the *encomienda* and all compulsory and unpaid labour by the indigenous people. The Spanish Kings subsequently banned the enslavement of the indigenous population (except in war) and issued the New Laws of 1542 that ordered that the natives be considered free and that the owners of the *encomiendas* could no longer demand any unpaid labour services from them. This also represented a power struggle between the Crown and the new colonial elites and in some cases, such as in Peru, even led to armed confrontations.

While from 1560 onwards numerous laws insisted that the Indigenous were free and could only work voluntarily and in exchange for wages, the demand for labour constantly grew with the consolidation of the colonial rule and the intensification of extractive activities in mining. The legal regime of confining the unrestricted exploitation of the local population (which in many regions did not recover from the initial

---

6 Seymour Drescher, "White Atlantic? The Choice for African Slave Labour in the Plantation Americas", in: David Eltis, Frank D. Lewis, and Kenneth L. Sokoloff (eds), *Slavery in the Development of the Americas* (Cambridge, 2004), pp. 31–69, at 43.

demographic catastrophe for a long time) was thus offset by a number of mechanisms of labour and tribute exaction. Since the late sixteenth century, the *repartimiento* (distribution) of indigenous labour became the general norm. This was a mandatory, paid labour draft based partially on pre-Hispanic forms of labour tribute. It was designed to last for specific time periods and it began to function for mining, public works, and building and construction activities in the cities. This entailed mobilizing the workforce from the rural communities of the vast territories of the previous pre-Hispanic empires, and it meant that the Spaniards continued to rely on indirect rule, using and recreating much of the traditional governmental structure at the local level.

The main export commodities on the mainland of the continent during almost three centuries were gold and silver. Silver, which entered into a continuous exchange between the Americas, Europe, Asia, and Africa enabled and fuelled the world trade of the epoch. Between 1500 and 1800, eighty percent of the world's silver was produced in Latin America. The two major silver mining centres were Potosí (today Bolivia) and northern central Mexico.

Mining in Potosí was mainly based on indigenous labour. After the Spanish conquest, the extraction process, smelting, casting in wind-blown furnaces (a traditional pre-Hispanic technique called *huayras*), and the sale of the silver in local markets were controlled by the indigenous population. It was a system of sharecropping. After 1570, however, important reforms were introduced. This led to the reorganization of the labour system, resorting to an old Inca system of labour tribute, the *mita* ('turn' or 'work'). This allowed a constant supply of labour, involving an indigenous labour force of 14,000 men per year, who were between eighteen and fifty years of age and recruited from seventeen provinces. The workers, called *mitayos*, went to Potosí with their families and laboured in the mines and mills for a year under the leadership of local indigenous authorities. The *mita* was complemented with another type of labourer, the *mingas*, i.e. persons who were paid by day or week. In fact, both groups overlapped, as the *mitayos* worked for one week out of three and therefore often performed labour as *mingas* during the second and third week.[7]

In contrast, Mexico had multiple silver mining locations in the northern central part of the colony around towns such as Zacatecas, Guanajuato, or Pachuca. When mining first begun, indigenous slaves were used. Over time, in Mexico, silver mining saw a complex and differentiated array of labour relations. On the one hand, there was the large majority of those who were forced to work there, including *indios*,

---

[7] Rossana Barragán Romano, "Dynamics of Continuity and Change: Shifts in Labour Relations in the Potosí Mines (1680–1812)", *International Review of Social History*, 61 (2016), Special Issue 24, pp. 93–114. For Potosí also see the following studies: Peter Bakewell, *Miners of the Red Mountain. Indian Labor in Potosí, 1545–1650* (Albuquerque, NM, 1984); and Jeffrey Cole, *The Potosí Mita, 1573–1700. Compulsory Indian Labor in the Andes* (Stanford, CA, 1985). For later periods, see: Enrique Tandeter, *Coercion and Market. Silver Mining in Colonial Potosí, 1692–1826* (Albuquerque, NM, 1993).

under the systems of *naboría* (a kind of serfdom) and *repartimiento*, as well as African slaves. On the other hand, there were free wage labourers, a group which varied constantly in size. The wage system included both cash payments and ore-sharing arrangements, called *pepena* or *partido*.[8] The year 1766 gave rise to a severe conflict about the *partido* in the mining town of Real del Monte. This conflict is sometimes considered the first strike in Latin America.[9]

Mining, of course, was not the only non-agrarian productive activity. The urban artisanal sector involved a complex array of workers of different socio-racial status: some trades were the domain of European immigrants and their descendants, others of indigenous artisans; in all trades, unfree labourers of varying origin could be involved. The Spanish Empire also saw the emergence of larger-scale manufacturing in the form of textile workshops (*obrajes*). These were sometimes cited as the first sprouts of an autochthonous Latin American industrialization, yet even in the recent debate about *labour intensive industrialization in global history*, which sets out to discuss alternative paths of industrial development beyond the European 'model', these are seen more as stinted enterprises, limited to the colonial context, than as first, proto-industrial steps.[10] *Obrajes* mainly developed in Puebla and Querétaro (Mexico), Quito (today Ecuador), and Cuzco (today Peru). They included almost all steps of wool cloth manufacturing and involved a heterogeneous mix of labour relations.

The great majority of the population, however, lived in rural areas. Subsistence production, indigenous communal land tenure, and smaller-scale production for local markets existed aside larger rural private estates, owned by Europeans and their descendants. Socio-racial correlations were not automatic, though: Indigenous peasants could produce substantial amounts for markets and larger estates could be limited to subsistence. The character of the latter, the *haciendas*, is a classic controversy of Latin American social history. Depending on the period and the location, the assessment changes from self-contained, autarchic entities representing a feudal, patriarchal order to dynamic, outward-looking capitalist enterprises producing for regional, interregional, or even intercontinental markets.[11]

---

8 John Monteiro, "Labour Systems", in: Victor Bulmer-Thomas, John H. Coatsworth, and Roberto Cortés Conde (eds), *The Cambridge Economic History of Latin America*. Vol. 1: *The Colonial Era and the Short Nineteenth Century* (Cambridge, 2006), pp. 185–234, at 226. On Mexican mining also see: Cuauthémoc Velasco Ávila, "Los trabajadores mineros en la Nueva España, 1750–1810", in: Enrique Florescano et al., *La clase obrera en la historia de México*. Vol. 1: *De la colonia al imperio* (México, DF, 1980), pp. 239–301.
9 See: Doris M. Ladd, *The Making of a Strike. Mexican Silver Workers' Struggles in Real del Monte 1766–1775* (Lincoln, NE, 1988).
10 Colin M. Lewis, "'Colonial' Industry and 'Modern' Manufacturing: Opportunities for Labour-Intensive Growth in Latin America, c. 1800–1940", in: Gareth Austin and Kaoru Sugihara (eds), *Labour-Intensive Industrialization in Global History* (London and New York, 2013), pp. 231–262, at 233f.
11 For an overview of these debates see: Eric Van Young, "Rural History", in: Moya, *Oxford Handbook of Latin American History*, pp. 309–341, at 312–318.

Understanding the nature of the labour involved was and still is the key issue in this debate. Indeed, the recruitment of labourers was the single most important challenge for these *haciendas* and took the most diverse forms, from traditional claims to labour services and the use of outright coercion, through tenancy and sharecropping arrangements, to the employment of seasonal labour. The conditions of these workers also varied according to the degree to which they were attached to the rural estates as permanent, seasonal, or casual labourers. Those living permanently on the estates had different names in each region, from *gañanes* in Mexico, through *inquilinos* in Chile, to *yanaconas* in the Andes. Many estates adopted a system of tenancy where peasants received a plot of land and had to work on the land of the owners in exchange. The seasonal and casual labourers (in most regions they were known as *peones*) complemented the requirements of the estates. Sometimes, the population decline could push up real wages but in other moments this circumstance led to the increased use of coercion, such as in debt peonage.[12] During the eighteenth century, one instrument to push peasants to work for wages was the so-called *repartos de bienes* y *mercancías*, which forced indigenous communities to buy certain goods at elevated prices from monopoly sellers. While earlier scholarship underlined the coercion and exploitation involved in the *repartos de bienes*, some recent studies reconsidered these to be a form of credit system and thus pointed to the opportunities they offered for articulating the Spanish and the indigenous economies.[13] In any case, coinciding with the prevalence of the *repartos de bienes* (and with a series of economic and political changes introduced by the colonial authorities), at the end of the eighteenth century three major insurrections took place in the Andean Region (associated with the names of Tomás Katari, Túpac Amaru, and Túpac Katari).[14]

Female labourers were directly or indirectly present in almost all of the labour arrangements described. As mentioned, tribute labour often involved many more people than those actually drafted, as women and children temporally migrated as well. In addition, female labour was particularly important in the cities in the domestic services but also in the urban markets: the markets in the Mexican, Guatemalan, and Andean cities were occupied by women.[15]

While indigenous forced labour was fundamental in the early Portuguese colonization of Brazil as well, the Portuguese were not able to build upon a previous im-

---

12 Monteiro, *Labor Systems*, p. 228.
13 Margarita Menegus (ed.), *El Repartimiento forzoso de mercaderías en México, Perú y Filipinas* (México, DF, 2000).
14 Sinclair Thomson, *We Alone Will Rule. Native Andean Politics in the Age of Insurgency* (Madison, WI, 2002); Sergio Serulnikov, *Revolution in the Andes. The Age of Túpac Amaru* (Durham, NC, 2013); Charles Walker, *The Tupac Amaru Rebellion* (Boston, 2016).
15 Karen Vieira Powers, *Women in the Crucible of Conquest. The Gendered Genesis of Spanish American Society, 1500–1600* (Albuquerque, NM, 2005); Irene Silverblatt, *Moon, Sun, and Witches. Gender Ideologies and Class in Inca and Colonial Peru* (Princeton, NJ, 1987); Susan Socolow, *Women of Colonial Latin America* (Cambridge, 2000).

perial structure and a territorially integrated system of labour tribute (such as the Spanish in the case of the Aztec and Inca empires). The mobilization of indigenous labour thus took the form of more direct coercion through the systematic capturing of people from the regions of the not-yet-colonized interior, resulting in a marked demographic decline in the indigenous population. Thus, with the beginning of a first sugar boom in the sixteenth century, African slaves became the fundamental workforce of the colony. It should always be born in mind, however, that in certain regions and moments indigenous forced labour continued to play an important role in Brazil during the entire colonial period.

African Slavery in Latin America

By the mid-sixteenth century, the transatlantic slave trade had established itself, with its well-known triangular dynamic of transporting commodities from Europe to Africa, enslaving people from Africa and taking them to the Americas, and transporting commodities from the Americas to Europe. Until 1800, the main centres of slavery were the island Hispaniola, the Brazilian coast, and the non-Spanish Caribbean where slaves worked in the sugar plantations and other export-oriented rural estates. Apart from this plantation slavery, however, slaves were present in all regions of Latin America performing all kinds of work.[16] While the numbers of actual African slaves living in Latin America (including those born there) still remain uncertain estimates, those of the slaves transferred in the middle passage have been approximated ever more precisely in recent research:[17] from 1500 until the final abolition in the second half of the nineteenth century about 12.5 million people were brought to Latin America and the Caribbean from different African regions, a perilous transfer which about 10.7 million survived. Most arrived in Brazil (ca. 4.8 million), while Spanish America received 1.2 million. While 780,000 arrived in Cuba (though the majority of them only in the nineteenth century), Hispaniola, Puerto Rica, and mainland Spanish America also saw considerable numbers in earlier periods. Even in those places where today's socio-cultural imagination does not acknowledge an Afro-American heritage (e. g. in Chile, the Rio de la Plata cities, and Mexico City), the presence of slaves was considerable.

---

16 A general overview of the development of African slavery in all regions of Latin America is offered in: Herbert Klein and Ben Vinson III, *African Slavery in Latin America and the Caribbean* (New York, 2007). For its origin and establishing see chapters 1 and 2.
17 To a high degree, this improvement was possible thanks to "Voyages: The Trans-Atlantic Slave Trade Database" (www.slavevoyages.org), a multi-institutional research cooperation which, from 2006, brought together many previous and ongoing endeavours in establishing numbers of slaves deported in the transatlantic slave trade. Numbers mentioned here are based on the tables available on the website.

In the regions of the Spanish Empire, the labour demand for African slaves grew in intensity from the last decades of the sixteenth century. This was due in part to the decline of the indigenous population but also to support some specific segments of the Spanish economy. African slaves and free blacks played a crucial role on estates that produced sugar (e.g. in Veracruz, Mexico), wine (in Peru on the Pacific coast), and wheat, in some of the silver and gold mines (e.g. in Barbacoas and Chocó, now in Colombia), in the above-mentioned *obrajes*, in urban domestic services (particularly in the big cities like Mexico, Lima, and Buenos Aires), in different specialized crafts, and in the shipbuilding industry.[18] In Brazil, slaves could also be found in activities other than plantation labour, from agriculture, cattle-breeding, or other food production to domestic services, crafts, or all kinds of transport labour, both on the coast and in the interior. A special variant of slavery in Brazil were the *escravos de ganho* (wage-earning slaves), who were ordered by their owners to seek wage labour (often at ports) and had to hand over a certain part of their earnings to them.[19] However, the majority of slaves in Brazil–as well as in those Spanish regions and Caribbean possessions by other powers where slave labour was the very foundation of the coastal or insular plantation economy–were put to work in often extremely arduous agricultural field labour. High mortality rates and constant resistance through flight and other activities testify to the hyper-exploitative character of this labour.

Although the first commercial sugarcane *ingenios* (cane plantations plus mills where the sugar cane was processed into exportable molasses or raw sugar) in the Americas were founded on the then Spanish island of Hispaniola (today Haiti and the Dominican Republic), it was Brazil's Northeast which emerged as the major centre of a slave-based sugar-plantation economy.[20] By 1600, more than sixty *engenhos* could be found in Pernambuco and around fourty in Bahia. These were complemented by smaller *lavradores de cana* that operated on smaller fields without mills and

---

18 Monteiro, *Labor Systems*, p. 208. For an example of the complicated coexistence of slavery and wage-labour in urban artisanal production, see: Lyman L. Johnson, "The Competition of Slave and Free Labor in Artisanal Production: Buenos Aires, 1770–1815", in: Tom Brass and Marcel van der Linden (eds), *Free and Unfree Labour: The Debate Continues* (Bern, 1997), pp. 265–280.
19 On labour and lives of urban slaves in Brazil, including the *escravos de ganho*, see for instance: Mary C. Karasch, *Slave Life in Rio de Janeiro, 1808–1850* (Princeton, NJ, 1987). On the wage-earning slaves' role in nineteenth-century urban contentiousness see: João José Reis, "'The Revolution of the Ganhadores': Urban Labour, Ethnicity and the African Strike of 1857 in Bahia, Brazil", *Journal of Latin American Studies*, 29 (1997), pp. 355–393.
20 Christopher Ebert, *Between Empires. Brazilian Sugar in the Early Atlantic Economy, 1550–1630* (Leiden and Boston, 2008); Daniel Strum, *The Sugar Trade: Brazil, Portugal and the Netherlands (1595–1630)* (Stanford, CA, 2013); Mary Eschberger Priante, *Escravos, mãos e pés do senhor de engenho. Economia açucareira no período colonial do Brasil* (Porto Alegre, 2004).

with less slaves. Together, these accounted for two thirds of the sugar produced in the Americas at the time.[21]

In the mid-seventeenth century, the centre of sugar-cane production began to shift again towards the Caribbean, where other European powers increasingly held possessions and introduced sugar plantations, most famously the French in the colony of Saint Domingue (the western part of the island Hispaniola). Meanwhile, the relative decline of slave-based sugar production in Brazil's Northeast was offset by a gold (and, to a lesser degree, diamond) boom in the centre and south of the country.[22] These changes and the constant influx of African slaves meant that by 1800 Brazil not only had the largest slave population in the Americas, it also saw the broadest diversity of the use of slave labour in both rural and urban activities. This, together with the considerable number of freed slaves and free-born Afro-Brazilians, gave rise to a variegated socio-racial constellation in Brazilian society.

In the Spanish Empire, the slave trade, which previously had been regulated through licenses and monopolies, was liberalized in 1789, resulting in the development of new centres of slave-based production in several regions: in Chocó (today Colombia) in the production of gold, in Venezuela in cacao, and in Puerto Rico and Cuba in coffee and, above all, sugar.[23] It was especially Cuba which experienced its heyday of a slave-based plantation economy only in the nineteenth century–a period in which both slave trade and slavery are supposed to have seen a decline and disappearance.

The decline of slavery as a social institution in the Americas and the beginning of the abolition of, first, slave trade (starting in 1807) and then of slavery itself, was protracted. Multiple factors influenced it, ranging from ideological (the emergence of a humanist abolition movement in Europe and the proliferation of Republican ideals after the French Revolution) through geopolitical (Latin American independence movements and the imposition of British hegemony over the Atlantic) to economic factors (the 'viability' of slave-based plantation complexes).[24] From a labour history point of view, however, it is important to stress that Afro-American slaves themselves played a major role in this process. It was initiated by a successful slave revolution

---

[21] Klein and Vinson, *African Slavery in Latin America and the Caribbean*, p. 44. For a comparative view about slavery in Brazil, Cuba, and the United States, see: Laird W. Bergad, *The Comparative Histories of Slavery in Brazil, Cuba, and the United States* (Cambridge, 2007).

[22] Klein and Vinson, *African Slavery in Latin America and the Caribbean*, pp. 53–57, 65–66. On gold mining, see: Kathleen J. Higgins, *'Licentious Liberty' in a Brazilian Gold-Mining Region. Slavery, Gender, and Social Control in Eighteenth-Century Sabara, Minas Gerais* (University Park, PA, 1999).

[23] See the classical study of Manuel Moreno Fraginals, *The Sugarmill. The Socioeconomic Complex of Sugar in Cuba 1760–1860* (New York, 1976 [Spanish original: 1964]). Another classic on Caribbean sugar cultivation remains: Sidney Mintz, *Sweetness and Power. The Place of Sugar in Modern History* (New York, 1985).

[24] Robin Blackburn, *The Overthrow of Colonial Slavery, 1776–1848* (London, 1988); Seymour Drescher, *From Slavery to Freedom. Comparative Studies in the Rise and Fall of Atlantic Slavery* (New York, 1999).

in Saint Domingue in 1791 (resulting in its independence as Haiti in 1804), which can be considered the most radical appropriation of the ideas promulgated during the French Revolution–an appropriation by a group of workers who had clearly not been addressed by these ideas. That event, its inspirational impact (on other slaves in the Americas) as well as provocation of fear (among the slave owners) had a large effect on the Latin American independence movement and on American politics until the last quarter of the nineteenth century. While slavery was successively abolished during the first half of the nineteenth century in most mainland Latin American countries and on numerous Caribbean islands, it was maintained in the USA, Puerto Rico, Cuba, and Brazil, leading to a marked increase in the number of slaves and a boom in slave-based plantation production in these countries. In the words of Ada Ferrer: "Slavery's expansion here must be viewed as part and parcel with its decline elsewhere."[25]

The boom of slavery and the related export commodities sugar (Cuba) and coffee (Brazil) in the age of slavery's 'official' decline has been the object of long scholarly debates. It led Dale Tomich to coin the term *second slavery* for the nineteenth century and to point to its central role in the development of (industrial) capitalism.[26] Contrary to older notions that slavery went into decline for purely economic reasons–because of its retrograde dependence on unrestrained exploitation and its supposed incompatibility with the maxims of capitalist profit maximization (investment in new technology, constant improvement of efficiency and the labour process, etc.)–more recent research has shown that ninteenth century slavery in the mentioned countries could go along with major technological improvements and efficiency-oriented procedures. This is true, for instance, in the case of the Cuban sugar industry, which by 1870 was producing around fourty percent of world output: in 1838 the first railroads were introduced in the rural areas, reducing transport costs and freeing large numbers of slaves from transport occupations. Also, steam-driven mills replaced animal powered processing, thus reorganizing sugar production in rural Cuba around the *centrales*, large factories in the field. These handed over sugar planting proper to smaller independent planters.[27]

Abolition came late in Cuba (1886) and was softened (for the slave owners) by an array of transitionary provisions (such as a long apprenticeships contracts, a de facto prolongation of unfreedom).[28] From the mid-nineteenth century on, the successive

---

[25] Ada Ferrer, "Cuban Slavery And Atlantic Antislavery", in: Josep M. Fradera and Christopher Schmidt Nowara (eds), *Slavery and Antislavery in Spain's Atlantic Empire* (New York, 2013), pp. 134–156, at 136.
[26] Dale Tomich and Michael Zeuske, "Introduction. The Second Slavery: Mass Slavery, World-Economy, and Comparative Microhistories", *Review. A Journal of the Fernand Braudel Center,* 31 (2008), pp. 91–100.
[27] Klein and Vinson, *African Slavery in Latin America and the Caribbean,* pp. 91–93.
[28] Rebecca J. Scott, *Slave Emancipation in Cuba. The Transition to Free Labor, 1860–1899* (Pittsburgh, PA, 1985).

international enforcement of the abolition of slave trade (including its trafficking form) and the constant acts of resistance from the slaves themselves as well as the considerable numbers of a free and/or manumitted Afro-Caribbean population led to attempts to complement or replace the slave population by other labourers, most prominently Chinese coolies.

In Brazil, second slavery also meant a geographical shift: the boom of coffee production in the southeast of the country led to a major internal slave trade. Abolition was a protracted process in Brazil as well, leading from the Free Womb Act in 1871 to the famous *Lei Áurea* (Golden Law) of 1888. The open resistance of slaves which was manifested by them fleeing the coffee plantations (which took the form of a mass-movement shortly before abolition) played a major role.[29]

The gamut of resistance by slaves in Latin America was broad and these acts started long before the combined effect of the Haitian Revolution and abolitionism offered a clear perspective for actually ending slavery. One fundamental act of defiance was flight. These *cimarrones* (maroons) would flee to inaccessible areas, often joining indigenous communities. Depending on proper geographical conditions, *cimarrones* were able to constitute stable communities (*quilombos, palenques*), in some cases even larger polities, such as the Quilombo dos Palmares in Brasil (crushed in 1695 by a colonial army), the Palenque de San Basilio in Colombia, or the *cimarrones* of Esmeraldas in Ecuador.[30]

Debates

Latin America and the Caribbean in colonial times and their variegated labour regimes have played a central role in a number of historiographic debates. Although these debates have mostly revolved around issues such as slavery or rural history, they have also included macro-controversies about the emergence and character of capitalism. As far as slavery is concerned, to a high degree the stakes still (or again) hinge upon *Capitalism and Slavery*, published in 1944 by the Jamaican historian Eric Williams which put forward the idea of a close nexus between the triangle trade, slave-based plantation economies, and the industrial revolution in Britain (resp. the capital accumulation needed to launch it). Another debate arose about Eric William's notion that slavery went into economic decline because of decreasing

---

[29] Emília Viotti da Costa, *Abolition. From Slavery to Free Labour* (São Paulo, 2013 [orig. in Portuguese 1982]). For the intricacies of protracted abolition and the role of slave resistance, see: Sidney Chalhoub, "The Politics of Ambiguity: Conditional Manumission, Labor Contracts, and Slave Emancipation in Brazil (1850s-1888)", *International Review of Social History*, 60, 2 (August 2015), pp. 161–191.
[30] See: Robert Nelson Anderson, "The 'Quilombo' of Palmares. A New Overview of a Maroon State in Seventeenth-century Brazil", *Journal of Latin American Studies*, 28, 3 (October 1996), pp. 545–566; Richard Price (ed.), *Maroon Societies. Rebel Slave Communities in the Americas* (Baltimore and London, 1979, 2nd edn).

profitability and 'backwardness'. A long list of research has instead stressed the peculiar modernity of slavery, especially where it continued in the nineteenth century (US South, Cuba, and Brazil), and its profitability and compatibility with modern technology and improved management methods.[31]

In the 1960s, Latin America saw the emergence of *dependency theory* (one of the few cases in which a major social science paradigm originated in the Global South). Despite its many variants, most of its proponents shared the idea that since its colonization Latin America was integrated into an emerging global market. This entailed a division of labour between world-regions which was characterized by the drive for capital accumulation, unequal exchange, and monopolies (imposed through the violence of colonial domination).[32] Labour relations in Latin America, whatever their form and mode, thus had to be analysed in terms of the essentially capitalist nature of the exchange between Latin America and Europe. Later *world-system analysis*, in many ways an extension and continuation of the dependency school, shared this fundamental notion of the compatibility of coercive, bonded, or enslaved labour with capitalism. Less well-known is the Latin American *mode of production* debate of the 1970s, which emerged as a critique of dependency currents and which tried to offer a more tiered and layered panorama of the interrelation of local labour regimes and commercial export dynamics.[33] Some proponents, such as Carlos S. Assadourian, also pointed to the notable (and geographically extended) internal dynamics of Latin American colonial economies, which enabled and catered for the mining complexes such as in Potosí. They proposed the existence of several modes of production in colonial Latin America, each based on specific forms of labour that were interrelated through so-called articulation.

More recently, a debate (in this necessarily extremely selective list of controversies) emerged in the context of historical institutional perspectives and their interest in *factor endowments*. As Acemoglu, Johnson, and Robinson saw it in their famous book *Why nations fail*,[34] colonialism in Latin America was fundamentally extractive

---

[31] Selwyn H.H. Carrington and Seymour Dresher, "Debate: Econocide and West Indian Decline, 1738–1806", *Boletín de Estudios Latinoamericanos y del Caribe*, 36 (June 1984), pp. 13–67; David Brion Davis, "Reflections on Abolitionism and Ideological Hegemony", *American Historical Review*, 92, 4 (1987), pp. 797–812; Thomas Bender (ed.), *The Antislavery Debate: Capitalism and Abolitionism as a Problem in Historical Interpretation* (Berkeley, CA, 1992); Selwyn H.H. Carrington, "Capitalism & Slavery and Caribbean Historiography: An Evaluation", *The Journal of African American History*, 88, 3 (2003), pp. 304–312.

[32] For the whole gamut of the debates, see: Cristóbal Kay, *Latin American Theories of Development and Underdevelopment* (London, 1989).

[33] Carlos Sempat Assadourian et al., *Modos de producción en América Latina* (Buenos Aires, 1973). Also see: Steve J. Stern, "Feudalism, Capitalism, and the World-System in the Perspective of Latin America and the Caribbean", *American Historical Review*, 93, 4 (October 1988), pp. 829–872.

[34] Daron Acemoglu and James Robinson, *Why Nations Fail. The Origins of Power, Prosperity, and Poverty* (New York, 2012). See also Daron Acemoglu, Simon Johnson, and James Robinson, "The Colonial Origins of Comparative Development: An Empirical Investigation", *American Economic Review*, 91, 5

(not least by exacting labour through coercion and slavery), giving rise to equally predatory institutions and, finally, to today's societies which are among the most unequal in the world. Contrary to that, colonialism in North America is presented as much more liberal, as accountable institutions, smallholding, free markets, etc. existed. While nobody would deny that Latin America still bears the marks of colonialism (not least in its labour relations), the particular opposition between the North and the South has been criticized as reductionist. It not only omits many of the complex nuances of economic and political arrangements in Latin America, it also ignores the important legacy of coercive practices in the North American colonies, from the marginalization of the indigenous population to the widespread use of indentured and slave labour.[35]

The long twentieth century

Agrarian Labour

The social and occupational trajectories of former slaves in Latin America and the Caribbean since the last decades of the nineteenth century constitute a proper field of research. The situation of the Afro-descendant population has seen both general trends—continued marginality and the social precarity of newly achieved freedom—as well many regional and sectional variations. Former slaves continued to work in sugar or coffee plantations as (often indebted) day labourers, moved towards subsistence agriculture, smallholding, or sharecropping, joined the marginal sectors of the urban working class, or became active in the (up until today) huge zone in which self-employment, informal work, and bare survival intersect.[36]

As mentioned, planters and public authorities had sought new ways to deploy workers on the plantations—even before the official end of slavery. In many regions, Asian coolies were recruited as replacement. While Indians were brought to British, French, and Dutch possessions in the circum-Caribbean, Chinese workers arrived

---

(December 2001), pp. 1369–1401, and Stanley Engerman and Kenneth Sokoloff, "Factor Endowments, Institutions, and Differential Paths of Growth Among New World Economies", in: Stephan Haber (ed.), *How Latin America Fell Behind* (Stanford, CA, 1997), pp. 260–304.

35 Regina Grafe and María Alejandra Irigoin, "The Spanish Empire and its Legacy: Fiscal Re-Distribution and Political Conflict in Colonial and Post-Colonial Spanish America", *Journal of Global History*, 1, 2 (2006), pp. 241–267; Gareth Austin, "The 'Reversal of Fortunes' and the Compression of History: Perspectives from African and Comparative Economic History", *Journal of International Development*, 20, 8 (2008), pp. 996–1027; John Coatsworth, "Structures, Endowments, and Institutions in the Economic History of Latin America", *Latin American Research Review*, 40, 3 (2005), pp. 126–144.

36 A graphic analysis of the situation in Cuba is offered in: Rebecca J. Scott and Michael Zeuske, "Property in Writing, Property on the Ground: Pigs, Horses, Land, and Citizenship in the Aftermath of Slavery, Cuba, 1880–1909", *Comparative Studies in Society and History*, 44, 4 (2002), pp. 669–699.

in substantial numbers in Cuba, Peru, Mexico, and Brazil.[37] In most cases, these workers were indentured and thus vulnerable to abuses and overexploitation, though their unfreedom and marginalization was not comparable to African-American slaves. In a later wave, from the 1900s on, Cuba and other locations also saw the massive recruitment of Afro-Caribbean workers from Haiti, Jamaica, etc. for work in cash-crop cultivation but also for large infrastructure works (railways etc.).[38] In other parts of Latin America, the demand for labour was met by European immigrants, especially in the cases of Brazil and Argentina. While Europeans in Brazil were meant to replace African slaves on coffee plantations, the migrants in Argentina were needed for the expanding agrarian sector (especially extensive cattle ranching) and the booming port cities. Argentina offered exceptionally high wages compared to the migrants's wages in their regions of origin (up to 200% higher than in Southern Europe, especially Italy and Spain, and Eastern Europe). The incentive for Europeans to become *colonos* on the coffee plantations in Brazil were less the wages but more the subsidized character of migration (including transport fees, housing, garden plots, etc.). In total, some 13 million Europeans arrived in Latin America from 1870 to 1930, though a remarkably high proportion of these migrants returned at some point or even migrated back and forth in regular, seasonal cycles (called *golondrinas*, birds of passage, in Argentina).[39]

While the previous existence of substantial slave labour can be seen as synonymous with an export-oriented cash-crop production in certain concentrated regions, it is important to bear in mind that the whole of Latin America experienced a boom in export-commodity production from the last third of the nineteenth century onwards. This forceful boom–the term *second conquest* has been used to describe it–included commodities from sugar, coffee, cacao, and bananas to guano, nitrate, rubber, henequen, and oil.[40] It affected both regions already connected to the world market as well as new ones. In that sense, Latin America can serve as a perfect example for the emerging research interest in *commodity frontiers*, i.e. the incorporation of agrarian areas into the domain of world-market production and the ensuing ecological pressures as well as challenges of mobilizing workers for this produc-

---

[37] Madhavi Kale, *Fragments of Empire. Capital, Slavery, and Indian Indentured Labor in the British Caribbean* (Philadelphia, PA, 1988); Lisa Yun, *The Coolie Speaks. Chinese Indentured Laborers and African Slaves in Cuba* (Philadelphia, PA, 2008); Walton Look Lai and Tan Chee-Beng (eds), *The Chinese in Latin America and the Caribbean* (Leiden and Boston, 2010).

[38] For an important 'debate opener' in this regard, see: Aviva Chomsky, *West Indian Workers and the United Fruit Company in Costa Rica, 1870–1940* (Baton Rouge, LA, 1994).

[39] Blanca Sánchez Alonso, "Labour and Immigration", in: Bulmer-Thomas, Coatsworth, and Cortés Conde, *Cambridge Economic History of Latin America*. Vol. 2, pp. 377–426, at 382–386.

[40] See: Stephen Topik (ed.), *The Second Conquest of Latin America. Coffee, Henequen, and Oil during the Export Boom, 1850–1930* (Austin, TX, 1998).

tion.⁴¹ In South America, this also involved a massive and often genocidal expansion of the postcolonial states into territories still inhabited by indigenous peoples, such as in Chile and Argentina towards the south or in Brazil towards the Amazon region.⁴² The commodity boom generally went along with political regimes that combined liberal economic policies with a repressive order and laid the foundations for the so-called *desarrollo hacia afuera* (outward-oriented development model) which lasted until Great Depression of the 1930s.

The export-oriented commodity boom involved numerous rearrangements in rural labour relations, not least in those former Spanish mainland countries in which a local indigenous or *mestizo* population constituted the majority. This meant, above all, a grand encroachment on the relatively broad base of communal and/or subsistence agriculture. While these processes took a great variety of forms and names and often continued to use colonial legal concepts and 'traditional' cultural forms, the most widespread generic labour relations in this sphere were, on the one hand, modes of giving access to land in exchange for labour on larger estates and, on the other, *debt peonage*, i.e. labour enforced through a system of advances and the ensuing state of accumulated debt. Regional and temporal specificities here abound (sometimes even working to the peasants's advantage), yet prototypical cases, such as Guatemala, point to the way debt peonage was entangled with racialized political ideologies (which denigrated anything *indio*) and repressive legal instruments, like anti-vagrancy laws, to create a general social surrounding that ensured a non-free agrarian labour force.⁴³ The well-known model of a fundamentally unequal and exploitative agrarian world consisting of great commercial estates (*latifundia*) lording over marginal smallholdings (*minifundia*) might be too simplistic for many empirical cases, yet its heuristic power for understanding the subcontinent *en gros* equally remains remarkable. It also constitutes the background for the fact that, during the twentieth century, Latin America became one of the world's most urbanized world-regions.

Peasant movements or outright revolts thus unsurprisingly constitute an important part of these worlds of agrarian labour. The many instances of mobilizations, however, have rarely been studied in an interregional and comparative way (either diachronically or synchronically).⁴⁴ Latin America has also seen important attempts

---

41 A notion coined by Jason W. Moore, see: Jason W. Moore, "Sugar and the Expansion of the Early Modern World-Economy: Commodity Frontiers, Ecological Transformation, and Industrialization", *Review. A Journal of the Fernand Braudel Center*, 23, 3 (2000), pp. 409–433.

42 For a social-historical emphasis among the extensive literature on this process in the Argentinian case, see for instance: Osvaldo Barsky and Jorge Gelman, *Historia del agro argentino. Desde la conquista hasta fines del siglo XX* (Buenos Aires, 2001), ch. V.

43 See: David McCreery, "Debt Servitude in Rural Guatemala, 1876–1936", *The Hispanic American Historical Review*, 63, 4 (1983), pp. 735–759.

44 For broader or comparative approaches, see for instance: Friedrich Katz (ed.), *Riot, Rebellion, and Revolution. Rural Social Conflict in Mexico* (Princeton, NJ, 1988); Pablo González Casanova (ed.), *Historia política de los campesinos latinoamericanos*. 4 vols (México, DF, 1984–1985); Henry Veltmeyer,

at agrarian reform, the most important being related to revolutionary upheavals: the reforms in Mexico in the 1930s which established a singularly modern form of *ejido* (communal land ownership) and which were a product of the gigantic agrarian mobilizations during the Mexican Revolution between 1910 and 1917, the Cuban Revolution of 1959, the Bolivian Revolution of 1952, and the attempts at agrarian reform launched in Chile under the *Unidad Popular* government (1970–1973). Up until today, some Latin American rural social movements rank among the internationally most iconic, such as the *Movimento dos Trabalhadores Sem Terra* (MST) (the landless labourers's movement) in Brazil, the *Neo-Zapatistas* in Mexican Chiapas, or the *Cocalero* movement in Bolivia. While in the case of the first, the 'socialist' and 'labour' identity has been at the forefront, in the latter two, the movements present themselves (or are generally perceived) in terms of their indigenous identity and the ensuing claims and aspirations.

The urban mélange

Since colonial times, urban spaces Latin America have seen a motley coexistence of different labour relations (from slavery through other unfree relations to free wage labour) and workers of all socio-racial status positions. This is especially true for the large port cities, such as Havanna, Veracruz, Lima, Buenos Aires, or Rio de Janeiro. The spaces where these labour activities have been taking place not only included workshops, offices, stores, the street, and public places, but also households, especially the residences of well-to-do-families. As mentioned, women have been very present both in households[45] and in markets. Urban plebeian groups consequently played an important role during the *independencia* struggles and were also able to intervene and secure claims in the post-colonial political constellations.[46] A series of studies have pointed out that, during the nineteenth century,

---

"La dinámica de las ocupaciones de tierras en América Latina", in: Sam Moyo and Paris Yeros (eds), *Recuperando la tierra. El resurgimiento de movimientos rurales en África, Asia y América Latina* (Buenos Aires, 2008), pp. 301–333; León Zamosc, Estala Martínez, and Manuel Chiriboga (eds), *Estructuras agrarias y movimientos campesinos en América latina, 1950–1990* (Madrid, 1997).

45 The history and present situation of domestic work in Latin America is a field of research of its own. Important cues since the 1990s can be found in: Elsa M. Chaney and Mary Garcia Castro (eds), *Muchachas No More: Household Workers in Latin America and the Caribbean* (Philadelphia, PA, 1989); Sandra Lauderdale Graham, *House and Street. The Domestic World of Servants and Masters in Nineteenth-Century Rio de Janeiro* (Austin, TX, 1992); Elizabeth Hutchison, *Labors Appropriate to Their Sex. Gender, Labor and Politics in Urban Chile, 1900–1930* (Durham, NC, 2001); Ann S. Blum, *Domestic Economies. Family, Work, and Welfare in Mexico City, 1884–1943* (Lincoln, NE, 2009).

46 It was especially in Argentina, resp. Buenos Aires, that independence happened as an outspokenly urban affair. For recent research, see: Lyman L. Johnson, *Workshop of Revolution. Plebeian Buenos Aires and the Atlantic World, 1776–1810* (Durham, NC, 2011); Gabriel Marco Di Meglio, ¡*Viva el*

different groups of workers continued to co-exist in Latin American cities (especially where slavery was in place until late) and that, in this period, the urban working population experienced profound shifts in terms of race (end of slave trade, beginning of European immigration) and gender (for instance, the displacement of women from their previously strong presence in retail).[47]

The formation of an urban industrial working class in Latin America took place later than in the North Atlantic and was embedded in the complicated occupational and social mélange mentioned. While classical labour history tended to focus on the formational element, more recent studies highlight the intermixture. Re-readings here are possible: for instance, Luis Alberto Romero's and Mirta Lobato's by now classic study of the working class formation in nineteenth-century Buenos Aires was, at the time of its publication, seen as an affirmation of the vanguard role of Buenos Aires in constituting the first fully free wage-labour society in Latin America;[48] in the light of current debates, however, its power lies more in showing how fluid the boundaries between day labour, petty commercial activities, (often makeshift) self-employment, domestic labour, productive activities within the household (e. g. in dressmaking), etc. were.

Cities also witnessed the most intense attempts by governments and local authorities to control and discipline the lower classes according to contemporary ideas of a modern, well-ordered city. Popular dwellings, street vending, day labouring at the harbour, the public presence and work of women, etc. could be subject to persecution based on laws and decrees against 'vagrancy' or 'prostitution'.[49]

During the twentieth century, Latin American cities, much like their North-Atlantic counterparts, became the focal point of industrial development, working class culture, the formation of unions, and labour-related political organizations, as well as state-policies benefitting these groups. Beyond this 'convergent' development, how-

---

bajo pueblo! La plebe urbana de Buenos Aires y la política entre la Revolución de Mayo y el rosismo (1810–1829) (Buenos Aires, 2016, 4th extended edn).

47 For artisanal workers in nineteenth-century cities in Mexico, see: Carlos Illades, *Estudios sobre el artesanado urbano del siglo XIX* (México, DF, 2001). For the manifold shifts among urban labourers in Rio de Janeiro see: Fabiane Popinigis and Henrique Espada Lima, "Maids and Clerks, and the Shifting Landscape of Labor Relations in Rio de Janeiro (1830s–1880s)", *International Review of Social History*, 62 (2017), Special Issue 25 [in print]. For political intersections or even interactions see: Marcelo Badaró Mattos, "Experiences in Common: Slavery and 'Freedom' in the Process of Rio de Janeiro's Working-Class Formation (1850–1910)", *International Review of Social History*, 55 (2010), pp. 193–213; Joan Casanovas, "Slavery, the Labour Movement and Spanish Colonialism (1850–1898)", in: Brass and van der Linden, *Free and Unfree Labour*, pp. 249–264.

48 Luis Alberto Romero and Hilda Sabato, *Los trabajadores de Buenos Aires. La experiencia del mercado, 1850–1880* (Buenos Aires, 1992).

49 For the case of Rio de Janeiro, see for instance: Lerice de Castro Garzoni, "At the Borders of Non-Work: Poor Female Workers and Definitions of Vagrancy in Early Twentieth-Century Rio de Janeiro", *International Review of Social History*, 60, 2 (2015), pp. 193–224; Cristiana Schettini, *'Que Tenhas Teu Corpo': uma historia social da prostituçao no Rio de Janeiro das primeiras décadas republicanas* (Rio de Janeiro, 2006).

ever, Latin American cities also 'diverged' as they spectacularly grew in size, receiving millions of internal migrants from the countryside who could not be absorbed by the urban labour markets and who swelled extensive irregular dwellings (*favelas, villas, barrios de miseria*, etc.). Its inhabitants have, especially since the second half of the twentieth century, accounted for a major part of the workforce in Latin American cities, moving with their labour in the difficult-to-define zone which is demarcated by day labouring, domestic services and care work in better-off households, precarious self-employment, criminal activities, or bare survival. They constitute what has been discussed since the 1960s as the *informal sector*, i.e. all economic activities outside of state regulation.[50] The debate about the informal sector has grown to fill libraries and offers many stimulating insights for labour historians. Still, expressly historiographical studies about the phenomenon remain relatively rare (though many anthropological studies include historical viewpoints). From a Global Labour History point of view, meanwhile, it seems important not to erect too rigid a distinction between 'formal' and 'informal' work, to point to the close interconnections between them (not only economically but also in relation to the persons and households involved), and to stress the historical continuities of the experience of urban precarity.

Industrial labour

The export oriented commodity production boom since the last third of the nineteenth century not only involved agricultural production but also instigated processes of industrial development in some regions. This was especially the case in Argentina, Chile, southern Brazil, and Mexico. The two main sectors of non-agrarian production since colonial times–mining and textiles–continued to be dominant,[51] complemented by new sectors such as food processing (canning, meat packing, etc.).

As mentioned, since the 1880s, the previous, often artisanal urban working classes sharply expanded through the arrival of European immigrants. The latter brought their political traditions with them, and soon mutual aid organizations, unions, and political groups emerged, ushering in the formation of a social group

---

50 For a recent overview, see: Alejandro Portes and William Haller, *La economía informal* (Santiago de Chile, 2014), available under: <http://www.cepal.org/es/publicaciones/6091-la-economia-informal>.
51 For a general overview of mining in Latin America in postcolonial states, see: Kendall W. Brown, *A History of Mining in Latin America. From the Colonial Era to the Present* (Albuquerque, NM, 2012), chs 5 and 6. On nitrate mining in Chile see: Julio Pinto, *Trabajos y rebeldías en la pampa salitrera. El ciclo del salitre y la reconfiguración de las identidades populares (1850–1900)* (Santiago de Chile, 1998). On early textile industries in Mexico see: Mario Trujillo Bodio, *Operarios fabriles en el Valle de México (1864–1884). Espacio, trabajo, protesta y cultura obrera* (México, DF, 1997). Also see the general overviews offered on Argentina, Brazil, Mexico, and Uruguay in: Lex Heerma van Voss, Els Hiemstra-Kuperus, and Elise van Nederveen Meerkerk (eds), *The Ashgate companion to the history of textile workers, 1650–2000* (Farnham, 2010).

which saw itself as part of a modern proletariat. While until World War I different currents of anarchism and, later, anarcho-syndicalism remained dominant, Latin America also saw a very early reception of Marx and Marxism (in Argentina since the 1870s) as well as socialist ideas.[52] Before World War I, a series of fundamental organizations such as the *Casa del Obrero Mundial* (COM) in Mexico, the *Federación Obrera Regional Argentina* (FORA), the *Socialist Party* (Argentina), and the *Partido Obrero Socialista* (Chile) had been established. Recently, research on these early working classes has gone beyond the mere reconstruction of political or ideological developments, focusing instead on the wider milieus, the everyday life components of political militancy,[53] and the transnational connections in the labour and political lives of these workers.[54]

Labour history as a field of enquiry unsurprisingly first emerged in Latin America out of the movements themselves; this historiography almost exclusively studied the political and ideological history of organizations.[55] Since the interwar period, Latin American labour also caught the attention of researchers from the North-Atlantic region. These often enough used highly problematic lenses when looking at phenomena which refused to follow Northern models. In the post-war period, a strong Anglophone research tradition emerged, which reflected varying intellectual and political concerns: from Robert J. Alexander's studies of political and labour organizations (deeply embedded in the cold war binary)[56] through Hobart Spalding's and Charles Bergquist's strongly comparative works[57] to the dynamic boom in labour history studies about Latin America since the 1980s, associated with historians such as Daniel James, John French, James Brennan, Peter Winn, Barbara Weinstein, etc. The

---

[52] Horacio Tarcus, *Marx en la Argentina. Sus primeros lectores obreros, intelectuales y científicos* (Buenos Aires, 2007).
[53] On Argentina, see for instance: Juan Suriano, *Paradoxes of Utopia. Anarchist Culture and Politics in Buenos Aires, 1890–1910* (Oakland, CA, 2010); Lucas Poy, *Los orígenes de la clase obrera argentina: huelgas, sociedades de resistencia y militancia política en Buenos Aires, 1888–1896* (Buenos Aires, 2014).
[54] See the contributions on Anarchists in Peru, Argentina, Brazil as well as in the labour and political circuits between the Caribbean, Mexico, and the USA in: Steven Hirsch and Lucien van der Walt (eds), *Anarchism and Syndicalism in the Colonial and Postcolonial World, 1870–1940. The Praxis of National Liberation, Internationalism, and Social Revolution* (Leiden and Boston, 2010).
[55] Abad de Santillán Diego, *La F.O.R.A.: Ideología y trayectoria del movimiento obrero revolucionario en la Argentina* (Buenos Aires, 1933); Jacinto Oddone, *Gremialismo proletario argentino* (Buenos Aires, 1949); Víctor Alba, *Historia del movimiento obrero en América Latina* (México, DF, 1964); Carlos Rama, *Historia del movimiento obrero y social latinoamericano contemporáneo* (Buenos Aires and Montevideo, 1967).
[56] Robert J. Alexander, *Labor Relations in Argentina, Brazil, and Chile* (New York, 1962); Robert J. Alexander, *Organized Labor in Latin America* (New York, 1965).
[57] Hobart A. Spalding Jr., *Organized Labor in Latin America: Historical Case Studies of Urban Workers in Dependent Societies* (New York, 1977); Charles Bergquist, *Labor in Latin America. Comparative Essays on Chile, Argentina, Venezuela, and Colombia* (Stanford, CA, 1986).

latter interacted (and still interact) with equally dynamic research efforts in Latin American countries themselves.

Though the genealogy of the debates is highly complex (and has seen trends and counter-currents as well as convergences and dissimilarities), a few characteristic features of the research from the late 1980s until 2005 can be highlighted: firstly, in this period labour history was very much framed in an either national or local perspective and the comparative as well as continental impetus of earlier studies was lost.[58] Secondly, cultural turn inspired readings made a full impact in the 1990s and subsequent studies were highly likely to have one or several of the corresponding catchwords in their title (culture, identity, subjectivity, everyday, *barrio*, etc.); this resulted in an impressive broadening and enrichment but also left the field mired in perennial (and from today's point of view quite worn) debates about 'culture' vs. 'structure'. Thirdly, questions of gender appeared early and forcefully, yet in the 1990s they were predominantly discussed in terms of identity and subjectivity, while the actual work done by women and their position in the broad gamut of labour relations has come into focus again only in the last ten years.[59] Fourthly, methodologically, it saw a strong oral and testimonial turn as well as a spatial shift away from factories and into the *barrios* and everyday life. While the emphasis of many of these studies was on the formation of cultural subjectivities, they also increased the visibility of the range of activities which enabled households and neighbourhoods to make ends meet. Conceptually, this entailed the rise of the notion of *popular sectors* and the attribute *popular*.[60] Fifthly, it continued to cultivate a focus on the political

---

[58] This was not, it should be remembered, a kind of methodological atavism but a reaction to the strong anti-localism of much of the previous dependency-inflected discussions. Besides, the studies about certain groups of workers such as coolies, cross-border migrant workers, etc. by default remained marked by broader perspectives.

[59] The literature on gender and labour has, fortunately, become very extensive; for savouring the shifts in concerns and perspectives since the 1990s, the following sequence of interventions might stand in as a proxy: Ann Farnsworth, *Dulcinea in the Factory. Myths, Morals, Men, and Women in Colombia's Industrial Experiment, 1905–1960* (Durham, NC, 2000); Thomas Miller Klubock, *Contested communities. Class, Gender, and Politics in Chile's El Teniente Copper Mine, 1904–1951* (Durham, NC, 1998); John D. French and Daniel James, *The Gendered Worlds of Latin American Women Workers. From Household and Factory to the Union Hall and Ballot Box* (Durham, NC, 1997); Mirta Zaida Lobato, *Historia de las trabajadoras en la Argentina (1869–1960)* (Buenos Aires, 2007); Andrea Andújar et al. (eds), *Vivir con lo justo. Estudios de historia social del trabajo en perspectiva de género. Argentina, siglos XIX y XX* (Rosario, 2016).

[60] For examples of studies which have introduced the attribute *popular* with great benefit, see: Gabriel Salazar, *Labradores, peones y proletarios. Formación y crisis de la sociedad popular chilena del siglo XIX* (Santiago de Chile, 1985); Luis Alberto Romero, "Los sectores populares en las ciudades latinoamericanas del siglo XIX: la cuestión de la identidad", *Desarrollo Económico*, 106 (1987), pp. 201–222. For a critical historical assessment of the move away from class and towards the 'popular' in the Argentine context, see: Lucas Poy, "Remaking *The Making*: E.P. Thompson's Reception in Argentina and the Shaping of Labor Historiography", *International Review of Social History*, 61, 1 (April 2016), pp. 75–93, at 79–84.

allegiance of workers, especially in relation to the 1940s until the 1970s, when many workers followed the different variants of Latin American populism.

While many of these concerns and interests are still in place and must be seen as lasting enhancements of the field, the last ten years have seen some shifts again, namely a return to a more decidedly social historical analysis (including attention to the inter-connected co-existence of different labour relations), a revived and revamped interest in the study of political organizations, and a higher sensitivity for the transnational dimensions in the lives of workers and the development of organizations.

The 1920s saw the emergence of Communist parties and organizations all over Latin America, and, though Communism remained a minority or even marginal phenomenon everywhere, its influence on pivotal sectors of industrial workers or trade unions, its wider social and cultural impact, as well as its long-term ideational power both over (curious) sympathizers and (determined) foes should not be underestimated.[61] In the 1930s, Latin America experienced a deep rupture in its basic economic setup: the Great Depression stalled the export-oriented commodity production and in a number of countries a new economic model, the so-called *desarrollo hacia adentro* (inward-oriented development) with its corresponding attempt to build national industries able to substitute the importation of both investment and consumer goods, successively emerged. There is no space here to discuss the highly uneven results of these policies, suffice to say that it led to a substantial growth in the number of industrial workers.

This deep change went along with the rise of a new political formation, populism, which combined charismatic leadership, (often massive) popular mobilizations, nationalist, eclectic, and anti-elitist ideologies, and the fostering and systematic incorporation of trade unions (while at the same time repressing any independent labour mobilization). Although it played a role in numerous Latin American countries, its iconic trinity remains the reigns of Lázaro Cárdenas in Mexiko (1934–1940), Juan D. Perón in Argentina (1943/45–1955), and Getúlio Vargas in Brazil (1930–1945; 1951–1954). Understanding the position of labour and allegiance of workers to these regimes has become one of the major topics, if not obsessions, of labour history from and about Latin America. Revisionisms and enhancements here abound, and interpretations have oscillated between views which see these regimes as alien to labour and as oppressive debauchers highjacking the autonomous traditions of workers and views that stress that populisms ably resonated with working class culture and identities and offered opportunities and platforms for advancing workers's con-

---

[61] For on overview of recent research on communism in Latin America, see David Mayer, "À la fois puissante et marginale: l'Internationale communiste et l'Amérique latine", in: *Monde(s). Histoire, Espaces, Relations*, 2016, Nr. 10, Special Theme "Dimension transnationale du communisme", ed. by Brigitte Studer and Sabine Dullin, pp. 109–128.

cerns and interests.[62] Milestones of the debate have especially been set in relation to Argentine Peronism: the debate started with the analysis of Gino Germani, one of the founding fathers of sociology as an academic discipline in Latin America, who stressed the demagogic manipulation of new, poor, and politically 'immature' layers of the working class. It was revised with the interpretations offered by Miguel Murmis, Juan Carlos Portantiero, etc. who revealed the degree to which long established unions and self-conscious and militant workers equally switched to Peronism.[63] Finally, it was fully reframed by the study by Daniel James that highlighted the congeniality of Peronism and workers's everyday worlds and subjectivities.[64] The latter was enhanced by further studies, often in-depth analyses of specific locales and oral sources.[65] Similar studies have pointed to the opportunities offered by *Varguismo* in Brazil.[66] In the case of Mexico, the challenge seems to consist less in the analysis of *Cardenismo* proper–as it was the most left-leaning of the populist regimes, professing a socialist ideology–yet more in analysing the allegiance of workers in the long subsequent reign of the state-party *Partido Revolucionario Institucional* (PRI) (which, soon after Cárdenas, broke with his left-wing aspirations).[67]

These debates about the aptitude of populisms for getting a grip on the imagination of workers and for advancing their interests can, however, eclipse the fact that from the 1960s on both industrial and political constellations started to change profoundly. In this process, countries varied greatly, yet there were also some common trends: firstly, the model of import-substituting industrialization began to show signs of stagnation or crisis (due to continued dependency on technology importation, the slow development of productivity, the dependency on a shield of protectionist policies, etc.). Some countries (Argentina, Brazil, and Mexico) responded with a partial (re-)opening to foreign investments which led to the establishment of new industries,

---

62 Gino Germani, *Política y sociedad en una época de transición, de la sociedad tradicional a la sociedad de masas* (Buenos Aires, 1962).
63 Miguel Murmis and Juan Carlos Portantiero, *Estudios sobre los orígenes del peronismo* (Buenos Aires, 1971).
64 Daniel James, *Resistance and Integration. Peronism and the Argentine Working Class, 1946–1975* (Cambridge, 1988).
65 Daniel James, *Doña María's story. Life History, Memory, and Political Identity* (Durham, NC, 2000); Mirta Zaida Lobato, *La vida en las fábricas. Trabajo, protesta y política en una comunidad obrera, Berisso (1904–1970)* (Buenos Aires, 2001).
66 John D. French, *The Brazilian Worker's ABC. Class Conflict and Alliances in Modern São Paulo* (Chapel Hill, NC, 1992); Alexandre Fortes et al. (eds), *Na luta por direitos. Estudos recentes em história social do trabalho* (Campinas, 1999). For an interpretation with an emphasis on the role of industrial employers see: Barbara Weinstein, *For Social Peace in Brazil. Industrialists and the Remaking of the Working Class in São Paulo, 1920–1964* (Chapel Hill, NC, 1996).
67 For two different ways to situate Cardenism, see: Alan Knight, "Cardenismo: ¿coloso o catramina?", and Ilán Semo, "El cardenismo revisado: la tercera vía y otras utopías inciertas", both in: María Moira Mackinnon and Mario Alberto Petrone (eds), *Populismo y neopopulismo en America Latina. El problema de la Cenicienta* (Buenos Aires, 1999), pp. 197–230 and 231–256. Also see: Norman Caulfield, *Mexican workers and the State. From the Porfiriato to NAFTA* (Forth Worth, TX, 1998).

especially in car manufacturing and other metal processing. At the same time, previous statist policies had led to a massive growth of state-employed workers, especially teachers and other education workers. Both groups constituted new and highly militant sectors of the working class. These moved within–yet also beyond–the perimeters set by populism and unions loyal to them. Secondly, the Cuban Revolution exerted a pervasive influence all over the continent, creating new organizations on the left yet also affecting all existing political formations, including trade unions.[68] Thirdly, the rise of military dictatorships was explicitly directed against the social unrest and politization of the 1960s, and its repressive policies included and all-out attack on all labour-related organizations. The impact of the Cuban Revolution, the failures of its professed revolutionary voluntarism, and the rise of anti-revolutionary military regimes in the longer run meant a shift in the general set-up of social mobilizations: the traditional left was crushed, the appeal of the revolutionary vanguardism of its more radical currents faded, and new, more grassroots forms of social movements appeared in the niches of oppression. This ushered in the so-called *new social movements* in the 1970s and early 1980s which were seen by many proponents as expressly non-labour-related; in reality, however, connections and intersections between 'old' labour and 'new' social movements were manifold.

One of the landmark events reflecting both industrial changes and a new working class militancy is the *Córdobazo* in May 1969, an uprising of workers, students, and other parts of the population in Córdoba, Argentina's second-largest industrial centre. It evolved from a general strike in the city's car industry.[69] It can not only be compared or related to the intervention of factory workers in Europe in 1968/1969 but also to workers's mobilizations during the Allende years in Chile.[70]

A major development of the 1970s was the formation of *new unionism* in Brazil. Its ability to combine effective trade union struggles with elements of more grassroots-oriented new social movements and the everyday sociability of workers in their neighbourhoods has been researched in depth.[71] As is well-known, it played

---

[68] For one of the rare continental analyses of this impact (including labour movements), see: Thomas C. Wright, *Latin America in the Era of the Cuban Revolution* (New York, 1991).
[69] James P. Brennan, *The Labor Wars in Córdoba, 1955–1976. Ideology, Work, and Labor Politics in an Argentine Industrial City* (Cambridge, MA, 1994); James P. Brennan and Mónica B. Gordillo, "Working Class Protest, Popular Revolt, and Urban Insurrection in Argentina: the 1969 Cordobazo", *Journal of Social History*, 27, 3 (Spring 1994), pp. 477–498.
[70] Peter Winn, *Weavers of Revolution. The Yarur Workers and Chile's Road to Socialism* (Oxford, 1986); Frank Gaudichaud, *Poder Popular y Cordones Industriales. Testimonios sobre el movimiento popular urbano, 1970–1973* (Santiago de Chile, 2004).
[71] Antonio L. Negro, *Linhas de montagem: o industrialismo nacional-desenvolvimentista e a sindicalizacão dos trabalhadores (1945–1978)* (São Paulo, 2004); Paulo Fontes and Francisco B. Macedo, "Strikes and Pickets in Brazil: Worker Mobilization in the 'Old' and 'New' Unionism, the Strikes of 1957 and 1980", *International Labor and Working Class History*, 83 (2013), pp. 86–111; Francisco Barbosa de Macedo, "Social Networks and Urban Space: Worker Mobilization in the First Years of 'New' Unionism in Brazil", *International Review of Social History*, 60, 1 (April 2015), pp. 33–71.

a major role in the country's re-democratization process at the beginning of the 1980s and the foundation of a new workers's party, the *Partido dos Trabalhadores* (PT) which, under Luís Inácio (Lula) da Silva, rose to national significance and later to government power (2003–2016).

The 1980s and 1990s witnessed a protracted crisis of industrial labour and labour movements: the ascendancy of neoliberalism brought de-industrialization on the one hand and the establishment of export-oriented, union-free, and highly exploitative special production zones (*maquiladoras*) on the other. With rising unemployment, precarization of formal employment, a further expansion of the informal sector, and the onset of a large stream of labour migration towards the USA (from Mexico and Central America), Europe (for instance from Ecuador), but also within Latin America, unions and labour-related organizations greatly weakened and the urban industrial working class, at least in its previously known form, depleted. This recomposition of the working class–which includes processes such as terciarization, precarization, feminization, and transnationalization–is continuing up until today.[72] At the same time, some remarkable countervailing tendencies have appeared since the beginning of the 2000s: the level of formal occupation rose again in numerous Latin American countries. In the context of a series of highly militant or even insurrectional mobilizations and the rise of expressly progressive projects to political power (ranging from the moderate, such as Lula in Brazil or Bachelet in Chile, to the more radical and contesting, such as Chávez in Venezuela or Evo Morales in Bolivia), government policies have used an economic boom (again largely based on export commodities) to reduce outright poverty, formalize employment, and raise minimum wages. For the first time in decades, inequality has decreased in Latin America.[73] While the tide of left-wing or progressive governments has started to recede again, trade unions in Latin America and labour-related political organizations confront an uneven situation. The structural weakening since the 1980s has not been made good–neither the working class nor its organizations could acquire previous levels of socio-ideological coherence again. At the same time, the major example of a labour-related party, Brazil's PT, which had been celebrated as a 'new type of party' due to its ability to give social movements ample space,[74] is currently not

---

[72] Enrique de la Garza Toledo, "La flexibilidad del trabajo en América Latina", in: Enrique de la Garza Toledo (ed.), *Tratado latinoamericano de sociología del trabajo* (México, DF, 2000), pp. 148–178; María Angélica Rodríguez Llona and Paula Vidal Molina (eds), *Transformacion(es) del trabajo, tiempo(s) de precariedad(es) y resistencia(s): algunas aproximaciones desde Latinoamérica* (Buenos Aires, 2013). For an influential theoretical intervention on the 'crisis of labour' see: Ricardo Antunes, *Adeus ao trabalho? Ensaio sobre as metamorfoses e a centralidade do mundo do trabalho* (São Paulo and Campinas, 1995). Also see the ILO regional annual reports: OIT/Oficina Regional para América Latina y el Caribe, *Panorama Laboral América Latina y el Caribe* (Lima, 1994 ff.).
[73] Branko Milanovic, "More or Less", *Finance and Development*, 48, 3 (September 2011), pp. 6–11, at 10.
[74] Michael Löwy, "A New Type of Party: The Brazilian PT", *Latin American Perspectives*, 14, 4 (Autumn 1987), pp. 453–464.

only in a deep crisis; during the years in power it also lost a considerable part of its previous movement components. The working class as formal-sector wage-earners engaged in urban industry or services thus seems splintered. This dire and conventionally pessimistic panorama, however, has to be contrasted with the remarkable instances of workers's militancy in many Latin American locations and the fact that Latin America is currently probably the only region in the world where the twentieth-century combination of liberationist and workers ideologies still is able to appeal to significant (though minority) numbers of the subjects addressed, i.e. to be appropriated by workers struggling both to improve their situation and to nurture a more general imagination of a better world.

In May 2017, a large Latin American labour congress, entitled "Work and Labourers–Past and Present", was held in La Paz, Bolivia; it resulted in the foundation of a new network of Latin American labour historians.[75] The papers presented reveal how far labour history in Latin America has continued to evolve from the 'state of the art' given in the overviews by John French and James Brennan ten years ago:[76] paid and unpaid activities were discussed on equal terms, the unemployed figured just as those in employment, rural labour was envisaged as a fundamental part of the worlds of labour, the free-unfree-continuum and its manifold intersections received ample attention, the work of women (especially in its informal, domestic, or self-employed forms) was analysed in numerous presentations, and the nexus of labour and migration (again) constituted a central concern. Also, the conference featured important temporal enhancements: both the colonial or immediate post-colonial eras as well as contemporary labour studies were included. The congress, however, has also shown that comparative, interregional, or transnational perspectives are still quite rare in labour history research from and about Latin America. The newly founded network, meanwhile, offers the opportunity that such perspectives are facilitated through one of its material preconditions: the closer collaboration of researchers from different countries in the region itself. With that, Latin American labour history thus might experience a further uplift in the coming years–not least by its regionalization and intra-continental linking.

---

[75] See <http://ctt2017.cis.gob.bo/inicio>. The provisional name of the network is Red Latinoamericana de Trabajo y Trabajador@as (RELATT).
[76] Brennan, "Latin American Labour History"; French, "Laboring and Middle-Class Peoples of Latin America".

Suggested reading

Bergad, Laird W. *The Comparative Histories of Slavery in Brazil, Cuba, and the United States* (Cambridge: Cambridge University Press, 2007).

Brennan, James P. *The Labor Wars in Córdoba, 1955–1976. Ideology, Work, and Labor Politics in an Argentine Industrial City* (Cambridge, MA: Harvard University Press, 1994).

Brown, Kendall W. *A History of Mining in Latin America. From the Colonial Era to the Present.* (Albuquerque, NM: University of New Mexico Press, 2012).

Chalhoub, Sidney. "The Politics of Ambiguity: Conditional Manumission, Labor Contracts, and Slave Emancipation in Brazil (1850s-1888)", *International Review of Social History*, 60, 2 (August 2015), pp. 161–191.

Chaney, Elsa M. and Mary Garcia Castro (eds). *Muchachas No More. Household Workers in Latin America and the Caribbean* (Philadelphia: Temple University Press, 1989).

Fontes, Paulo. *Migration and the Making of Industrial São Paulo* (Durham, NC: Duke University Press, 2016, 2nd edn).

Fortes, Alexandre et al. (eds). *Na luta por direitos. Estudos recentes em história social do trabalho* (Campinas: Editora da UNICAMP, 1999).

French, John D. and Daniel James. *The Gendered Worlds of Latin American Women Workers. From Household and Factory to the Union Hall and Ballot Box* (Durham, NC: Duke University Press, 1997).

French, John D. *The Brazilian Worker's ABC. Class Conflict and Alliances in Modern São Paulo* (Chapel Hill, NC: The University of North Carolina Press, 1992).

Garza Toledo, Enrique de la (ed.). *Tratado latinoamericano de sociología del trabajo* (México, DF: El Colegio de México etc., 2000).

James, Daniel. *Resistance and integration. Peronism and the Argentine Working Class, 1946–1975* (Cambridge: Cambridge University Press, 1988).

Karasch, Mary C. *Slave Life in Rio de Janeiro, 1808–1850* (Princeton, NJ: Princeton University Press, 1987).

Klein, Herbert and Ben Vinson III. *African Slavery in Latin America and the Caribbean* (New York: Oxford University Press, 2007).

Lobato, Mirta Zaida. *Historia de las trabajadoras en la Argentina (1869–1960)* (Buenos Aires: Edhasa, 2007).

Look Lai, Walton and Tan Chee-Beng (eds). *The Chinese in Latin America and the Caribbean* (Leiden and Boston: Brill, 2010).

Mintz, Sidney. *Sweetness and Power. The Place Of Sugar In Modern History* (New York: Viking Penguin, 1985).

Portes, Alejandro and William Haller. *La economía informal* (Santiago de Chile: CEPAL, 2014), available under: <http://www.cepal.org/es/publicaciones/6091-la-economia-informal>.

Schwartz, Stuart. *Slaves, Peasants, and Rebels. Reconsidering Brazilian Slavery* (Urbana, IL: University of Illinois Press, 1996).

Scott, Rebecca J. *Slave Emancipation in Cuba. The Transition to Free Labor, 1860–1899* (Princeton, NJ: Princeton University Press, 1985).

Serulnikov, Sergio. *Revolution in the Andes. The Age of Túpac Amaru* (Durham, NC: Duke University Press, 2013).

Socolow, Susan. *Women of Colonial Latin America* (Cambridge: Cambridge University Press, 2000).

Suriano, Juan. *Paradoxes of Utopia. Anarchist Culture and Politics in Buenos Aires, 1890–1910* (Oakland, CA: AK Press, 2010).

Topik, Stephen (ed.). *The Second Conquest of Latin America. Coffee, Henequen, and Oil during the Export Boom, 1850–1930* (Austin, TX: University of Texas Press, 1998).

Vieira Powers, Karen. *Women in the Crucible of Conquest. The Gendered Genesis of Spanish American Society, 1500–1600* (Albuquerque, NM: University of New Mexico Press, 2005).

Winn, Peter. *Weavers of Revolution. The Yarur Workers and Chile's Road to Socialism* (Oxford: Oxford University Press, 1986).

Bryan D. Palmer
2.5. Canada and the United States

How histories get written changes with the ebb and flow of particular contexts. As Marx and Engels well knew, instability characterizes both thought and practice in bourgeois times: "All fixed, fast, frozen relations, with their train of ancient and venerable prejudices and opinions, are swept away, all new-formed ones become antiquated before they can ossify."[1]

Few fields have felt this pressure of quickening change and destabilization more than North American working-class history in the past half century. Over the course of recent decades the shifting analytic ground of studies in this area has been evident in all manner of ways. Research into and analysis of labour's past in Canada and the United States, for instance, was reborn in the 1960s and 1970s.[2] Working-class history was often regarded as a vanguard of the cutting edge of an ascendant social history in the 1970s and early-to-mid 1980s, but thereafter it quickly found itself a field relegated to apparent disarray and crisis, frustrated in its search of an elusive, perhaps impossible, synthesis.[3]

An untenable, exaggerated binary opposition was introduced into historiographic commentary. Studies accenting agency and resistance, however much they gestured to structures of determination, were questioned, even chastised, for their illu-

---

[1] Karl Marx and Frederick Engels, "Manifesto of the Communist Party", *Selected Works* (Moscow, 1968), p. 38.
[2] For comment, often illuminating important contentions, see David Brody, "The Old Labor History and the New: In Search of An American Working Class", *Labor History*, 20 (1979), pp. 111–126; David Montgomery, "The Conventional Wisdom", *Labor History*, 13 (1972), pp. 107–136; Montgomery, "To Study the People: The American Working Class", *Labor History*, 21 (1980), pp. 485–512; Robert Ozanne, "Trends in American Labor History", *Labor History*, 21 (1980), 513–521; Gregory S. Kealey, "Looking Backward: Reflections on the Study of Class in Canada", *History and Social Science Teacher*, 16 (1981), pp. 213–222; Kealey, "Labour and Working-Class History in Canada: Prospects in the 1980s", *Labour/Le Travail*, 7 (1981), pp. 95–126; David J. Bercuson, "Through the Looking-Glass of Culture: An Essay on the New Labour History and Working-Class Culture in Recent Canadian Historical Writing", *Labour/Le Travail*, 7 (1981), 95–126; Kenneth McNaught, "E.P. Thompson vs. Harold Logan: Writing About Labour and the Left in the 1970s", *Canadian Historical Review*, 62 (1981), pp. 141–168; Bryan D. Palmer, "Working-Class Canada: Recent Historical Writing", *Queen's Quarterly*, 86 (1979/1980), pp. 594–616; Palmer, "Canada", in: Joan Allen, Alan Campbell, and John McIlroy (eds), *Histories of Labour. National and International Perspectives* (London, 2010), 196–230.
[3] The short-lived quest for synthesis was perhaps abandoned at the height of postmodernist influence in the late 1980s and early 1990s, as historians were admonished to abandon master narratives. On the original appeal see Herbert G. Gutman, "The Missing Synthesis: Whatever Happened to History", *The Nation*, 233 (1981), 553–554; Alan Dawley, "A Preface to Synthesis", *Labor History*, 29 (1988), 363–377; Carrol J. Moody and Alice Kessler-Harris (eds), *Perspectives on American Labor History: Problems of Synthesis* (DeKalb, Illinois, 1989); Bryan D. Palmer, "Canadian Controversies", *History Today*, 44 (1994), pp. 44–49.

mination of class struggle, their emphasis on how the "weapons of the weak"[4] revealed a fundamental class difference that animated wide-ranging research into working-class life and leisure and creative reinterpretation of economic, social, cultural, and political history.[5] This was represented by critics as exaggerated wish fulfillment, a romanticization of the working-class past sometimes labelled "culturalism."[6] By the mid-to-late 1990s, the so-called "new" labour history was being judged rather harshly, dismissed as "old hat": an authorial social construction premised on what had not happened in the past being written into a presentist history as what was.[7] Along the way, as all that once seemed solid melted into the air of critical rejoinder and skepticism, much that, in past times, apparently appeared holy, was profaned.

At issue was always the politics of interpretation. The material circumstances of late capitalism, pressured by new, but predictable, crises, unleashed a confusing

---

[4] James C. Scott, *Weapons of the Weak: Everyday Forms of Peasant Resistance* (New Haven, CT, 1985), appeared late in the production of these labour histories, but was congruent with the approaches developing at the time. See also, Scott, *Domination and the Arts of Resistance: Hidden Transcripts* (New Haven, CT, 1990).

[5] The undeniable influence of E.P. Thompson, *The Making of the English Working Class* (London, 1963) was paramount, but in the United States the different approaches of Herbert G. Gutman and David Montgomery registered decisively. See, especially, Gutman, *Work, Culture and Society in Industrializing America* (New York, 1976) and Montgomery, *Workers' Control in America: Studies in the History of Work, Technology, and Labor Struggles* (New York, 1979). A subsequent collection of essays indicated the range of studies that emerged in this period: Michael H. Frisch and Daniel J. Walkowitz (eds), *Working-Class America: Essays on Labor, Community, and American Society* (Urbana, IL, 1983). An especially influential and representative statement was Alan Dawley and Paul Faler, "Working-Class Culture and Politics in the Industrial Revolution: Sources of Loyalism and Rebellion", *Journal of Social History*, 9 (1976), pp. 466–480. In Canada comparable texts would perhaps be Gregory S. Kealey and Peter Warrian (eds), *Essays in Canadian Working-Class History* (Toronto, 1976); Bryan D. Palmer, *A Culture in Conflict: Skilled Workers and Industrial Capitalism in Hamilton, Ontario, 1860–1914* (Kingston and Montreal, 1979); Kealey, *Toronto Workers Respond to Industrial Capitalism, 1867–1892* (Toronto, 1980).

[6] Salient early texts include Elizabeth Fox-Genovese and Eugene D. Genovese, "The Political Crisis of Labor History", *Journal of Social History*, 10 (1976), pp. 205–220; Richard Johnson, "Edward Thompson, Eugene Genovese, and Socialist-Humanist History", *History Workshop*, 6 (1978), pp. 79–100; Bercuson, "Through the Looking Glass of Culture"; McNaught, "E.P. Thompson vs. Harold Logan"; Ian McKay, "Historians, Anthropology, and the Concept of Culture", *Labour/Le Travailleur*, 8/9 (1981–1982), pp. 185–241; Daniel Drache, "The Formation and Fragmentation of the Canadian Working Class, 1820–1920", *Studies in Political Economy*, 15 (1984), pp. 43–89; Lawrence T. McDonnell, "'You Are Too Sentimental': Problems and Suggestions for a New Labor History", *Journal of Social History*, 17 (1984), pp. 629–654; Michael Kazin, "A People Not a Class: Rethinking the Political Language of the Modern US Labor Movement", in: Mike Davis and Michael Sprinker (eds), *Reshaping the US Left: Popular Struggles in the 1980s* (London, 1988), pp. 257–286; Kazin, "The Historian as Populist", *New York Review of Books*, 35 (12 May 1988), pp. 48–50; "A Symposium on *The Fall of the House of Labor*", *Labor History*, 30 (1989), pp. 92–197.

[7] See, for instance, Nick Salvatore, "Herbert Gutman's Narrative of the American Working Class", *International Journal of Politics, Culture, and Society*, 12 (1998), pp. 43–80.

swirl of change that embraced the market ideology of neoliberalism and the radical relativism of postmodernism and its linguistic turn. Both the institutions of the labour movement and entrenched intellectual-political understandings of class came under forceful attack. The resilience and resources of the left retreated. For some spokespersons in the seemingly victorious capitalist west, the ostensible ultimate demise of "socialism" with the implosion of the Soviet Union spelled nothing less than "the end of history."[8]

Small wonder that scholars began to approach the history of class experience differently.[9] Alternative approaches to what many dismissed as an out-dated "proletarian model" emerged: gender historians questioned the masculinizing of labour studies; critical theory's discourse-driven linguistic turn interrogated foundational understandings of production's materiality and the determinative boundaries it established for class formation.[10]

Lenard R. Berlanstein, writing in 1993, provided a post-mortem: "Recently, the collapse of communism, the ostensible universal enchantment with the marketplace as liberator, and the strength of ethnic over class identities do not lend credence to the role of the working class as an agent of change. At the same time, flourishing women's movements have cast doubt on the claims of a male-dominated left to

---

8 Francis Fukuyama, "The End of History?", *The National Interest* (Summer 1989), pp. 3–18, and the sophisticated engagement with this and related texts in Perry Anderson, "The Ends of History", in: Anderson, *A Zone of Engagement* (London, 1992), pp. 279–375.

9 Gareth Stedman Jones, *Languages of Class: Studies in English Working-Class History, 1832–1982* (Cambridge, 1983), was an early and suggestive statement. For critiques see, Ellen Meiksins Wood, *The Retreat from Class. A New 'True Socialism'* (London 1986); Bryan D. Palmer, "The Poverty of Theory Revisited; or, Critical Theory, Historical Materialism, and the Ostensible End of Marxism", *International Review of Social History*, 38 (1993), pp. 133–162. For a different critique, more quintessentially "American", see Jefferson Cowie and Nick Salvatore, "The Long Exception: Rethinking the Place of the New Deal in American History", *International Labor and Working-Class History*, 74 (2008), pp. 3–32, responded to usefully in David Montgomery, "The Mythical Man", pp. 56–62. See, for a more recent elaboration, Jefferson Cowie, *The New Deal and the Limits of American Politics* (Princeton, 2016).

10 For the United States see the development of statements on gendered labour history in Susan Levine, "Class and Gender: Herbert Gutman and the Women of Shoe City", *Labor History*, 29 (1988), pp. 344–355; Mari Jo Buhle, "Gender and Labor History", and Alice Kessler-Harris, "A New Agenda for American Labor History: A Gendered Analysis and the Question of Class", in: Moody and Kessler-Harris (eds), *Perspectives on American Labor History*, pp. 55–79, 217–234; Ava Baron, "Gender and Labor History: Learning from the Past, Looking to the Future", in: Baron (ed.), *Work Engendered: Toward a New History of American Labor* (Ithaca, NY, 1991), pp. 1–46; Ruth Milkman, *On Gender, Labor, and Inequality* (Urbana and Chicago, 2016). In Canada, note Joy Parr, *The Gender of Breadwinners: Women, Men, and Change in Two Industrial Towns, 1880–1950* (Toronto, 1990); Franca Iacovetta and Mariana Valverde (eds), *Gender Conflicts: New Essays in Women's History* (Toronto, 1992); and Joan Sangster, *Through Feminist Eyes: Essays on Canadian Women's Histories* (Athabasca, Alberta, 2011). Highly influential, and indicative of the ways in which gender analysis and the linguistic turn might coincide, was Joan Scott, "Gender: A Useful Category of Historical Analysis", *American Historical Review*, 91 (1986), pp. 1053–1075.

speak for the emancipation of all people. The changed political climate forces historians to wonder if they have been posing the right questions."[11] Almost a decade later, similar positions were also being espoused by Elizabeth Faue, a gender historian of labour who concluded in 2002 that the analytic failures of Marxism, postmodernism, and masculine-centered accounts of the workplace, in conjunction with the reconfiguration of post-Iron Curtain societies, left class, as an interpretive category, wanting in both substance and audience: "More and more class to me looks less like a structure and more like an empty vessel into which all pour content. It exists even now in mainstream American culture as an origin story that has lost its claim on the popular imagination. Since the dismantling of the Soviet bloc, it has lost in scholarly sectors as well."[12]

Contesting crisis

To be sure, there were commentators who refused to see labour history as having entirely succumbed, taking the opportunity, as did Ira Katznelson, to insist that, "assessed by the standards of the craft of history, more excellent work is being done now than ever before. Read as an empirical genre, irrespective of trends in the world or normative commitments, labour history has never been better, more diverse or richly textured. Impressively, it is the site of important epistemological debates. Further, labour history has extended its domain to include subjects such as drink, crime, leisure, sexuality and the family it once either ignored or relegated to the periphery of its concerns." Katznelson conceded that, in William Sewell's words, labour history was mired in some "continuing intellectual doldrums", and his impression was that the field had suffered a loss of élan, directionality, and intellectual purpose. That said, the field was not in crisis, and Katznelson offered a way forward, via the "new institutionalism" of political science and sociology, whereby labour historians could return to Geoff Eley's and Keith Nield's earlier provocation to revitalize the study of the political. For Katznelson this might productively be engaged by addressing the "bourgeois" dimensions of subjects such as law and the state, both of which had considerable purchase on working-class lives.[13]

---

11 Lenard R. Berlanstein, "Introduction", in: Berlanstein (ed.), *Rethinking Labor History. Essays on Discourse and Class Analysis* (Urbana and Chicago, 1993), p. 5. My own response to these developments was obviously different: Bryan D. Palmer, *Descent into Discourse. The Reification of Language and the Writing of Social History* (Philadelphia, 1990).
12 Elizabeth Faue, "Retooling the Class Factory: United States Labour History After Marx, Montgomery, and Postmodernism", *Labour History,* 82 (2002), pp. 109–119.
13 Ira Katznelson, "The 'Bourgeois' Dimension: A Provocation About Institutions, Politics and the Future of Labor History", *International Labor and Working-Class History,* 46 (1994), pp. 7–32; William Sewell, "Toward a Post-materialist Rhetoric for Labor History", in: Berlanstein, *Rethinking Labor History,* p. 16; Geoff Eley and Keith Nield, "Why Does Social History Ignore Politics?", *Social History,* 5 (May 1980), pp. 249–271.

So dominant had assessments of the waning of working-class history in the 1990s become a decade later that Katznelson's push to critically engage with labour history in 1994 was dubbed a mourning, cited one-sidedly, conveying an exaggerated assessment of interpretive malaise.[14] Sven Beckert would write of the denouement of labour history's American golden age in ways that structured the demise politically. During the "heyday" of labour history in the 1970s and 1980s, Beckert asserted, writing in the field was "still explicitly or implicitly informed by one question, namely Werner Sombart's famous 'Why is there no socialism in the United States'?" Beckert explained that, "With the labour movement found wanting, workers' collective identities, especially as expressed in the realm of culture, increasingly moved to the center of attention. The inability to find a socialist project among the American working class that matched, a cynic might say, the perhaps exaggerated expectations of historians, led scholars ultimately to make do with collective picnics in the park." Needless to say, this retrospective (and jaundiced) view of the history of the working class was unsustainable, and Beckert concludes that by the 2000s "graduate students and their mentors had lost enthusiasm for the history of workers and their institutions."[15]

Charting the new course

Within this declension deconstruction, the drift to new interpretive panaceas proliferated. They have changed with striking rapidity over the course of the last four decades. An astute commentator on the signs in the street of American working-class historiography, Leon Fink, offers a series of mappings and prognoses. At the end of the 1980s Fink was still hopeful of the possibilities inherent in analysis of working-class culture, broadly conceived, concluding that, "For labour historians, the study of culture always begins with the study of possibility, with the assumption

---

14 Contrast what Katznelson actually says in the opening paragraph of "The 'Bourgeois' Dimension", with how the essay is quoted in Leon Fink, "What is to be Done – In Labor History?", *Labor History*, 43 (2002), p. 419.
15 Sven Beckert, "History of American Capitalism", in: Eric Foner and Lisa McGirr (eds), *American History Now* (Philadelphia, 2011), pp. 317–318. Beckert's generalization about Sombart's influence is obviously a caricature of American labour history written during this period. The essays in Frisch and Walkowitz, *Working-Class America*, which present characteristic work in the field in the early 1980s, contain barely a reference to Sombart, and that allusion is in passing and is critical. (Sean Wilentz, "Artisan Republican Festivals and the Rise of Class Conflict in New York City, 1788–1837", pp. 64, 76.) To the extent that comment on Sombart and the question of why there was no socialism in America, or "American exceptionalism", was addressed in this period of labour history's "heyday", commentary ran in the direction of critique of Sombart, rather than a fixation on his concerns. See Eric Foner, "Why Is There No Socialism in the United States", *History Workshop Journal*, 17 (1984), pp. 57–80; Sean Wilentz, "Against Exceptionalism: Class Consciousness and the American Labor Movement, 1790–1920", *International Labor and Working-Class History*, 26 (1984), pp. 1–24; Leon Fink, "Looking Backward: Reflections on Workers' Culture and Certain Conceptual Dilemmas within Labor History", in: Moody and Kessler-Harris, *Perspectives on American Labor History*, p. 6.

that there is 'life below'. Rather than bring down the final curtain on culturalism, let us instead have the second act." A few years later, under the onslaught of increasingly vociferous complaint that labour history's search for synthesis had stalled, that accent on the cultural was judged an inadequate response to "a sober neo-realism on the limits of the American labour tradition." Focus on the masculinist elements of a workplace-defined culture, Fink suggested, blinded historians to the profound ways in which class was gendered. In 1993, Fink thus backed tentatively away from the preoccupation with synthesis, and refocused the cultural, asserting that "gendered histories" not only endowed the culturalist current of labour history with "a tougher, more self-critical angle of analysis", but promised a heralded "second act" of working-class research, in which the central theme would be "Gender". Almost a decade later, in 2002, Fink provided a wish-list of subjects that needed exploration, some of them actually reminiscent of Katznelson's "new institutionalist" and "bourgeois" dimension: occupations and occupational culture; class-inflected counter-narratives of political history; race, slavery, and unfree labour systems; business history with the labour left in; micro-histories of labouring people, revealed through studies of memory, community, or biography; classic class conflicts reimagined; and immigrant and migrant workers. Finally, in 2011, Fink offered an optimistic statement on "how a field survived hard times", detailing, in his view, labour history's resilience in the face of the organized trade union movement's decline and the demise of 1960s-style mobilizations for progressive social change. Neoliberalism's ravages aside, Fink saw two "nutritive supplements" sustaining labour history through tough times. First, a fresh focus on "multidimensional borderlands", in which former peripheral regions and work sites were studied, explorations that often involved transnational inquiries, new regional studies of frontier zones within the United States,[16] and occupational histories far removed from traditional concerns with fac-

---

16 Fink suggested that research trajectories within United States labour history "drifted in focus from the urban-industrial centres of the East Coast and Midwest toward the extractive or transport centers of the west", citing Thomas G. Andrews, *Killing for Coal. America's Deadliest Labor War* (Cambridge, MA, 2008); John P. Enycart, *The Quest for 'Just and Pure Law': Rocky Mountain Workers and American Social Democracy, 1870–1924* (Stanford, CA, 2009); and Theresa A. Case, *The Great Southwest Railroad Strike and Free Labor* (College Station, TX, 2010), a list that could also include many other titles, including Ruth Milkman, *L.A. Story: Immigrant Workes and the Future of the U.S. Labor Movement* (New York, 2006) and the more recently-published James J. Lorence, *Palomino: Clinton Jencks and Mexican-American Unionism in the American Southwest* (Urbana and Chicago, 2013). It is, however, unclear if such a research shift actually occurred, given continued publication on other regions, and, in fact, the longstanding record of research on workers in the frontier west. There remained interest, of course, in New York, Philadelphia, Detroit, Chicago, and the Midwest, with many important studies appearing, among them: Rosemary Feuer, *Radical Unionism in the Midwest, 1900–1950* (Urbana and Chicago, 2006); Peter Cole, *Wobblies on the Waterfront: Interracial Unionism in Progressive Era Philadelphia* (Urbana and Chicago, 2007); John B. Jentz and Richard Schneirov (eds), *Chicago in the Age of Capital: Class, Politics, and Democracy during the Civil War and Reconstruction* (Urbana and Chicago, 2012); Lisa Phillips, *A Renegade Union: Interracial Organizing and Labor Radicalism* (Urbana and Chicago, 2013). In Canada, while publication of labour studies in all regions has been ongoing,

tory, mine, and mill. Second, labour history had been revived, relatedly, by new refusals to take "for granted a neat division among slavery, contract, and 'free' labour systems."[17]

These surveys of the historiography, spiced with interpretive insights and provocations, constitute a useful guide to where labour history has been over the last few decades, and prophetic suggestion of where it is going.[18] To read Fink's essays, which constitute something of a bellwether of the field, is to appreciate that what is new in the current conjuncture is the shift in sensibilities associated with the different concerns of contemporary historians, compared with their predecessors who were writing in the 1970s and 1980s, advocates of the so-called "new" labour history.

The analytic paradigm of this earlier fruitful period, according to Fink, was ordered by a dual inspiration. On the one hand, a humanistic interest in ordinary working people and the diversity and richness of their cultural lives took the study of workers in many positive and imaginative directions. On the other hand, all of this lent new purpose and passion to labour history, recasting understandings of the institutions, politics, and struggles that had long been regarded as central to the oppositional substance of class under capitalism. These two "identifiable sources of inspiration" had produced a library of impressive studies by the 1990s, and published research would continue to appear, but by this late date Fink suggests that the shelf life of this project "had largely expired."[19] What new kind of shelf now supports the study of labour? What is the state of the art of labour history as a field?

---

there is no discernible decline in interest in central Canadian cities, as evidenced in two recently-published studies: Craig Heron, *Lunch-Bucket Lives: Remaking the Workers' City* (Toronto, 2015) and Bryan D. Palmer and Gaetan Heroux, *Toronto's Poor: A Rebellious History* (Toronto, 2016).

17 Fink, "Looking Backward", esp. p. 23; Fink, "Culture's Last Stand: Gender and the Search for Synthesis in American Labor History", *Labor History*, 34 (1993), pp. 178–189; Fink, "What is to be Done – In Labor History?" pp. 419–424; Fink, "The Great Escape: How a Field Survived Hard Times", *Labor: Studies in Working-Class History of the Americas*, 8 (2011), pp. 109–115. Some of these essays are reproduced in Fink, *In Search of the Working Class: Essays in American Labor History and Political Culture* (Urbana and Chicago, 1994).

18 See my earlier plea for a more appreciative sense of the different schools of labour historiography, and especially conventional writings, in Bryan D. Palmer, "Fin-de-Siècle Labour History in Canada and the United States: A Case for Tradition", in Jan Lucassen (ed.), *Global Labour History: A State of the Art* (Bern, 2006), pp. 195–226. Fink gestures toward the necessity of a reconsideration of more traditional writings in the field in "John R. Commons, Herbert Gutman, and the Burden of Labor History", *Labor History*, 29 (1988), pp. 313–322, but opportunities to address Commons and older published histories with new developments in the field are seldom taken. As Fink outlines the importance of new studies of labour on the American frontier and of recent works addressing slavery as a form of unfree labour, for instance, it bears mentioning that the first two volumes of the multi-volume *Documentary History of American Industrial Society* (Cleveland, 1910–1911), edited by John R. Commons, Ulrich B. Phillips, Eugene A. Gilmore, Helen L. Sumner, and John B. Andrews, with prefaces and introductions by Richard T. Ely and John B. Clark, addressed "Plantation and Frontier, 1649–1863."

19 Fink, "The Great Escape", pp. 109–110.

Continuities amid change

Such questions are not easy to answer. There is much art in labour history, but little state, although this intended pun should not be misinterpreted as meaning that studies of the class policies and practices of the apparatus of governance are few, for they have been a rich site of labour historiographies in both Canada and the United States for some time.[20] Indeed, addressing the state at junctures where policies intersect with the movements and mobilizations of labouring people has long orchestrated studies of immigration, deportation, gender, law, and class conflict, illuminating their related histories.[21] In the scholarship of Joan Sangster and Stephen Meyer, such work can reach deep into the cultural intricacies of gendered workplace cultures, exposing a raw underside of masculine-feminine divides that are nonetheless lived out within boundaries established by class.[22] It can also address the pursuit of equity in ways that highlight the importance of a class struggle for gendered citizen-

---

[20] See, for instance, Christopher L. Tomlins, *The State and the Unions: Labor Relations, Law, and the Organized Labor Movement in America, 1880–1960* (Cambridge, 1985); Tomlins, *Freedom Bound: Law, Labor, and Civic Identity in Colonizing English America, 1580–1865* (New York, 2010); William E. Forbath, *Law and the Shaping of the American Labor Movement* (Cambridge, MA, 1991); Alan Dawley, *Struggles for Justice: Social Responsibility and the Liberal State* (Cambridge, MA, 1991); Melvyn Dubofsky, *The State and Labor in Modern America* (Chapel Hill, NC, 1994); Joseph A. McCartin, *Labor's Great War. The Struggle for Industrial Democracy and the Origins of Modern American Labor Relations, 1912–1921* (Chapel Hill, NC, 1998); McCartin, *Collision Course: Ronald Reagan, the Air Traffic Controllers, and the Strike that Changed America* (New York, 2011); Paul Craven, *'An Impartial Umpire': Industrial Relations and the Canadian State, 1900–1911* (Toronto, 1980); Bob Russell, *Back to Work? Labour, State, and Industrial Relations in Canada* (Scarborough, Ontario, 1990); Leo Panitch and Donald Swartz, *Assault on Trade Union Freedoms: From Wage Controls to Social Contract* (Aurora, Ontario, 1993); Peter McInnis, *Harnessing Labour Confrontation: Shaping the Postwar Settlement in Canada* (Toronto, 2002); Reg Whitaker, Gregory S. Kealey, and Andy Parnaby, *Secret Service Policing in Canada from the Fenians to Fortress America* (Toronto, 2012).

[21] To cite only some examples of studies addressing Canada: Barbara Roberts, *Whence They Came: Deporatation from Canada, 1900–1935* (Ottawa, 1988); Franca Iacovetta with Paula Draper and Robert Ventresca, *A Nation of Immigrants: Women, Workers, and Communities in Canadian History, 1840s-1960s* (Toronto, 1998); Judy Fudge and Eric Tucker, *Labour Before the Law. The Regulation of Workers' Collective Action in Canada, 1900–1948* (Toronto, 2001); Donna Gabaccia and Franca Iacovetta (eds), *Women, Gender, and Transnational Lives: Italian Workers of the World* (Toronto, 2002); Iacovetta, *Gatekeepers: Reshaping Immigrant Lives in Cold War Canada* (Toronto, 2006); David Goutor, *Guarding the Gates: The Canadian Labour Movement and Immigration, 1872–1934* (Vancouver, 2007); Jennifer A. Stephen, *Pick One Intelligent Girl: Employability, Domesticity, and the Gendering of Canada's Welfare State, 1939–1947* (Toronto, 2007); Reinhold Kramer and Tom Mitchell, *When the State Trembled: How A.J. Andrews and the Citizens' Committee Broke the Winnipeg General Strike* (Toronto, 2010); Joan Sangster, *Transforming Labour: Women and Work in Postwar Canada* (Toronto, 2010); Eric Tucker and Judy Fudge (eds), *Work on Trial: Canadian Labour Law Struggles* (Toronto, 2010).

[22] Stephen Meyer, *Manhood on the Line. Working-Class Masculinities in the American Heartland* (Urbana and Chicago, 2016); Joan Sangster, "Just Horseplay? Masculinity and Workplace Grievances in Fordist Canada, 1947–1970s", *Canadian Journal of Women and the Law*, 26 (2014), pp. 330–364.

ship, associated with the writings of Alice Kessler-Harris, Dorothy Sue Cobble, Nancy MacLean, and others.[23] As in the case of MacLean, this orientation dovetails nicely with attention to race and civil rights mobilizations, where the struggles of African Americans, Asian Americans, and Mexican Americans have often proceeded as class movements that exercised an impact on the state, labour relations, and understandings of citizenship,[24] an experience that also had its Canadian particularities.[25]

Much, if not all, of this writing was perfectly congruent with the general development of the field of labour history as it had evolved from the 1970s into the 1990s, in spite of the ostensible crisis afflicting the study of the working-class past. To be sure, there were detours that took new directions, some associated with a postmodernist-inflected culturalism[26] that had little to do with the attraction to a combative

---

23 Kessler-Harris's pioneering survey, *Out to Work. A History of Wage-Earning Women in the United States* (New York, 1982) was later complemented with *In Pursuit of Equity: Women, Men, and the Quest for Economic Citizenship in Twentieth Century America* (New York, 2002), and a collection of essays, *Gendering Labor History* (Urbana and Chicago, 2007). See, as well, Dorothy Sue Cobble, *The Other Women's Movement: Workplace Justice and Social Rights in Modern America* (Princeton, NJ, 2005); Dennis Deslippe, *Rights, Not Roses: Unions and the Rise of Working-Class Feminism* (Urbana and Chicago, 2000); Nancy MacLean, "The Hidden History of Affirmative Action: Working Women's Organizations in the Workplace Struggles of the 1970s and the Gender of Class", *Feminist Studies*, 25 (1999), pp. 43–78.
24 Nancy MacLean, *Freedom is not Enough: The Opening of the American Workplace* (Cambridge, MA, 2006). The literature on race and class is voluminous, far too extensive to cite adequately. But consider the following influential monographs, many of them relatively recently published: Vicki L. Ruiz, *Cannery Women, Cannery Lives: Mexican Women, Unionization, and the California Food Processing Industry, 1930–1950* (Albuquerque, NM, 1987); Ruiz, *From Out of the Shadows: Mexican Women in Twentieth-Century America* (New York, 1999); Robert Korstad, *Civil Rights Unionism: Tobacco Workers and the Struggle for Democracy in the Twentieth-Century South* (Chapel Hill, NC, 2003); Mae Ngai, *Impossible Subjects: Illegal Aliens and the Making of Modern America* (Princeton, NJ, 2005); William P. Jones, *The Tribe of Black Ulysses. African American Lumber Workers in the Jim Crow South* (Urbana and Chicago, 2005); Miriam Pawel, *The Union of their Dreams: Power, Hope, and Struggle in Cesar Chavez's Farm Worker Movement* (New York, 2009); and the immense contribution of Michael K. Honey, including *Going Down Jericho Road: The Memphis Strike, Martin Luther King's Last Campaign* (New York, 2007); Honey (ed.), *'All Labor Has Dignity': Martin Luther King, Jr.*(Boston, 2011); and Honey, *Black Workers Remember: An Oral History of Segregation, Unionism, and the Freedom Struggle* (Los Angeles, 2012). See also David R. Roediger and Elizabeth D. Esch, *The Production of Difference. Race and Management of Labor in U.S. History* (New York, 2012).
25 See, for instance, Ross Lambertson, *Repression and Resistance: Canadian Human Rights Activists, 1930–1960* (Toronto, 2005); Carmela Patrias, *Jobs and Justice: Fighting Discrimination in Wartime Canada, 1939–1945* (Toronto, 2012); Dominique Clément, *Human Rights in Canada* (Waterloo, 2016).
26 One example of this trend would be the extremism of a focus on gender performativity evident in attempts to recast the nature of class struggles in the needle trades in Daniel E. Bender, *Sweated Work, Weak Bodies: Anti-Sweatshop Campaigns and Languages of Labor* (New Brunswick, New Jersey, 2004). Bender would also contribute an essay, "Sensing Labor: The Stinking Working Class After the Cultural Turn", to Donna Haverty-Stacke and Daniel J. Walkowitz (eds), *Rethinking U.S. Labor History: Essays in the Working-Class Experience, 1756–2009* (New York, 2010), pp. 243–265 that revealed a problematic tendency in this new culturalist turn. Shorn of the kind of political sensibilities, rooted

working-class culture that captivated so much of a post-1960s generation of labour historians in Canada and the United States, inspired by E. P. Thompson, Herbert G. Gutman, David Montgomery, and Alice Kessler-Harris. But the extensive output of North American labour historians in the 1990s and into the first decade of the 21st century more often than not built on past accomplishments, however varied, rather than breaking decisively from them, embedding what had often seemed points of contention around subjects like gender and race into the fabric of labour's history, increasingly understood in complex, but not entirely unfamiliar, ways.[27]

Detailed examinations of strikes as the most obvious expression of working-class discontent clearly remained relevant, for instance. They revealed the powerful class forces, sustained by state power, that were arrayed against insurgencies of labour, even as some workers were recruited to turn against their struggling counterparts, acting as strike breakers.[28] Violence was never far removed from this picture. Yet turning the other cheek, studies of working-class religion have recently proliferated, especially in the United States,[29] and there have been significant forays into the in-

---

in outrage at the denigration of the poor, that grounded earlier studies of the physical degradation of outcast sectors of the working class, evident in pioneering statements such as Louis Chevalier, *Laboring Classes and Dangerous Classes in Paris During the First Half of the Nineteenth Century* (New York, 1973), Bender's article, as its title suggests, carried within it more than a whiff of complacency and condescension.

27 See the collection of essays in Bryan D. Palmer and Joan Sangster (eds), *Labouring Canada. Class, Gender, and Race in Canadian Working-Class History* (Don Mills, Ontario, 2008).

28 J. Anthony Lukas, *Big Trouble. A Murder in a Small Western Town Sets Off a Struggle for the Soul of America* (New York, 1997); Stephen L. Endicott, *Bienfait. The Saskatchewan Miners' Struggle of 1931* (Toronto, 2002); Stephen H. Norwood, *Strikebreaking and Intimidation. Mercenaries and Masculinity in Twentieth-Century America* (Chapel Hill, NC, 2002); Bryan D. Palmer, *Revolutionary Teamsters: The Minneapolis Truckers' Strikes of 1934* (Leiden and Boston, 2013).

29 Jarod Roll, *Spirit of Rebellion: Labor and Religion in the New Cotton South* (Urbana and Chicago, 2010); Erik S. Gellman and Jarod Roll, *The Gospel of the Working Class: Labor's Southern Prophets in New Deal America* (Urbana and Chicago, 2011); William A. Mirola, *Redeeming Time: Protestantism and Chicago's Eight-Hour Movement, 1866–1912* (Urbana and Chicago, 2015); Christopher D. Cantwell, Heath W. Carter, and Nannie Giodano (eds), *The Pew and the Picket Line: Christianity and the American Working Class* (Chicago, 2016); Mathew Pehl, *The Making of Working-Class Religion* (Urbana and Chicago, 2016); Elizabeth Fones-Wolf and Ken Fones-Wolf, *Struggle for the Soul of the Postwar South: White Evangelicals and Operation Dixie* (urbana and Chicago, 2016); and the interesting statements by a number of working-class historians in Nick Salvatore (ed.), *Faith and the Historian: Catholic Perspectives* (Urbana and Chicago, 2007). There is no comparable output on working-class religion in Canada, although older studies such as Richard Allan, *The Social Passion. Religion and Social Reform in Canada, 1914–1928* (Toronto, 1971) and Ramsay Cook, *The Regenerators. Social Criticism in Late Victorian Canada* (Toronto, 1975), have been supplemented with Nancy Christie and Michael Gauvreau, *A Full-Orbed Christianity: The Protestant Churches and Social Welfare in Canada, 1900–1940* (Montreal and Kingston, 2001); Paula Maurutto, *Governing Charities: Church and State in Toronto's Catholic Archdiocese, 1850–1950* (Montreal and Kingston, 2003); Richard Allan, *The View From the Murney Tower: Salem Bland, the Late Victorian Controversies, and the Search for a New Christianity* (Toronto 2008); Janis Thiessen, *Manufacturing Mennonites: Work and Religion in Post-War Manitoba* (Toronto, 2013).

tellectual history of labour.[30] New work sites have been probed with heightened sensitivities to gender and race,[31] as have workers' celebrations of May Day and Labour Day.[32] Appreciations of the struggles of the poor, the unemployed, and the wageless, orchestrated less by resistance to the extraction of surplus than by fighting for minimums of survival, have helped to realign understandings of class formation with appreciations of dispossession. This both broadens a sense of what constitutes class and offers, especially in the work of Canadian social historian Todd McCallum, a sense of how capitalism was perceived by certain marginalized groups, who were often able to creatively push the envelope of resistance.[33] Especially in Canada, where histories of aboriginality in the cauldron of colonialism are now arguably at the cutting edge of recent historiography, the involvement of indigenous peoples in labouring activity has recently received important new treatment.[34] And much of the writing on the revolutionary left, where there has been a particular recent in-

---

30 Note especially Steve Fraser and Joshua B. Freeman (eds), *Audacious Democracy: Labor, Intellectuals and the Social Reconstruction of America* (Boston, 1997); Rosanne Currarino, *The Labor Question in America. Economic Democracy in the Gilded Age* (Urbana and Chicago, 2011); Jeffrey Sklansky, "William Leggett and the Melodrama of the Market", in: Michael Zakim and Gary J. Kornblith (eds), *Capitalism Takes Command. The Social Transformation of Nineteenth-Century America* (Chicago, 2012), pp. 199–222; Leon Fink, *The Long Gilded Age. American Capitalism and the Lessons of the New World Order* (Philadelphia, 2015).
31 Among two areas of rich recent study are agricultural labour and work associated with airlines. See Cindy Hahamovitch, *The Fruits of Their Labor. Atlantic Coast Farmworkers and the Making of Migrant Poverty, 1870–1945* (Chapel Hill, NC, 1997); Matt García, *A World of Its Own. Race, Labor, and Citrus in the Making of Greater Los Angeles, 1900–1970* (Chapel Hill, NC, 2001); Kathleen Mapes, *Sweet Tyranny: Migrant Labor, Industrial Agriculture, and Imperial Politics* (Urbana and Chicago, 2009); McCartin, *Collision Course*; Liesl Miller Orenic, *On the Ground. Labor Struggle in the American Airline Industry* (Urbana and Chicago, 2009); Joan Sangster and Julia Smith, "Beards and Bloomers: Flight Attendants, Grievances, and Embodied Labour in the Canadian Airline Industry, 1960s-1980s", *Gender, Work, and Organization*, 23 (2016), pp. 183–199.
32 Craig Heron and Steve Penfold, *The Workers' Festival: A History of Labour Day in Canada* (Toronto, 2005); Donna Haverty-Stacke, *America's Forgotten Holiday: May Day and Nationalism, 1867–1960* (New York, 2009).
33 See Tobias Higbie, *Indispensable Outcasts: Hobo Workers and Community in the American Midwest, 1880–1930* (Urbana and Chicago, 2003); Todd DePastio, *Citizen Hobo. How a Century of Homelessness Shaped America* (Chicago, 2003); and the particularly imaginative study, Todd McCallum, *Hobohemia and the Crucifixion Machine: Rival Images of a New World in 1930s Vancouver* (Athabasca, Alberta, 2014); Palmer and Heroux, *Toronto's Poor*; and for conceptual statements, Michael Denning, "Wageless Life", *New Left Review*, 66 (2010), pp. 79–97; Bryan D. Palmer, "Reconsiderations of Class: Precariousness as Proletarianization", in: Leo Panitch, Greg Albo, and Vivek Chibber (eds), *The Socialist Register, 2014: Registering Class – 50 Years, 1964–2014* (London, 2014), pp. 40–62.
34 Paige Raibmon, *Authentic Indians. Episodes of Encounter from the Late Nineteenth-Century Northwest Coast* (Durham, North Carolina, 2005); Andrew Parnaby, *Citizen Docker. Making a New Deal on the Vancouver Waterfront, 1919–1939* (Toronto, 2008). As in the case of Keith Thor Carlson, *The Power of Place, the Problem of Time. Aboriginal Identity and Historical Consciousness in the Cauldron of Colonialism* (Toronto, 2010), some of this writing actually addresses slavery and class distinctions *within* First Nations.

terest in anarchism as well as important new studies of communism, has relevance for histories of labour in both the United States and Canada.³⁵

Beyond this, however, lay arguably the three most significant developments in approaching labour history in new ways. All have emerged after 2000, and all are related. These developments accent the transnational dimensions of labouring life, pushing historians to see across national boundaries rather than isolating workers within particular, limited, regionalized states; situate class within the multiplicity of socio-economic relations associated with a broad contextualization designated "capitalism"; and insist on stretching the study of the working class beyond the wage labour market into sectors of coerced, "unfree", regimes of exploitation, such as slavery. These fresh turns involve approaching the working class differently, often researching its development on broader canvases that demand methodologies somewhat different than those that served the "new" labour history of the post-1960s decades well. Perhaps most importantly, these new studies of labour exhibit a different sensibility toward agency and resistance than was often on offer in earlier studies associated with the renaissance of labour history in the decades immediately following the 1960s.

---

35 Chicago's anarchists and the police who clashed with them at the Haymarket events of 1886 are the subject of two controversial studies by Timothy Messer-Kruse, *The Trial of the Haymarket Anarchists. Terrorism and Justice in the Gilded Age* (New York, 2011) and *The Haymarket Conspiracy. Transatlantic Anarchist Networks* (Urbana and Chicago, 2012). Note, as well, James Green, *Death in the Haymarket. A Story of Chicago, the First Labor Movement, and the Bombing that Divided Gilded Age America* (New York, 2007); Sam Mitrani, *The Rise of the Chicago Police Department: Class and Conflict, 1850–1994* (Urbana and Chicago, 2014); Tom Goyens, *Beer and Revolution: The German Anarchist Movement in New York City, 1880–1914* (Urbana and Chicago, 2007); Kenyon Zimmer, *Immigrants Against the State: Yiddish and Italian Anarchism in America* (Urbana and Chicago, 2015); Travis Tomchuk, *Transnational Radicals. Italian Anarchists in Canada and the U.S., 1915–1940* (Winnipeg, 2015). Recent studies of the revolutionary left include Bryan D. Palmer, *James P. Cannon and the Origins of the American Revolutionary Left, 1890–1928* (Urbana and Chicago, 2007); Randi Storch, *Red Chicago: American Communism at the Grassroots, 1928–1935* (Urbana and Chicago, 2009); Jeffrey B. Perry, *Hubert Harrison: the Voice of Harlem Radicalism, 1883–1918* (New York, 2009); Jacob A. Zumoff, *The Communist International and US Communism, 1919–1939* (Boston and Leiden, 2014); Donna Haverty-Stacke, *Trotskyists on Trial: Free Speech and Political Persecution Since the Age of FDR* (New York, 2015); Ian McKay, *Reasoning Otherwise: Leftists and the People's Enlightenment in Canada, 1890–1920* (Toronto, 2008); Stephen L. Endicott, *Raising the Red Flag: The Workers' Unity League of Canada, 1930–1936* (Toronto, 2012); Ester Reiter, *A Future Without Hate or Need: The Promise of the Jewish Left in Canada* (Toronto, 2016). Social democracy has a more robust presence in Canadian history than in that of the United States. See James Naylor, *The Fate of Labour Socialism: The Co-operative Commonwealth and the Dream of a Working-Class Future* (Toronto, 2016).

Recent related paths of labour history: the transnational, the capitalist, and the unfree[36]

In an age of globalization, as new social movements arose in the aftermath of the post-Seattle World Trade Organization protests of 1999, labour historians began to accent the transnational in their studies.[37] In so doing they necessarily confronted issues of labour recruitment and displacement that were central to capital's obvious mobility, a subject of longstanding interest as evidenced in Canadian studies of "labour continentalism", the economics of trade unionism's "foreign domination", or the earlier mid-nineteenth century social dislocation associated with communities of peripatetic canal diggers, subjects explored, respectively, by Robert Babcock, Sally Zerker, and Peter Way. More recent histories of related phenomenon, situating labour studies in the direct orbit of capitalism's global imperatives, include Jefferson Cowie's 1999 account of Radio Corporation of America's decades-long quest for cheap labour and Bryan D. Palmer's exploration of the colonization of the eastern Ontario "backcountry" by the Goodyear tire enterprise in 1990.[38] The cluster of important recent monographs emanating from United States and Canadian working-class historians' invigorated interest in cross-border studies reveal much about the movements of labour and capital, their respective places in forging the bonds of econo-

---

36 Given space considerations what follows is an abbreviated discussion, in which a full critical engagement with contemporary trends is sidestepped. I am currently preparing a more sustained discussion, tentatively titled, "The Mind Forg'd Manacles of Contemporary Labor History."

37 An initial phase of global or transnational labour history is usefully summarized in two recent texts: Jan Lucassen (ed.), *Global Labor History: A State of the Art* (Bern, 2006); Marcel van der Linden, *Workers of the World: Essays Toward a Global Labor History* (Leiden and Boston, 2008). In the United States, the transnational turn in labour history is apparent in Leon Fink (ed.), *Workers Across the Americas. The Transnational Turn in Labor History* (New York, 2011). Canadian historians of the working class have not gravitated as decisively toward transnationalism, largely because they have always situated their studies of the working class within understandings of immigration streams, so-called international unionism, and the creation of Dominion settler societies, formed at the interface of national and international developments. See, for instance, the joint 1996 publication of the Canadian journal *Labour/Le Travail*, 38 (Fall 1996) and the Australian journal *Labour History*, 71 (November 1996). The co-published issues closed, moreover, with a statement by Charles Bergquist, "Postscript: Comparative Research on the 'New World Order'", pp. 278–288. Enthusiasm for the project of transnational studies is clearly apparent among social historians. See, for instance, Karen Dubinsky, Adele Perry, and Henry Yu (eds), *Within and Without the Nation* (Toronto, 2015); Karen Dubinsky, Sean Mills, and Scott Rutherford (eds), *Canada and the Third World: Overlapping Histories* (Toronto, 2016).

38 Robert H. Babcock, *Gompers in Canada. A Study of American Continentalism Before the First World War* (Toronto, 1975); Sally Zerker, *The Rise and Fall of the Toronto Typographical Union, 1832–1972. A Case Study of Foreign Domination* (Toronto, 1982); Peter Way, *Common Labor. Workers and the Digging of North American Canals, 1760–1860* (New York, 1993); Jefferson Cowie, *Capital Moves. RCA's Seventy-Year Quest for Cheap Labor* (Ithaca, New York, 1999).; Bryan D. Palmer, *Capitalism Comes to the Backcountry. The Goodyear Invasion of Napanee* (Toronto, 1994).

mies and empires, and the contradictory experiences of class collectivity, on the one hand, and fragmentations of labour, on the other.[39]

If globalization spawned labour history transnationalism, economic crisis induced working-class historians to reflect more consciously on the downturns and panics endemic to capitalism, situating workers within these persistent slumps and depressions.[40] But the new shelf that would support and sustain labour histories in this context was an odd one. Even as capitalism foundered, and class and its injuries, no longer quite so hidden, seemed forced into the public discourse,[41] a revival of labour history could, apparently, only take place through a kind of consumer rebranding. Thus a truly new labour history was to be launched under the auspices of a somewhat commodified "history of capitalism." Sven Beckert offered the view that an older historiography of workers constituted little more than a narrowing field that had "reached an impasse", a subject "in need of new perspectives." By embracing "the history of capitalism", Becker insisted, United States labour historians could "link … their work … to the concerns of a broader field that is arguably central to the American historical profession."[42]

Beckert's fine study *Empire of Cotton: A Global History* (2015), has many attributes and is a welcomed addition to our understanding of a commodity that figured decisively in the making of the modern world. A chapter on the "global reconstruction" of the cotton economy at the time of the American Civil War and its immediate

---

39 Leon Fink, *The Maya of Morganton. Work and Community in the Neuvo New South* (Chapel Hill, NC, 2003); Fink, *Sweatshops at Sea. Merchant Seamen in the World's First Globalized Industry from 1812 to the Present* (Chapel Hill, NC, 2011); Aviva Chomsky, *West Indian Workers and the United Fruit Company in Costa Rica, 1870–1940* (Baton Rouge, 1996); Chomsky, *Linked Labor Histories: New England, Columbia, and the Making of a Global Working Class* (Durham, 2008); Julie Greene, *The Canal Builders: Making America's Empire at the Panama Canal* (New York, 2009); Jacob A.C. Remes, *Disaster Citizenship: Survivors, Solidarity, and Power in the Progressive Era* (Urbana and Chicago, 2016).
40 Leon Fink, Joseph A. McCartin, and Joan Sangster (eds), *Workers in Hard Times: A Long View of Economic Crises* (Urbana and Chicago, 2014).
41 Note the response to the 2007–2008 financial meltdown: "Is Class Back?" *The Economist*, 15 December 2008; Michelle Golderberg, "A Generation of Intellectuals Shaped by 2008 Crash Rescues Marx from History's Dustbin", *Tablet*, 14 October 2013; Ross Douthat, "Marx Rises Again", *New York Times Sunday Review*, 19 April 2014. Thomas Piketty, *Capital in the Twenty-First Century* (Cambridge, MA, 2013) obviously achieved something of its stature on the basis of increasing obviousness of class inequality and the ravages of economic recession. See Timothy Shenk, "Thomas Piketty and the Millennial Marxists on the Scourge of Inequality", *The Nation*, 5 May 2014.
42 Beckert, "History of American Capitalism", p. 315. On the marketing of this new commodity see Jennifer Schuessler, "In History Departments, It's Up with Capitalism", *New York Times*, 6 April 2013; "Interchange: The History of Capitalism", *Journal of American History*, 101 (2014), pp. 503–536. The push towards the new history of capitalism has registered weakly, if at all, in Canada, perhaps because of a much stronger tradition of indigenous political economy and a radical nationalist concern with subordination to dominant capitalist metropoles. See, for a recent critical comment on this national tradition, Paul Kellogg, *Escape from the Staples Trap: Canadian Political Economy After Left Nationalism* (Toronto, 2015).

aftermath repeatedly explores "new systems of labor", addressing freed slaves and sharecroppers as the objects of intensifying capitalist coercion and discipline. The next chapter, focused on the "destructions" that followed with the rapid rise of industrial capitalism and its ramifications within "cotton's empire" explores how in the United States, India, Egypt, China and elsewhere metropolitan capital integrated rural production and urban manufacturing, a process of consolidation in which states orchestrated contract law, property rights, transportation systems, and imperial control over territories the better to rationalize and extend markets and discipline labour.[43] Transnationalism and capitalism, as sites of labour recruitment and organization, subordination and struggle, meet in Beckert's exploration of cotton's contested relations of production, in which an empire of exchange consolidated within a new global order.

This "history of capitalism" approach, as Beckert's study suggests, is pushing historians to explore class at the conjuncture of slavery, wage labour, and survival in early America. The analytic accent of such research tends to highlight the disciplines of work and the market, exploring how workers cultivated mechanisms of adaptation within these structures, rather than other robust agencies of class initiative, in which overt struggle and varied forms of resistance offered explicit challenge.[44] Michael Zakim's and Gary J. Kornblith's edited collection, *Capitalism Takes Command* (2014), for instance, reveals how "a new set of questions ... guide historical inquiry: not 'Who built America?' but rather 'Who sold America?' or perhaps more to the point, 'Who financed those sales?' The subsequent essays show the fruitfulness of such an approach, but also expose the vulnerabilities of a volume lacking any contribution invested in that once-classic hallmark of the history of capitalism: *proletarianization*." [45]

As Beckert notes, this new orientation differs from the social histories of labour appearing previously: "Workers are seen as much less autonomous and powerful than in the accounts of an earlier generation of historians, perhaps expressing

---

[43] Sven Beckert, *Empire of Cotton: A Global History* (New York, 2015), pp. 274–349.
[44] See, for instance, Seth Rockman, *Scraping By. Wage Labor, Slavery, and Survival in Early Baltimore* (Baltimore, 2008).
[45] Zakim and Kornblith, *Capitalism Takes Command*, commented on by Seth Rockman, "What Makes the History of Capitalism Noteworthy?", *Journal of the Early Republic*, 34 (2014), pp..439–466, esp. pp. 464, 453. The shift away from "Who built America?" is an obvious reference to the suggested value of distancing scholarship from the Gutman-inspired and Stephen Brier/Joshua Brown continued American Social History Project, whose major attempt to synthesize working-class history first appeared as American Social History Project, *Who Built America? Working People and the Nation's Economy, Politics, Culture, and Society:* Volume 1 – *From Conquest and Colonization Through Reconstruction and the Great Uprising of 1877* (New York, 1989): Volume 2 – *From the Gilded Age to the Present* (New York, 1992).

among other things the darker prospects of labour in the twenty-first century."[46] Given this emphasis on labour's subordination, it is not surprising that a third new path in working-class history is the study of "unfree" labour. Recent North American research has often turned to the padrone system, prisons and the chain gang, and coolie/indentured labour.[47]

It is in the study of slavery, interpreted as a capitalist regime of work organization ordered by the lash that drove profits to soaring highs, where "new methods of labour management" receive perhaps their most imaginative reconstruction. Rightly seeing the history of slavery as a history of labour, works structured around understandings such as Walter Johnson's and Edward E. Baptist's "slave labour capitalism" not surprisingly adopt an approach to agency, resistance, and struggle congruent with those who have studied workers within "the history of capitalism" framework. Neither historian of slaves as labourers thinks there is much to be gained by attempting to write histories that address the agency of these coerced workers. Rather, says Johnson, historians should "re-immerse ourselves in the nightmare of History rather than resting easy while dreaming that it is dawn and we have awakened." Baptist is no more open to charting the contours of slave agency; he wants little to do with histories of resistance because the hard horrors of slavery were too all consuming to allow much of that. "From those who survived" slavery, Baptist declares unequivocally, plantation capitalism "stole everything", with slave lives "ripped asunder so that their market value could be extracted." This is a labour history of exploitation's excesses, one that countenances no illusions that those who were truly naught might someday be all.[48] It is not pushing argument too far to suggest that these new histories of "capitalism/labour/slavery" present working slaves in ways that historicize the exploited and oppressed usefully, albeit with a surfeit of determination and an underwhelming, somewhat skewed accounting of agency.

---

[46] Beckert, "History of American Capitalism", pp. 325–326, citing Rockman, *Scraping By*; Way, *Common Laborers*; and Gunther Peck, *Reinventing Free Labor: Padrones and Immigrant Workers in the North American West, 1880–1930* (New York, 2000).

[47] Alex Lichtenstein, *Twice the Work of Free Labor. The Political Economy of Convict Labor in the New South* (New York, 1996); Peck, *Reinventing Free Labor*; Scott Reynolds Nelson, *Steel Drivin' Man* (New York, 2006); Moon-Ha Jung, *Coolies and Cane. Race, Labor, and Sugar in the Age of Emancipation* (Baltimore, 2006); Ted McCoy, *Hard Time: Reforming the Penitentiary in Nineteenth-Century Canada* (Althabasca, Alberta, 2012). For indentured labour in Canada the experience of early *voyageurs* and *couriers de bois* is instructive. See Edith Burely, *Servants of the Honourable Company. Work, Discipline, and Conflict in the Hudson's Bay Company, 1770–1879* (Toronto, 1997); Carolyn Podruchny, *Making the Voyageur World: Travelers and Traders in the North American Fur Trade* (Lincoln, Nebraska, 2006); Giles Havard, *Histoire des couriers de bois: Amérique du Nord, 1600–1840* (Paris, 2016).

[48] Walter Johnson, *River of Dark Dreams: Slavery and Empire in Cotton Kingdom* (Cambridge, MA, 2013); Edward E. Baptist, *The Half Has Never Been Told: Slavery and the Making of American Capitalism* (New York, 2014), esp. pp. xix, 113, 142, 147, 188. Sven Beckert, "Slavery and Capitalism", *The Chronicle of Higher Education*, 12 December 2014. For Johnson's repudiation of agency see "On Agency", *Journal of Social History*, 37 (2003), pp. 113–124.

Conclusion

Labour histories, as this overview of recent writing on Canada and the United States suggests, are overwhelmingly oppositional in their politics of interpretation. The field was born as a critique of the most arbitrary excesses of class power, as it was wielded from above against those below.[49] Over time, and within any given period of contested class relations, there will inevitably be a diversity of oppositional possibilities, and labour history has always been a field where liberal, social democratic, feminist, Marxist, anarchist and other voices of dissenting analysis clash interpretively. A part of labour history's robust and resilient nature is precisely that it contains this analytic and political diversity, spawning serious debate. This has always leavened and enlivened the intellectual nature of an oppositional field.

If, indeed, we recognize, as we should, that men and women do make their own history, but not entirely as they please, it is incumbent upon all labour historians to at least agree that history is made at the interface of objective constructs/constraints and subjective creations/aspirations, the place where apparent destiny and the project of desire meet, and often conflict. Neither side is untouched by the other. To be sure, if the past writing of labour histories is instructive, it is likely the case that different histories will line up on one interpretive side of this ever-present, understandable, divide or the other. The subject studied, the methodologies and conceptual frameworks adopted, the canvass on which the general or the particular part of labour's history is painted, with strokes broad and bold or fine and finite, not to mention the politics of interpretation, all influence how specific writing in the field leans. Let us do our best to insure that while we tilt in one direction, our hands waving in analytical animation, we at least ground our feet in ways acknowledging the other way of addressing at our subject. Labour history, as a field of study, needs this two-sidedness if it is to continue to play a small role in contributing, however marginally, to a new and more humane future.

---

49 John R. Commons, "American Shoemakers, 1648–1895: A Sketch of Industrial Evolution", *Quarterly Journal of Economics*, 24 (November 1909), pp. 39–84 still repays rereading.

Suggested reading

Burely, Edith. *Servants of the Honourable Company. Work, Discipline, and Conflict in the Hudson's Bay Company, 1770–1879* (Toronto: Oxford University Press, 1997).

Cobble, Dorothy Sue. *The Other Women's Movement: Workplace Justice and Social Rights in Modern America* (Princeton, NJ: Princeton University Press, 2005).

Cowie, Jefferson. *Capital Moves. RCA's Seventy-Year Quest for Cheap Labor* (Ithaca, NY: Cornell University Press, 1999).

Fink, Leon (ed.). *Workers Across the Americas. The Transnational Turn in Labor History* (New York: Oxford University Press, 2011).

Fink, Leon, Joseph McCartin, and Joan Sangster (eds). *Workers in Hard Times: A Long View of Economic Crises* (Urbana and Chicago, IL: University of Illinois Press, 2014).

Fink, Leon. *Sweatshops at Sea: Merchant Seamen in the World's First Globalized Industry from 1812 to the Present* (Chapel Hill, NC: NC: University of North Carolina Press, 2011).

Fink, Leon. *The Maya of Morgantown: Work and Community in the Neuvo South* (Chapel Hill, NC: University of North Carolina Press, 2003).

Frisch, Michael H. and Daniel J. Walkowitz (eds). *Working-Class America: Essays on Labor, Community, and American Society* (Urbana, IL: University of Illinois Press, 1983).

Fudge, Judy and Eric Tucker. *Labour Before the Law: The Regulation of Workers' Collective Action in Canada, 1900–1948* (Toronto: University of Toronto Press, 2001).

Gabaccia, Donna and Franca Iacovetta (eds). *Women, Gender, and Transnational Lives: Italian Workers of the World* (Toronto: University of Toronto Press, 2002).

Goutor, David. *Guarding the Gates: The Canadian Labour Movement and Immigration, 1872–1934* (Vancouver: UBC Press, 2007).

Gutman, Herbert G. *Work, Culture and Society in Industrializing America* (New York: Alfred Knopf, 1976).

Hahamovitch, Cindy. *The Fruits of Their Labor. Atlantic Coast Farmworkers and the Making of Migrant Poverty, 1870–1945* (Chapel Hill, NC: University of North Carolina Press, 1997).

Heron, Craig. *Lunch-bucket Lives: Remaking the Workers' City* (Toronto: Between the Lines, 2015).

Honey, Michael K. *Going Down Jericho Road: The Memphis Strike, Martin Luther King's Last Campaign* (New York: W.W. Norton, 2007).

Iacovetta, Franca. *Gatekeepers: Reshaping Immigrant Lives in Cold War Canada* (Toronto: Between the Lines, 2006).

Kealey, Gregory S. and Bryan D. Palmer, *Dreaming of What Might Be: The Knights of Labor in Ontario, 1880–1900* (Cambridge and New York: Cambridge University Press, 1983).

Kealey, Gregory S. *Toronto Workers Respond to Industrial Capitalism, 1860–1892* (Toronto: University of Toronto Press, 1980).

Kessler-Harris, Alice. *Out to Work. A History of Wage-Earning Women in the United States* (New York: Oxford University Press, 1982).

McCartin, Joseph. *Collision Course: Ronald Reagan, the Air Traffic Controllers, and the Strike that Changed America* (New York: Oxford University Press, 2011).

Montgomery, David. *Workers' Control in America: Studies in the History of Work, Technology, and Labor Struggles* (New York: Cambridge University Press, 1979).

Moody, Carrol J. and Alice Kessler-Harris (eds). *Perspectives on American Labor History. Problems of Synthesis* (DeKalb, IL: University of Northern Illinois Press, 1989).

Palmer, Bryan D. and Joan Sangster (eds). *Labouring Canada. Class, Gender, and Race in Canadian Working-Class History* (Don Mills, Ontario: Oxford University Press, 2008).

Palmer, Bryan D. *Capitalism Comes to the Backcountry. The Goodyear Invasion of Napanee* (Toronto: Between the Lines, 1994).

Panitch, Leo and Donald Swartz, *Assault on Trade Union Freedoms. From Wage Controls to Social Contract* (Aurora, Ontario: Garamond Press, 1993).

Parr, Joy. *The Gender of Breadwinners: Women, Men, and Change in Two Industrial Towns, 1880–1950* (Toronto: University of Toronto Press, 1990).

Sangster, Joan. *Through Feminist Eyes. Essays in Canadian Women's Histories* (Edmonton: AU Press, 2011).

Sangster, Joan. *Transforming Labour. Women and Work in Postwar Canada* (Toronto: University of Toronto Press, 2010).

Tomlins, Christopher L. *The State and the Unions: Labor Relations, Law, and the Organized Labor Movement in America, 1880–1960* (Cambridge: Cambridge University Press, 1985).

Tucker, Eric and Judy Fudge (eds). *Work on Trial. Canadian Labour Law Struggles* (Toronto: Irwin Law for the Osgoode Society for Canadian Legal History, 2010).

Way, Peter. *Common Labor. Workers and the Digging of North American Canals, 1760–1860* (Baltimore, MD: Johns Hopkins University Press, 1997).

Susan Zimmermann
2.6. Eastern Europe

This chapter gives a glimpse into past and present historiographies of labour in East Central Europe, South-eastern Europe, and Eastern Europe including the post-Soviet territories. The focus is on writings on the history of labour in Eastern Europe, or the region so defined, between the early modern period and 1989–1991. I have considered here only what has been published since the 1960s, and the emphasis is on labour from the nineteenth century onwards. My aim has been to explore how that historiography has contributed to the development of an inclusive type of global labour history – or contains the potential to do so. I therefore present here a selective and somewhat generous reading[1] of the scholarship discussed, foregrounding two interconnected aspects. I shall explore to what extent and in what ways the literature has been attentive to some of those groups of workers, and to some of those forms of work and labour, and labour conditions and relations that have often been rendered marginal in classical labour history. In addition, I shall discuss how the literature has invoked trans-local, transnational, comparative, or universal horizons, and in particular how it has characterized and explained local or regional characteristics of the history of labour with reference to such broader horizons.

Foregrounding those two themes might suggest an undue lack of emphasis on the inherent value – indeed the indispensability – to any project intended to advance global labour history of regional historiography on its own account. However, this chapter will demonstrate that the chosen focus, at least in the case of Eastern Europe, allows a re-evaluation of important traditions and trajectories of such regional historiography from a global perspective. The related argument evolves from my interest in a third thing that has guided me through this essay – the question of whether and how the new global labour history has been affected by or partaken in increasingly globalized and often asymmetric circuits of knowledge. I wonder what the effect has been of the corresponding adulation or even fetishization of some scholarship on the one hand, and the devaluation of much Eastern European scholarship and its producers on the other. In this essay I shall seek to counteract such harmful possibilities.

After an introductory section on the relevant waves of labour historiography, I shall discuss how the literature has addressed „special" groups of workers and „special" forms of labour. I have paid attention to concepts and horizons, with the particular aim of including comparative studies, and I read the literature produced during both waves as situated knowledge production.

---

[1] A presentation by Alexandra Ghit (European Social Science History Conference, Valencia 2016) first drew my attention to this concept.

Waves

Eastern European historiography has been important to the process by which labour history developed from the 1960s to the end of state socialism in 1989–1991 into a more respectable and internationally accepted branch of research. This I shall refer to as „Wave One". Within state-socialist Europe, research into the history of the working class and the labour movement was at the core of the state-promoted agenda for historical research. For example, in Hungary,[2] among other countries in the region, key institutions regarded both the large-scale opening of the archives after 1945 and explicit promotion of research into the modern capitalist epoch as important means of generating support for systemic change to socialism. After Stalin's death there were a great many institutions and publications dealing with many aspects of the history of labour. The *Revue Roumaine d'histoire*, established in 1962 and before long published several times a year, had before the end of the decade addressed a diverse range of topics. Articles appeared on the 1907 peasant revolt in an international context, the „heroic struggles" of railway and petroleum workers against the fascistization of the country in 1933, Lenin's address to the workers and peoples of Austria-Hungary in 1918, the steps towards the unification of Romania as mirrored in socialist thinking, and the contribution of the labour and socialist movement to unification. The journal examined the fight of Romanian workers for the liberation of Ernst Thälmann, looked at relations between Romanian and French workers and socialists between 1880 and 1900, and dissected socialist international relations in South-eastern Europe at the end of the nineteenth and the beginning of the twentieth centuries. Karl Marx featured, too, with the Romanians' struggle for social emancipation and national liberation, and there was a recounting of the diffusion of knowledge about Marx's *Capital* in Romania in the late nineteenth century. For earlier periods the journal gave space to pieces on the guilds in Moldova and Walachia in the tenth to the seventeenth century. Later, in 1979, came a study of international and Romanian activities aimed at the rationalization of labour and production in the interwar period, and in 1981 a cluster of articles on the social and legal history of peasants. In 1986 a study was included about Italian workers in Romania before World War I.[3]

While historiographical accounts of different countries agree that labour history blossomed in terms of published output and broadened and diversified thematically, they disagree widely as to the extent of scholarly, thematic, and conceptual openness

---

2 Péter Gunst, *A magyar történetírás története* (Debrecen, 1995), p. 191.
3 The list is exhaustive in terms of the contributions on labour history included in the journal. The language of the journal was predominantly French.

and achievement.⁴ More historiographical research needs to be done before substantial comparisons across the region and globally are possible.

The early and strong presence in Eastern Europe of labour history at the core of the historian's profession and of national research infrastructures had visible repercussions internationally, as did its centrally designed and vividly discussed research agenda. In the context of the Cold War and against the background of a growing international presence from the later 1950s onwards of „undogmatic" Marxist and socialist historians from Western countries and the de-petrification of Eastern European historical research, the Eastern European challenge contributed to making social and labour history more attractive in the West from the 1960s onwards. By 1989 the activities developed by the International Conference of Labour and Social History (ITH) had been documented in seventeen volumes, bringing together labour history writing from both sides of the Iron Curtain (including a number of contributions on the history of labour in the Global South) since 1964. The contributors showed a strong focus on the history of the labour movement in all its variations, including its international dimensions and its relationships to colonialism, imperialism, and war. They also tackled themes such as the involvement of women, the historical geography of Marxism, the question of workers' consciousness, the status of the working class in various contexts, labour migration, and the „problems of the emergence and political formation of the working class". The volumes also give extensive bibliographical information as well as information about research institutions, sources, and documentation, and they repeatedly document the discussion of research methods.⁵

Scholarship produced and published in state-socialist Europe between the 1960s and the 1980s followed and co-shaped the dominant trends of the period, such as writing labour history as the social history of the constitution, and the position of the working class. Flagship journals of the historical profession likewise addressed that large theme repeatedly as well as dealing with the more classical history of the labour movement. In 1978 *Acta Poloniae Historica*, published in Western languages, dedicated a whole volume to labour history. It included contributions on historiography, differentiation and integration, „cultural heritage" and the political attitudes of the working class.⁶ The highly variable character and uneven development of the working class was made clear in Jürgen Kuczynski's forty-volume *Die Geschichte der Lage der Arbeiter unter dem Kapitalismus* [History of the Position of the Workers under Capitalism] published between 1960 and 1972. That monumental work included a volume on women workers in Germany since 1700 and another that gave *Eine Weltübersicht über die Geschichte der Lage der Arbeiter* [Global Overview on the History of the Po-

---

4 Andrei Sokolov, „The Drama of the Russian Working Class and New Perspectives for Labour History in Russia", in: Jan Lucassen (ed.), *Global Labour History: A State of the Art* (Bern, 2006), pp. 399–411, gives a detailed account of the development of labour history in the Soviet Union.
5 https://search.socialhistory.org/Record/COLL00300, last accessed 20 March 2017.
6 *Acta Poloniae Historica*, 38 (1978).

sition of the Workers] (1963 and 1967 respectively).⁷ Miklós Lackó's carefully researched and methodologically reflective *Ipari munkásságunk összetételének alakulása: 1867–1949* [The Evolution of the Composition of our Working Class 1867–1949] (1961) similarly focused on the variable character and uneven development of the history of labour, exploring the social origin, composition, and stratification of the Hungarian industrial working class and describing the various types of workers belonging to this class. Besides statistical and other primary material, the study used the author's own sociographic encounters with many workers. For instance, it paid attention to how the gender and national composition of the workforce was related to the division between skilled and unskilled workers, migratory processes, geographic differentiation, and the development of the labour movement. Lackó was careful to refer closely to his rich data to underline again and again that the industrial labour force had been of „mixed" composition, and highlight the „transitional forms" of wage labour. He pointed out, too, that „double-residence" or „perpetual fluctuation" of large parts of the Hungarian working class between agriculture and industry persisted well into the interwar period. Lackó gave some explanatory background in rather schematic sections on economic development⁸ and the unequal „international division of labour" in Europe.⁸ Meanwhile, in the 1960s the Soviet Union saw the multi-volume publication of *Istoriya Komministicheskoj Partii Sovietskogo Sojuza* [The History of the Communist Party of the Soviet Union] and then, in 1981, the launch of the nine-volume *Istoriia rabochego klassa SSSR* and *Istoriia sovetskogo rabochego klassa* [History of the Working Class of the USSR], which offered valuable data and accumulated knowledge within the confines of a restrictive ideology.⁹

Among Western academics the Wave One period similarly brought the heyday of the by-now classic variants of the social history of the working class, some of which was oriented more towards structure while other versions also explored workers' agency. That context was conducive to scholarship on Eastern European labour, too, and the Anglo Saxon tradition of Russian and Soviet studies in particular generated important work on the history of labour in Russia and the Soviet Union.¹⁰ For pre-socialist Russia the work of Reginald E. Zelnik, among others, was groundbreaking.¹¹

---

7 Jürgen Kuczynski, *Studien zur Geschichte der Lage der Arbeiterin in Deutschland von 1700 bis zur Gegenwart*, Die Geschichte der Lage der Arbeiter unter dem Kapitalismus, 40 vols, vol. 18 (Berlin, 1963), idem, *Eine Weltübersicht über die Geschichte der Lage der Arbeiter*, Die Geschichte der Lage der Arbeiter unter dem Kapitalismus, 40 vols, vol. 37 (Berlin, 1967).
8 Miklós Lackó, *Ipari munkásságunk összetételének alakulása: 1867–1949* (Budapest, 1961), especially pp. 11 ff., 30–33, 138 f.
9 Sokolov, „The Drama of the Russian Working Class", p. 407.
10 The introduction in Donald Filtzer et al. (eds), *A Dream Deferred. New Studies in Russian and Soviet Labour History* (Bern, 2008), and Lewis Siegelbaum, „Workers and Industrialization", in: Ronald Grigor Suny (ed.), *The Twentieth Century*, vol. 3, *The Cambridge History of Russia* (Cambridge, 2006), pp. 440–467, provide good overviews of research and scholarship in the pre- and post-1991 periods.
11 Reginald E. Zelnik, *Labor and Society in Tsarist Russia. The Factory Workers of St. Petersburg 1855–1870* (Stanford, CA, 1971).

Regarding the Soviet period, there were important studies on the entanglement of and tensions between economic policies, including the wider contexts and pressures generating them, on the one hand, and on the other hand labour relations broadly conceived.[12] The scholarship also discussed issues such as the living conditions of the working population.

If, in the West, postmodern and cultural turns caused a crisis in the conception of labour history as the social history of the working class, in Eastern Europe 1989–1991 marked a rupture both much harsher and more tangible. In most of East Central and South-eastern Europe the decline was steeper than in Western Europe in terms of both the devaluation of all earlier scholarship on the history of labour and the virtual disappearance of any related themes or subjects from the research agenda until well into the 2000s. Within and in relation to Russia and certain of the former Soviet territories, and perhaps Poland and the Czech Republic, things never reached quite such a pass as they did in the rest of East Central and in South-eastern Europe during the 1990s. In Russia the degradation of the inherited research infrastructure and institutions was less pronounced, and that might be because the denigration of the state-socialist past or some aspects of it was more contested there than elsewhere. In addition, the Anglo Saxon tradition of Russian and Soviet studies in the 1990s profited greatly from the opening up of many archives, and especially in that period this tradition functioned as the prime platform preventing the complete disappearance of Russian labour history. In that context, the International Institute of Social History in Amsterdam also played a visible role. As a result, the output of internationally visible scholarship on the history of labour in Russia and the Soviet Union continued throughout the 1990s.[13]

Since the 2000s, accompanied by both a visible brain drain from East to West and pronounced if asymmetric internationalization of research and scholarly infrastructures within and beyond Europe, we have seen the beginning of a new wave of interest in labour history all over Eastern Europe; this I shall refer to as „Wave Two". With regard to many countries in the region, the resurgence so far has been characterized by a strong focus on labour under state socialism and state socialism as a quintessentially

---

12 Donald Filtzer, *Soviet Workers and Stalinist Industrialization. The Formation of Modern Soviet Production Relations, 1928–1941* (London etc., 1986).
13 For example, Lewis H. Siegelbaum and Ronald Grigor Suny, *Making Workers Soviet: Power, Class, and Identity* (Cambridge, 1994). Sokolov, „The Drama of the Russian Working Class", especially pp. 413–417, gives concrete information on the activities of Western scholars and institutions in this period and their role for developments in Russia. In his 2006 survey article on pre- and post-1989–1991 Anglo-Saxon scholarship on labour in the Soviet Union, Lewis Siegelbaum basically describes the publications appearing in the 1990s as a late outlet of the earlier „romance" of this scholarship with the Soviet worker. Siegelbaum claims that from the late 1980s onwards class as a category of analysis was „dislodge[d] ... from its privileged position" in Anglo-Saxon historiography on labour in the Soviet Union, and that scholarship largely turned away from its earlier interest in workers and labour. Lewis H. Siegelbaum, „The Late Romance of the Soviet Worker in Western Historiography", *International Review of Social History*, 51, 3 (2006), pp. 463–481, esp. 476–478.

labour-oriented social formation.[14] For the time being, there is more research going on into the beginnings and the ending of state socialism, including the transition, than there is on the period between the 1960s and the mid-1980s.[15] Similarly, new studies on labour in the decades before the Eastern expansion of National Socialism are still rare for East Central and South-eastern Europe.[16] A particularly neglected large theme within Wave Two is the history of workers' organizations and labour movements in Eastern Europe. However, recently a number of cross-country and transnational studies have begun to carve out new terrain with regard to workers' organizations and labour movements too.[17] In general Eastern Europe's new labour history has not yet become very visible within nor integrated into the new global labour history.

---

14 Important cross-country collections of articles were published in *Bohemia: A Journal of History and Civilisation in East Central Europe*, 42, 2 (2001), „Sozialgeschichtliche Kommunismusforschung"; Peter Hübner, Christoph Klessmann, and Klaus Tenfelde, *Arbeiter im Staatssozialismus: Ideologischer Anspruch und soziale Wirklichkeit* (Cologne, 2005); *International Labor and Working-Class History*, 68 (2005), „Labor in Postwar Central and Eastern Europe". *Mitteilungsblatt des Instituts für Soziale Bewegungen*, 37 (2007), „Sowjetische Bergleute und Industriearbeiter – Neue Forschungen", assembles studies on Russian and other post-Soviet territories. Important reviews and bibliographical essays in English and not contained in any of these collections include: Peter Heumos, „Workers under Communist Rule: Research in the Former Socialist Countries of Eastern-Central and South-Eastern Europe and in the Federal Republic of Germany", *International Review of Social History*, 55, 1 (2010), pp. 83–115; Tuong Vu, „Workers under Communism: Romance and Reality", in: Stephen A. Smith (ed.), *The Oxford Handbook of the History of Communism* (Oxford, 2013), pp. 471–487.
15 Recent examples dealing with the period from the 1960s onwards include Eszter Bartha, *Alienating Labour: Workers on the Road from Socialism to Capitalism in East Germany and Hungary* (New York, 2013), and Eeva Keskülä, „Fiddling, Drinking and Stealing: Moral Code in the Soviet Estonian Mining Industry", *European Review of History/ Revue européenne d'histoire*, 20, 2 (2013), pp. 237–253. The collections cited above also include a few examples of research with a focus on the „middle" period, notably by Lenka Kalinová and Eszter Zsófia Tóth.
16 Examples include Rudolf Kučera, *Život na příděl. Válečná každodennost a politiky dělnické třídy v českých zemích 1914–1918* (Prague, 2013). On pre-Soviet Russia (and the Soviet Union) see Filtzer et al., *A Dream Deferred*.
17 In relation to the Yugoslav territories and the border region with Italy, Sabine Rutar, „Towards a Southeast European History of Labour: Examples from Yugoslavia", in: *idem* (ed.), *Beyond the Balkans: Towards an Inclusive History of Southeastern Europe* (Münster, 2013), pp. 337–342, 348–353, discusses in detail some of this work, including her own. Craig Phelan (ed.), *Trade Unionism since 1945: Towards a Global History*, vol. 1 (Oxford, 2009); Stefan Müller, „West German Trade Unions and the Policy of Détente (1969–1989)", *Moving the Social. Journal of Social History and the History of Social Movements*, No. 52 (2014), pp. 109–137.

Agricultural labour

The period before 1989 gave rise to the detailed study of many forms of agrarian labour,[18] including the labour force that seemed to have been lingering somewhere between an agricultural way of life and various forms of proletarianization. In the most basic sense, that was simply because in the nineteenth and the first half of the twentieth centuries agrarian labour in the broad sense of the term had been the dominant form of labour in most regions of Eastern Europe. In Russia in 1900 eighty per cent of the population were peasants, and they never acknowledged any claim to land by anyone who did not work it.[19] In addition, in many places agrarian labour had been associated with exploitation and misery, and repeatedly with labour struggle and radicalism. As state socialism and thus Wave One came to its end, historiography had created differentiated knowledge about the varieties of labour relations involving agrarian labour, the related history of agrarian unrest and rebellion, and the comparative history of agrarian development. Some of this historiography referred to the history of agrarian labour as shaped by both pan-European and global economic developments and divisions of labour, and local politics, when discussing developments in Eastern Europe.[20]

Other factors more specific to Eastern Europe contributed to the strength of the historiography of agricultural labour. In some cases peasant studies, conceived of as a branch of historical studies separate from the more mainstream history of the labour movement, flourished because less mainstream historians, especially those inclined to favour populist conceptions of national history, prioritized that field of study. There, one could do detailed „thick" social history of „the people". In parallel, the study of peasant-workers and all varieties of agrarian labour was facilitated by one of the most schematic dogmas of Eastern European Marxism Leninism, namely the concept of the „alliance of the workers and the peasants". Among other things, that concept was rooted in the idea that the protracted transition to capitalism in the region meant that peasant-workers had formed an important basis for revolution. Last but not least, the circumstances and position of the Eastern European agrarian population were at the

---

18 For more on the Hungarian case, see Susan Zimmermann, „The Agrarian Working Class Put Somewhat Center Stage: An Often Marginalized Group of Workers in the Historiography of Labor Written in State-Socialist Hungary", *European Journal of History* (under review).
19 Esther Kingston-Mann, „Transforming Peasants in the Twentieth Century: Dilemmas of Russian, Soviet and Post-Soviet Development", in: Suny, *Twentieth Century*, p. 412.
20 Examples involving comparative or cross-national dimensions include Emil Niederhauser, *A nagybirtok és a parasztság Kelet-Európában a polgári forradalmak után* (Debrecen, 1961); T(ibor) Kolossa, *Beiträge zur Verteilung und Zusammensetzung des Agrarproletariats in der Österreichisch-Ungarischen Monarchie*, vol. 51, Studia Historica, Separatum (Budapest, 1961); Ákos Egyed, Lajos Vajda, and Ion Cicalá, *Munkás- és parasztmozgalmak Erdélyben 1905–1907* (Bucharest, 1962); Péter Gunst (ed.), *Kelet-Európa agrárfejlödése a századfordulón (1880–1914)* (Budapest, 1989).

core of the debate on the development of Eastern Europe, which will be reviewed further below.

The fact that during Wave One most authors consistently attached the label „feudal remnant" to some forms of agricultural labour and called others „transitional" still did not limit their interest in exploring how various forms of labour mingled and affected each other. A monumental 1960s publication dealing with the history of the peasantry in Hungary between 1848 and 1914 pursued an inclusive research agenda in that it included those strata of the agrarian population which were outside all means of production and those who, alongside their smallholdings, fell back on wage labour. Such individuals would be traditional cottars, servants, so-called *summás* workers, who were seasonal workers often from distant regions who brought their own tools and were recruited for a fixed period of time. Others might be inhabitants of the problem zone where the world of agrarian labour was experiencing „disintegration". The latter included workers still connected to or based in their villages but working at the margins of or outside that sphere. Examples of such workers are the pick and shovel men, or *cubics*, and forestry workers, and those who broke out of the village setting by seeking refuge from it in migration within and beyond their country, but especially overseas. As István Szabó, doyen of Hungarian peasant history, summarized it, „The concept of the peasantry in this larger sense is – eminently dissimilar class bonds notwithstanding – defined and bound together by economic, social, lifestyle-related, and cultural indicators".[21]

Wave Two added new studies on agrarian labour, even though interest in the subject was now more often reduced to something of a sideshow in peasant studies more generally. There are new studies on policies such as collectivization, yet they hardly touch upon the transformation of labour and livelihood that came with collectivization.[22] Leonard G. Friesen's study, to mention one publication on rural transformation in an earlier period in Southern Ukraine, includes a brief discussion of how, before the mid-nineteenth century, new production strategies and changes to crops resulted in a shortage of labour and functioned as a push towards hired labour; in later decades this created tensions around labour control and between local and migratory labour.[23]

---

21 The quotation is from Szabó's 1961 foundational conceptual study, reprinted in István Szabó, *Jobbágyok-parasztok. Értekezések a magyar parasztság történetéből* (Budapest, 1976); idem, *A parasztság Magyarországon a kapitalizmus korában 1848–1914* (Budapest, 1965).
22 An example is the otherwise substantial volume by Constantin Iordachi and Arnd Bauerkämper (eds), *The Collectivization of Agriculture in Communist Eastern Europe: Comparison and Entanglements* (Budapest and New York, 2014).
23 Leonard Friesen, *Rural Revolutions in Southern Ukraine: Peasants, Nobles, and Colonists, 1774–1905* (Cambridge, MA, 2008).

Women's paid work

There is abundant evidence that women and girls in modern Eastern Europe have long been substantially involved in gainful employment. In 1853 women – many of them peasant-migrants – owned 107 (11 per cent) of all registered enterprises in Moscow and the Moscow district.[24] In the second half of the nineteenth century many girls under the age of ten worked between April and September as goose watchers on the Great Hungarian Plain, spending those long months in remote hamlets far away from their parents.[25]

Three themes have been of key importance in making women's paid work visible and revealing its role in the gendered division of labour in Eastern European societies. First is women's role in farming and agriculture; second, the contested process of women's initial entry into the paid labour force in the nineteenth and the early decades of the twentieth centuries; and, third, scholarship has considered women's mass entry into and work within the non-agricultural sectors of the labour market under state socialism.[26] Historical research into those three large themes has developed unevenly, and there is still little reflection on broader implications beyond Eastern Europe of the findings of that research, and little comparative thinking on the subject.

The history of women's work under the impact of pre-state-socialist industrialization has been studied from a number of perspectives. Working women were to be found in factories in increasing numbers and proportions in many places, yet domestic service, too, proved to be a persistent source of paid work for women. In 1910 in the Hungarian kingdom domestic servants comprised forty per cent of the non-agricultural female workforce, and the figure was the same even in the capital city, a fast growing industrial hub with close to a million inhabitants. Figures were similarly high in partitioned and interwar Poland. Everywhere, the female labour force suffered from enormous women-specific wage discrimination and unequal access to the labour market as compared with men, with particular restrictions on access to learned professions and other skilled work. In addition, working women were discriminated against by social policy legislation largely because their work, for instance as domestic

---

[24] Boris B. Gorshkov, „Serfs on the Move: Peasant Seasonal Migration in Pre-Reform Russia, 1800–61", *Kritika: Explorations in Russian and Eurasian History*, 1, 4 (2000), pp. 627–656, at 649.
[25] Lajos Kiss, *A szegény asszony élete* (Budapest, 1943), pp. 6–31; the book was reprinted several times in Hungary under state socialism.
[26] Christine Schindler (ed.), *Der Forschungsstand zum Thema „Klasse und Geschlecht" in Zentral- und Osteuropa* (Vienna, 1993), gives a good bibliography on studies of women's work, including historical studies, in Albania, Bulgaria, CIS/USSR (including many works on non-Russian territories), Poland, Czechoslovakia, and Hungary during Wave One and in the early 1990s. Krassimira Daskalova and Susan Zimmermann, „Women's and Gender History", in: Irina Livezeanu and Árpád von Klimó (eds), *The Routledge History of East Central Europe since 1700* (London and New York, 2017), pp. 272–315, gives up-to-date information on the history and historiography of women's work in East Central and South-eastern Europe.

servants, was not considered „real work", and because they were strongly represented among the informal, casual, and seasonal labour force not covered by those policies. In trade unions and the labour movement they were confronted with strong masculinism and once again marginalized. Steve Smith's careful comparison of women's strikes in St Petersburg before 1917 and Shanghai before 1927 points to possible relationships between the often violent and elemental character of those strikes and the marginal position of women in the organized labour movement. Smith discusses relationships among female workers and between male and female workers, as well as employers' manipulations of those relations.[27]

A substantial portion of the new scholarship on the history of women's paid work under state socialism has focused on the mobilization of women for paid labour and their legal treatment. There has been a good deal of attention focused on women in highly feminized or „unusual" sectors of the labour market, such as the textile or mining industries, and women's involvement in particular institutions of state-socialist labour, such as Stakhanovism. There has been interest, too, in how their involvement in paid work and later the demise of the state-socialist world of labour has affected women's self-identification and status in society at large.[28] Working women under state socialism were consistently confronted with discrimination and masculinist attitudes both on the shop floor and elsewhere. In the pursuit of their interests and depending on circumstances, women workers therefore mobilized both the state-socialist women's emancipation discourse and the ideological tropes that challenged

---

27 Barbara Alpern Engel, *Between the Fields and the City: Women, Work, and Family in Russia, 1861–1914* (Cambridge, 1994); Anna Żarnowska and Andrzej Szwarc (eds), *Kobieta i praca. Wiek XIX I XX* (Warsaw, 2000); Anna Żarnowska, *Workers, Women, and Social Change in Poland, 1870–1939* (Aldershot, 2004); Susan Zimmermann, *Divide, Provide and Rule. An Integrative History of Poverty Policy, Social Policy, and Social Reform in Hungary under the Habsburg Monarchy* (Budapest and New York, 2011); Zsuzsa Fonó, *Az ipari nőmunkások helyzetéről a századfordulón* (Budapest, 1974); Zsuzsa Fonó, *A magyar munkásnők helyzete és szervezettsége a két világháború között* (Budapest, 1978); Steve Smith, „Class and Gender: Women's Strikes in St Petersburg, 1895–1917 and in Shanghai, 1895–1927", *Social History*, 19, 2 (1994), pp. 141–168.

28 Examples include: Mary Buckley, *Mobilizing Soviet Peasants: Heroines and Heroes of Stalin's Fields* (Lanham, MD, 2006); Melanie Ilic, *Women Workers in the Soviet Interwar Economy: From „Protection" to „Equality"* (New York, 1999); Eszter Zsófia Tóth, „Shifting Identities in the Life Histories of Working-Class Women in Socialist Hungary", *International Labor and Working-Class History*, Mo. 68 (2005), pp. 75–92; Chiara Bonfiglioli, „Gender, Labour and Precarity in the South East European Periphery: The Case of Textile Workers in Štip", *Contemporary Southeastern Europe*, 1, 2 (2014), pp. 7–23; Malgorzata Fidelis, *Women, Communism, and Industrialization in Postwar Poland* (Cambridge, 2010); Diane P. Koenker, „Men against Women on the Shop Floor in Early Soviet Russia: Gender and Class in the Socialist Workplace", *American Historical Review*, 100, 5 (1995), pp. 1438–1464; Tanja Penter, *Kohle für Stalin und Hitler. Arbeiten und Leben im Donbass 1929 bis 1953* (Essen, 2010); Daniela Koleva (ed.), *Negotiating Normality. Everyday Lives in Socialist Institutions* (New Brunswick, NJ, 2012).

that discourse.²⁹ Research has now begun to address topics related to those groups of women, who faced particular hardship or differential treatment compared with other women in the world of work, such as the Romnja, and to look at how women combined different types of work.³⁰ So far, however, far less attention has been given to the matter of the management and control of women's paid work, its specific status and function in the state-socialist world of work, and the consequences for women's work when labour became increasingly involved with the global economy – which in many parts of state-socialist Europe happened well before the demise of state socialism. While it is clear that a large proportion of women workers tended to remain in unskilled or semi-skilled occupations, more research is necessary to explore fully and think through the stratification of the state-socialist working class, including its gendered dimension.³¹ Women's agricultural work under state socialism is another subject that has been far too little studied.³²

Unfree labour

Research on unfree labour in Eastern Europe has focused on three main themes. They are second serfdom and agrarian labour in later periods, coerced labour under National Socialism, and coerced labour within the Gulag system and other forms of direct labour coercion in state-socialist Europe. Other themes, such as German labour force policies in occupied Poland and Lithuania during World War I, or convict labour in Siberia in tsarist Russia, have been addressed by substantial yet so far rather isolated monographs.³³

The debate on the second serfdom and its long-term consequences in Eastern Europe, which has continued throughout the period under consideration here, can be considered a most lively intervention in and relevant contribution to global labour history. More recent studies dealing with the subject tend to emphasize intra-regional and even local variety.³⁴ Whatever their position in the debate, many relevant authors, including the most „revisionist" ones, some of whom tend to deny the very existence of

---

29 Éva Fodor, *Working Difference. Women's Working Lives in Hungary and Austria, 1945–1995* (Durham and London, 2003), pp. 141–145; Jill Massino, „Constructing the Socialist Worker: Gender, Identity and Work under State Socialism in Brașov, Romania", *Aspasia*, 3, 1 (2009), pp. 131–160.
30 For a review see Susan Zimmermann, „Gender Regime and Gender Struggle in Hungarian State Socialism", *Aspasia*, 4, 1 (2010), pp. 1–24.
31 Mark Pittaway, *From the Vanguard to the Margins. Workers in Hungary, 1939 to the Present* (Leiden and Boston, 2014).
32 Beatrice Farnsworth and Lynne Viola (eds), *Russian Peasant Women* (New York and Oxford, 1992), assembles some classic studies.
33 Christian Westerhoff, *Zwangsarbeit im Ersten Weltkrieg* (Paderborn, 2012); Elzbieta Kaczynska, *Das größte Gefängnis der Welt. Sibirien als Strafkolonie zur Zarenzeit* (Frankfurt am Main, 1994).
34 For an excellent recent overview on the debate, with many references to empirical works, see Markus Cerman, *Villagers and Lords in Eastern Europe, 1300–1800* (Basingstoke, 2012).

second serfdom, agree that agrarian labour from the sixteenth to the nineteenth century was characterized by more and more protracted „unfreeness" in many regions of Eastern as compared with Western Europe. However, once transatlantic slavery and the abolition of slavery as a form of coerced labour associated with Western European powers and developments is brought into the picture, the historical East-West unbalance in terms of the unfreedom or freedom of labour is thoroughly disrupted.[35]

For decades, the conceptual debate consistently situated the history of unfree serf labour in Eastern Europe within a pan-European or even global setting. Authors writing in the liberal tradition maintained that the lack of freedom of labour was one of the root causes of the economic backwardness of Eastern Europe, or that it certainly helped exacerbate it. By contrast, Marxist historians such as Zsigmond Pál Pach have argued that the „'second edition' of serfdom" in Hungary was generated as a result of the „world market relationships arising since the sixteenth century", which created a „disadvantageous, economically dependent situation". The limited development of commodity production and the fact that the transition from feudalism to capitalism was „delayed" in comparison to Western Europe and „different, occurring under particular circumstances" were both consequences of that foundational relationship. Pach discusses, too, the various forms and combinations of the employment and bonding of such labour, and the decreasing role of paid labour within that setting in the seventeenth century – basing what he says on empirical material and, of course, stressing that agrarian wage labour at that time was not free labour in the „double sense" of labour under capitalism.[36] World-system analysis would later be built on the work of authors such as Pach and the Polish historian Witold Kula.

More recently, research on agrarian unfreedom has become more comparative and tends to think of more and less constrained agrarian labour in different world regions as a continuum. These newer studies have also questioned unfreedom's economically constraining or thoroughly negative effects.[37] Reference to trans-regional connections in co-producing labour relations, including second serfdom and other forms of agrarian unfreedom that characterized Eastern Europe from the early modern period to the nineteenth century, is visibly in retreat, while recent research on developments within Eastern Europe is methodologically and conceptually sophisticated. Examples include the study by T.K. Dennison and Sheilagh Ogilvie, which, comparing two serf estates in early modern Bohemia and pre-emancipation Russia, argues that serf communities were important in shaping social and labour relations on their estates and forging relationships with overlords and other authorities. The authors

---

35 Alessandro Stanziani has done much to advance this perspective; a good summary can be found in Alessandro Stanziani, „Russian Serfdom: A Reappraisal", *Ab Imperio*, 2 (2014), pp. 71–99, especially 92f.
36 Zsigmond Pál Pach, *Die ungarische Agrarentwicklung im 16–17. Jahrhundert. Abbiegung vom westeuropäischen Entwicklungsgang* (Budapest, 1964), especially pp. 37f., 74–80, 92.
37 Stanziani, „Russian Serfdom: A Reappraisal", argues that both before and after the abolition of serfdom in Russia in 1861 economic growth had been higher than previously assumed.

suggest that their findings should caution everyone against making generalizations about the positive effects of horizontal social capital on overall economic performance.[38] Markus Cerman, discussing the new research on varieties of constrained labour in early-modern East Central and Eastern Europe, concluded that „it is not always possible to distinguish clearly between individual forms of labour constraints and 'free' wage labour in practice".[39]

In parallel, and beginning with Peter Kolchin's by now classic 1987 study on American slavery and Russian serfdom, a number of publications have restaged the classic debate, discussing unfreedom in Eastern Europe with reference to the context of colonial slavery and unfree labour in the West. For Kolchin, constrained labour in Russia and slavery in the American South, both labelled „non-capitalist productive systems", were responses to the growing interest of landlords and plantation owners in commerce and the market opportunities for them when combined with the scarcity of labour in the regions of agricultural expansion.[40] More recently, Alessandro Stanziani, while confirming the insight that historically market development could and often did rely on coerced labour, has presented a different argument. Constraints on labour in Russia from the seventeenth to the nineteenth century were much more multifaceted and combined more flexibly with wage labour than previously thought. There was more movement away from constraining labour before 1861, and constraints were not abruptly lifted by abolition. Such flexibility, together with „relaxing legal constraints", explains the similarly revisionist and much more optimistic estimations of economic growth and market development in Russia in the period. Stanziani explicitly denies the relevance of „developing markets in the West" as a potential „origin of increasing bondage in the East".[41] While in fact none of the above arguments is related to the question of intra-European or global economic interaction – nor would they be required to be – Stanziani thereby ensures that his argument must be read as focusing on intra-Russian explanations for degrees and development of labour coercion. At the same time, he describes Eastern European unfree labour as an extreme variant of a continuum between East and West and clearly distinguishes the labour system in Russia from colonial slavery.

At present then, thinking globally about unfree agrarian labour in Eastern Europe appears to entail two conceptual moves. The paradigm of Eastern European particu-

---

38 T.K. Dennison and Sheilagh Ogilvie, „Serfdom and Social Capital in Bohemia and Russia", *Economic History Review*, 60, 3 (2007), pp. 513–544.
39 Markus Cerman, „Constrained Labour in Early-Modern Rural East-Central and Eastern Europe: Regional Variation and its Causes", in: Alessandro Stanziani (ed.), *Labour, Coercion, and Economic Growth in Eurasia, 17th-20th Centuries* (Leiden, 2013), pp. 189–214, here 214.
40 Peter Kolchin, *Unfree Labor. American Slavery and Russian Serfdom* (Cambridge, MA, 1987), especially pp. 17–31, 359 ff. One recent volume bringing together research into the history of unfree labour in Eastern Europe with developments elsewhere in „Eurasia" is Stanziani, *Labour, Coercion, and Economic Growth in Eurasia*.
41 Alessandro Stanziani, *Bondage. Labor and Rights in Eurasia from the Sixteenth to the Early Twentieth Centuries* (New York, 2014), especially pp. 138 f.; *idem*, „Russian Serfdom: A Reappraisal".

larity has been replaced by recognition of the intra-Eastern European and global diversity of labour relations and the shifting local varieties and combinations of freedom and unfreedom. The Eastern European historiography and debate on unfree agricultural labour has made a lasting contribution to this changing landscape of research in regional and global labour history. At the same time, many authors no longer systematically include either the asymmetric economic division of labour in global capitalism or trans-regional market forces as important factors to be investigated when wishing to explain the emergence or prolongation of unfree labour in Eastern Europe – and by implication across the globe. In recent years we have thus witnessed a double shift in research on the history of unfree labour in Eastern Europe. The unfolding of more global and inclusive deep research into the forms and historical persistence of unfree labour has been combined with reduced interest in the relationship between the global and regional development of capitalism on the one hand and the history of unfree labour on the other. Yet the importance of that relationship to the global study of labour is epitomized by the theme addressed in the following section.

On the move

Important long-term features of the history of labour in Eastern Europe have been the instability, fluidity, and volatility of the work and labour relations of ordinary people, and that has long been recognized. A very important element of this history has been geographical mobility, including for seasonal work and other forms of temporary migration within and across political and national borders, as well as mass long-distance migration and considerable re-migration. Ulf Brunnbauer recently argued that migration has been a key defining characteristic of the overall modern history of Balkan societies, including the repercussions from emigration on the societies of origin.[42] For both Russia and East Central Europe it is safe to adopt that diagnosis without hesitation. Two recent essays, by Aleksandr V. Gevorkyan and Serguey Ivanov[43] covering the seventeenth to the nineteenth and the twentieth to the twenty-first centuries respectively, together give an insightful overview of the manifold migration movements so foundational for the Russian Empire.

As compared with other aspects of the history of migration in, from, and to Eastern Europe, there are fewer studies on the impact on the countries of origin of the large-scale emigration of labour out of the region. At times, emigration took on dramatic

---

42 Ulf Brunnbauer, *Globalizing Southeastern Europe. Emigrants, America, and the State since the Late Nineteenth Century* (Lanham etc., 2016).
43 Aleksandr V. Gevorkyan, „Russia, Migration 17th-19th Century", in: Immanuel Ness (ed.), *The Encyclopedia of Global Human Migration* (Chichester, 2013), vol. 5, pp. 2665–2671; Serguey Ivanov, „Russian Internal Migration, Early 20th Century to Present", in: *ibid.*, pp. 2671–277.

proportions, and useful studies of its effect on the world of work within the region are especially lacking.⁴⁴

The large-scale mobility of the agrarian masses and other ordinary people took different forms in different parts of Eastern Europe. In the Habsburg Empire there was more pronounced internal migration within Austria as compared with Hungary (including Croatia). The populations on the eastern and southern peripheries of the empire were included in other migration circuits that tended to cross borders. Between the 1870s and the 1920s up to four million people emigrated from Austria and Hungary, sometimes accompanied by sizeable return migration, with women making up consistently more than forty per cent of emigrants. The territories of partitioned Poland saw a similarly dramatic migration wave following, as Ewa Morawska has argued, the „Western penetration" and the end of serfdom in the nineteenth century. The dramatic decrease in the size of many peasant holdings, the destruction of traditional rural handicrafts as a complementary source of income, and the development of transport all contributed to the process. Taking border-crossing and internal migration together, between 1860 and 1914 approximately ten million individuals were on the move – a third of the population. In the years before World War I annually more than half a million workers from Austrian and Russian Poland left for Germany as seasonal migrants.⁴⁵ The large-scale migration processes in East Central Europe brought many workers from peasant backgrounds into the quickly growing cities within the regions, and migration history has explored, among other things, the relationship between that phenomenon and local working-class cultures and labour movements in these cities.⁴⁶

The Balkans saw significantly less emigration than did Austria-Hungary, at least if we exclude Croatia and Slovenia, both of which belonged to the Habsburg Monarchy. However, as the nineteenth century ended, overseas migration gained ground dramatically in the Balkans, too, certainly when compared to the more traditional migration between the different Balkan polities and to other parts of the Ottoman Empire. Persistent large wage differentials between the region and Western destinations of emigration, falling travel costs, and locally closed borders all made important contributions to a considerable exodus from the Balkans. The tradition of itinerant labour

---

44 See, however, Dirk Hoerder, Horst Rössler, and Inge Blank (eds), *Roots of the Transplanted* (New York, 1994); Brunnbauer, *Globalizing Southeastern Europe*.
45 Emigration from Galicia of course is included in the numbers for both Austria-Hungary and partitioned Poland. Annemarie Steidl, „On Many Roads: Internal, European, and Transatlantic Migration in the Habsburg Monarchy, 1850–1914" (*Habilitation*, University of Vienna, 2014); idem, „Ein ewiges Hin und Her. Kontinentale, transatlantische und lokale Migrationsrouten in der Spätphase der Habsburgermonarchie", *Österreichische Zeitschrift für Geschichtswissenschaft*, 19, 1 (2008), pp. 15–42; Ewa Morawska, „Labor Migrations of Poles in the Atlantic World Economy, 1880–1914", in: Dirk Hoerder and Leslie Page Moch (eds), *European Migrants: Global and Local Perspectives* (Boston, 1996), pp. 170–208.
46 Anna Żarnowska, „Rural Immigrants and Their Adaptation to the Working-Class Community in Warsaw", in: Hoerder et al., *Roots of the Transplanted*, vol. 2, pp. 289–304; Péter Sipos, „Migration, Labor Movement and Workers' Culture in Budapest, 1867–1914", in: *ibid.*, pp. 155–171.

included seasonal migration from mountain villages or semi-sedentary lifestyles connected to animal husbandry – rather reminiscent of our goose-watching girls on the Great Hungarian Plain – and it had long been „a mainstay of economic life in the Balkans". In due course the tradition of itinerant labour was to become an important generator of long-distance migration.⁴⁷

For a long-term perspective on Russia we must highlight a number of large-scale types of mobility. All the relevant types of mobility were connected with or even based on corresponding immobility regimes, in other words they depended on foundational legal and administrative restrictions and controls on mobility. Organized politics of the settlement and resettlement of agrarian labour, aimed at sustaining and stabilizing imperial expansion, took on unprecedented dimensions from the late eighteenth century onwards. Between the seventeenth and nineteenth centuries „the scale [of human migration] was immense and the process slow", including large-scale colonization projects in Siberia, the Far East, and the Caucasus, so that „in the end, the Russian Empire stood as the rightful heir to that era".⁴⁸ Both before and after the end of serfdom in 1861 these settlement policies combined with more pronounced and individualized mobility from village to village, estate, town, and city. Millions of peasants, male and female, temporarily and often in seasonal rhythm, left their villages to work, some of them far away, as labourers, craftsmen, traders, and entrepreneurs. In the mid-nineteenth century, in the central provinces, over a five-year period roughly a quarter of adult male peasants received permission to migrate temporarily, although the actual proportion of peasants on the move in any given year was considerably higher. One result was the notorious irregularity and instability of the urban workforce.⁴⁹ Steve Smith argues that the agency and changing identity of masses of peasants migrating throughout the decades to St Petersburg and Shanghai respectively played an important role in the revolutionary processes that later went on in both Russia and China.⁵⁰ From the second half of the nineteenth century, border-crossing migration into the Russian Empire, notably from the north-western Iranian province of Azerbaijan, became a mass phenomenon. An estimated 200,000 to 300,000 people, a considerable proportion of them women, crossed Russia's Asian frontiers every year, often for seasonal agricultural work, craftsmen's work, and trade. Considerable numbers of Persians toiled in the Baku oil industry, and as foreigners the migrants

---

47 Brunnbauer, *Globalizing Southeastern Europe*, especially chs 1 and 2; Holm Sundhaussen, „Southeastern Europe", in: Klaus J. Bade *et al.* (eds), *The Encyclopedia of Migration and Minorities in Europe: From the 17th Century to the Present* (Cambridge, 2011), pp. 163–181.
48 Gevorkyan, „Russia, Migration 17th-19th Century", p. 2670; Richard Hellie, „Russia and Belarus", in: Bade *et al.*, *Encyclopedia of Migration and Minorities in Europe*, pp. 181–192.
49 Gorshkov, „Serfs on the Move", also gives the more extensive earlier literature on the post-emancipation period.
50 S.A. Smith, *Revolution and the People in Russia and China: A Comparative History* (Cambridge, 2008).

suffered particular discrimination.⁵¹ Ramin Taghian's careful study illuminates how the Central Asian or Russian experience of so many workers reverberated in the history of the Iranian socialist movement and the Constitutional Revolution in Iran from 1905.⁵²

As a result of large-scale state-led industrialization and collectivization of the agrarian world, migration remained an important feature of the history of labour within the Soviet political sphere. In addition, the borderlands of the Soviet empire, including the republics of Moldova, Armenia, and Georgia, to varying degrees remained net immigration zones until as late as the 1960s or 1970s. In parallel, new types of mobility control and restriction were set in motion, such as the introduction of compulsory internal passports in 1932.⁵³ The control of internal mobility was an important feature of state-socialist policies all over Eastern Europe after 1945.

The study of migration and Eastern Europe can make important contributions to global labour history. First of all it helps to decentralize the global history of labour and labour migration by focusing on migration from, within, and, for the earlier periods in particular, to the region as a permanent and pronounced feature of the history of Eastern Europe. It also sheds light on the connection between modern economic development within and trans-regional divisions of labour beyond Eastern Europe on the one hand, and the mobilization of labour in the region on the other. Within the region, industrialization processes and efforts were dynamic, although before the advent of state socialism they were often insular too. However, these processes and efforts were one of the root causes that set Eastern European labour in motion. For example, Peter Kriedte has recently argued that in the first half of the nineteenth century power elites in Congress Poland, making use of a border protected by a tariff barrier, systematically generated eastward immigration of skilled workers in order to promote the beginnings of a textile industry.⁵⁴ The exodus of millions of people from the agrarian world could not have happened without a great agrarian transformation, which often came with pronounced wage pressure on agrarian labour in Eastern Europe. In the nineteenth and early twentieth centuries the changes were in large

---

51 Hassan Hakimian, „Wage Labor and Migration: Persian Workers in Southern Russia, 1880–1914", *International Journal of Middle East Studies*, 17, 4 (1985), pp. 443–462.
52 Ramin Taghian, *Grenzgänger des Sozialismus. Die transnationale Dimension der frühen sozialistischen Bewegung im Iran (1905–1911)* (Vienna, 2014). Habib Ladjevardi, *Labor Unions and Autocracy in Iran* (New York, 1985), also touches on these migrations and interactions, and pursues a transnational perspective in relation to later decades too.
53 Lewis H. Siegelbaum and Leslie Page Moch (eds), *Broad is my Native Land. Repertoires and Regimes of Migration in Russia's Twentieth Century* (Cambridge, 2014); Siegelbaum, „Workers and Industrialization", pp. 446f.; Attila Melegh, *Diverging Historical Development of Migration in Southeastern Europe since 1950* (Budapest, 2013), especially pp. 26f.; Dirk Hoerder, *Migrations and Belongings 1870–1945* (Cambridge, MA, 2012), especially pp. 35–39.
54 Peter Kriedte, „Migration, Gewerbepolitik und Industrialisierung. Die letzte Phase der West-Ost-Wanderung und die Anfänge des mittelpolnischen Textilindustriereviers (1815–1850)", *Zeitschrift für Ostmitteleuropa-Forschung*, 61, 2 (2012), pp. 163–218.

measure an offshoot of the integration of Eastern European agriculture in trans-European and global markets, and of liberal political reform. The large-scale emigration that followed was directed not only towards the West; it included, for example, the relocation of more than 100,000 Ukrainians to Siberia alone in the second half of the nineteenth century. The great movement that followed the abolition of serfdom in 1861 and gained even more momentum as a result of the Stolypinian agrarian reform after the turn of the century was encouraged and orchestrated by the tsarist government, which promised access to land to this impoverished agricultural population in the faraway region.[55] A not insignificant factor that contributed to setting Eastern European labour on the move was that the trans-European and global integration of agriculture caused agrarian labour in the region to become dependent on international and faraway business cycles. The strong emigration movement itself also had important, though insufficiently studied, effects on the places of origin, in terms of both agrarian labour relations and wages and the availability of remittances – or lack of them.[56]

Second, besides economics politics have always been at the core of the history of migration in the region. State-led settlement and colonization policies were emphasized in particular and over long periods under the Russian Empire, while in the state-socialist period, even though there were policies of bringing industrial employment to people living in remote places, state-led economic development endeavours were built everywhere on the mobilization of labour across space. After 1945, when the rest of Europe saw another large labour-centric migration wave, the state-socialist regimes everywhere (with the exception of Yugoslavia) strictly controlled and regulated Eastern European labour emigration, especially to the West. Even in net-emigration countries such as Hungary, Romania, Bulgaria, and Albania the net emigration ratios remained low compared with those for some other countries in economically similar positions. In those rare instances, when control was relaxed or restrictions were selectively lifted the resulting migration waves, such as that after the 1956 uprising in Hungary or the Jewish emigration from Poland and the Soviet Union between the end of the 1960s and the 1980s, were driven by both political motives and the search for a better life in the West.[57] For the most part, under state socialism labour migration was contained within the Eastern bloc and managed through closely controlled migration accords within

---

[55] „Ukraine", in: Bade *et al.*, *Encyclopedia of Migration and Minorities in Europe*, p. 198; Vladimir Shaidurov, „Ukrainians in Western Siberia in the Second Half of the 19th – Early 20th Century: Specific Features Characterizing Their Resettlement and Economic Adaptation", *Acta Histriae*, 24, 2 (2016), pp. 313–336, especially 319–325.
[56] Brunnbauer, *Globalizing Southeastern Europe*, especially pp. 118–126.
[57] Melegh, *Diverging Historical Development of Migration*, p. 16; Dariusz Stola, *Kraj bez wyjścia? Migracje z Polski 1949–1989* (Warsaw, 2010); Ruth Moshkovitz, „'Ich bin nur froh, dass die Sowjetunion uns nicht zurückgenommen hat.' Bucharisch-jüdische (Re-)Migration nach Wien im Kontext transnationaler Vergeschlechtlichung und Rassifizierung" (Diplomarbeit, University of Vienna, 2016).

Eastern Europe, and from the 1960s with countries in the communist Global South.⁵⁸ The organized intake of labour from the Global South, for instance through the Czech-Vietnamese labour exchange programme inaugurated in 1967,⁵⁹ indicates both the state-socialist endeavour of building an alternative world system, and the insatiable hunger for labour that characterized the heyday of state-led state-socialist economic development. It is probable that the need for new cheap labour played a role in generating these programmes, as integration into the world economy increased.

This picture of labour migration under state socialism raises a number of questions especially about the relationship between the politics of labour migration on the one hand and trans-European and global economic disparities and polarization on the other. Was political control of migration in state-socialist Europe more likely to succeed when economic catching-up was successfully under way, or did it work because of the strong „visible hand" of the socialist state? Did keeping the labour force at home contribute to the economic catch-up? Comparatively speaking, what were the consequences for the development of the home countries and societies of a mass exodus of the labour force in cases such as those of Greece, Spain, and Yugoslavia? These questions might be productively addressed by future research. In more general terms, the study of labour on the move could benefit from close attention to the relationship between the various waves of „untying" and mobilizing it and the changing forms of controlling it.⁶⁰ Nor, of course, should we forget discrimination against migrant labour in terms of wages, rights, and welfare in the hubs of modern economic development, and the fates and fortunes of economic and social development in Eastern Europe as key factors shaping the dynamics of labour migration and the experience of workers in and from Eastern Europe.

Social reproduction and subsistence labour

In most of the historiography reviewed for this essay both the labour of social reproduction and non-commodified subsistence labour, while repeatedly mentioned and often regarded as given, are either not considered to be work or not mapped and discussed in conceptual terms within a framework of labour history. Yet it can be argued that a focus on unpaid labour for social reproduction and on subsistence la-

---

58 Dorota Praszłowicz, „Poland", in: Bade et al., *The Encyclopedia of Migration and Minorities in Europe*, p. 148; Alena K. Alamgir, „Recalcitrant Women: Internationalism and the Redefinition of Welfare Limits in the Czechoslovak-Vietnamese Labor Exchange Program", *Slavic Review*, 73, 1 (2014), pp. 133–155.
59 Alena Alamgir, „Race is Elsewhere: State-Socialist Ideology and the Racialisation of Vietnamese Workers in Czechoslovakia", *Race and Class*, 54, 4 (2013), pp. 67–85.
60 Andrea Komlosy's „State, Regions, and Borders: Single Market Formation and Labor Migration in the Habsburg Monarchy, 1750–1918", *Review*, 27, 2 (2004), pp. 135–177, discusses some of these connections, with a focus on Cisleithanian Austria.

bour is not only a basic requirement for developing more inclusive perspectives on the history of all labour. In addition, it contains the potential to develop a deeper understanding of the history of commodified labour (regardless of its status and ties with social policy measures). Many characteristics of and developments in the world of paid labour can be more adequately understood if explored from the perspective of their connection with unpaid labour. The commodification of formerly unpaid labour, as well as the lack of it, has in fact had important ramifications for the history of paid labour.

A number of studies on Russian and early Soviet industrialization, on home industries, and on women's work under state socialism have already laid some groundwork for such a broadened view of the history of labour. Much has been written about the Russian peasant-proletariat. The social reproduction of Russian factory workers, which remained connected to the village and agrarian labour, was in part ensured through their own and their families' subsistence labour.[61] Gijs Kessler has argued that from a long-term global and comparative perspective the complementarity of subsistence and wage labour, so visible as a defining feature of Russian labour history, no longer appears to be an Eastern European particularity. By contrast, the Soviet period stood out globally for a particularly pronounced decrease in the proportion of individuals and households who combined gainful employment and subsistence labour.[62] At least in its initial decades the enforced state-socialist industrialization project that formed the backdrop of that development resulted in a dramatic squeeze on labour for social reproduction. That was especially true because women were drawn into the labour force in unprecedented numbers and proportions. While men were unwilling to participate more equally in unpaid „women's work" for social reproduction, the state-socialist regimes did not invest sufficiently in the transformation of unpaid work for social reproduction into paid labour, for instance in social services, canteens, and the like.[63] The tense connection between the labours of social reproduction and the increasing involvement of the population in paid labour stood at the core of some of the hardship of early state socialism. This hardship was important in generating both anti-communist attitudes and action, and the policies of repression deployed so thoroughly in the period. From yet another perspective it can be argued that however much it suffered from the squeeze discussed above, unpaid domestic labour enabled „cheap" industrialization in the Soviet Union and other state-socialist

---

61 Victoria E. Bonnell (ed.), *The Russian Worker. Life and Labor under the Tsarist Regime* (Berkeley, 1983); Gijs Kessler, „The Rural–Urban Nexus in Russian Labour History, 1860s – 1930s: Suggestions for a Global, Comparative Perspective", in: Marcel van der Linden and Prabhu P. Mohapatra (eds), *Labour Matters: Towards Global Histories. Studies in Honour of Sabyasachi Bhattacharya* (New Delhi, 2009), pp. 207–225.
62 Gijs Kessler, „Wage Labour and the Household Economy: A Russian Perspective, 1600–2000", in: Marcel van der Linden and Leo Lucassen (eds), *Working on Labor. Essays in Honor of Jan Lucassen* (Leiden and Boston, 2012), pp. 353–369.
63 Zimmermann, „Gender Regime and Gender Struggle".

countries. In both urban and rural contexts work on quasi-private plots of land generated resources indispensable for survival, especially in very hard times. The reintroduction in the Soviet Union of such plots in the middle of the brutal drive to agrarian dispossession and collectivization of the 1930s has been described as an „extraordinary and rare concession from the Stalinist state" brought about by rural resistance that was led by women. As an ubiquitous feature of life under state socialism, the private plot helped to keep wages low so that more resources could be transferred to the accumulation fund used to finance catch-up industrialization.[64]

What were the repercussions of the connection between agrarian subsistence labour and industrial wage work embodied by the peasant-worker on both industrial development and subsistence labour in tsarist Russia? What was the overall role of the quasi-private agricultural plot in the state-socialist development project? My own admittedly limited review of the vast literature on the Russian peasant-worker and agrarian labour under state socialism was in part directed by those large questions. Beyond the work of Teodor Shanin on late imperial Russia and the very beginnings of the socialist period[65] and the debate around it – now long in abeyance – I have encountered no systematic interest in translating what is an enormous subject into manageable research projects.

At the same time, many of the studies I have reviewed for this essay on work in the industrialized and industrializing societies of Eastern Europe can be read in new ways if we place at centre stage the role played by the unpaid labours of social reproduction and subsistence in shaping the world of gainful labour. A few glimpses must suffice here. When women workers went on strike in St Petersburg before 1917 the few gender-specific demands they raised were to do with working hours and matters of maternity.[66] That points up the fact that the dissimilar involvement of women and men in social reproduction had discernible repercussions on how men and women related differently to the world of paid work. A study of early state socialism in Poland reveals that a number of woman-specific problems in the world of paid labour can be explained with reference to the association of women's paid labour with their unpaid work for the family.[67] In some parts of the Habsburg Monarchy cottage industries in combination with subsistence agriculture were important for survival, while under the impact of

---

64 Gijs Kessler, „A Population under Pressure: Household Responses to Demographic and Economic Shock in the Interwar Soviet Union", in: Filtzer *et al.*, *A Dream Deferred*, pp. 315–342, especially 342, and the other contributions in Section III of that volume'; Kingston-Mann, „Transforming Peasants in the Twentieth Century"; Ildikó Asztalos Morell, *Emancipations Dead-End Roads? Studies in the Formation and Development of the Hungarian Model for Agriculture and Gender, 1956–1989* (Uppsala, 1999); Susan Bridger, „Soviet Rural Women: Employment and Family Life", in: Farnsworth and Viola, *Russian Peasant Women*, pp. 271–293.
65 Teodor Shanin, *The Awkward Class. Political Sociology of Peasantry in a Developing Society, Russia 1910–1925* (Oxford, 1972).
66 Smith, „Class and Gender".
67 Natalia Jarska, „Gender and Labour in Post-War Communist Poland: Female Unemployment 1945–1970", *Acta Poloniae Historica*, 110 (2014), pp. 49–85.

economic liberalization and industrialization that type of work was extremely exploited and its vulnerability, especially when detached from agricultural production, became highly visible.[68]

The examples touched upon in this section suggest that the labour of social reproduction needs to be taken properly into consideration when we try to explain the agency of workers and their families on the one hand and the business and development strategies of employers and states on the other. In the later decades of state socialism governments and employers did more than was done in many other parts of the world to „socialize" social reproduction. We might well advance our conceptual understanding of patterns of modern economic development and potential alternatives to capitalism by advancing the comparative study of such policies, including their repercussions for the world of labour and society at large.

Concepts, connections, directions

Many of the phenomena and research examples reviewed in this essay could have been discussed in multiple sections, and the agricultural *summás* workers in Hungary under the Habsburg Monarchy epitomize them. Women formed part of the labour „gangs" in which the *summás* workers were organized but could never be leaders of them. Each individual *summás* worker was involved in different types of labour and labour relations, did wage work, and owned some of the means of production. These workers were bound to fulfil long-term labour contracts and migrated regularly, some of them to distant places to engage in gainful employment. Many *summás* workers were of ethnic backgrounds different from local workers, or spoke a different language. Every *summás* worker was integrated into overlapping cycles of social reproduction, namely at the faraway estate that, during the work season, fed him or her and the „gang" to which she or he belonged, and in the village back home. However, the explanation for the persistence and change over time of *summás* work is less obvious. It is difficult to see clearly whether and how pan-European and global connections were involved in and shaped the history of *summás* work. The place of that sort of work in global labour history deserves further research, and dominant concepts and debates in the new global history give barely any direct guidance. As Wave Two of Eastern European labour historiography gains momentum, questions such as these thus offer promising research avenues.

Among the things the new research can build upon is empirical knowledge produced during Wave One, the period between the 1960s and the demise of state socialism. Even in a less than generous reading, that was a time when a vast stock of more

---

68 Andrea Komlosy, „Austria and Czechoslovakia: The Habsburg Monarchy and its Successor States", in: Lex Heerma van Voss, Els Hiemstra-Kuperus, and Elise van Nederveen Meerkerk (eds), *The Ashgate Companion to the History of Textile Workers, 1650–2000* (Farnham, 2010), pp. 43–75; Lackó, *Ipari munkásságunk összetételének alakulása*.

complex historiographies of labour was built up in Eastern Europe. This insight is not meant to imply that today's researchers should be more excited or affirmative about the scholarship produced during Wave One. Rather, I see my approach as an invitation to all of us to interrogate some of the new global labour history more critically, especially, I would argue, for its scant interest in the role that both unequal global economic integration and social reproduction have played in the history of labour in all regions of the world.

From a historiographical point of view it would be worthwhile, then, to think comparatively about the histories of labour already written and still to be written in the West, the Global South, and Eastern Europe. Rather than aiming for comparative value judgement such an endeavour could contribute to our understanding of the impact of the global constellation at a given time in labour history writing. Undoubtedly some of the new transnational and global labour history has lacked critical reflection on its own relationship to the globalization we are seeing today. By contrast, such a layer of added reflection, whenever pursued, has certainly generated more insight and has served to caution us all against complacency. For example, in the new Eastern European historiography of labour, studies on workers' agency under state socialism have emerged in critical response to the totalitarian paradigm so prevalent in the post-1989 European historiography in both the East and West. These studies[69] have begun to generate important new insights and will potentially generate a rethink of workers' agency and labour movements in capitalist contexts too. Developing research on this great theme might therefore help give the global labour history of our own days a more critical edge.

---

69 Examples include Chris Ward, *Russia's Cotton Workers and the New Economic Policy. Shop-Floor Culture and State Policy 1921–1929* (Cambridge, 1990); Bartha, *Alienating Labour*; Pittaway, *From the Vanguard to the Margins*; Alena K. Alamgir, „'Inappropriate Behavior': Labor Control and the Polish, Cuban and Vietnamese Workers in Czechoslovakia", in: Marsha Siefert (ed.), *Labor in State Socialist Europe after 1945: Contributions to Global Labor History* (forthcoming); Peter Heumos, „Strikes in Czechoslovakia from 1945 to 1968: Cross-System Aspects and the Debate over the Causes of the Collapse of State Socialism", in: Siefert, *Labor in State Socialist Europe after 1945*.

Suggested reading

Bartha, Eszter. *Alienating Labour: Workers on the Road from Socialism to Capitalism in East Germany and Hungary* (New York and Oxford: Berghahn, 2013).
Bonnell, Victoria E. (ed.). *The Russian Worker. Life and Labor under the Tsarist Regime* (Berkeley, CA: University of California Press, 1983).
Buckley, Mary. *Mobilizing Soviet Peasants: Heroines and Heroes of Stalin's Fields* (Lanham, MD: Rowman & Littlefield, 2006).
Cerman, Markus. *Villagers and Lords in Eastern Europe, 1300–1800* (Basingstoke: Palgrave Macmillan, 2012).
Engel, Barbara Alpern. *Between the Fields and the City. Women, Work, and Family in Russia, 1861–1914* (Cambridge: Cambridge University Press, 1994).
Farnsworth, Beatrice and Lynne Viola (eds). *Russian Peasant Women* (New York and Oxford: Oxford University Press, 1992).
Fidelis, Malgorzata. *Women, Communism, and Industrialization in Postwar Poland* (Cambridge: Cambridge University Press, 2010).
Filtzer, Donald A. *Soviet Workers and Stalinist Industrialization. The Formation of Modern Soviet Production Relations, 1928–1941* (London: Pluto Press, 1986).
Filtzer, Donald A. *Soviet Workers and Late Stalinism. Labour and Restoration of the Stalinist System after World War II* (Cambridge: Cambridge University Press, 2002).
Filtzer, Donald A. *Soviet Workers and De-Stalinization, The Consolidation of the Modern System of Soviet Production Relations, 1953–1964* (Cambridge: Cambridge University Press, 1992).
Filtzer, Donald A. *Soviet Workers and the Collapse of Perestroika. The Soviet Labour Process and Gorbachev's Reform, 1985–1991* (Cambridge: Cambridge University Press, 1994).
Goodwin, Lawrence. *Breaking the Barrier. The Rise of Solidarity in Poland* (New York: Oxford University Press, 1991).
Haraszti, Miklós. *Worker in a Workers' State*. Trans. Michael Wright (New York: Universe Books, 1978).
Ilic, Melanie. *Women Workers in the Soviet Interwar Economy: From „Protection" to „Equality"* (New York: Palgrave, 1999).
Kolchin, Peter. *Unfree Labor. American Slavery and Russian Serfdom* (Cambridge, MA: Harvard University Press, 1987).
Lomax, Bill (ed.). *Hungarian Workers' Councils in 1956* (New York: Columbia University Press, 1990).
Murphy, Kevin. *Revolution and Counterrevolution. Class Struggle in a Moscow Metal Factory* (New York and Oxford: Berghahn, 2005).
Petrungaro, Stefano. „The Fluid Boundaries of 'Work'. Some Considerations Regarding Concepts, Approaches, and South-Eastern Europe", *Südost-Forschungen*, 72 (2013), pp. 271–286.
Pittaway, Mark. *From the Vanguard to the Margins. Workers in Hungary, 1939 to the Present* (Leiden and Boston: Brill, 2014).
Rabinovitch, Alexander. *The Bolsheviks Come to Power. The Revolution of 1917 in Petrograd* (Chicago: Haymarket Books, 2004).
Rutar, Sabine. „Towards a Southeast European History of Labour: Examples from Yugoslavia", in: idem (ed.), *Beyond the Balkans: Towards an Inclusive History of Southeastern Europe* (Münster: LIT, 2013), pp. 325–356.
Shanin, Teodor. *The Awkward Class. Political Sociology of Peasantry in a Developing Society, Russia 1910–1925* (Oxford: Clarendon Press, 1972).
Smith, S.A. *Revolution and the People in Russia and China: A Comparative History* (Cambridge: Cambridge University Press, 2008).

Stanziani, Alessandro (ed.). *Labour, Coercion, and Economic Growth in Eurasia, 17th-20th Centuries* (Leiden and Boston: Brill, 2013).

Ward, Chris. *Russia's Cotton Workers and the New Economic Policy. Shop-Floor Culture and State Policy 1921–1929* (Cambridge: Cambridge University Press, 1990).

Żarnowska, Anna. *Workers, Women, and Social Change in Poland, 1870–1939* (Aldershot: Ashgate, 2004).

Zelnik, Reginald E. *Labor and Society in Tsarist Russia. The Factory Workers of St. Petersburg 1855–1870* (Stanford, CA: Stanford University Press, 1971).

Zimmermann, Susan. *Divide, Provide and Rule: An Integrative History of Poverty Policy, Social Policy, and Social Reform in Hungary under the Habsburg Monarchy* (Budapest and New York: Central European University Press, 2011).

Andrea Komlosy
2.7. Western Europe

This contribution evaluates research on work and labour, looking at the period when concepts of a new global history began to emerge. Although counter-cyclical state policies tended to postpone that history's momentum, the paradigm dates from the 1970s in Europe and North America, in line with the transition from the post-World-War-II Fordist welfare state towards the end of industrial mass production that formed its foundation. We are dealing therefore with a rather longer period of twenty years, until the 1990s, when neo-liberal policies and the globalization of commodity chains became widespread. Both types of European welfare state were affected, although in different ways. In the capitalist West the decline of industry and the end of what was considered "standard" employment happened more gradually and went hand in hand with the decline of traditional labour history. Meanwhile, in the socialist COMECON states the collapse of the system in 1989–1991 marked a sudden rupture terminating a social model that had been defined by labour.[1] Traditional labour history, which had played a prominent role in state socialism, lost its institutions, funding, and legitimation. The two systems had already begun to interact in the 1970s, when Eastern European state enterprise served as extended workbenches for Western firms and joint ventures were set up in Poland, Hungary, and Romania. However, after 1989, Eastern Europe was transformed according to the interests of Western companies, and many East European firms were unable to compete and closed down. In other cases, privatization broke up integrated production lines and retained labour-intensive operations that supplied Western companies with cheap but still in many cases skilled labour. Moreover, acquisitions and greenfield investment increased the role of contract manufacture, which allowed Western companies to compete with Asian firms and maintain their control of global commodity chains. Car manufacturing is a good example of the shift from a low level of East European domestic-label production to just-in-time piece suppliers for West European, US, and Korean companies.[2]

From the 1990s onwards established industrial regions all over Europe faced strong competition from global peripheries where labour and production costs were lower. The Global South acquired a new role as industrial mass production

---

[1] GDR sociologists and historians proposed the term "workers' society" (*arbeiterliche Gesellschaft*): Helga Schultz, "Das sozialistische Projekt und die Arbeiter. Die DDR und die Volksrepublik Polen im Vergleich", in: *idem* and Hans-Jürgen Wagener (eds), *Die DDR im Rückblick. Politik, Wirtschaft, Gesellschaft, Kultur* (Berlin, 2007), pp. 224–243, at 227.

[2] Andrea Komlosy, "Systemtransformation als Krisenmanagement. Der RGW-Umbruch im globalen Kontext, 40 Jahre danach (1973–2013)", in: Dariusz Adamczyk and Stephan Lehnstaedt (eds), *Wirtschaftskrisen als Wendepunkte. Ursachen, Folgen und historische Einordnungen vom Mittelalter bis zur Gegenwart* (Osnabrück, 2015), pp. 337–376, at 365f.

was outsourced to free production zones in Central America, South-east Asia, Turkey, Maghreb, and later to China and Eastern Europe. Such regions offered not only cheap labour but also subsidies, tax exemptions, and the absence of labour protection and social legislation. In the West, the relocation of huge parts of mass production to the Global South led to a shift from manufacturing to the service sector. That allowed Western companies to overcome the profit squeeze of the 1970s and to upgrade and strengthen their research and value-adding operations. Innovation was linked to rationalization, but that contributed in turn to structural unemployment. Technological adjustment favoured regional polarization, delinking former industrial regions that were now being placed in great despair. Layoffs and closures led to a vicious circle of declining infrastructure and education, pushing the mobile workforce to migrate. Textile regions in Catalonia, Normandy, Lancashire, or Lower Austria were affected as much as mining and regions of heavy industry such as Wales, Yorkshire, the English Midlands, Wallonia, the Saar-Lorraine region, the Rhine-Ruhr, or Upper Styria. What in the West took several years and was eased, if not overcome, by regional and social programmes came suddenly to Eastern Europe when the socialist system was dissolved. Vast industrial regions suffered decline and many workers lost their jobs, whereupon considerable numbers of them turned to alcohol as employment became a makeshift thing and labour was forced to migrate. Relocations of Western multinationals into the privatized industrial landscape could not make up for the losses, and in the West and East alike informalization, precarity, and deregulation gained ground. For a growing number of workers a transformation had come to what had been regulated and socially secure workplaces, turning them into permanent battlefields for jobs, opportunities, or social transfers.

New challenges for historical research

The new landscape of global competition that was enabled by neoliberal deregulation at the national and international levels left its imprint on academia too. Neoliberal social science paved the way for the introduction of reforms, preparing public opinion and interpreting the changes. Other non-liberal social scientists pointed to social consequences, increasing gaps, impoverishment, and a loss of solidarity and cohesion that could be understood only in a global context. At first, historians were rarely involved in analysing transformation and globalization. It was a time when the "cultural turn" had shifted the focus of many historians from studying social structures and longitudinal perspectives to looking at single cases and discourse analysis. The French journal *Annales. Histoire, Sciences Sociales* will serve as an example. As a 1930s flagship of a new type of history that adopted methods of the social sciences, such as typology, global outreach, and *longue durée*, it changed direction in the early 1980s – "just at the moment when ... its results were taken as authoritative well beyond the boundaries of the profession and the 'territory of the historian' seemed capable of indefinite enlargement" – as Jacques Revel observed in his manifesto of micro-history.³ Micro-history, historical anthropology, and cultural studies flourished while social and economic history became less attractive.

Even historians who were still attached to social and economic structures and conflicting interests changed their methods and approaches because they realized that the changing global environment had affected how they should assess historical developments. This was the birth of global history, embedded in a "spatial turn". It might be built on older world history, but it was more aware of the former's inherently Eurocentric teleology. All world regions and world cultures ought to be studied on their own terms in their mutual entanglement and hierarchical relations – to sum up the programme that required the collaboration of various experts and disciplines from all over the world.⁴ Work and labour was just one of the fields that were changing in the light of new global approaches to history.

With regard to work and labour, global history opened a new research agenda that went beyond previous studies of labour relations and labour movements. Work and labour should not be reduced to commodified free labour. The global angle opened historians' eyes to non-paid labour (subsistence, homework), small-scale agriculture, craft, home and self-employed labour, forced labour (serfdom, slavery, indentured labour), and formal and informal labour. Those forms of labour and their representatives – peasants, serfs, servants, slaves, homeworkers, craftsmen/women, housewives, industrial workers, clerks, and so on – were considered working characters who deserved equal analysis in their own specific contexts. Moreover, the global perspective helped historians to realize that all those labour relations coexisted within individual people according to age and status, within households, within regions, and on a global scale.

Since the 1970s world-system analysis had emphasized the synchronicity of different labour relations as a principal feature of capitalism. It could be understood only in its global, unequal composition and resulted from the functional division of labour in different zones of the global economy.⁵ Global labour history pleaded for a

---

3 "… au moment où … ses résultats s'imposaient bien au-delà des frontières de la profession et où le 'territoire de l'historien' paraissait pouvoir s'élargir indéfinitivement". Jacques Revel (ed.), *Jeux d'échelles. La micro-analyse à l'expérience* (Paris, 1996), p. 18. See *Annales. Histoire, Sciences Sociales* or *Quaderni storici* since the 1980s.
4 *Annales. Histoire, Sciences Sociales* devoted a special issue to the global turn. See issue 56, 1 (2001), "Une histoire à l'échelle globale", edited by Serge Gruzinski and Sanjay Subrahmanyam, where an attempt is made to reconcile micro and global history. See also Matthias Middell and Katja Naumann, "Global History and the Spatial Turn: From the Impact of Area Studies to the Study of Critical Junctures of Globalization", *Journal of Global History*, 5, 1 (2010), pp. 149–170.
5 Immanuel Wallerstein has become the most prominent social scientist identified with "world-systems analysis". The approach was developed in a collective endeavour, inspired by the cross-cutting institutionalization of social sciences and area studies at the École des Hautes Etudes en Sciences Sociales (EHESS) in Paris, with which Wallerstein has been associated since the 1970s. World-systems analysis grew from his collaboration with Fernand Braudel, who became the moving spirit of Waller-

deep analysis of each type of labour and of labour relations to see how they were interrelated and how they affected social relations.⁶ It was evident that types of labour and labour relations varied according to age, gender, ethnicity (or race), and location in the international division of labour. Specialists in those fields were therefore invited to contribute to a cooperative agenda.⁷

In spite of its cooperative and global claims, world systems and global labour history was a Western project primarily based in Great Britain, the Netherlands, and the United States.⁸ It could therefore be seen as a transatlantic or perhaps more precisely a North Atlantic project. The main institutional pillars were at State University of New York at Binghamton,⁹ at the École des Hautes Etudes (EHESS) Paris, at the London School of Economics (LSE),¹⁰ and above all at the International Institute of Social History (IISG) in Amsterdam. The IISG played a leading role in developing a research agenda, establishing international research projects and networks, and encouraging global labour research in various world regions.¹¹ It was

---

stein's Fernand Braudel Center for the Study of Economies, Historical Systems, and Civilizations at SUNY Binghamton.

6 Marcel van der Linden, *Workers of the World. Essays Toward a Global Labor History* (Leiden and Boston, 2008); Marcel van der Linden and Leo Lucassen (eds), *Working on Labor. Essays in Honor of Jan Lucassen* (Leiden and Boston, 2012).

7 Barbara Duden and Karin Hausen, "Gesellschaftliche Arbeit, geschlechtsspezifische Arbeitsteilung", in: Annette Kuhn and Gerhard Schneider (eds), *Frauen in der Geschichte* (Düsseldorf, 1979), pp. 11–33; Maria Mies and Veronika Bennholdt-Thomsen, *The Subsistence Perspective. Beyond the Globalised Economy* (London, 1989); Wilma A. Dunaway, "The Semiproletarian Household over the Longue Durée of the Modern World-System", in: Richard E. Lee (ed.), *The* Longue Durée *and World-System Analysis* (Albany, NY, 2012), pp. 97–136.

8 In Jan Lucassen (ed.), *Global Labour History. A State of the Art* (Berne, 2006), presenting the state of the art of global labour history, Dick Geary's contribution on "Labour History in Western Europe from c. 1800" was confined to Britain, France, and Germany.

9 The Fernand Braudel Center at SUNY Binghamton, founded by Terence Hopkins and Immanuel Wallerstein in 1976, initiated a number of working groups that laid the foundation for systematic explorations of global relations. See the programmatic article by Terence K. Hopkins and Immanuel Wallerstein, "Patterns of Development of the Modern World-System", *Review*, 1, 2 (1977), pp. 111–145. Since the 1990s, world-systems analysis has embarked on different conceptual paths, leading to a multiplication of places, journals, and institutions of research. Meanwhile, adaptations, revisions, and new departures took place, taking into account the view of critics and recent developments in global studies.

10 The Global Economic History Network (GEHN) is based at the London School of Economics and was coordinated by Patrick O'Brien from 2003 to 2007. Like EHESS it can build on an institutionalized network of social scientists and area studies. Its work is published by Cambridge University Press and other major publishing houses. *The Journal of Global History* (Cambridge University Press) is a product of this network.

11 Compare the founding document by research directors Marcel van der Linden and Jan Lucassen, *Prolegomena for a Global Labour History* (1999), and the annual reports documenting ongoing research activities and publications ever since: www.socialhistory.org, last accessed 13 February 2017. The IISG set up affiliates responsible for document collection all over the Global South and in Russia, initiating local and cooperative research projects. Moreover, it supported the development of regional

able to build on the IISG's vast collections on the history of labour and other social movements. When global labour history was implemented as a key research agenda, the institute developed active strategies to bring documents from non-European regions into the collections and to employ non-European scholars to rectify its lack of knowledge of the Global South. IISG scholars contributed to the formation of an international community of labour historians from all over the world who rely on multiple language skills but communicate in English to exchange and accumulate regional expertise. The IISG, its staff, and scholars were important agents in promoting a global shift in labour research worldwide.[12]

Looking back at the regional focus of global labour research reveals various waves. In a first wave of exploration of the Global South, Latin America was at the foreground. Latin America offered a vast amount of evidence of how indigenous people, slaves, and colonial settlers interacted to extract resources to be used for European manufacture. The transatlantic trade triangle, consisting of African slaves working on American plantations and fed by indigenous forced labour and the rise of industrial capitalism in Western Europe, was one of the main features of global studies.[13] With the exception of the slave trade, African studies was a rather marginal subject while European activities in Asia were often included in the colonial paradigm of colonial extractivism encountered in the Americas.

In the late 1990s a second wave of historical research emphasized the independent development of trades and manufacture in various Asian regions instead of attributing leadership to European companies and skills. Asian regions were "discovered" for their competitive advances in technology and the quality of their manufacture. The specific combination of export textile trades and local agrarian production in rural households from West to East Asia fed the paradigm of a "labour

---

networks of global labour history, coordinated by the IISG and its partners. Major projects involving international participation dealt with specific groups of workers (at the docks, or in textiles, sugar cane, oil, for example) or work conditions (of children, soldiers, migrants), or aimed at the collection of data (on wages, prices, the typology of labour relations) for long-term comparative analyses. In 2007 a Global Collaboratory on the History of Labour Relations was initiated. Its first main goal is to provide statistical insights into the global distribution of all types of labour relations (systematically including women and child labour) in five historical cross-sections: 1500, 1650, 1800, 1900, [Africa: 1950], and 2000. The second main goal will be the explanation of shifts signalled in labour relations worldwide. See https://collab.iisg.nl/web/LabourRelations. The findings of the various projects are published by major publishing houses. See, for example, the *Studies in Global Social History* edited by Marcel van der Linden, and the *Studies in Global Migration History* edited by Dirk Hoerder (published by Brill, Leiden/Boston). See also the *International Review of Social History* (Cambridge University Press).

12 The output of global labour history is huge. A good way to keep up to date are the calls, reports, and reviews on the web forum history.transtransnational within the framework of H-Soz-u-Kult and Clio-online: http://geschichte-transnational.clio-online.net/transnat.asp?lang=en.

13 See the survey of the literature on Atlantic history by Ulrike Schmieder, "Aspekte der Forschungsgeschichte zum Atlantischen Raum", in: *idem* and Hans-Heinrich Nolte (eds), *Atlantik. Sozial- und Kulturgeschichte in der Neuzeit* (Vienna, 2010), pp. 226–254.

intensive" and industrious mode of production.[14] Andre Gunder Frank rejected the narrative of the "European World System", to which he had contributed in earlier days. Frank had realized it was Eurocentric, and urged "reorientation". He now acknowledged Asia's leading role in a multi-centric world system until the eighteenth century (India, the Ottoman Empire) or the nineteenth century (China).[15]

For both narratives Latin America was a source for extraction with the help of slaves and indentured servants. The indigenous population were also exterminated, assimilated, displaced, and marginalized. According to the new interpretation the transatlantic triangle was linked to Asian trade and American silver and gold, allowing European merchant companies to import and re-export Asian-manufactured goods globally. The "European miracle", a supposed exceptionalism based on the continuity of European civilization leading from Greek Antiquity to the Renaissance and Enlightenment, was called into question and then replaced by the paradigm of the "Great Divergence"[16] signalled by the rise of Western European hegemony at the expense of Asia at the beginning of the nineteenth century. Situating Asia at the core of "industrious" manufacture had repercussions on the conventional way of assessing the "industrial" revolution. Only recently have studies of African labour transcended the boundaries of area studies and entered the realm of global labour history.[17]

Assessing Europe in the global history of work

Notwithstanding a vivid debate that questioned conventional knowledge, terms, and concepts of industry and labour in the emerging global history networks, "Europe" was usually considered synonymous with "Western Europe". It was symbolized by the "European banana", stretching from the northern parts of France and Italy to

---

[14] The "industrious" mode of production is seen as a way of raising productivity in crafts and putting-out industries. It was common in many export trades all over the world, before the factory-based "industrial" mode became dominant in the nineteenth century. In many Asian regions, mainly in East Asia, industrious production survived, representing an autonomous path towards modern industry, finally merging with the industrial system. Compare Jan de Vries, *The Industrious Revolution. Consumer Behaviour and the Household Economy, 1650 to the Present* (Cambridge, MA, 2008), and Gareth Austin and Kaoru Sugihara (eds), *Labour-Intensive Industrialization in Global History* (London, 2013).
[15] Andre Gunder Frank, *ReORIENT. Global Economy in the Asian Age* (Berkeley, CA, 1998). Frank's revisions of the European origins of the capitalist world system gave way to controversial discussions, reflected in reviews, books, and journal articles. He proposed to replace the intrinsically Eurocentric notion of capitalism with capital accumulation, realized by competitive advantages in exchange processes.
[16] The term was coined by Kenneth Pomeranz, *The Great Divergence. China, Europe, and the Making of the Modern World Economy* (Princeton and Oxford, 2000).
[17] Andreas Eckert, "Capitalism and Labor in Sub-Saharan Africa", in: Jürgen Kocka and Marcel van der Linden (eds), *Capitalism: The Reemergence of a Historical Concept* (London, 2016), pp. 165–186.

Germany, the Netherlands, and England. Taking the Genovese, Dutch, French, and English trajectories as models for types of development, it was almost impossible to assess composite monarchies such as the Holy Roman Empire, the Habsburg Empire in Central, Eastern, and South-eastern Europe, the Russian Empire in Eastern Europe, or the Ottoman Empire in South-eastern Europe. It was equally difficult to address their imperial legacies in their smaller national successor states.[18]

Those parts of Europe certainly represented different political and economic systems that were interrelated with Western Europe by unequal divisions of labour similar to the intercontinental ones. But they showed, too, different patterns of integration at the global level. The Hanse established a medieval system of unequal exchange with north-eastern Europe. The Italian state republics and France were the first to set up colonial networks in the Mediterranean and the Black Sea, and they served as models for the Spanish and Portuguese transatlantic plantation systems after the eastern Mediterranean came under Ottoman rule. From 1600 onwards Dutch and English trading companies carried out commercial activities, interlinking Atlantic, Asian, Mediterranean, North Sea, and Baltic trade by their respective maritime and communication capacities. They set up a system of commodity chains that relied on and profited from the combination of different labour regimes in the various regions. When merchant capital was replaced by domestic industrial interests connected to the political economy of the state, the equilibrium between Asia and Europe gradually gave way to European dominance.

Indeed, the hierarchical interactions set up by colonialism and imperialism are mirrored in colonial history. The academic communities tread paths paved by trade or conquest and previously used for investment, exchange, migration, and all sorts of transfers. Global history follows the tracks beaten by colonialism, area studies often concentrating on the "golden eras" of the respective states and empires. That is why research in Spain and Portugal concentrates on Latin America and the slave trade; in France on Caribbean and African history; in the Netherlands on Caribbean, South African, and Indonesian history; and in Great Britain on North America, the Caribbean, India, Africa, and the Commonwealth. Each area and each period is linked with specific labour regimes, including chattel slavery, indentured labour, sharecropping, and free farming. After decolonization the new states developed anti-colonial counter-narratives. It is no surprise that the impetus to place colonial and anti-colonial area studies under the common heading of global interconnections began in the United States, for after it had succeeded Great Britain as global leader during World War II the US relied not on territorial domination of colonies but on control of global flows.

Concentration on specific regions was the result of cultural and language competence too. Empirical research requires language skills, and among other legacies of

---

[18] Competing concepts and subdivisions of Europe are discussed in Thomas Ertl, Andrea Komlosy, and Hans-Jürgen Puhle (eds), *Europa als Weltregion. Zentrum, Modell oder Provinz?* (Vienna, 2014).

colonialism[19] colonial borders survive in the linguistic reach of English, French, Spanish, Portuguese, or Dutch. With the hegemonic rise of the United States, English has acquired global dominance in the Western world of science, and other Western languages have been marginalized. Since 1990 English has even replaced Russian as the lingua franca in the former European COMECON states. While for a long time French, Spanish, and Portuguese scholars found it difficult to accept linguistic Anglicization and wished to continue to emphasize their own national languages, Dutch and to a lesser extent Scandinavian scholars easily adopted English as their academic working language, thereby improving their international visibility.

Central European regions do not fit into the pattern of imperialism with overseas colonies – or did so only for short periods.[20] Compared with the Western states and empires bordering the Atlantic, they did not acquire colonies and accounted for relatively small shares of intercontinental trade. As long as labour history dealt with domestic work and labour relations in agriculture, crafts and industry, trade unions, and labour movements, Central European narratives were comparable with similar projects in Western Europe. But when the domestic framework was challenged by global history, Central European scholars took up the agenda that had been set in Western Europe and the United States. German, Austrian, and Scandinavian schools and universities very soon included in their curricula the history of European colonialism and its impact on non-European regions. Those schools profited from their supposedly neutral position to learn about and investigate all kinds of colonial activities. They did not deny that their own regions had profited from colonial extraction and unequal exchange through trade, but concentrated on those aspects of North-South relations where being part of the Global North did not require direct colonial conquest, or interference.

When, in the course of doing global history, basic terms and concepts were re-evaluated, it ceased to be possible to assume a position of colonial non-involvement.[21] Instead of acquiring overseas colonies and participating in the slave trade,

---

19 "Coloniality" refers to racial and epistemological hierarchies shaped by colonial domination which remain effective after decolonization. See, for example, Walter D. Mignolo, *Local Histories/Global Designs. Coloniality, Subaltern Knowledges, and Border Thinking* (Princeton, NJ, 2000). Equally, coloniality has been placed in a position of power by the hierarchical structures and inequalities of global capitalism.

20 Successor states, too, of former colonial sea powers such as Portugal and Spain that later underwent decline and peripheralization have difficulty defining their role in history. It is beyond the scope of this article to address them however.

21 According to Jürgen Osterhammel's definition of colonialism (*Colonialism: A Theoretical Overview* (Princeton, NJ, 2010)), the concept can easily be applied to the domination of internal peripheries by an imperial core, as well as to the attitudes of cultural superiority that legitimate dominance. Following the European perception of West and East Asian cultures as backward or primitive, Edward Said coined the term "orientalism", which had transcended its regional meaning and become a general term for legitimizing "civilizing" missions by reference to cultural or economic deficiencies. See Edward W. Said, *Orientalism. Western Concepts of the Orient* (New York, 1978).

the Habsburg Monarchy and Prussia, and later the German Reich, pursued a policy of conquest and quasi-colonial dominance in competition with the Russian and Ottoman empires when they expanded into Eastern and South-eastern Europe in the eighteenth century. They transformed their new territorial acquisitions into internal colonies, or peripheries. The Habsburgs conquered provinces of the Ottoman Empire and acquired former Venetian provinces, and the Habsburgs and Prussians conquered the Kingdom of Poland-Lithuania.[22] During World War I the territorial conquest of lands, crops, and labour power, from the Baltic regions to Belarus, Russian Poland, Ukraine, and Serbia, was again a principal military objective of imperial Germany and Austria. Occupations followed economic aims, which required the mobilization of the local population to work on large agricultural estates and in forestry and mining. In times of war, labour mobilization in frontier zones meant coercion under military law. While Habsburg Austria-Hungary had no overseas colonies, Germany had taken part in the "Scramble for Africa", acquiring German East Africa and German South-West Africa at the Berlin Africa Conference of the Great Powers in 1884. In 1878 the Berlin Balkan Conference had already agreed zones of Great Power influence in the Balkans, attributing to Austria-Hungary the right to occupy the Ottoman province of Bosnia-Herzegovina, which was then transformed into a military and economic frontier zone serving Austro-Hungarian interests.

Under the rubric of global history, National Socialist expansion is also discussed within the framework of the colonial competition that encouraged the Nazi leadership to catch up in the race for colonies in Eastern and South-eastern Europe, Africa, and the Near East. From a global perspective the Holocaust, property confiscation, labour coercion, and compensation for victims can no longer be discussed in isolation as a matter for the Germans; instead it has to be seen as a phenomenon that requires the acknowledgement of comparison and interaction with other cases of genocide, labour enforcement, and expulsion.[23]

Finally, Germany and Austria, which now belonged to the European core, together became the driving forces of EU enlargement in the 1990s, insisting to East European candidates for accession to the EU that they must dismantle the labour regulations and social protection that had been established under communism.

It was even more difficult to match Eastern Europe to the Western stereotype of global history. East Central Europe is a region that has always shifted between West-Central European and Russian interests.[24] Joining, or hoping to join, the Euro-

---

[22] Nolte organized several conferences on internal peripheries. See Hans-Heinrich Nolte (ed.), *Internal Peripheries in European History* (Göttingen, 1991); idem (ed.), *Europäische innere Peripherien im 20. Jahrhundert* (Stuttgart, 1997); and idem (ed.), *Innere Peripherien in Ost und West* (Stuttgart, 2002).
[23] Aleida Assmann and Sebastian Conrad (eds), *Memory in a Global Age: Discourses, Practices and Trajectories* (Basingstoke, 2010); Berthold Unfried, *Vergangenes Unrecht. Entschädigung und Restitution in einer globalen Perspektive* (Göttingen, 2014).
[24] South-eastern Europe is facing similar problems with regard to competing and overlapping legacies of Ottoman, Habsburg, and Russian influence and domination.

pean Union highlighted its identification with the West and entrenched its borders with Russia and the post-Soviet world. The new member states did indeed become part of the West, although in a dependent status that was often contested by their older, more socialist- or nationalist-inclined populations – especially in rural areas. By contrast, in young academia, becoming part of the West was a thing to be welcomed most warmly. As social matters in general and labour history in particular were topics related to the old regime, they were no longer considered attractive. Based on the official rejection of communist ideas, which in some countries were forbidden under new constitutions, labour research institutions faced political pressure, loss of funding, or even dissolution.[25] The situation was therefore favourable neither to labour history nor to critical assessments of the capitalist transformation. Colonization and external domination were attributed to the Soviet Union, and after its dissolution to Russia alone. The peripheralizing effects of West-Central European occupation and exploitation of the region before and after the Soviet period did not fit into the new self-images of countries that now saw themselves as members of the European core. They wished to distance themselves from the post-Soviet world and from old orientalizing stereotypes. In the case of Western Ukraine, conquered by Habsburg Austria in 1772 to become the province of Galicia, the striving for Westernization had consequences for the historical perception of the Habsburg period. In order to mark the distance from the Soviet influence that was attributed entirely to Russia and the Russians, the Habsburg past came to be applauded as a civilizing mission, used for nostalgic propaganda and tourism as well as being reassessed in academia.[26]

Eastern Europe entering global labour history

From the 2000s onwards social issues in the new EU member states could no longer be neglected in the social sciences. A new generation of scholars began to raise critical questions about transformation, including contemporary and historical aspects of work and labour. In the globalized framework of academic mobility, individual careers can no longer be associated with Western or Eastern Europe. However, because of the socioeconomic gap between West and East we face a semipermeable situation. Young scholars from Eastern Europe strive to work with Western institutions and

---

25 See Susan Zimmermann (Ch. 2.7) in the present volume. A dramatic way of excluding scholars from academic life was devised in the German Democratic Republic. West German scholars took the opportunity to escape the precariousness of academic life and voluntarily took over the jobs of the scholars who had been sacked. See Stefan Bollinger, Ulrich van der Heyden, and Mario Keßler, *Ausgrenzung oder Integration? Ostdeutsche Sozialwissenschaftler zwischen Isolierung und Selbstbehauptung* (Berlin, 2004).
26 Exhibition and catalogue "Mythos Galizien" (Wien Museum and International Cultural Center Cracow, 2015) represent both the production of nostalgia and its critical assessment.

projects. Apart from Eastern Germany, where, after the change of system, academic posts in the humanities were taken over by West Germans, there has been no comparable eastward movement and East European scholars and institutions take part in international research projects funded by Western institutions. The matters raised by Western and Eastern academia include the following labour-related topics.[27]

Historical transformation research

If we include the 1970s, when trade and industrial cooperation between Eastern and Western Europe began to gather momentum, the transformation spans more than forty years. The dismantling of labour protection and social security, the commodification of labour for Western investment in the form of outsourcing, and the mobilization and control of migrant labour were crucial things to be investigated in regional, local, and branch studies with regard to cycles, ruptures, particularities, and shared features.[28] Roughly put, there were three attitudes that reflected the fragmentation of societies. First there was an approving approach that blamed governments and population for deficiencies and lack of cooperation with EU programmes and institutions. Second was a reformist approach intended to improve implementation, then a critical approach in which the structural inequalities of the world system were assessed. As well as all that, consideration was given to the conditions of accession as the main factor in the ongoing economic peripheralization and social disparity within the East European states that accompanied – and by some indicators exceeded – the gaps in international development.[29]

---

[27] The publications selected mirror the author's personal choice and limited language skills.
[28] For example, Regina Barendt and Bettina Musiolek, *Workers' Voices. The Situation of Women in the Eastern European and Turkish Garment Industries* (Meißen, 2005); Eszter Bartha, *Alienating Labour. Workers on the Road from Socialism to Capitalism in East Germany and Hungary* (Oxford and New York, 2013); Dorothee Bohle and Béla Greskovits, "Capitalism without Compromise: Strong Business and Weak Labor in Eastern Europe's New Transnational Industries", *Studies in Comparative International Development*, 41, 1 (2006), pp. 3–25; Jan Drahokoupil, "The Politics of the Competition State: The Agents and Mechanisms of State Transnationalization in Central and Eastern Europe", in: László Bruszt and Ronald Holzhacker (eds), *The Transnationalization of Economies, States, and Civil Societies: New Challenges for Governance in Europe* (New York, 2009), pp. 135–155; Hannes Hofbauer, *EU-Osterweiterung. Historische Basis – ökonomische Triebkräfte – soziale Folgen* (Vienna, 2007); Philipp Ther, *Die neue Ordnung auf dem alten Kontinent. Eine Geschichte des neoliberalen Europa* (Frankfurt am Main, 2014), to list just a few.
[29] Hofbauer, *EU-Osterweiterung*; Dariusz Adamczyk, "Vom Kommunismus zur EU-Integration. Polens Entwicklung nach dem Kollaps des Monopolsozialismus", in: Hans-Heinrich Nolte (ed.), *Transformationen in Osteuropa und Zentralasien: Polen, die Ukraine, Russland und Kirgisien* (Schwalbach am Taunus, 2007). See also the Hofbauer-Adamczyk debates on the prospects of Poland's catching up in the *Zeitschrift für Weltgeschichte*, 6, 2 (2005), pp. 115–125, and 13, 2 (2012), pp. 75–94.

State socialism – rise and decline

There arose among historians a new interest in the transition to state socialism. Unlike research into the Cold War, the focus was on the everyday aspects of social life and work in a planned economy rather than on the takeover of political power and ideological confrontation. The question was, "How did the priority given to work and the worker affect labour relations, social status, cohesion, and social advancement?"[30] In spite of the official rhetoric that defined work as gainful employment, subsistence gardening, households, and the informal economy played an important role compensating for problems of short supply and difficulties with the distribution of consumer goods.[31] Labour migration under socialism followed different rules than in the West. East German factories along the river Oder used to employ Polish workers;[32] Czechoslovakia and East Germany, the technologically most advanced COMECON states, exchanged machinery for workers from Vietnam, Algeria, Mozambique, Cuba, and China, who were engaged to work for a certain period in Czech and German companies, in turn serving as suppliers of consumer goods for their families and as agents of knowledge transfer back home. How did those guest workers integrate on the shop floor and in community life?[33]

Within the international economic history network established by Alice Teichova at the universities of Bratislava, Cracow, Prague, and Vienna, one of the things economic historians and institutions all over the region were studying was how East-West cooperation took place across the Iron Curtain in different periods.[34] In recent years there has been increasing interest among East European scholars in exploring labour relations in state-socialist enterprises.[35]

---

[30] Peter Hübner and Klaus Tenfelde (eds), *Arbeiter in der SBZ-DDR* (Essen, 1999); Peter Hübner, Christoph Klessmann, and Klaus Tenfelde (eds), *Arbeiter im Staatssozialismus: Ideologischer Anspruch und soziale Wirklichkeit* (Cologne, 2005); Schultz, "Das sozialistische Projekt und die Arbeiter".

[31] Ute Gerhard, "Die staatlich institutionalisierte 'Lösung' der Frauenfrage: Zur Geschichte der Geschlechterverhältnisse in der DDR", in: Hartmut Kaelble, Jürgen Kocka, and Hartmut Zwahr (eds), *Sozialgeschichte der DDR* (Stuttgart, 1994), pp. 383–403.

[32] Polish contract work in Eastern Germany has frequently been addressed in projects at the Viadrina European University in Frankfurt (Oder), and documented in a book series (*Frankfurter Studien zur Grenzregion*), edited by Helga Schultz et al. Volumes include Helga Schultz and Alan Nothnagle (eds), *Grenze der Hoffnung. Geschichte und Perspektiven der Grenzregion an der Oder* (Berlin, 1996), and Katarzyna Stokłosa, *Grenzstädte in Ostmitteleuropa. Guben und Gubin 1945 bis 1995* (Berlin, 2003).

[33] For an overview, see Jörg Roesler, "Auf dem Weg zum Einwanderungsland. Zur Situation der Vertragsarbeiter in der DDR während der 1970er und 1980er Jahre", *Standpunkte*, 16 (Berlin, 2012).

[34] Gertrude Enderle-Burcel et al., *Gaps in the Iron Curtain. Economic Relations between Neutral and Socialist Countries in Cold War Europe* (Cracow, 2009) gives country-based evidence on economic relations between neutral and socialist countries in Cold War Europe. The work's main concern is with trade and investment, while labour relations are widely neglected.

[35] See, for instance, Goran Musić, *Yugoslavia: Workers' Self-Management as State Paradigm* (Chicago, 2011); Sabine Rutar, "Towards a Southeast European History of Labour: Examples from Yugoslavia",

Eastern Europe in the international division of labour

After the end of socialism, the widespread ideological satisfaction that Eastern Europe had joined the West did not prevent the region from new peripheralization. Regional and social polarization, unemployment, poverty, precarious labour conditions, brain drain and care drain, lack of skilled labour in education and health care – from that perspective older debates on social and economic deficiencies and the structural dependency on West Central Europe reappeared on the agenda, oscillating among "backwardness", "peripheralization", and "orientalization" while looking for moments of agency from both local governments and ordinary citizens.

The role of "second serfdom", which, according to Marxist historiography, followed the peripheral integration of East Central Europe into the early modern world economy and that had inspired world-system analysis,[36] was revised and replaced by more regional differentiation and a gradual approach to the borders between different agrarian systems. Certain scholars rejected a world-economic impact on regional developments,[37] while empirical case studies by others brought new evidence of peripheralization.[38]

A similar controversy came up with regard to industrial catching up in the second half of the nineteenth century. Could backwardness be overcome by the joint efforts of private investment and state support, as modernization theory claims,[39] or did the structural dependency laid out by early modern functional integration into

---

in: Sabine Rutar (ed.), *Beyond the Balkans. Towards an Inclusive History of Southeastern Europe* (Münster, 2015), pp. 323–356, for former Yugoslavia.

36 Marian Małowist, "The Economic and Social Development of the Baltic Countries from the 15th to the 17th Centuries", *Economic History Review*, Second Series, 12, 2 (1959), pp. 177–189, for Poland; Zsigmond Pál Pach, *Die ungarische Agrarentwicklung im 16–17. Jahrhundert. Abbiegung vom westeuropäischen Entwicklungsgang* (Budapest, 1964), for Hungary; Christoph Schmidt, *Leibeigenschaft im Ostseeraum* (Cologne, 1997), in a comparative approach to the Baltic Sea region.

37 Markus Cerman, *Villagers and Lords in Eastern Europe, 1300–1800* (Basingstoke, 2012), on Eastern Europe and Russia; idem and Hermann Zeitlhofer, *Soziale Strukturen in Böhmen. Ein regionaler Vergleich von Wirtschaft und Gesellschaft in Gutsherrschaften, 16.–19. Jahrhundert* (Vienna and Munich, 2002), in the framework of a collaborative research project on "Social structures in Bohemia"; Alessandro Stanziani, *Bondage. Labor and Rights in Eurasia from the Sixteenth to the Early Twentieth Centuries* (New York and Oxford, 2014), on Russia. The results confirm those of Larry Wolff's provocative book *Inventing Eastern Europe. The Map of Civilization on the Mind of the Enlightenment* (Stanford, 1995), which includes the concept of peripheralization in the process of "invention".

38 Dariusz Adamczyk, *Silber und Macht. Fernhandel, Tribute und die piastische Herrschaftsbildung in nordosteuropäischer Perspektive (800–1100)* (Wiesbaden, 2016) on Poland; Klemens Kaps, *Ungleiche Entwicklung in Zentraleuropa. Galizien zwischen überregionaler Verflechtung und imperialer Politik (1772–1914)* (Vienna, 2015), on Habsburg Galicia.

39 See, for example, David F. Good, "The Economic Lag of Central and Eastern Europe: Income Estimates for the Habsburg Successor States, 1870–1910", *Journal of Economic History*, 54, 4 (1994), pp. 869–891.

Western structures produce only a second wave of dependent accumulation, as is supposed in world-system approaches?[40]

Studies on Eastern Europe, in comparison or in entanglement with Western regions, had become a prominent topic, and students and scholars all over Europe produced a large amount of new evidence. International research projects were initiated by universities in, for example, Leipzig,[41] Frankfurt an der Oder,[42] and Vienna,[43] all of which have long traditions of Eastern European studies. Conferences were organized, study programmes set up, and material published in cooperation with East European partners. But work and labour, although often addressed, were rarely the topics of investigation, so that in fact much research is still overshadowed by the neglect of social questions that has been a result of the cultural turn in the humanities and social sciences and the collapse of state socialism.

In the course of growing international interest, Eastern Europe overcame its role as the other, backward, belated half of Europe, which has raised questions of connections with the rest of the world. A few examples will illustrate a trend of including Eastern Europe in global history projects and debates.[44] There are a growing number of studies exploring the composition of exports, imports, and trade partners, allowing assessment of labour relations that reflect equality and inequality of trade.[45]

---

40 For example, Andrea Komlosy, "Regionale Ungleichheiten in der Habsburgermonarchie: Kohäsionskraft oder Explosionsgefahr für die staatliche Einheit?", in: Nolte, *Innere Peripherien in Ost und West*, pp. 95–109, on internal peripheries in the Habsburg Monarchy; Kaps, *Ungleiche Entwicklung*, on Habsburg Galicia; Susan Zimmermann, *Divide, Provide and Rule. An Integrative History of Poverty Policy, Social Policy, and Social Reform in Hungary under the Habsburg Monarchy* (Budapest and New York, 2011), on Hungary, approaching work and labour through the history of poverty and policy.
41 Gesellschaft für Kultursoziologie (journal: *Kultursoziologie*, Welttrends Verlag; *Leipziger Jahrbücher Osteuropa in Tradition und Wandel*); Geisteswissenschaftliches Zentrum Geschichte und Kultur Ostmitteleuropa (GWZO).
42 Viadrina European University, Frankfurt (Oder), Department of Social and Economic History. See the book series *Frankfurter Studien zur Wirtschafts- und Sozialgeschichte Osteuropas*, Berlin Verlag.
43 Various projects at the Departments for Eastern European and Economic and Social History, Slavic Studies, Anthropology and Social Sciences, including the doctoral programme "Austrian Galicia and its Multicultural Heritage", https://dk-galizien.univie.ac.at/english/, last accessed 10 October 2016; Forschungsplattform Osteuropaforum https://sowi.univie.ac.at/forschung/forschungsplattformen/wiener-osteuropaforum/, last accessed 10 October 2016.
44 For example, the Global and European Studies Institute (GESI, University of Leipzig) programme on "East Central Europe in transnational perspective"; joint European Master's in "Global History from a European Perspective", including universities in Leipzig, London, Roskilde, Vienna, and Wrocław; Masters' programmes in Global Studies at the Freie University Berlin and Humboldt University Berlin. By making GESI Leipzig the organizing body of the European Network in Universal and Global History (ENIUGH), Eastern European colleagues became part of the network building from the beginning. In global history journals, such as *Comparativ* (Leipzig) and *Zeitschrift für Weltgeschichte* (Hanover), articles on Eastern Europe in global and comparative perspectives are frequent.
45 Trade analyses cover the period from early medieval trade between the Baltic regions and the Arab world, when Baghdad was at the core of the global economy, showing that the orientation to-

Moreover, Eastern Europe has become a major region for global migration studies.[46] Last but not least, the concept of "second serfdom" was liberated from an academic cul-de-sac by comparison with the concept of "second slavery", which had been developed to distinguish between an early period of chattel slavery that gave way to more intensive exploitation of slave labour with the rise of the factory system and the demand for cotton, sugar, and other raw materials.[47] Although there is no consensus about what different types of forced labour might have in common, the isolated way of studying serfdom, slavery, or forced labour in labour camps and prisons has given way to comparative approaches.[48] Until recently, slavery along the frontiers between the Christian and Muslim worlds had received little attention, but now new studies dealing with stabilizing and destabilizing impacts on border societies have engendered comparison with transatlantic slavery.[49]

---

wards Western Europe followed the decline of the Arab world (Adamczyk, *Silber und Macht*). For later periods, it proved useful to extend bilateral trade relations by interrelating them with one other – see, for example, Klemens Kaps, "Internal Differentiation in a Rising European Semi-Periphery: Cameralist Division of Labor and Mercantile Polycentrism: Two Different Models of Political Economy in Eighteenth-Century Habsburg Central Europe", *Review*, 36, 3–4 (2013), pp. 315–350, for the entanglement of Habsburg Galicia and Lombardy within a polycentric empire.

46 Ulf Brunnbauer, *Globalizing Southeastern Europe: Emigrants, America, and the State since the Late Nineteenth Century* (Lanham, 2015), for South-east Europe; Ewa Morawska, "Labor Migrations of Poles in the Atlantic World Economy, 1880–1914", in: Dirk Hoerder and Leslie Page Moch (eds), *European Migrants: Global and Local Perspectives* (Boston, 1996), pp. 170–208, for Poland; handbooks (Hoerder and Moch, *European Migrants*) and encyclopaedias (Klaus Bade et al. (eds), *The Encyclopedia of Migration and Minorities in Europe: From the 17th Century to the Present* (Cambridge, 2011)) cover historical migration from all parts of Eastern Europe. Recent developments such as care chains are investigated in light of earlier labour migrations of servants, agricultural labourers, or permanent migrants from Eastern to Western Europe. See, for example, Helma Lutz, *Vom Weltmarkt in den Privathaushalt. Die neuen Dienstmädchen im Zeitalter der Globalisierung* (Opladen and Farmington Hills, 2007).

47 Manuela Boatca, "Second Slavery versus Second Serfdom: Local Labor Regimes of the Global Periphery", in: Said Arjomand (ed.), *Social Theory and Regional Studies in the Global Age* (New York, 2013), pp. 361–388.

48 *Zeitschrift für Weltgeschichte*, Special Issue, 3, 2 (2002); Claus Füllberg-Stolberg, "Zwangsarbeit in der Moderne. Vergleichende Überlegungen", *ibid.*, pp. 71–88. On this see also De Vito's chapter (4.3) on convict labour in the present volume.

49 See, for example, Andrzej Gliwa, "Krise durch Plünderung. Die zivilisatorische und ökonomische Entwicklung im Grenzgebiet des Osmanischen Reiches und der polnisch-litauischen Adelsrepublik", in: Adamczyk and Lehnstaedt, *Wirtschaftskrisen als Wendepunkte*, pp. 289–318, on Tartar raids; Alison Frank-Johnson, "The Children of the Desert and the Laws of the Sea: Austria, Great Britain, the Ottoman Empire, and the Mediterranean Slave Trade in the Nineteenth Century", *American Historical Review*, 117, 2 (2012), pp. 410–444, on the Austrian Lloyd involvement in slave transports to the Ottoman Empire.

Multiple approaches to research on work and labour

While the requirements of funding contribute to the merging of individual scholars into trans-national communities, language and habit prevent dialogue between different epistemic communities. We shall look here at three communities that all deal with work and labour. First will be the museology of work and labour, second its social and economic history, and third the new global history. Finally, we shall consider the potential of labour research to serve as a means of dialogue and cooperation among them.

Museology of work and labour

There is an old tradition in European anthropology of addressing social change by collecting symbolic items from the past, exhibiting them in museums, and thereby coming to terms with the transition to a new period. It began in the nineteenth century when, to preserve the memory of the world of artisans and old village life, their artefacts were transferred to local museums as industrial manufacturing replaced traditional handicrafts. Then, another wave of musealization took place from the 1970s onwards, when industrial manufacturing disappeared because of computer-aided rationalization or outsourcing. Former factories, mines, workplaces, industrial districts, and workers' housing were saved from destruction by turning them into museums, heritage zones, and historical entertainment parks.[50] Open-air museums, or *Skansens*,[51] which represented traditional peasant work all over Europe were joined by museums and heritage trails commemorating industrial labour. The trend began in the former industrial regions of Great Britain, with their rich heritage of architecture, machinery, and artefacts. They attracted former employees, who could show their worlds of labour and reassert their otherwise lost identities as workers.[52] As with the adoption of the factory system in about 1800 in continental Europe and following Great Britain's example, labour museums and industrial heritage spread all over Europe, blossoming wherever enterprises had closed, and old build-

---

50 Hildegard K. Vieregg, *Geschichte des Museums* (Munich, 2008); Peggy Levitt, *Artifacts and Allegiances. How Museums Put the Nation and the World on Display* (Berkeley, CA, 2015).
51 The name of the first open-air museum (Sweden, 1880s) has become a trademark.
52 The Ironbridge Gorge Museum Trust, founded in 1967, includes thirty-five historic sites, including the Museum of the Gorge, the recreated Victorian town of Blists Hill, and the Coalbrookdale Museum. This project can be seen as the starting point and reference for many other European projects to preserve memories of industrial labour, technology, and social relations. http://www.ironbridge.org.uk/about-us/ironbridge-gorge-museum-trust/, last accessed 10 October 2016.

ings considered worthy of preservation were turned into museums.[53] Often such memorials were established on the initiative of communities and local associations, relying on individual enthusiasm and voluntary work. Bigger projects support permanent staff, collection departments and strategies with changing exhibitions, and education programmes. Many serve as pilot institutions and models for smaller projects.

While architects care for the conservation of the buildings, cultural anthropologists and historians develop concepts of presenting, interpreting, and visualizing for visitors the transition from the industrial to the post-industrial era. Projects like that are purely local, but in dealing with a European trend they address a general problem. As they contribute to finding new forms of income and identity for former industrial regions, they become part of the tourism industry, making it easier to raise funds and secure publicity, at the risk of turning what was a harmful process of industrial closures, rationalization, and job loss into something like an industrial Disneyland, as if there had only ever been fun and romanticism.

In spite of the tension between commerce and conservation, labour museums and trails have engendered research into labour conditions in regions, industries, and even specific companies, contributing to the rise of a professional network of museum experts. Focusing on everyday life, they document not only the work done in factories, fields, and mines, they also include in their agenda housing, housework, gardening, social care, workers' culture, and political organization. Taking place outside academic institutions, the research carried out in museums, exhibitions, and industrial heritage trails is often neglected in academia. In fact, such efforts rescue documents, artefacts, and memories of work that deserve high esteem. They serve as a link between collection, conservation, research, and public education. Most national museums of technology and industry nowadays include consideration of the history of labour, reorganizing collections and exhibitions with a special focus on work.[54] Local labour museums often rely on the benevolent cooperation of former factory owners or workers, and when such experts are no longer available in person labour museums will face a serious challenge. In response, public support for private museums can help to improve concepts and marketing, bridging the gap between voluntary and professional work in the field.

---

53 For an overview of major labour museums, see the homepage of the International Association of Labour Museums http://worklab.info/, last accessed 10 October 2016. Information on small local museums can be found on various regional websites.
54 The Technical Museum Vienna (opened 2011) hosts a ground-breaking exhibition "On Labour", presenting historical Austrian artefacts against the background of current technical change, globalization, and the challenge of redefining work.

Social and economic history

In the interwar period social and economic history split from economics and political history and became established as a historical sub-discipline with separate academic departments and journals. Since then it has specialized further in the conditions and relations of labour under changing historical conditions, but since the 1990s labour-related topics have lost their attraction for students and scholars. Those subjects have been replaced by questions of identity that were no longer related to class struggles and conflicts of interest but to diversity, which became an appealing approach. However, there was no establishment of links between matters of gender or ethnicity and economic interests, nor between labour relations and social inequalities in a changing global environment. The unity of social, economic, and cultural aspects that was characteristic of the profile of social and economic history in the early days of the sub-discipline were eroded, giving way to fragmentation into different epistemic communities. Cultural historians emphasized "discourse" and "representation", avoiding contact with the "real world". For their part social historians with an interest in material culture were reluctant to admit the impact of discourse on society. Both sorts of historians had difficulties in making theoretical assessments of changes wrought on their specific milieus by new social and economic environments on a global scale. It was due mainly to the rise of globalist and feminist approaches that the history of work and labour could be placed into a new and appealing conceptual framework. Based on a broad notion of work and labour that went beyond the factory and the proletarian household, and acknowledging the variety of labour relations beyond the industrialized cores of the global economy, older research on the industrial era could open itself up to a broader acknowledgement of shifting technological and economic cycles. Fresh eyes noted changing regional participation and leadership, and saw the impact they had on the definition and perception of work and labour. Institutions like the International Conference of Labour and Social History (ITH), with its annual conferences, held in Linz since 1964,[55] and the International Research Centre "Work and Human Lifecycle in Global History" (re:work) at Humboldt University,[56] founded in 2009, offered new arenas, programmes, incentives, funding, and collaborative workplaces for global labour studies. In both cases the International Institute of Social History (IISG), represented by Marcel van der Linden, who was once its research director, played an important role in reconciling old and new approaches to labour history.[57]

---

[55] http://www.ith.or.at/start/d_index.htm, last accessed 10 October 2016. For the reorientation of this labour research institution towards global connections, see Marcel van der Linden (ed.), *Labour History Beyond Borders: Concepts and Explorations* (Leipzig, 2010).
[56] https://rework.hu-berlin.de/en/news.html, last accessed 10 October 2016.
[57] Karl Heinz Roth, "Ein Enzyklopädist des kritischen Denkens: Marcel van der Linden, der heterodoxe Marxismus und die Global Labour History", *Sozial.Geschichte Online*, 9 (2012), pp. 116–244.

New global history

With the rise of a global approach to social, cultural, and economic history, the dead ends of classic Eurocentric narratives could be avoided. Asking questions from the perspective of non-European regions required rethinking old concepts. In the case of the Industrial Revolution, a key topic both for industrial and labour history, the idea of a British beginning and advance, rooted in the internal conditions and dynamics of British society, could no longer be claimed in light of the leading position of Asian manufacture, which British merchant companies had imported and distributed worldwide from the sixteenth to the eighteenth centuries until domestic producers began their own successful industrial catching up with the help of centralized mechanical production in factories.[58] Similarly, the catching up done by other industrializing regions on the European continent cannot be explained unless the changing global conditions of the British advance are taken into account. Furthermore, another key concept, that of capitalism and the relationships of production to commodification and the accumulation of capital, appears in a new light and raises new questions if it is looked at from a global instead of a national perspective.[59]

The epistemic potential of work and labour

Among the challenges that might contribute to a renewal of social, cultural, and economic history, work and labour have the potential to serve as links crossing existing borders and reassembling fragmentation among epistemic communities. First, the concept of work and labour has to be delinked from its reduction to paid labour and employment and be opened up to all kinds of activities that are necessary for human life.[60] Second, the debate about how people assess work requires historical context, in other words its social, spatial, and temporal background. Work must be seen in discursive, relational categories instead of one fixed one.[61] Third, if we in-

---

[58] Sven Beckert, *Empire of Cotton: A Global History* (New York, 2014); Andrea Komlosy, *Arbeit. Eine globalhistorische Perspektive. 13.–21. Jahrhundert* (Vienna, 2014); van der Linden, *Workers of the World*.

[59] Jürgen Kocka and Marcel van der Linden (eds), *Capitalism: The Reemergence of a Historical Concept* (London, 2016).

[60] Jürgen Kocka and Claus Offe (eds), *Geschichte und Zukunft der Arbeit* (Frankfurt am Main and New York, 2000); Josef Ehmer and Catharina Lis (eds), *The Idea of Work in Europe from Antiquity to Modern Times* (Farnham, 2009).

[61] In the project "The Production of Work" (POW, http://pow.univie.ac.at/, last accessed 10 October 2016) at the University of Vienna, local studies have investigated in depth the discourses between public authorities and workers from 1880 to the 1930s, thus establishing notions of what work was in the public consciousness and what it ought to be, in contrast to activities not regarded as work. See also Sigrid Wadauer, Thomas Buchner, and Alexander Mejstrik (eds), *The History of Labour Inter-*

clude all parts of the world and adopt a *longue durée* perspective we will have the tools necessary to launch a global history of work. Moreover, the IISG Collaboratory on the Global History of Labour Relations, 1500–2000, has been preparing a taxonomy and database to be able to assess the changing composition and distribution of labour relations from the 1500s to the 2000s, so preparing the ground for embedding case studies into a global quantitative framework.[62]

In that broad sense there is rarely a question that is not related to work, for – if seen through the prism of a broad concept of work – other topics will appear in a new light.[63] Identity, social stratification, class, gender, age, migration, education, social inequality, and social movements all show intersections with work, allowing connections to be made among all those topics. Work establishes relations with other academic disciplines, too, from the social and technical sciences to the humanities. Making work a key concept turned out to be just as beneficial when looking at transdisciplinary and international centres and networks of global labour research. Examples there are the networks of global labour history that take shape at the regional level in Africa, India, Latin America, and Europe, or at the global level with the institutional backing of the IISG in Amsterdam, re:work in Berlin, the ITH in Austria, and the Global and European Studies Institute (GESI) in Leipzig – to name just some of the European driving forces of such endeavours. Work is the key subject of the online journal *Workers of the World*, which deals with strikes and social conflicts and involves scholars from all over the world.[64]

Awareness of work's great relevance to power relations and the struggle to maintain or overcome inequality in subsistence, income, status, and fulfilment is a broad avenue to historical research. Historians undoubtedly need such awareness if they are to make any impact on key questions of social change, both in the community and at state level, and in their consideration of international relations and the global inequalities that always rely on unequal access to work and education, unequal pay, and labour conditions. Work is a moral category in all world religions, philosophies, and political concepts. The question of whether it should be sought and acquired or got rid of is contested. Is it a source of satisfaction, or only of income and thereby access to social security? Work is a key category of both utopian and dystopian thinking from Thomas More to Aldous Huxley; it is addressed in numerous contemporary novels, films, and artistic works. Evaluating historical utopias is therefore an important part of investigating the historical variety of concepts and realizations of work.[65]

---

mediation: Institutions and Finding Employment in the Nineteenth and Early Twentieth Centuries (New York and Oxford, 2015).
62 https://collab.iisg.nl/web/labourrelations, last accessed 10 October 2016.
63 See my synopsis of various approaches to global labour history in Andrea Komlosy, "Work and Labor Relations", in: Kocka and van der Linden, *Capitalism*, pp. 33–70.
64 https://workersoftheworldjournal.wordpress.com/, last accessed 10 October 2016.
65 Andreas Heyer, *Die Utopie steht links!* (Berlin, 2006) gives a chronological overview of prominent utopian writings. Felix Wemheuer, "Dining in Utopia: An Intellectual History of the Origins of the Chi-

Assessing changing concepts and discourses about work can enrich the debate about the future of work that comes up against the obvious deficiencies of our global economic order with regard to its ability to satisfy needs and hopes.

Conclusion

This article supports the idea that the historiography of work cannot be separated from work's transformation and the concomitant altered labour conditions and relations. The relocation of industrial mass production to newly industrializing countries since the 1970s and the decline and neoliberal restructuring of economies and labour in capitalist Western and communist East European states affected how work and labour were perceived and interpreted both in present times and from a historical perspective. While the "cultural turn" diverted scholarly interest towards questions of identity and representation, the "spatial turn" has emphasized location and place, opening the way to studying regional imbalances, social inequality, and the synchronicity of various types of labour at different places in globalized commodity chains.

Initiatives towards global labour history originated from academic institutions in countries that were either directly involved in colonizing activities or played leading roles as cores of the capitalist world economy. In Eastern Europe, labour history, including the history of international labour movements, enjoyed prominence under state socialism, but lost its attractiveness after the transformation. Interest and activity were revived only when scholars were able to establish connections between transformations at local, national, and global levels, so that they could then assess contemporary and historical processes of peripheralization.

When state industry was dismantled in the 1990s and replaced by production sites in the framework of transnational production and care chains, Western Europe's borders with the eastern part of the continent became porous. Eastern Europe was transformed into a peripheral part of what was always seen as "The West", on the one hand facing a continuing process of military and political as well as economic enlargement, but on the other seeing Western labour markets open up for migrants. In academia, Western institutions and programmes exert a particular pull for young scholars, who enthusiastically mutate into a sort of transnational species of mobile cosmopolitans, often obliged to accept flexibility and precarious working conditions as they beat the paths of their academic careers.

---

nese Public Dining Halls", in: Matthias Middell and Felix Wemheuer (eds), *Hunger and Scarcity under State-Socialism* (Leipzig, 2012), pp. 277–302, relates Chinese attempts to socialize cooking and eating to influences of European utopian thinking.

Suggested reading

Bade, Klaus et al. (eds). *The Encyclopedia of Migration and Minorities in Europe: From the 17th Century to the Present* (Cambridge: Cambridge University Press, 2011).
Barendt, Regina and Bettina Musiolek. *Workers' Voices. The Situation of Women in the Eastern European and Turkish Garment Industries* (Meißen: Evangelische Akademie, 2015).
Bartha, Eszter. *Alienating Labour: Workers on the Road from Socialism to Capitalism in East Germany and Hungary* (Oxford and New York: Berghahn, 2013).
Brunnbauer, Ulf. *Globalizing Southeastern Europe: Emigrants, America, and the State since the Late Nineteenth Century* (Lanham, MD: Rowman and Littlefield, 2016).
Cerman, Markus. *Villagers and Lords in Eastern Europe, 1300–1800* (Basingstoke: Palgrave Macmillan, 2012).
Ehmer, Josef and Catharina Lis (eds). *The Idea of Work in Europe from Antiquity to Modern Times* (Farnham: Ashgate, 2013).
Hoerder, Dirk and Leslie Page Moch (eds). *European Migrants: Global and Local Perspectives* (Boston, MA: Northeastern University Press, 1996).
Komlosy, Andrea. *Work. The Last 1000 Years* (London and New York: Verso, 2017).
Małowist, Marian. "The Economic and Social Development of the Baltic Countries from the 15th to the 17th Centuries", *Economic History Review*, Second Series, 12, 2 (1959), pp. 177–189.
Nolte, Hans-Heinrich (ed.). *Internal Peripheries in European History* (Göttingen: Muster-Schmid Verlag, 1991).
Stanziani, Alessandro. *Bondage. Labor and Rights in Eurasia from the Sixteenth to the Early Twentieth Centuries* (New York and Oxford: Berghahn, 2014).
Wolff, Larry. *Inventing Eastern Europe. The Map of Civilization on the Mind of the Enlightenment* (Stanford, CA: Stanford University Press, 1995).
Zimmermann, Susan. *Divide, Provide and Rule. An Integrative History of Poverty Policy, Social Policy, and Social Reform in Hungary under the Habsburg Monarchy* (Budapest and New York: Central European University Press, 2011).

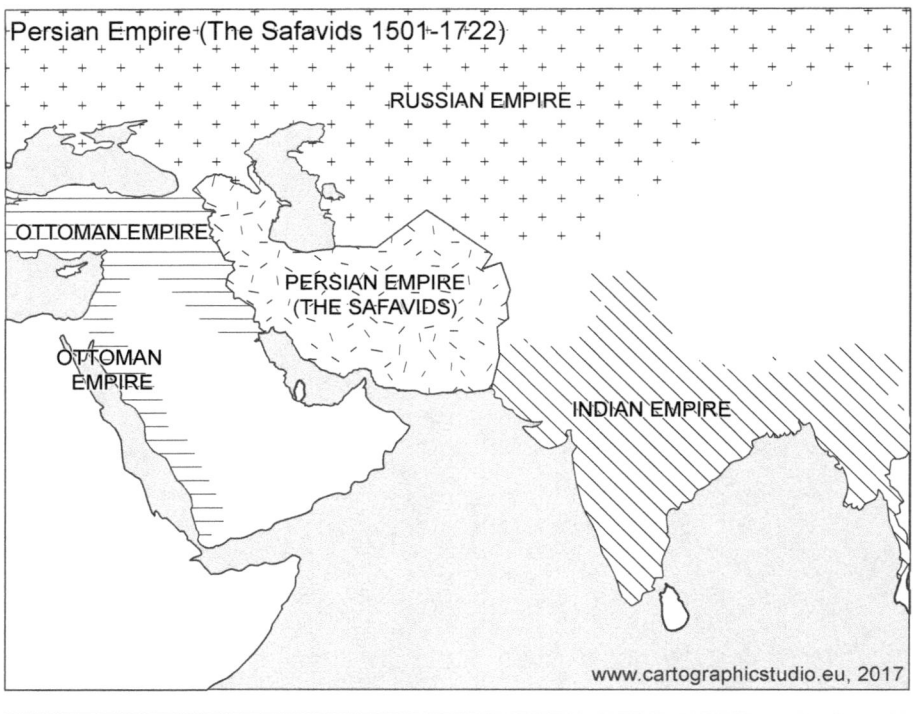
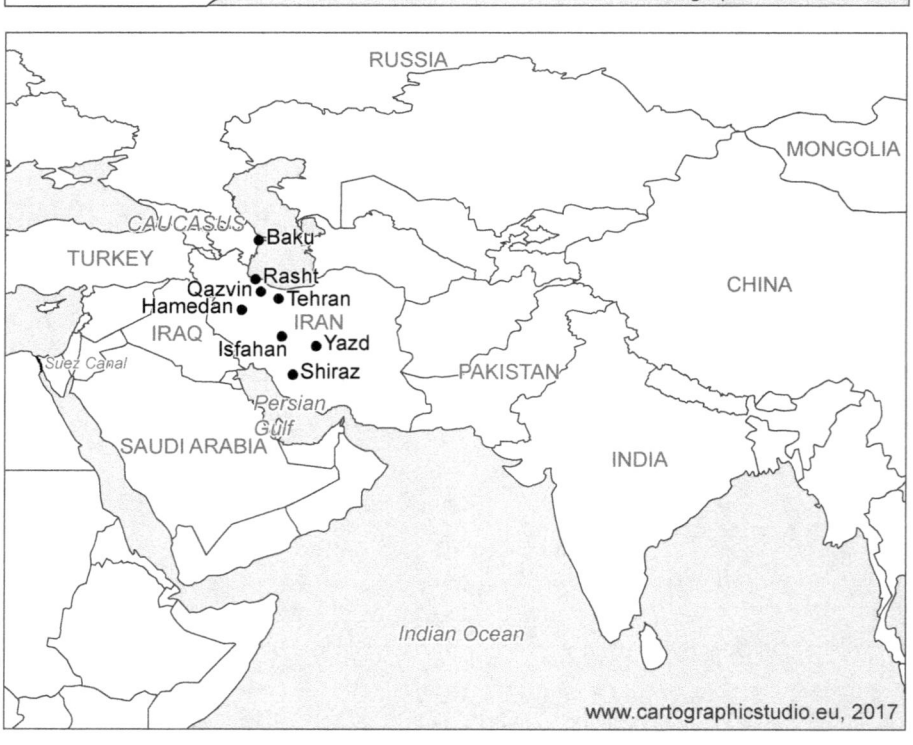

Touraj Atabaki
2.8. Iran (Persia)*

For historians and social scientists studying the emergence and development of capitalism in Persia (renamed Iran in 1935), the formation of the Safavid Empire (1501–1722) marks a turning point. Unifying much of the ancient Persian plateau under a single centralized state, the Safavids transformed an essentially agro-tribal order into a more sedentary and urbanized society. Moreover, by introducing Shiite Islam as the state religion, the Safavid rulers not only refashioned the collective identity of the empire's subjects against the neighbouring Sunni Caliphate of the Ottoman Empire, it also crafted a more homogeneous populace, more easily ruled by the patriarchal despotic state. The rather long period of political stability caused social and economic sustainability in the empire. Furthermore, the process of sedentarization of the nomadic commonalty, along with political stability, led the Safavid dynasty to derive most of its revenue from agriculture and trade.

What made the status of Safavid Persia in the age of global interaction (1450–1750) significant was the link, if not the integration, between its developing national market and the expanding world market ruled by the European kingdoms. Here the sea-based traders, especially the British and Dutch East India companies, functioned as the commercial agents, accommodating Persia within the emerging commercial capitalist order. According to one eyewitness account, "the Hollanders and the English bring their ready money, and some certain commodities which they either take up in Europe, or go to the Indies for, and sell them there to very good profit", and on return "they buy of the Persian saints purfled with gold or silver, silk-stuffes and cottons of the country, Persian Tapestry, [etc.]"[1]

In this period, the manufactured commodities of Persia finding their way onto the world market included silks of various kinds, coarse cotton cloths, carpets, gold and silver enamelled work, military arms and metalwork, leather, and glassware. These commodities were produced in workshops in cities such as Isfahan, Shiraz, Yazd, Hamadan, Qazvin, and Rasht, and some engaged more than one hundred labourers, with a distinct division of labour.[2]

The demise of the Safavid Empire in the early eighteenth century, when global industrialization and integration was inaugurating a new age of industrial revolution (1750–1900), paved the way for the return of tribal politics and created a rupture in

---

* I would like to thank Ervand Abrahamian, Mohammad Maljoo, and Eskandar Sadeghi-Boroujerdi for their helpful comments on the first draft of this paper.
1 J.A. de Mandelslo, *The Voyages and Travells of the Ambassadors Sent by Frederick Duke of Holstein ...* (London, 1662), in: Charles Issawi (ed.), *The Economic History of Iran, 1800–1914* (Chicago and London, 1971), pp. 11–12.
2 Mohamad-Reza Fashahi, *Takvin-e Sarmayehdari dar Iran* [The Development of Capitalism in Iran] (Tehran, 1981), p. 16. Issawi, *Economic History of Iran, 1800–1914*, p. 262.

the development of capitalism in Persia. The political disintegration and economic eclipse lasted for almost a century, and it was only at the turn of the nineteenth century and with the foundation of the Qajar Empire (1796–1925) that Persia returned to the political territoriality of Safavid Persia. However, the frontiers of the newly founded empire soon proved to be unsustainable in an age when the emerging colonial powers were perpetually engaged in expanding their territorial dominance.

For Persia, the 1813 and 1828 treaties – the outcome of the two long military confrontations with the Tsarist Empire – saw not only the total surrender of its territory in the Caucasus, but also a gradual, albeit significant, political and socioeconomic transformation. The political concessions, commercial capitulations, and economic penetration that were the direct consequences of the military defeats led the country's economy to become more dependent on the international market and its fluctuations. The decline of the domestic and external value of the Iranian currency, the non-export agricultural products, the traditional crafts and local industries, the increase in the level of the country's foreign trade, the commercialization of agriculture, and the rise in the production of cash crops were all the direct result of linking the Persian economy to the world market.[3] The outcomes of this linkage were class dislocation and population displacement, which were intensified with the gradual increase in the country's population from five or six million in 1800 to about ten million by 1914.[4] Such changes brought about a new pattern of consumption and subsequently changed social norms, social stratification, and the traditional power structure. Persia's economic decline was deepened further in 1869 by the excavation of the Suez Canal, which provided easier access to the Indian Ocean for European navigation. At the same time, the importance of the Tabriz–Trebizond route diminished. The closure of this route, which for centuries had been the most important route joining Europe to the Indian subcontinent, was an extra burden for the Persian economy, which was already going through drastic economic decline.

Persia entered the twentieth century with a semi-colonial status. Britain and Tsarist Russia were two major powers that considered Persia as the backyard of their political and economic interests. Reaction to this semi-colonial status made the twentieth century a century of revolutions for Persia. The first revolution, the Constitutional Revolution (1905–1909), led to drastic changes in socioeconomic and sociocultural conditions aimed at crafting a new political order for the country, ending the monarchical regime, introducing law and order, establishing accountability in the exercise of power, both political and economic, and considering all (at this point only male) citizens equal before the law. Modernization of society through the industrialization of the country's economy was another target of the revolution. However, the Constitutional Revolution soon faced severe obstacles, first due to the lack

---

3 Homa Katouzian, *The Political Economy of Modern Iran* (London, 1981), p. 27.
4 Issawi, *Economic History of Iran, 1800–1914*, p. 20.

of a central state, then to the coercive policies of Tsarist Russia, and later the outbreak of the First World War.

The discovery of oil in southern Persia in 1908 coincided with the Constitutional Revolution and boosted the geostrategic significance of the country. When the outbreak of the First World War terminated the European "hundred years' peace", as Karl Polanyi called it,[5] the global shift from coal to oil in technology, military, and industry had enormous implications for the strategic significance of Persia and the Persian Gulf as a region that contained the world's largest oil deposits. Oil was an impressive strategic and socially produced commodity, and, globally, oil capitalism replaced the financial capitalism of the nineteenth century, continuing somehow to dominate the entire twentieth century.

The pivotal position of Persian oil in the First World War refashioned the country's destiny throughout the twentieth century. Two coups d'état in 1921 and 1953 and the second revolution in 1977–1979 were all, in one way or another, associated with oil. However, while the oil industry remained a major industry throughout the twentieth century and an icon of industrialization and urbanization for Persia, the twentieth century amounted to more than oil for Persia. If the First World War turned Persia into a battleground of the great powers and caused some discontinuity in the process of economic development and the practice of constitutionalism, in the world that emerged from the First World War, Persia, like its other neighbours Tsarist Russia and Ottoman Turkey, appeared with a different cap. The coup d'état of 1921 paved the way for the inauguration of the Pahlavi dynasty (1925–1979), instituting a vast array of authoritarian political and economic modernization policies in Persia. The Pahlavi modern state accommodated many of the constitutionalists' demands, with the exception of avoiding autocracy.

There is consensus among the economic historians of modern Persia in taking the Constitutional Revolution and the outbreak of the First World War as the terminus of the early development of capitalism in Persia,[6] dividing the fifty-four years of Pahlavi rule that followed into a period of formation of industrial capitalism (1925–1963) and a period of expansion in capitalist relations (1963–1978).[7]

---

[5] Karl Polanyi, *The Great Transformation. The Political and Economic Origins of Our Time* (Boston, 2001), p. 5. The adjective "European" needs to be appended to Polanyi's "hundred years' peace", otherwise the notion would be Eurocentric. During this "hundred years", the world witnessed many colonial wars outside Europe.

[6] Fashahi, *Takvin-e Sarmayehdari dar Iran*; Issawi, *Economic History of Iran 1800–1914*.

[7] Mohamad Reza Sodagar, *Roshd-e Ravabet-e Sarmayehdari dar Iran. Marhaleh Enteghali* [The Development of Capitalist Relations in Iran: The Period of Transition] (Tehran, 1978); *idem*, *Roshd-e Ravabet-e Sarmayehdari dar Iran. Marhaleh Gostaresh* [The Development of Capitalist Relations in Iran: The Period of Expansion] (Tehran, 1990).

History and the historiography of labour and the working class

Twenty years after *The Making of the English Working Class* appeared, the historiography of Iran eventually became acquainted with E.P. Thompson's innovative work, due to the efforts of Ervand Abrahamian.[8] This first acquaintance with Thompson was in 1982, as a result of the publication of *Iran Between Two Revolutions*, a class analysis of the history of twentieth-century Iran and its two revolutions of 1905–1909 and 1977–1979.[9] In 1982, when Abrahamian's book appeared, it was not only Iranian Marxist activists who were puzzled by the outcome of the revolution. Marxist academics, too, began to question the essentialist and teleological narrative provided by cruder versions of historical materialism, as they struggled to discern the social base of the 1977–1979 Revolution that brought the political clergy to power. Under the influence of Thompson's neo-Marxist approach, Abrahamian opened up a new horizon, where class needed to be understood within the broader context of hegemonic culture and in social contention with other classes. The Thompsonian effect not only refashioned social and labour historiography in the Global North, in the Global South, too, it crafted a new labour history undeniably distinct from the old one. If, as Marcel van der Linden characterized it, the old labour history was "institutional, focused on the description of organizational developments, political debates, leaders and strikes", the new labour history "attempted to *contextualise* workers' struggles" through recovering "not just labour processes and everyday culture, but gender, ethnicity, race and age [...] along with household structures, sexuality, and informal politics."[10]

In my revisiting the history and historiography of labour and the Iranian working class, I identify two historiographical currents, exemplifying the old and new labour histories. While in both currents one finds traces of the other, it is the absence or presence of the Thompsonian effect that crucially distinguishes them from one another.[11]

---

8 E.P. Thompson, *The Making of the English Working Class* (London, 1963).
9 Ervand Abrahamian, *Iran Between Two Revolutions* (Princeton, NJ, 1982).
10 Marcel van der Linden, "Labour History: The Old, the New and the Global", *African Studies*, 66, 2–3 (2007), p. 169.
11 One of the earliest work on guilds in Iran is *Resaleh-e Sanaeyeh* [Book of Artefact], written by Mirza Abulqasem Astrabadi-Fendereski (1563–1640), where the author briefly describes the positions of artisans and craftsmen in Safavid Persia and the interdependency of the townsmen who work as members of a certain guild. Mirza Abulqasem Astrabadi-Fendereski, *Resaleh-e Sanaeyeh* [Book of Artefact], edited and annotated by Hassan Jamshid (Tehran, 2008). *Resaleh-e Sanaeyeh* was not the only treatise on guilds and on labour working for guilds in pre-industrial Persia. In his Ph.D. dissertation, Mehdi Keyvani provides a survey of all available sources. Mehdi Keyvani, *Artisans and Guild Life in the Later Safavid Period: Contributions to the Social-Economic History of Persia* (Berlin, 1982). Following this broad literature survey, Keyvani studies the social, political, cultural, and religious functions

To begin with the first current, the background to writing on labour in Persia (Iran) broadly goes back to the nineteenth century and largely to industrial labour. Scholarly research on the history of agricultural labour is rare. A pioneer in this field was Ann Lambton, who published two influential books on land tenure: *Landlord and Peasant in Persia* (1953; expanded edition, 1991), and *The Persian Land Reform, 1962–1966* (1969).[12] But in later years the topic has mostly been neglected, except for the study by Farhad Kazemi and Ervand Abrahamian, who examined the non-revolutionary peasantry in modern Iran.[13] Later, Farhad Kazemi published a comparative study on the revolutionary peasantry in Iran, Iraq, and Turkey in an edited volume on peasants and politics in the Middle East.[14] In the same volume, Ahmad Ashraf wrote an article on agrarian relations in the pre- and post-revolution eras, opening a venue for a better understanding of the class composition of the Iranian 1977–1979 Revolution.[15]

The formation of Persia's industrial working class dates to the second half of the nineteenth century and had its origins, ironically, outside the political frontiers of Persia. The migration of Persian labouring poor in search of employment began in the mid-nineteenth century. Imperial Russia, India, the Ottoman Empire, and north and west Africa were the most favoured destinations for migration. Of these destinations, Tsarist Russia, with its flourishing economy in the late nineteenth century,[16] attracted many of the Iranian labouring poor, largely from central and north-

---

of each guild and examines their relations with merchants and the state in late seventeenth-, early eighteenth-century Persia. However, while the position of masters in the guilds has been adequately described in Keyvani's study, what is missing in his work and similar studies is the position of apprentices or labourers working in the guilds during this period. W.M. Floor, "The Guilds in Iran – An Overview from the Earliest Beginnings till 1972", *Zeitschrift der Deutschen Morgenländischen Gesellschaft*, 125, 1 (1975), pp. 99–116. Idem, *Guilds, Merchants, & Ulama in Nineteenth-Century Iran* (Washington, 2009). Kuznetsova's work on guilds could be considered an exception, since she draws on Russian, Armenian, and Georgian sources and conveys a picture of the labourer (she refers to the *muzdvar*, the correct spelling of which is *muzdur*, one who is paid, hired worker, labourer) in eighteenth- and nineteenth-century Persia. N.A. Kuznetsova, "Materialy k kharakterstike remeslennogo provizvodstva v iranskom grode XVIII-nachala XIX veka", in: Issawi, *Economic History of Iran 1800–1914*, pp. 285–292.

12 Ann Lambton, *Landlord and Peasant in Persia: A Study of Land Tenure and Land Revenue Administration* (London, 1953; expanded edition 1991); idem, *The Persian Land Reform, 1962–1966* (Oxford, 1969).
13 Farhad Kazemi and Ervand Abrahamian, "The Nonrevolutionary Peasantry of Modern Iran", *Iranian Studies*, 11, 1–4 (1978), pp. 259–304.
14 Farhad Kazemi, "Peasant Uprisings in Twentieth-Century Iran, Iraq, and Turkey", in: idem and John Waterbury (eds), *Peasants and Politics in the Modern Middle East* (Gainesville, FL, 1991), pp. 101–124.
15 Ahmad Ashraf, "State and Agrarian Relations Before and After the Iranian Revolution, 1960–1990", in: Kazemi and Waterbury, *Peasants and Politics in the Modern Middle East*, pp. 277–311.
16 By the late nineteenth century the Baku oilfield supplied ninety-five per cent of Russia's consumer oil and held the second largest oil deposits in the world after the United States. On Russian state-oriented industrialization, see M.E. Fakus, *The Industrialisation of Russia, 1700–1914* (London, 1972).

ern Persia. By the time of the Russian Revolution of 1917, there were hundreds of thousands of Persian migrant workers, chiefly working in the Baku oil and mining industries, and constructing roads and railroads in the southern regions of the empire, the Caucasus, and Central Asia.

Soviet historians were pioneers in writing about these migrant workers. By exploiting the rich archive of the Tsarist administration of the Caucasus, Belova and Strigunov provided a detailed empirical account of Persian migrant workers in the Caucasus.[17] Following those Soviet historians, it was Hassan Hakimian who examined Persian labour migration to southern Russia within the framework of the Persian political economy of the late nineteenth and early twentieth centuries.[18]

By the turn of the century, and within the political frontiers of Persia, industrialization was slowly but surely taking place, giving birth to a new cluster of industrial workers in the country. The "slow development of large-scale industry took place against a background of lack of integration in the world economy, and a generally low level of custom duties (about 4–5 percent) on imported manufactures, not to mention a series of political changes."[19] Following the path of the early Soviet labour historians, in 1963 Abdullaev published his book on industrialization and the emergence of the Iranian working class in the late nineteenth and early twentieth centuries.[20] Although Abdullaev's analytical framings, imbued with Soviet essentialism, exemplified more than anything else the Soviet-Stalinist perception of historical materialism, one should not underestimate his major contribution to a better understanding of the formation of the working class in Iran, especially when one is engaged with facts and figures. His work remains a major work of reference for labour historians.

Willem Floor is another historian who has studied the size, composition, and working conditions of Persia's working class during the last two decades of the nineteenth century.[21] If Abdullaev's major references derive from Tsarist-Russian accounts and statistics, with Floor it is the accounts and narratives of European travellers as well as diplomatic sources, chiefly British, that craft his historiography. However, the component common to both these studies is the absence of Persian sources, chiefly documents to be found in the central and local archives, or, even more imperative, the petitions sent to the king, local authorities, and institutions by labourers. Furthermore, if in Abdullaev's narrative of labour life and work the formation of the working class and the construction of its consciousness is shaped by the develop-

---

[17] N.K. Belova, "Ob otchodnichestve iz severozapadnego Irana v kontse XIX-nachale XX veka", *Voprosy istorii*, 10 (1959); I.V. Strigunov, *Iz storii formirovaniia Bakinskogo proletariata* (Baku, 1960).
[18] Hassan Hakimian, "Wage Labour and Migration: Persian Workers in Southern Russia, 1880–1914", *International Journal of Middle East Studies*, 17, 4 (1985), pp. 443–462.
[19] Julian Bharier, *Economic Development in Iran 1900–1970* (London, 1971), p. 171.
[20] Z.A. Abdullaev, *Promyshlennost I zarozhdenie rabochego klassa Irana v kontse XIX-nachale XX vv* (Baku, 1963).
[21] Floor, *Guilds, Merchants, and Ulama in Nineteenth-Century Iran*.

ment of capitalism and the process of class conflict and class struggle, for Floor, labour in Persia during this period never constituted a class, but rather a cluster in the larger entity of ruled people or *ro'aya:* "labour had no say in or control over its own destiny, neither about the direction of the course it was on, nor about the pace at which it was to proceed."[22]

The global and regional movement for social progress, modernism, and ultimately constitutionalism, which had been developing since the mid-nineteenth century, culminated in a series of revolutions in Tsarist Russia (1906), Persia (1905–1909), and Ottoman Turkey (1908). In all these countries, within the constitutional movement there was a core of radical political activists whose reading of constitutionalism went beyond empowering individual autonomy, human agency, and imposing limits to state authority on the application of the law; they demanded a unified legal system.[23] With an unequivocal social democratic platform, and associated to some extent with the Second International of Socialist and Labour Parties (1889–1916), Iranian social democrats founded their party, the Social Democratic Party (Ejtema'iyun-'Amiyun) prior to the Constitutional Revolution. Following the revolution, they created the Democrat Party of Iran (Hezb-e Demokrat-e Iran) and pursued their activities in the Iranian parliament.[24] The outbreak of the First World War and the Russian Revolution radicalized these social democrats, and finally, in June 1920, after arduous endeavours, they founded the Communist Party of Iran (Hezb-e Komonist-e Iran).[25]

With the birth of the Communist Party of Iran, a party affiliated to the Third International (the Comintern), a new school of labour studies and labour historiography gradually emerged in Persia. Refashioned by Marxism-Leninism, and revisiting the history of late nineteenth- and early twentieth-century Persia through the lens of class and class conflict, the agency of the Iranian working class in modern Persian history was highlighted. Sultanzadeh, one of the founders of the Communist Party of Iran and an active member of the early Comintern, contributed to this historiography.[26] In his first scholarly book, *Contemporary Persia*, published in 1922, based on his fieldwork, he

---

22 Ibid., p. 21.
23 Ali Gheissari, "Constitutional Rights and the Development of Civil Law in Iran, 1907–1941", in: H.E. Chehabi and Vanessa Martin (eds), *Iran's Constitutional Revolution: Popular Politics, Cultural Transformations and Transnational Connections* (London, 2010), pp. 69–79, at 72.
24 For the history of early social democratic organizations, see Abdolhossein Agahi, "Piramun-e Nakhostin Ashna'i-ye Iranian ba Marxism" [On the Early Acquaintances of Iranians with Marxism], *Donya*, 3 (1962).
25 For the development of the early socialist movement in Iran, see Touraj Atabaki, "Missing Labour in the Metanarratives of Practicing Modernity in Iran: Labour Agency in Refashioning the Discourse of Social Development", in: David Mayer and Jürgen Mittag (eds), *Interventions: The Impact of Labour Movements on Social and Cultural Development* (Leipzig, 2013), pp. 171–195.
26 For the early Soviet-constructed school of oriental and Iranian studies, see Touraj Atabaki and Lana Ravandi-Fadai, "Iranshenasi-e Sorkh" [Red Iranian Studies], *Iran-Nameh, A Quarterly of Iranian Studies*, 2 (2015), pp. 174–190.

presented his analysis of Persia's agrarian economy, as well as of the development of capitalism in the country. Along with this analysis, he described the social status of both the agrarian and the urban labourers in the country's economy since late nineteenth century.[27] In another book, published in 1924, Sultanzadeh once more studied the development of the Iranian working class and linked it to political developments in Iran after the First World War, and the rise to power of Reza Khan, whom Sultanzadeh praised as the representative of the "nationalist bourgeoisie" – a position consistent with the Comintern and Soviet view on Iran and neighbouring Turkey in this period.[28]

Before continuing our review of labour histories and historiographies in twentieth-century Persia, prior to the First World War and in the interwar period, it might be interesting to refer to the first labour novel published in Persian. *Workers in Bleak Times*, written in 1923–1925 by Ahmad Ali Khodadadeh, is a narrative of a poor agrarian labourer fleeing from the unbearable working and living conditions in the village in search of work in the city. The narrative, which takes the form of a literary travelogue, a common genre in Persian literature at that time, meticulously describes and distinguishes the everyday life of the poor labourer (*ranjbar*) from that of the worker (*kargar*) and even the poor labour worker (*kargr-e ranjbar*), who, according to the author, falls into the category of slaves.[29]

Histories of labour and the working class in the period prior to the Second World War had been compiled by others, Marxist and non-Marxist. At the core of all these histories, without exception, lies organized labour and the narratives of the movement to unionize the working class. Shokrollah Mani's *A Concise History of the Labour Movement in Iran* is an excellent example; even today, it is an important first-hand account of the unionization movement in Iran.[30] In the 1960s and 1970s, with reference to chronicles such as Shokrollah Mani's narrative and other accounts derived from the Communist Party of Iran and the Comintern archive, Tudeh Party historians in exile[31] compiled studies on the history of the communist and working-class movements in Iran.[32] What makes these studies distinct is the perception of Tudeh Party his-

---

27 A. Sultanzadeh, *Sovremennaya Persia* [Contemporary Persia] (Moscow, 1922).
28 *Idem*, *Persia* [Persia] (Moscow, 1924).
29 Ahmad Ali Khodadadeh, *Rooz-e Siyah-e Kargar* [Workers in Bleak Times], edited by Nasser Mohajer and Asad Seyf (Paris, 2016), pp. 293–294.
30 Shokrollah Mani, *Tarikhcheh Nehzaht Karigari dar Iran* [A Concise History of the Labour Movement in Iran] (Tehran, 1946).
31 The Tudeh Party of Iran was founded in 1941 to substitute for the Communist Party of Iran, the majority of whose leadership had been purged in the Soviet Union during the Stalinist reign of terror.
32 Ali Shamide, *Rabochi I profsoyouzhoe dbizhehy v irane v 1960–1953* [Workers and Union Movement in Iran 1906–1953] (Baku, 1967); *idem*, *Iranda fahle ve hemkarlar hereketi 1941–1946* [Workers and Union Movement in Iran 1941–1946] (Baku, 1961); Abdolsamad Kambakhsh, "Nazari beh Panjah Sal Fa'aliyat-e Hezb-e Tabaqeh Kargar dar Iran" [A Reflection on Fifty Years of Activity by the Working Class Party in Iran], *Donya*, 2 (1970), pp. 2–15; Ardashes Avanesiyan, *Safahati chand az Jonbesh Kargari va Komonisti Iran dar Dowran Avval Reza Shah* [Pages on the Workers and Communist Movements

torians concerning labour history. For these historians, labour history is the history of factory-based organized labour associated with the communist movement. Ardashes Avanesiyan, a leading member of the Communist Party and later of the Tudeh Party, refers to this association in the following words:

> In practice, workers' unions in Iran were different from the common West European trade unions. Put differently, the Communist Party did not emerge from the union movement; instead, it was the party that forged the foundations of the unions. This led to a revolutionary sprit and tradition among Iranian unions.[33]

This argument was later challenged by other Marxian historians. Atabaki has questioned the association between union and party in Iranian labour history, as narrated by Avanesiyan. In one of his articles, he also examined how, since the early days of the Comintern's formation, and in the Stalinist labour historiography, the Comintern's position on the labour movement often associated party with union. Furthermore, he argued that in the same school of historiography selective amnesia led to independent unions not associated with political parties being ignored.[34] In their joint study on the labour movement prior to the Second World War, Jalil Mahmudi and Nasser Sa'idi share Atabaki's verdict.[35]

For decades, the historiography of labour in Iran had been considered the territory of communist historians. However, with the publication of Habib Ladjevardi's *Labour Unions and Autocracy in Iran* in 1985, the historiography of labour and the working class in Iran was enriched by the work of a new, non-Marxist scholar.[36] Although the core of Ladjevardi's book covers the period 1941–1953, in his introduction and postscript the author loosely expands his work on the Constitutional Revolution and the end of the Pahlavi era. Tracing labour activism, Ladjevardi focuses on and limits his analysis to organized labour, and chiefly the period when they are undertaking more salient and confrontational forms of activity. In Ladjevardi's study it is difficult to find an account of either non-unionized labour or any other form of labour protest, such as sending petitions or other repertoires of peaceful protest. However, one cannot underestimate the two noteworthy achievements of Ladjevardi's work. Firstly, he takes a distinct approach and eschews studying the labour move-

---

in Iran during the First Period of Reza Shah's Reign] (Leipzig, 1978); Abdolhossein Agahi, "60 Sal az Tarikh Tasis Hezb Komonist Iran Gozasht" [60 Years On from the Foundation of the Communist Party of Iran], *Donya*, 3 (1980), pp. 30–63; Mehdi Keyhan, "Hafdad sal Jonbesh Sandikaii dar Iran" [Seventy Years of Trade-Union Movement in Iran], *Donya*, 2 (1980), pp. 28–41.
33 Avanesiyan, *Safahati chand az Jonbesh Kargari va Komonisti Iran*, p. 7.
34 Touraj Atabaki, "L'Organisation syndicale ouvrière en Iran, de 1941 à 1946", *Soual*, 8 (1988), pp. 35–60; idem, "The Comintern, the Soviet Union and Labour Militancy in Interwar Iran", in: Stephanie Cronin (ed.), *Iranian-Russian Encounters: Empires and Revolutions since 1800* (London and New York, 2013), pp. 298–323.
35 Jalil Mahmudi and Nasser Sa'idi, *Shuq-e Yak Khiz-e Boland* [Towards a Subtle Rise] (Tehran, 2002).
36 Habib Ladjevardi, *Labour Unions and Autocracy in Iran* (Syracuse, NY, 1985).

ment as subordinate to the political; instead, he gives a rather independent agency to the labour movement. Secondly, he draws on considerable and diverse sources, Persian and non-Persian, chiefly the diplomatic accounts derived from the United States and the British archives. Absent of course are the major sources on Iran from Soviet archives.

The labour history of pre-Second World War Iran saw two other publications in the 1980s: Farhang Qasemi's book *Trade Unions in Iran 1905–1941*,[37] and *Labour Unions, Law, and Conditions in Iran (1900–1941)* by Willem Floor.[38] Both were distinguished by their non-Marxian approach. As is clear from the titles of these two studies, organized labour and their activities comprise the core of the authors' analyses. However, what makes Qasemi's analysis different from Floor's is Qasemi's approach to the notion of labour agency in the labour movement. Although he highlights the political dependency of the labour movement, chiefly with respect to social democracy, socialist and communist political groups and parties, in analysing the background of labour activists he presents examples of what might be called a rather indigenous initiative in this movement. For Floor, the independent agency of labour is questionable, since "the trade unions were started and led by men whose material and cultural background made them members of the middle class", and

> the workers in general had neither the time and energy, nor the understanding and capability to organize labour activities let alone a labour movement. These members of the intelligentsia, being Marxist moreover, considered the labour problem as being an integral part of the socio-economic and political system in which imperialism and capitalism were the moving forces.[39]

One should not underestimate the novelty of Floor's work. Furthermore, he draws on a wide range of primary and secondary sources, mostly in European languages, which he exploits in order to depict the working and living conditions of labour, such as the cost of living, wages, hygiene and nutrition, working hours, and safety. Furthermore, Floor presents a detailed account of labour regulation and legislation in Iran during the first four decades of the twentieth century.

Under the shadow of E.P. Thompson

As noted earlier, it was with Ervand Abrahamian that the social and labour historiography of Iran became cognizant of E.P. Thompson and his *The Making of the English Working Class*. Although Abrahamian published only one study explicitly on la-

---

[37] Farhang Qasemi, *Sandikalism dar Iran 1284–1320* [Trade Unionism in Iran 1905–1941] (Paris, 1985).
[38] Willem Floor, *Labour Unions, Law, and Conditions in Iran (1900–1941)* (Durham, 1985).
[39] *Ibid.*, p. 2.

bour,⁴⁰ in his writings on the history of modern Iran, labour is visibly present throughout his work. Abrahamian's first and most prominent study, *Iran Between Two Revolutions*, is a well-researched, documented, and analytical social history of twentieth-century Iran. This grand work educated a generation of students of the social history of Iran. It encompasses a large section on labour history from the early twentieth century to the Revolution of 1977–1979. Abrahamian's social and cultural analysis of working-class history, and this can be said of other social forces he analyses in his book, has to a large extent been influenced by the British Marxist Historians school of *Past & Present:* Dona Torr, Christopher Hill, Eric Hobsbawm, and especially E.P. Thompson:

> The underlying premise throughout the book will be E.P. Thompson's neo-Marxist approach that the phenomenon of class should be understood not simply in term of its relation to the mode of production (as orthodox Marxist have often argued), but, on the contrary, in the context of historical time and of social friction with other contemporary classes.⁴¹

With Ervand Abrahamian, many young social and labour historians working on Iran became acquainted with Thompson and his seminal work, although it has only recently been translated into Persian.⁴² In an article published in 2013 on the occasion of the fiftieth anniversary of the publication of *The Making of the English Working Class*, Abrahamian highlighted Thompson's legacy as "shunning grand theory, broad generalizations and abstract hair-splitting, E.P. [Thompson] appealed to historians eager to immerse themselves into the past, and draw larger conclusions only after searching through a mass of empirical information."⁴³

In 2003 Touraj Atabaki and Marcel van der Linden edited a dossier of the *International Review of Social History* entitled "Twentieth Century Iran: History from Below".⁴⁴ It included three papers on the twentieth-century history of Iran's working class. In his article Kaveh Ehsani examined the role of labourers, migrants, women, and petty functionaries in the making and shaping of the city of Abadan during the twentieth century.⁴⁵ What is significant in Ehsani's work is that he does not confine his study solely to workers in the oil industry in Abadan, and he unearths the resist-

---

40 Ervand Abrahamian, "The Formation of the Proletariat in Modern Iran, 1941–1953", Working Paper, Fernand Braudel Center for the Study of Economies, Historical Systems, and Civilizations (1978).
41 Idem, *Iran Between Two Revolutions*, p. 6.
42 E.P. Thompson, *Takvin-e Tabaqeh Kargar dar Engelestan* [The Making of the English Working Class], translated by Mohammad Maljoo (Tehran, 2017).
43 Ervand Abrahamian, "Voice of the Discontented", *History Workshop Journal*, 76, 1 (2013), pp. 256–258, at 257.
44 *International Review of Social History*, 48, 3 (2003), pp. 353–455.
45 Kaveh Ehsani, "Social Engineering and the Contradictions of Modernization in Khuzestan's Company Town: A Look at Abadan and Masjed-Soleyman", *International Review of Social History*, 48, 3 (2003), pp. 361–399.

ance among the Abadanis at large in their struggle to redefine the urban space of the company town and make it their own. The second article in that volume was Atabaki's study on the transnational aspects of working-class formation.[46] Having located documents from various Tsarist, Soviet, and Iranian archives, he studied the history of everyday life of the Iranian labouring poor and working class on the margins of the Tsarist Empire prior to the 1917 Russian Revolution. By focusing on the everyday life of migrant labour and on the crafted inclusive culture and political activism in the town to which they migrated, Atabaki highlighted the multiple identities of migrant workers, their class, ethnic, linguistic, and political loyalties, and examined how, within a certain political reality, one identity could take precedence over another. Finally, there was Willem Floor's article on the work, labour relations, and living conditions of labourers at the brick kilns of South Tehran.[47] In his study, Floor underlined the appalling working and living conditions of these labourers, partly urbanized, partly transient rural, who were among the poorest of the Iranian labouring class. He also examined labour activism among the brick-kiln workers by comparing six strikes between July 1953 and April 1979.

In another project, and in a comparative study examining the accommodation and resistance among subalterns in Persia and the Ottoman Empire to authoritarian modernization, Atabaki, inspired by E.P. Thompson's study of time and labour discipline, studied the advent of the public mechanical clock and the introduction of measured time among urban labour since sixteenth century. This essay continued by examining the earliest wave of industrialization, advancing a new perception of time, of teamwork, of organization, and cooperation, as well as the early labour legislation that severely enforced the new work discipline.[48]

In 2010, at the International Institute of Social History and in the context of the grand global labour history,[49] a research project was launched on the social history of labour in the Iranian oil industry. With a aim of developing an empirical and qualitative study of labour and the working class during the one-hundred-year history of the Iranian oil industry (1908–2018) and relying on the theoretical and analytical tools provided by the new labour history, the project focused on five main areas: the composition of the labour force (ethnicity, gender, and age); the process of labour formation (recruitment, skills, training, and education); labour relations (wages and labour discipline); labour migration, mobility, and integration; and living conditions / quality of life (housing, nutrition, hygiene, health, and leisure).

---

46 Touraj Atabaki, "Disgruntled Guests: Iranian Subaltern on the Margins of the Tsarist Empire", *International Review of Social History*, 48, 3 (2003), pp. 401–426.
47 Willem Floor, "The Brickworkers of Khatunabad: A Striking Record (1953–1979)", *International Review of Social History*, 48, 3 (2003), pp. 427–455.
48 Touraj Atabaki, "Time, Labour-Discipline and Modernization in Turkey and Iran: Some Comparative Remarks", in: idem (ed.), *The State and the Subaltern: Modernization, Society and the State in Turkey and Iran* (London, 2007), pp. 1–16.
49 https://socialhistory.org/en/research/global-labour-history.

So far, this project has resulted in two Ph.D. dissertations[50] and numerous articles; a book is in the pipeline. In the autumn of 2013, *International Labor and Working-Class History* published a special section on the social history of Iranian oil workers.[51] Contributions in this section included an essay by Touraj Atabaki on the formation of the working class in the oil industry.[52] In that essay he examined the early formation of oil workers, who were recruited primarily from among the tribal and village-based labouring poor and subjected to the labour discipline of an advanced industrial economy; this eventually contributed to the formation of the early clusters of modern Iran's working class. On the formation of workers' consciousness he joined Zachary Lockman in arguing that working-class formation is as much a discursive as it is a material process.[53] Questioning the validity of the conventional structuralist, objectivist definition of the worker and working class, Atabaki argued that, after the lengthy process of recruitment and subjection to a new labour discipline, working people in the Iranian oil industry ended up with a new image of themselves as a distinctive group with a collective social identity. An image that is an iconic vision of group solidarity – one that brings people together through the cultural contestations of their everyday life, forging not only a collective class consciousness but also other forms of consciousness – a kind of practical consciousness, derived from social representation as well as social recognition.[54]

Maral Jefroudi was another contributor to this edited volume. She authored a study of the "Long Sixties", when the Iranian government, while introducing top-down economic and social reforms, also installed formidable barriers to independent trade unionism. In her article Jefroudi challenges the prevailing narrative in Iranian historiography that describes this period as one where state repression and/or structural deficiencies within the working class prevented workers from pursuing collective radical action. Instead, she argues that, on the contrary, it was the objective and subjective conditions of their class that led workers to engage in forms of collective action that would not antagonize the government nor jeopardize the benefits they had accrued as a result of social reforms. Furthermore, she maintains that, in general, workers' repertoires of collective action should be contextualized and analysed

---

50 Robabeh Motaghedi, "The Impact of the Oil Industry on Changing of the Subaltern Social Life in Southern Iranian Oilfields (1908–1932)" (Ph.D. dissertation, Alzahra University, 2013); Kaveh Ehsani, "The Social History of Labor in the Iranian Oil Industry: The Built Environment and the Making of the Industrial Working Class (1908–1941)" (Ph.D. dissertation, Leiden University, 2014).
51 Touraj Atabaki (ed.), "Writing the Social History of Labor in the Iranian Oil Industry", *International Labor and Working-Class History*, 84 (2013), pp. 154–217.
52 Touraj Atabaki, "From '*Amaleh* (Labor) to *Kargar* (Worker): Recruitment, Work Discipline and Making of the Working Class in the Persian/Iranian Oil Industry", *International Labor and Working-Class History*, 84 (2013), pp. 159–175.
53 For Lockman's argument see Zachary Lockman, "Imagining the Working Class: Culture, Nationalism, and Class Formation in Egypt, 1899–1914", *Poetics Today*, 15, 2 (1994), pp. 158–159.
54 Atabaki, "From '*Amaleh* (Labor) to *Kargar* (Worker)", pp. 170–173.

qualitatively rather than being juxtaposed with some idealized form of radical activism.[55]

Peyman Jafari's study of oil workers in the 1970s, a decade that ended with the Iranian Revolution of 1977–1979, was also published in this volume. Jafari's contribution to the history of the oil workers and revolution provided a picture of the institutional, socioeconomic, political, and cultural conditions among Iranian oil workers in the years preceding the Iranian Revolution and drew out the factors that explain their participation in that revolution. While questioning the prevailing notion of a "labour aristocracy" constructed by the oil workers, Jafari explores the mechanisms that contributed to the formation of control, conflict, and consent in the oil industry, and shows how these mechanisms created grievances among oil workers that resonated with the grievances of the subaltern classes in society at large.[56]

The history of oil workers, workers' migration, mobility, and transregional integration was examined in a number of articles. The agency of Indian migrant workers in the Iranian oil industry during the first half of the twentieth century, their ethno-religious identities, the recruitment process, their working conditions, terms of contract, and their experiences once they had been hired were studied in a recent publication by Atabaki.[57] The labour transregional integration during the First World War was the subject of a study conducted by Atabaki and Ehsani. They studied the global shift to oil from coal during the First World War, which paved the way for the new politico-economic regime of Fordism, characterizing mass industrial production and consumption under scientific labour management.[58]

Still on the same social history of labour track, Serhan Afacan wrote a Ph.D. on the social history of labour in the Iranian textile industry,[59] from the inception of the Constitutional Revolution until the end of Reza Shah's reign in 1941. What made Afacan's research very significant was not only his vast use of labourers' petitions, but also his view and conceptualization of labour, which went beyond the traditional and formal organized labour and collective labour action. In addition to studying factory workers, Afacan restored the agency of those workers employed in craft industries, as

---

[55] Maral Jefroudi, "Revisiting 'The Long Night' of Iranian Workers: Labor Activism in the Iranian Oil Industry in the 1960s", *International Labor and Working-Class History*, 84 (2013), pp. 176–194. Maral Jefroudi is a Ph.D. candidate affiliated to the oil project at the International Institute of Social History.
[56] Peyman Jafari, "Reasons to Revolt: Iranian Oil Workers in the 1970s", *International Labor and Working-Class History*, 84 (2013), pp. 195–217. Peyman Jafari is a Ph.D. candidate affiliated to the oil project at the International Institute of Social History.
[57] Touraj Atabaki, "Far from Home, But at Home: Indian Migrant Workers in the Iranian Oil Industry", *Studies in History*, 31, 1 (2015), pp. 85–114.
[58] Touraj Atabaki and Kaveh Ehsani, "Oil and Beyond: Expanding British Imperial Aspirations, Emerging Oil Capitalism, and the Challenge of Social Questions in the First World War", in: Helmut Bley and Anorthe Kremers (eds), *The World During the First World War* (Essen, 2014), pp. 261–287.
[59] Serhan Afacan, "State, Society and Labour in Iran, 1906–1941: A Social History of Iranian Industrialization and Labour with Reference to the Textile Industry" (Ph.D. dissertation, Leiden University, 2015).

well as considering throughout his study the diverse aspects of workers' lives other than their worksite experiences.

Missing gender components in the main trends in Iranian historiography, including the social historiography, Valentine Moghadam highlighted women's economic participation in Iran's "long twentieth century". According to Moghadam, Iranian peasants and working-class women have constituted a vast reserve of cheap labour not much different from child labour. Moreover, in her classification of labour, Moghadam brings domestic labour, servitude, and prostitution to the core of her missing agency in the historiography, although this very importance reference is never given adequate space in her study.[60] More on women's agency in the labour historiography and with a specific reference, Stephanie Cronin in her revisiting of the workers strike in the oil refinery of Abadan in 1929, when a large number of the strikers were brought to custody, highlights the position of wives of the striking workers when they rushed to the street, not only demanding the immediate discharge of their spouses, but also iterating their demands.[61]

Arriving at the 1977–1979 Revolution and the post-revolution period, Asef Bayat was a pioneer in conducting extensive fieldwork among workers in Tehran and the north-western city of Tabriz from 1980 to 1981.[62] As well as examining industrial relations in Iran, Bayat revisited post-revolution Iran through the lens of workers, and it is this that makes his study essential reading. His interviewees took part in the revolution, bringing down the monarchy, and set up councils (*Shura*) to control, though partially and temporarily, the workplaces, chiefly large factories. Some years later, in a chapter for Zachary Lockman's edited volume, Bayat introduced a new agency into the Iranian labour historiography: "Labor history, however, is not solely the domain of labor researchers; social historians, political scientists, leftist activists, and religious (Islamic) authorities have also commented on the history and behavior of the working classes."[63]

Another academic analysis of Iranian working-class agency in the 1977–1979 Revolution and after has been undertaken by Ahmad Ashraf. In his highly meticulous study, which is both quantitative and qualitative, he analyses the economic

---

[60] Valentine M. Moghadam, "Hidden from History? Women Workers in Modern Iran", *Iranian Studies*, 33, 3–4 (2000), pp. 377–401.
[61] Stephanie Cronin, "Popular Politics and the Birth of the Iranian Working Class: The 1929 Abadan Oil Refinery Strike", *Middle Eastern Studies*, 5 (2010), pp. 699–732.
[62] Asef Bayat, *Workers and Revolution in Iran: A Third World Experience of Workers' Control* (London, 1987). Valentine M. Moghadam is another historian who has studied working-class participation in the Iranian Revolution. Taking the city of Tabriz as her case study, she explores the reasons for the late conversion of Tabrizi's working class to revolutionary protest; it was, she argues, due to their relatively privileged status. See Val Moghadam, "Industrial Development, Culture and Working-Class Politics: A Case Study of Tabriz Industrial Workers in the Iranian Revolution", *International Sociology*, 2, 2 (1987), pp. 151–175.
[63] Asef Bayat, "Historiography, Class, and Iranian Workers", in: Zachary Lockman (ed.), *Workers and Working Classes in the Middle East: Struggles, Histories, Historiographies* (London, 1994), p. 165.

changes and developments that Iran experienced in the 1970s and the early post-revolutionary period and questions the revolutionary makeup of the Iranian working class.[64]

In a distinctive genre, through an interview with Amir, a truck driver, born in 1921, and his family, Fakhreddin Azimi gives a pictorial account of the Iranian labouring poor in the twentieth century. Amir Agha's narrative of everyday life prior to the Second World War and during the war, when Iran was occupied by Allied Forces, as well as his assessments of political movements and parties in the post-war period leading up to the 1977–1979 Revolution, is one of the few recollections by working people of the social and political changes that Iran went through in the twentieth century.[65]

The history of the Iranian working class in the post-revolutionary period is the subject of a study by Haideh Moghissi and Saeed Rahnema.[66] By reviewing the evolution of the Iranian working-class movement in the twentieth century, Moghissi and Rahnema arrive at the post-1977–1979 Revolution. The authors examine the configuration of the working people and give a detailed account of the employment, occupation, and gender composition of labour in mid-1990s. Finally, Moghissi and Rahnema turn to the Islamic government's "contentious preoccupations" labour policy since its establishment, and the resistance it encountered from the independent working-class movement and the civil society movement at large.

On post-revolutionary labour activism and the civil rights movement, Peyman Jafari has written two studies. In the first, he looks at the transformations in workers' socioeconomic conditions and labour activism during four distinctive periods: the Iran-Iraq War (1980–1988), the economic reconstruction under Ali Akbar Hashemi Rafsanjani (1989–1997), the reforms under Mohammad Khatami (1997–2005), and Mahmoud Ahmadinejad's neo-populism (2005–2013).[67] In the second, Jafari situates these transformations within processes of class re-formation, arguing that labour activism has become increasingly connected to broader forms of civil society activism and demands related to democratization, women's rights, and ecological sustainability.[68]

No review of studies by those engaged with the history of labour and the working class in Iran (Persia) would be complete without mentioning the documentary pub-

---

[64] Ahmad Ashraf, "Kalbod-shekafi Enqelab: Naqsh Kargaran San'ati dar Enqelab-e Iran" [Autopsy of Revolution: The Role of Industrial Workers in the Iranian Revolution], *Goftogou*, 55 (2010), pp. 55–123.
[65] Fakhreddin Azimi, "Amir Agha: An Iranian Worker", in: Edmund Burke, III (ed.), *Struggle and Survival in the Modern Middle East* (Berkeley, CA, 1993), pp. 290–304.
[66] Haideh Moghissi and Saeed Rahnema, "The Working Class and the Islamic State in Iran", *Socialist Register*, 37 (2001), pp. 197–218.
[67] Peyman Jafari, "Rupture and Revolt in Iran", *International Socialism*, 124 (2009), pp. 95–136.
[68] Sina Moradi (pseudonym), "Labour Activism and Democracy in Iran", Working Paper 22, Humanist Institute for Cooperation with Developing Countries, The Hague (July 2013).

lications by Cosroe Chaqueri. Although Chaqueri chiefly researched and published on the socialist and communist movements in Iran, his reprinted documents on the conditions of the working class in Iran from the early twentieth century to the 1977–1979 Revolution remain a major source for labour and social historians of modern Iran. These documents are derived from the national and diplomatic archives of the United States, Britain, Germany, and France, and to a lesser extent the former Marx-Engels-Lenin Institute in Moscow, and also include leaflets and pamphlets published by various political groups and parties.[69]

Labour historians and social historians of work studying modern Iran benefit from fictional prose narratives by Iranian novelists and short-story writers.[70] The surveying and analysis of this literature is the subject of another study and beyond the scope of the present essay. However, one cannot avoid mentioning just a few characteristic prototypes in this genre, by writers such as Ebrahim Golestan,[71] Ahmad Mahmoud,[72] Mahmoud Dowlatabadi,[73] Nasser Taghvai,[74] and last but not least Nasim Khaksar.[75]

Conclusion

To conclude this essay, and looking back at the almost one hundred years since the first chronicles and histories of labour and the working class in Iran (Persia) were written, surely one can acknowledge that Iranian labour historiography refashioned itself by adopting new theoretical and methodological avenues developed in the field of global labour history. For much of these one hundred years, the historiography of labour and the working class was associated with the history of the socialist movement. Moreover, crafted by an essentialist and teleological longing to revisit the past, the historiography of labour in Iran failed for a long time to explore new trajectories, where workers were more than urban, non-migrant, organized, factory-based, free, salaried, and Muslim males. Tracing the multiple identities of the working class has undoubtedly confronted the historian of Iranian labour and the working class with new challenges.

---

[69] Cosroe Chaqueri (ed.), *The Condition of the Working Class in Iran: A Documentary History*, 4 vols (Paris, 1989).
[70] For a survey of Persian fictional prose, see Faramarz Soltani, *Adabiyat-e Kargari. Iran dar Qarn-e Mo'aser* [Proletarian Literature: Iran in the Contemporary Century] (Tehran, 2008).
[71] Ebrahim Golestan, *Azar, Mah-e Akhar-e Paiz* [Azar, the Last Month of Autumn] (Tehran, 1969).
[72] Ahmad Mahmoud, *Bandar* [Harbour] (Tehran, 1993); *Hamsayeh-ha* [The Neighbours] (Tehran, 1974).
[73] Mahmoud Dowlatabadi, *Kelidar* (Tehran, 1977–1984).
[74] Nasser Taghvai, *Tabestan-e Haman Sal* [The Summer of That Year] (Tehran, 1969).
[75] Nasim Khaksar, *Man Midanam Bacheh-ha Doust Darnd Bahar Biyayad* [I Know Children Love the Spring to Come] (Tehran, 1973); idem, *Giyahak* (Tehran, 1979).

Suggested reading

Abrahamian, Ervand. *Iran Between Two Revolutions* (Princeton, NJ: Princeton University Press, 1982).
Ashraf, Ahmad. "State and Agrarian Relations Before and After the Iranian Revolution, 1960–1990", in: Farhad Kazemi and John Waterbury (eds), *Peasants and Politics in the Modern Middle East* (Gainesville, FL: University Press of Florida, 1991), pp. 277–311.
Atabaki, Touraj (ed.). "Writing the Social History of Labor in the Iranian Oil Industry", *International Labor and Working-Class History*, 84 (2013), pp. 154–217.
Atabaki, Touraj. "Time, Labour-Discipline and Modernization in Turkey and Iran: Some Comparative Remarks", in: *idem* (ed.), *The State and the Subaltern: Modernization, Society and the State in Turkey and Iran* (London, 2007), pp. 1–16.
Atabaki, Touraj. "Disgruntled Guests: Iranian Subaltern on the Margins of the Tsarist Empire", *International Review of Social History*, 48, 3 (2003), pp. 401–426.
Atabaki, Touraj and Marcel van der Linden (eds). "Twentieth Century Iran: History from Below", *International Review of Social History*, 48, 3 (2003), pp. 353–455.
Azimi, Fakhreddin. "Amir Agha: An Iranian Worker", in: Edmund Burke, III (ed.), *Struggle and Survival in the Modern Middle East* (Berkeley, 1993), pp. 290–304.
Bayat, Asef. *Street Politics. Poor People's Movements in Iran* (New York: Columbia University Press, 1997).
Bayat, Asef. *Workers and Revolution in Iran: A Third World Experience of Workers' Control* (London: Zed Books, 1987).
Chaqueri, Cosroe. *Origins of Social Democracy in Modern Iran* (Seattle, WA: University of Washington Press, 2001).
Chaqueri, Cosroe (ed.). *The Condition of the Working Class in Iran: A Documentary History*, 4 vols (Paris: Antidote, 1989).
Chehabi, H.E. and Vanessa Martin (eds). *Iran's Constitutional Revolution: Popular Politics, Cultural Transformations and Transnational Connections* (London: I.B. Tauris, 2010).
Cronin, Stephanie. "Popular Politics and the Birth of the Iranian Working Class: The 1929 Abadan Oil Refinery Strike", *Middle Eastern Studies*, 5 (2010), pp. 699–732.
Floor, Willem. *Guilds, Merchants, & Ulama in Nineteenth-Century Iran* (Washington, DC: Mage Publishers, 2009).
Floor, Willem. *Labor and Industry in Iran, 1850–1941* (Washington, DC: Mage Publishers, 2009).
Floor, Willem. *Labour Unions, Law, and Conditions in Iran (1900–1941)* (Durham: Centre for Middle Eastern and Islamic Studies, 1985).
Jafari, Peyman. "Rupture and Revolt in Iran", *International Socialism*, 124 (2009), pp. 95–136.
Kazemi, Farhad. "Peasant Uprisings in Twentieth-Century Iran, Iraq, and Turkey", in: *idem* and John Waterbury (eds), *Peasants and Politics in the Modern Middle East* (Gainesville, FL: University Press of Florida, 1991).
Kazemi, Farhad and Ervand Abrahamian. "The Nonrevolutionary Peasantry of Modern Iran", *Iranian Studies*, 11, 1–4 (1978), pp. 259–304.
Keyvani, Mehdi. *Artisans and Guild Life in the Later Safavid Period: Contributions to the Social-Economic History of Persia* (Berlin: Klaus Schwarz, 1982).
Ladjevardi, Habib. *Labour Unions and Autocracy in Iran* (Syracuse, NY: Syracuse University Press, 1985).
Lambton, Ann. *Landlord and Peasant in Persia: A Study of Land Tenure and Land Revenue Administration* (London: Oxford University Press, 1953; expanded edition London: I.B. Tauris, 1991).
Lambton, Ann. *The Persian Land Reform, 1962–1966* (Oxford: Clarendon Press, 1969).

Moghadam, Valentine M. "Hidden from History: Women Workers in Modern Iran", *Iranian Studies*, 33, 3–4 (2000), pp. 377–401.

Moghadam, Val. "Industrial Development, Culture and Working-Class Politics: A Case Study of Tabriz Industrial Workers in the Iranian Revolution", *International Sociology*, 2, 2 (1987), pp. 151–175.

Moghissi, Haideh and Saeed Rahnema. "The Working Class and the Islamic State in Iran", *Socialist Register*, 37 (2001), pp. 197–218.

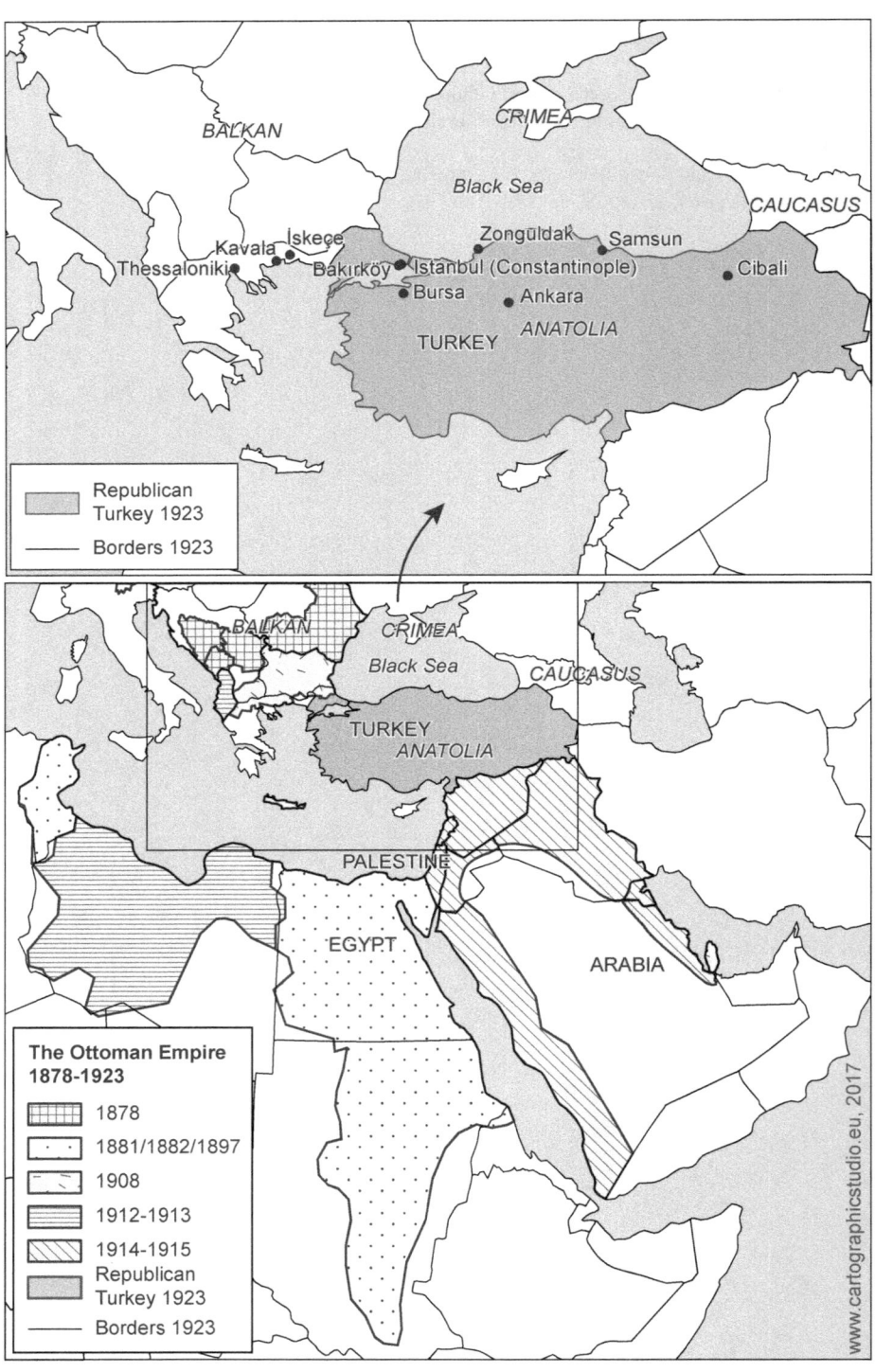

Gavin D. Brockett and Özgür Balkılıç
2.9. The Ottoman Middle East and Modern Turkey

The globalization of the "new" labour history ushered in by E.P. Thompson's *The Making of the English Working Class* began in the 1990s. Initially it featured scholarship on Asia, Africa, and Latin America while the region we know as the "Middle East" did not figure prominently. Since 2000, when since the International Institute for Social History in Amsterdam celebrated its 65th anniversary with a conference on Global Labour History, however, scholars have begun to publish widely on the social history of the Middle East and that has included studies related to workers, the working class and labour movements. Indeed in recent years there has been a steady growth in the number of articles by a new generation of Middle East scholars in journals devoted to labour history, as well as an increase in the number of articles about labour in journals dedicated to the Middle East. Monographs may be few and far between, but the foundational research on which they will be based in the future is most certainly underway in universities both in the Middle East and beyond.

The very term "Middle East" increasingly poses a problem not only because of post-modern, post-colonial critiques of assumptions long held in western academia, but because those who live in the region rarely if ever identify with the term. Whatever their ethnic or national identity, there is little evidence that people from Morocco to Iran see themselves as part of the cohesive entity that has become commonly referred to as the Middle East. Today, as scholars from these countries make important contributions to the social sciences and humanities – writing in both English and in their native languages – they prefer to be identified with their countries of origin or with specific ethnic communities. Well versed in their fields they make important contributions both methodologically – often able to locate and work with sources to a degree that others cannot – and theoretically. They bring to their subjects a distinct perspective that is invaluable to the continued growth and development of global labour history.

The birth of modern nation-states in the Middle East in the first half of the twentieth-century gave rise to powerful nationalist narratives notable for a deceptive simplicity that denied not only the complex social and cultural elements that constituted each country, but also the historical legacy of the Ottoman Empire which had incorporated the region for centuries before. However it is fair to say that the expansion of social history as a field within Middle East studies has been integral to the disruption of these narratives: recognition of a common Ottoman past and a deeper understanding of social and economic forces challenges a representation of history that so far has been dominated by national politics and a narrow group of elite actors. Significantly the emergence of Middle Eastern social history has coincided with increasingly profound political changes underway throughout the region. Just what will comprise the new histories that must – sooner or later – replace the old narratives as a result of the tumult that has engulfed the region since 2011 remains to be seen.

Ottoman labour history

The Ottoman Empire was a dynamic multi-ethnic, multi-religious state centred on the city of Istanbul (Constantinople) following its capture in 1453. Ruled by what was originally the Turkish "Ottoman" dynasty, at its height in the sixteenth-century it incorporated diverse regions that included the Anatolian peninsula; the Balkans and much of south eastern Europe; the Crimea and the Caucasus; the Fertile Crescent, Arabia and North Africa. Gradually the historiography of what was one of the most important empires in world history has shifted away from a focus upon elites in Istanbul, first to their counterparts in the provinces, and then, more recently, to ordinary people both in Istanbul and beyond. Increasingly we see that over the six hundred years of its existence, the Ottoman Empire's history encompassed an extraordinary range of experiences that can be understood from a rich variety of perspectives.

Historians of the Ottoman Empire are indebted to the late Halil İnalcık (1916 – 2016), whose vast oeuvre is unparalleled. Significantly, Inalcik not only altered our understanding of the Ottoman state and its institutions, but laid the groundwork for an Ottoman social history that would extend beyond the imperial court in Istanbul to incorporate people of all types throughout the empire's diverse provinces. As he noted in 1978, İnalcık had been deeply influenced by the *Annales* school as well as the seminal work of the demographer Ömer Lutfi Barkan.[1] Together with the social historian Suraiya Faroqhi and the economic historian Huri Islamoğlu, İnalcık trained multiple generations of Ottoman social historians whose burgeoning work is now reshaping our understanding of the Mediterranean world and the Middle East.[2]

Within the corpus of literature devoted to Ottoman social history is an impressive array of studies that reflect the priorities of the new labour history and that contribute to the foundation on which global labour history itself must be based. Contrary to the long-dominant notion of Ottoman "decline" and economic stagnation after the sixteenth century – one derived from Ottoman political narratives viewed through an Orientalist lens – this research offers rich insight into the lives of people and the nature of their work. Guilds as an expression of "organized labour", and slave labour, for example, have become popular fields of research promoted by both estab-

---

[1] Halil İnalcık, "The Impact of the *Annales* School on Ottoman Studies and New Findings", *Review* 1, 3–4 (Winter-Spring 1978), pp. 69–96.
[2] For a recent discussion of the state of Middle East social history see the roundtable discussions in the *International Journal of Middle East Studies*, 46 (2014).

lished and younger historians.³ As is so important in Ottoman studies, these topics are now understood in terms of specific regions, social groups and time periods, making possible in the future comparisons within the empire as well as with other forms of organized and unfree labour in other parts of the world.

Gender too has become an important analytical framework, and various studies illustrate the axes along which Ottoman labour history is now being written. Madeline Zilfi argues for the significance of previously invisible women as slave labour in the eighteenth and nineteenth centuries throughout the empire. By contrast, Fariba Zarinebaf-Shahr concentrates on Istanbul and women who contributed to the urban imperial economy in various sectors, and the challenges this posed to the established guild system.⁴ A recent edited volume on women in the latter years of the Ottoman Empire includes three essays, each with a noteworthy focus: one concentrates on minority women (Armenian) working in theatre; a second adopts a provincial perspective when examining Thessaloniki women employed in tobacco workshops; while the third considers ethno-religious distinctions among women employed to produce fezes both in factories and at home in Istanbul.⁵

Just as social history has shifted the focus beyond Istanbul as metropolitan centre, so too a major contribution of Ottoman labour history is to provide new narratives that elaborate on lived experiences of work in the provinces. The contribution of the environmental historian Alan Mikhail is particularly promising in this regard.⁶ His focus upon eighteenth and nineteenth-century Egypt explores the changing relationship between human and animal labour in the context of widespread disease that led to human labour becoming much cheaper than that of animals. At a time when wealthy provincial elites were accumulating more land and establishing their independence from Istanbul, this transformation led to the emergence of corvée

---

3 Onur Yıldırım, "Ottoman Guilds in the Early Modern Era", *International Review of Social History*, 53 (2008), Supplement 16, pp. 73–93; Cengiz Kırlı, "A Profile of the Labor Force in Early Nineteenth-Century Istanbul", *International Labor and Working Class History*, 60 (2001), pp. 125–140; Ehud Toledano, *As If Silent. Bonds of Enslavement in the Islamic Middle East* (New Haven, CT, 2007); Eve Troutt Powell, *Tell This in my Memory. Stories of Enslavement from Egypt, Sudan and the Ottoman Empire* (Stanford, 2012); Paul Auchterlonie, "Surviving as a Slave: The Economic Reality of Life as a European Slave in Ottoman North Africa, 1600–1820", *Maghreb Review: Majallat al-Maghrib*, 40, 4 (2015), pp. 445–472.

4 Madeline Zilfi, *Women and Slavery in the Late Ottoman Empire: The Design of Difference* (Cambridge, 2010); Fariba Zarinebaf-Shahr, "The Role of Women in the Urban Economy of Istanbul, 1700–1850", *International Labor and Working Class History*, 60 (2001), pp. 141–152.

5 See: Hasmik Khalapyan, "Theater as Career for Ottoman Armenian Women, 1850–1910"; E. Tutku Vardağlı, "Searching for Women's Agency in the Tobacco Workshops: Female Tobacco Workers of the Province of Selanik"; and M. Erdem Kabadayı, "Working from Home: Division of Labor among Female Workers of Feshane in Late Nineteenth Century-Istanbul", in: Duygu Köksal and Anastasia Falierou (eds), *A Social History of Late Ottoman Women: New Perspectives* (Leiden and Boston, 2013).

6 Alan Mikhail, "Unleashing the Beast: Animals, Energy, and the Economy of Labor in Ottoman Egypt", *American Historical Review*, 118 (2013), pp. 317–348; Alan Mikhail, "Labour and Environment in Egypt since 1500", *International Labor and Working Class History*, 85 (2014), pp. 10–32.

and the establishment of vast contingents of forced labour to undertake the development of infrastructure related to transportation and irrigation.

Mikhail's use of a wide variety of sources that included local Egyptian court records and estate inventories to reconstruct the history of rural peasants and transformations in labour relations is indicative of the direction Ottoman labour history is now taking. Less than two decades ago, Donald Quataert pointed out the difficulties of overcoming an elite-centred focus infused by the modernization paradigm, but much has happened in the intervening years. Imperial sources rarely paid sufficient attention to the "stuff of labour history" in terms of information about workers, their wages and their social relations.[7] However, as social history has opened up new sources so too labour historians are using them as well. The challenge of course comes from efforts to develop sufficient data sets that can be used to make generalizations not only within the immediate locale but across a province or the entire empire in order to make comparisons with circumstances in other polities around the globe.[8]

Donald Quataert and Middle East labour history

That historians of the Ottoman Empire are now tackling these challenges can be attributed in large part to the influence of Quataert (1941–2011), whose research concentrated on the tumultuous late nineteenth and early twentieth-centuries. Aggressive colonial expansion on the part of European powers combined with nascent nationalist movements in the Balkans severely reduced the amount of territory over which the Ottomans could claim control. Nationalism began to gain currency among Muslims and Christians even in the Anatolian heartland and Arab provinces. A political system undergoing transformation resulted in intense elite rivalries as well as challenges to the very sovereignty of the Sultan. At which time, incorporation of the empire into the world economy had considerable impact on both farmers and urban labourers leading to considerable social unrest and forms of collective action that burst onto the public scene with the Young Turk Revolution of 1908, and that would foreshadow the emergence of labour movements in Ottoman successor states in the twentieth century.[9]

---

[7] Donald Quataert, "Labor History and the Ottoman Empire, c. 1700–1922", *International Labor and Working Class History*, 60 (2001), pp. 93–109.

[8] For instance the work of Hülya Canbakal is particularly interesting as she has participated in the International Institute for Social History's Global Collaboratory on Labour Relations. Hülya Canbakal, *Society and Politics in an Ottoman Town: Ayntab in the 17th Century* (Leiden and Boston, 2006).

[9] Reşat Kasaba, *The Ottoman Empire and the World Economy: The Nineteenth Century* (Albany, NY, 1988). E. Attila Aytekin, "Peasant Protest in the Late Ottoman Empire: Moral Economy, Revolt and the Tanzimat Reforms", *International Review of Social History*, 57, 2 (2012), pp. 191–227.

As a recent issue of *Comparative Studies of South Asia, Africa and the Middle East* demonstrates, Quataert's influence was profound.[10] Without his efforts Ottoman labour history would still be very much in its infancy. A professor at SUNY Binghamton, Quataert was dedicated to "history from below" and he trained numerous future scholars to examine the lives of ordinary workers, artisans and peasants through the creative use of primary sources that extended beyond official records typically found in the imperial Ottoman archives. Quataert's research initially concentrated on manufacturing and popular resistance to economic disruption at the end of empire.[11] Towards the conclusion of his career, however, he had the good fortune to stumble across a substantial trove of Ottoman records related to the lives of coal miners in the Black Sea city of Zonguldak in the nineteenth and early twentieth centuries.[12] In between, Quataert authored a number of seminal works on Ottoman social and economic history.[13]

Quataert set the agenda for Ottoman and Turkish labour history, working closely with colleagues at the International Institute for Social History in Amsterdam. In 1995, he and Eric Jan Zürcher co-edited *Workers and the Working Class in the Ottoman Empire and the Turkish Republic, 1839–1950* in which they established the importance of a labour framework for overcoming the normally discrete histories of the Ottoman Empire and republican Turkey.[14] The one did not inevitably dissolve into the other; rather, the study of workers, labour organizations, and collective action by workers allows scholars to explore both continuities and distinctions between the two polities. In that early volume, Quataert called for a broader research agenda to include the difficult topic of ethnicity at a time when the very foundations of the Ottoman state were under siege. Since that time, Quataert has inspired scholars to pursue an ever-wider variety of subjects related to labour as evident in two issues of *International Labour and Working Class History* (ILWCH) that he edited. In 2001, this included articles related to coal heavers in Egypt, female workers in Istanbul, coal miners in Zonguldak, and the very question of how to define the Ottoman "work-

---

10 See a set of articles devoted to the memory of Quataert in *Comparative Studies of South Asia, Africa and the Middle East* 34, 1 (2014). Included in this is the text of a lecture delivered by Quataert shortly before his death in which he describes his life-long commitment to social and labour history: "History from Below and the Writing of Ottoman History."
11 Donald Quataert, *Social Disintegration and Popular Resistance in the Ottoman Empire, 1881–1908: Reactions to European Economic Penetration* (New York, 1983); Quataert, *Ottoman Manufacturing in the Age of the Industrial Revolution* (Cambridge, 1993); Quataert, *Manufacturing in the Ottoman Empire and Turkey, 1500–1950* (Albany, NY, 1994).
12 Donald Quataert, *Miners and the State in the Ottoman Empire. The Zonguldak Coalfield, 1822–1920* (New York, 2006).
13 Donald Quataert and Halil İnalcık (eds), *An Economic and Social History of the Ottoman Empire, 1300–1914* (Cambridge, 1994).
14 Donald Quataert and Erik Jan Zürcher (eds), *Workers and the Working Class in the Ottoman Empire and the Turkish Republic, 1839–1950* (London, 1995).

er."[15] In 2011, just before he died, Quataert coedited with Prasannan Parthasarathi an issue devoted to migrant labour, showing just how far the field had come since Quataert had begun his work in the 1960s.[16]

Late Ottoman labour history

In Middle East history, one of the most enduring debates concerns the question: at what point did nation-state formation in fact begin and the viability of an Ottoman Empire end? Contrary to the religious-nationalist rhetoric of recent decades, "Turkey" does not have an exclusive claim over the Ottoman legacy, nor was its emergence inevitable with the demise of the empire. Rather it was born out of popular resistance to European plans to divide and claim parts of Anatolia between 1919 and 1922, and the new Turkish state soon found definition in *opposition* to its Ottoman heritage. The inter-war years were characterized by authoritarian government led by Mustafa Kemal Atatürk (1923–1938), during which time public dissent from the official ethnic nationalism was not tolerated. Neither religious, ethnic-minority, nor class-based labour movements had the freedom to engage in national politics.

After 1945, political changes led to a multi-party system that has remained the norm despite numerous interventions by the military in an effort to stabilize the country amidst volatile and sometimes violent political and social conflict. Leftist intellectuals and labour organizations both contributed to, and were the victims of, the tumult. Initially there was an expansion of leftist media that supported a labour movement determined to remain loyal to the Turkish nation. In the context of the Cold War, however, these were quickly censored as agents of communism. The 1960s and 1970s witnessed increasingly intense conflict between leftists and ultra-nationalists as well as an increasingly active labour movement that organized strikes at factories, especially in Istanbul. Ultimately a military coup in 1980 resulted in the harsh suppression of both leftists and labour activists, and the emergence of a new religious-nationalist ideology upon which the success of Turkey's ruling Justice and Development Party since 2002 has been based.

Labour history offers one means to trace the contours of the transformation from empire to nation state, not only in Turkey but in all Ottoman successor states. Viewed from the perspective of ordinary people engaged in various forms of work to sustain

---

[15] The following articles appeared in Number 60 (Fall 2001) of *ILWCH*: Donald Quataert, "Labor History and the Ottoman Empire, c. 1700–1922"; Donald Quataert and Yüksel Duman, "A Coal Miner's Life during the Late Ottoman Empire"; Fariba Zarinebaf-Shahr, "The Role of Women in the Urban Economy of Istanbul, 1700–1850"; Cengiz Kırlı, "A Profile of the Labor Force in Early Nineteenth-Century Istanbul"; and, John Chalcraft, "The Coal Heavers of Port Sa'id: State-Making and Worker Protest, 1869–1914."

[16] See Prasannan Parthasarathi and Donald Quataert, "Migrant Workers in the Middle East: Introduction", *International Labor and Working Class History*, 79 (2011), pp. 4–6.

their own existence, the picture becomes far richer – and more complex – than the nationalist narratives would suggest. The extent of literature on labour history in each of these states varies considerably but the new generation of scholars inspired by the likes of Donald Quataert is fast making its mark. At the global labour history conference organized by the International Institute for Social History in 2000, Zachary Lockman effectively delineated labour historiography as it related specifically to Palestine, Israel and Egypt.[17] Since that time there has been a noticeable growth in the labour historiography of these countries. Subjects of study range from an interest among historians in forced labour – labour battalions in World War I in particular – to questions concerning ethnicity, gender and labour, as well as those about the relationship between labour and the Arab Spring.[18] Particularly noteworthy is recognition that labour migration is relevant both today and historically: migration of ethnic groups *to* Gulf countries or Israel for instance, as well as migration of people from many Middle Eastern countries – especially from, but not limited to, Turkey – to parts of Europe.[19]

More recently, in 2009, Touraj Atabaki and Gavin Brockett edited a volume[20] that introduced the new generation of Turkish labour historians whose work contrasts distinctly with the essays published in the volume edited by Quataert and Zürcher

---

[17] Zachary Lockman, "Reflections on Labour and Working-Class History in the Middle East and North Africa" in Jan Lucassen (ed.), *Global Labour History. A State of the Art* (New York, 2006), pp. 117–146.

[18] Kyle J. Anderson, "The Egyptian Labor Corps: Workers, Peasants, and the State in World War I", *International Journal of Middle East Studies*, 49, 1 (2017), pp. 5–24; F. Umut Beşpinar, "Questioning Agency and Empowerment: Women's Work-Related Strategies and Social Class in Urban Turkey", *Women's Studies International Forum*, 33, 6 (2010), pp. 523–532; Barbara Curli, "Dames Employées at the Suez Canal Company: The 'Egyptianization' of Female Office Workers, 1941–56", *International Journal of Middle East Studies*, 46, 3 (2014), pp. 553–576; Sami Zemni, Brecht de Smet and Koenraad Bogaert, "Luxemburg on Tahrir Square: Reading the Arab Revolutions with Rosa Luxemburg's *The Mass Strike*", *Antipode*, 45, 4 (2013), pp. 888–907; Joel Beinin, "Egyptian Workers and January 25th: A Social Movement in Historical Context", *Social Research*, 79, 2 (2012), pp. 323–348; Moshe Sharabi, "The Meaning of Work among Jews and Arabs in Israel: The Influence of Ethnicity, Ethnic Conflict, and Socio-Economic Variables", *International Social Science*, 61, 202 (2010), pp. 501–510.

[19] Liat Kozma, "Women's Migration for Prostitution in the Interwar Middle East and North Africa", *Journal of Women's History*, 28, 3 (Fall 2016), pp. 93–113; Linda Andersson and Mats Hammarstedt, "Ethnic Enclaves, Networks and Self-Employment among Middle Eastern Immigrants in Sweden", *International Migration*, 53, 6 (2015), pp. 27–40; Bina Fernandez, "Traffickers, Brokers, Employment Agents, and Social Networks: The Regulation of Intermediaries in the Migration of Ethiopian Domestic Workers to the Middle East", *International Migration Review*, 47, 4 (2013), pp. 814–843; Marko Valenta and Jo Jakobsen, "Moving to the Gulf: An Empirical Analysis of the Patterns and Drivers of Migration to the GCC Countries, 1960–2013", *Labor History*, 57, 5 (2016), pp. 627–648; Adrianna Kemp and Rebecca Raijman, "Bringin in State Regulations, Private Brokers and Local Employers: A Meso-Level Analysis of Labor Trafficking in Israel", *International Migration Review*, 48, 3 (2014), pp. 604–642.

[20] Touraj Atabaki and Gavin D. Brockett (eds), *Ottoman and Republican Turkish Labour History*. International Review of Social History Supplement 17 (Cambridge, 2009).

in 1995. These new historians may themselves have been inspired by public debate and activism on university campuses, however of equal if not more importance was the opportunity they had had to engage with the intellectual trends of global labour history outside of their country.[21] Indeed most of today's new generation of Turkish labour historians were heavily influenced by Donald Quataert if not trained by him. Many studied at SUNY Binghamton, while others worked at the International Institute for Social History or studied at the Atatürk Institute for Modern Turkish History at Boğaziçi University.[22]

In the last two decades these scholars have published studies of labour history spanning the final years of the Ottoman Empire and the rise of an active labour movement in Turkey through the 1970s. Significantly, the one period that has largely been neglected is the 1920s when Atatürk was consolidating his hold over the new Turkey. A number of the scholars work on both polities and so we see similar, if not identical characteristics in the scholarship.

Among the scholars of the late Ottoman Empire there is a desire to explain large scale economic, political, cultural and social transformations that impacted but were also shaped by ordinary people rather than simply by political and social elites. Their studies concentrate on workers of all sorts: male and female, skilled and unskilled, Turkish-Muslim and non-Turkish-Muslim, migrant and local employees. These were employed in different factories, companies, and mines including: the Cibali Regie Factory; the Imperial Naval Arsenal in Istanbul; several tobacco factories in İstanbul, İskeçe, Kavala, Thessalonika and Samsun;[23] the Fez Factory in İstanbul; and the Zonguldak mines.[24] Typically the history narrated is that of working class identity formation as workers engaged in acts of resistance that asserted their rights against those of the state.[25]

---

21 Çetinkaya argues that ideology and political activism on university campuses is the primary force behind the emergence of the labour history in Turkey. Y. Doğan Çetinkaya, "Sefaletten İhyaya: Türkiye İşçi Sınıfı Tarihi ve E. P. Thompson", [From Poverty to Rejuvenation: History of the Working Class in Turkey and E. P. Thompson] *Tarih ve Toplum*, 17 (Spring 2014), pp. 201–221.
22 Leading scholars at the Atatürk Institute were trained by Quataert at SUNY Binghamton.
23 Can Nacar, "Labor Activism and the State in the Ottoman Tobacco Industry", *International Journal of the Middle East Studies*, 46, 3 (2014), pp. 533–551; Nacar, "The Regie Monopoly and Tobacco Workers in Late Ottoman Istanbul" *Comparative Studies of South Asia, Africa and the Middle East*, 34, 1 (2014), pp. 206–219; Nacar. "Tobacco Workers in the Late Ottoman Empire: Fragmentation, Conflict and Collective Struggle" (PhD Dissertation, State University of New York at Binghamton, 2010); E. Tutku Vardağlı, "Searching for Women's Agency in the Tobacco Workshops: Female Tobacco Workers of the Province of Selanik"; Vardağlı, "Tobacco Labor Politics in the Ottoman Thessaloniki Province: Cross-Communal and Cross-Gender Relations" (PhD Dissertation, Boğaziçi Üniversitesi, 2011); Akın Sefer, "From Class Solidarity to Revolution: The Radicalization of Arsenal Workers in the Late Ottoman Empire", *International Review of Social History*, 58, 3 (December 2013), pp. 395–428.
24 Nurşen Gürboğa, *Mine Workers, the Single Party Rule, and War* (İstanbul, 2009).
25 Nurşen Gürboğa "The Şirket-i Hayriye Pension Fund, Right to Retirement and Labor Control (1893–1932)", in: Selim Karahasanoğlu and Deniz Cenk Demir (eds), *History from Below. A Tribute in Memory of Donald Quataert* (İstanbul, 2016).

Unlike studies of republican Turkey, those that concentrate on the end of empire do explore the importance of ethno-religious and gender identities. They do so as they consider the intersection between these factors and the experiences of workers: their relations with employers; their sense of belonging to an emerging labour movement; their shared experiences on the shop-floor in the work place; the hierarchy of work in different environments; and their solidarity and/or fragmentation in the context of collective resistances. Gülhan Balsoy, for example, explains how gender values affected labour relations and were reproduced in the Cibali Fez Factory by looking at the women's photographs taken while they were working on the shop floor. When analyzing the hierarchy and organization of work in the factory, she asserts that the factory departments and labour process were mainly organized according to gender.[26] Can Nacar focuses on ethno-religious networks in understanding the labour movement in the tobacco industry in the late Ottoman Empire;[27] while Erdem Kabadayı concludes that religious and gender identities accounted for the divisions of labour in the Feshane fez factory based on an analysis of the workers' wage ledgers.[28]

Republican Turkish labour history

Compared with studies on the last years of the Ottoman Empire, labour historiography related to the Republican Turkey is less prolific as well as less well-developed, due in part to the limited availability of sources. However it is in studies of republican Turkish labour that we also see clearly the impact of this new generation's agenda: to reject earlier old-school historians who had argued that working class consciousness did not emerge until the 1960s, and that employees – in state enterprises that dominated large-scale industry in the 1930s – constituted their own "labour aristocracy" that allegedly undercut class identities.[29] Instead the new genera-

---

26 Gülhan Balsoy, "Gendering Ottoman Labour History: The Cibali Régie Factory in the Early Twentieth Century", in: Atabaki and Brockett, *Ottoman and Republican Turkish Labour History*, pp. 45–68.
27 Can Nacar, " 'Our Lives Were Not As Valuable As An Animal': Workers in State –Run Industries in World-War-II Turkey", in: Atabaki and Brockett, *Ottoman and Republican Turkish Labour History*, pp. 143–167.
28 M. Erdem Kabadayı, "Working for the State in a Factory in Istanbul: The Role of Factory Workers' Ethno-Religious and Gender Characteristics in State-Subject Interaction in the Late Ottoman Empire" (Ph.D. Dissertation, Ludwig Maximilian University, 2008); Kabadayı. "Working from Home: Division of Labor among Female Workers of Feshane in Late Nineteenth-Century Istanbul"; Kabadayı, "Working in a Fez Factory in Istanbul in the Late Nineteenth Century: Division of Labour and Networks of Migration Formed along Ethno-Religious Lines", in: Atabaki and Brockett, *Ottoman and Republican Turkish Labour History*, pp. 69–91.
29 Yıldırım Koç, *Türkiye İşçi Sınıfı Tarihi: Osmanlı'dan 2010'a* [History of the Working Class in Turkey: From the Ottomans to 2010] (Ankara, 2010); M. Şehmus Güzel, *İşçiler Örgütleniyor (1939–1950)* [The Workers are Organizing] (İstanbul, 2016).

tion not only argues for the existence of workers as important social actors in political and social events, but they also examine how workers perceived, experienced and acted upon different stages in the emergence of capitalist social relations. The foci of these scholars include both the state's changing role in reconfiguring social relations – such as defining its subjects as citizens and granting certain rights to them – and, how collective groups of workers took shape as a result of all these transformations. Thus, their commitment to explain workers' s roles in the complex social order as well as a shared consciousness among workers is a radical departure from the previous generation of labour historians who generally asserted the existence of a pre-defined and ideal worker consciousness which was assumed to be devoted to overthrowing capitalism as defined by a narrow reading of socialist ideology.

When analyzing agricultural labour, the primary scholarly objective has been to explain the ways in which small landholders – as the most important group of peasants – lived through marketization of the rural economy and the state's increasing efforts to regulate rural life at a time when governments hoped to cultivate political support among peasants even as they were beginning to migrate to urban centres.[30] However, the majority of scholarship devoted to labour history in Turkey has concentrated on the industrial labour force. Once again the Zonguldak mines are the subject of study: they offer the opportunity to explore a number of themes, including forced convict labour and migrant labour.[31] However it is the variety of studies devoted to factories that is noteworthy. Görkem Akgöz and Can Nacar explore state-owned enterprises in the Bakırköy cotton factory and Sümerbank and Etibank companies between 1930 and 1950.[32] By contrast, Özgür Balkılıç and Can Taştan deal with class formation and conflicts in the new private metal hardware sector, again, after World War II: Balkılıç's unit of study is the whole metal sector in Istanbul between 1945 and 1970, while Taştan's study is of one important factory of the sector, namely Arçelik Factory, from the beginning of its foundation in the mid-1950s to 1980.[33]

---

[30] Murat Metinsoy, "İkinci Dünya Savaşı Yıllarında Devlet ve Köylüler: Hububat Alımları, Toprak Mahsülü Vergisi ve Köylü Direnişi", *Tarih Ve Toplum*, 15 (Autumn 2012), pp. 127–146; Sinan Yıldırmaz, *Politics and Peasantry in Post-War Turkey: Social History, Culture and Modernization* (London, 2016); Yıldırmaz, "From "Imaginary" to "Real": A Social History of Peasantry in Turkey (1945–1960)" (PhD Thesis, Boğaziçi Üniversitesi, 2009).

[31] Ali Sipahi, "Convict Labor in Turkey, 1936–1953: A Capitalist Corporation in the State?", *International Labor and Working Class History*, 90 (2016), pp. 244–265; Erol Kahveci, "The Condition of the Ottoman Mine Labour and Its Impact on the Republican Period", *Middle Eastern Studies*, 51, 5 (2015), pp. 711–726; Kahveci, "Migration, Ethnicity, and Divisions of Labour in the Zonguldak Coalfield, Turkey", *International Review of Social History*, 60, 2 (2015), pp. 207–226.

[32] Nacar, "'Our Lives Were Not As Valuable As An Animal'"; Görkem Akgöz, "Many Voices of a Turkish State Factory: Working at Bakırköy Cloth Factory" (PhD Dissertation, University of Amsterdam, 2012).

[33] Özgür Balkılıç, "For the Union Makes Us Strong: The Istanbul Metal Workers and Their Struggle For Unionization in Turkey, 1947–1970" (PhD Dissertation, Wilfrid Laurier University, 2015); Onur Can

Hakan Koçak's study spans a much longer time span: he focuses on the Paşabahçe Glass Factory from its establishment in the mid-1930s in Istanbul to the present.[34] Finally, Barış Alp Özden's study adopts a much broader focus to explore daily practices and public discourses among Istanbul's working class between 1945 and 1960. His study devotes particular attention to the lived experiences of workers beyond their factories.[35]

State-led industrial enterprises had a measured impact on Turkish society prior to 1935, but it was after World War II that the impact of industrialization was most notable especially in terms of unprecedented levels of internal migration from the countryside to provincial urban centres, and from the provinces to Istanbul. Each of these studies takes into account the place of migrant workers in the Turkish labour. They consider the realities experienced by both local and migrant workers who lived in the vicinity of their workplaces, and the bitter housing problem facing newcomers. Workers responded to these challenges by building squatter houses around the factories, and these in turn fostered their class solidarity. The resulting neighbourhoods and rising new class culture in these spaces became important networks through which workers formed their own identities and further consolidated their sense of unity. [36]

These studies place a considerable emphasis on the implementation of modern management and organizational techniques, as well as state legal structures regulating industrial enterprises; by contrast those that focus on the late Ottoman period concentrate more on efforts to discipline labour and coercively maintain a work force in order to operate industrial enterprises. The important point is that historians of republican Turkey not only analyze how these interventions were devised by state-bureaucratic elites and private employers, but they also question how they were actually implemented in the work places. This allows consideration of how workers perceived, resisted and/or used such interventions for their own purposes. For example, they analyze employers' changing managerial tactics, including work place organizations and workers' incentives to influence the labour force, as well as various tactics by workers to resist individually or collectively. They also weave their narratives around the institutionalization of labour relations and new legal regulations after the foundation of the Republic by looking at how the workers perceived all these transformations, both challenging them and capitalizing upon them simultaneously to improve their own work and life conditions.

Taştan, "Türkiye'de Metal Sektöründe Fabrika Rejimi Mücadeleleri: 1960–1980 Dönemi Arçelik Örneği" (PhD Dissertation, Ankara Üniversitesi, 2016).
34 M. Hakan Koçak, *Camın İşçileri: Paşabahçe İşçilerinin Sınıf Olma Öyküsü* (İstanbul, 2014).
35 Barış Alp Özden, "Working Class Formation in Turkey, 1946–1962" (PhD Dissertation, Boğaziçi Üniversitesi, 2011).
36 Barış Alp Özden, "Health, Morality and Housing: The Politics of Working Class Housing in Turkey, 1945–1960", *New Perspectives on Turkey*, 49 (2013), pp. 91–120

Consequently, we learn a considerable amount about not only the workplace but also about the very real challenges workers faced in daily life whether in terms of obtaining adequate housing or health care, even if the workers' families themselves remain largely obscured from view. In addition to their shared problems at work and in daily life, different factors – such as their place of origin, gender, and structures of hierarchy in the work place – had an impact on working class identity. At times these factors might foster a collective identity among all workers, while at others they might support more specific group identities that would interfere with an over-arching shared consciousness. While this might have led a failure of collective action in some instances, the tendency is for researchers to concentrate on how these different factors forged workers' collective identities and led to the success of their actions.

To write this history and to give voice to ordinary people, these scholars have had to resort to a variety of non-conventional sources that include: photographs and post-cards; petitions and police archives; oral history databases and interviews; factory inspectors' reports; memoirs; foreign consular reports; newspapers and journals; factory documents in company archives; trade union archives and publications; parliamentary records; provincial yearbooks; and census data. However, the availability of these resources for particular periods and particular enterprises varies greatly. For example, Özgür Balkılıç, in his study of workers employed in the private metal sector in Istanbul after the Second World War, could not locate what surely would have been invaluable sources such as factory archives and Ministry of Labour archives; what he was able to find in terms of both state archival material and documents from union archives was limited. The result being a very incomplete picture of the daily life of workers in the factory and at home, as well as a limited understanding of the thoughts and experiences of those who played a less role prominent in collective action. By contrast, Görkem Akgöz was extremely fortunate to have access to substantial materials in state archives – not typically available to the researcher – with relation to the Bakırköy textile factory in Istanbul. Examining workers' petitions, speeches and personal accounts, she is able to reconstruct with some success the personal lives of workers and their engagement with discourses of both nation building and class politics.

All in all, this new generation of historians has had as its main concern the illumination of the real, tangible experiences of the labouring classes in the past. They narrate the ways in which ordinary people worked within and pushed against structural constraints in an industrializing Turkey. They have granted workers human agency, as such making significant strides towards fulfilling Quataert's agenda of doing history from below in order to gain a more comprehensive picture of late Ottoman and early republican Turkish history.

Global Labour History in Turkey

As practitioners of the new labour history, they work in opposition to the Eurocentric modernization paradigm that assumed power was largely reserved for the state and a few among the elite. Gradually they are formulating explanations for the emergence of working class identities and consciousness beginning in the last decade of Ottoman rule and continuing through the first decades of the Turkish Republic. In so doing they are beginning to engage the larger global discourse about labour history that includes not only collective action in the workplace but life beyond it and even beyond the workers themselves. Their conclusions will enable historians of Turkey to enter into conversation with colleagues whose interests may be in other parts of the world but who look to make comparisons and understand differences.

Global labour history in the Turkish context, however, has a long way to go when current scholarship is viewed in light of the agenda set out by its leading proponent, Marcel van der Linden, almost twenty years ago.[37] The nation-state remains very much the primary framework for analysis and comparative work remains rare. This applies whether we are talking about comparisons between workplaces or industries within Turkey, or between workplaces in Turkey and those in other countries. To be sure scholars are conscious that they must acknowledge the transnational contexts of unions and companies, but a willingness or ability to engage the broader field is limited. Similarly, the scholarship is marked by a rather sterile commitment to history alone: engagement with other disciplines such as sociology or ethnology is extremely rare. Finally these scholars are working not from a wealth of data, but typically from fragmentary records that are hard come by. In Turkey records related to labour and industrial enterprises are extremely difficult to find: state archives make available only very limited collections related to state enterprises, while all too often the records related to private enterprises have not survived.

Whether or not the highly centralized university system in Turkey can nurture this new generation of labour historians and enable them to achieve success at furthering their research in the years to come remains to be seen. They have been heavily influenced by developments in historical methods and theory beyond Turkey, but they contribute knowledge and skills of their own to the global discourse about labour history. It is perhaps no coincidence that the most promising work in Turkish labour history is that of a scholar who has worked closely with the International Institute for Social History and been an active participant in its Global Collaboratory on Labour Relations. Erdem Kabadayı, now at Koç University in Istanbul, is the recipient of a European Council Research Grant that will fund the collection and analysis of Ottoman and Turkish labour-related data from the mid-nineteenth century to 2000.

---

37 Among the many publications in which van der Linden established this agenda was: Marcel van der Linden, "Labour History: The Old, The New and the Global", *African Studies*, 66, 2–3 (August-December 2007), pp. 169–180.

Already he has engaged with questions of gender and ethno-religious identity. His work is also comparative: his publications include a seminal article that compares urban labour in Ankara, Bursa, and Thessalonika; and another that compares early republican Turkey with Greece.[38] If this is the future of Turkish engagement with Global Labour History, then it is in good hands.[39]

---

38 M. Erdem Kabadayı, "Working for the State in Urban Economies of Ankara, Bursa, and Salonica: From Empire to Nation State, 1840s-1940s", *International Review of Social History* 61, 2 (2016), pp. 213–241; Kabadayı and Kate Elizabeth Creasey, "Working in the Ottoman Empire and in Turkey: Ottoman and Turkish Labor History within a Global Perspective", *International Labor and Working Class History*, 82 (2012), pp. 187–200; Leda Papastefanaki and Kabadayı, "Introduction", in Kabadayı and Papastefanaki (eds), *Working in Greece and Turkey: A Comparative Labour History from Empires to Nation States, 1840–1940* (New York, forthcoming); Kabadayı, "The Shifts in Occupational Structure and Urban Economic Change in Turkey in the Twentieth Century" in: Osamu Saito and Leigh Shaw-Taylor (eds), *Occupational Structure and Industrialization in a Comparative Perspective* (forthcoming).
39 The title of Kabadayı's ERC project is: "Industrialisation and Urban Growth from the mid-nineteenth century Ottoman Empire to Contemporary Turkey in a Comparative Perspective, 1850–2000".

Suggested Reading

Anderson, Kyle J. "Lost and Found, then Lost Again? The Social History of Workers and Peasants in the Modern Middle East", *History Compass*, 14, 12 (2016), pp. 582–593.

Atabaki, Touraj and Gavin D. Brockett (eds). *Ottoman and Republican Turkish Labour History*. International Review of Social History Supplement 17 (Cambridge: Cambridge University Press, 2009).

Beinin, Joel. *Workers and Peasants in the Modern Middle East* (Cambridge: Cambridge University Press, 2001).

Canbakal, Hülya. *Society and Politics in an Ottoman Town. Ayntab in the 17th Century* (Leiden and Boston: Brill, 2006).

Clement, Anne. "Rethinking 'Peasant Consciousness,' in Colonial Egypt: An Exploration of the Performance of Folksongs by Upper Egyptian Agricultural Workers on the Archaeological Excavation Sites of Karnak and Dendera at the Turn of the Twentieth Century (1885–1914)", *History and Anthropology*, 21, 2 (2010), pp. 73–100.

Faroqhi, Suraiya. *Artisans of Empire. Crafts and Craftspeople under the Ottomans* (London: I.B. Tauris, 2009).

Faroqhi, Suraiya. *Subjects of the Sultan. Culture and Daily Life in the Ottoman Empire* (London: I.B. Tauris, 2000).

Islamoğlu-Inan, Huri (ed.). *The Ottoman Empire and the World Economy* (Cambridge: Cambridge University Press, 1987).

Jones, Kevin. "Unmaking the Middle Eastern Working Classes: Labour and the Politics of Historiography", *Social History*, 40, 2 (May 2015), pp. 145–156.

Kahveci, Erol, Nadir Sugur and Theo Nicols (eds). *Work and Occupation in Modern Turkey* (New York: Routledge, 1996).

Lockman, Zachary (ed.). *Workers and Working Classes in the Middle East: Struggles, Histories, Historiographies* (Albany, NY: SUNY Press, 1994).

Madeline Zilfi, *Women and Slavery in the Late Ottoman Empire: The Design of Difference* (Cambridge: Cambridge University Press, 2010).

Paschale, Ghazaleh. "Trading in Power: Merchants and the State in 19th Century Egypt", *International Journal of Middle East Studies*, 45, 1 (2013), pp. 71–91.

Quataert, Donald and Erik Jan Zürcher (eds). *Workers and the Working Class in the Ottoman Empire and the Turkish Republic, 1839–1950* (London: I.B. Tauris, 1995).

Quataert, Donald. *Miners and the State in the Ottoman Empire. The Zonguldak Coalfield, 1822–1920* (New York: Berghahn, 2006).

Teoman, Özgür and Muammer Kaymak. "Commerical Agriculture and Economic Change in the Ottoman Empire during the Nineteenth Century: A Comparison of Raw Cotton Production in Western Anatolia and Egypt", *Journal of Peasant Studies*, 35, 2 (2008), pp. 314–334.

Yıldırmaz, Sinan. *Politics and Peasantry in Post-War Turkey: Social History, Culture and Modernization* (London: I.B. Tauris, 2016).

Zürcher, Erik-Jan (ed.). *Fighting for a Living. A Comparative History of Military Labour, 1500–2000* (Amsterdam: Amsterdam University Press, 2013).

3. Types of Work

Eric Vanhaute

3.1. Agriculture

Peasants are workers of the land. They live in rural, agricultural households that have direct access to the land they work, either as common users, tenants, or smallholders. They are organized in family bonds, village communities, and social groups, which we call peasantries. These bonds pool different forms of income and meet a major portion of their subsistence needs via networks of production, exchange, credit, and protection. Most of the time, peasantries have been ruled by other social groups that extract a surplus either via rents, via market transfers, or through control of public power (taxation). Key terms are (a degree of) household and local autonomy, direct access to land and labour resources, flexible strategies of income-pooling, household-based village structures, and surplus extraction outside local control.[1] Differences between peasants, market-driven farmers, and industrial or entrepreneurial farming must be understood on a continuous scale. The primacy of subsistence production, household labour, and local community relations is the main discriminating variable. As a rule, peasant labour relations comprise a mix of activities, including subsistence farming, market production, and agricultural and non-agricultural wage labour. Peasantries are not undifferentiated social entities; they include middle and small peasant farmers, and self-employment and waged labour in combination with subsistence farming. Because peasant households combine multiple income strategies, peasantries cross all categories in the taxonomy of *the Global Collaboratory on the History of Labour Relations*, except the group of 'non-working'.[2]

Peasantries have been the largest and most important social group in human history. Until the end of the twentieth century, agricultural work was the main profession around the world. Although employment growth in agriculture has slowed, farming remains the world's largest economic sector. Still more than thirty percent of the world population, about 2.5 billion people, is economically dependent on agricultural production as a source of income. Agriculture employs over 1.3 billion people throughout the world, or close to forty percent of the global workforce. This goes

---

[1] This equals Eric Wolf's 'fund of rent' that distinguishes the peasant from the 'primitive cultivator'. In his book *Peasants* (Englewood Cliffs, 1966) Wolf asserts that after ensuring their own survival, peasants must put any surplus to three uses: 1) Ceremonial fund (social and religious activities), 2) Replacement fund (repair/replacement for future production), 3) Rent fund (payment for use of land and/or equipment). See also Eric Vanhaute, "Peasants, Peasantries and (De)peasantization in the Capitalist World-system", in: Salvatore J. Babones and Christopher Chase-Dunn (eds), *Routledge Handbook of World-systems Analysis* (London and New York, 2012), pp. 313–321.
[2] https://collab.iisg.nl/web/labourrelations.

up to seventy-five percent in the poorer nations.[3] Most of these men and women work as peasant farmers or as agricultural wage labourers. Both in developing and developed countries, peasant farming remains the predominant form of agriculture in the food production sector.[4] According to the Food and Agriculture Organization of the United Nations (FAO), today more than 570 million farms exist throughout the world, from which more than ninety percent are managed and operated by a family and predominantly rely on family labour—carried out by both women and men.[5] Peasant or family farms remain by far the most prevalent form of agriculture in the world. Estimates suggest that they occupy around seventy to eighty percent of farm land and produce more than eighty percent of the world's food in value terms. The vast majority of the world's farms are small or very small, and in many lower-income countries farm sizes are becoming even more miniscule. Worldwide, farms of less than one hectare account for seventy-two percent of all agricultural holdings but control only eight percent of all agricultural land. In contrast, only one percent of all farms in the world are larger than fifty hectares, but they control sixty-five percent of the world's agricultural land. Of the world's 570 million farms, almost seventy-five percent are in Asia (thirty-five percent in China, twenty-four percent in India), nine percent in sub-Saharan Africa, four percent in Latin America and the Caribbean, and four percent in high-income countries.

Rural labour markets are much more extensive and differentiated than often perceived. They include a small stratum of commercially-oriented smallholders and owners of medium- and large-sized farms, and a growing mass of wage labourers, many of whom still cling to small plots of land as part of their livelihoods. This is a large, poorly paid, footloose reserve army of labour, either confined to local labour markets, or part of a migratory labour force reliant on seasonal and casual wage labour, in both agriculture and the rural nonfarm sectors.[6] According to the International Labour Organization (ILO), roughly 500 million agricultural workers are employed as casual and temporary workers by small and large growers. This includes women and children, both constituting up to thirty percent of the total group. Rural wage workers are engaged in a highly diverse range of work experiences and conditions, often mixing agricultural and non-agricultural activities as well as wage labour and subsistence activities on small plots. It is difficult to identify distinct groups based on the continuum from small peasant families relying predominantly on subsistence agriculture, over self-employed labour, to households of landless wage labourers.

---

3 FAO, *State of Food and Agriculture 2015*; http://www.fao.org/publications/sofa/2015/en.
4 FAO, *Towards stronger family farms, 2014*; http://www.fao.org/3/a-i4171e.pdf.
5 FAO, *The State of Food and Agriculture 2014. Innovation in family farming*; http://www.fao.org/3/a-i4040e.pdf.
6 Carlos Oya, *Rural Labour Markets in Africa: The Unreported Source of Inequality and Poverty* (Department of Development Studies, SOAS); https://www.soas.ac.uk/cdpr/publications/dv/file63653.pdf.

While the number of workers in agriculture is expected to decline over time, the share of the working poor in the sector will rise. Particularly in the Global South, the inherently uncertain nature of agricultural work continues to promote subjection to volatile prices, low wages, deficient labour regulations, dangerous working conditions, and a high incidence of child and forced labour. This coincides with a process of feminization of agriculture, referring to women's increasing participation in the agricultural labour force, whether as independent producers, as unremunerated family workers, or as agricultural wage workers. Today, women comprise an average of forty-three percent of the agricultural labour force in developing countries, varying considerably across regions from twenty percent or less in Latin America to fifty percent or more in parts of Asia and Africa. Nonetheless, women farmers control less land and have more restricted access to inputs, seeds, and credits. Less than twenty percent of landholders are women. Gender differences in access to land and credit still affect the relative ability of female and male farmers and entrepreneurs to invest and benefit from new economic opportunities.[7]

The world of today mirrors a major trend in historical capitalism. Capitalist expansion induced a highly divergent range of labour regimes and systems of recruiting, organizing, and reproducing labour. Most regimes combine subsistence with commodity production; fully proletarianized wage labour still only makes up a minority today.[8] These labour systems include so-called free (waged, unbound) labour, forced labour (by tribute, taxation, and forced labour service) and semi-proletarian labour (wage labour plus subsistence production). Many researchers have stressed the centrality of coercion in the massive group of *subaltern workers*, including peasant populations. Every person whose labour power is sold or hired out to another person under economic or non-economic compulsion belongs to this class of subaltern workers, regardless of whether he or she is a free labourer or owns/controls part of the means of production.[9] Within the variety of labour regimes that exist, boundaries are flexible and sometimes vague. Moreover, individual relations are embedded in household-based and group-based networks. 'The partiality of wage labour' is especially clear from a household perspective, since a large majority of households has never been solely dependent on wage labour incomes.[10] Non-wage labour has been an essential part of capitalist reproduction; it produces 'cheap labour', it creates part of the surplus, and it absorbs part of the costs (of care and reproduction).

---

7 http://www.unwomen.org/en/what-we-do/economic-empowerment/facts-and-figures.
8 Immanuel Wallerstein, "Class Conflict in the Capitalist World-economy", in: Immanuel Wallerstein, *The Capitalist World-economy* (Cambridge, 1979), pp. 283–293; Marcel van der Linden, *Workers of the World. Essays toward a Global Labor History* (Leiden and Boston, 2008), pp. 291–292.
9 Van der Linden, *Workers of the World*, pp. 33–35.
10 Wilma A. Dunaway, "The Centrality of the Household to the Modern World-system", in: Babones and Chase-Dunn (eds), *Routledge Handbook of World-systems Analysis* (London and New York, 2012), pp. 453–459; Joan Smith and Immanuel Wallerstein (eds), *Creating and Transforming Households. The Constraints of the World-economy* (Cambridge, 1992).

Peasant worlds and peasant work

The minimum social conditions for farming include access to land, labour, tools, and seeds. Historically, the principal social units through which the means of farming have been secured were the rural household and the village household system, both varying greatly in size, composition, and social relations through time and space. For a long time, intellectuals aimed to describe and understand the 'distinctness' of the peasantry, to explore the 'essence' of the peasant, the "countryman working on the land", and "member of the class of farm labourers and small farmers".[11] Disdain towards the peasants has been part of the discourse of the wealthy, the powerful, and the literate in the West for a long time.[12] The dualistic and biased images of the rural versus non-rural worlds can be traced back to the origin of the concepts of *pagensis/paysan(ne)/paisano(a)/peasant*, meaning from the pays, the countryside. In the Anglo-Saxon version peasant continues to keep its narrow meaning, basically pointing at the eras of so-called feudalism, and referring to social groups from the (far away) past. Even in its broadest usage, such as *campesino(a)* in Latin America, peasants have been viewed as remnants of the past.[13] In nineteenth and twentieth century modernization thinking, the peasant as a kind of archetypical rural producer represented the starting point on the axis of evolution: the traditional community and the opposite of modernity. Western-based historiography has long developed and described the 'anti-modern' model of a 'familistic' (family-based) society as a relatively undifferentiated economy of family farms and rural crafts and services, structured by internal agencies such as family, kinship, and village. In the 1960s and 1970s, the rediscovery of the works of the Russian agrarian economist and rural sociologist Alexander V. Chayanov (1888–1937) triggered a new wave of peasant studies and a renewed debate about the nature of peasant societies. The rural anthropologist Eric Wolf and rural sociologist Theodor Shanin, amongst others, moved this debate beyond a-historical and dichotomist representations.[14] The question is not whether peasants are naturally conservative, values-rational, safety-oriented investors in their land and labour or whether they tend to be risk-taking, market-oriented maximizers. They were and continue to be both. They are "rural cultivators whose

---

11 *Oxford Advanced Learner's Dictionary.*
12 Paul Freedman, *Images of the Medieval Peasant* (Stanford, CA, 1999). "The point is that farmers figure as examples, as stereotypes, that had nothing to do with the daily work experience and actual living conditions of real people." Catharina Lis and Hugo Soly, *Worthy Efforts. Attitudes to Work and Workers in Pre-Industrial Europe* (Leiden and Boston, 2012), p. 159.
13 Annette Desmarais, *Globalization and the Power of Peasants. La Vía Campesina*, (Halifax, 2007), pp. 195–198.
14 Wolf, *Peasants*; Teodor Shanin, "Measuring Peasant Capitalism", in: E.J. Hobsbawm et al. (eds), *Peasants in History. Essays in Honour of Daniel Thorner* (Oxford, 1980), pp. 89–104; Teodor Shanin, "Introduction. Peasantry as a Concept", in: Teodor Shanin (ed.), *Peasants and Peasant Societies. Selected readings* (Oxford and New York, 1987).

surpluses are transferred to a dominant group of rulers that uses the surpluses both to underwrite its own standard of living and to distribute the remainder to groups in society that do not farm but must be fed for their specific goods and services in return."[15] That is why peasants—contrary to Eric Wolf's primitive cultivators—only exist within a social formation: peasantries, and within a class relationship: the subordination to lords, government/state authorities, and regional or international markets which involve surplus extraction and social differentiation.

Peasant households are basic economic units and the gateway to the wider world. They pursue an agricultural livelihood by combining subsistence and commodity production, through direct access to nature, land, labour, and commodities. Together with extended families, kinship, and village societies they are the vital nodes of production, consumption, reproduction, socialization, welfare, credit, and risk-spreading. Peasant worlds are built on peasant work. Work includes any human effort adding use value to goods and services.[16] In the last three centuries, the use value of work has been increasingly defined in terms of economic independence; economic activities taking place in manifold and extended subsistence networks are increasingly labelled as worthless or even as forms of idleness.[17] The differentiation between work and non-work is an invention of industrial society, together with a growing emphasis on different social meanings of work and on different gender roles. This fixation has seriously affected our view of peasant worlds and peasant work. The economic roles that different household and community members take on are not fixed nor permanent. They signify a transient social relationship, one that can be replaced rather quickly by other sources of labour and income. That is why the dividing lines between paid and non-paid work, between workers in the rural and non-rural worlds, between visible (registered) and hidden labour, and between free and unfree labour are fuzzy at best.[18] Peasant labour should be understood within the dialectics between humans and nature, to put it with the famous words of Marx: "Labour is, in the first place, a process in which both man and Nature participate, and in which man of his own accord starts, regulates and controls the material re-actions between himself and Nature. [...] By this acting on the external world and changing it, he at the same time changes his own nature."[19] Through these sets of relations work/nature is transformed into value, which can be appropriated via coercive (non-economic) means, or capitalized as commodified labour-

---

15 Wolf, *Peasants*, pp. 3–4.
16 Chris Tilly and Charles Tilly, *Work Under Capitalism* (Boulder, CO, 1998), p. 22.
17 Lis and Soly, *Worthy Efforts*, e.g., p. 3, p. 569.
18 Marcel van der Linden, "The Promise and Challenges of Global Labor History", *International Labor and Working-Class History*, 82 (Fall 2012), pp. 57–76.
19 Karl Marx. *Capital. Volume One. Part III: The Production of Absolute Surplus-Value. Chapter Seven: The Labour-Process and the Process of Producing Surplus-Value. Section 1: The Labour-Process or the Production of Use-Values* [https://www.marxists.org/archive/marx/works/1867-c1/ch07.htm].

power.[20] In the end, the valorization of labour-power always causes the appropriation of unpaid work/energy from nature, including human/peasant work.

Peasant transformation and the agrarian question

Peasantries create societies, and societies create peasantries. Surplus production from the land is a precondition for large-scale societal change. Societal change is necessary to group the agricultural producers into peasantries. Agricultural-based economic systems facilitate vaster communal units and extended village networks. This provokes profound changes in the structure of social relations, population growth, and village and supra-village institutions.[21] Like every social formation, peasantries develop as sets of social relationships. Peasant transformation has often been framed in dichotomous and predominantly a-historical models.[22] Market versus non-market relations, economic versus cultural forms of exchange, modern versus traditional societal arrangements – a long tradition of rural sociology is grafted upon these dichotomies. Concepts as traditional, survival, subsistence, or informal economies have not been very helpful to understand social change in a world-historical context. They freeze peasants's history in dualistic frames and fail to grasp the dynamics and changes within peasant societies. When survival and subsistence refer to self-supporting at a level at which the bare minimum is produced and there is little or no surplus, peasant economies do not fit these typologies. On the contrary, they are rooted in a wide variety of reciprocal exchanges, that integrate different spaces in networks of mutual obligations, and regional and extra-regional market transactions and public retributions. Ultimately, peasantry has often been considered to be a class whose significance inevitably diminishes with the further development of capitalism.

---

20 Jason Moore, "Cheap Food and Bad Climate. From Surplus Value to Negative-Value in the Capitalist World-Ecology", *Critical Historical Studies*, 2, 1 (2015), p. 3. [http://www.jasonwmoore.com/uploads]

21 Paul Brassley and Richard Soffe, *Agriculture. A Very Short Introduction* (Oxford, 2016); Marcel Mazoyer and Laurence Roudart, *A History of World Agriculture. From the Neolithic Age to the Current Crisis* (London and Sterling, VA, 2006).

22 These models are framed in the tradition of modernization theories, de/prescribing a progressive transition from a 'pre-modern' or 'traditional' to a 'modern' society; see e. g., Jan K. Coetzee, J. Graaff, G. Wood, F. Hendricks, *Development: Theory, Policy and Practice* (Cape Town, 2002). Barrington Moore Jr., *Social Origins of Dictatorship and Democracy. Lord and Peasant in the Making of the Modern World* (Boston, 1966) argued the centrality of struggle between classes of pre-capitalist landed property and (peasant) agrarian labour in the differential paths of state formation in the modern world. Seth LaAnyane, *Economics of Agricultural Development in Tropical Africa* (Chichester, 1985), highlights the stereotypes of modernization theory.

3.1. Agriculture — 223

For more than a century, debates about this 'agrarian question' have been dominated by two groups of protagonists.[23] On the one hand, the *disappearance thesis* defends that the inevitable expansion of capitalism will lead to the extermination of the peasantry. Following Lenin and Kautsky, the former, more or less undifferentiated class of peasants is transformed into new, distinct groups: capital owners (capitalist farmers) and wage labourers. On the other hand, advocates of the *permanence thesis* argue that, according to Chayanov's peasant mode of production, peasant societies have a distinct developmental logic that supports the survival of the peasantry within capitalism. A central question behind this debate is if and how peasants, who made up the vast majority of the population in former agrarian societies, thereby sustaining and reproducing both themselves and the dominant classes and institutions, still can be perceived as a social group within the contemporary globalizing and de-ruralizing world. Do peasantries still constitute a general (and generic) social group, determined by a set of distinct qualities, from household subsistence over village solidarity to social/ecological harmony, as opposed to other social groups such as rural proletarians and market-oriented farmers?[24] The search for 'peasant essentialism' has been apparent in both historical (peasants as pre-capitalist survivors) and contemporary (agrarian populism) analyses. Post-modern and globalization studies have often amplified the thesis of *the end of peasantries* while sometimes dismissing the concept of the peasant altogether.

Both the teleological (disappearance as social group) and the essentialist (survival as a *sui generis* group) views have been suffering from a-historical and often functionalistic presumptions.[25] Historically, the processes of peasant transformation have neither been unilinear nor have they taken fixed forms of social differentiation over time and space. In this sense peasantry is an open process that interacts within multiple forms and scales of conflict and interaction and leaves room for different levels of autonomy. The concepts of *peasantization, de-peasantization* and *re-peasantization* refer to the ongoing processes of creation, decline, adaptation, and resistance. Throughout history, peasantries have been the historical outcome of labour and income processes that are constantly adjusted to surrounding conditions, such as fluctuations of markets, state control, technical innovations, demographic trends, and environmental changes. Rural populations become peasants by degree and relinquish their peasant status only gradually over time.[26] However, the combined processes of overburdening, restricting, and reducing peasant spaces have considerably

---

[23] Farshad Araghi, "Global Depeasantization, 1945–1990", *The Sociological Quarterly*, 36 (1995), pp. 601–632.
[24] Henry Bernstein, "Farewells to the Peasantry", p. 10; Henry Bernstein, *Class Dynamics of Agrarian Change* (Halifax and Winnipeg, 2010), pp. 110–112.
[25] John R. Owen, "In Defense of the 'Peasant'", *Journal of Contemporary Asia*, 35, 3 (2005), pp. 368–385.
[26] Deborah Fahy Bryceson, Cristobal Kay and Jos Mooij (eds), *Disappearing Peasantries? Rural Labour in Africa, Asia and Latin America* (London, 2000).

weakened their material basis in the last few centuries. The concept of de-peasantization refers to this multi-layered processes of erosion of an agrarian way of life. It is increasingly difficult to combine subsistence and commodity agricultural production with an internal social organization based on family labour and village community settlement.[27] This has triggered a further diversification of rural coping mechanisms, including petty commodity production, rural wage labour, seasonal migration, subcontracting to national and multinational corporations, self-employment, remittances, and transregional and transnational income transfers. So-called de-peasantization very often hides more diversified and more precarious labour and income strategies developed by the peasantry. Moreover, processes of de-agrarianization in the core zones often coincide with the creation of new peasantries in the periphery. Recent forces of de-agrarianization are triggered by the enforcement of neo-liberal policies and structural adjustment programmes. In many parts of the periphery, vulnerability has switched from a temporary to a structural state of being. This is countered by the intensification of old and the introduction of new forms of livelihood diversification such as taking up non-farming activities and relying on non-farming income transfers.[28]

Peasant frontiers and peasant regimes

The survival and persistence of peasantries in a globalizing and ever more commodified world has been puzzling social scientists for a long time now. Time and again, the demise of the peasant was announced by intellectuals, capitalists, reformers, and development planners alike.[29] The very notion of peasants and peasantries confronts us with the flaws of traditional/orthodox economic development theories. The mainstream image of the fate of peasants and peasantries is still based on the standard story of the much-praised English road to capitalist agriculture, and the concurrent disintegration of peasant societies. Recent history has shown that the English and Western European experience of the dissolution of peasant societies within the context of expanding industrial and welfare economies is not and cannot be the general example for the rest of the world. When we look beyond the old premises of westernized development, we see a very different picture. It is a picture of vast, family-based, rural, and agricultural economies, in which diversified production chains

---

27 Deborah Fahy Bryceson, *African Rural Labour, Income Diversification and Livelihood Approaches. A Long-term Development Perspective* (Leiden: African Studies Centre, 1999), p. 175.
28 Frank Ellis, "Agrarian Change and Rising Vulnerability in Rural Sub-Saharan Africa", *New Political Economy*, 11, 3 (2006), pp. 387–397.
29 For example, in his acclaimed book *The Age of Extremes*, Eric Hobsbawm wrote that "the most dramatic and far-reaching social change of the second half of this century, and the one which cuts us off for ever from the world of the past, is the death of the peasantry". Eric Hobsbawm, *Age of Extremes. The Short Twentieth Century 1914–1991* (London, 1994), p. 289.

and multiple strategies of risk minimization are pooled with locally and regionally anchored income and exchange systems.[30]

The fate of rural societies in the past and today cannot be understood in a singular manner. Understanding multiple trajectories of peasant change requires new historical knowledge about the role of peasantries within long-term and worldwide economic and social transformations. Peasantries across the world have followed different trajectories of change and have developed divergent repertoires of accommodation, adaptation, and resistance. The expansion of civilizations, states, imperialism, socialism, and global capitalism triggered different paths of peasant transformation, of processes of peasantization, de-peasantization, and re-peasantization. Peasants's history is the history of the struggle over the fruits of their labour. In agricultural societies, social relations are built on the returns of the land to support and reproduce institutions and norms that define new rules of ownership, inheritance, transmission, and control. Peasants gain a substantial part of their income from direct access to products that are a result of the input of their labour on the land; any loss implies a notable decline in their living standards. Peasantries not only feed civilizations, empires, states, and economies. They support their ecological and social resilience and fuel their expansion. Gradual processes of incorporation disclose new supplies of labour, land, and nature, which are mobilized in new production processes.[31] The incorporation of rural zones and the creation of new peasantries have been central to the expansion of global capitalism. In most societal settings, these zones are integrated as loci of appropriation of the produce of land and labour and as peripheral spaces of production, exploitation, and recreation. Peasantries are thus primary frontiers in societal expansion. Their partial incorporation as producers of new surpluses instigates mixed, complex, and often opposing processes of restructuring, generating a multiplicity of rural frontier zones. Capitalist incorporation and expansion is fuelled by the opening of the *Great Frontier*, a metaphor for an intensifying and interconnected world-wide set of new and shifting frontiers. This instigates an intensifying process of exhaustion of both land and labour, and the appropriation of new frontiers of what Jason Moore coins as *uncapitalized nature*. New frontiers are opened, their 'free gifts' (of land, labour, nature) identified, mapped, secured, and appropriated.[32] This massive process of creating new commodity frontiers

---

[30] See, amongst others, Miguel Altieri and Clara Nicholls, *Agroecology and the Search for a Truly Sustainable Agriculture* (Berkeley, CA, 2005); Philip McMichael, "Peasants Make Their Own History, But Not Just as They Please ...", *Journal of Agrarian Change*, 8, 2–3 (2008), pp. 205–228; Jan Douwe Van der Ploeg, "The Peasantries of the Twenty-first Century: The Commoditisation Debate Revisited", *The Journal of Peasant Studies*, 37, 1 (2010), pp. 1–30.

[31] Jason Moore, "Cheap Food and Bad Money. Food, Frontiers, and Financialization in the Rise and Demise of Neoliberalism", *Review (Fernand Braudel Center)*, 33, 2–3 (2010), pp. 225–261, at 245; Edward B. Barbier, *Scarcity and Frontiers. How Economies Have Developed through Natural Resource Exploitation* (Cambridge, 2011), p. 7.

[32] Moore, "Cheap Food and Bad Climate", pp. 20–21.

and the gradual commodification of the global countryside have opened up an unseen bounty of nature, land, and labour's rewards, fuelling globalizing capitalism.

Peasant change has often been understood from a post-hoc perspective. It gets its meaning from the outcome we measure. Agrarian and farming systems are an influential ordering tool in agricultural and rural history. Research concentrates on the organization, functioning, and outcomes of subsequent systems, with a strong focus on ecology, technology, and farming practices. This often results in models of evolution, classification, and differentiation of agrarian systems in a given region or within in the world.[33] Social-ecological agrosystems describe rural production networks as sets of region-specific social power relations shaping the economic reproduction of a given geographical area. They are the theoretical expression of historically constituted and geographically localized types of agriculture and ecological and social (re)production systems.[34] In a global-comparative context, these typologies are frequently based on Eurocentric models and understood in *a priori* historical sequences. This risks creating new myths that underpin existing power relations and legitimizing discourses both in academic knowledge and in applied fields such as development work.[35] Time and again, bottom-up research discloses that agrarian and peasant regimes cannot be predicted from environmental, demographic, or evolutionary contexts.

In order to make sense of social change in a broad time/space span we can frame social realities in a genealogy of evolving and changing *peasant regimes*.[36] The peasant regime is a tool to contextualize and understand how peasantries in a certain time/space are (internally) organized and (externally) embedded. Each regime embodies an institutionalization of economic, social, political, cultural, and ecological forces that structures internal and external peasant relations. It organizes forms and relations of production, reproduction, exchange, and extraction. It defines how these

---

[33] See, for example, Mazoyer and Roudart, *History of World Agriculture*, pp. 21–23; Guy M. Robinson, *Geographies of Agriculture. Globalisation, Restructuring and Sustainability* (Harlow, 2004), pp. 1–29; Mark B. Tauger, *Agriculture in World History* (London and New York, 2010), pp. 2–3.

[34] Erik Thoen, "'Social Agrosystems' as an Economic Concept to Explain Regional Differences. An Essay Taking the Former County of Flanders as an Example (Middle Ages-19th Century)", in: B.J.P. van Bavel and P. Hoppenbrouwers (eds), *Landholding and Land Transfer in the North Sea Area (Late Middle Ages-19th Century)* (Turnhout, 2004), pp. 47–66; Erich Landsteiner and Ernst Langthaler (eds), *Agrosystems and Labour Relations in European Rural Societies (Middle Ages–Twentieth Century)* (Turnhout, 2010).

[35] Mats Widgren, "Four Myths in Global Agrarian History", in: M. Bondesson, A. Jarrick and J. Myrdal (eds), *Critical Studies in World History* (Lund, forthcoming); online manuscript: https://stockholmuniversity.box.com/shared/static/bp0kb081zlko2onfunx1zbzeuekxr4bm.pdf.

[36] I borrow the concept of genealogy from Michel Foucault, "Nietzsche, Genealogy, History", in: Michel Foucault, *Language, Counter-Memory, Practice: Selected Essays and Interviews* (Ithaca, NY, 1980), pp. 139–164. "Genealogy [...] rejects the meta-historical deployment of ideal significations and indefinite teleologies [...]. Genealogy does not pretend to go back in time to restore an unbroken continuity [...]. Genealogy does not resemble the evolution of a species and does not map the destiny of a people." (pp. 140, 146).

relations are ordered and represented (or legitimized) via structures of power and forms of hegemony. A genealogy of peasant regimes claims that episodes of restructuring and transition are bounded by more stable periods of regulation and organization, albeit in a non-determined way. The genealogy of societal regimes provides a global comparative-historical lens on the social, economic, political, and ecological relations of agrarian empires and global capitalism.[37] It aims at a non-hierarchical, non-evolutionary, and non-deterministic interpretation of global social change. Despite huge differences in time and space, these peasant regimes are mostly defined by gradual peasant incorporation into wider social systems, indirect political control, and coerced extraction of land and labour surpluses via taxes, tributes, rents, and confiscations.[38] The invention of private property and the commodification of the countryside mark the beginning of capitalist expansion, accelerating in the long sixteenth century. Within capitalism, peasant regimes are premised on new forms of enclosure of land and labour. Direct incorporation thoroughly altered ecological relations and changed the rules of the game. This resulted in a greater diversification of systems of access to nature, land, and labour, of systems of production, and reproduction, and of survival and coping mechanisms.

Agrarian change and the peasant question in global capitalism

Fernand Braudel famously characterized the early modern world as "one vast peasantry, where between eighty and ninety percent of the people lived from the land and from nothing else."[39] He distinguished between three main types of agricultural societies: "nomads and stockbreeders", "peoples practicing a still deficient form of agriculture, primarily peasants using hoes", and what he labelled as "civilizations; relatively dense populations possessing multiple assets and advantages: domestic animals, swing-ploughs, ploughs, carts, and above all, towns."[40] As a general rule, Braudel wrote, the civilizations played and won. They took over 'cultures' and 'prim-

---

[37] Philip McMichael, *Food Regimes and Agrarian Questions* (Halifax and Winnipeg, 2013), pp. 1–12; Robert Boyer, *The Regulation School. A Critical Introduction* (New York, 1990). The regulation school studies the transformation of social relations in the context of changing regimes of accumulation: patterns in the way production, circulation, consumption, and distribution organize and expand capital and stabilize the economy over time.

[38] See for example: Colin Renfrew and Paul Bahn (eds), *The Cambridge World Prehistory*. 3 vols (Cambridge, 2014); Michael E. Smith (ed.), *The Comparative Archeology of Complex Societies* (Cambridge, 2011); Graeme Barker, *The Agricultural Revolution in Prehistory. Why did Foragers become Farmers?* (Oxford, 2006); Peter Bellwood, *First Farmers* (Oxford, 2005).

[39] Fernand Braudel, *The Structures of Everyday Life. The Limits of the Possible* (London, 2002), p. 49.

[40] Ibid., p. 57.

itive peoples' and what was perceived as 'unoccupied territory'.[41] This generally happened via widespread peasant colonization, such as the East frontier towards the east of the Elbe, Siberia and the steppes between the Volga and the Black Sea; and the western frontier in North America. Successful frontier movements are backed by expanding state power, pushing back what James Scott labelled *non-state spaces*, or *state-preventing societies*, peoples that "have not yet been fully incorporated into nation-states."[42] Quoting Scott again, "The founding of agrarian states, then, was the contingent event that created a distinction, hence a dialectic, between settled, state-governed population and a frontier penumbra of less governed or virtually autonomous peoples." The objective of this 'last enclosure' "has been less to make them productive than to ensure that their economic activity was legible, taxable, assessable, and confiscatable, or failing that, to replace it with forms of production that were."[43] According to Scott, these peoples were not archaic residues, they were "barbarians by design", created by states. They – temporarily – escaped the status of *core peasantries*, practicing fixed field agriculture, tied to the land through redefined property entitlements, and living in permanent settlements and patriarchal family bonds.[44]

The incorporation of non-capitalist, rural worlds into a capitalist world economy animated several intensive and long-standing academic debates, all addressing the peasants and the fruits of their labour. A key concept within the debate on the transformation of pre-capitalist societies has been primitive accumulation, defined as extra-economic coercion and dispossession, distinct from the market-derived compulsion of economic forces characteristic of capitalist exploitation.[45] Typically, different models of accumulation, and different paths of agrarian transition towards capitalism have been identified. These include: the English path (original transition to capitalist farming, with the disposition of the peasantries), the Prussian path (feudal landed property transformed itself into capitalist commodity production, turning peasants into wage-workers), the American path (capitalism developed within the peasant sector through a process of socio-economic differentiation, turning smallholders into petty commodity producers), and the East Asian path. In Japan and South Korea, for example, peasant surpluses were used to finance capitalist industrialization without a transition to agrarian capitalism (in the English sense). This differentiation begs the question about the range of possible connections between the

---

41 *Ibid.*, p. 98.
42 James C. Scott, *The Art of Not Being Governed. An Anarchist History of Upland Southeast Asia* (New Haven, CT, and London, 2009), pp. ix–x.
43 *Ibid.*, pp. 4–5.
44 *Ibid.*, pp. 8–9.
45 Bernstein, *Class Dynamics of Agrarian Change*, pp. 27–32.

development of capitalism and peasant transformation.⁴⁶ Initially, this debate focused on class transformation within the European countryside, and capital's subordination of landed property. Lenin defended the inevitability of capitalist transition in agriculture following the same basic pattern.⁴⁷ Peasants became locked into commodity production by the 'dull compulsion of economic forces', the commodification of their subsistence. This triggered a differentiation of the peasantry into distinct—rich, middle, and poor—rural classes. In his *Die Agrarfrage* (1899), Karl Kautsky explored the impact of capitalism on agrarian societies, the role of agriculture during capitalist development, and the political role (or lack thereof) of the peasantries in radical social change.⁴⁸ Though the book follows a standard, teleological conception of capitalist development, Kautsky questioned the prescribed evolution towards large-scale, wage-labour based production in agriculture. Peasant agriculture can, in fact, be functional according to the dynamics of capitalist accumulation. In the end, Kautsky supported the view of an increasing polarization of classes in agrarian society and the attendant concentration of rural property. In response, Chayanov tried to demonstrate that capitalist class polarization was not an inevitable outcome of capitalist transformation. He argued that the peasantry could play a significant role as individual family farmers within modern (socialist) societies, for example through the establishment of cooperatives.⁴⁹ The rediscovery of his research in the 1960's inspired a powerful wave of peasant studies, illustrating the resilience of peasant farming, the regional specificity of agrarian change, and the diversity of forms of dispossession and control of peasant labour.⁵⁰

The transformation of the countryside, and especially the transformation of rural property relations, has taken centre stage in a range of debates on the origins of agrarian capitalism.⁵¹ This process of transforming 'peasants into farmers' started

---

46 Terence J. Byres, "The Landlord Class, Peasant Differentiation, Class Struggle and the Transition to Capitalism: England, France and Prussia Compared", *The Journal of Peasant Studies*, 36, 1 (2009), pp. 33–54.
47 Vladimir Ilyich Lenin, *The Development of Capitalism in Russia. The Process of the Formation of a Home Market for Large-Scale Industry* (1899, https://www.marxists.org/archive/lenin/works/1899/devel).
48 Karl Kautsky, *The Agrarian Question*, 2 vols (London, 1988. Orig. 1899).
49 Alexander V. Chayanov, *The Theory of Peasant Economy* (Madison: University of Wisconsin Press, 1986. Orig. 1924).
50 "Following its translation, Chayanov's work became enormously influential in the Anglophone academy, not least as an inspiration of neo-populist analysis of peasants and agricultural development." Henry Bernstein and Terence J. Byres, "From Peasant Studies to Agrarian Change", *Journal of Agrarian Change*, 1, 1 (2001), pp. 1–56, at 5.
51 Maurice Dobb et al., *The Transition from Feudalism to Capitalism. A Symposium* (London, 1954); Rodney Hilton (ed.), *The Transition from Feudalism to Capitalism* (London, 1976); T.H. Aston and C.H.E. Philpin (ed.), *The Brenner Debate. Agrarian Class Structure and Economic Development in Pre-industrial Europe* (Cambridge, 1985); Ellen Meiksins Wood, *The Origin of Capitalism* (New York, 1999); Peter Hoppenbrouwers and Jan Luiten van Zanden (eds), *Peasants into Farmers? The Transformation of Rural Economy and Society in the Low Countries (Middle Ages–19th Century) in Light of the*

in a specific time and place, England in the Late Middle Ages, setting in motion a capitalist dynamic, and a growing subjection of rural producers to market imperatives. The differentiation of the English peasantry deprived direct producers of their non-market access to the means of their production and reproduction, creating a growing market dependence of producers, as well as appropriators.[52] Capitalism, with all its very specific drives for accumulation and profit maximization, was born in the countryside; it required not a simple extension or expansion of barter and exchange but a complete rupture in peasant societies. With a distinct twist, the Danish economist Ester Boserup described peasant transformation towards agrarian intensification as a process of economic growth. She defined population pressure as a major cause of change in land use, agricultural technology, land tenure systems, and settlement forms. Farmers were induced to adopt more intensive cropping systems and, hence, to innovate.[53]

Studies on 'the agrarian question', although bringing in peasant transformation as a constitutive process in modern social change, substantiated a distorted, often teleological view on 'the end of peasantries'. In addition, most of this work is dismissive of peasants's social consciousness and agency, resembling Marx's famous qualification of the rural underclasses as a 'sack of potatoes'. From the 1960's, this structuralist view provoked new bottom up research, focusing, among others, on peasant agency in social movements.[54] These studies repeatedly show that peasant mobilization was not only part of the transition from pre-capitalist to capitalist societies, but remains a major social force in the modern capitalist world.[55] This reassessment of peasant studies has been criticized because of its alleged 'populist postmodernism', aiming to reconstruct previously hidden subaltern voices, re-essentializing a distinct

---

Brenner Debate (Turnhout, 2001); Bas van Bavel, *Manors and Markets. Economy and Society in the Low Countries 500–1600* (Oxford, 2010).
52 Wood, *Origin of Capitalism*, p. 53.
53 Ester Boserup, *The Conditions of Agricultural Growth: The Economics of Agrarian Change under Population Pressure* (London, 1965).
54 See e.g. Eric Hobsbawm, *Primitive Rebels. Studies in Archaic Forms of Social Movement in the 19th and 20th Century* (Manchester, 1959); Eric Wolf, *Peasant Wars of the Twentieth Century* (New York, 1969); James C. Scott, *Weapons of the Weak. Everyday Forms of Peasant Resistance* (New Haven, CT, and London, 1985); Gerrit Huizer, *Peasant Unrest in Latin America: Its Origins, Forms of Expression and Potential* (Amsterdam, 1970); Eric Stokes, *The Peasant and the Raj. Studies in Agrarian Society and Peasant Rebellion in Colonial India* (Cambridge, 1980); Herbert P. Bix, *Peasant Protest in Japan, 1590–1884* (New Haven, CT, 1986); Christopher R. Boyer, *Becoming Campesinos. Politics, Identity, and Agrarian Struggle in Postrevolutionary Michoacán, 1920–1935* (Stanford, CA, 2003); Eric Vanhaute, "Globalizing Local Struggles. Localizing Global Struggles. Peasant Movements from Local to Global Platforms and Back", *Workers of the World. International Journal on Strikes and Social Conflict*, 1, 5 (2014), pp. 114–129.
55 Annette Aurelie Desmarais, *La Via Campesina: Globalization and the Power of Peasants* (Chicago, IL, 2007); Desmarais, "Conflict in the Contemporary Rural World. New Interpretations of an Old Problem", *Workers of the World. International Journal on Strikes and Social Conflict*, 1, 5 (2014).

'peasantness' in the rural worlds.[56] This debate addresses not only the questions of agrarian change and economic growth but the very essence of (modern/capitalist/socialist) development itself, and the agency of peasant consciousness and peasant mobilization. These agrarian and peasant questions received a major platform in the *Journal of Peasant Studies*, founded in 1973.[57] From the start, peasant change and peasant differentiation became the pervasive themes, thus transcending the limitations of inward-looking peasant studies. Peasant change has been researched in a wide range of subjects such as pre-capitalist agrarian formations, transitions to capitalism in the industrialized and non-industrialized countries, projects of socialist agrarian transition, experiences of colonialism in the imperialist periphery and contradictory processes of development/underdevelopment in poor countries after the end of colonial rule. In 2001, the *Journal of Agrarian Change* (JAC) joined the *Journal of Peasant Studies* (JPS). Both journals remain committed to the promotion of "critical thinking about social structures, institutions, actors and processes of change in and in relation to the rural world" (JPS) and the "investigation of the social relations and dynamics of production, property and power in agrarian formations and their processes of change, both historical and contemporary" (JAC). Increasingly, research into rural power relations between classes and other social groups includes perspectives on gender relations, technological change, and ecological and global transformations.

The transformation of the global countryside

The incorporation and redefinition of rural zones in the last few centuries has continuously redefined and recreated peasant regimes. The outcome of the configuration of power relations, i.e. the social distribution of land and labour, differed wildly over time and space. The expansion of the Great Frontier required a more direct intervention in peasant institutions and practices of allocation and use of land and labour.[58] This frontier-based development of new resources necessitated a permanent restructuring of peasant land and labour regimes, generating significant differences over space and time. In the peasant question, land and labour rights have been the prime subject of expropriation and negotiation.[59] These processes have never been

---

56 Tom Brass, *Peasants, Populism, and Postmodernism. The Return of the Agrarian Myth* (London, 2000); Brass, *Class, Culture and the Agrarian Myth* (Leiden and Boston, 2014).
57 Bernstein and Byres, "From Peasant Studies to Agrarian Change", pp. 1–56.
58 Barbier, *Scarcity and Frontiers*, p. 418; Bernstein, *Class Dynamics*, p. 43.
59 Philip McMichael, "Peasant Prospects in the Neoliberal Age", *New Political Economy*, 11, 3 (2006), pp. 407–418; Farshad Araghi, "The Great Global Enclosure of Our Times. Peasants and the Agrarian Question at the End of the Twentieth Century", in: Fred Magdoff, John Bellamy Foster and Frederick H. Buttel (eds), *Hungry for Profit. The Agribusiness Threat to Farmers, Food and the Environment* (New York, 1999), pp. 145–160.

absolute or complete. Capitalism's tendency towards generalised commodity production has created immense disparities on a global level; uneven commodification has always been at the heart of historical capitalism.[60] For example, nineteenth century colonialism in India and twentieth century colonialism in Africa engendered processes of systemic peasantization that supported the colonial governments's agricultural commodity export goals.[61] Spurred by colonial taxation, African agrarian producers increasingly produced agricultural commodities in conjunction with their subsistence production. Alternatively, they exported male labour based on circular migration. The major expansion of peasant and commodity frontiers redesigned rural societies and fuelled both state and capitalist growth. This transformation of the global countryside gained momentum after 1850.[62] Until the nineteenth century, most world regions produced agricultural commodities by peasant labour. It took massive state efforts to integrate this labour into a global capitalist production system. For example, the expansion of capitalist cotton agriculture from the last third of the nineteenth century was a direct result of powerful interventions of the state, first and foremost through a redefinition of property rights, redistributing land away from village societies and nomadic peoples.[63] The transformation of the countryside through the commodification of land and labour spread capitalist social relations, including private credit and private ownership of land. This momentous process of making peasants into cultivators and eventually consumers of commodities was supported by the spread of a variety of labour regimes, such as sharecropping, family yeoman farming, and proletarian agricultural labour. It was also supported by new forms of coercion through taxation, compulsory crops, debt-bondage etc. By the end of the nineteenth century, sharecropping and tenant farming had become the dominant mode of mobilizing agricultural labour. In many parts of the world, integration into the capitalist world market went hand in hand with widespread re-peasantization—not straightforward proletarianization. Meanwhile, the expansion of grain and meat production in settler economies and the expansion of tropical export crops in colonial Asia and Africa coincided with massive de-agrarianization and de-peasantization and more diversified, capital-intensive farming in Europe.

The globalization of farming and food consumption in the twentieth century reinforced the highly differential impacts on societies in the North and South, through

---

60 Immanuel Wallerstein, *Historical Capitalism with Capitalist Civilization* (London and New York, 1995), pp. 13–43.
61 Jan Breman, *Of Peasants, Migrants and Workers. Rural Labour Circulation and Capitalist Production in West India* (Oxford, 1985); Jan Breman, *Labour Migration and Rural Transformation in Colonial India* (Amsterdam, 1990); Fred Cooper, Allen Isaacman, Florencia Mallon, William Roseberry, and Steve Stern, *Confronting Historical Paradigms. Peasants, Labor, and the Capitalist World System in Africa and Latin America* (Madison, WI, 1993); Gareth Austin, *Labour, Land and Capital in Ghana. From Slavery to Free Labour in Asante, 1807–1956* (Rochester, 2005).
62 Sven Beckert, *Empire of Cotton. A Global History* (New York, 2014), p. 184.
63 Ibid., p. 297.

new international divisions of labour and increased trade in agricultural commodities. The commodification and marginalization of peasant subsistence in the South coincided with the expansion of export crops like coffee, cocoa, tea, sugar, cotton, and palm oil, the promotion of high value commodities like horticultural products, and the expansion of large-scale production of soy, sugar, and grains. The working poor of the South were increasingly forced to pursue their reproduction through insecure and oppressive wage employment and/or a range of precarious small scale and 'informal economy' survival activities, including marginal farming. Moreover, livelihoods were pursued across different spaces of the social division of labour: urban and rural, agricultural and non-agricultural, wage employment and marginal self-employment.[64] Coercion remained central in the twentieth century colonial worlds, permanently recasting social structures, and mobilizing labour in different ways. In many places constraints to mobilize sufficient workers for large plantations stimulated systems of share-cropping. The recasting of the countryside spread to the Soviet Union, China, and India, making these regions part and parcel of the new geography of global capitalism. By the mid twentieth century, governments and capital had transformed the global countryside.[65] Developmentalist projects integrated peasantries as part of nationalist movements and as citizens of new states. Since they no longer needed the state to turn rural cultivators into commodity growers, from the 1980's capitalists increasingly turned away from state intervention. The neoliberal revolution created new frontiers of market expansion in the countryside, instigating a new phase in its revolutionary transformation.

Developments that have often been regarded as historical processes of de-peasantization were, in essence, part of the spread of more diversified labour and income strategies of the peasantries. Due to intensifying economic and social uprooting, for an important portion of the world's population these survival strategies have become more important than ever. Some authors have coined these revived multi-level strategies of survival, autonomy, and resistance as a recreation of peasant strategies. This argument has revived the classic peasant question, that has been raised to query the role and fate of peasantries within the process of capitalist transition. It essentially entails political questions that "reflect the very structure of the society", although "it was a question posed *about* the peasantry, not necessarily *of* or *by* them."[66] In a non-Western and global context, this socio-economic peasant question (peasantry as a class) becomes complexly entangled with the socio-cultural indigenous question (indigenousness as a cultural identity). The labels *peasant* and *indigenous* refer to a set of claims that may coincide or overlap with various other identities (gender, class, linguistic, national). However, peasant and indigenous identities have increasingly

---

64 Bernstein, *Class Dynamics*, pp. 87, 111.
65 Beckert, *Empire of Cotton*, p. 376.
66 William Roseberry, "Beyond the Agrarian Question in Latin America", in: Fred Cooper *et al.* (eds), *Confronting Historical Paradigms. Peasants, Labor, and the Capitalist World System in Africa and Latin America* (Madison, WI, 1993), pp. 321–323.

become overlapping and reinforcing categories of *peripherality*, an umbrella stigma of the poor and the marginalized in today's globalizing world. In turn, these global processes generate new forms of *peripheral consciousness*.[67] The locality and the community are reinforced; sometimes they are reinvented as a basic framework for both peasant and indigenous identities. Battles related to the contested peasant and indigenous claims to land, territory, and resources, which usually have a communal rather than an individual nature, are a central instigator. For peasantries, land has been and continues to be the main basis of negotiation and interaction with other sectors of society because its use has direct implications for their exchange relations (products derived from that land) and for their power relations (the regulation of access to the land). The communal level remains a central space for self-determination, negotiation, and resistance. This combination of autonomy and intermediation converts 'the communal' into a crucial gateway to both different and independent 'local histories' and to interaction within larger, incorporative, and global systems.[68]

---

[67] Eduardo Devés-Valdés, "The World from Latin America and the Peripheries", in: Douglas Northrop (ed.), *A Companion to World History* (Chichester, 2012), pp. 466, 469–474.
[68] James V. Fenelon and Thomas D. Hall, *Indigenous Peoples and Globalization* (Boulder, CO, 2009); Walter D. Mignolo, *The Darker Side of Western Modernity. Global Futures, Decolonial Options* (Durham, NC, 2011); Saturnino M. Borras Jr., "Agrarian Change and Peasant Studies: Changes, Continuities and Challenges. An Introduction", *Journal of Peasant Studies*, 36, 1 (2009), pp. 5–31.

Suggested readings

Aston, Trevor H. and C.H.E. Philpin (eds). *The Brenner Debate. Agrarian Class Structure and Economic Development in Pre-industrial Europe* (Cambridge: Cambridge University Press, 1985).
Barbier, Edward B. *Scarcity and Frontiers. How Economies Have Developed through Natural Resource Exploitation* (Cambridge: Cambridge University Press, 2011).
Beckert, Sven. *Empire of Cotton: A Global History* (New York: Alfred A. Knopf, 2014).
Bernstein, Henry and Terence J. Byres. "From Peasant Studies to Agrarian Change", *Journal of Agrarian Change*, 1, 1 (2001), pp. 1–56.
Bernstein, Henry. *Class Dynamics of Agrarian Change* (Halifax and Winnipeg: Fernwood Publishing, 2010).
Boserup, Ester. *The Conditions of Agricultural Growth. The Economics of Agrarian Change under Population Pressure* (London: G. Allen and Unwin, 1965).
Brass, Tom. *Peasants, Populism, and Postmodernism. The Return of the Agrarian Myth* (London: Routledge, 2000).
Braudel, Fernand. *The Structures of Everyday Life. The Limits of the Possible* (London: Phoenix Press, 2002).
Breman, Jan. *Of Peasants, Migrants and Workers. Rural Labour Circulation and Capitalist Production in West India* (Oxford: Oxford University Press, 1985).
Bryceson, Deborah, Cristobal Kay and Jos Mooij (eds). *Disappearing Peasantries? Rural Labour in Africa, Asia and Latin America* (London: Intermediate Technology Publications, 2000).
Chayanov, Alexander V. *The Theory of Peasant Economy* (Madison: University of Wisconsin Press, 1986. Orig. 1925).
Cooper, Fred, et al. *Confronting Historical Paradigms. Peasants, Labor, and the Capitalist World System in Africa and Latin America* (Madison: University of Wisconsin Press, 1993).
CORN Publication Series (Comparative Rural History of the North Sea Area; Turnhout: Brepols, 1999–2014; 15 vols).
Hobsbawm, Eric J. et al. (eds). *Peasants in History. Essays in Honour of Daniel Thorner* (Oxford: Oxford University Press, 1980).
Kautsky, Karl. *The Agrarian Question*, 2 vols (London: Zwan Publications, 1988. Orig. 1899).
Mazoyer, Marcel and Laurence Roudart. *A History of World Agriculture. From the Neolithic Age to the Current Crisis* (London: Earthscan, 2006).
McMichael, Philip. *Food Regimes and Agrarian Questions* (Halifax and Winnipeg: Fernwood Publishing, 2013).
Moore, Barrington Jr. *Social Origins of Dictatorship and Democracy. Lord and Peasant in the Making of the Modern World* (Boston: Beacon Press, 1966).
Moore, Jason W. *Capitalism in the Web of Life. Ecology and the Accumulation of Capital* (London: Verso, 2015).
Scott, James C. *Weapons of the Weak. Everyday Forms of Peasant Resistance* (New Haven, CT, and London: Yale University Press, 1985).
Shanin, Teodor (ed.). *Peasants and Peasant Societies. Selected Readings* (Oxford and New York: Basil Blackwell, 1987).
Tauger, Mark B. *Agriculture in World History* (London and New York: Routledge, 2010).
Van der Ploeg, Jan Douwe. *The New Peasantries. Struggles for Autonomy and Sustainability in an Era of Empire and Globalisation* (London: Earthscan, 2008).
Weis, Tony. *The Global Food Economy. The Battle for the Future of Farming* (London: Zed Books, 2007).
Wolf, Eric. *Peasants* (Englewood Cliffs: Prentice Hall: 1966).
Wood, Ellen Meiksins. *The Origin of Capitalism* (New York: Monthly Review Press, 1999).

Ad Knotter
3.2. Mining

From early on, and all over the world, mining has been a crucial activity in human society.[1] It supplied minerals for making tools, weapons, and utensils. Precious metals such as gold and silver were won for their beauty and value, and for the supply of money. Coal was used by craftsmen and manufacturers, or in households for heating. Until well into the eighteenth century, mining developed at a slow pace. From the late eighteenth century industrial and transport revolutions resulted in the development of mining operations on a grander scale, at first of coal and iron ore, and later also of such metals as copper, lead, and tin. The mining of such precious minerals as silver, gold, and diamonds expanded as well. Mining became a global industry. In the following account I have selected some of the most important issues in the global history of labour in mining: migration, mobility, and control of the labour force; the variety of labour relations between proletarian and forced labour; gender; and industrial relations. To mobilize and attach workers to mining sites all over the world, mine management used various mechanisms of control in a broad array of labour relations. Unfree labour in different forms, ranging from debt bondage and indenture to convict labour and outright slavery, existed side by side with wage labour and subcontracted self-employment. Migrants were mobilized from nearby and far away, often resulting in an ethnically stratified labour force in the mines. Mining is generally perceived as an exclusively male and pre-eminently masculine domain, but historically in many districts women were employed in mining as well, while in others they were relegated to the home to perform reproductive tasks and fully support the male members of the miners' household. Although the image of mining as a strike-prone industry may not be fully warranted, in the twentieth century miners were at the forefront of radical movements and policies in many countries.

Labour relations in European mining from the fifteenth to the eighteenth century

In the medieval and early modern period, important mining developments took place in Central Europe, especially in the Alpine areas (Tirol), the Harz region, Saxony, Bohemia, and Hungary, where gold, silver, lead, copper, and iron were mined. In the

---

[1] For a short overview, see John Temple, *Mining. An International History* (London, 1972). For early developments in China, see Joseph Needham, *Science and Civilisation in China. Volume 5. Chemistry and Chemical Technology. Part XIII. Mining*, by Peter J. Golas (Cambridge, 1999). For a general overview on the Americas since pre-Columbian times, see Helmut Waszkis, *Mining in the Americas. Stories and History* (Cambridge, 1993).

fifteenth and sixteenth centuries, the scale of mining enterprises grew. Large sums of money were needed to develop mines, to pay for the drainage machines, and the sinking of deeper shafts. Mines were often owned by absentee shareholders (such as the famous Fugger family from Augsburg), who supplied the capital and collected the profits. A clear distinction emerged between the owners and the workers, resulting in a loss of privileges for both self-employed and wage labourers.[2] This led to sometimes violent disputes, which, according to the German mining historian Klaus Tenfelde, anticipated "a thoroughly modern dispute behaviour in industrial relations".[3] After the mid-fifteenth century collective actions of miners in the Saxon and Bohemian ore mountains became more frequent, for instance in Freiberg (1444–1469), Altenberg (1469), Schneeberg (1496–1498), and Joachimsthal (1517–1525). In the sixteenth century there were large miners' revolts in Bohemia, Saxony, and the Alpine regions, sometimes in connection with the so-called Peasants' War.[4]

Since medieval times iron, tin, and copper ores had been mined in other European areas as well. A salient example is tin mining in Cornwall. Originally, "free tinners" had worked their own leased property or formed small partnerships. In the seventeenth century a rapid increase in production proletarianized an ever larger section of the population. Miners were employed by specific forms of subcontracting, based on a sum per cubic foot or on the value of the ore sent to the surface. The lack of manifestations of class identity and trade unionism until the late nineteenth century is sometimes attributed to this "tribute system", as miners in this system considered themselves little entrepreneurs rather than workers. At that time, the tin mines in Cornwall were in decline, but in the wake of British colonization and global-mining operations, demand for Cornish mining skills provided opportunities all over the world. Tens of thousands left the region, not just to populate the developing mining districts of the world, but also to dominate them as senior and middle managers. In this way, Cornish mineworkers played a crucial part in the global expansion of mining during the nineteenth and early twentieth centuries. In spite of late trade union-

---

[2] For a recent overview of labour relations in late-medieval German mining, see Hans-Joachim Kraschweski, "Arbeitsverhältnisse im spätmittelalterlichen Bergbau", and Andreas Bingener, Christoph Bartels, and Michael Fessner, "Soziale Entwicklungen – von der Bruderschaft zur Knappschaft", in: Christoph Bartels and Rainer Slotta (eds), *Geschichte des deutschen Bergbaus. Band I. Der alteuropäische Bergbau. Von den Anfängen bis zur Mitte des 18. Jahrhunderts* (Münster, 2012), pp. 297–305 and 409–420.
[3] Klaus Tenfelde, "Streik als Fest. Zur frühneuzeitlichen Bergarbeiterkultur", in: Richard van Dülmen and Norbert Schindler (eds), *Volkskultur. Zur Wiederentdeckung des vergessenen Alltags (16.–20. Jahrhundert)* (Frankfurt am Main, 1984), pp. 177–202, 188.
[4] *Ibid.*, pp. 189–192; Uwe Schirmer, "Das Erzgebirge im Ausstand. Die Streiks in den Revieren zu Freiberg (1444–1469), Altenberg (1469), Schneeberg und Annaberg (1469–1498) sowie in Joachimsthal (1517–1525) im regionalen Vergleich", and Adolf Laube, "Bergarbeiter- und Bauernbewegungen in Deutschland von der Mitte des 15. Jahrhunderts bis zum Ende des Bauernkriegs 1525/26", in: Angelika Westermann and Ekkehard Westermann (eds), *Streik im Revier. Unruhe, Protest und Ausstand vom 8. bis 20. Jahrhundert* (St. Katharinen, 2007), pp. 65–93 and 113–135.

ism in their home country, in the British settler colonies they were often pioneers in labour organization.⁵

Of paramount importance for early modern European industry were the supplies of Swedish and Russian iron ore, mined respectively in the Bergslagen region west of Stockholm, and in the Ural mountains. The labour forces in these regions were quite different. In Sweden, production was in the hands of small landowning households. Members divided the hours of work between tasks performed in the mine, charcoal burning, transportation of pig iron, and agricultural work. In the seventeenth century it was only around certain mines that a small population of more or less specialized miners came into existence. In the Urals, serfs or conscripted so-called state peasants were employed, coerced to work in the mines and the ironworks as part of their labour duties.⁶

In several places in Europe, coal has been mined since the Middle Ages. Before industrialization, markets were predominantly local, unless transport was cheap, as it was for Newcastle coal from the Durham and Northumberland coalfields, which was sold all around the North Sea. For this reason, and because of rising energy needs in Britain itself, the British coal industry expanded earlier than its European counterparts. The supply of coal in Britain has been identified as a major prerequisite for its industrialization in the late eighteenth century.⁷ From a labour history perspective the debate about disciplining the workforce is perhaps the most interesting. In early modern Britain, two systems of control stand out: the "yearly bond" in the north-east of England, and the "colliery serfdom" in the Scottish coalfields. In eighteenth-century Durham and Northumberland, "annual bonds" (the obligation to work in the mine during a full year) were widely used to track down and legally punish those who left before the end of the contracted period. British labour historians

---

5 Roger Burt, "Industrial Relations in the British Non-Ferrous Mining Industry in the Nineteenth Century", *Labour History Review*, 71, 1 (2006), pp. 57–79; idem, "Cornwall as a Social Mining Region", in: Angelika Westermann (ed.), *Montanregion als Sozialregion. Zur gesellschaftlichen Dimension von "Region" in der Montanwirtschaft* (Husum, 2012), pp. 239–252; Gill Burke, "The Cornish Diaspora of the Nineteenth Century", in: Shula Marks and Peter Richardson (eds), *International Labour Migration. Historical Perspectives* (London, 1984), pp. 57–75; John Rule, *Cornish Cases. Essays in Eighteenth and Nineteenth Century Social History* (Southampton, 2006).

6 Anders Florén, "Social Organization of Work and Labour Conflicts in Proto-Industrial Iron Production in Sweden, Belgium and Russia", in: Catharina Lis, Jan Lucassen, and Hugo Soly (eds), *Before the Unions. Wage Earners and Collective Action in Europe, 1300–1850*, Supplement 2 *International Review of Social History*, 39 (1994), pp. 83–113; Anders Florén and Göran Rydén, with Ludmila Dashkevich, D.V. Gavrilov, and Sergei Ustiantsev, "The Social Organisation of Work at Mines, Furnaces and Forges", in: Maria Ågren (ed.), *Iron-Making Societies. Early Industrial Development in Sweden and Russia, 1600–1900* (New York and Oxford, 1998), pp. 61–139.

7 E.A. Wrigley, *Continuity, Chance and Change. The Character of the Industrial Revolution in England* (Cambridge, 1988); idem, *Energy and the English Industrial Revolution* (Cambridge, 2010); Kenneth Pomeranz, *The Great Divergence. China, Europe and the Making of the Modern World Economy* (Princeton, 2000).

have been debating this phenomenon from an early date.⁸ Perhaps the most convincing explanation is provided by James Jaffe: because management was not (yet) able to control the labour process at the point of production, it at least tried to control the labour market.⁹

Although quite different from the yearly bonds in the coalfields of north-east England, Scottish "colliery serfdom" as a system of life-long bondage (like feudal serfs) was designed to guarantee local labour supply as well. It was established in 1606, consolidated in the seventeenth century, and after a first act of emancipation in 1775 not abolished completely until 1799. The "independent colliers" of the Scottish coalfields in the nineteenth century, brought to life by labour historian Alan Campbell,¹⁰ perceived their eighteenth-century forbearers as "degraded slaves", but this picture has been nuanced in research on the agency of the "collier serfs", who were far from docile, subdued, or deferential, and who were able to act collectively. Paradoxically, the self-perception of "independence", it is argued, may well have originated before the abolition of serfdom.¹¹

A global industry

Although mining activities can be traced in many parts of the world long before European expansion, a globally connected mining industry only emerged in the era of colonialism and imperialism from the sixteenth to the twentieth century. Methods to exploit and process metals and minerals had been developed in pre-conquest America, Asia, and Africa, but mining was small scale, primitive, and based only on read-

---

8 Sydney Webb, *The Story of the Durham Miners (1662–1921)* (London, 1921), pp. 7–15; T.S. Ashton and J. Sykes, *The Coal Industry of the Eighteenth Century* (Manchester, 1929), pp. 70–99; Robert Colls, *The Pitman of the Northern Coalfield. Work, Culture and Protest, 1790–1850* (Manchester, 1987), pp. 64–73.
9 James A. Jaffe, *The Struggle for Market Power. Industrial Relations in the British Coal Industry 1800–1840* (Cambridge, 1991), pp. 49–50, 100–104.
10 Alan B. Campbell, *The Lanarkshire Miners. A Social History of their Trade Unions 1775–1874* (Edinburgh, 1979), pp. 9–12; Alan Campbell and Fred Reid, "The Independent Collier in Scotland", and Alan B. Campbell, "Honourable Men and Degraded Slaves: A Comparative Study of Trade Unionism in Two Lanarkshire Mining Communities, c. 1830–1874", in: Royden Harrison (ed.), *Independent Collier. The Coal Miner as Archetypal Proletarian Reconsidered* (Hassocks, 1978), pp. 54–74 and 75–113.
11 Christopher A. Whatley, "'The Fettering Bonds of Brotherhood': Combination and Labour Relations in the Scottish Coal-Mining Industry c. 1690–1775", *Social History*, 12, 2 (1987), pp. 139–154; idem, "Scottish 'Collier Serfs' in the 17th and 18th Centuries: A New Perspective", and a rejoinder by Alan Campbell, "18th Century Legacies and 19th Century Traditions: The Labour Process, Work Cultures and Miners' Unions in the Scottish Coalfields Before 1914", in: Ekkehard Westermann (ed.), *Vom Bergbau- zum Industrierevier* (Stuttgart, 1995), pp. 217–238 and 239–255. See also Rab Houston, "Coal, Class and Culture: Labour Relations in a Scottish Mining Community, 1650–1750", *Social History*, 8, 1 (1983), pp. 1–18.

ily available materials.¹² The Europeans brought not only a lust for profit, but also more accomplished techniques to gain from mining. The wish to extract more of the earth's riches was a driving force behind the Spanish exploration and conquest of the "New World". The iconic mining site of early modern colonialism is the Potosí silver mine in today's Bolivia, "perhaps the world's most famous mining district".¹³ From the sixteenth century onwards, it was Spanish America's, and indeed the world's, greatest silver producer. In the seventeenth century, with around 160,000 inhabitants it was one of the world's biggest cities as well. The flow of bullion from the New World allowed Europe to balance its trade with Asia and in this way contributed to the formation of an integrated world economy.¹⁴

Potosí is infamous for its extreme forms of coercion to secure workers, the so-called *mita* system of forced and tributary Indian labour.¹⁵ Male inhabitants in the wide surroundings were obliged to work at the mines on a rotational basis. This was combined with forms of wage labour and self-employment of workers mining on their own account in their "free time". In a recent history of Potosí mining, working on one's own was considered an act of resistance,¹⁶ but it also made working in the mines attractive for coerced workers. More than 10,000 people had to migrate every year to the Potosí mines from thousands of places, and brute force had to be combined with more subtle mechanisms to ensure the workers' compliance, i.e. the opportunity to gain a supplementary income by self-employment.¹⁷ The mandatory conscription affected only men, but wives and children moved with them to Potosí, where they assisted by sorting and transporting the ore.¹⁸ In the eighteenth century the number of *mitayos* diminished, also proportionally, but the system of forced labour ceased to exist only after Bolivia's independence (1825). It was then replaced by a system of subcontracting. In the nineteenth century, agro-mining companies

---

12 Needham, *Science and Civilisation in China. Mining*; Waszkis, *Mining in the Americas*.
13 Kendall W. Brown, *A History of Mining in Latin America. From the Colonial Era to the Present* (Albuquerque, 2012), p. xii; for a concise overview, see Renate Pieper, "Die Reviere von Hochperu und Neuspanien als Sozialregionen (16.–18. Jahrhundert)", in: Westermann, *Montanregion als Sozialregion*, pp. 253–266.
14 Andre Gunder Frank, *ReORIENT. Global Economy in the Asian Age* (Berkeley, 1998).
15 Peter Bakewell, *Miners of the Red Mountain. Indian Labor in Potosí, 1545–1650* (Albuquerque, 1984); Enrique Tandeter, *Coercion and Market. Silver Mining in Colonial Potosí, 1692–1826* (Albuquerque, 1993).
16 Brown, *History of Mining in Latin America*, ch. 4.
17 Rossana Barragán Romano's review of Brown, *A History of Mining in Latin America*, *International Review of Social History*, 60, 2 (2015), pp. 287–290, 290.
18 Pascale Absi, "Lifting the Layers of the Mountain's Petticoats. Mining and Gender in Potosí's Pacamama", in: Jaclyn J. Gier and Laurie Mercier (eds), *Mining Women. Gender in the Development of a Global Industry, 1670 to 2005* (Basingstoke, 2006), pp. 58–70, 59.

owned haciendas as well as silver mines and obliged their tenants (*peons*) to work in the mines.[19]

Potosí was not the only mine in Latin America exploited by the early modern colonizers. Silver mining was developed in several sites in Mexico too. Mexican mining appears to have been based mainly on wage labour by so-called *mestizos* (of mixed descent, while the coerced Potosí *mitayos* were indigenous Indians).[20] The production of gold and diamonds centred on Brazil. Diamond deposits were discovered in the Brazilian Minas Gerais district in the 1720s. The miners were mostly African slaves, and the discovery of these deposits was followed by a massive increase in unfree labour.[21] The exploitation of the Brazilian diamond mines set off a rearrangement of the global diamond trade, which until that time had been an Indian monopoly. In India's diamond fields miners worked in small units, but because of the labour-intensive production process the total number of workers could be several tens of thousands in each field. Men dug the pits and took out the earth, which was then carried away in baskets by women and children to be dried and then sieved and searched to discover the diamonds. Miners were contract labourers who worked for wages in cash. Most of them were impoverished peasants, who moved seasonally from agricultural areas to the mines.[22]

In the nineteenth and twentieth centuries the European colonial powers stepped up their rush to exploit available resources globally. Capital was invested in the mining of coal, metals, and minerals in every corner of the world. Africa became the stage of major raids to exploit its geological riches. Some notorious examples in Southern Africa are diamond mining after the Kimberley strike of 1868 and its subsequent development by the British colonizer Cecil Rhodes and his De Beers Consolidated Mines Company (formed in 1888), and gold mining starting to develop in the Witwatersrand Basin in the mid-1880s, extending into Southern Rhodesia. In 1917 the Anglo-American Corporation of South Africa was formed as a gold mining company. In 1926 it became the majority stakeholder in the De Beers company as well, and in the years to follow it began mining copper in Northern Rhodesia (today's Zambia). The Central African Copperbelt stretched from Northern Rhodesia into Katanga (part of Belgian Congo). The Katanga fields were developed in the beginning of the twentieth century by the British company Tanganyika Concessions Ltd (indirectly

---

19 Erick D. Langer, "The Barriers to Proletarianization: Bolivian Mine Labour, 1826–1918", in: Shahid Amin and Marcel van der Linden (eds), *"Peripheral" Labour? Studies in the History of Partial Proletarianization*, Supplement 4 *International Review of Social History*, 41 (1996), pp. 27–51, 38–48.
20 John Tutino, *Making a New World. Founding Capitalism in the Bajío and Spanish North America* (Durham, 2011). See also Peter J. Blakewell, *Silver Mining in Colonial Mexico, Zacatecas 1546–1700* (Cambridge, 1971).
21 Karin Hofmeester, "Working for Diamonds from the 16th to the 20th Century", in: Marcel van der Linden and Leo Lucassen (eds), *Working for Labor. Essays in Honor of Jan Lucassen* (Leiden, 2012), pp. 19–46, 37.
22 *Ibid.*, pp. 25–27.

also a creation of Cecil Rhodes). In 1906, this company merged with the Belgian Comité Spécial du Katanga, dominated by the Société Générale de Belgique, to form the Union Minière du Haut-Katanga.[23]

Colonial status was no prerequisite for foreign exploitation of mineral resources, as becomes clear in the mining history of nineteenth- and twentieth-century Latin America. The famous El Teniente Copper Mine in Chile, for instance, was originally owned by Chilean families, but, copper becoming in high demand with the development of electricity, in 1904 the American Smelting and Refining Company (controlled by Rockefeller) stepped in. In 1908 the mine was bought by the Guggenheim brothers and merged with their US copper mines into the Kennecott Copper Corporation. Copper mining expanded during World War I and in the 1920s. Miners were recruited by agents (*enganchadores*), mainly among rural workers (*campesinos*) in the agricultural regions of southern and central Chile.[24] In Peruvian mining of (mainly) copper, the Cerro de Pasco Corporation, formed in 1902 by an American syndicate composed of, among others, J.P. Morgan, became the dominant force.[25]

Tin is another mineral exploited for the global market. As the substantial Cornish deposits in Britain were gradually depleted, the sources in Malaysia, Indonesia, and Bolivia were brought into production networks that eventually spanned the entire globe. In the interwar years Congo and Nigeria became important producers.[26] The labour history of tin mining has been studied in several areas,[27] particularly in Bolivia.[28] Originally mined as a by-product of silver, Bolivian tin mining grew rap-

---

23 Charles Perrings, *Black Mineworkers in Central Africa. Industrial Strategies and the Evolution of an African Proletariat in the Copperbelt, 1911–41* (New York, 1979).
24 Thomas Miller Klubock, *Contested Communities. Class, Gender, and Politics in Chile's El Teniente Copper Mine, 1904–1951* (Durham, NJ, 1998), pp. 20–38.
25 Dirk Kruijt and Menno Vellinga, *Labor Relations and Multinational Corporations. The Cerro de Pasco Corporation in Peru (1902–1974)* (Leiden, 1979); Josh DeWind, *Peasants become Miners. The Evolution of Industrial Mining Systems in Peru, 1902–1974* (New York, 1987).
26 Mats Ingulstad, Andrew Perchard, and Espen Storli (eds), *Tin and Global Capitalism. A History of the Devil's Metal, 1850–2000* (London, 2014).
27 In Nigeria British companies began tin mining in 1906: Bill Freund, *Capital and Labour in the Nigerian Tin Mines* (Harlow, 1981); see also *idem*, "Labour Migration to the Northern Nigerian Tin Mines, 1903–1945", *Journal of African History*, 22, 1 (1981), pp. 73–84. In Malayan tin mining European companies replaced Chinese owners in the 1910s and 1920s: Amarjit Kaur, *Wage Labour in Southeast Asia since 1840. Globalization, the International Division of Labour and Labour Transformations* (London, 2004), pp. 27–58; *idem*, "Race, Gender and the Tin Mining Industry in Malaya, 1900–1950", in: Kuntala Lahiri-Dutt and Martha Macintyre (eds), *Women Miners in Developing Countries. Pit Women and Others* (Aldershot, 2006), pp. 73–88. In Indonesia tin mining was developed by the Dutch Billiton Company: Jurrien van den Berg, "Tin Island: Labour Conditions of Coolies in the Billiton Mines in the Nineteenth and Early Twentieth Centuries", in: Vincent J.H. Houben and J. Thomas Lindblad (eds), *Coolie Labour in Colonial Indonesia. A Study of Labour Relations in the Outer Islands, c. 1900–1940* (Wiesbaden, 1999), pp. 209–229.
28 A classic (anthropological) study is June C. Nash, *We Eat the Mines and the Mines Eat Us. Dependency and Exploitation in Bolivian Tin Mines* (New York, 1993).

idly in the 1890s, and by 1900 Bolivia had become one of the largest producers in the world. The industry was dominated by foreign capital, mainly from Chile, but also from Britain and the USA. High levels of capitalization brought about great changes in labour conditions. Migration of full-time wage labourers to the tin mines in northern Potosí largely severed the links between the peasantry in the surrounding countryside, but on the remaining agro-mining complexes in the southern part the presence of peasant-miners on the estates retarded full proletarianization.[29]

Coal mining is another global industry with enormous impact on labour relations in different parts of the world. To a great extent nineteenth- and early twentieth-century globalization, including colonialism, depended on a transport and industrial revolution, based on coal as a supplier of energy. With rising energy needs coal mining expanded globally. Wherever in the world coal was found, even in the most desolate and remote areas, mines were opened, and to enable exploitation mine operators had to find, mobilize, and direct workers to these sites.[30]

Mobilizing labour

An urgent quest for labour characterizes the history of mining everywhere and drove varying constellations of labour relations. At the start, experienced miners were recruited from other mining areas. Migration trajectories, return and circular migration, resulting in ethnic diasporas of skilled miners, can be traced in many mining districts. Much of the global expansion of mining in the nineteenth and twentieth centuries could be achieved only because of the migration of skilled groups of workers from Great Britain (like the Cornish miners, mentioned above). They introduced mining skills and techniques, and often continued to hold privileged positions afterwards. Migration trajectories of British miners can be traced in almost every mining area in the British Empire, but also in other parts of the world. Transference of experience and technological skills, acquired in the British mines, was essential for the development of the US mining industry for instance.

Early migration of skilled groups of workers to introduce mining skills was supplemented by waves of inexperienced migrants, both from the surrounding countryside and from more distant places, regions, and countries. The mobilization of labour for the mines was often closely linked to the transition from agriculture to industry, the creation of a wage labour market, and the formation of a mining proletariat. These processes were not easy or straightforward. Workers had to be found who could be coerced or motivated to move, changing not only places, but their entire way of life. Cross-border migratory labour connected mining districts, regions, and

---

29 Langer, "The Barriers to Proletarianization", pp. 49–50.
30 Ad Knotter and David Mayer (eds), *Migration and Ethnicity in Coalfield History: Global Perspectives*, Special Issue 23, *International Review of Social History*, 60 (2015).

countries, and mobilized new groups of workers of a variety of national and ethnic descent. Ethnic (minority) groups were mobilized from outside, but also from within national states and empires. Telling examples in coal mining in the nineteenth and early twentieth centuries are: Flemish workers to the Walloon coalfields in Belgium, Irish to Scotland in the UK (before Irish independence), Poles to the Ruhr area in the German empire (before Polish independence), African-Americans from the south to Virginia and Alabama in the US, migrants from the French colonies in the Maghreb (Algeria and Morocco) to France, and Koreans to the Hokkaidō and Chikuhō coalfields in Japan (Korea then being part of the Japanese empire). Their mobilization as miners reflected the low status of work in the mines, and also the position of migrants as secondary workers within the mines.[31]

Gold rushes are perhaps anomalies in the "normal", more gradual build-up of a migrant labour force in mining, but they nevertheless exemplify the extraordinary push mining developments could give to migration and the formation of multicultural communities.[32] The gold rushes to California and Australia in the mid-nineteenth century were followed by one to South Africa in the late 1880s. The growth of gold mining caused the development of Johannesburg and the Witwatersrand, nowadays the prime metropolitan area of South Africa. Coal was exploited at Witbank too. As the coal mines produced mainly for the gold industry, they were often owned by gold-mining companies. Their recruitment agency, the Witwatersrand Native Labour Association (WNLA), popularly known as "Wenela", constructed an extensive recruiting network across the three southern provinces of Portuguese Mozambique, both for the gold mines and the collieries.[33] By 1910, 100,000 men from all over Southern Africa had come to work in the gold mines. Their numbers grew to 300,000 by 1940, and 500,000 by 1985.[34]

There is a wealth of research on African labour in the mines in Southern Africa, and some important debates in global labour history have been triggered by seminal publications on this issue. The South African migration system was founded on the premise that men would migrate as wage labourers and women would remain behind to work in the fields. In this way male wages could be kept low as they did not include the costs of reproduction at home. Starting from the oscillation of African

---

31 Ad Knotter, "Migration and Ethnicity in Coalfield History: Global Perspectives", in: *ibid.*, pp. 13–39.
32 Susan Lee Johnson, *Roaring Camp. The Social World of the California Gold Rush* (New York, 2000).
33 The mobilization of migratory labour for the South African gold mines has been the subject of numerous studies. See, among others, Ruth First, *Black Gold. The Mozambican Miner, Proletarian and Peasant* (Manchester, 1983); Alan Jeeves, *Migrant Labour in South Africa's Mining Economy. The Struggle for the Gold Mines' Labour Supply, 1890–1920* (Kingston, Ont., 1985); T. Dunbar Moodie (with Vivienne Ndatshe), *Going for Gold. Men, Mines, and Migration* (Berkeley, 1994). On the migrant labour in the collieries, see Peter Alexander, "Oscillating Migrants, 'Detribalised Families', and Militancy: Mozambicans on Witbank Collieries, 1918–1927", *Journal of Southern African Studies*, 27, 3 (2001), pp. 505–525.
34 Moodie, *Going for Gold*, p. 1.

migratory wage labourers between the mines and subsistence agriculture of the peasant families left behind, the South African Marxist sociologist Harold Wolpe was able to historicize the rather abstract concept of "articulation of modes of production" in the writings of Louis Althusser and his followers in the 1970s,[35] a concept which for a while also captured the imagination of early modern European labour historians.[36] A second very influential work is Charles van Onselen's *Chibaro*, which showed that in the mines of Southern Rhodesia (today's Zimbabwe) the particular form of contract labour designated to control African migratory labour in "prison-like conditions" was perfectly compatible with the development of capitalism in Southern Africa.[37] This recruitment system was dismantled, however, when market forces were sufficiently developed to push workers to the mines in large numbers.[38]

The importance of oscillating migrants working seasonally in the mines has been established in numerous studies on mining labour in several parts of the world. By recruiting peasant-migrants from the land, labour supply and the agrarian seasons were interconnected. Two salient examples include the Jahria coalfield in India (opened in the 1890s),[39] and the Donbass mining region in the Ukraine (opened in the 1870s). The Ukrainian population being persistently reluctant to enter the mines, Russian migrants and migratory workers formed the rank and file of the min-

---

35 Harold Wolpe, "Capitalism and Cheap Labour-Power in South Africa: From Segregation to Apartheid", *Economy and Society*, 1, 4 (1972), pp. 425–456; idem (ed.), *The Articulation of Modes of Production. Essays from Economy and Society* (London, 1980).
36 It became particularly relevant in debates on so-called proto-industry and its relationship with the peasant family in the 1970s and 1980s: Peter Kriedte, Hans Medick, and Jürgen Schlumbohm, *Industrialisierung vor der Industrialisierung. gewerbliche Warenproduktion auf dem Land in der Formationsperiode des Kapitalismus* (Göttingen, 1977). The debate has subsided, if only because the application of the Marxist concept of mode of production to the peasant or family economy is not self-evident. Cf. Ad Knotter, "Problems of the 'Family Economy': Peasant Economy, Domestic Production and Labour Markets in Pre-industrial Europe", in: Maarten Prak (ed.), *Early Modern Capitalism. Economic and Social Change in Europe, 1400–1800* (London, 2001), pp. 135–160. From a Marxian perspective, "partial proletarianization" would perhaps be more apt to designate the links between wage labour and the peasantry. Cf. Amin and van der Linden, *"Peripheral" Labour?*
37 Charles van Onselen, *Chibaro. African Mine Labour in Southern Rhodesia, 1900–1933* (London, 1976).
38 Ibid., pp. 116–119.
39 Dilip Simeon, *The Politics of Labour under Late Colonialism. Workers, Unions and the State in Chota Nagpur 1928–1939* (New Delhi, 1995); idem, "Coal and Colonialism: Production Relations in an Indian Coalfield, c. 1895–1947", in: Amin and van der Linden, *"Peripheral" Labour?*, pp. 83–108. C.P. Simmons, "Recruiting and Organizing an Industrial Labour Force in Colonial India: The Case of the Coal Mining Industry, c. 1880–1939", *The Indian Economic and Social History Review*, XIII, 4 (1976), pp. 455–485; idem, "Seasonal Labour Oscillation in the Indian Coal Mining Industry before Independence", in: Marc Gaborieau and Alice Thorner (eds), *Asie du Sud. Traditions et changements. Sèvres 8–13 juillet 1978* (Paris, 1979), pp. 477–482.

ing labour force.[40] Likewise, in Peru, when the Cerro de Pasco Corporation began mining, the labour force consisted of peasant workers who were primarily engaged in subsistence agriculture. In the early days of mining the company tried to control the seasonal flow of workers through a debt labour system known as *enganche* (the hook). Company-commissioned *enganchadores* (labour contractors) advanced loans to peasants, who had to repay them by working in the mines. The company set wages so low that workers were often unable to pay for their living expenses or repay their *enganche* debts.[41]

Controlling labour

The Peruvian example of the *enganche* system makes clear that mobilizing and controlling labour were inextricably intertwined. Once mobilized to do the heavy work in the remote mining sites, companies had to find ways to prevent the workforce from leaving. In Malaysian and Indonesian tin mining labour control of the predominantly Chinese workers was primarily achieved through the mechanism of indenture: mine owners or coolie brokers paid the travel costs and expenses of the migrant worker in exchange for a contractual obligation for a specified period – usually three years. Wages were so low, that paying back the costs plus interest at the end of this three years was often impossible, so the worker had to be indentured for a further period. Women were usually employed as *dulang* washers (or panners), not as miners. They stood in water all day long to recover the tin, which was then deposited in large sluice boxes. During the period 1911–1947 women *dulang* washers formed between eleven and twenty per cent of the total workforce.[42]

These kinds of systems of coercion and dependency were not confined to migrant labour. In the coalfields of British India (Bengal), mine owners had purchased large tracts of land near the pits and had developed a service tenancy arrangement, whereby peasants were granted a small piece of land in return for working a certain number of days in the company mine instead of paying rent, on pain of eviction.[43] In this way the colliery owners were able to bind a permanent supply of mining labour. The system had been applied by early starters in the Indian coalfields and persisted

---

[40] Theodore H. Friedgut, *Iuzovka and Revolution. Vol. I. Life and Work in Russia's Donbass, 1869–1924* (Princeton, 1989).
[41] DeWind, *Peasants become Miners*. The *enganche* system of indebted labour was also used to mobilize and control plantation labour in Peru, and has elicited a more general debate on the character of debt bondage as unfree labour. Cf. Tom Brass, "The Latin American *Enganche* System", in: *idem*, *Towards a Comparative Political Economy of Unfree Labour. Case Studies and Debates* (Abingdon, 1999), pp. 182–202.
[42] Kaur, *Wage Labour in Southeast Asia since 1840*, pp. 37–49; *idem*, "Race, Gender and the Tin Mining Industry".
[43] Simmons, "Recruiting and Organizing an Industrial Labour Force", pp. 463–471; Simeon, *The Politics of Labour under Late Colonialism*, p. 26.

into the 1950s. For more recently established enterprises, control of the migratory peasant-miners was achieved by means of subcontracting. Labour contractors were responsible for the entire labour process, from the hiring of the labour force to the cutting and loading of coal. A contractor recruited relatives and personal friends from his home village or thereabout, and made every effort to ensure that his "gang" would return to a particular mine next year. He advanced train fares, food, and money to his co-villagers, later to be deducted from wages earned, obliging workers to stay with him and to work at a particular colliery.[44]

Systems of subcontracting were widely used elsewhere as well. Labour for the Nigerian tin mines was recruited by a "network of contractors and other parasitic intermediaries".[45] In Chinese coal mining until the 1920s the largest part of the labour force, up to between sixty and eighty per cent, were recruited by contractors. Apart from supplying labour, many contractors also had to provide most of the materials to work the mine.[46] A similar recruiting system existed for the Russian seasonal miners in the Ukrainian Donbass. Agents went to the villages to persuade peasants to work in the mines, paying their travel and living expenses. These advances were later deducted from wages, keeping the worker in debt from the beginning.[47] Also in Japan, a system of recruitment by labour contractors was generally used in coal and other mines. A contractor hired several groups of ten to twenty mineworkers from farming backgrounds, provided lodging, and supervised labour underground. On behalf of the mine owners the contractors had complete authority over the workforce, both at work and in daily life. They recruited the miners, supervised them at the production site, and controlled their life at their lodges.[48]

In other cases blunt force was used to recruit people to work in the mines and stay there. Especially in the start-up of mining operations, various forms of forced labour were quite common. We find several examples in Chinese coal mining well into the twentieth century, be it in the form of convict labour, debt servitude, or servile labour.[49] In the Dutch Indies (Indonesia), the labour shortage at the start of the Ombilin coal mines (West Sumatra) was "solved" by the forced employment of convict labourers, both political and criminal prisoners, from other parts of the colony. Convict and contract labourers dominated the growing number of miners until the first half of the 1920s.[50] In the nineteenth-century southern USA, convict labour of (pre-

---

44 Simeon, *The Politics of Labour under Late Colonialism*, pp. 27, 149; Simmons, "Recruiting and Organizing an Industrial Labour Force", pp. 471–482.
45 Freund, "Labour Migration", p. 83.
46 Tim Wright, "'A Method of Evading Management' – Contract Labor in Chinese Coal Mines before 1937", *Comparative Studies in Society and History*, 23, 4 (1981), pp. 656–678.
47 Friedgut, *Iuzovka and Revolution. Vol. I*, pp. 234, 260–263, 269–271.
48 Nimura Kazuo, *The Ashio Riot of 1907. A Social History of Mining in Japan* (Durham, NC, 1997), pp. 161–178.
49 Tim Wright, *Coal Mining in China's Economy and Society 1895–1937* (Cambridge, 1984), p. 165.
50 Erwiza, "Miners, Managers and the State: A Socio-Political History of the Ombilin Coal-Mines, West Sumatra, 1892–1996 (Ph.D. dissertation, University of Amsterdam, 1999), pp. 36–41. See also

dominantly) African-Americans was regularly used in the coal mines of Georgia, Tennessee, and Alabama after the abolition of slavery (the employment of slaves had been common in the mines before).[51] They often remained in the mines after they had been released. In this way the system offered both an instrument for disciplining the black labour force and for securing a steady flow of cheap labour for the mines.

In Japan, labour scarcity at the start of the Hokkaidō coal mines (from 1882) was also solved by convict labour. After 1894 this was replaced by a system of recruitment by labour contractors. After 1939 coercive mobilization of Koreans in the mines and other industries became important in the Japanese war economy. Between 1939 and 1945 more than 300,000 Koreans were sent to Japanese mines, most against their will.[52] Like the Japanese, the Nazi-German war economy used forced labour on a massive scale during World War II, both in Germany itself and in the European occupied territories.[53] In this system ethnic discrimination and forced labour were closely interrelated, as most of the deployed workers were so-called *Ostarbeiter* and prisoners of war from Poland, Ukraine, and Russia, whom the Nazis considered to be of an inferior "race".

But mining companies used not only "the stick" by forcefully pushing labour into the mines, they could also use "the carrot" of seduction by offering facilities for workers and their families. This seems to have been the case in Northern Rhodesian / Zambian copper mining.[54] To alleviate the shortage of labour caused by the labour demand and relatively high wages elsewhere in Southern Africa, the copper mining companies allowed wives at worksites to attract male workers. Proletarian families living on the company compounds were much more common here than elsewhere in Southern Africa, where migratory labour based in rural household formation prevailed. In the Congolese part of the Copperbelt as well, by the 1920s the circular migration of young men began to give way to family migration. Mining companies adopted policies designed to support family life to stabilize the labour

---

Erwiza Erman, "Generalized Violence: A Case Study of the Ombilin Coal Mines, 1892–1996", in: Freek Colombijn and Thomas J. Lindblad (eds), *Roots of Violence in Indonesia. Contemporary Violence in Historical Perspective* (Leiden, 2002), pp. 105–131.

51 Ronald L. Lewis, *Black Coal Miners in America. Race, Class, and Community Conflict, 1780–1980* (Lexington, 1987), pp. 3–35; Alex Lichtenstein, *Twice the Work of Free Labor. The Political Economy of Convict Labor in the New South* (London, 1996).

52 Ken C. Kawashima, *The Proletarian Gamble. Korean Workers in Interwar Japan* (Durham, NC, 2009), pp. 25–45; Michael Weiner, *Race and Migration in Imperial Japan* (London and New York, 1994), pp. 112–113, 133–135, 150, 205.

53 Klaus Tenfelde and Hans-Christoph Seidel (eds), *Zwangsarbeit im Bergwerk. Der Arbeitseinsatz im Kohlenbergbau des Deutschen Reiches und der besetzten Gebiete im Ersten und Zweiten Weltkrieg, Band I: Forschungen* (Essen, 2005).

54 George Chauncey Jr., "The Locus of Reproduction: Women's Labour in the Zambian Copperbelt, 1927–1953", *Journal of Southern African Studies*, 7, 3 (1981), pp. 135–164; Jane L. Parpart, *Labor and Capital on the African Copperbelt* (Philadelphia, 1983); idem, "The Household and the Mine Shaft: Gender and Class Struggles on the Zambian Copperbelt, 1926–64", *Journal of Southern African Studies*, 13, 1 (1986), pp. 36–56.

force and to compete more effectively for workers. Workers and their families were provided with accommodation, food rations, health care, and schools.[55]

Likewise, during the 1920s, Kennecott Copper Corporation, the American owner of Chile's El Teniente Copper Mine, implemented a set of social welfare policies, which complemented traditional coercive forms of labour control to combat high levels of turnover. The programme aimed to reform workers' social and cultural lives and to train a permanent, reliable workforce. Part of this reform was the support of nuclear families formed by a male wage earner and a female housewife. Fathers and husbands were supposed to be tied down by family responsibilities, which would make them a more disciplined workforce. Social workers were hired to pay home visits and to teach women domestic skills so that they would be able to administer the family wage more efficiently.[56]

Paternalism, as this strategy of intervention in workers' family lives is commonly called in European labour history,[57] entailed a wide variety of efforts to create an environment in which a worker would comply with the harsh labour conditions in the mines, thus limiting the need to resort to external means of coercion and control. Companies subsidized a wide range of social services, such as housing, pension schemes, schools, and churches, to attract workers and to encourage them to settle down with their families. Paternal welfare provisions were designed to link the worker closer to the company, and were combined with control and the maintenance of discipline, reaching into the family lives of the workers. Although the above examples show that paternalism was a strategy among mine owners in different parts of the world, it was most prevalent in European and North American mining.[58]

Gendering labour

In 1975, the British sociologist Martin Bulmer gave an overview of "sociological models of the mining community". All characteristics of this "community" were related to the men's work. There was only scant reference to the female members of the community, and the one time women were mentioned they did not seem to have a life of

---

[55] John Higginson, *A Working Class in the Making. Belgian Colonial Labor Policy, Private Enterprise, and the African Mineworker, 1907–1951* (Madison, 1989), pp. 61–85.

[56] Thomas Miller Klubock, "Working-Class Masculinity, Middle-Class Morality, and Labor Politics in the Chilean Copper Mines", *Journal of Social History*, 30, 2 (1996), pp. 435–463, 436–437.

[57] See, among others, on France, Peter Stearns, *Paths to Authority. The Middle Class and the Industrial Labor Force in France, 1820–48* (Urbana, 1978), and, on the British textile industry, Patrick Joyce, *Work, Society and Politics. The Culture of the Factory in Later Victorian England* (New Brunswick, 1980).

[58] On France: Donald Reid, "Industrial Paternalism: Discourse and Practice in Nineteenth-Century French Mining and Metallurgy", *Comparative Studies in Society and History*, 27, 4 (1985), pp. 579–607. For an example from the United States, see Crandall A. Shifflett, *Coal Towns. Life, Work, and Culture in Company Towns of Southern Appalachia, 1880–1960* (Knoxville, 1991).

their own: "the woman's activities are centred on the home, in providing for husband and children".[59] This view was not only ahistorical, as many women, both in Europe and other parts of the world, have been employed as workers in mining, and many miners' wives and daughters have held jobs outside mining, it was also gender biased, as Angela John remarked in her study on women workers in Victorian coal mining: "their position has tended to be viewed solely in terms of the wife's back-up support for the male miner. Admittedly this was vital, but accounts of mining communities have not only forgotten the single woman and the widow, but have internalised the male miners' 'eye view'".[60] Or, in the words of Kuntala Lahiri-Dutt and Martha Macintyre: "Women in mining communities are not seen as active participants [...] [but] as miners' wives, staying at home and supporting their working class men".[61]

However much this may be true, in many mining communities in Europe, North America, and elsewhere there was a strict gender division of labour, at least during the twentieth century: women were supposed to support and care for male miners in the reproductive sphere, to enable them to do the demanding work underground. The routine of the household revolved around the routine of the pit and the needs of the miners.[62] While separated, male and female domains were complementary and mutually dependent. To enable the worker to perform the highly rationalized labour in the mines, organized in day and night shifts, it was the mining companies' preferred solution to relegate reproductive tasks to the miners' wives and keep them at home. Concern for the miner's family was part and parcel of the paternalist policies of these companies, directed at the families at large, and the reproductive tasks of the miners' wives in particular. The complementarity of male and female roles in wage and unpaid domestic labour had negative effects on opportunities for women, both married and unmarried, especially daughters, to find paid work in the labour market. The one-sidedness of the division of labour was thus perpetuated. Only in districts where mining was interspersed with, for instance, textile industry, could women find a job

---

59 M.I.A. Bulmer, "Sociological Models of the Mining Community", *The Sociological Review*, 23, 1 (1975), pp. 61–92, 87. See also Norman Dennis, Fernando Henriques, and Clifford Slaughter, *Coal is Our Life. An Analysis of a Yorkshire Mining Community* (London, 1956). For a secondary analysis of this mining community from a deliberately less gender-biased perspective, see Dennis Warwick and Gary Littlejohn, *Coal, Capital and Culture. A Sociological Analysis of Mining Communities in West Yorkshire* (London, 1992).
60 Angela V. John, *By the Sweat of Their Brow. Women Workers at Victorian Coal Mines* (London, 1980), pp. 14–15.
61 Kuntala Lahiri-Dutt and Martha Macintyre, "Where Life is in the Pits (and Elsewhere) and Gendered", in: *idem, Women Miners in Developing Countries*, pp. 1–22, 2.
62 Cf. Valerie Hall, *Women at Work, 1860–1939. How Different Industries Shaped Women's Experiences* (Woodbridge, 2013). See also Griselda Carr, *Pit Women. Coal Communities in Northern England in the Early Twentieth Century* (London, 2001).

more easily. In other cases, women sought income in "informal" activities, like gardening or lodging.[63]

The corollary of this strict division of labour was the development of an outspoken ideology of manhood and an image of masculinity attached to the mining profession. Part of this was a particular idea of values deemed "masculine", such as physical strength, capacity for hard labour, toughness, rough sports such as football, and, most of all, the strict observance of a gendered division of labour. George Orwell, writing about the mining communities in northern England in his famous novel *The Road to Wigan Pier* (1936), emphasized that even when unemployed a man would rarely do "a stroke of housework" for fear he "would lose his manhood".[64] While this attitude was supported by paternalist company policies, it was also very much part of the self-image of the miners, and of their representation in politics, unionism, literature, and other works of art, at least in the twentieth century.

In earlier periods, however, women had been employed in the mining industry in several parts of Europe, both below and above ground. In early modern German mining, women were employed above ground in picking, sorting, hammering, and washing the ore.[65] In coal mining, in the system of pillar and stall the employment of women was often part of a family concern: the male collier working at his post as a hewer was assisted by his wife and children.[66] The women's main task was to work as drawers: pulling sledges or tubs along the pit floor to the bottom shaft. It is an image made familiar by the French writer Emile Zola in his great novel *Germinal* (1884–1885) on the miners in northern France. One of the female characters, Catherine Maheu, works together in a team of male and female workers. Women worked underground as hauliers (*hiercheuses*). Both in France and in Belgium work in the coal mines was organized in this way, until underground labour for women was prohibited by law in 1892. Above ground, women continued to work as *hiercheuses*, *trieuses* (sorting coal), and *lampenistes*.[67] In Britain, working the mines in underground family teams was common in the eighteenth and early nineteenth centuries. By the 1840s, female colliery labour appears to have been declining slowly, and to have become concentrated in more clearly defined areas. The British Mines Act of 1842 excluded women from working underground, but, like in France and Belgium,

---

[63] Notorious examples can be found in Chauncey, "The Locus of Reproduction".

[64] George Orwell, *The Road to Wigan Pier* (London, 1936), p. 75, cited by Ben Clarke, "'Noble Bodies': Orwell, Miners, and Masculinity", *English Studies*, 89, 4 (2008), pp. 427–446, 433.

[65] Cristina Vanja, "Bergarbeiterinnen. Zur Geschichte der Frauenarbeit im Bergbau, Hütten- und Salinenwesen seit dem späten Mittelalter. Teil I: Spätes Mittelalter und frühe Neuzeit", *Der Anschnitt. Zeitschrift für Kunst und Kultur im Bergbau*, 39 (1987), pp. 2–15.

[66] Idem, "Teil II: Die Entwicklung im 19. und 20. Jahrhundert", ibid., 40 (1988), pp. 128–143.

[67] Leen Roels, *Het tekort. Studies over de arbeidsmarkt voor mijnwerkers in het Luikse kolenbekken vanaf het einde van de negentiende eeuw tot 1974* (Hilversum, 2014). In Germany, by contrast, it was uncommon for women to work in the mines. See Christina Vanja, "Mining Women in Early Modern European Society", in: Thomas Max Safley and Leonard N. Rosenband (eds), *The Workplace before the Factory. Artisans and Proletarians, 1500–1800* (Ithaca, NY, 1993), pp. 100–117, 100.

in several districts (such as Lancashire) family labour groups simply reformed to encompass work above ground by women known as "pit brow lasses".⁶⁸

In other parts of the world, women working underground in family teams persisted well into the twentieth century. In the Indian coalfields of Jharia and Raniganj, in 1924 almost fifty per cent of the women underground were working with their husbands, thirty per cent with relatives, and the remaining twenty per cent on their own.⁶⁹ Man and wife often worked in pairs: the man cutting, and the wife together with children and other kin loading, carrying, and hauling the coal. This was common as long as teamwork around the hewer, working at different posts in the room-and-pillar system, was prevalent. These were miners from the local "tribal" population of so-called Adivasi. A decline in the number of women working underground since the 1920s has been associated with the introduction of mechanized production techniques, both in coal cutting and transport, leading to the rationalization of production and the introduction of long-wall mining in a shift system, and the recruitment of male migrant labour for these mechanized mines. In 1929 underground labour by women was prohibited under the Indian Mines Act (within ten years).⁷⁰

Until the late 1920s, such a system of family labour in underground teams could also be found in Japan, especially in the Kyushu coal mines in the south (much less so in the Hokkaidō mines in the north). The so-called *hitosaki* (a pair working team for mining) consisted of a *sakiyama* (male hewer "at the working face") and an *atoyama* (a female haulier "backstage in the pit"). In 1924 there were more than 68,000 female labourers in the coal mines nationwide, of whom 48,000 (seventy-one per cent) were working underground. Family work persisted as long as traditional stall-and-pillar mining prevailed. After the mid-1920s, mechanization of the production process and the replacement of stall-and-pillar by long-wall mining resulted in mass dismissals, especially of women. In 1928 female miners were prohibited from working underground by law.⁷¹

---

68 John, *By the Sweat of Their Brow*, pp. 20–25.
69 Peter Alexander, "Women and Coal Mining in India and South Africa, c1900–1940", *African Studies*, 66, 2–3 (2007), pp. 201–222, 206.
70 *Ibid.*, pp. 207–209. See also Shashank S. Sinha, "Patriarchy, Colonialism and Capitalism: Unearthing the History of *Adivasi* Women Miners of Chotanagpur", and Kuntala Lahiri-Dutt, "Mining Gender at Work in the Indian Collieries: Identity Construction by *Kamins*", in: Lahiri-Dutt and Macintyre, *Women Miners in Developing Countries*, pp. 89–108, and 163–181; Kuntala Lahiri-Dutt, "Kamins Building the Empire: Class, Caste, and Gender Interface in Indian Collieries", in: Gier and Mercier, *Mining Women*, pp. 71–87.
71 Sachiko Sone, "Japanese Coal Mining: Women Discovered", in: Lahiri-Dutt and Macintyre, *Women Miners in Developing Countries*, pp. 51–72; Regine Mathias, "Female Labour in the Japanese Coal-Mining Industry", in: Janet Hunter (ed.), *Japanese Women Working* (London and New York, 1993), pp. 99–121; Yutaka Nishinarita, "The Coal-Mining Industry", in: Masanori Nakamura (ed.), *Technology Change and Female Labour in Japan* (Tokyo, 1994), pp. 59–96.

Industrial relations, strike propensity, and political radicalism: an isolated mass?

I would guess that few sociological theories have been more thoroughly deconstructed than the idea of "the isolated mass" as an explanation of differences in "interindustry propensity to strike". In an endlessly cited and recycled article, published in 1954, Clark Kerr and Abraham Siegel argued that strike rates among geographically and socially isolated, cohesive, homogeneous groups of workers such as miners were higher than among other workers. Mining was one of those industries tending to "direct workers into isolated masses", which by themselves were supposed to be highly strike prone.[72]

Almost from the start, the thesis generated considerable controversy and an extensive secondary literature, perhaps because it was such an easy target.[73] Criticisms of the Kerr-Siegel hypothesis, apart from revealing shortcomings of the data and statistics, argued that industries such as mining, considered typical for the "isolated massness" of their workers, were in fact much less so; differences within industries were not accounted for; other possible explanations of strike behaviour, such as workplace characteristics, were neglected; it was not clear if the "isolated mass" was a necessary or sufficient condition for strikes to occur; the mobilizing or pacifying role of trade unions remained unaccounted for; the approach did not allow for changes in strike propensity over time; and the strike behaviour of miners varied greatly in different countries. While in Germany miners' unions were extraordinarily strong, with union densities in the 1950s and 1960s at around ninety per cent, strike propensity – probably for this reason – was quite low.[74] Shorter and Tilly even concluded that, historically, strike propensity in France was much higher among "integrated" than among "isolated" workers.[75]

In spite of the many criticisms, the Kerr-Siegel hypothesis continued to influence attempts to explain strike behaviour among coal miners, especially in Great Britain, well into the 1980s. Therefore, in the 1990s, Roy Church and Quentin Outram felt justified in subjecting the relationship between the "isolated mass" and strike propen-

---

[72] C. Kerr and A. Siegel, "The Interindustry Propensity to Strike – An International Comparison", in: A. Kornhauser, R. Dubin, and A.M. Ross (eds), *Industrial Conflict* (New York, 1954), pp. 189–212.
[73] Gaston V. Rimlinger, "International Differences in the Strike Propensity of Coal Miners: Experience in Four Countries", *Industrial and Labor Relations Review*, 12, 3 (1958/59), pp. 389–405; P.K. Edwards, "A Critique of the Kerr-Siegel Hypothesis of Strikes and the Isolated Mass: A Study of the Falsification of Sociological Knowledge", *The Sociological Review*, 25:3 (1977), pp. 551–574.
[74] Klaus Tenfelde, "Radikal, militant? Forschungen über Bergarbeiterstreiks im 20. Jahrhundert", in: Westermann and Westermann, *Streik im Revier*, pp. 381–404.
[75] Edward Shorter and Charles Tilly, *Strikes in France, 1830–1968* (Cambridge, 1974), pp. 287–295: "The Kerr-Siegel 'isolation' hypothesis and France's experience".

sity in British coalfield history to systematic statistical testing.[76] Their conclusion was that the Kerr-Siegel hypothesis did help to explain variations in strike behaviour in interwar England and Wales between collieries, but that there was no linear relationship: "massed isolation" facilitated but by no means guaranteed high levels of strike activity. The main explanatory factor was the size of the workplace: bigger collieries were more strike prone than smaller ones. More importantly from a historical point of view was their conclusion about the inability of the model to offer an explanation of variation over time: collieries that have gone on strike frequently have rarely done so with any temporal consistency. Specific historical factors thus need to be added for the isolation of the miners' community to have any value in explaining strike behaviour.

The argument of "isolation" has been broadened by Klaus Tenfelde to explain the political radicalization of miners and other workers in specific historical contexts in the interwar years, but without the essentially static interpretation of the Kerr-Siegel model.[77] To explain communist success in some isolated German communities, he added a historical dimension by introducing the argument of a recent, sudden industrialization (*punktuelle Industrialisierung*). His argument can be combined with French research stressing the generational factor: radicalization could be found among second-generation migrants in this kind of newly established local community.[78] This is consistent with a more general critique of the "isolated mass" thesis and its corollary of the "occupational community": miners generally moved quite frequently, and supposedly homogeneous miners' communities were in fact highly diversified.[79]

Although from this perspective a universal relationship cannot be established, in many countries miners were in the forefront of radical politics. This could take several forms, both socially and politically, and in different political manifestations. The British Labour Party started its parliamentary representation in the early twentieth century from a regional base in the coalfield areas.[80] Miners in African colonies such as Zambia and Nigeria were in the forefront of national liberation movements.[81]

---

[76] Roy Church, Quentin Outram, and David N. Smith, "The 'Isolated Mass' Revisited: Strikes in British Coal Mining", *The Sociological Review*, 39, 1 (1991), pp. 55–87; Roy Church and Quentin Outram, *Strikes and Solidarity. Coalfield Conflict in Britain 1889–1966* (Cambridge, 1998), pp. 132–158: "Conflictual context? The 'isolated mass' revisited".

[77] Klaus Tenfelde, "Social Consequences of Isolated Industrialization: The Case of Germany", in: Sakari Hänninen et al. (eds), *Meeting Local Challenges – Mapping Industrial Identities* (Helsinki, 1999), pp. 108–121.

[78] Ad Knotter, "'Little Moscows' in Western Europe: The Ecology of Small-Place Communism", *International Review of Social History*, 56, 3 (2011), pp. 475–510.

[79] Knotter, "Migration and Ethnicity in Coalfield History", pp. 35–38.

[80] P.J. Taylor and R.J. Johnston, *Geography of Elections* (Harmondsworth, 1979), p. 398.

[81] Thomas Rasmussen, "The Popular Basis of Anti-Colonial Protest", in: William Tordoff (ed.), *Politics in Zambia* (Berkeley, 1974), pp. 54–55; Carolyn A. Brown, *"We Were All Slaves". African Miners, Culture, and Resistance at the Enugu Government Colliery* (Portsmouth, NH, 2003).

During the twentieth century tin miners played a decisive role in altering the political structure of Bolivia.[82] In Spanish Asturias coal miners took the lead in a memorable uprising in the 1930s and in the opposition against the Franco regime in the 1970s. The communist-led Comisiones Obreras had its origins there.[83]

Especially in the 1930s and 1940s, many mining regions became communist strongholds. Communist parties considered miners "archetypical proletarians" and were often able to mobilize them around this identity.[84] Perhaps the Soviet hero Stakhanov is the ultimate symbol of the communist image of coal miners as tough proletarians. Nevertheless, communist or other radical political influences among miners cannot be ascribed to a kind of supposedly inherent or essential characteristic of their work or community. It always resulted from a specific configuration of political and class forces in specific moments in time. In French Nord-Pas-de-Calais coal-mining communist influence originated in the Popular Front and Resistance era between 1936 and 1944; it managed to survive the harsh repression during the 1948 miners' strike,[85] in contrast to the German Ruhr area, where interwar and postwar communist influence among miners melted away into a dominant social democratic electorate in the late 1940s.[86] In spite of their relative insignificance as a political party in Britain, communists were very influential in British miners' unionism, and had several strongholds in the South Wales and Scottish coalfields.[87]

Communist influence among miners was not restricted to Europe. In Australia, communism was firmly implanted in the coalfields of New South Wales.[88] In Chile, the communists had their major base in the mining areas: in 1947 they re-

---

[82] Robert L. Smale, *"I Sweat the Flavor of Tin". Labor Activism in Early Twentieth Century Bolivia* (Pittsburgh, 2010).

[83] Adrian Shubert, *The Road to Revolution in Spain. The Coal Miners of Asturias 1860–1934* (Urbana and Chicago, 1987); Holm-Detlev Köhler, *Asturien. Der Niedergang einer industriellen Region in Europa* (Essen, 1998).

[84] Marc Lazar, "Le mineur de fond: un exemple de l'identité du PCF", *Revue française de science politique*, 35, 2 (1985), pp. 190–205. For the masculine connotation of this identity, see Hanna Diamond, "Miners, Masculinity and the 'Bataille du Charbon' in France 1944–1948", *Modern and Contemporary France*, 19, 1 (2011), pp. 69–84.

[85] Marion Fontaine and Xavier Vigna, "La grève des mineurs de l'automne 1948 en France", *Vingtième siècle. Revue d'histoire*, 121 (2014), pp. 21–34.

[86] Till Kössler, *Abschied von der Revolution. Kommunisten und Gesellschaft in Westdeutschland 1945–1968* (Düsseldorf, 2004).

[87] Chris Williams, *Democratic Rhondda. Politics and Society, 1885–1951* (Cardiff, 1996); Alan Campbell, "Communism in the Scottish Coalfields, 1920–1936", *Tijdschrift voor Sociale Geschiedenis*, 18 (1992), pp. 168–190. See also Nina Fishman, *Arthur Horner. A Political Biography*, 2 vols (London, 2010).

[88] Ellen McEwen, "Coalminers in Newcastle, New South Wales: A Labour Aristocracy?", and Andrew Reeves, "'Damned Scotsmen': British Migrants and the Australian Coal Industry, 1919–49", in: Eric Fry (ed.), *Common Cause. Essays in Australian and New Zealand Labour History* (Sydney, 1986), pp. 77–92 and 93–106; Martin Mowbray, "The Red Shire of Kearsley: 1944–1947: Communists in Local Government", *Labour History*, 51 (1986), pp. 83–94.

ceived seventy-one per cent of the coal miners' vote, and fifty-five per cent of the vote of the copper workers (nationally this was eighteen per cent).[89] I end this overview with the remarkable history of China's "Little Moscow" Anyuan,[90] not only because of the political and cultural configurations of communist implantation in this coal-mining town in the 1920s, but also because of the way memories of this episode were politicized during the Cultural Revolution to symbolize an authentically Chinese revolutionary tradition, above all encapsulated by the then famous painting "Chairman Mao goes to Anyuan". China is now experiencing a huge energy transformation from coal to renewable energy. Like in Europe, mining and mine labour will soon be something of the past – and of memory cultures and the writing of history.

Conclusion

In the traditions of European labour history mining has been privileged in the research of proletarian labour and anti-capitalist social movements. The "global turn" in labour history has made it clear that the idea of the miner as an "archetypal proletarian" was both Eurocentric and ahistorical however. Historically and globally, a broad array of labour relations existed in mining next to wage labour, sometimes in the same location. Studies of mining labour in different parts of the world exemplify the many variations in labour relations in capitalist development. They have led to generalizations about the articulation of different types of labour relations in forms of free and unfree labour, partial proletarianization, subcontracting, seasonal migration, and the gendered nature of reproductive labour, and also about the interconnectedness of labour mobilization and labour control. The debate on these themes has the potential to yield a more comprehensive view of global labour history in general, or at least to stimulate global comparative research of labour relations in other industrial sectors from a global perspective.

---

89 James Petras and Maurice Zeitlin, "Miners and Agrarian Radicalism", *American Sociological Review*, 32, 4 (1967), pp. 578–586, 579–580; on the Chilean coalfields see also Jody Pavilack, *Mining for the Nation. The Politics of Chile's Coal Communities from the Popular Front to the Cold War* (University Park, PA, 2011).
90 Elizabeth Perry, *Anyuan. Mining China's Revolutionary Tradition* (Berkeley, CA, 2012).

Suggested reading

Blakewell, Peter J. *Miners of the Red Mountain: Indian Labor in Potosí, 1545–1650* (Albuquerque, NM: University of New Mexico Press 1984).

Brown, Carolyn A. *"We Were All Slaves". African Miners, Culture, and Resistance at the Enugu Government Colliery* (Portsmouth NH: Heinemann, 2003).

Brown, Kendall W.A. *History of Mining in Latin America. From the Colonial Era to the Present* (Albuquerque: University of New Mexico Press, 2012).

Church, Roy, and Quentin Outram. *Strikes and Solidarity. Coalfield Conflict in Britain 1889–1966* (Cambridge: University Press, 1998).

First, Ruth, *Black Gold. The Mozambican Miner, Proletarian and Peasant* (Manchester: Palgrave Macmillan, 1983)

Freund, Bill. *Capital and Labour in the Nigerian Tin Mines* (Harlow: Longman, 1981).

Gier, Jaclyn J. and Laurie Mercier (eds). *Mining Women. Gender and the Development of a Global Industry, 1670 to the Present* (Basingstoke: Palgrave Macmillan, 2006).

Higginson, John. *A Working Class in the Making. Belgian Colonial Labor Policy, Private Enterprise, and the African Mineworker, 1907–1951* (Madison, WI: University of Wisconsin Press, 1989).

Kaur, Amarjit. *Wage Labour in Southeast Asia since 1840: Globalisation, the International Division of Labour and Labour Transformations* (London: Palgrave Macmillan, 2004).

Knotter, Ad and David Mayer (eds). *Migration and Ethnicity in Coalfield History: Global Perspectives*, Special Issue 23, *International Review of Social History* 60 (2015).

Kruijt, Dirk and Menno Vellinga. *Labor Relations and Multinational Corporations: The Cerro de Pasco Corporation in Peru (1902–1974)* (Leiden and Boston: Brill, 1979).

Lahiri-Dutt, Kuntala and Martha Macintyre (eds). *Women Miners in Developing Countries: Pit Women and Others* (Aldershot: Ashgate, 2006).

Miller Klubock, Thomas. *Contested Communities: Class, Gender, and Politics in Chile's El Teniente Copper Mine, 1904–1951* (Durham, NC: Duke University Press, 1998).

Moodie, Dunbar (with Viviane Ndatshe). *Going for Gold: Men, Mines, and Migration* (Berkeley, CA: University of California Press, 1994).

Nash, June C. *We Eat the Mines and the Mines Eat Us. Dependency and Exploitation in the Bolivian Tin Mines* (New York: Columbia University Press, 1993).

Golas, Peter J. *Mining*. Part XIII of Joseph Needham, *Science and Civilisation in China. Volume 5. Chemistry and Chemical Technology* (Cambridge: Cambridge University Press, 1999).

Nimura, Kazuo. *The Ashio Riot of 1907. A Social History of Mining in Japan* (Durham, NC: Duke University Press, 1998).

Perry, Elizabeth. *Anyuan: Mining China's Revolutionary Tradition* (Berkeley CA: University of California Press, 2012).

Simeon, Dilip. *The Politics of Labour Under Late Colonialism: Workers, Unions and the State in Chota Nagpur 1928–1939* (New Delhi: South Asia Books, 1995).

Tandeter, Enrique. *Coercion and Market. Silver Mining in Colonial Potosí, 1692–1826* (Albuquerque: University of New Mexico Press 1993).

Tutino, John. *Making a New World. Founding Capitalism in the Bajı́o and Spanish North America* (Durham: Duke University Press, 2011).

Van Onselen, Charles. *Chibaro. African Mine Labour in Southern Rhodesia, 1900–1933* (London: Pluto Press, 1976).

Wright, Tim. *Coal Mining in China's Economy and Society 1895–1937* (Cambridge: Cambridge University Press, 1984).

Prasannan Parthasarathi
3.3. Textile Industry

Introduction

The manufacture of textiles has been a critical dimension of labour history. The ubiquity of textile production—clothing being one of the three material essentials for humans, along with food and shelter—meant that large numbers of men and women devoted their lives to the making of cloth. Textiles and the raw materials needed for their manufacture were traded extensively and formed an important part of local, regional, and global commerce. Although it is difficult to confirm quantitatively, anecdotal evidence suggests that cloth was the single largest manufactured good in world trade till well into the nineteenth and perhaps even twentieth century. For these reasons, the editors of the authoritative study of textile workers around the world write, "The relevance of a global history of textile production over a long period of time is clear: textile products cater for a basic human need, they are among the most important goods fabricated and traded by mankind and have thus played a central role in human activities throughout history."[1]

This paper uses the prism of textile workers to examine four critical themes in labour history. First, textile manufacturing is an excellent vantage point from which to trace changes in the organization and forms of work from the sixteenth century to the present. Textiles have been made, and continue to be made, in a bewildering variety of settings and social relationships, from dispersed rural manufacturing in households to centralized computer-driven factories. Second, the making of textiles raises profound questions about the division of labour between men and women and inequalities between the sexes. Before the mechanization of textile manufacturing, the almost universal divide between spinning and weaving in which the former was allocated to women and the latter to men meant that the activity which was typically the highest value-added portion of the process was monopolized by men. After mechanization, inequality between the sexes was reproduced in factories around the world. Third, the textile trades were an important site for worker resistance, which raises fundamental questions of worker subjectivity. The Luddites, for instance, were drawn from the ranks of stocking knitters in England. In the nineteenth and twentieth centuries, textile workers formed the backbone of strikes and opposition to governments around the world. Finally, textile workers are critical for a global labour history. For centuries, the vibrant global trade in textiles shaped

---

[1] Els Hiemstra-Kuperus, Lex Heerma van Voss and Elise van Nederveen Meerkerk, "Textile Workers Around the World. 1650–2000: Introduction to a Collective Work Project", in: Lex Heerma van Voss, Els Hiemstra-Kuperus and Elise van Nederveen Meerkerk (eds), *The Ashgate Companion to the History of Textile Workers, 1650–2000* (Farnham, 2010), pp. 1–13, at 1.

cloth manufacturing around the world. Booms in some regions have been matched by busts in others. And this global trade sparked momentous changes in the process of textile manufacture as well as worker politics, a striking example of which is the so-called Arab Spring in Egypt in 2011. This chapter takes each of these themes in turn.

The organization of textile manufacturing

In 1500 textile manufacturing in many parts of the world was dominated by guilds or guild-like institutions. Europe and the Ottoman Empire possessed classic guild forms, which were associations of urban artisans that controlled prices and quality of cloth as well as the entry into the craft. These institutions were also self-governing and possessed leaders and statutes. Artisans in cloth in India, China and Japan, although not organized in classic guilds, possessed guild-like organizations which had many of the powers of European and Ottoman guilds. In Mexico, as well, guilds were formed after the Spanish conquest.[2] Drawing on this diverse evidence, Bo Gustafsson concluded that guilds were a "generally occurring city-based industrial form of production in all pre-industrial/pre-capitalist economies."[3]

In the sixteenth and seventeenth centuries commercial expansion in Europe, and the growing demand for cloth, led to an expansion of textile manufacturing in rural areas, which lay outside the control of urban guilds. Although this growth in rural manufacturing had been the subject of historical research for many years, as indicated by Joan Thirsk's classic article "Industries in the Countryside", the phenomenon received widespread attention after the publication of an important article by Franklin Mendels, who dubbed the phenomenon "proto-industrialization" or the first phase of the industrialization process.[4]

The growing demand for cloth and a mercantile desire to obtain the commodity at lower prices were behind the shift of manufacturing to the countryside. The cheap labour of rural men, women and children was substituted for more expensive urban, male, guild workers. The guilds of Europe challenged this merchant move to elude their monopoly on production, but history was to be with the merchants and this

---

[2] Jeffrey Bortz, "Mexican Textile Workers: From Conquest to Globalization", in: Heerma van Voss, Hiemstra-Kuperus and van Nederveen Meerkerk, *Ashgate Companion*, pp. 333–361, at 338.
[3] Bo Gustafsson, "The Rise and Economic Behaviour of Medieval Craft Guilds", in his *Power and Economic Institutions: Reinterpretations in Economic History* (Aldershot, 1991), pp. 69–70, cited in Lars K. Christensen, "Institutions in Textile Production: Guilds and Trade Unions", in: Heerma van Voss, Hiemstra-Kuperus and van Nederveen Meerkerk, *Ashgate Companion*, pp. 749–771, at 750.
[4] Joan Thirsk, "Industries in the Countryside", in F. J. Fisher (ed.), *Essays in the Economic and Social History of Tudor and Stuart England* (Cambridge, 1961), pp. 70–88; Franklin Mendels, "Proto-Industrialization: The First Phase of the Industrialization Process", *Journal of Economic History*, 32, 1 (1972), pp. 241–261.

shift was part of the larger complex of changes often associated with the rise of capitalism. Historians have challenged central elements of the proto-industrialization thesis, however.

A number of scholars have questioned the universalism of its claims, which are implied in the portrayal of proto-industrialization as the first phase of industrialization. Specialists on regions such as the Middle East and South Asia have argued that proto-industrialization is not appropriate for describing the evolution of textile manufacturing outside Europe. Donald Quataert, the historian of the Ottoman Empire, writes, "Embedded in the pairing of the terms proto-industrialization and industrialization remains a sense of success or failure, approval for economies that successfully industrialized and disappointment in those that did not. This procedure seems rather judgmental to me and thus I am not entirely comfortable with the term."[5] Frank Perlin systematically critiqued the term from the vantage point of South Asia and found it wanting for its teleological assumptions. In its place, Perlin proposed the concept of commercial manufactures, which he argued more accurately depicted the transformation in textile manufacturing on a global scale.[6] This was, of course, the growing importance of mercantile interests in the textile trades as demand from long-distance markets grew in the seventeenth and eighteenth centuries. Merchants and manufacturers began to enter into relations with textile workers, whether spinners or weavers or specialists in finishing cloth, to obtain goods of specific type, quality and price. These took the form of putting out systems in which materials were distributed to what could at times be vast networks of producers and commercial advance systems in which money was given to producers for their subsistence and purchase of materials. While the former was common in Europe, the latter prevailed in regions such as South Asia. The growth of commercialized systems for the manufacture of cloth laid the foundations for conflict between mercantile and worker interests, which will be taken up in due course. (In this period, self-financed production by peasant households to meet commercial demands also took place, which was the case in the lower Yangzi region of the Qing Empire.[7])

Even in Europe, proto-industrialization did not automatically lead to industrialization and there are countless cases of proto-industrial success and industrial failure. For this reason proto-industrialization is often seen as a superfluous or unnecessary category, "a concept too many" in the words of D. C. Coleman.[8] However, in

---

5 Donald Quataert, "Proto-industrialization and Industrialization and 'Modernity' in a Global Perspective", in: Heerma van Voss, Hiemstra-Kuperus and van Nederveen Meerkerk, *Ashgate Companion*, pp. 577–595, at 579.
6 Frank Perlin, "Proto-Industrialization and Pre-Colonial South Asia", *Past and Present*, 98 (1983), pp. 30–95.
7 Robert Cliver, "China", in: Heerma van Voss, Hiemstra-Kuperus and van Nederveen Meerkerk, *Ashgate Companion*, pp. 103–139, at 108.
8 D. C. Coleman, "Proto-Industrialization: A Concept Too Many", *Economic History Review*, 36, 3 (1983), pp. 435–448.

the European context, proto-industrialization did point to the changing relations of production in textile manufacturing in which the power, influence and autonomy of workers who had been organized in guilds began to wane.

While it is important to recognize that by the eighteenth century, especially in Europe, the work of textile manufacturing, both urban and rural, could be characterized by long hours, low earnings, and repetitive and tedious work, the degradation of work and workers worsened with the coming of the factory system. The centralization of work had long antecedents. There were large workshops in Europe and the Ottoman Empire and in Mughal India some textile manufacturing for the state and nobility was undertaken in *karkhanas*, in which state officials organized production. The karkhanas, however, were set up for the making of high value cloths (as well as other goods) in order to directly supervise the workers and prevent the embezzlement of costly raw materials.[9]

The modern factory emerged in Western Europe in the wake of industrialization and the mechanization of textile manufacturing. While there is certainly a technological component in the reorganization of production into central points—the power demands of some machines such as Arkwright's waterframe make it difficult to operate them in homes or cottages—that is not the full story. Stephen Marglin has argued forcefully that the factory was an effort to monitor and discipline workers in order to increase the profits of the merchant or manufacturer, now capitalist.[10] In dispersed systems of production, which characterized the putting out system, it could be difficult to get the workers to put in the effort that capitalists wanted. In a classic paper, E. P. Thompson described the uneven rhythms that characterized pre-industrial work in which the work week was populated by Saint Mondays, frequent breaks, and bouts of drinking.[11] Dispersed producers possessed more power to steal raw materials and produce goods that were subpar in quality.[12] The factory resolved these contradictions for the cloth manufacturer. Workers were brought under the discipline of the employer and while embezzlement was not eliminated altogether, it became more difficult. The factory was then a quintessentially modern disciplinary institution, a point that Michel Foucault acknowledged.[13]

---

9 Irfan Habib, "Potentialities of Capitalistic Development in the Economy of Mughal India", *Journal of Economic History*, 29, 1 (1969), pp. 32–78, at 59, 68–9.
10 Stephen A. Marglin, "What Do Bosses Do? The Origins and Functions of Hierarchy in Capitalist Production", *Review of radical political economics*, 6 (1974), pp. 60–112.
11 E. P. Thompson, "Time, Work-Discipline and Industrial Capitalism", *Past and Present*, 38 (1967), pp. 56–97.
12 John Styles, "Embezzlement, Industry and the Law in England, 1500–1800", in: Maxine Berg, Pat Hudson and Michael Sonenscher (eds), *Manufacture in Town and Country before the Factory* (Cambridge, 1983), pp. 173–210; Prasannan Parthasarathi, *The Transition to a Colonial Economy. Weavers, Merchants and Kings in South India, 1720–1800* (Cambridge, 2001), pp. 25–6.
13 Michel Foucault, *Discipline and Punish. The Birth of the Prison*. Trans. Alan Sheridan (New York, 1977).

Despite the modernity of the factory, centralized production in textiles has not eliminated decentralized or dispersed production, which continues to exist to this day. Nor has mechanization spelt the end of hand-powered methods of textile manufacture. Some forms of hand production disappeared quite quickly in the face of machine competition, the most striking being the spinning of yarn which in many cases was unable to compete against the dramatic price reductions that machinery wrought. However, in weaving and finishing hand methods persist. In some cases, these hand methods endure because of worker choices—the craft was the source of livelihood and to abandon it would have meant economic uncertainty and quite possibly unemployment. For others, the craft was a source of meaning and to give it up would be tantamount to rejecting oneself and one's heritage. Such actions from below may be identified from Britain to India and China and elsewhere.[14]

While not minimizing these worker choices, decentralized production has also persisted because of the decisions of merchants and manufacturers. Rajnarayan Chandavarkar showed this in striking fashion for British India during the Great Depression of the 1930s. After the collapse of the agrarian economy, Indian towns and cities had plentiful supplies of unemployed men and women who could be put to work on a very cheap basis. Textile capitalists opted to employ this labour in dispersed production rather than investing in factories because it was both cheaper and more flexible. When demand for cloth increased or decreased, workers could be hired or fired more easily with decentralized systems than centralized.[15] Not all of this dispersed production was conducted on the basis of hand machinery. Douglas Haynes has shown that in western India small workshops were established on the basis of inexpensive power machinery, some of it used powerlooms discarded by the mills of Bombay.[16] By the twentieth century, textile manufacturing was organized in a remarkable number of ways.

This continues to be case even in the twenty-first century, where rural-based manufacturing co-exists with highly automated computer-driven spinning and weaving. In a case that is reminiscent of Joan Thirsk's "Industries in the Countryside", in the Indian state of West Bengal, the embroidery of saris, an important element in the finishing of cloth in that region, is shifting from its urban home in Kolkata to rural villages. Because of a growing demand for low-cost embroidered saris, merchants and manufacturers have established putting out networks to take advantage of cheap labour in the countryside, putting highly skilled urban artisans out of

---

14 Quataert, "Proto-industrialization and Industrialization", pp. 590–594.
15 Rajnarayan Chandavarkar, "Industrialization in India before 1947: Conventional Approaches and Alternative Perspectives", *Modern Asian Studies*, 19, 3 (1985), pp. 623–668.
16 Douglas Haynes, *Small Town Capitalism in Western India. Artisans, Merchants and the Making of the Informal Economy, 1870–1960* (Cambridge, 2012).

work.[17] The flexibility, innovativeness, and sheer drive for profit of textile manufacturers are something to behold.

Male and female textile workers

Textile manufacturing, perhaps more than any other industry, gave rise to stark inequalities between the sexes. Whether in dispersed production or centralized, in many parts of the world the making of textiles was characterized by a strict sexual division of labour in which the lucrative tasks within the manufacturing process were monopolized by men. There were of course exceptions to this general rule. In North America before industrialization women were involved in all stages of the production process and in Argentina and Mexico weaving was women's work. However, in most parts of the world, women spun and men wove. Women and children also assisted in the preparatory and ancillary work around weaving.[18]

Evidence from a number of places suggests that in the pre-industrial era girls and women dominated the ranks of spinners. Quantitative data on employment is limited and imprecise. However, the data which exists suggests that in the Netherlands in the sixteenth to eighteenth centuries 51 to 92 per cent of spinners were female. In lower Austria, the figure was up to 80 per cent.[19] In many regions of India spinning was considered women's work and men refused to do it. In the nineteenth-century South Indian jails, in order to cover their keep, the British put prisoners to work in the manufacture of textiles. The male prisoners were amenable to learning to weave, which was the preserve of men, but refused to spin on the grounds that it was a woman's job.[20]

Because there were so many spinners, in the pre-industrial era the bulk of textile workers were female. Spinning was less productive than weaving and for each weaver several spinners were required to work distaffs and wheels to produce adequate supplies of yarn. The ranks of spinners were swelled further by the fact that many spinners did not work full time but rather in snatches during free moments in the day or in the agricultural off-seasons. Maxine Berg has described the former when she argues that the distaff survived because it "could tap labour not otherwise in

---

17 Durba Chattaraj, "Globalization and Ambivalence: Rural Outsourcing in Southern Bengal", *International Labor and Working Class History*, 87 (2015), pp. 111–136.
18 Janet Hunter and Helen Macnaughtan, "Gender and the Global Textile Industry", in: Van Voss, Hiemstra-Kuperus and van Nederveen Meerkerk, *Ashgate Companion*, pp. 703–724, at 707–708. It should be noted that in Qing China, as well as parts of Europe and the Middle East, commercial production of high-value cloth (silk in the Chinese case) was a male occupation and the domestic production, including weaving, of low-value goods (cotton again in China) was done by women.
19 Elise van Nederveen Meerkerk, Lex Heerma van Voss and Els Hiemstra-Kuperus, "The Netherlands", in: Heerma van Voss, Hiemstra Kuperus and van Nederveen Meerkerk, *Ashgate Companion*, pp. 363–395, at 374; Hunter and Macnaughtan, "Gender and the Global Textile Industry", p. 705.
20 Parthasarathi, *Transition to a Colonial Economy*, p. 59.

use—that of feeble old women and young children, and the hands of women not otherwise in use when walking, talking, tending animals or watching over children."²¹ She has further argued that such a rhythm distinguished female work from that of males, who did not face a double bind of both market and domestic work and were able to exert greater control over their schedules in the manner that E. P. Thompson described in his classic article on time and work discipline.²²

The latter, the seasonality of spinning, is evident in South India where the work of making yarn was concentrated in areas that had a long agricultural off-season. In ecological zones where there was plentiful irrigation, and thus shorter periods in which there was not much agricultural work, there was little spinning. However, in unirrigated or rain-fed areas, the long dry months when there was no cultivation gave ample time for spinning. In these dry areas, agricultural output was also more uncertain and spinning provided a form of insurance in bad seasons. It was work that could be taken up when there were harvest shortfalls and at such moments so many hands turned to spinning that yarn prices could fall at times of dearth when food prices rose.²³

In Britain, the division of labour in which women spun and men wove, the latter being the more remunerative part of the production chain, was justified either by arguments that women's fingers were more nimble, thus more appropriate for spinning, or that spinning was unskilled work. Weaving, on the other hand, was perceived as a preserve of masculine knowledge and ability. Maxine Berg has noted, however, that "the very definitions of skilled and unskilled labour have at their root social and gender distinctions of far greater significance than any technical attribute."²⁴

A sexual division of labour persisted in the industrial era. Young women, as well as children, became the backbone of textile factory labour forces around the world. Janet Hunter and Helen Macnaughtan write, "During and following the process of industrialization, a significant majority of textile factory operatives around the world were characterized as female, young and initially of rural origin."²⁵ This was the case in many parts of Europe, East Asia, and the Americas and in some of these places the factory girl became synonymous with the manufacture of textiles.

The introduction of machinery made it possible to replace more expensive male workers with cheaper female. However, this was a slow and uneven process. In early industrial Britain, for example, men dominated in early mule spinning factories. They were well-paid and militant workers and according to Alan Fowler, "The self-actor spinning machine was developed in the 1820s by Richard Roberts as a response to this problem with the specific aim of substituting female for male operatives as

---

21 Maxine Berg, *The Age of Manufactures, 1700–1820* (London, 1985), p. 140.
22 Ibid., pp. 172–4.
23 Parthasarathi, *Transition to a Colonial Economy*, p. 59.
24 Berg, *Age of Manufactures*, p. 150.
25 Hunter and Macnaughtan, "Gender and the Global Textile Industry", p. 705.

women were seen as more tractable as well as providing cheaper labour."[26] This effort failed, however, and men continued to dominate spinning. They were simultaneously an elite class of workers and the supervisors of male and female assistants on the factory floor. In weaving, however, after the introduction of the powerloom women dominated that sector of factory production. Women were preferred in British mills because they could be paid less than men and they were also thought to be more docile.[27] Between 1850 and 1871 the wages of male self-actor spinners rose by 8s. 3d. while those of women weavers increased by only 3s.[28]

On the other side of Eurasia, when textile factories were first established in Japan in the 1870s and 1880s they employed both men and women, but over time the workforce was feminized. Men were retained for tasks that required skill or strength, but women came to predominate in all other areas. Women were preferred for their docility and lower wages, but the recruitment of female labour, especially in the countryside, was also a product of the rapid growth of textile factories, which greatly increased the demand for workers. Rural households were willing to part with young females because they were seen as less critical for production on the farm but many left the mills after they married.[29] A strikingly similar system emerged in the early nineteenth century textile factories of New England, in the northeastern part of the United States.[30]

India was the exception to the general rule that women workers predominated in textile factories. In the Bombay cotton industry some 20 per cent of the work force was female in 1885. (By contrast at that time the Lancashire cotton industry was 60 per cent female.) The bulk of these women in the Bombay mills were concentrated in reeling and winding where they worked with hand-driven machinery. It was thought to be inappropriate for women to use power-driven machinery so the tasks of running those, primarily spinning machines, was restricted to men. Women were not even allowed to repair power-driven machines.[31] A roughly similar situation pre-

---

[26] Alan Fowler, "Great Britain: Textile Workers in the Lancashire Cotton and Yorkshire Wool Industries", in: Heerma van Voss, Hiemstra-Kuperus and van Nederveen Meerkerk, *Ashgate Companion*, pp. 231–252, at 237.
[27] Ibid., p. 238.
[28] E. J. Hobsbawm, "The Labour Aristocracy", in: *Labouring Men. Studies in the History of Labour* (New York, 1964), pp. 346–347.
[29] Hunter and Macnaughtan, "Japan", in: Heerma van Voss, Hiemstra-Kuperus and van Nederveen Meerkerk, *Ashgate Companion*, pp. 318–319.
[30] Mary H. Blewett, "USA: Shifting Landscapes of Class, Culture, Gender, Race and Protest in the American Northeast and South", in: Heerma van Voss, Hiemstra-Kuperus and van Nederveen Meerkerk, *Ashgate Companion*, pp. 531–557, at 534.
[31] Hatice Yıldız, "Parallels and Contrasts in Gendered Histories of Industrial Labour in Bursa and Bombay 1850–1910", *The Historical Journal*, First View, https://www-cambridge-org.proxy.bc.edu/core/journals/historical-journal/article/div-classtitleparallels-and-contrasts-in-gendered-histories-of-industrial-labour-in-bursa-and-bombay-18501910a-hreffns01-ref-typefnadiv/28BC4   A3926943CDF0994EF0C890AB545, accessed on 7 February 2017.

vailed in the jute mills of Calcutta, where between 1911 and 1950 the proportion of women in the work force was around 15 per cent, in contrast to the predominance of females in Dundee, Scotland, the other major center of jute manufacturing in the world.[32]

There is a final important point about men and women and textile manufacturing which has to do with the transition from dispersed production to factory. In that transition a number of world regions suffered deindustrialization. While historians have tempered the rapidity of the decline of industry in places such as China, the Ottoman Empire and India, there is little doubt that there was significant loss of manufacturing. The deindustrialization debate with its focus on weaving has had a male bias, however. Women textile workers were likely to have borne the consequences of deindustrialization in these places, simply due to the fact that they were concentrated in hand spinning, the textile activity which was hardest hit by mechanization. While some numbers of weavers adopted machine-spun yarn and survived, spinning was largely wiped out by the end of the nineteenth century. The loss of this income must have hit women hard and affected their social power and position, but this question remains under-studied and is in need of further serious examination.[33]

Resistance and subjectivity

Textile workers loom large in accounts of worker resistance and subjectivity. Recall the famous passage from E. P. Thompson's *The Making of the English Working Class:* "I am seeking to rescue the poor stockinger, the Luddite cropper, the 'obsolete' hand-loom weaver, the 'utopian' artisan, and even the deluded follower of Joanna Southcott, from the enormous condescension of posterity."[34] Two of these, the stockinger and the weaver, fall squarely within the textile trades. And both were central in Thompson's account of the making of working class consciousness in England between the 1790s and 1832. Of weavers, Thompson wrote, "The Lancashire radicalism of 1816–20 was in great degree a movement of weavers, and the *making* of these later

---

[32] Samita Sen, *Women and Labour in Late Colonial India. The Bengal Jute Industry* (Cambridge, 1999), p. 5.
[33] Prasannan Parthasarathi, "Historical Issues of Deindustrialization in Nineteenth-Century South India", in: Giorgio Riello and Tirthankar Roy (eds), *How India Clothed the World. The World of South Asian Textiles, 1500–1850* (Leiden, 2009), pp. 415–435 and Nirmala Bannerjee, "Working Women in Colonial Bengal: Modernization and Marginalization", in: Kumkum Sangari and Sudesh Vaid (eds), *Recasting Women. Essays in Indian Colonial History* (New Brunswick, NJ, 1989), pp. 269–301. Craig Muldrew has documented the important contribution that earnings from spinning made to household incomes in seventeenth and eighteenth century England. See his "'Th'ancient Distaff' and 'Whirling Spindle': Measuring the Contribution of Spinning to Household Earnings and the National Economy in England, 1550–1770", *The Economic History Review*, 65 (2012), pp. 498–526.
[34] E. P. Thompson, *The Making of the English Working Class* (New York, 1964), p. 12.

leaders was in communities of this kind."³⁵ And resistance to the new order played no small role in that process. The Luddites, who Thompson explores in detail, were drawn from the ranks of croppers and framework-knitters who feared unemployment and loss of status as a consequence of mechanization.

While the worker subjectivity that Thompson explores was new—it was the articulation of class consciousness—it was preceded by and built upon long traditions of resistance and community consciousness in England to which textile workers were key contributors. Adrian Randall has brought out this pre-history in the case of machine breaking, which was found in the woolen cloth industry in the decades before the emergence of Luddism. For Randall, custom and community were the foundations upon which resistance was built. He writes, "It was the structure and customs of the woollen industry which shaped community as a dynamic force for social cohesion and resistance to change."³⁶

With his emphasis on custom, Randall builds upon the important work of John Rule for whom custom was central in understanding work and workers in eighteenth-century English industry. According to him, custom was critical for labourers in "determining the expectations from work"; "conditioning their attitudes in practices in performing it"; and "defining their relationships with their employers."³⁷ And Rule shows that custom played a key role in weaver struggles against merchant-manufacturers in the West Country of England throughout the eighteenth century and in their efforts to organize themselves for more effective action.³⁸ Randall and Rule focus on urban, male, textile labourers, but Maxine Berg has argued that a powerful community culture resting on custom was found among rural textile workers. She writes that in the mid-eighteenth century "dispersed production and a workforce scattered over many parishes did not prevent the cotton check weavers [of Lancashire] from organizing."³⁹ Berg believes that similar community networks, often based on neighborhoods, existed among women textile workers as well, but the limitation of the sources makes it impossible to establish this with certainty.

Powerful community organizations of textile workers existed outside Europe as well. In South India, there is evidence for the corporate organization of weavers going back to medieval times. Marriage, worship at temples, and common residency in neighborhoods of towns and villages created and sustained these community ties. Weaver corporate organization did not exist only at the local level, but extended to

---

35 *Ibid.*, pp. 294–295. Emphasis in original.
36 Adrian Randall, *Before the Luddites. Custom, Community and Machinery in the English Woollen Industry, 1776–1809* (Cambridge, 1991), p. 7. For a rigorous examination of community and collective action, see Craig Calhoun, *The Question of Class Struggle. Social Foundations of Popular Radicalism during the Industrial Revolution* (Chicago, 1982).
37 John Rule, *The Experience of Labour in Eighteenth-Century English Industry* (New York, 1981), p. 194.
38 *Ibid.*, pp. 158–164.
39 Berg, *Age of Manufactures*, p. 161.

the regional as well. These were maintained through ties of caste, marriage, pilgrimage and patronage of temples.[40] Weavers activated both local and regional corporate organizations in the late eighteenth century to mount a series of spectacular protests against the newly formed English East India Company state and its attempts to restructure the cloth procurement system. The Company state sought to reduce weaver autonomy and power, which called forth powerful efforts to resist from weavers. The idiom of custom (*mamool*) was also found in South India where the East India Company was seen as upending a longstanding customary order that shaped relations between weavers and the merchants who financed cloth production.[41]

These pre-industrial notions of custom and community continued to inform the subjectivities and the resistance of textile workers in the era of the factory, but they were of course mixed with new political ideas as well. The case of weavers in Lyons, who were seeking to organize a trade union in 1828, is instructive. According to Eric Hobsbawm, these weavers "naturally organized their society of 'Mutualists' on the revolutionary model. Thus they described their foundation year as 'Year One of Regeneration', an obvious echo of Jacobinism", but this was combined with organization into small conspiratorial groups which may have owed something to the 'old Compagnonnages."[42] Hobsbawm concludes that "it is mere antiquarianism to think of the [labour] movement of the 1870s, or even of the 1830s in terms of, say, the early hatters' and curriers' trade societies. However, historically speaking, the process of building new institutions, new ideas, new theories and tactics rarely starts as a deliberate job of social engineering. Men live surrounded by a vast accumulation of past devices, and it is natural to pick the most suitable of these, and to adapt them for their own (and novel) purposes."[43]

Another source of textile worker solidarity which had a long life was the neighborhood. Berg in the case of England and Parthasarathi in the case of South India have pointed to the important role that neighborhoods played in worker organization in the eighteenth century. Jumping to the interwar years of the twentieth century, Rajnarayan Chandavarkar has shown that the social ties formed in the neighborhoods of Bombay were critical in the forging of remarkable mill worker cohesion. Chandavarkar writes, "Historians of labour have generally regarded the workplace as the decisive arena for the development of the political consciousness and political action of the working class. However, ... the associations forged in the neighbourhood provided an important base for wider social and political organization."[44] It was such organization and solidarity that made it feasible for workers to mount spectacular acts of resistance such as the general strikes of 1928–29 which mobilized

---

[40] Parthasarathi, *Transition to a Colonial Economy*, pp. 31–4.
[41] Ibid., chap. 4.
[42] E. J. Hobsbawm, "Labour Traditions", in: *Labouring Men*, p. 438.
[43] Ibid., p. 437.
[44] Rajnarayan Chandavarkar, *The Origins of Industrial Capitalism in India. Business Strategies and the Working Classes in Bombay, 1900–1940* (Cambridge, 1994), pp. 237–238.

over 150,000 workers and crippled work at more than 80 cotton mills for a period of eighteen months.[45]

Textile workers and global history

The fate of textile workers in the centuries after 1500 cannot be understood fully without a global lens. Although there is little evidence for the development of a consciousness of being part of a "world working class" among textile labourers, the global trade in cloth shaped the economics and politics of textile manufacturing around the world.[46]

Cloth entered into long-distance trade because of its high value and low weight and the global exchange of cloth grew steadily in the centuries after 1500 when New World silver fueled a boom in world trade. From the perspective of textile workers, the half millennium from 1500 to the present may be divided into three periods. The first runs roughly from 1500 to 1780. In this period the most important cloth exporting regions lay in India. The second, from 1780 to the eve of World War I, represented a shift in textile manufacturing for export from Asia to Northwestern Europe as a result of the British Industrial Revolution. Finally, from 1913 to the present world textile manufacturing returned to Asia, but on very different foundations than in early modern times.

Till the twentieth century cotton accounted for the bulk of the textiles that were traded globally. In 1913 cotton represented 80 per cent of global fiber consumption and even in 1990 when synthetic fibers had grown in popularity, and came to represent 38 per cent of world fiber use, cotton still accounted for 48 per cent.[47] In the centuries before 1780 the preeminence of cotton meant that the regions that accounted for the bulk of textile exports lay in Asia, most importantly in India. This export trade was not only in luxury goods, but for many centuries included lower priced cloths which fit the budgets of middling and lower class buyers.[48]

India had long been the home of sophisticated cotton manufacturing and its textile workers possessed abundant knowledge and skill as well as the ability to cater to the tastes of diverse markets. Indian knowledge extended from the spinning of yarn in a variety of counts for different purposes. The yarn for the manufacture of muslins

---

[45] Rajnarayan Chandavarkar, "Questions of Class: The General Strikes in Bombay, 1928–29", *Contributions to Indian Sociology*, 33, 1–2 (1999), pp. 205–237.
[46] The term "world working class" comes from Marcel van der Linden, "The Promise and Challenges of Global Labor History", *International Labor and Working Class History*, 82 (2012), pp. 57–76, at 67.
[47] Prasannan Parthasarathi, "Global Trade and Textile Workers", in: Heerma van Voss, Hiemstra-Kuperus and van Nederveen Meerkerk, *Ashgate Companion*, pp. 561–576, at 561. For discussions of cotton, see Giorgio Riello, *Cotton: The Fabric that Made the Modern World* (Cambridge, 2013) and Sven Beckert, *Empire of Cotton: A Global History* (New York, 2014).
[48] Parthasarathi, "Global Trade and Textile Workers", p. 563.

was particularly impressive for its fineness and strength and the cloth that was made from it was extolled around the world.[49] While India was famous for its complex weaves (ikats and fine brocades come to mind immediately), the bulk of the export goods were simply woven. However, they were remarkable for their colors, which could be created in the loom itself with dyed yarns—such as the checks and stripes which were widely demanded in West Africa—or by painting and printing on white cloth. Here, the knowledge of dyeing that these Indian craftsmen possessed was unmatched in the world and they produced fabrics in which the colors were not only fast but were also reputed to become more beautiful after repeated washings.[50]

In the seventeenth and eighteenth centuries European observers focused less on the knowledge of Indian workers and more on the low prices of the textiles to explain their success in global markets. These observers attributed the cheapness of the cloth to the abysmal and exploited conditions under which Indian workers laboured, which translated into very low wages. Daniel Defoe wrote, "The People who make all these fine Works are to the last Degree miserable, their Labour of no Value, their Wages would fright us to talk of it, and their way of Living raise a horror in us to think of it."[51] The exploitation of Indian workers became a rallying cry for textile labourers in Europe to oppose the import of the cloth and in response to spectacular protests against imports—in London weavers ripped cotton gowns off the backs of women in the streets—states across Europe restricted the entry of these goods.[52]

While the lowness of Indian wages has been questioned, the debate over comparative standards of living between India and other parts of the world continues.[53] What is more widely accepted as a consequence of the global turn in economic history is that the challenge of Indian cottons sparked a response in Europe in the form of mechanization. The European-wide process of imitating Indian goods began with cloth printing and then extended to spinning and weaving. This entailed the development of knowledge, sometimes obtained from India itself, and at other times developed independently. The crucial breakthrough was the British invention of machinery which could spin yarn that matched the Indian for strength and quality. These machines were the waterframe and then the mule.[54]

---

[49] For a discussion of these cloths see Prasannan Parthasarathi, *Why Europe Grew Rich and Asia Did Not: Global Economic Divergence, 1600–1850* (Cambridge, 2011), p. 33–34.
[50] Ibid., pp. 27–34.
[51] Daniel Defoe, *A Plan of the English Commerce* (London, 1728, repr. Oxford, 1928), pp. 49–50.
[52] Beverly Lemire, *Fashion's Favourite. The Cotton Trade and the Consumer in Britain, 1660–1800* (Oxford, 1991), pp. 34–36; Parthasarathi, *Why Europe*, chap. 5.
[53] Prasannan Parthasarathi, "Rethinking Wages and Competitiveness in the Eighteenth Century: Britain and South India", *Past and Present*, 158 (1998), pp. 79–109; Stephen Broadberry and Bishnupriya Gupta, "The Early Modern Great Divergence: Wages, Prices and Economic Development in Europe and Asia, 1500–1800", *Economic History Review*, n.s., 59 (2006), pp. 2–31; Parthasarathi, *Why Europe*, pp. 37–46.
[54] For an account of this see Parthasarathi, *Why Europe*, chap. 4.

With these inventions the center of gravity in textile manufacturing, and thus cloth export, moved from India to northwestern Europe and in the nineteenth century Britain became the workshop of the world. These inventions also gave birth to the new industrial order based on machinery, power, and the factory, which created a new class of labourers, the industrial working class. Over the next two centuries, wherever some form of protection could be erected from external competition this form of production was replicated around the world, forging not only a new economic system but also a new political order in which textile labourers played a pivotal role in trade unions, labour parties, and the struggle for alternative futures.

In several parts of the world, where protection from imports was not politically feasible, the expansion of textile manufacturing in northwestern Europe had a deleterious impact, producing deindustrialization and a reduction in the size of the textile labour force. In Mexico, due to cheap imports from Britain, textile workers went from comprising half of Mexico City's population in 1788 to one-third in 1842. In the Ottoman Empire, imports of cheap British yarn led to a sharp reduction in the ranks of spinners and by 1900 hand-spun yarn only accounted for a quarter of total yarn consumption. Similar stories may be told about China and India. In the case of India, in 1900–1901, nearly two billion yards of cotton cloth were imported from Britain.[55] Forced to compete against machine-made yarn and cloth, textile workers in these regions were immiserated, laying the foundations for future sweating as described by Rajnarayan Chandavarkar, Douglas Haynes, and others.[56]

A global textile order in which northwestern Europe, and in particular Britain, dominated the world trade in cloth remained in place till World War I. In the case of jute, Calcutta challenged the Scottish city of Dundee's reign even before the war, but in the much larger cotton industry it was not till the interwar period that India and Japan began to challenge British dominance in major markets, most critically China.[57] The economic depression of the 1930s and World War II smashed that British-led order and in the post-war period a new global textile regime emerged. In in the decades between 1945 and 1980 textile manufacturing grew around the world, from Argentina, Uruguay, India and China, to Turkey.[58]

From the 1980s, however, new pressures of global competition pushed textile manufacturing back into low-wage countries. From the United States, textile factories shifted across the border to Mexico. In the case of Japan, cotton mills were moved to China where cheap labour and modern technology created a formidable global competitor. India, Bangladesh and Pakistan were other nations where textile manufacturing expanded rapidly and by 1998 China and South Asia together accounted for about a third of the world's production of cotton yarn. The return to Asia is reminiscent of the pre-industrial period, but it rests on radically different foundations. While

---

[55] Parthasarathi, "Global Trade and Textile Workers", pp. 569–571.
[56] Chandavarkar, *Origins of Industrial Capitalism*; Haynes, *Small Town Capitalism*.
[57] Jim Tomlinson, *Dundee and the Empire: "Juteopolis" 1850–1939* (Edinburgh, 2014).
[58] Parthasarathi, "Global Trade and Textile Workers", p. 572

pre-industrial Asian manufacturing prowess rested on high standards of living and worker knowledge, the twentieth-century version rested on low wages and a deskilled labour force.[59]

Exports from these Asian centers had an impact on textile industries around the world and the United States, Japan, Argentina all lost employment as a consequence of lower price imports.[60] In a striking echo of the eighteenth century, however, imports of textiles from South Asia (and this time Southeast Asia as well) contributed to economic dislocation and loss of jobs in Egypt. According to Joel Beinin, the strike waves that gripped Egypt for several years, and contributed to the Arab Spring protests of 2011, were organized by textile workers who were thrown out of work by lower cost imports from the South and Southeast Asia.[61]

Conclusion

The work of textile manufacturing raises a number of central questions in labour history. The organization of production, and thus the nature of work and the relationship between workers and merchants and employers, looms large and textiles were made in a variety of settings, from households to small workshops and large factories and in both rural and urban settings. The manufacture of textiles also rested on deep sexual divisions of labour, but these divisions could vary widely across space and time. And in general, men monopolized the higher paying jobs, while women were deemed as unskilled and docile and given the less remunerative. Textile workers were also politically organized and resisted transformations in the market as well as organization of production and payment which they deemed to be disadvantageous. And in the last several centuries textile workers have been at the heart of spectacular movements of protest. Finally, a study of textile workers is incomplete without a global perspective. The trade in cloth and the movement in production from one place to another have been and continue to be significant.

In this complex world of textile manufacturing there are no universals. The making of cloth looks different in different places and in different time periods. Nor is there a single direction of change. Decentralized production has given way to centralized, only to return to decentralized. And in many places in the last two hundred years household production has existed alongside factory, at times in close proximity. The only certainty is that textiles will continue to be manufactured, for the need for cloth will never disappear.

---

59 *Ibid.*, p. 574.
60 *Ibid.*
61 Joel Beinin, "Workers and Egypt's January 25th Revolution", *International Labor and Working Class History*, 80 (2011), pp. 189–196.

Suggested reading

Beckert, Sven. *Empire of Cotton: A Global History* (New York: Alfred Knopff, 2014).
Berg, Maxine. *The Age of Manufactures, 1700–1820* (London: Fontana, 1985).
Bortz, Jeff. *Revolution Within the Revolution. Cotton Textile Workers and the Mexican Labor Regime, 1910–1923* (Stanford, CA: Stanford University Press, 2008).
Breman, Jan. *Making and Unmaking of an Industrial Working Class. Sliding Down the Labour Hierarchy in Ahmedabad, India* (New Delhi: Oxford University Press, 2004).
Canning, Kathleen. *Languages of Labor and Gender. Female Factory Work in Germany, 1850–1914* (Ithaca, NY: Cornell University Press, 1996).
Dublin, Thomas. *Women at Work. The Transformation of Work and Community in Lowell, Massachusetts, 1826–1860* (New York: Columbia University Press, 1993).
Faison, Elyssa. *Managing Women. Disciplining Labor in Modern Japan* (Berkeley, CA: University of California Press, 2007).
Gómez Galvarriato, Aurora. *Industry and Revolution. Social and Economic Change in the Orizaba Valley, Mexico* (Cambridge, MA: Harvard University Press, 2013).
Gulvin, Clifford. *Tweedmakers. A History of the Scottish Fancy Woolen Industry 1600–1914* (Newton Abbot: David & Charles; New York: Barnes & Noble, 1973).
Hareven, Tamara K. and Randolph Langenbach. *Amoskeag: Life and Work in an American Factory-city* (Hanover, NH: University Press of New England, 1995).
Hareven, Tamara K. *Family Time and Industrial Time. The Relationship between the Family and Work in a New England Industrial Community* (Lanham, MD: University Press of America, 1993).
Haynes, Douglas. *Small Town Capitalism in Western India. Artisans, Merchants and the Making of the Informal Economy, 1870–1960* (Cambridge: Cambridge University Press, 2012).
Heerma van Voss, Lex Els Hiemstra-Kuperus and Elise van Nederveen Meerkerk (eds). *The Ashgate Companion to the History of Textile Workers, 1650–2000* (Farnham: Ashgate, 2010).
Honig, Emily. *Sisters and Strangers. Women in the Shanghai Cotton Mills, 1919–1949* (Stanford, CA: Stanford University Press, 1986).
Kidd, Yasue Aoki. *Women Workers in the Japanese Cotton Mills, 1880–1920* (Ithaca, NY: China-Japan Program, Cornell University, 1978).
Liu, Tessie P. *Weaver's Knot. The Contradictions of Class Struggle and Family Solidarity in Western France, 1750–1914* (Ithaca, NY: Cornell University Press, 1994).
Marks, Paula Mitchell. *Hands to the Spindle, Texas Women and Home Textile Production, 1822–1880* (College Station: Texas A&M University Press, 1996).
McLaurin, Melton Alonza. *Paternalism and Protest. Southern Cotton Mill Workers and Organized Labor, 1875–1905* (Westport, CT: Greenwood, 1971).
Mendels, Franklin. "Proto-Industrialization: The First Phase of the Industrialization Process", *Journal of Economic History*, 32, 1 (1972), pp. 241–261.
Murphy, Eamon. *Unions in Conflict. A Comparative Study of Four South Indian Textile Centres, 1918–1939* (New Delhi: Manohar, 1981).
Perlin, Frank. "Proto-Industrialization and Pre-Colonial South Asia", *Past and Present*, 98 (1983), pp. 30–95.
Potwin, Marjorie Adella. *Cotton Mill People of the Piedmont. A Study in Social Change* (New York, AMS Press 1968).
Scholliers, Peter. *Wages, Manufacturers, and Workers in the Nineteenth-Century Factory. The Voortman Cotton Mill in Ghent* (Oxford and Washington, DC: Berg Publishers, 1996).
Shehata, Samer S. *Shop Floor Culture and Politics in Egypt* (Albany: SUNY Press, 2009).

Thirsk, Joan. "Industries in the Countryside", in: F. J. Fisher (ed.), *Essays in the Economic and Social History of Tudor and Stuart England* (Cambridge, 1961), pp. 70–88.

Thompson, E.P. "Time, Work-Discipline and Industrial Capitalism", *Past and Present*, 38 (1967), pp. 56–97.

Tomlinson, Jim. *Dundee and the Empire: "Juteopolis" 1850–1939* (Edinburgh: Edinburg University Press, 2014).

Tsurumi, E. Patricia. *Factory Girls. Women in the Thread Mills of Meiji Japan* (Princeton, NJ: Princeton University Press, 1990).

Walker, William MacReady. *Juteopolis. Dundee and its Textile workers 1885–1923* (Edinburgh: Scottish Academic Press, 1979).

Walkowitz, Daniel J. *Worker City, Company Town. Iron and Cotton-worker Protest in Troy and Cohoes, New York, 1855–84* (Urbana, IL: University of Illinois Press, 1978).

Winn, Peter. *Weavers of Revolution. The Yarur Workers and Chile's Road to Socialism* (New York: Oxford University Press, 1986).

Peter Cole and Jennifer Hart
3.4. Trade, Transport, and Services

The movement of people and goods sits at the core of global history, shaping the rise and fall of empires, trading systems, and cultural exchange in various forms over at least the last several thousand years. Among scholars of world history, these historical realities have fueled long-running debates over what C.A. Bayly calls "the birth of the modern world". The labourers who facilitated this long history of movement and exchange, operating at the crossroads of trade networks and state power, also sit at the intersection of these scholarly debates about world history and labour history. Their histories are an integral part of global labour history, as both workers in their own right and vital connections between different regimes of labour on local and global scales.

While labour for trade, transport, and services dates back to the earliest systems of economic exchange and labour diversification, these forms of work were concentrated and organized in new and unprecedented ways in the context of the growth of global capitalism, beginning in the 16th century. Workers in trade, transport, and services participated directly in the growth of this global economic system, transporting goods and people around the world, as part of the infrastructure of what scholars like Immanuel Wallerstein, Giovanni Arrighi, and Janet Abu-Lughod term a "world system". These workers also facilitated the participation of others in that system—as producers, traders, and consumers. And yet, trade, transport, and services also provided opportunities for work that challenged the implicit power structures within that emerging global capitalist order.

Labourers in the fields of trade, transport, and services, then, belonged to what John Urry calls a "mobility-system": the comprehensive system of infrastructures, technologies, policies, cultures, sociabilities, movements, economies, and institutions through which people interact and goods are exchanged. Labourers in these industries are "mobile workers" through both the physical movement implicit in their labour as individuals, as well as the ways in which they facilitate the movements of others through participation in broader systems of transportation and trade. As such, these mobile workers often mediated between binary categories—local and global, formal and informal, traditional and modern, stable and precarious—which too often shape histories of labour and capitalism. Operating across and in between these boundaries, mobile workers shaped the global system even as they embraced very local economic cultures.[1]

The expansion and contraction of industrial economies in the 19th and 20th century exposed the inequalities inherent in the structures and practices of global capitalism. The centrality of mobile work to industrial growth meant that these workers

---

[1] John Urry, *Mobilities* (Cambridge, 2007).

were always in demand. However, the constantly shifting technology of industrial economies also meant that their work was inherently precarious. Some mobile workers seized the possibilities and risks of precarity in order to maximize profits and seize control of sectors within local economies. Some successful workers established prosperous and stable lives through their manipulation of risk or created the freedom to pursue non-economic interests by strategically pursuing precarious work. Others sought stability in the formal sector, organizing themselves into labour unions and workers associations, which set standards for working conditions and pay. Still others moved between these two spheres of work in response to changing economic conditions.

By highlighting the mobility of labourers in trade, transport, and services, then, we decentre Western narratives that privilege formal-sector wage labour. Instead we argue that a full understanding of mobile labour requires a truly global perspective, which acknowledges the inherent precarities of the global capitalist system, from its earliest times to the present, as part of an ongoing negotiation about the nature of work and the movement of people and goods. Fortunately, research in labour and working-class history has become less Eurocentric and more global in recent years. Nevertheless, it is impossible to thoroughly explore the historiography of these multiple, interlocking industries, around the world, from approximately 1500 to the present, so this essay will highlight some key texts and themes interwoven among the trade, transport, and service industries. In particular, trade-related labour is woven throughout discussions of the transport and service industry. By doing a global survey, we can discover many similarities across countries and societies. Recently, moreover, the growing influence of neoliberal policies have resulted in increasing commonalties among countries across the world, in the Global North and South, in advanced industrial and less developed economies.

Transport

A globalized world resting upon trade and labour has existed for many centuries and those working in transportation stood at its centre. Transportation is all about interconnections and interconnectedness, be it on oceans, roads, rails, canals, or rivers.[2] In no small part thanks to maritime labour history, a growing trend in History and other academic disciplines is to see the world as deeply interconnected—centuries prior to contemporary globalization—with oceans and other waterborne routes as highways rather than dividing lines; however, as Kären Wigen writes:

---

[2] These points also are made in the wonderful introduction to Stefano Bellucci, Larissa Rosa Correa, Jan-Georg Deutsch, and Chitra Joshi, "Labour in Transport: Histories from the Global South, c. 1750–1950", *International Review of Social History* 59, special issue 22 (2014), pp. 1–10.

"[...] seascapes loom large in the public imagination. Yet on the mental maps of most scholars, oceans are oddly occluded. Geographically marginal to the grids of academic inquiry, the watery world seems to fall between our conceptual cracks as well. When not ignored altogether, maritime topics are routinely relegated to subfields on shipping or migration, pirates or fisheries. That ocean basins are sliced in half on our classroom maps only reinforces their academic invisibility."[3]

More precisely, those who work in maritime transport, including those engaged in the most menial of tasks, contributed fundamentally to an increasingly globalized world, starting with the European age of exploration in the late 15th century. Workers aboard ships and in ports exchanged information and ideas while also moving an exponentially increasing amount of commodities and people. This reality continues to present day. As Allan Sekula and Noël Burch declare in their film *Forgotten Space*, "the sea remains the crucial space of globalization. Nowhere else is the disorientation, violence, and alienation of contemporary capitalism more manifest, but this truth is not self-evident, and must be approached as a puzzle, or mystery, a problem to be solved". Even in the 21st century, 90 % of goods are moved, for at least part of their journeys, by ship.[4]

Many workers aboard ships and in ports possessed long histories of radicalism, often forsaking their national, religious, and racial identities for more cosmopolitan, militant, and even revolutionary ones. Even when committed to their national identities, sailors and dockworkers often acted against those in power, acting through systems of colonialism, racism, and capitalism. Peter Linebaugh and Marcus Rediker remain perhaps the most widely known proponents of this view. As they argue in *The Many Headed Hydra: Sailors, Slaves, Commoners and the Hidden History of the Revolutionary Atlantic,* from the 15th through 18th century Atlantic world, sailors, slaves, pirates, labourers, market women, and indentured servants embraced radical ideals of freedom and acted accordingly. In their book the so-called dispossessed—they would say the world's first proletariat—stand at the centre of the making of the modern world. They convincingly argue that many of the most important ideas about political and human rights were not developed by European philosophers but, rather, by slaves and servants, pirates, and labourers, men and women. Linebaugh and Rediker, of course, are just two of many other scholars of (maritime) labour involved in the growing trends among historians and other scholars to cross national boundaries in their studies, i.e. thinking beyond nation-states or transnationally.[5]

---

3 Jerry H. Bentley, Renate Bridenthal, and Kären Wigen (eds), *Seascapes, Maritime Histories, Littoral Cultures, and Transoceanic Exchanges* (Honolulu, 2007), p. 1.
4 Allan Sekula and Noël Burch, directors, *The Forgotten Space* (Doc.Eye Film, 2010), pdf: http://www.icarusfilms.com/new2012/fs.html (June 13, 2014); Alice Mah, *Port Cities and Global Legacies. Urban Identity, Waterfront Work, and Radicalism* (New York, 2014), p. 1.
5 Peter Linebaugh and Marcus Rediker, *The Many Headed Hydra. Sailors, Slaves, Commoners and the Hidden History of the Revolutionary Atlantic* (Boston, 2000).

So, too, in the 19th and 20th centuries sailors and dockers played vital roles in history. For instance, Gopalan Balachandran studies South Asian seafarers, themselves a diverse lot with varied interests, who sought to break negative stereotypes that restricted their employment inside the British maritime system during the era of high imperialism. Risa L. Faussette describes the radicalism of West Indian longshoremen in the same era, who experienced an explosion of global trade and imperialism in the wake of industrialization. Similarly, Alan Gregor Cobley argues Caribbean seamen profoundly influenced both labour and black political organizing, from the 18th century into the 20th. The British demand for maritime labourers drew in these former slaves from the Caribbean who, in turn, helped shape various social movements, including maritime unions and Pan-Africanism throughout the Atlantic world, much like what Linebaugh and Rediker discuss. Across the world, in China, dockworkers and sailors organized into proto-unions, participated in the Communist Party, and contributed to growing militancy prior to the 1949 revolution. Earlier, in the West African colony of the Gold Coast, canoe men used their boats to ferry goods like cocoa from the beaches of trading towns like Accra to ships waiting in the deeper waters along the coast. Canoe men, who viewed their transport work as a temporary break from their regular work as fishermen, organized informal associations and used their position as casual labourers to control the conditions of their work, even as European trading interests increasingly sought to control commerce along the coast in the 18th and 19th centuries. Boatmen in early colonial eastern India worked under similar contracts along the Ganga River, building on practices that dated back to the Mughal Empire but reinterpreted through Indian interaction with the English East India Company. The British colonial government introduced regulations for the contract system, driven by the complaints of passengers and the demands of labour mobilization. The pressure to standardize and regulate labour associated with transport and trade in other ports like Mombasa, Kenya, led colonial officials to use their increasing political, juridical, and economic power to transform the casual labour of African dockworkers into a new class of wage labourers, defined by the regularity and "respectability" of their work.[6]

While sailors were important, those who loaded and unloaded ships—called dockers, dockworkers, longshoremen, or stevedores—provided essential links, cul-

---

[6] Gopalan Balachandran, *Globalizing Labour? Indian Seafarers and World Shipping, c. 1870–1945* (Delhi and Oxford, 2012); Risa L. Faussette, "Race, Migration, and Port-City Radicalism: West Indian Longshoremen and the Politics of Empire, 1880–1920", in: *Seascapes*, pp. 169–185; Alan Gregor Cobley, "That Turbulent Soil: Seafarers, the 'Black Atlantic,' and Afro-Caribbean Identity", in: *Seascapes*, pp. 153–68; Jean Chesneaux and Richard C. Kagan, "The Chinese Labour Movement: 1915–1949", *International Social Science Review*, 58, 2 (1983), pp. 78–79; Peter Gutkind, "The Canoemen of the Gold Coast (Ghana): A Survey and an Exploration in Precolonial African Labour History", *Cahiers d'études africaines*, 29 (1989), pp. 339–376; Nitin Sinha, "Contract, Work, and Resistance: Boatmen in Early Colonial India, 1760s-1850s", *International Review of Social History*, Special Issue, 59 (2014), pp. 11–43; Fred Cooper, *On the African Waterfront. Urban Disorder and the Transformation of Work in Colonial Mombasa* (New Haven, CT, 1987).

turally, materially, and politically between sea and land. The most important survey remains the two-volume *Dock Workers: International Explorations in Comparative Labour History, 1790–1970* that includes about forty essays on different ports and themes. In their introduction, Sam Davies and Klaus Weinhauer contend "this important occupational group" must be "considered in a comparative fashion on an international scale". Yet despite such logic and that anthology's vital contributions, historian Jordi Ibarz's quite extensive, very recent survey of two hundred historical studies on dockers—written in English, French, Portuguese, and Spanish—reveals many gaps including: (1) almost all histories of dockers focus on a single port, (2) very few studies of African ports exist, (3) very few comparative studies exist, (4) no comparison of North-South ports exist, (5) very few studies examine both the casual and decasual eras of a port, (6) almost no port or dock labour studies combine the traditional and container eras, and (7) and very few studies examine dockworkers in the container era, period, despite the fact that this technology revolutionized all modes of transportation thereby making the explosion of trade in recent decades possible.[7]

As more historians embrace a "maritime turn", the appreciation for the importance of the maritime world upon cultural, economic, political, and social relations within and between societies will only increase. Even today, though, a disappointing omission has been studies exploring the truly revolutionary impacts of containerization on labour; indeed, the editors of *Dock Workers* consciously ended their project with the advent of containerization. For that matter, the history of seafarers remains something of a "black hole", neither well integrated into the labour histories of specific nations nor receiving the sort of desperately needed, global, comparative treatment that characterizes the scholarship on dockers.

An investigation of dock labour also points to additional categories of transport labourers, whose work is often obscured by a focus on industrialized and mechanized labour in the 19th and 20th centuries. The trade routes across the Sahara and around the Indian Ocean, documented as early as the 1st century, were dominated by head carriers or caravan porters in Africa and India, for example, who transported goods in caravans, connecting producers to domestic and long-distance trade routes. Particularly in areas where diseases like the tsetse fly made it impossible to use draft animals, carriers served as the primary means of long distance transport. Similar flag post relay mail runners carried mail for the British colonial administration in colonies like British Southern Cameroon through the mid-20th century. Some of these forms of transport labour persisted into the 21st century, often operating alongside new forms of industrialized labour and transgressing boundaries of

---

[7] Sam Davies and Klaus Weinhauer, "Towards a Comparative International History of Dockers", in: Sam Davies, *et al.* (eds), *Dock Workers: International Explorations in Comparative Labour History, 1790–1970*, Vol. 1 (Aldershot: Ashgate, 2000), p. 3; Jordi Ibarz, "Recent Trends in Dock Workers History", paper presented at the European Social Sciences History Conference, Valencia, Spain, 2016 (in possession of the authors).

trade, transport, and services. Rickshaws, hammocks, and cask rolling represented variations on the carrier model, and these technologies often circulated through the networks of 19th century European empire. Carriers often were drawn from both free/waged and unfree labour into the 19th century, and they were deployed across a wide array of private, state, and military sectors. In India these labourers were identified as part of an underclass of "coolies". As African historian Stephen Rockel notes, however, carrier labour in some regions of East Africa developed into a highly organized form of wage labour, defined by both the mobility and stability of their work.[8]

In the global south, rickshaw pullers were particularly notable. Jim Warren argues that "rickshaw coolies" played a crucial role in the development of Singapore in the late 19th and first half of the 20th centuries for they transported the palm oil, rubber, tin, and tobacco grown and processed across Malaysia through the British port of Singapore. As this port hub grew, tens of thousands of poor men arrived in the booming seaport from overcrowded southeast China to take up the backbreaking but essential trade of rickshaw pullers. Similarly, Tim Wright writes of rickshaw pullers in early 20th century Shanghai. As in Singapore and throughout Asia, these workers occupied a crucial node of transport in densely packed industrial and trading centers, moving both cargo and people. Given the seemingly unlimited supply of labour from rural China, Shanghai's rickshaw pullers faced incredible downward pressure on their low wages; they also suffered at the hands of rickshaw owners who con-

---

[8] Stephen Rockel, *Carriers of Culture: Labor on the Road in Nineteenth-Century East Africa* (Portsmouth, NH, 2006); Devon Dear, "Holy Rollers: Monasteries, Lamas, and the Unseen Transport of Chinese-Russian Trade", *International Review of Social History*, Special Issue, 59 (2014), pp. 69–88; Lipokmar Dzuvichu, "Empire on their Backs: Coolies in the Eastern Borderlands of the British Raj", *International Review of Social History*, Special Issue, 59 (2014), pp. 89–112; A.G. Hopkins, *An Economic History of West Africa* (New York, 1973); Komla Tsey, *From Headloading to the Iron Horse. Railway Building in Colonial Ghana and the Origins of Tropical Development* (Cameroon, 2012); Kwabena Akurang-Parry, "Colonial Forced Labor Policies for Road-Building in Southern Ghana and International Anti-Forced Labor Pressures, 1900–1940", *African Economic History*, 28 (2000), pp. 1–25; John Parker, *Making the Town. Ga State and Society in Early Colonial Accra* (Portsmouth, NH, 2000); Radhika Singha, "Finding Labor from India for the War in Iraq: The Jail Porter and Labor Corps, 1916–1920", *Comparative Studies in Society and History*, 49, 2 (2007), pp. 412–445; Jim Warren, "The Singapore Rickshaw Pullers: The Social Organization of a Coolie Occupation, 1880–1940", *Journal of Southeast Asian Studies*, 16, 1 (March 1985), pp. 1–15; Jan Breman and E. V. Daniel, "The Making of a Coolie", *Journal of Peasant Studies*, 19, 3–4 (1992), pp. 268–295; Paulo Cruz Terra, "Free and Unfree Labour and Ethnic Conflicts in the Brazilian Transport Industry: Rio de Janeiro in the Nineteenth Century", *International Review of Social History*, Special Issue, 59 (2014), pp. 113–132; Walter Gam Nkwi and Mirjam de Bruijn, "'Human Telephone Lines': Flag Post Mail Relay Runners in British Southern Cameroon (1916–1955) and the Establishment of a Modern Communication Network", *International Review of Social History*, Special Issue, 59 (2014), pp. 211–235; Chitra Joshi, "Dak Roads, Dak Runners, and the Reordering of Communication Networks", *International Review of Social History* (Special Issue: Labor in Transport: Histories from the Global South [Africa, Asia, and Latin America], c. 1750–1950), 57, 1 (April 2012), pp. 169–189; Tim Wright, "Shanghai Imperialists versus Rickshaw Racketeers: The Defeat of the 1934 Rickshaw Reforms", *Modern China*, 17, 1 (January 1991), pp. 76–111.

trolled the licenses as well as the equipment thereby further squeezing these workers.⁹

Similarly, railroads proved absolutely vital to the economic development of countries within and outside of the networks of imperialism, industrialization, and global capitalism in the 19th and early 20th centuries, and railway workers possess long histories of organizing and militancy. Indeed, railroads proved essential for expanding global capitalism in the 19th and 20th centuries as railroad workers emerged as among the most visible, well organized, and powerful workforces in many countries. In his global survey of railroad labour, Shelton Stromquist argues that despite railroading's technological uniformity, the historical development of railroads followed certain distinctive patterns in what he categorized as metropolitan (Western Europe), colonies (in Asia, Africa, and Latin America), and settler colonies (including the USA and Canada, Australasia, and parts of Latin America). Stromquist further contends that railroad employment was both segmented (many distinct trades) and stratified (skilled and unskilled). Interestingly, while railways often served the imperialist agenda of European and US powers, railroad workers repeatedly challenged such authority in both settler societies and colonial ones. In the United States in the late 19th century, railroad workers led mammoth strikes including America's first national strike, nicknamed the Great Upheaval of 1877; in 1894, perhaps the US' largest strike erupted when hundreds of thousands of railroad workers, led by American Railway Union and future Socialist Party leader, Eugene V. Debs. This latter strike originated among workers who built Pullman rail cars then joined by hundreds of thousands of other railroad workers who boycotted, in solidarity with Pullman workers, all Pullman cars around the nation. The Pullman boycott drastically impaired the national economy for several weeks until the president dispatched soldiers to break it, confirming the power of organized railway workers and centrality of railroads to industrial economies.¹⁰

Railway workers in African colonies also demonstrated their potential to disrupt. In African colonies, railways were almost exclusively associated with resource extraction, transported valuable agricultural and mineral products from interior production zones to coastal ports, provided revenue for colonial coffers, and funneled primary commodities to the West as essential components of industrial manufacturing. When African railway workers like those in colonial French West Africa engaged in massive strikes in 1947–48, the economic pressure of the strike forced important concessions from colonial officials who controlled the railways in the region, but also

---

9 Jim Warren, "The Singapore Rickshaw Pullers: The Social Organization of a Coolie Occupation, 1880–1940", *Journal of Southeast Asian Studies*, 16, 1 (1985), pp. 1–15; Tim Wright, "Shanghai Imperialists versus Rickshaw Racketeers: The Defeat of the 1934 Rickshaw Reforms", *Modern China*, 17, 1 (1991), pp. 76–111.
10 Shelton Stromquist, "Railroad Workers and the Global Economy: Historical Patterns", in: Jan Lucassen (ed.), *Global Labour History: A State of the Art* (Bern, 2006); idem, *A Generation of Boomers. The Pattern of Railroad Labor Conflict in Nineteenth-Century America* (Urbana, IL, 1987).

served as the foundation for much broader demands for independence within French West Africa and across the continent. African historian Frederick Cooper argues that the economic power of railway workers at this nexus of transport and trade inspired a new language of decolonization rooted in the experiences of mobile labour and a critique of colonialism and global capitalism. This connection between leftist politics and labour mobilization among railway workers was also evident in early twentieth century strikes in independent countries like Brazil.[11]

As potentially powerful as they were, railroad workers and unions sometimes were forces of conservatism, more interested in preserving what wealth and status they possessed than promoting radical change. Eric Arnesen demonstrates how white American railroaders occasionally organized across racial divides in mixed race organizations but, far more commonly, tried their utmost to deny black workers equal access to jobs and unions. Accordingly, black workers organized their own unions, most famously the Brotherhood of Sleeping Car Porters (BSCP), though they also fought (against unions and employers while appealing to the government) for equal access. Pullman porters, overwhelmingly black, actually straddled the transport and service worker divide, labouring aboard railroads while serving the needs and whims of white passengers. Of course, ethnic-based patterns hardly were unique to US railroad employment; Ottoman railroads hired European and Ottoman Christians for white-collar jobs and Ottoman Muslims for most blue-collar tasks. Yet the BSCP might be best known for collaborating with the broader civil rights movement for racial equality—similar to African railway workers whose actions contributed to anti-colonial struggles in French West Africa or dockers in Guinea-Bissau's leading port, Pidgiguiti, whose 1959 strike contributed to the formation of a militant liberation movement in Guinea and the Cape Verde Islands with links to Angola, as well.[12]

The conservative inclination to preserve existing status and roles also manifested itself in debates over the gendering of work. In Nigeria, Lisa Lindsay details the ways in which colonial officials transformed wage labour into a male domain through a study of African railway workers. By reframing the conditions of work for African railway employees within the framework of the nuclear family, colonial officials empowered the "male breadwinner" as the target of wage labour. This system both de-

---

[11] Frederick Cooper, "'Our Strike': Equality, Anticolonial Politics and the 1947–1948 Railway Strike in French West Africa", in: James D. Le Suer (ed.), *The Decolonization Reader* (New York, 2003); idem, *Decolonization and African Society. The Labour Question in French and British Africa* (Cambridge, 1996). Also see Cooper, *On the African Waterfront*; Guilherme Grandi, "The First Great Railway Strike: Rereading the Early Labour Movement in Sao Paulo", *International Review of Social History*, Special Issue, 59 (2014), pp. 161–183.

[12] Eric Arnesen, *Brotherhoods of Color. Black Railroad Workers and the Struggle for Equality* (New York, 2001); Beth Tompkins Bates, *Pullman Porters and the Rise of Protest Politics in Black America, 1925–1945* (Chapel Hill, NC, 2001); Donald Quataert, "Labor History and the Ottoman Empire, c. 1700–1922", *International Labor and Working-Class History*, 60 (October 2001), pp. 93–109, at 104; Basil Davidson, *No Fist Is Big Enough to Hide the Sky. The Liberation of Guinea Bissau and Cape Verde. Aspects of an African Revolution* (London, 1981), pp. 16–17.

nigrated women's work and relied on the continued involvement of women as providers and earners in the "informal economy", often providing necessarily labour in local and long-distance markets as carriers or traders. While more interested in Japanese passengers using modern transport technologies, Alisa Freedman examines how (male) consumers perceived female transportation workers, like bus drivers, in early 20th century Tokyo. What these workers shared with other transportation and service industry workers in the modern era was being overworked and underpaid employees of large, powerful corporations. Thus, like many other transportation workers, they might work in mobility but their lives were anything but upwardly mobile. In fact, the choice by Japanese transportation operators to hire female workers was not uncommon. Margaret Walsh notes, "the global search for cheap labour is another factor that has propelled women into the fields of international and local travel, tourism, and transportation".[13] As women found their way into occupations traditionally seen as male, it forced reexaminations by male workers and historians alike. For instance, dockwork—along with workers aboard ships—were historically associated with masculinity. Not surprisingly, then, these workforces often incorporated notions of manliness into occupational identities. Dockers—from Liverpool to Turku, Finland, to Portland, Oregon (USA)—supposedly were manly because they worked in physically demanding and dangerous occupations. Hence, men resisted the hiring of women on the docks because they supposedly were not strong or brave enough to handle the work but also because women doing "men's work" undermined dockers' identity.[14]

Transport workers in cities also played important roles in labour, urban, and political history. Anton Rosenthal writes of streetcar (trolley or tram) workers in Montevideo who engaged in public strike actions that improved their own lots as well as promoted radical, democratic visions that challenged the ruling elite and their notions of "progress". If less radical, Philadelphia streetcar workers' strikes and unionism also greatly impacted the lives of residents and economic trajectory of one of America's great industrial cities, as James Wolfinger demonstrates. Transportation

---

[13] Lisa Lindsay, *Working with Gender. Wage Labor and Social Change in Southwest Nigeria* (Portsmouth, NH, 2003); Claire Robertson, *Sharing the Same Bowl. A Socioeconomic History of Women and Class in Accra, Ghana* (Bloomington, IN, 1984); Gracia Clark, *Onions Are My Husband. Survival and Accumulation by West African Market Women* (Chicago, 1995); Alisa Freedman, *Tokyo in Transit. Japanese Culture on the Rails and Road* (Stanford, CA, 2011), p. 244 and ch. 4; Margaret Walsh, "Gender and the History of Transportation Services: A Historiographical Perspective", *Business History Review*, 81, 3 (2007), pp. 545–562, at 545.

[14] Pat Ayers, "The Making of Men: Masculinities in Interwar Liverpool", in: Margaret Walsh (ed.), *Working Out Gender. Perspectives from Labour History* (Aldershot, 1999), pp. 66–83; William W. Pilcher, *The Portland Longshoremen. A Dispersed Urban Community* (New York, 1972); Ava Baron, "Masculinity, the Embodied Male Worker, and the Historian's Gaze", *International Labor and Working Class History*, 69 (Spring 2006), pp. 143–146. Tapio Bergholm mostly writes in Finnish but see his paper, "After Harmaja We Are All Bachelors", European Labour History Network, Torino, Italy, December 2015: https://helsinki.academia.edu/TapioBergholm.

workers and their unions frequently were attacked for being a "special interest" and interfering with residents' commutes and employers' profits though, really, what they posited was an alternate vision of urban life. Workers labouring in the public's view and sphere frequently asserted their power and vision.[15] In colonial cities across Africa, Asia, and Latin America, transport workers often settled near infrastructure hubs, disrupting European plans to limit access to urban areas. Far from mere labour, these transport workers—along with their counterparts in the trade and services sectors—established vibrant cultural economies around markets and ports and created new forms of sociability and identification that redefined urban life.[16]

Motor transport workers faced similar challenges and pressures within communities of circulation and exchange. The introduction of usable and reliable motor vehicles in the early part of the 20th century provided an alternative form of public transport technology, which proved more mobile and adaptable. Motor transport workers in places as diverse as Ghana, South Africa, India, Mexico, and the United States used this new technology to create a diverse array of transport systems, from bus and taxi services to long-haul trucking. As part of a broader system of public transportation and public infrastructure, motor transport workers often found themselves heavily regulated. Companies or the state, which provided necessary technology, training, and wages, employed some of these workers. However, motor transport technology also freed many workers from the centralized infrastructure of the railway, taking advantage of the relatively low-cost of vehicles to create their own businesses. In Ghana and Nigeria, many people worked as owner-operators within a loosely organized transport system. These entrepreneurial systems echoed the bus and taxi companies closely associated with public transportation in the United States and Europe, even as they often rejected their model of centralized company ownership and wage labour.[17]

The global spread of motor transport technologies often reconfigured the technological and cultural relationships between producers and consumers, rooted in the particularities of local mobility cultures and values. In the United States, for instance, Cotten Seiler argues that motor transportation became closely associated with narratives of individualism and the "freedom of the road", spawning a new sort of road-oriented cultural economy. Drive-in movie theaters and restaurants, roadside motels, and suburban sprawl reshaped an American society rooted in an

---

[15] Anton Rosenthal, "The Arrival of the Electric Streetcar and the Conflict over Progress in Early Twentieth-Century Montevideo", *Journal of Latin American Studies*, 27, 2 (1995), pp. 319–341; James Wolfinger, *Running the Rails. Capital and Labor in the Philadelphia Transit Industry* (Ithaca, NY, 2016).
[16] Cooper, *On the African Waterfront*; Marian Aguiar, *Tracking Modernity. India's Railway and the Culture of Mobility* (Minneapolis, 2011); Ritika Prasad, *Tracks of Change. Railways and Everyday Life in Colonial India* (Cambridge, 2016); Teresa van Hoy, *A Social History of Mexico's Railroads. Peons, Prisoners, and Priests* (New York, 2008).
[17] Jennifer Hart, *Ghana on the Go. African Mobility in the Age of Motor Transportation* (Bloomington, IN, 2016).

assumed ubiquity of private car ownership. This assumption meant that those without vehicles—and those who served them—were associated with poverty. Outside of major urban centres, where population density made private car ownership impractical, public transportation deteriorated throughout much of the United States in the 20th century. Public transit workers, likewise, experienced decreased wages, job security, and status, i.e. growing precariousness due to systematic disinvestment encouraged by corporations in the motor transport industry (auto and truck manufacturers, oil producers, tire companies, etc.).[18]

In Great Britain and across Europe, motor transportation was less appealing as a form of public transportation, as the dense settlements of more compact European cities and extensive railway infrastructure made motor vehicles not only unnecessary but, in many cases, impractical.[19] However, workers in European colonies and many other places quickly grasped the potential of motor transport technology. Drivers used motor vehicles to fill in the gaps left by limited, export-oriented railway infrastructure, connecting rural and urban areas in comprehensive public transportation systems that carried both goods and passengers. In facilitating the circulation and exchange of people, ideas, and products, drivers embodied a new form of working class cosmopolitanism that often differed from the privilege and status of Western-educated elites. Drivers also created cosmopolitan cultures among the communities along their routes. As in the United States, motor transport technologies created new social, economic, and cultural possibilities. In Ghana, Gracia Clark argues that female market traders established special relationships with drivers, capitalizing on the speed and convenience of motor transport to engage in new forms of long-distance trade while still maintaining their domestic responsibilities. Polly Hill argues that Ghanaian cocoa farmers reinvested their profits in motor vehicles, using them to transport their produce to coastal ports and bypassing the colonial railways. In Tanzania, garages emerged along roadsides and in neighborhoods, catering to the technological needs of vehicle owners but also creating imaginative spaces where "tinkerers" could build unique vehicles using customized and spare parts. Across Latin America, Asia, and Africa, drivers decorated their vehicles, using colorful designs and popular slogans to express their own aspirations and that of their passengers.[20]

---

18 Cotten Seiler, *A Republic of Drivers. A Cultural History of Automobility in America* (Chicago, 2008); *Taken for a Ride*, dir. by Jim Klein and Martha Olson (New Day Films, 1996); Kenneth T. Jackson, *Crabgrass Frontier. The Suburbanization of the United States* (New York, 1985).
19 Wolfgang Schivelbusch, *The Railway Journey. The Industrialization of Time and Space in the 19th Century* (Los Angeles, 1987); Jo Guldi, *Roads to Power. Britain Invents the Infrastructure State* (Cambridge, MA, 2012).
20 Kristen Ross, *Fast Cars, Clean Bodies: Decolonization and the Reordering of. French Culture* (Cambridge, MA, 1995); Gracia Clark, *Onions Are My Husband*; Polly Hill, *The Migrant Cocoa Farmers of Southern Ghana. A Study in Rural Capitalism* (Cambridge, 1963); Joshua Grace, "Modernization Bubu. Cars, Roads, and the Politics of Development in Tanzania, 1870s to 1980s" (Ph.D.: Michigan State University, 2013).

Particularly in industrialized economies, long-haul trucking emerged as a distinct category of motor transport labour as early as the 1930s. In the United States, Shane Hamilton explores cartelization in trucking industry from the 1930s into the 1970s and 1980s, the rise of the powerful Teamsters Union that represented most drivers in trucking, and the subsequent efforts that resulted in "independent contractors" remaking the industry and nation's economy, thereby facilitating the rise of Wal-Mart, America's most powerful corporation, and more broadly today's low-price, low-wage economy. However, the distinctiveness of U.S. long-haul trucking assumed a distinction between passenger and goods transport that certainly was shared across most Western and industrialized economies, but which was considerably more blurred in colonial and postcolonial economies, where production and circulation was often controlled by small-scale farmers and traders who traveled with their goods. European colonial governments often sought to reinforce, legislate, and police these distinctions. In places like colonial Ghana, where Africans controlled the profitable cocoa and palm oil industries, drivers frequently carried both goods and passengers in an effort to respond to the needs of their clients and to maximize their own profits. They also moved freely between different categories of driving work—long-haul trucking, passenger transport, and taxis; formal sector wage employment and self-employed, entrepreneurial work—creating a complex, adaptable, and fiercely independent motor transport system that continues to inform postcolonial economic development.[21]

In recent decades, aviation has taken off, mostly to move people but also some cargo. Aviation sector workers, accordingly, have increased in numbers and influence over the last sixty years. As Geraint Harvey and Peter Turnbull write about the contemporary aviation industry, "The global economic impact of civil aviation is estimated to be around US$3.5 trillion, equivalent to 7.5 per cent of world GDP". Strict divisions of labour exist between highly skilled and, often, well paid pilots and mechanics, and those who load and unload cargo and serve as flight crew. Like other transport sectors, civil aviation is well organized with some workers in craft unions and others in industry-wide ones. For instance, in the USA, pilots, flight attendants, mechanics, and baggage handlers all have unionized but in separate organizations though they maintain alliances to improve wages and working conditions. The most infamous moment in US aviation labour history occurred in 1981, when President Ronald Reagan fired unionized air traffic controllers engaged in an (illegal) strike; the high-pressure nature of their jobs and desire to remain in the middle class had been hindered by severe limits placed upon public sector workers includ-

---

[21] Shane Hamilton, *Trucking Country. The Road to America's Wal-Mart Economy* (Princeton, 2008); Jennifer Hart, *Ghana on the Go*; Jennifer Hart, "Motor Transportation, Trade Unionism, and the Culture of Work in Colonial Ghana", *International Review of Social History*, Special Issue, 59 (2014), pp. 185–209; Jennifer Hart, "'One Man, No Chop': Licit Wealth, Good Citizens, and the Criminalization of Drivers in Postcolonial Ghana", *International Journal of African Historical Studies*, 46, 3 (2013), pp. 373–396.

ing controllers. Setbacks aside, the more than five million workers in civil aviation, globally, comprise a vital sector of the global economy.[22]

Today, ships, railroads, and trucks constitute the field of "logistics" or what Anna Tsing calls "supply chain capitalism". Among the most important works centreing labour in the recent history of global transportation is Edna Bonacich and Jake B. Wilson's *Getting the Goods*, a study of the nation's most important port, Los Angeles-Long Beach. This port serves as a window into the modern logistics industry, the gateway for goods shipped through an efficient, intermodal freight system in which containers move from factories in Asia to consumers in the United States. Since, clearly, the logistics industry has contributed mightily to the "global race to the bottom", by supplying Wal-Mart and other big-box retailers, appreciating this subject is essential to a labour history of global trade and transport.[23]

Trade and service

Wage labour regimes required new forms of service labour to cater to individuals who increasingly relied on institutions outside of the home to provide basic services. In many cases, the labour of service workers overlapped with the labour associated with transport and trade. Further blurring the lines between these industries, trade, service, and transportation often came together in port cities. These convergences not only applied to wage labourers but also employers and managers as Çağlar Keyder, Y. Eyüp Özveren and Donald Quataert write, "The merchant communities of the [Ottoman] port cities were well organized and well educated", both helpful in protecting and asserting their class interests vis-à-vis their workers but also in relation to the state.[24]

Paul E. Johnson's classic *Shopkeeper's Millennium* examines the rising bourgeois class of Rochester, New York in the first half of the 19th century, at the start of large-scale industrialism. As throughout pre-industrial societies, the people who hired other workers also were workers themselves, i.e. skilled craftsmen (generally men). Such artisans hired other workers (journeymen and apprentices) but also sold their own finished goods to consumers. Industrialization resulted in a separa-

---

[22] Geraint Harvey and Peter Turnbull, "The Impact of the Financial Crisis on Labour in the Civil Aviation Industry", (Geneva, 2009), pp. iii, 1; Liesl Miller Orenic, *On the Ground. Labor Struggle in the American Airline Industry* (Urbana, IL, 2009); Joseph A. McCartin, *Collision Course. Ronald Reagan, the Air Traffic Controllers, and the Strike that Changed America* (New York, 2011).
[23] Anna Tsing, "Supply Chains and the Human Condition", *Rethinking Marxism*, 21, 2 (2009), pp. 148–176; Edna Bonacich and Jake Wilson, *Getting The Goods. Ports, Labor, and the Logistics Revolution* (Ithaca, NY, 2008).
[24] E.P. Thompson, *The Making of the English Working Class* (London, 1963), 1966; Çağlar Keyder, Y. Eyüp Özveren and Donald Quataert, "Port-Cities in the Ottoman Empire: Some Theoretical and Historical Perspectives", *Review* (Fernand Braudel Centre), 16, 4 (Fall 1993), pp. 519–558, at 555.

tion between production and retailing and, thereby, increased the number of traders as well as sharpening the divisions between employers and employees.[25]

In the same era, the dawn of industrial capitalism, Walter Johnson studies another preindustrial institution, the slave trading market, when human beings were commodified as chattel slaves, as property. In *Soul by Soul*, Johnson examines New Orleans, America's largest slave market. He discusses the traders, buyers, and slaves who belonged to a single system, in which slave traders sold human beings as slaves to "masters" (employers), laying bare the brutal economics of this sort of trading and —as in many workplaces—the many interdependencies. More typical of labour histories are those studying employees.[26]

Susan Porter Benson explores an important service workplace born of industrialization, the modern department store. In *Counter Cultures: Saleswomen, Managers, and Customers in American Department Stores, 1890 – 1940* Benson connects class and gender to write a social history of women sales clerks. Wage-earning female salesclerks, their all-male managers, and upper-class women who viewed such stores as places of "recreation and sociability" belonged to an interlocking network not entirely different from the slave market described by Johnson. Benson's work remains a standard for those interested in the labour history of workers in sales.[27]

Of course, retail labour varied widely in different countries. In 20th century South Africa, for instance, the state created a segmented and bifurcated market based upon gender, skill, and race. The legal system privileged white and male workers yet that did not stop female workers from attempting to improve their conditions, both through greater government protection as well as unionism. For workers such as these, and indeed across the global South, where access to wage labour was limited and where salaries were often quite low, precarity has always existed. Even wage labourers in countries like South Africa or Ghana sought to supplement their meager wages with entrepreneurial work like farming, trade, or other small business ownership, which they pursued outside of their formal sector jobs, often with the help of additional family labour. Retail workers in industrialized societies, who have increasingly been forced into more casual and precarious labour, e. g. hired through labour brokers, irregular and limited working hours, now more closely resemble conditions in South Africa.[28]

---

25 Paul E. Johnson, *A Shopkeeper's Millennium. Society and Revivals in Rochester, New York, 1815 – 1837* (New York, 1978; reprint 2004).
26 Walter Johnson, *Soul by Soul. Life Inside the Antebellum Slave Market* (Cambridge, MA, 2001).
27 Susan Porter Benson, *Counter Cultures. Saleswomen, Managers, and Customers in American Department Stores, 1890 – 1940* (Urbana, IL, 1986).
28 Bridget Kenny, "The Regime of Contract in South African Retailing: A History of Race, Gender, and Skill in Precarious Labour", *International Labor and Working-Class History*, 89 (2016), pp. 20 – 39; Franco Barchiesi, "Wage Labour, Precarious Employment, and Social Inclusion in the Making of South Africa's Postapartheid Transition", *African Studies Review*, 51, 2 (2008), pp. 119 – 142, at 124; Ralph Callebert, "Working Class Action and Informal Trade on the Durban Docks, 1930s – 1950s",

Perhaps more than other wage labour sectors, service industries often drew heavily on the labour of women, who transferred domestic skills expertise in caretaking—work that today is still associated with women, but which was firmly rooted in 19th century conceptions of gendered divisions of labour and the morality of the private sphere—into the workplace. In many cases, the presence of women in the workplace created conflicts along the lines of gender and labour, as Dorothy Sue Cobble explores in *Dishing It Out: Waitresses and Their Unions in the Twentieth Century*, which discusses how American women simultaneously fought against their fellow (male) workers for inclusion in male-dominated unions and (male) employers in order to improve their economic conditions. When able to unionize, waitresses drastically improved their wages and conditions though their battles against sexist, male workers, in and out of unions, hindered their efforts to challenge their male employers. Cobble positions waitresses at the centre of the rise of a service-oriented economy in which the feminization of the workforce also occurred; of course, this process continues to this day. Similarly, Marianne Debouzy studies the approximately 25,000 McDonald's workers in France. Just as Eric Schlosser demonstrated for U.S. fast food workers in his popular history *Fast Food Nation*, McDonald's Corporation strives to keep its French workers—generally quite young—out of unions despite the French tradition of heavily unionized, working-class militancy. McDonald's, like Wal-Mart, depends on a low-wage workforce to maintain profitability with a business model based upon low profit margins.[29]

As with the world's most famous fast food corporation, Wal-Mart arose as the largest and most powerful retailer and, accordingly, has drawn the attention of a growing number of labour historians. In *The Retail Revolution: How Wal-Mart Created a Brave New World of Business*, Nelson Lichtenstein argues that Wal-Mart created its own corporate subculture rooted in its birthplace, the Ozark region of Arkansas, one of the whitest, most homogeneous parts of the USA. Founder Sam Walton frequently claimed "his" workers were "a family", and Lichtenstein describes how the company created a corporate culture built upon a particular ideological take on family and religion that—concurrently—was built upon a largely-female workforce that suffered low wages, job insecurity, and pervasive corporate control. In contrast to Henry Ford's motor company, Wal-Mart operates upon the premise that it is cheaper to hire and train new workers than pay existing "associates" good wages and develop career-long workers. Similarly, Bethany Moreton's book *To Serve God and Wal-Mart: The Making of Christian Free Enterprise* focuses upon the mostly female, married,

---

Journal of Southern African Studies, 38, 4 (2012), pp. 847–861; Hart, "Motor Transportation"; Robertson, *Sharing the Same Bowl*.

29 Judith Walkowitz, *City of Dreadful Delight. Narratives of Sexual Danger in Late-Victorian London* (Chicago, 2013); Dorothy Sue Cobble, *Dishing It Out. Waitresses and Their Unions in the Twentieth Century* (Urbana, IL, 1991); Eric Schlosser, *Fast Food Nation. The Dark Side of the All-American Meal* (New York, 2001), ch. 3; Marianne Debouzy, "Working for McDonald's, France: Resistance to the Americanization of Work", *International Labor and Working-Class History*, 70 (2006), pp. 126–142.

white workers who embodied the transition in America (and other industrial societies) to two-income households and an economy dominated by services, not manufacturing. Moreton contends Wal-Mart workers embraced a "reproducerism" that celebrated traditional feminine traits of caring and service though men controlled nearly all of the managerial positions.[30]

Wal-Mart's success was not solely based on its "associates" but also a highly sophisticated, global system that manufactured cheap goods, especially in China, and pioneered bar-code-based, computerized shipping. In an earlier, edited collection, *Wal-Mart: The Face of Twenty-First-Century Capitalism* (2006), Nelson Lichtenstein echoes Peter Drucker that every era has a dominant business the shapes society in its own image. In recent decades Wal-Mart typifies giant retail corporations dominate and dictate global supply chains and, hence, global capitalism. Thomas Adams' essay explains how Wal-Mart's authoritarian management, fierce anti-unionism, and low-wage model became prevalent; by contrast, department stores used to be much more heavily unionized. Ellen Rosen's contribution highlights managerial speedups, systematic understaffing, and "wage theft" (i.e. when workers continue working beyond their assigned shift, off the clock and without pay). Along with pro-corporate, neoliberal policies, ever more workers toil in low-wage, import dependent, retail sales. Companies like Wal-Mart have supplanted the manufacturing firms of the Fordist era as the mobility of retail capital dominate labour(ers) far less mobile.

As mammoth retail corporations like Tesco and Wal-Mart expand into new markets, workers and their organizations respond differently. In India, for instance, many millions of family-run shops and street vendors historically dominated local trade—and still do to some extent. However, as multinational corporations entered urban India, it being much more integrated into global capitalism, the greatly expanding retail workforce unionized and, simultaneously, collaborated with international labour networks and federations. Interestingly, these transnational alliances promote retail workers' rights but also allied with traditional traders, themselves resisting encroachment and competition. Events in India, in terms of transnational networks of retail workers and unions, parallel other nations in the Global South. Yet, as in other industries, corporations generally have far more power and ability to shift production and distribution networks; meanwhile, human labourers remain far more place-bound for socio-cultural, economic, and political reasons. Despite this uphill struggle, workers in retail increasingly attempt to form transnational alliances—following the lead of maritime workers who created the International Transport Workers Federation as early as 1896.[31]

---

[30] Nelson Lichtenstein, *The Retail Revolution. How Wal-Mart Created a Brave New World of Business* (New York, 2009); Bethany Moreton, *To Serve God and Wal-Mart. The Making of Christian Free Enterprise* (Cambridge, MA, 2009).

[31] Martin Franz, "The Potential of Collective Power in a Global Production Network: Unicome and Metro Cash & Carry in India", *Erdkunde*, 64, 3 (2010), pp. 281–290; Debashish Bhattacherjee, *Organ-*

As a subsection of trade, retail workers typify work in contemporary times. Bridget Kenny, an expert on South African retail, insightfully notes that studies on precariousness "has come to describe the subjective experience of the [current] time, a zeitgeist of sorts". Workers in sales, she highlights, are an especially apt workforce to examine if one truly is interested with precariousness: "Retail is used as a case because it has become a powerful symbol of contingent employment globally, for its reliance on part-time, low-wage, and insecure employment now and as a sign of erosion of hard-fought gains by the labour movement". However, Kenny punctures this balloon by observing, "When one examines precariousness from the perspective of the Global South where insecurity for many has always been a core feature of labour markets and economies, less readily does this presumption fit".[32]

In the Global South, the instability and weakness of the wage labour market—a weakness that was inscribed in many ways in the global inequalities produced through the very economic structures and relationships of capitalism and colonialism that grew in the 18th and 19th centuries—inspired the growth of a large informal economy. Some associate the informal economy with the illegality and immorality of a "black market" or shadow economy. However, as Brian Larkin argues, in much of the global South the informal economy constitutes a large and vibrant sector of legitimate economic enterprise that often fills the gaps left by a weak formal sector. The informal sector flourishes particularly across the fields of trade, transport, and services. Market women, food sellers, drivers, hawkers, and many others operate small businesses, ensuring that desired goods and services reach consumers. In their search for economic security, individuals working in the informal sector often engage in multiple sorts of work simultaneously, blurring the boundaries between formal and informal, local and global. In countries like Ghana, Nigeria, South Africa, and India, these informal economic activities often build on precapitalist systems of exchange adapted to reflect the new opportunities and insecurities of capitalism. In industrial economies, however, many look to emerging service and transport industries like Uber as an expansion of the informal economy in response to more recent precarianization.[33]

---

ized *Labour and Economic Liberalization. India: Past, Present, and Future* (Geneva, 1999); Harold Lewis, "The International Transport Workers Federation (ITF) 1945–1965. An Organizational and Political Anatomy" (Ph.D.: University of Warwick, 2003), ch. 2.
32 Kenny, "Regimes of Contract in South African Retailing", p. 20.
33 Keith Hart, "Informal Income Opportunities and Urban Employment in Ghana", *The Journal of Modern African Studies*, 11, 1 (1973), pp. 61–89; Brian Larkin, *Signal and Noise. Media, Infrastructure, and Urban Culture in Nigeria* (Durham, NC, 2008); Robert Neuwirth, *Stealth of Nations. The Global Rise of the Informal Economy* (New York, 2012); Sudhir Venkatesh, *Off the Books. The Underground Economy of the Urban Poor* (Cambridge, MA, 2009); Kaveri Gill, *Of Poverty and Plastic. Scavenging and Scrap Trading Entrepreneurs in India's Urban Informal Economy* (Oxford, 2012).

Conclusions

We welcome the ongoing embrace of comparative, transnational, and global methods by historians and other scholars that, most likely, will continue. In particular, those who study workers, labouring culture, and worker organizations stand to gain a great deal from changing their lenses and gazing at the past in new ways. As we suggest, there are myriad opportunities to reframe old orthodoxies previously bound by nation-states by engaging in transnational and comparative studies of the labour of trade, transport, and services. Considerations of these forms of mobile labour push us to reconsider the emphasis placed on formal sector wage labour. In the process, these histories highlight a shared history of precarity lying at the centre of global capitalism.

Suggested reading

Balachandran, Gopalan. *Globalizing Labour? Indian Seafarers and World Shipping, c. 1870–1945* (Delhi and Oxford: Oxford University Press, 2012).

Bellucci, Stefano, Larissa Rosa Correa, Jan-Georg Deutsch and Chitra Joshi (eds). "Labour in Transport: Histories from the Global South, c. 1750–1950", *International Review of Social History* 59, special issue 22 (2014).

Benson, Susan Porter. *Counter Cultures: Saleswomen, Managers, and Customers in American Department Stores, 1890–1940* (Urbana: University of Illinois Press, 1986).

Bonacich, Edna and Jake Wilson. *Getting The Goods. Ports, Labor, and the Logistics Revolution* (Ithaca, NY: Cornell University Press, 2008).

Cobble, Dorothy Sue. *Dishing It Out: Waitresses and Their Unions in the Twentieth Century* (Urbana: University of Illinois Press, 1991).

Cooper, Fred. *On the African Waterfront: Urban Disorder and the Transformation of Work in Colonial Mombasa* (New Haven, CT: Yale University Press, 1987).

Davies, Sam et al., *Dock Workers: International Explorations in Comparative Labour History, 1790–1970*, 2 volumes (Aldershot: Ashgate, 2000).

Gill, Kaveri. *Of Poverty and Plastic: Scavenging and Scrap Trading Entrepreneurs in India's Urban Informal Economy* (Oxford: Oxford University Press, 2012).

Hart, Jennifer. *Ghana on the Go. African Mobility in the Age of Motor Transportation* (Bloomington, IN: Indiana University Press, 2016).

Hoy, Teresa van. *A Social History of Mexico's Railroads. Peons, Prisoners, and Priests* (New York: Rowman and Littlefield, 2008).

Kerr, Ian J. *Building the Railways of the Raj* (Delhi: Oxford University Press, 1995).

Lichtenstein, Nelson. *The Retail Revolution. How Wal-Mart Created a Brave New World of Business* (New York: Metropolitan, 2009).

Linebaugh, Peter and Marcus Rediker. *The Many Headed Hydra. Sailors, Slaves, Commoners and the Hidden History of the Revolutionary Atlantic* (Boston: Beacon, 2000).

Orenic, Liesl Miller. *On the Ground. Labor Struggle in the American Airline Industry* (Urbana: University of Illinois Press, 2009).

Rockel, Stephen. *Carriers of Culture. Labor on the Road in Nineteenth-Century East Africa* (Portsmouth, NH: Heinemann, 2006).

Rosenthal, Anton. "The Arrival of the Electric Streetcar and the Conflict over Progress in Early Twentieth-Century Montevideo", *Journal of Latin American Studies*, 27, 2 (1995), pp. 319–341.

Stromquist, Shelton. *A Generation of Boomers: The Pattern of Railroad Labor Conflict in Nineteenth-Century America* (Urbana: University of Illinois Press, 1987).

Walsh, Margaret. "Gender and the History of Transportation Services: A Historiographical Perspective", *Business History Review*, 81, 3 (2007), pp. 545–562.

Warren, Jim. "The Singapore Rickshaw Pullers: The Social Organization of a Coolie Occupation, 1880–1940", *Journal of Southeast Asian Studies*, 16, 1 (1985), pp. 1–15.

Therese Garstenauer
3.5. Administrative Staff

This chapter will describe and discuss the social position, work, and conditions of employment of a group that has been called *ambtenaren*, *Beamte*, *chinovniki*, *civil servants*, *fonctionnaires*, *guān*, *mülkiye*, *quipucamayocs*, and otherwise in various times and places. These terms are not synonymous, but in a very general way they denote similar phenomena. Many of the terms had not come into general use before the late eighteenth century. For an overview that spans a period from 1500 to the present, it is therefore useful, difficult as it may be, to find a more general term for this group. Following Jos C.N. Raadschelders' suggestion, we will use the Weberian term administrative staff (*Verwaltungsstab*), encompassing "all those working for those in political power at all times".[1] The work performed by this staff includes a wide range of tasks, such as clerical work, auditing and accounting, tax collection, advising the ruler, judicial activities, policing, and other public tasks, from menial activities to prestigious ones. In some of these functions, they represented the interface between the subjects and the ruler or the citizens and the state respectively.

A global history of administrative staff as such has yet to be written, although the personnel also figure in seminal works on the histories of empires, bureaucracies, and public administration spanning many epochs and cultures.[2] In the academic field of public administration, the necessity of comparative approaches has been acknowledged for some time and has engendered a number of prolific international research projects. Notably, from the early 1990s on scholars from the universities of Leiden and Indiana have been collaborating on the project "Civil service systems in comparative perspective", developing a neo-institutional conceptual basis (of which historical development is one crucial component) and empirical applications thereof.[3]

This chapter also draws on a recent volume on empires and bureaucracies which, covering an impressive range of cultures and time periods, looks at bureauc-

---

[1] Jos C.N. Raadschelders, "Changing European Ideas about the Public Servant: A Theoretical and Methodological Framework", in: Fritz Sager and Patrick Overeem (eds), *The European Public Servant: A Shared Administrative Identity?* (Colchester, 2015), pp. 15–34, 15.

[2] See, for example, S.N. Eisenstadt, *The Political Systems of Empires* (London, 1963); E.N. Gladden, *A History of Public Administration: From the Eleventh Century to the Present Day*, 2 vols (London, 1972); Henry Jacoby, *The Bureaucratization of the World* (Berkeley, CA, 1973); and Ferrell Heady, *Public Administration: A Comparative Perspective*, 6th edn (New York, 2001).

[3] Frits van der Meer, "Civil Service Systems in Western Europe: An Introduction", in: *idem* (ed.), *Civil Service Systems in Western Europe*, 2nd edn (Cheltenham etc., 2011), pp. 1–11, 4. See also Hans A.G.M. Bekke, James L. Perry, and Theo A.J. Toonen (eds), *Civil Service Systems in Comparative Perspective* (Bloomington etc., 1996), and Sager and Overeem, *European Public Servant*.

racies as an essential component of imperial rule.[4] Whereas the evolution of the civil service in Europe is strongly related to the growing role of the state and the development of centralized national states, administration within empires follows different rules.

Although this chapter is supposed to present a global view of the history of administrative staff, it will start with Max Weber's clearly Eurocentric criteria of bureaucratic and patrimonial rule and organization.[5] Given the lack of more globally oriented ones so far, these concepts will serve as a basis. In the following section, the cases of China, the Ottoman Empire, Western Europe, Russia, and the United States, and some aspects of colonial and postcolonial administration will be addressed. It will thus become clear that the history of administrative staff has many facets, and research perspectives need to be expanded. This should be done not as comparative history in a traditional sense, but as a "history that compares", i.e. "meaningful comparisons across time and between cultures" without "sweeping the particular under the global".[6] The final section will briefly address developments in the twentieth and twenty-first centuries, particularly the internationalization and globalization of public administration.

Patrimonial and bureaucratic rule and staff

The Weberian ideal types of patrimonial and bureaucratic rule and the corresponding staff are a useful framework for making sense of various forms of administrative staff in different contexts, not only for want of a framework developed especially for global history. It is, however, crucial to understand them as ideal types, not as prescriptive models. Traits of both types can coexist in one context – and they do, even in today's apparently highly rationalized European public administration ("old boys' networks" as a recruiting ground for higher public office for example).[7] Furthermore, a transition from patrimonial organization towards modernization by means of bureaucratization is not always a necessary – and necessarily successful – linear development, as examples from late colonial administration have shown.[8]

Patrimonialism has been described as a "broad concept referring to several different types of administrative forms usually associated with traditional authority, including the use of kin, slaves, patronage, feudalism, prebendalism, local notables,

---

[4] Peter Crooks and Timothy H. Parsons (eds), *Empires and Bureaucracy in World History: From Late Antiquity to the Twentieth Century* (Cambridge, 2016).
[5] Max Weber, *Wirtschaft und Gesellschaft*, 5th edn (Tübingen, 1980), pp. 124–140.
[6] Frederick Cooper, "Race, Ideology, and the Perils of Comparative History", *American Historical Review*, 101, 4 (1996), pp. 1122–1138, at 1135.
[7] Jos C.N. Raadschelders, *Handbook of Administrative History* (New Brunswick, 2012), p. 160.
[8] Peter Crooks and Timothy H. Parsons, "Empires, Bureaucracy and the Paradox of Power", in: *idem, Empires and Bureaucracy in World History*, pp. 3–28, at 20.

sale of offices, and tax farming."[9] The patrimonial ruler is related to his subordinates and officials through arbitrary decisions of the moment, and he grants powers to his officials, or commissions them to perform set tasks. Decisions are taken either on the basis of the authority of particular received legal norms or precedents, or entirely as arbitrary decisions on the part of the ruler. Household officials and favourites are often recruited on a purely patrimonial basis from among slaves or serfs. Qualification for office depends upon the ruler's personal judgement of quality among his household officials, retainers, or favourites, who are usually supported and equipped in the ruler's household and from his personal stores. The ruler himself, or those who act in his name, conduct the affairs of government when and if they consider it appropriate.[10]

By contrast, the bureaucratic organization is characterized by continuous administrative activity and the application of formal rules and procedures. Offices are clear and specialized, and organized in a hierarchical manner. The use of written documents and an adequate supply of means (desks, paper, etc.) are a matter of course. Officials do not own their offices and are submitted to procedures of rational discipline and control. Within bureaucratic organizations, office is held by individual functionaries who are subordinate and appointed, and must have expertise. They are assigned by contractual agreement in a tenured (secure) position, and fulfil their office as their main or only job. They work in a career system and are rewarded with a regular monetary salary and pension, according to rank. Furthermore, they are promoted according to seniority, and work under formal protection of their office.[11]

Looking at historical examples, we naturally find that ideal types never fully apply; instead, we find combinations of more or less of the criteria mentioned above, sometimes in surprising ways. The administration of *Tahuantinsuyu*, the empire ruled by the Incas until the late sixteenth century, efficiently gathered statistical information regarding demographics and commodities using a mnemonic system of knots (*quipus*), mastered by specialized staff called *quipucamayocs*.[12] Thus, a culture without alphabetic writing achieved higher levels of information retrieval than a

---

[9] Edgar Kiser and Audrey Sacks, "African Patrimonialism in Historical Perspective: Assessing Decentralized and Privatized Tax Administration", *The Annals of the American Academy of Political and Social Science*, 636 (2011), pp. 129–149, 130.
[10] See Reinhard Bendix, *Nation-Building and Citizenship. Studies of Our Changing Social Order* (Berkeley, CA, 1969), p. 130.
[11] This condensed list of criteria (based on Weber, *Wirtschaft und Gesellschaft*, pp. 124–140) was compiled by A. van Braam, "Bureaucratiseringsgraad van de plaatselijke bestuursorganisatie van Westzaandam ten tijde van de Republiek", *Tijdschrift voor Geschiedenis*, 90, 3–4 (1977), pp. 457–483, quoted in Jos C.N. Raadschelders and Mark R. Rutgers, "The Evolution of Civil Service Systems", in: Bekke et al., *Civil Service Systems in Comparative Perspective*, pp. 67–99, 92.
[12] Chris Given-Wilson, "Bureaucracy without Alphabetic Writing: Governing the Inca Empire, c. 1438–1532", in: Crooks and Parsons, *Empires and Bureaucracy in World History*, pp. 81–101.

"modern" administration such as that in British colonies in Africa in the mid-twentieth century.[13]

China

Bureaucracy is neither a European invention, nor is its development confined to the early modern era.[14] A global approach to the history of administrative staff cannot ignore the impressive history of the civil service in the various dynasties of China.[15] Already in the fifth century BC, "modern" rules such as salaries for officials, graded by rank and high enough that they did not need their office to be a further source of income, existed. The performance of officials was evaluated by their superiors, and they could be demoted or dismissed for corruption, failure to collect enough taxes, antagonizing the local populace, and similar irregularities. More rapid promotion and promotion to more important posts served as reward for excellent performance. Officials were never assigned to their home prefectures and were frequently transferred.[16] The keys to the success of ruling a vast empire over centuries were written rules that allowed administrative rules to be recreated even after the collapse of a dynasty, and the high prestige of serving the government.[17]

The examinations the origins of which can be traced back to the Qin dynasty and were in use until 1905 as one of its most salient features will be highlighted here. In a time when European administrative staff were recruited on a purely patrimonial basis, Chinese officials had to pass a formal exam that required specialized knowledge and skills. The examinations were a role model for British civil service reforms in the nineteenth century.[18] Given the timeframe of this volume, our focus will be on the shape of the examinations in the late Ming and Qing dynasties.

Those who wanted to succeed in the examinations had to be fluent in the Mandarin-spoken dialect and classical Chinese. They had to be familiar with the Confu-

---

13 Crooks and Parsons, "Empires, Bureaucracy and the Paradox of Power", p. 20.
14 "Bureaucratic systems developed in all instances where large groups of men existed in large areas creating the need for a central agency to deal with problems." Jacoby, *Bureaucratization*, p. 9. See, too, Eisenstadt, *Political Systems*, p. 11.
15 Patricia Ebrey criticizes Max Weber's referring to a unitary Chinese empire and suggests understanding it as a succession of states/empires in China. See Patricia Ebrey, "China as a Contrasting Case: Bureaucracy and Empire in Song China", in: Crooks and Parsons, *Empires and Bureaucracy in World History*, pp. 31–53, 31.
16 Ibid., p. 41.
17 Ibid., p. 52.
18 Ssu-yü Têng, "Chinese Influence on the Western Examination System", *Harvard Journal of Asiatic Studies*, 7, 4 (1943), pp. 267–312. The Chinese model (and the Prussian one) also influenced the introduction of a civil service examination in Japan in the nineteenth century, interestingly at a time when its own reputation was in decline. See Robert M. Spaulding, *Imperial Japan's Higher Civil Service Examinations* (Princeton, NJ, 1967), p. 3.

cian Four Books and Five Classics, and with dynastic histories. The mere extent of this curriculum required several years of preparation. During the Ming and Qing it was furthermore required that all candidates' essays be composed in "styles known as 'eight-legged essays' (*pa-ku-wen*), a genre infamous among examination candidates and baffling for merchants, peasants, and artisans unschooled in elite discourse." [19] Furthermore, candidates had to be adept at the art of calligraphy.

The examinations were in principle a meritocratic institution that was theoretically open to all. In practice, over ninety per cent of the population were excluded: peasants, artisans, clerks, Buddhists, and Taoists, and women in general[20] could not participate. Sons of merchants were legally excluded until the Ming dynasty. Apart from this, sons of families with limited traditions of literacy had little chance of succeeding in the competition, owing to their lack of linguistic and cultural resources.[21] As a consequence, "the educational system designed for the civil service in China served to defend and legitimate the differentiation of Chinese society into autocratic rulers (even if non-Chinese in origin), Confucian gentry-officials, and illiterate or non-classically literate commoners."[22] In the course of the nineteenth century, the adequacy of the traditional examination criteria (along with the reputation of the civil service) was called into question.

In the twentieth century, the development of the civil service in China was affected by two revolutions, a foreign invasion, and years of civil war.[23] From 1911 onwards, examinations with more modern requirements than before were in use. In the 1920s and 1930s, civil service reforms led to the development of a professionalized and "protected"[24] service that came to an abrupt halt with the Japanese invasion in 1937.[25] With the founding of the People's Republic of China, in principle everyone became an employee of the state. Today, white-collar workers who work for government agencies (excluding the service unit sector, e.g. education, telecommunication, state-owned enterprises) are counted as civil servants in China, as are politicians.[26]

---

19 Benjamin A. Elman, "Political, Social, and Cultural Reproduction via Civil Service Examinations in Late Imperial China", *The Journal of Asian Studies*, 50, 1 (1991), pp. 7–28, at 21.
20 In early modern China, there were literate women who left behind a large amount of writing. See Daria Berg, *Women and the Literary World in Early Modern China, 1580–1700* (Abingdon, 2013), p. 3. Stories of talented girls who pass the exam disguised as men were popular in fiction. See Bonnie G. Smith, "Civil Service", in: *idem* (ed.), *The Oxford Encyclopedia of Women in World History* (Oxford etc., 2008), pp. 398–401, at 399.
21 Elman, "Reproduction", pp. 17 ff.
22 *Ibid.*, p. 23.
23 John P. Burns, "The Civil Service System of China: The Impact of the Environment", in: *idem* and Bidhya Bowornwathana (eds), *Civil Service Systems in Asia* (Cheltenham etc., 2001), pp. 79–113, at 82.
24 See the section on Western Europe.
25 Burns, "Civil Service System", p. 84.
26 *Ibid.*, p. 81.

Ottoman empire

Traditional historiography has it that after its heyday under Süleyman the Magnificent the Ottoman Empire was in a steady decline that eventually led to its end in 1922. Such a biased perspective has been criticized, and attention has been directed to how well it actually functioned, focusing rather on transformation, experimentation, and reform than decline.[27]

Early modern Ottoman society was divided into the subject population (*reaya*) and the ruling elite (*askerî*). The elite group for its part consisted of three subgroups: the military-administrative (*seyfiye*), the religious-judicial (*ilmiye*), and that of the scribal service (*kalemiye*). Career lines of individuals could also cross between these groups. *Kalemiye* in the central administration were a small group (about 110 in the 1530s).[28] They were recruited from ranks of *askerî*, either as descendants or through patronage networks of *ilmiye*, servants, or bureaucratic families. Young men entered the service as apprentices and could rise through the ranks due to merit and patronage.[29] Administrative staff worked primarily in the financial administration and the state chanceries. Members of the former had to master, among other skills, a special script (*siyakat*) that was in use until the eighteenth century.[30]

As a consequence of Süleyman's conquests, the size of the administrative apparatus increased tenfold in comparison with earlier centuries. Tax farming increasingly replaced the fief (*tımar*) system. Despite its general patrimonial structure, by the end of the sixteenth century bureaucratic features in Ottoman rule had developed: "administrators and judges were appointed from the capital on a rotating basis, rules of office were codified and passed down, training was formalized, career lines and hierarchies were present, and universalistic principles as well as an 'ethos' of office were all in evidence."[31]

In the nineteenth century, wide-ranging reforms of government, military, law, and education took place under the name *Tanzimat* (reorganization). Legal and administrative systems from Western states (France and Switzerland for example) were borrowed in order to modernize the state, thus breaking the monopolies of the religious institutions in the fields of law and education. Bureaucrats were agents as well as objects of the reforms. Members of the administrative staff were now referred to as *mülkiye* (civil servants), who enjoyed security of tenure due to the reforms.[32] A special

---

[27] Karen Barkey, "The Ottoman Empire (1299–1923): The Bureaucratization of Patrimonial Authority", in: Crooks and Parsons, *Empires and Bureaucracy in World History*, pp. 102–126, at 115.
[28] Colin Imber, *The Ottoman Empire 1300–1650* (New York, 2002), p. 169.
[29] Barkey, "Ottoman Empire", pp. 113f.
[30] Suraiya Faroqhi, *Approaching Ottoman History. An Introduction to the Sources* (Cambridge, 1999), p. 72.
[31] Barkey, "Ottoman Empire", p. 108.
[32] Carter Vaughn Findley, *Bureaucratic Reform in the Ottoman Empire. The Sublime Porte, 1789–1922* (Princeton, 1980), p. 157.

vocational high school for civil administration (*Mekteb-i Mülkiye*) was founded in 1859.[33] The administrative staff increased in size considerably: from about 1,000 at the end of the eighteenth century to between 50,000 and 100,000 at the end of the nineteenth as the state took over tasks (including education, orphanages, and hospitals) formerly undertaken by religious groups or communities.[34] With the end of the Ottoman Empire, the new republic proclaimed in 1923 by Mustafa Kemal Atatürk retained about eighty-five per cent of the existing administrative staff in its service.[35]

Western Europe

The five-phase model of the evolution in Western European administration at the level of central government presented in the following was elaborated by Jos C.N. Raadschelders and Mark R. Rutgers.[36] Its purpose here is to describe and explain which factors led to expansion and changes in this administration, beginning with the stage of medieval *personal servants* of a lord gradually turning into *state servants* and later *public servants*. In the nineteenth century, the civil service became a *protected service* within specific legal regulations and, later on, an increasingly *professional service*. The periodization of the phases is not clear-cut, since we are dealing with a gradual development.

In the first phase, administrative staff were basically *personal servants* of a lord. Raadschelders traces the roots of contemporary government in Western nations to the High Middle Ages, when church and state became separated in practice and government was moving to centre stage in the regulation of society.[37] The tasks of government in medieval and early modern times were to safeguard the internal and external order in its territory and regulate relationships between citizens. "To this end, they replaced standing armies, developed a judicial system, refined a tax system, created more or less specialized organizations, and issued a series of charters and ordinances that delineated the boundaries within which citizens were supposed to act."[38] The administrative staff, existing in small numbers only, were one of three groups of servants to the king (or regional lord), i.e. court, army, and scribal servants. The hierarchical organization of the church served as an important influence and role model for the nascent public administration.[39] Whereas in France and Eng-

---

[33] Carter Vaughn Findley, *Ottoman Civil Officialdom. A Social History* (Princeton, 1989), p. 114.
[34] Findley, *Bureaucratic Reform in the Ottoman Empire*, pp. 167 f.
[35] Dankwart A. Rustow, "The Military: Turkey", in: Robert E. Ward and Dankwart A. Rustow (eds), *Political Modernization in Japan and Turkey* (Princeton, 2015), pp. 352–388, at 388.
[36] Raadschelders and Rutgers, "Evolution".
[37] Raadschelders, *Handbook*, p. 138.
[38] Ibid. p. 137.
[39] Raadschelders and Rutgers, "Evolution", p. 71.

land, state formation took place centred on the central authority of the king, in the Holy Roman Empire this development originated in the territories.[40]

From the early modern period on, administrative staff turned into *state servants*. The most important factors taking effect in this period were the territorial expansions of states, the growing role of the state in international relations, and the rise of absolutism and mercantilism, along with centralization of communal functions in government bodies.[41] From the sixteenth century onwards laypersons, mostly non-noble doctors of law, instead of clerics, were increasingly hired for important administrative offices. In many European countries, university training in law and the liberal arts gained importance for preparing competent administrative staff. The exception was England, where training took place in Inns of Court.[42] Additional examinations were introduced in the course of the eighteenth century.[43] In the sixteenth to the eighteenth century the academic fields of cameralistic and police science, and related subjects dealing with state administration, developed in various European countries.[44] The emergent professionalization notwithstanding, remuneration for the services of administrative staff was still a mix of salary, emoluments, and sinecures; provision for old age and for sick public servants and their dependants was granted only occasionally. Patronage and corruption were common, and job security was not guaranteed for state servants.[45] Venality of office was common in many European countries (most of all in France, where acquisition of office could also lead to ennoblement, the so-called *noblesse de robe*), both as sale of office by individuals and as a source of income for the state.[46] "Bureaucracy" as an invective was coined by Vincent de Gournay in 1759, referring to misuse or excessive exertion of power by the administrative staff.[47]

When not the state, but the public, the citizenry, was to be served, the group under investigation in this chapter became truly *public servants*. The period between 1780 and 1820 was a crucial one for the establishment of the modern civil service in many European states as a result of peaceful or violent reorganization.[48] The reforms introduced by Napoleon I in France had an influence on many European countries,

---

40 Hans Hattenhauer, *Geschichte des Beamtentums* (Cologne, 1980), p. 43.
41 Raadschelders, *Handbook*, p. 151; Raadschelders and Rutgers, "Evolution", p. 78.
42 Jens Bruning, "Beamtenausbildung", in: Friedrich Jaeger (ed.), *Enzyklopädie der Neuzeit*, vol. 1 (Stuttgart, 2005), pp. 1121–1125, at 1122 f.
43 In Germany, for example, one needed to pass the state *Gymnasium* with its final exam (*Abitur*), which qualified graduates for university study. After studying law, candidates had to pass a first state examination, work as a *Referendar*, and then pass a second state examination. Only then was one a fully trained civil servant. See Bruning, "Beamtenausbildung", pp. 1123 f.
44 Cf. Alain Desrosières, *La Politique des Grands Nombres. Histoire de la Raison Statistique*, ch. 1, "Le Préfet et le Géomètre" (Paris, 1993), pp. 26–59.
45 Raadschelders and Rutgers, "Evolution", p. 77.
46 Koenraad Wolter Swart, *Sale of Offices in the Seventeenth Century* (The Hague, 1949).
47 Raadschelders, *Handbook*, p. 142.
48 Ibid., pp. 151 f.

particularly in the realm of local government. Changes occurred in the structure and processes in which public servants worked as well as in the conditions of their appointment. When a constitutional foundation to the state and its public sphere was established, a separation of politics from administration took place. Legislation became the prerogative of political officials, whereas tasks were executed by administrative staff. The state took over additional roles, which required more administrative personnel, which called for a clearer departmentalization of the administrative apparatus. The use of written documents in administrative practice increased considerably. Unlike before, offices could no longer be inherited or sold. Rank systems linked to criteria for promotion were established, along with regular salaries and pensions for public servants and their dependants.[49]

In the course of the nineteenth century, the administrative staff, like other citizens, discovered that they had not only duties, but also rights. They became aware of their crucial role within the development of society and demanded rights, in the realm of job security for example. In exchange for security and protection, administrative staff could act as loyal and neutral servants of the public, turning public service into *protected service*.[50] Except for a few pioneers, such as the kingdom of Bavaria, which had implemented legal frameworks protecting the administrative staff as early as 1805, elsewhere such regulations were introduced only after the 1850s.[51] Access to public office became more open in principle – although poorer families could usually not afford to have a son take the long and costly path to a secure position in the civil service.[52] It was also in this period that women were first admitted to public employment, although rather as exceptions (as a means of subsistence for widows or orphans of public servants for example) and in subaltern positions. Restrictions to women's participation were also due to restricted access to the education required for higher administrative positions.[53]

With the duties and rights of administrative personnel well established, the civil service assumed its modern form of *professional service* (in Raadschelders and Rutgers' phase model) in the twentieth century. Political and economic crises, particularly in the first half of the century, affected members of the civil service, for example in the form of the reduction in staff in the interwar period, or purges on political or racist grounds during the period of National Socialist rule, but they did not call into question the institution of civil service as such. Professionalization has manifested itself through educational provision, open exams and competition, and the provision

---

[49] Raadschelders, "Changing European Ideas", pp. 22ff.
[50] Raadschelders, *Handbook*, p. 152.
[51] Hattenhauer, *Beamtentum*, pp. 182ff.
[52] *Ibid.*, pp. 250ff.
[53] There are major differences between states in this respect. In Spain, women were not admitted to the civil service until 1918. Before 1946, Frenchwomen "were generally not admitted to the administrative branches of the civil service because they were seen as not able to reason". Smith, "Civil Service", p. 399.

of specialized management staff.[54] The twentieth century saw a remarkable growth in the number of administrative staff, in numbers and as a proportion of the total labour force. The main reasons for this development are the nationalization of large industries after World War I and the expansion of the welfare state.[55]

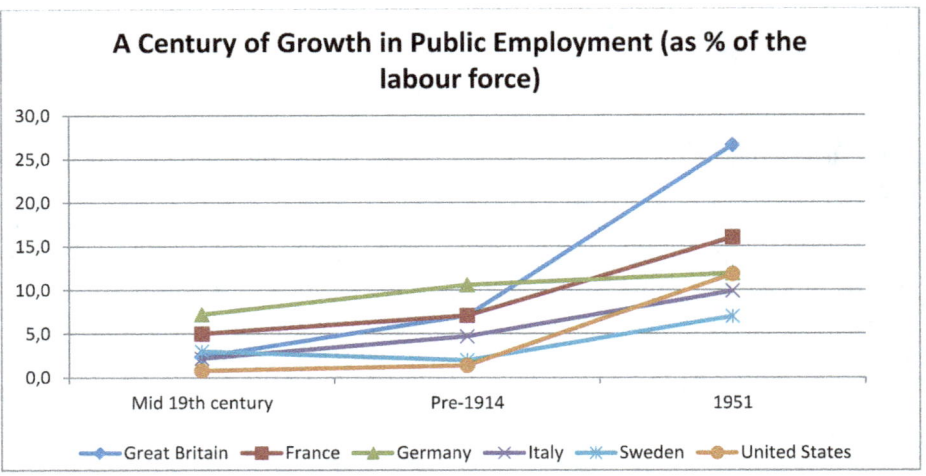

Source: Based on the table in Raadschelders, *Handbook*, p. 146.

The automation of public administration, i.e. the implementation of information technology and computer applications from the 1960s onwards,[56] has considerably changed the work performed by administrative staff. Beginning with the late 1970s, reforms of the public service have been performed under labels such as "New Public Management" and have challenged traditional tenets of this profession. These reforms imply

> the disaggregation of public service organisations into separate units, related by contractual or semi-contractual arrangements; a shift to greater outsourcing of, and competition in, the delivery of public services; a stress on private sector styles of management; explicit standards and measures of performance linked to a greater emphasis on output controls; a stress on discipline and parsimony in resource use; and a service and client orientation.[57]

---

54 Raadschelders and Rutgers, "Evolution", p. 87.
55 Raadschelders, *Handbook*, p. 144.
56 *Social Europe: The Computerization of Public Administration*, Supplement 4/88 (Luxembourg, 1988), p. 4.
57 David Clark, "Public Service Reform: A Comparative West European Perspective", *West European Politics*, 23, 3 (2000), pp. 25–44, at 25.

However, despite the perceived omnipresence of such discourses, there is yet little empirical evidence for actual changes in the culture and practices of public administration.[58]

Russia

The history of administrative staff in Russia is specific because of constellations such as – compared with Western Europe – the early centralization of power, the relatively weak position of the nobility in relation to the tsar, and a close connection between social order and administrative ranks. From the late fifteenth century on, Muscovian rulers, beginning with Ivan III, established a centralized bureaucracy to serve the fiscal, military, and judicial needs of the state. Its personnel (*prikaznye liudi*) had to be literate (unlike most members of the elite) and have administrative skills. They could advance in professional rank if they performed well *and* had the proper connections. The government agencies (*prikazy*) of seventeenth-century Muscovy featured some of the characteristics of Weberian bureaucracy, including written rules, regular procedures, functional differentiation, and reward for merit, albeit in a patrimonial environment.[59]

The nobility had been required before to serve the state in the military or in the civil service, but it was a novelty when Peter I decreed mandatory lifelong service for noblemen. With the table of ranks (*tabel' o rangakh*) issued in 1722, he instituted a new order for military, court, and the civil service, consisting of a system of fourteen classes (*klassy*) in which one's rank (*rang*) was determined by one's title (*chin*) within the class. Those who entered were usually promoted after a certain period in service. On reaching the eighth class, commoner civil servants were raised to the peerage. To a certain extent, serving the state permitted social mobility, although in the course of the eighteenth century a number of social and professional groups were declared ineligible, including peasants, soldiers, merchants (in the second half of the eighteenth century), and those obliged to pay the poll tax.[60] After Peter I's reign the obligation on the part of noblemen to enter service was reduced to twenty-five years and finally abolished in 1762. Still, the moral obligation remained, due to a long and deeply ingrained tradition.[61] Mere copyists and aides were outside the system of the table of

---

[58] Raadschelders, "Changing European Ideas", pp. 27 f.
[59] Marshall Poe, "The Central Government and its Institutions", in: Maureen Perrie (ed.), *The Cambridge History of Russia Vol. I: From Early Rus' to 1689* (Cambridge, 2006), pp. 435–463, at 453 f.
[60] James Hassell, "Implementation of the Russian Table of Ranks during the Eighteenth Century", *Slavic Review*, 29, 2 (1970), pp. 283–295, at 286. At the beginning of the twentieth century, the majority of the bureaucratic elite still originated from the old hereditary nobility. See Dominic Lieven, "The Elites", in: *idem* (ed.), *The Cambridge History of Russia Vol. II: Imperial Russia, 1689–1917* (Cambridge, 2006), pp. 225–244, at 227.
[61] Hassell, "Table of Ranks", p. 289.

ranks. Women were barred from a career in the civil service.⁶² Unlike in other European states, venality of office was not common in Russia.⁶³

Under Catherine II, in 1755 local government was newly organized within a framework of provinces (*gubernii*) and districts (*uezdy*), each provincial capital having a salaried staff headed by a governor, which considerably increased the number of administrative staff.⁶⁴ The striking differences between officials in the central administration and provincial administrators have been emphasized.⁶⁵ The latter were notorious for corruption. Susanne Schattenberg has argued that they must not be evaluated using the criteria of rational bureaucratic administration, but rather as patrimonial civil servants who had to make ends meet with inadequate salaries and operate within their relevant networks of patronage.⁶⁶ Mikhail Speranskiy, son of a village priest who had a career in the civil service and who also held political office, attempted to reform the civil service. His plans to introduce an examination for civil servants in 1809 were thwarted by that very group, and this incident was the first occasion on which they acted as a specific interest group.⁶⁷

As elsewhere, the number of administrative staff increased impressively throughout the nineteenth century, especially in the provincial administration. Whereas in 1796 there were 15,000 to 16,000 officials for a population of approximately thirty-six million (c. 0.04%), in 1851 there were over 74,000 officials for a population of about sixty-nine million (c. 0.1%); by 1903 there were about 385,000 officials for a population of one hundred and twenty-nine million (c. 0.3%).⁶⁸

After the October Revolution, the Soviet rulers, in theory, tried to do away with the bureaucracy and its protagonists altogether. In practice, state administration proliferated throughout the Soviet era. The positions and personnel of the Communist Party were interleaved with those of the state administration. The insertion of state and party agencies into the national economy during the 1920s and 1930s was a proc-

---

62 Barbara Alpern Engel, *Women in Russia, 1700–2000* (Cambridge, 2004), p. 117. Ladies-in-waiting were included in the rank system of court service, otherwise married women were counted among the same class as their husbands.
63 Hassell, "Table of Ranks", p. 291.
64 Victor Lieberman, *Strange Parallels: Southeast Asia in Global Context, c. 800–1830, Volume 2, Mainland Mirrors: Europe, Japan, China, South Asia, and the Islands* (Cambridge etc., 2009), p. 302.
65 A.V. Obolonskii, "Na Sluzhbe Gosudarevoi: K Istorii Rossijskoj Chinovnichestva", *Obshchestvennye Nauki i Sovremennost'*, 5 (1997), pp. 63–76, at 73.
66 Susanne Schattenberg, *Die korrupte Provinz. Russische Beamte im 19. Jahrhundert* (Frankfurt am Main, 2008).
67 Hassell, "Table of Ranks", p. 295.
68 P.A. Zaionchkovskii, *Pravitel'stvennii Apparat Samoderzhavnoi Rossii* (Moscow, 1978), p. 221; the percentage calculations are mine.

ess so universal and pervasive that it has been summarized in the phrase "society becomes bureaucracy".[69]

United States

The United States represents a special case in the history of administrative staff, starting as settlements with little need for administration and gradually turning into a global power. America's national bureaucracy did not "spring full-grown from the head of the First Continental Congress in 1775"; its fundamental nature, and structure, began to develop then.[70]

In Frederick Mosher's classic periodization of administration in the United States,[71] the first phase is called "government by gentlemen" (1789–1829). After the experience with British administration, there was no striving for a bureaucratic apparatus. In the late eighteenth century departments headed by single officials, appointed by the president, were created. The bureaucracy was small and its functions were to collect customs and excise taxes, and to deliver the mail.[72] This phase was characterized by limited political participation and nepotism. Officials were recruited according to patronage and, to some extent, on merit. Entry to this early public administration was limited to the gentry, i.e. white male landowners. Gradually, distrust of this "aristocracy" in government and administration grew. In 1829, President Jackson introduced the so-called spoils system, assuming that the "duties of all public officers are [...] so plain and simple that men of intelligence may readily qualify themselves for their performance" and "that much more is lost by the long continuance of men in office than is generally to be gained by their experience".[73] Jobs were given to persons with the right political loyalties, and little emphasis was put on job-related competence. Rotation in office was frequent, particularly when new presidents assumed power. This phase, called "government by the common people" (1829–1883), did indeed create more egalitarian access to positions in public administration. It was also in this era (1861) that the first female clerks were hired by federal agencies.[74]

---

[69] Don K. Rowney and Eugene Huskey, "Introduction: Russian Officialdom since 1881", in: *idem* (eds), *Russian Bureaucracy and the State: Officialdom from Alexander III to Vladimir Putin* (Houndsmills, 2009), pp. 1–19, 8.
[70] Michael Nelson, "A Short, Ironic History of American National Bureaucracy", *The Journal of Politics*, 44, 3 (1982), pp. 747–778, at 749.
[71] Frederick Mosher, *Democracy and the Public Service* (New York, [1968] 1982), pp. 315ff.
[72] Nelson, "History", p. 756.
[73] *Ibid.*, p. 759.
[74] Cindy Sondik Aron, *Ladies and Gentlemen of the Civil Service. Middle-Class Workers in Victorian America* (New York, 1987), p. 70.

Unintentionally, the spoils system encouraged bureaucratization and the growth of the state apparatus (for example, by requiring more positions to be created due to there being fewer competent and experienced staff). Efforts to prevent corruption and embezzlement also prevented efficient administrative work. After the assassination of President Garfield by a frustrated office seeker in 1881, the spoils system was abolished.

The next phase, dubbed "government by the good" (1883–1906), is characterized by the implementation of the Pendleton Act, which introduced new rules for the civil service. It stipulated that recruitment should be merit-based, candidates had to pass specific entrance exams, and policy and politics were to be separated from their administration. A bipartisan Civil Service Commission was established, whose three members were appointed by the president and which recruited civil servants from among the best examinees. The implementation of new technologies – telephones, typewriters, and even primitive counting machines – in the last two decades of the nineteenth century was associated with a clear feminization of tasks performed using the new instruments.[75]

The phase of "government by the efficient" (1906–1937) relied on maintaining the merit system with political neutrality and distinguished itself by emphasizing efficiency in government operations based on scientific management. This movement, which started specifically at the municipal level, intensified the specialization of work for the government and the standardization of job positions.[76] As a consequence of the Great Depression and the New Deal, the role of the state and, thus, also of the administrative staff changed. In the phase of "government by managers" (1937–present), not only efficiency but also performance, outcomes, and responsibility became important criteria for the work of public employees. The boundaries between administrative and political activities became blurred. A major reform took place in 1978 with the implementation of the Civil Service Reform Act. It reduced the scope of civil service positions at the top levels of government agencies, creating instead a Senior Executive Service. Major policymaking positions were to be outside the neutral and permanent civil service. Political activities on the part of federal civil servants were no longer banned.[77] Whether a more recent phase of "government by citizens, experts and results" (1995-present), as suggested by Milakovich and Gordon, describes reality or rather a desideratum remains to be seen.[78]

---

[75] *Ibid.*, p. 86. In European public administration, such developments took place several decades later. See Stefan Nellen, "Mechanisierte Sekretäre. Verwaltung im Zeichen der Schreibmaschine", in: Peter Becker (ed.), *Sprachvollzug im Amt. Kommunikation und Verwaltung im Europa des 19. und 20. Jahrhunderts* (Bielefeld, 2011), pp. 247–274.
[76] Mosher, *Democracy*, pp. 80 f.
[77] Mordecai Lee, "US Administrative History: Golem Government", in: B. Guy Peters and Jon Pierre (eds), *The SAGE Handbook of Public Administration* (Los Angeles, 2012), pp. 215–227, at 223.
[78] Michael E. Milakovich and George J. Gordon, *Public Administration in America* (Boston, 2009), p. 317.

Colonial and postcolonial administration

In the following, the focus will mainly be on European colonies in South America (including the Spanish Main), India, and Africa. The Spanish administration in its colonies in the Americas was installed in the course of the sixteenth century. Each kingdom was headed by a viceroy, who oversaw along with the exiguous military establishment "a network of subordinate captains-general and governors" of the provinces.[79] The agencies were a mixture of imported Spanish models and, to some extent, local offices and practices and were in charge of asserting royal authority, jurisdiction, and tax collection (partly directly collected, partly outsourced to tax farmers). This relatively small and simple bureaucracy remained rather stable until the seventeenth century, when the whole Spanish empire suffered a crisis. The eighteenth century saw the administration in Spanish America being reformed and expanded: taxes were now collected only by royal collectors, and new cadres of officials were created. Recruitment was often based on patrimonial networks.[80] Sale of *audiencias* (superior law courts) and other offices by the king was common.[81]

For most of its time, the colonial administration in European colonies in Asia had been rather small and undifferentiated. Before the nineteenth century, administration was by and large in the hands of chartered companies such as the East India Company,[82] whose main aim was to maximize profits. After the revolt of 1857, the governance of India was transferred from the company to the crown. The officers of the Indian Civil Service (ICS) were supposed to manifest gentlemanly qualities such as "virtue, courage, honesty, loyalty, generosity, modesty", yet de facto these standards were not always met.[83] Service in the ICS was not too popular and prestigious, so it was hard to find qualified British personnel. Indian personnel were recruited, starting in the late nineteenth century, but it was not until after World War I that Indians participated in any great number.[84] Before 1922, ICS examinations were held in London only. The number of British civil servants in India was rather small – about 900 in the late nineteenth century, compared with 300 Dutch civil servants on Java (with

---

[79] Christopher Storrs, "Magistrates to Administrators, Composite Monarchy to Fiscal-Military Empire: Empire and Bureaucracy in the Spanish Monarchy c. 1492–1825", in: Crooks and Parsons, *Empires and Bureaucracy in World History*, pp. 291–317, at 300.
[80] Ibid., pp. 312f.
[81] M.A. Burkholder and D.S. Chandler, "Creole Appointments and the Sale of Audiencia Positions in the Spanish Empire under the Early Bourbons, 1701–1750", *Journal of Latin American Studies*, 4, 2 (1972), pp. 187–206.
[82] The term "civil servants" was first used in the late eighteenth century to distinguish the civilian from the military personnel of the company. See Hans A.G.M. Bekke *et al.*, "Introduction: Conceptualizing Civil Service Systems", in: *idem*, *Civil Service Systems in Comparative Perspective*, pp. 1–10, at 1.
[83] Dana Heath, "Bureaucracy, Power and Violence in Colonial India", in: Crooks and Parsons, *Empires and Bureaucracy in World History*, pp. 364–390, at 371.
[84] Ibid., pp. 374f.

only one-tenth of the population of India) in the same period.[85] By 1945 Indians had moved into a dominant position in the ICS and made up more than half of its staff.[86]

The spate of annexations ("scramble for Africa") beginning in the 1880s took place in an era when in Europe the modern bureaucratic administration was developing rapidly. However, the administration in European colonies in Africa had little to do with Weberian rational bureaucracy – rather, it was inspired by the rule of chartered companies until after World War I – and was based on indirect rule. For example, the British Colonial Office advised the colonial secretary and supervised the colonial civil service, but it exercised little direct authority over local district officers, soldiers, and settlers.[87] Colonial rule was enforced through local authorities – the chiefs (the "street-level agents of colonial rule"[88]). The administration typically consisted of some understaffed technical departments, the field administration, and subordinate non-European clerks, artisans, and assistants, etc.[89] Colonial officers, combining executive and judicative functions, had more opportunities for uncontrolled exercise of power than their colleagues in European administrations. Their privileges (official residence, cars, servants, etc.) were scarcely merit-based, but primarily markers of social distinction.[90] The ideal colonial civil service did not excel in administrative or technical knowledge, but was a generalist who "developed his habits of 'rigorous mental exercise' by studying Greek and Latin at Oxford or Cambridge".[91]

Ironically, the decline of the colonial administration and rule occurred along with attempts to modernize and rationalize this administration. African popular resistance to these attempts played a direct role in accelerating the process. After World War II the production of raw materials was increased to fund Britain's reconstruction. In the course of the reforms, the number of colonial personnel grew, to some extent also because of the increasing numbers employed by the police, army, and intelligence-gathering services.[92] Officially, there was no racial segregation, and all employees received equal pay. But the reality was different. Even by the 1950s, Africans were not yet eligible for senior positions in the colonial service.[93]

---

85 H.L. Wesseling, *The European Colonial Empires, 1815–1919* (Abingdon, 2013), p. 49.
86 David C. Potter, "Manpower Shortage and the End of Colonialism: The Case of the Indian Civil Service", *Modern Asian Studies*, 7, 1 (1973), pp. 47–73, at 72.
87 Timothy H. Parsons, "The Unintended Consequences of Bureaucratic 'Modernization' in Post-World War II British Africa", in: Crooks and Parsons, *Empires and Bureaucracy in World History*, pp. 412–434, at 414.
88 Thomas Bierschenk and Jean-Pierre Olivier de Sardan, "Ethnographies of Public Services in Africa: An Emerging Research Paradigm", in: idem (eds), *States at Work. Dynamics of African Bureaucracies* (Leiden and Boston, 2014), pp. 35–56, at 41
89 Parsons, "Consequences", p. 415.
90 Bierschenk and Olivier de Sardan, "Ethnographies", p. 40.
91 Parsons, "Consequences", p. 416
92 Ibid., pp. 429 ff.
93 Ibid., p. 428.

At the same time, in many African states independence movements grew stronger. In 1945, the Fifth Pan-African Congress, held in Manchester, insisted on the "immediate right to self-determination for all colonial people".[94] Colonial administrators did not expect independence to be given in the immediate future and did not prepare for it. The new African states of the 1950s and 1960s had a strong commitment to the goals of independence, to improving the quality of life of their populations by providing infrastructure and services with the help of a competent, strong, and well-equipped civil service. The senior staff inherited from the colonial administration were in some cases helpful in localizing staff (a process that took rather long). Yet, the favourable conditions in the early postcolonial administration did not last for more than a decade.[95] In the 1980s and 1990s, many African countries reformed their civil service, inspired by the New Public Management approach, often as part of programmes facilitated by the World Bank and the IMF.[96] These efforts have largely failed, often due to insufficient knowledge of local organizational processes and practices.[97]

Administrative staff beyond national confines

With the emergence of international organizations such as the League of Nations (1920) and the United Nations (1945), and supranational ones such as the European Union (1958) and the Organization of African Unity (1963), a new kind of administrative staff emerged that is no longer responsible to one state or empire. Ideally, these civil servants should shed their national loyalties and consider, when carrying out their work, only the interests of the international organization that employs them. They should be impartial and independent, the latter being guaranteed by job security. Furthermore, they should be recruited first and foremost on the basis of merit, although a certain amount of geographical representation also comes into play.[98] In practice, these ideals were and are often hard to maintain. Recent developments such as multi-level governance, replacing traditional hierarchical structures by networks involving actors from national, supranational, and sub-national levels, and non-governmental organizations across national borders, pose new challenges for

---

[94] *Ibid.*, p. 419.
[95] Ladipo Adamolekun, "Africa: Rehabilitating Civil Service Institutions – Main Issues and Implementation Progress", in: Jos C.N. Raadschelders *et al.* (eds), *The Civil Service in the 21st Century: Comparative Perspectives* (Houndsmills, 2007), pp. 82–104, at 82f.
[96] Kempe Ronald Hope, Sr., "The New Public Management: Context and Practice in Africa", *International Public Management Journal*, 4 (2001), pp. 119–134, at 128.
[97] Bierschenk and Olivier de Sardan, "Ethnographies", pp. 44f.
[98] Norman A. Graham and Robert S. Jordan (eds), *The International Civil Service: Changing Role and Concepts* (New York etc., 1980).

administrative staff.⁹⁹ The new shape that bureaucratic administration has been taking on in the era of globalization – a global landscape of work cells separated by movable panels and connected via fibre-optic cables, scattered across continents, and losing its national segmentary character – has been dubbed *cubicle land*.¹⁰⁰

Conclusion

With Max Weber's ideal types as a rough guideline, this chapter has given an overview of the various shapes assumed by administrative staff over the last five centuries in various contexts. Working for one's lord, the empire, the state, or the public has been a prestigious position more often than not. Yet, it has also been one that has attracted criticism (deservedly or undeservedly), especially in relation to the privileges that the occupational group of modern civil servants have attained over the centuries. Despite all negative images and all efforts to reduce and privatize the state apparatus, the administrative staff in service of the state (still being "the only actor that can make binding decisions for a whole population"¹⁰¹) will likely continue to exist – and keep on adapting to new conditions.

---

99 Caspar F. van den Berg and Theo A.J. Toonen, "National Civil Service Systems and the Implications of Multi-Level Governance: Weberianism Revisited?", in: Raadschelders *et al.*, *The Civil Service in the 21st Century*, pp. 103–120.
100 Klaus Schlichte, "Cubicle Land: On the Sociology of Internationalized Rule", InIIS Working Paper, No. 38 (2012), https://www.google.nl/url?sa=t&rct=j&q=&esrc=s&source=web&cd=1&cad=rja&uact=8&ved=0ahUKEwixqr36yozSAhXPyRoKHbLbBEgQFgghMAA&url=http%3A%2F%2Fwww.iniis.uni-bremen.de%2Flib%2Fdownload.php%3Ffile%3Dd08ca01288.pdf%26filename%3DAP_38_2012.pdf&usg=AFQjCNEayFyn5HE56uriaYKRFGGUnUShzQ, last accessed on 11 November 2016, p. 4.
101 Raadschelders, "Changing European Ideas", p. 17.

Suggested reading

Aron, Cindy Sondik. *Ladies and Gentlemen of the Civil Service: Middle-Class Workers in Victorian America* (New York: Oxford University Press, 1987).
Burns, John P. and Bidhya Bowornwathana (eds). *Civil Service Systems in Asia* (Cheltenham: Edward Elgar, 2001).
Crompton, Rosemary and Gareth Jones. *White Collar Workers. Deskilling and Gender in Clerical Work.* (London: Macmillan, 1984).
Crooks, Peter and Timothy H. Parsons (eds). *Empires and Bureaucracy in World History. From Late Antiquity to the Twentieth Century* (Cambridge: Cambridge University Press, 2016).
Davies, Margery. *Women's Place is at the Typewriter: Office Work and Office Workers, 1870–1930* (Philadelphia: Temple University Press, 1982).
Findley, Carter Vaughn. *Ottoman Civil Officialdom. A Social History* (Princeton, NJ: Princeton University Press, 1989).
Freeman, Carla. *High Tech and High Heels in the Global Economy: Women, Work, and Pink-Collar Identities in the Caribbean* (Durham, NC: Duke University Press, 2000).
Graham, Norman A. and Robert S. Jordan (eds). *The International Civil Service: Changing Role and Concepts* (New York: Pergamon Press, 1980).
Heller, Michael. *London Clerical Workers, 1880–1914: Development of the Labour Market* (London and Brookfield: Pickering and Chatto, 2011).
Jacoby, Henry. *The Bureaucratization of the World* (Berkeley, CA: University of California Press, 1973).
Lowe, Graham S. *Women in the Administrative Revolution. The Feminization of Clerical Work* (Toronto: University of Toronto Press, 1987).
Marsh, Robert M. *The Mandarins. The Circulation of Elites in China, 1600–1900* (Glencoe, IL: Free Press, 1961).
Raadschelders, Jos C.N. *Handbook of Administrative History* (New Brunswick, NJ: Transaction Publishers, 2012).
Raadschelders, Jos C.N. et al. (eds), *The Civil Service in the 21st Century. Comparative Perspectives* (Houndsmills: Palgrave Macmillan, 2007).
Rowney, Don K. and Eugene Huskey (eds). *Russian Bureaucracy and the State. Officialdom from Alexander III to Vladmir Putin* (Houndsmills: Palgrave Macmillan, 2009).
Spaulding, Robert M. *Imperial Japan's Higher Civil Service Examinations* (Princeton, NJ: Princeton University Press, 1967).
Strom, Sharon Hartman. *Beyond the Typewriter. Gender, Class, and the Origins of Modern American Office Work, 1900–1930* (Urbana, IL and Chicago: University of Illinois Press, 1992).
Swart, Koenraad W. *Sale of Offices in the Seventeenth Century* (The Hague: Martinus Nijhoff, 1949).
Têng Ssu-yü. "Chinese Influence on the Western Examination System", *Harvard Journal of Asiatic Studies*, 7, 4 (1943), pp. 267–312.
Valli, Linda. *Becoming Clerical Workers* (Boston and London: Routledge and Kegan Paul, 1986).
Van der Meer, Frits (ed.). *Civil Service Systems in Western Europe*, 2nd edn (Cheltenham, 2011).
Weber, Max. *Economy and Society.* 2 volumes (Berkeley, CA: University of California Press, 2013).

4. Labour Relations

Karin Hofmeester
4.1. Introductory Remarks*

To better understand the diverse forms of labour relations worldwide, in 2007 the International Institute of Social History (IISH) in Amsterdam set up the Global Collaboratory on the History of Labour Relations. The first phase of this project (2007–2012) involved data mining.[1] A large group of international scholars met during workshops, worked together online, and developed a large number of datasets containing data on the occurrence of all types of labour relations in all parts of the world during five cross sections in time: 1500, 1650, 1800, 1900 (and, for Africa, 1950 too), and 2000, thereby also developing a new taxonomy of labour relations based on a shared set of definitions.[2] The second phase of the project sets out in search of explanations for shifts in labour relations as well as for the possible patterns observed therein. We look for causes and consequences of shifts in labour relations by looking in depth at possible explanatory factors, such as the role of the state; demography and family patterns; the role of economic institutions; and mechanisms that determine shifts in and out of self-employment.[3]

Efforts to classify work according to the different human relations involved are not new. The oldest are the distinctions between man and woman, master and servant, and between slave owner and slave. Alongside these distinctions came the no-

---

* Part of this article is based on the working paper by Karin Hofmeester, Jan Lucassen, Leo Lucassen, Rombert Stapel, and Richard Zijdeman, "The Global Collaboratory on the History of Labour Relations, 1500–2000: Background, Set-Up, Taxonomy, and Applications" (October 2015), available at http://hdl.handle.net/10622/4OGRAD.
[1] For the data and their accompanying methodological papers, see https://datasets.socialhistory.org/dataverse/labourrelations.
[2] This project has been made possible by generous grants from the Gerda Henkel Stiftung in Düsseldorf as well as from the Netherlands Organization for Scientific Research (NWO) and the International Research Centre "Work and Human Lifecycle in Global History" at Humboldt University in Berlin (re: work). Further, separate grants were made available for conferences held by a number of subgroups, for example in Portugal, Turkey, and India. For more information on the project and its participants, see https://collab.iisg.nl/web/labourrelations.
[3] These factors are explored in a series of dedicated workshops. Papers from the first workshop, on the role of the state, have been published in Karin Hofmeester, Gijs Kessler, and Christine Moll-Murata (eds), "Conquerors, Employers, and Arbiters: States and Shifts in Labour Relations, 1500–2000" Special Issue of *International Review of Social History*, 61:S24 (2016). A number of papers from the workshop on demography and family patterns have been published as a special section of *The History of the Family*, 22:1 (2017). Papers presented at the workshop on economic institutions will be published in Karin Hofmeester and Pim de Zwart (eds), *Colonialism, Institutional Change and Shifts in Global Labour Relations* (forthcoming).

DOI 10.1515/9783110424584-016

tion of "class society" developed by various nineteenth-century thinkers, of whom Karl Marx is the most well known, and those inspired by him. Central to this line of thinking is the rise of the proletariat, i.e. wage-dependent workers. The German scholar Werner Sombart (1863–1941) was perhaps the first to attempt to apply this concept to the entire occupational population of a country (in this case the German Empire in 1905).[4] Sociologists and historians subsequently tried to apply these categories to the entire population of Europe (except Russia) for the past five centuries.[5] Ethnographers, geographers, and archaeologists (some of whom referred to Karl Marx) compared labour relations in market economies in the West and those in the rest of the world, sometimes (as Karl Polanyi and anthropologists inspired by him tended to do) stressing especially the differences.[6] Finally, irrespective of time and place, historical and contemporary occupational census takers, sociologists, and historians have increasingly struggled with definitions of work, influenced in part by the emerging feminist movement, which stressed the importance of the often unobserved work of women and children.

One of the most comprehensive definitions of work has been provided by the sociologists Charles and Chris Tilly:

> Work includes any human effort adding use value to goods and services. [...] Prior to the twentieth century, a vast majority of the world's workers performed the bulk of their work in other settings than salaried jobs as we know them today. Even today, over the world as a whole, most work takes place outside of regular jobs. Only a prejudice bred by Western capitalism and its industrial labor markets fixes on strenuous effort expended for money payment outside the home as "real work", relegating other efforts to amusement, crime, and mere housekeeping.[7]

All these lines of thinking have inspired the members of the Collaboratory to develop a new encompassing classification of labour relations, one necessary for long-term global comparisons, using the following definition: labour relations define for or with whom one works and under what rules. These rules (implicit or explicit, written or unwritten) determine the type of work, type and amount of remuneration, working hours, degrees of physical and psychological strain, as well as the degree of freedom and autonomy associated with the work. The Collaboratory's classification of labour relations claims a much wider validity than traditional occupational censuses do, because it is intended to cover the whole world, from 1500 and in principle also for earlier periods. At the same time, it pays tribute to a long historical pedigree of ideas,

---

[4] Werner Sombart, *Das Proletariat. Bilder und Studien* (Frankfurt am Main, 1906).
[5] Charles Tilly, "Demographic Origins of the European Proletariat", in: David Levine (ed.), *Proletarianization and Family History* (Orlando [etc.], 1984), pp. 1–85.
[6] Jan Lucassen, "Outlines of a History of Labour", IISH Research Paper 51 (2013), available at http://socialhistory.org/en/publications/outlines-history-labour (commenting upon Weber, Polanyi, Chayanov, and others).
[7] Charles Tilly and Chris Tilly, *Work under Capitalism* (Boulder, CO, 1998), p. 22.

and it intends to offer an analytical instrument for comparing labour relations globally. The following steps were taken to arrive at this taxonomy of labour relations.

Taxonomy of labour relations, units of analysis: individual, household(s), polity, and market

People usually do not work alone. Seldom do they work only for themselves. In the first place, most *individuals* work the larger part of their lives for a *family*, defined as a group of kin or a *household*, who pool their income and mostly live and eat together. The activities of all members can thus be assumed to constitute a collective.[8] They coordinate their activities, so we can speak of a collective strategy, also called "household living strategy".[9] This consists of the mutual division of tasks according to skills, gender, age, and marriage strategy. Taking the *individual* as a nucleus, we distinguish the *household* as the first goal of production. Sometimes groups of individuals or households share tasks, in which case we speak of *communities*. When communities share a form of government whose leadership has the power or mandate to establish and maintain rules pertaining to labour, we speak of a *polity*. When we call the *household* (or several, united in a community) the first goal, the *polity* logically forms the second, and the *market* the third. This brings us to the following taxonomy:

---

[8] For the seasonality, see the "work cycle" in Jan Lucassen, *Migrant Labour in Europe, 1600–1900: The Drift to the North Sea* (London, 1987).

[9] Also known as "coping strategies". See Theo Engelen, "Labour Strategies of Families: A Critical Assessment of an Appealing Concept", *International Review of Social History*, 47, 3 (2002), pp. 453–464; and J. Kok (ed.), *Rebellious Families: Household Strategies and Collective Action in the Nineteenth and Twentieth Centuries* (New York and Oxford, 2002).

Taxonomy of Labour Relations

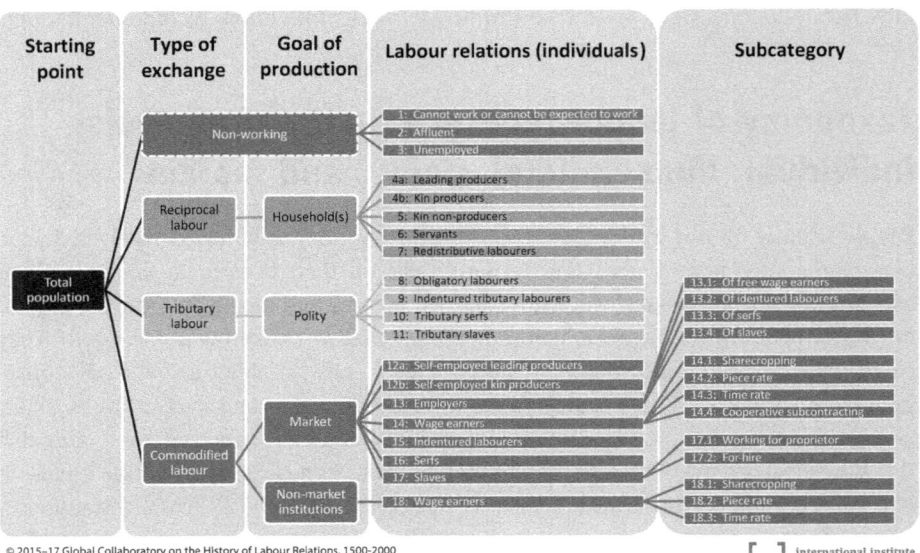

© 2015–17 Global Collaboratory on the History of Labour Relations, 1500-2000
http://www.historyoflabourrelations.org

{ } international institute of social history

In order to classify the total population ("Starting point", column 1) according to this taxonomy, we applied the following logic. We stress that this taxonomy should primarily be considered a tool to characterize individuals (whose labour relations are listed in column 4). The scheme should therefore be read from right to left and enables us to shed some light on the character of that society within a given place and period.

First, the taxonomy distinguishes between those who are able to work and those unable to work (the category non-working in our taxonomy). This has at least two advantages: it forces one to be aware of what work is; and it covers the entire population, thus explicitly also taking working women and children into account. As a consequence, in the day-to-day practice of historical research it compels scholars to test the demographic logic of their results, as all categories together should equal the total population. In addition, it provides a basic critique of a large number of historical occupational censuses, which systematically under-register female work and work in the household in general.

Next, in column 2, it distinguishes between the three types of exchange in organizing the exchange of goods and services. These types of exchange are linked with the three levels of analysis listed in column 3, which reflect the target of production: the household and/or community, the polity, or the market. The principles on which this exchange takes place are *reciprocity* (work done for other members of the same household or a group of households that form a community), *tribute giving* (work based on obligations vis-à-vis the polity), and market exchange in which labour is "*commodified*" (i.e. where the worker sells their capacity to work – or, in the case of unfree labour, the owner sells the worker itself).

For the past five hundred years, in most parts of the world reciprocal labour outside the household has no longer been the sole category. This is true even if we concede that "self-sufficiency", which occurs in labour relations 4a and 4b of our taxonomy, can include small-scale market transactions that aim at sustaining households rather than at accumulating capital by way of profiting from exchange value.[10]

All other, more subtle, distinctions fall within these four main categories (non-working, reciprocal labour, tributary labour, and commodified labour). They are based on various considerations, including the character of the entities that organize labour (households, communities, polities, or markets), the degree of freedom, and methods of remuneration. These subcategories are explained in detail in the appendix to this chapter. The Collaboratory fully recognizes that individuals might experience different labour relations at the same time. In those cases (serfs who are permitted to perform wage labour part of the year), the researcher may attribute a primary labour relation to the main activity (as defined by hours spent) and a second or even a third to the subsidiary activity. Even more importantly, research so far has shown that shifts in labour relations mostly take the form of shifts in such combinations, especially in the short run.

Shifts in labour relations

By using the taxonomy, shifts in labour relations can be signalled and followed over time and place. The preliminary outcomes of this project suggest that in the long run, the share of the population engaged in commodified labour increased at the expense of reciprocal labour and tributary labour. Commodified labour started earlier than expected (in 1500 some ten per cent of the world population we have data for had commodified labour relations as their primary labour relation), but at the same time reciprocal labour lasted longer than previously assumed (in 2000 ten per cent of the total world population still had reciprocal labour relations as their primary labour relation; this can largely be explained by the fact that we consider working for the household as reciprocal labour).[11]

---

10 Marcel van der Linden, *Workers of the World. Essays Toward a Global Labor History* (Leiden and Boston, 2008), pp. 315–316, referring to G.A. Cohen, *Karl Marx's Theory of History: A Defence* (Oxford, 1978). See also Akira Hayami, Osamu Saitô, and Ronald P. Toby (eds), *The Economic History of Japan 1600–1990*, Vol. 1: *Emergence of Economic Society in Japan 1600–1859* (Oxford, 2004), who argue in a similar sense for a broader concept of "self-sufficiency" that allows for market production as long as accumulation is not the basic goal of such transactions.
11 For an overview of countries and cross sections included in the Collaboratory, as well as data on which part of the world population is covered, percentages of labour relations per country, continent and the world as a whole per cross section, and for a visualization of all data as hierarchical tree-map

The biggest shift from reciprocal to commodified labour seems to have taken place between 1800 and 1900, especially in Europe and Asia, going hand in hand with an increase in the size of the non-working population. The South American countries included in the Collaboratory dataset show a more or less stable percentage of people in reciprocal and commodified labour relations in 1800 and 1900, though of course the nature of commodified labour changed from slavery to various less unfree forms of commodified labour. In the various sub-Saharan African countries we studied, reciprocal labour prevailed both in 1800 and in 1900, though it decreased from some seventy-five per cent to fifty per cent in favour of commodified labour, which seemed to have shifted from slavery to other forms of less unfree commodified labour relations, including self-employment.

Another important finding is that, from early on, many individuals and households pooled various types of labour relations – combining commodified labour with reciprocal labour, for example, as was the case with Spanish farmers in 1800, who combined self-employment with reciprocal labour.[12] Russia is a very special case in this respect. Here, in 1800, farmers combined both tributary labour (as serfs) with reciprocal labour relations, as they worked their own land and were part-time wage workers.[13] In the Deccan in India, self-employment in farming and manufacturing was often combined with work for the community, a combination that seemed to remain stable even between 1900 and 2000.[14]

Often, shifts in labour relations manifest themselves as shifts in combinations of labour relations. In Spain, in 1900, farmers still combined two types of work, though now both were commodified: they worked as self-employed farmers on their own plot of land and as wage earners on other people's land.[15] Shifts within the larger category of commodified labour from 1800 to 1900 could, and often did, manifest themselves as shifts in combinations of labour relations. Within the combination of self-employment and wage work, the ratio shifted from more self-employment

---

graphs, see https://socialhistory.org/en/projects/labourrelations/treemap. For a preliminary overview of some of these data, see also Karin Hofmeester, "Self-employment as Category in the Global Collaboratory on the History of Labour Relations, 1500–2000", Paper prepared for the workshop "Self-Employment in Historical Perspective", 15–16 December 2016, IISH, Amsterdam. Unless stated otherwise, data mentioned in this article can be found in dataverse as mentioned in reference 1 and via the above mentioned link.

12 José-Miguel Lana-Berasain, "Labour Relations in Spain, 1800, 1900 and 2001: A Methodological Approach", p. 13 and dataset. See for the dataset and the methodological paper, *idem*, "Spain 1800,1900,2000 [Global Collaboratory on the History of Labour Relations 1500–2000 Dataset]", http://hdl.handle.net/10622/CH6ZP5, IISH Dataverse, V1.

13 Gijs Kessler, "Wage Labor and the Household Economy: A Russian Perspective, 1600–2000", in: Marcel van der Linden and Leo Lucassen (eds), *Working on Labor. Essays in Honor of Jan Lucassen* (Leiden, 2012), pp. 353–369, at 362–363.

14 Jan Lucassen and Rombert Stapel, "Shifts in Labour Relations in India 1800–2000", Paper for the Early Modern Panel, X. International Conference on Labour History, The Association of Indian Labour Historians, V.V. Giri National Labour Institute, Noida, India, 22–24 March 2014, pp. 32–35.

15 Lana-Berasain, "Labour Relations in Spain".

to more wage work. Between 1900 and 1950 wage labour seems to have grown considerably worldwide, especially in sub-Saharan countries, where colonial economic activities stimulated wage labour (not always free wage labour) at the cost of self-employment. By 2000 this trend had been reversed, certainly in sub-Saharan African countries but, so it seems, also in Asian and European countries.

Though these results are still very sketchy and partial, they do give some indication of the potential of the Collaboratory's approach for studying the various forms of labour relations worldwide.

Appendix: Definitions of Labour Relations

Non-working:

As a starting point for each geographical unit and cross section, we take the entire population and subsequently determine what part is not, as a rule, working, and, consequently, what part is working (these "calculations" will often be based on estimates rather than precise data). The non-working population is divided into the following three categories:

1. *Cannot work or cannot be expected to work:* those who cannot work, because they are too young (≤ 6 years), too old (≥ 75 years),[16] disabled, or are studying.

2. *Affluent:* those who are so prosperous that they do not need to work for a living (rentiers, etc.), and consequently actually do not work. This also goes for their spouses if all their productive and reproductive tasks are taken over by servants, nannies, etc. There are, of course, affluent people, owners of big companies, who are wealthy enough to stop working but nevertheless choose to continue to work. If they are employers, these people should be assigned to labour relation 13 instead of 2.

3. *Unemployed:* although unemployment is very much a nineteenth- and, especially, twentieth-century concept, we do distinguish between those in employment and those wanting to work but who cannot find employment.

Working:

Reciprocal labour:

Persons who provide labour for other members of the same household and/or community are subsumed within the category **Reciprocal labour.**

---

[16] These minimum and maximum ages are very much culturally determined. The age brackets chosen will always be indicated in the database and explained in the methodological paper.

Within the household:

4a. Leading household producers: heads of self-sufficient households (these include family-based and non-kin-based forms). Self-subsistence can include small market transactions, but only if most (at least eighty per cent) of total household income is earned through self-subsistence labour. Heads of households have labour relation 4a.

4b. Household kin producers: subordinate kin, including spouses (men and women) and children of the above heads of households, who are mainly self-subsistent and who contribute to the maintenance of the household by performing productive work for that household.

5. Household kin non-producers: subordinate kin, including spouses (men and women) and children of heads of households, who can support the household (under either reciprocal or commodified labour relations). These spouse and kin dependants are free from productive work, but they contribute to the maintenance of the household by performing reproductive work for the household, i.e. especially child rearing, cooking, cleaning, and other household chores. In all other cases spouses and kin producers in the categories named have income-generating activities essential for the survival of the household, i.e. labour relations 12a, 12b, 13, 14, or 18, and will have one of these labour relations themselves.

6. Reciprocal household servants and slaves: subordinate non-kin (men, women, and children) contributing to the maintenance of self-sufficient households. This category does not include household servants who earn a salary and are free to leave their employer of their own volition (i.e. labour relation 14), but it does include servants in autarchic households, monasteries, and palaces. They may work under all shades of conditions, from enforcement (including pawnship) to a desire to receive patronage. These conditions may change from one generation to another.[17]

Within the community:

7. Community-based redistributive labourers: persons who perform tasks for the local community in exchange for communally provided remuneration in kind, such as food, accommodation, and services, or a plot of land and seed to grow food on their own. Examples of this type of labour include working under the Indian *jajmani* system, hunting and defence by Taiwanese aborigines, or communal work among nomadic and sedentary tribes in the Middle East and Africa. In the case of the *jajma-*

---

[17] First-generation slaves might be commodified, whereas their children might no longer be considered slaves and might be working for the household on conditions that were more free, as was the case with children of slave women and free Ashanti men. See Gareth Austin, *Labour, Land and Capital in Ghana: From Slavery to Free Labour in Asante, 1807–1956* (Rochester, NY, 2005), pp. 106–134, 174–180, 481–490, 498–500.

ni workers in South Asia, hereditary structures form the basis of the engagement, while in parts of Africa or Taiwan the criteria for fulfilling community-based labour are gender and age (in Taiwan, for example, males between six and forty).

Tributary labour:

Persons who are obliged to work for the polity (often the state, though it could also be a feudal or religious authority). Their labour is not commodified but belongs to the polity. Those workers are included in the category **Tributary labour.**

8. *Obligatory labourers:* those who have to work for the polity, and are remunerated mainly in kind. This category includes those subject to civil obligations (corvée labourers, conscripted soldiers and sailors), and work as punishment, i.e. convicts. Yet the obligatory work can also be an entitlement that enjoys middle or high social standing, such as the European or Indian nobility, the samurai in Japan, or banner people in Qing China.

9. *Indentured tributary labourers:* those contracted to work as unfree labourers for the polity for a specific period of time to pay off a debt or fine to that same polity.

10. *Tributary serfs:* those working for the polity because they are bound to its soil and bound to provide specified tasks for a specified maximum number of days, for example state serfs in Russia.

11. *Tributary slaves:* those who are owned by and work for the polity indefinitely (deprived of the right to leave, to refuse to work, or to receive compensation for their labour). One example is forced labourers in concentration camps.

Commodified labour:

Work done on the basis of market exchange in which labour is "commodified", i.e. where the worker or the products of his work are sold. The category **Commodified labour** is subdivided into those working for the market and those working for public institutions *that may nevertheless produce for the market* (though not for the gain of private individuals).

For the market, private employment:

12a. *Self-employed leading producers:* those who produce goods or services for the market (for example, peasants, craftsmen, petty traders, transporters, as well as those in a profession) with fewer than three employees, possibly in cooperation with

12b. *Self-employed kin producers:* household members including spouses and children who work together with self-employed leading producers who produce for the market. All members of a family working under a putting-out system should be counted as self-employed producers.[18]

13. *Employers:* those who produce goods or services for market institutions by employing more than three labourers. The number after the dot is an attribute that says something about the freedom or unfreedom of the employees.

   13.1 Employers who employ free wage earners.
   13.2 Employers who employ indentured labourers.
   13.3 Employers who employ serfs.
   13.4 Employers who employ slaves.

14. *Market wage earners:* wage earners (including the temporarily unemployed) who produce commodities or services for the market in exchange mainly for monetary remuneration. A subdivision is made by type of remuneration.

   14.1 Sharecropping wage earners: remuneration is a fixed share of total output.
   14.2 Piece-rate wage earners: remuneration at piece rates.
   14.3 Time-rate wage earners: remuneration at time rates.
   14.4 Cooperative subcontracting workers at piece rates.

15. *Indentured labourers for the market:* those contracted to work as unfree labourers for an employer for a specific period of time to pay off a private debt. They include indentured European labourers in the Caribbean in the seventeenth and eighteenth centuries, and indentured Indian, Chinese, and Japanese workers after the abolition of slavery.

16. *Serfs working for the market:* those bound to the soil and bound to provide specified tasks for a specified maximum number of days for private landowners, for example serfs working on the estates of the nobility.

17. *Slaves who produce for the market:* those owned by their employers (masters). They are deprived of the right to leave, to refuse to work, or to receive compensation for their labour. Here we do not distinguish between the different ways individuals may become enslaved (sale, pawning, etc.). We do, however, differentiate between:

   17.1 Slaves working directly for their proprietor, for example productive work by plantation slaves, and domestic slavery in households producing for the market.
   17.2 Slaves for hire, for example for agricultural or domestic labour (as a rule they may keep a small part of their earnings, while the largest part goes to the owner).

For non-market institutions:

18. *Wage earners employed by non-market institutions* (that may or may not produce for the market), such as the state, state-owned companies, the Church, or production

---

[18] As long as they are ≥ 6 and ≤ 75 (or other age indications for too young or too old to work as documented for the cross section that is specifically analysed).

cooperatives, who produce or render services for a free or a regulated market. A subdivision is made by type of remuneration:

18.1 Sharecropping wage earners: remuneration is a fixed share of total output.
18.2 Piece-rate wage earners: remuneration at piece rates.
18.3 Time-rate wage earners: remuneration at time rates.

Eileen Boris
4.2. Subsistence and Household Labour

The peasant and the housewife represent two nodes of subsistence relations of production, both connected to but distinct from market economies. Dismissed by Marx and Engels as unproductive labourers for generating use rather than exchange value, they became in the 1970s and 1980s vibrant objects of analysis. Observed German feminist theorist Veronika Bennholdt-Thomsen in 1981, "within the present world economy, housewives and peasants (men and women) reproduce labour power for capital without compensation." They engage in "*subsistence production*, since it is here that human life and vital capacity to work are continuously produced and reproduced."[1] Or, as US anthropologist Jane Collins and sociologist Martha Gimenez noted a decade later, "domestic labor—whether in the homes of industrialized nations or the farms and *favelas* of developing nations—had to be understood in relation to unfolding processes of capital accumulation."[2]

Development studies, neo-Marxist world systems theory, and Marxist feminist inquiries into what became known as reproductive labour gained prominence during the late 20th century as ways to rethink fundamental relations between households and economies. In the context of new versions of the dispossession of people from their land and livelihoods and in light of freedom struggles in both the West and the "Third World", the emerging field of "women and development" sought to turn the subsistence labour of rural women into income generating activities to liberate such women from the family. In practice, development schemes actually disinvested rural women from independent sources of livelihood.[3] Critics offered self-organization as an antidote to the hardships of self-employment, while struggling for recognition of domestic labour as work.[4]

This chapter addresses forms of subsistence and household labour that are linked in being essential for the maintenance of life, but usually not performed for a wage. "The producers themselves are in charge of the work of reproducing their own labour and that of their family; capital does not assume any responsibility for it", explained Bennholdt-Thomsen in the *Journal of Peasant Studies*, a publication

---

[1] Veronika Bennholdt-Thomsen, "Subsistence Production and Extended Reproduction", *Journal of Peasant Studies*, 9, 4 (1982), pp. 241–254, at 246–247.
[2] Jane L. Collins and Martha Gimenez (eds), *Work Without Wages. Domestic Labor and Self-Employment within Capitalism* (Albany, 1990), p. x.
[3] Ester Boserup, *Women's Role in Economic Development* (New York, 1970); Kate Bedford, *Developing Partnerships. Gender, Sexuality, and the Reformed World Bank* (Minneapolis, 2009); Sarah A. Radcliffe, *Dilemmas of Difference. Indigenous Women and the Limits of Postcolonial Development Policy* (Durham, 2015).
[4] For example, Lourdes Benería (ed.), *Women and Development. The Sexual Division of Labor in Rural Societies* (New York, 1982).

that with its first issue in 1973 announced a field of historically-inflected scholarship.[5] Kinship as an organizing feature has appeared as a central component of subsistence relations over time and space since households have deployed the labour of their inhabitants, blood or fictive, free or unfree, to generate survival of the unit. When defined as housework—cooking, cleaning, caring, and socializing the next generation into class and culture—family labour emerged as a distinct form of subsistence work first among the urban middle classes in the industrialized West as a product of the gendered ideology of domesticity, class conceptions of propriety, and the structural need for consumption.[6]

For many people, even in Western nations, the removal of production from dwelling places was incomplete; the transformation of raw materials into consumable items supplemented wages, salaries, and rents. Commodities made in dwellings subsequently circulated from their place of fabrication to be sold like any other good. Indeed, with British and subsequent textile-based industrialization in North America and then worldwide, the putting out system generated "invisible threads" that tied the home to the mill as an extension of the factory.[7] If one was a housewife, then taking in lace or minding children could be justified as pin-money or just a way to be busy rather than necessary production.[8]

Categories of subsistence labour rarely have existed as pure types, sufficient unto themselves. Their configurations since 1500 have taken distinct forms across the globe, disrupted and reshaped by empire, colonialism, nation-building, development and underdevelopment, and various manifestations of globalization that have created capitalist world systems.[9] Colonializing states have deployed force (as with war), destroyed ecological balances (as with over depletion of resources), disrupted family formation (as through gendered migration) and monetized social relations (as with community ceremonies) so to replace "reproductive forms of subsistence production through the expansion of commodity production."[10] Modernization theorists conceive of each "new nation" moving through a similar process of development, leaving behind subsistence for commodified market relations, but the world

---

[5] Bennholdt-Thomsen, "Subsistence Production and Extended Reproduction", p. 245.
[6] Frans W.A. van Poppel, Hendrik P. van Dalen and Evelien Walhout, "Diffusion of a Social Norm: Tracing the Emergence of the Housewife in the Netherlands, 1812–1922", *The Economic History Review*, New Series, 62 (2009), pp. 99–127; Jan de Vries, *The Industrious Revolution: Consumer Behavior and the Household Economy, 1650 to the Present* (New York, 2008).
[7] Karl Marx, *Capital*, vol. I (New York, 1967), p. 461; Eileen Boris, *Home to Work. Motherhood and the Politics of Industrial Homework in the United States* (New York etc., 1994).
[8] Maria Mies, *The Lace Makers of Narsapur* (London, 2012).
[9] Wilma A. Dunaway (ed.), *Gendered Commodity Chains. Seeing Women's Work and Households in Global Production* (Stanford, 2014).
[10] Georg Elwert and Diana Wong, "Subsistence Production and Commodity Production in the Third World", *Review* (Fernand Braudel Center), 3 (1980), pp. 501–522, at 506.

in which such change occurs was never static.¹¹ Historians recognize that while processes might appear similar, power within the global economy has shifted over time and space since 1500.

The standard story about subsistence production begins with hunter-gathers and early agriculturalists, moves onto serfs under feudalism, and dwells on peasants.¹² Though recognizing the sexual division of labour within these types, such analysis once considered the household as a unit without sufficiently interrogating gendered and generational relations. In contrast, feminist critique not only highlights power relations within the family and home but also investigates the structural impact of the unwaged labour of wives, mothers, daughters, and other women, that is, how tending to household members in the labour force has relieved the employer or capitalist from compensating the waged worker sufficiently to purchase such services on the market, thus aiding in the subsequent extraction of surplus value from the labour of paid workers. Engendering the "Great Transformation" in the magisterial *Caliban and the Witch*, Italian historical theorist Silvia Federici rethinks the dispossession of subsistence relations of production by attributing the domination of women's bodies through their violent appropriation, as seen in witchcraft persecutions, to the same political economy that fenced in the commons, blocking access to the land on which rural people of all sorts depended upon. Understanding control over the land and over the female body as integral to the spread of capitalism, Federici discovers a historical pattern in the squeezing of European peasantry, the conquest of the Americas, the slave trade, and the penetration of multinational corporations into the global South. However, unlike modernization theorists, she understands that the first enclosure produced a world in which subsequent enclosures have proceeded.¹³

The claim that the peasant and the housewife resemble each other, or that subsistence producers of the past stand in a similar relation to capitalism of their day as those of more recent times, requires refinement. Class and power have mattered. Bennholdt-Thomsen suggests that the "first-world" housewife has shared more with the "third world" peasant than she does with the "third world" housewife who relies on a staff of servants (this incorrectly assumes that the Western housewife employs no "help.")¹⁴ The connection between past and present, peasant and housewife, must appear as relational: what German sociologist Maria Mies named as "housewifization" developed with colonization and the extraction of surplus from peasants

---

11 Dean C. Tipps, "Modernization Theory and the Comparative Study of Societies: A Critical Perspective", *Comparative Studies in Society and History*, 15 (1973), pp. 199–226.
12 Marshall Sahlins, *Stone Age Economics* (New York, 1972); Claude Meillassoux, *Maidens, Meal and Money. Capitalism and the Domestic Community* (New York, 1981); Frederick Engels, *The Origin of the Family, Private Property and the State*, 1884 (London, 2010).
13 Silvia Federici, *Caliban and the Witch* (Brooklyn, 2004).
14 Bennholdt-Thomsen, "Subsistence Production and Extended Reproduction", p. 244.

around the world.[15] The third world woman of the late 20th century seems similar to the enslaved African and indigenous women of the Americas and the colonized women of Asia in being they who become "'integrated' in the world economy as producers of labour-power to be used and 'consumed' in the industrialized regions; they further produce commodities for export."[16] But the world economy of the 17th and 18th centuries differs from the 21st. In the making of people who migrate to labour for low wages, the mothers of the global South are doubly exploited for their household labour. But this same labour—through remittances or actual foodstuffs, care, and clothing—has sustained their communities, suggesting the power of household relations of production as a resource for not only survival but also for resistance.[17]

Drawing from a plethora of scholarship on subsistence and household relations of production, this chapter links theoretical and conceptual discussion of these categories to their historical manifestations. It considers classic literature on subsistence production and explicates the necessary persistence of such relations in other forms of production, as well as the impact of access to resources for sustainable subsistence practices. After parsing the chief arguments of the domestic labour debate, it more briefly turns to the figure of the housewife in relation to household relations of production in the industrialized West. The conclusion looks at the emergence of "women and development" as an intellectual arena where feminists of various persuasions addressed subsistence and household production in the global South during the last third of the twentieth century.

Subsistence beyond a sackful of potatoes

The writings of Marx and Engels remain a starting point to discuss household relations of production. The wide use of the very concept of subsistence highlights the flexibility of the term and its usefulness in describing a range of social formations. Historical specificity nuances theoretical discussions of subsistence by underscoring the centrality of producing life on a daily basis for the continuance, if not thriving, of human societies. Feminist theorists particularly have complicated discussions of subsistence relations of production.

For Marx, subsistence relations of production were essential but insufficient for what amounts to an evolutionary vision of change. He infamously referred to French

---

[15] Maria Mies, *Patriarchy and Accumulation on a World Scale: Women in the International Division of Labour* (London, 1986).
[16] Silvia Federici, "Reproduction and Feminist Struggle in the New International Division of Labor", in: Mariarosa Dalla Costa and Giovanna F. Dalla Costa (eds), *Women, Development and Labor of Reproduction. Struggles and Movements* (Trenton, NJ, 1999), p. 50.
[17] Rhacel Parreñas, *Servants of Globalization: Migration and Domestic Work*, 2nd edition (Stanford, 2015); Ton van Naerssen, Lothar Smith, Tine Davids and Marianne H. Marchand, (eds), *Women, Gender, Remittances and Development in the Global South* (Farnham, Surrey etc., 2015).

peasants as "the great mass [...] formed by simple addition of homologous magnitudes much as potatoes in a sack form a sackful of potatoes." Near self-sufficiency defined the peasant family, which "directly produces the major part of its consumption." Without specialization (though there existed an internal division of labour, sexual and generational, that Marx hardly noticed), peasant society lacked development: "no diversity of talents, no wealth of social relations."[18] It was, in short, primitive, backward, and doomed to obsolescence.

However, Marx understood the transformation of the peasant from a worker-proprietor into a wage labourer, along with the severing of the serf from the lord and the land, as a precondition for the growth of capitalism. "The So-Called Primitive Accumulation" occurred "when 'great masses of men are suddenly and forcibly torn from their means of subsistence and hurled as free and 'unattached' proletarians on the labour market. The expropriation of the agricultural producer, of the peasant, from the soil, is the basis of the whole process."[19] The means of expropriation varied: enclosing the commons, whether in early modern Europe or 20th century Nigeria; damming rivers and diminishing game animals through settler encroachment on indigenous lands; usurping customary rights of squatters through legal titles; relocating peasantry, as to "planned villages" under Tanzanian "*Ujamaa* Socialism;" cordoning off of hunting and grazing lands for tourist wildlife parks throughout Africa.[20]

Writing on "the peasant question", Engels associated the peasant with subsistence relations of production: labour undertaken by the family for the household. (Whether just by family, however defined, appears more complicated, especially in societies of slavery, indenture, and other forms of unfree labour.) He predicted that the European peasantry could not maintain viability because of debt, taxes, loss of supplemental handicraft production, failure of crops, too few draft animals, and inheritance practices that divided the land.[21] The peasant economy, however, lingered, even in Europe; only after WWII with deliberate social policies in both West and East Germany, for example, did subsistence farms end.[22] Indeed, peasants long depended on subsistence production because other sources of livelihood, such as wages earned from temporary migration, proved inadequate—the case throughout Latin America even after commercial agriculture had become dominant in the 1970s.

---

18 Karl Marx, "The Eighteenth Brumaire of Louis Bonaparte" (1852), in: Robert Tucker (ed.), *The Marx-Engels Reader*, 2nd edition (New York, 1976), p. 608.
19 Marx in *Capital*, vol. 1 as quoted in Michael Duggett, "Marx on Peasants", *Journal of Peasant Studies*, 2, 2 (1975), pp. 159–182, at 167.
20 Federici, *Caliban and the Witch*, pp. 68–72; David Rich Lewis, "Changing Subsistence, Changing Reservation Environments: The Hupa, 1850–1980s", *Agricultural History*, 66 (1992), pp. 34–51; Tony Waters, *The Persistence of Subsistence Agriculture: Life Beneath the Level of the Marketplace* (Lanham, 2007), pp. 179, 201.
21 Nirmal Kuman Chandra, "The Peasant Question from Marx to Lenin: The Russian Experience", *Economic and Political Weekly*, 37 (May 18–24, 2002), pp. 1927–1938, at 1929 and 1933.
22 Veronika Bennholdt-Thomsen and Maria Mies, *The Subsistence Perspective. Beyond the Globalized Economy* (London, 1999), pp. 84–86.

Under ninetieth century regimes of colonialism, indigenous peoples also combined subsistence production with wage labour, crafts marketing, and self-commodification, as when charging tourists for photographing them or observing their rituals[23]

Rather than fulfilling basic needs through purchase of commodities, Marxist and modernization theorists alike agree, subsistence regimes produce for use, absorbing the outcome of household labour. But just because subsistence societies consume their production did not mean they eschewed relations of exchange. Writing in the 1920s and 1930s, the Russian agrarian economist A.V. Chayanov judged peasants as non-capitalists, who entered the market to purchase necessary goods or services rather than to increase wealth. With needs fulfilled, they would cease working. But without adequate resources, they would tighten their belts and intensify self-exploitation. The extent of work connected to the number of producers related to consumers (the too young or old) in the household.[24] As German historian Hans Medick argued in 1976, "the family functioned *objectively* as an internal engine of growth in the process of proto-industrial expansion precisely because *subjectively* it remained tied to the norms and rules of behavior of the traditional familial subsistence economy", that is, the ways that the household regulated its consumption and marshaled all members for labour.[25]

British sociologist Teodor Shanin, an interpreter of Chayanov, has emphasized the leveling mechanisms within such communities that constitute subsistence exchange: rules of behavior that led to sharing or giving away surplus that cemented relationships, affirmed culture and fulfilled obligations.[26] Mutual exchange of labour facilitated ground clearing, harvesting, and house building outside of market relations throughout the world. Such cooperative labour in North America among European settlers, who sometimes conveyed enslaved Africans to "frontier" settlements, occurred while occupying territory previously held by indigenous peoples.[27] "Moral economy" rather than profit governed some of these societies, even if the genocidal practices of settler colonialism or the forced labour of bondage hardly appears

---

[23] Michael Painter, "The Value of Peasant Labour Power in a Prolonged Transition to Capitalism", *The Journal of Peasant Studies*, 13 (1986) pp. 221–239; Paige Raibmon, *Authentic Indians. Episodes of Encounter from the Late-Nineteenth-Century Northwest Coast* (Durham, NC, 2005).
[24] A.V. Chayanov, *The Theory of Peasant Economy* (Madison, WI, 1966).
[25] Hans Medick, "The Proto-Industrial Family Economy: The Structural Function of Household and Family during the Transition from Peasant Society to Industrial Capitalism", *Social History*, 1, 3 (October 1976), pp. 291–315, at 300 and 308.
[26] Teodor Shanin, "The Nature and Logic of the Peasant Economy I: A Generalization", *The Journal of Peasant Studies*, 1 (1973), pp. 63–80; "The Nature and Logic of the Peasant Economy II: Diversity and Change; III Policy and Intervention", *The Journal of Peasant Studies*, 1 (1974), pp. 186–206. See also, Goran Hyden, *Beyond Ujamaa in Tanzania. Underdevelopment and an Uncaptured Peasantry* (Berkeley, CA, 1980). Notions of the "gift" build upon Marcel Mauss, *The Gift. The Form and Reason for Exchange in Archaic Societies* (New York, 1990; originally published in 1950).
[27] Waters, *Persistence of Subsistence Agriculture*, provides much evidence from the 1500s to the 2000s.

"moral." Into the late 20th century, peasants in Oaxaca, Mexico, for example, came together to confirm social belonging through festivals and participation in community projects.[28]

Though focused on pre-capitalist formations, economic anthropologists, American Marshall Sahlins and French Claude Meillassoux, have stressed the importance of kinship in ordering subsistence relations of production. As Sahlins explained, "its own inner relations, as between husband and wife, parent and child, are the principal relations of production in society. The built-in etiquette of kinship statuses, the dominance and subordination of domestic life, the reciprocity and cooperation, here make the 'economic' a modality of the intimate."[29] Nineteenth century St. Kilda, Scotland exemplifies such processes. Its division of labour resembled work organization among European peasants in which women cared for children and gardens; they made cheese, spun wool, and sewed. Men wove cloth in the winter and otherwise worked outside the home in the fields, here they also sheared sheep and fished in a sustainable relationship with the environment.[30] German immigrants to Nebraska's Great Plains in the 1880s clung to subsistence farming, in which women raised poultry and knitted stockings.[31] Peasant households throughout East Central Europe, many of which worked land they did not own, also produced necessities for daily life—with a variegated sexual division of labour that sometimes saw women, when relieved of family labour, engaged in tasks elsewhere defined as men's work.[32] The Aymara in Southern Peru provide further evidence of a "flexible sexual division of labor [...] according to what seems the most advantageous strategy at a particular time" when their region became more enmeshed in global capitalist markets in the 1970s. Women as well as men left the home for seasonal wage labour.[33]

Meillassoux stressed the domestic mode of production as one of reproduction of the household and community. In "primitive" societies, *"power [...] rests on control over the means of human reproduction—subsistence goods and wives*—and not over the means of material production."[34] The social and economic structure of peasantry actually coincided with the predominance of the paternal household head determin-

---

[28] Matthew Day Whittle, "The Culture of Collaboration: the Resilience of the Peasantry in San Pablo Coatlan, Oaxaca, Mexico" (Ph.D., University of California, Santa Barbara, 2013).
[29] Sahlins, *Stone Age Economics*, p. 77.
[30] Waters, *Persistence of Subsistence Agriculture*, pp. 77–78.
[31] Linda Schelbitzki Pickle, *Contented Among Strangers: Rural German-speaking Women and Their Families in the Nineteenth-Century Midwest* (Urbana, IL, 1996), p. 70.
[32] Krassimira Daskalova and Susan Zimmermann, "Women's and Gender History", in: Irina Livezenau and Arpad von Klimo (eds), *The Routledge History of East Central Europe since 1700* (London, 2017), pp. 272–316.
[33] Michael Painter, "Changing Relations of Production and Rural Underdevelopment", *Journal of Anthropological Research*, 40, 2 (Summer 1984), pp. 271–292, at 281.
[34] Meillassoux, *Maidens, Meal and Money*, p. 49.

ing the labour of others.³⁵ In an extensive review of nonindustrial societies throughout the world, anthropologists Alice Schlegel and Herbert Barry III found that "where men control women's subsistence, men also control their sexuality—licitly through an insistence on virginity, illicitly through rape."³⁶ Étienne Cantin similarly concludes for China that during the Ming and Qing dynasties, in determining "women's work, marriages and persons, women could be made to yield resources convertible into property belonging to men" as they consumed less than they produced beyond the subsistence needs of households.³⁷ Allocation of women's labour in India peasant households in the first decades of the 19th century was one factor that stymied Anglo attempts to enhance cotton production for the world market. Women clung to their hand *churka* gins as part of a household strategy to maintain the family division of labour, maximize food production and minimize the risk to the peasant household by controlling the extent of cotton manufacturing.³⁸

Though most women's work stood outside the public sphere, consumed by the household, the sexual division of labour led to "female economies" in which women controlled the selling of surplus goods. An adage of 1534 underscored the significance of women's labour: "'A woman cannot get her living honestly with spinning on the distaff, but it stoppeth a gap.'"³⁹ Oaxacan women transferred tortilla-making skills into home-based businesses; West African and Caribbean women also displayed comparable strategies to earn cash for taxes and school fees.⁴⁰ Elder men retained power in post-colonial rural Mali, for example, but women inherited their own fields, which they used to enhance economic security of their children by producing crops either for direct consumption or for easy exchange. Time to farm depended on other household work, especially raising children, while actual labour did not necessarily translate into greater autonomy.⁴¹

By absorbing the cost of individual and family maintenance, subsistence production has enabled other relations of production, regimes of unfree as well as free labour. Plantation owners had the enslaved cultivate crops for their own use, either for direct consumption or exchange, sometimes with the masters themselves who would

---

35 Shanin, "The Nature and Logic of the Peasant Economy 1", pp. 67–69.
36 Alice Schlegel and Herbert Barry III, "The Cultural Consequences of the Female Contribution to Subsistence", *American Anthropologist*, New Series, 88, 1 (March 1986), pp. 142–150, at 147.
37 Étienne Cantin, "Modes of Production, Rules for Reproduction and Gender: the Fabrication of China's Textile Manufacturing Workforce Since the Late Empire", *Third World Quarterly*, 30, 3 (2009), pp. 453–468, at 456–457.
38 Sven Beckert, *Empire of Cotton: A Global History* (New York, 2014), pp. 70, 128–131; Christopher M. Florio, "From Poverty to Slavery: Abolitionists, Overseers, and the Global Struggle for Labor in India", *Journal of American History*, 102, 4 (March 2016), pp. 1005–1024, at 1022.
39 Quoted in Medick, "Proto-Industrial Family Economy", p. 311.
40 Whittle, "The Culture of Collaboration", pp. 314–315; Gina Ulysse, *Downtown Ladies. Informal Commercial Importers, a Haitian Anthropologist, and Self-Making in Jamaica* (Chicago, 2007).
41 Laurence Becker, "The Collapse of the Family Farm in West Africa? Evidence from Mali", *The Geographical Journal*, 156 (1990), pp. 313–322.

pay for chickens or produce. The availability of provisioning grounds, often on marginal plots of land, was widespread in the Caribbean and where the task system prevailed in North America, as with rice production.[42] In early 19th century Cuba, frontier regions saw subsistence plots, which persisted in tobacco areas.[43]

Other forms of racialized enterprise sought to offset the cost of worker maintenance through women's unpaid labour. In the 1930s, while South African mines separated men from their rural households, Northern Rhodesian companies encouraged the presence of wives and other women to service the workforce through cooking, laundry, and sex. Some mines provided plots to grow foodstuffs, purchasing the resulting harvest to feed single men more cheaply. Temporary wives throughout Africa, and in the Caribbean, undertook subsistence in the midst of capitalist extraction of natural resources.[44]

Self-provisioning carried over to post-emancipation plantations and became particularly important for coffee production. Into the mid 20th century, estate owners and merchants in the Sao Paulo region of Brazil, Columbia, Venezuela, Central Costa Rica, and for a time in Puerto Rico relied on peasant self-exploitation. The *colonato* family labour system, a "coffee and food-crop" combination, provided these ruling classes with "a measure of flexibility in the face of price slumps on the world market that they would not have enjoyed with wage labour", historian Verena Stolcke documents. Guatemala and El Salvador, in contrast, forced indigenous labour to work on plantations, destroying their rights to the land and seeking to undermine their culture and resistance.[45] Peru offers another variation. Subsistence production allowed Peru to develop a coffee industry after WWII by reducing the cost of reproducing families who remained in the highlands. Land reform between 1969–1975 kept communal ownership inalienable, restricting individual accumulation even while cordoning off acquisition from outsiders—thus effectively "subsidiz[ing] the cost of maintaining and reproducing labor, which must seek economic opportunities outside of the communities."[46]

Historian Sven Beckert observes that the subsistence activities of "Indian peasants, like their counterparts in Anatolia, western Africa, and elsewhere, had shaped a

---

42 Sidney Minz, *Caribbean Transformations* (Chicago, 1974); B.W. Higman, *Slave Population and Economy in Jamaica, 1807–1834* (Kingston, 1995); Ira Berlin and Philip D. Morgan, *The Slaves' Economy: Independent Production by Slaves in the Americas* (London, 1991).
43 William Morgan, "The Internal Economy of Cuban Tobacco Slavery", *Slavery and Abolition*, 37 (2016), pp. 284–306.
44 George Chauncey Jr., "The Locus of Reproduction: Women's Labour in the Zambian Copperbelt", *Journal of Southern African Studies*, 7, 2 (April 1981), pp. 135–164, at 135, 139; Luise White, *The Comforts of Home. Prostitution in Colonial Nairobi* (Chicago, 1990); Kamala Kempadoo, *Sexing The Caribbean. Gender, Race, and Sexual Labor* (New York, 2004).
45 Verena Stolcke, "The Labors of Coffee in Latin America: The Hidden Charm of Family Labor and Self-Provisioning", in: William Roseberry, Lowell Gudmundson, and Mario Samper Kutschbach (eds), *Coffee, Society, and Power in Latin America*, (Baltimore etc., 1995), pp. 65–93, especially p. 81, p. 85.
46 Painter, "Changing Relations of Production", p. 288.

world in which they could resist the onslaught of European merchant capital", increasing their reliance on the U.S. South and its system of slavery before the Civil War. Indian peasants reserved the best soil for consumable crops, refused new technologies, and retained rights to the land.[47] Certainly liberated Haitians resisted waged as well as forced labour in the 1820s by having their own land, organized into the extended family *lakou* system. Here a number of houses encircled a common center, emphasizing independence without discouraging communal exchanges for larger tasks like home construction or some harvests.[48] Even under slavery, subsistence cultivation provided "spaces of autonomy" that challenged systems of bondage and provided material conditions for resistance, whether funds to purchase freedom or foodstuffs to maintain protests. As historian William A. Morgan concludes, "that autonomous activity ranging from surplus production used for consumption to the production of marketable goods was happening within the constraints of slavery means that enslaved individuals were using an internal economy to push the boundaries and limitations of their enslavement."[49] When Jamaica instituted a liminal system of apprenticeship between 1834–1838 prior to emancipation, the formerly enslaved refused continuous labour, insisting on customary practices, including provisioning grounds and gardens allotted for their own use, in negotiations with sugar plantation managers.[50]

Production for use transformed the meaning of the stretch-out of unfree woman's days. As black feminist theorist Angela Davis contended in a path-breaking 1972 article, "in the infinite anguish of ministering to the needs of the men and children around her … [the black woman] was performing the *only* labour of the slave community which could not be directly and immediately claimed by the oppressor." The black woman wove "into the warp and woof of domestic life a profound consciousness of resistance." Rather than a symbol of drudgery, household labour became the means of retaining group humanity and, thus, the desire for freedom.[51] Northern Rhodesian women a century later would transform subsistence plots into self-employment, winning through their beer brewing, gardening, and other labours greater independence from their men, as well as some overall household maneuverability against employers.[52] Wherever workers could return to family plots, they could protest industrial conditions without fear of starvation.[53] Joining together in

---

[47] Beckert, *Empire of Cotton*, 131.
[48] Laurent DuBois, *Haiti: The Aftershocks of History* (New York, 2012), pp.106–108.
[49] Morgan, "The Internal Economy", 285.
[50] Kenneth Morgan, "Labour Relations during and after Apprenticeship: Amity Hall, Jamaica, 1834–1840", *Slavery and Abolition*, 33 (2012), pp. 457–478.
[51] Angela Davis, "Reflections on the Black Women's Role in the Community of Slaves", *The Massachusetts Review*, 13 (Winter-Spring 1972), pp. 86–87.
[52] Chauncey, "The Locus of Reproduction", p.144.
[53] Stolcke, "The Labors of Coffee in Latin America"; Thomas Dublin, *Transforming Women's Work. New England Lives in the Industrial Revolution* (Ithaca, NY, 1994), pp. 29–118.

household activities, women obtained "a source of power and protection" through their "intense female sociality and solidarity", lost under the sexual division of labour under capitalism.[54]

The worth of domestic labour

Even without monetization, the worth of domestic labour seems apparent under systems of subsistence and proto-industrialization. But what was the value of housework under capitalism? The Marxist tradition recognized reproductive labour, though Engels claimed that women's emancipation required leaving unwaged domestic labour for employment outside of the home. Lenin referred to "domestic slavery" from the conditions of "petty housework", which "chains her to the kitchen and the nursery" where "she wastes her labour on barbarously unproductive, petty, nerve-racking, stultifying and crushing drudgery."[55] The logical conclusion was the full socialization of housework, the dream of early 20th century US feminist Charlotte Perkins Gilman as well as late 20th century black Communist feminist Angela Davis.[56] Despite greater provision of nurseries and legal gender equality, state socialist countries never fully achieved socialization of domestic labour, though Bulgaria made the most headway in the 1970s.[57] Market economies would socialize household labour through commodification that maintained the illusion of a private sphere by transferring essential tasks from the family into waged work in the service sector or bringing paid workers into the home to substitute their labour for that of the housewife's.[58]

Beginning in the late 1960s, Marxist and socialist feminists debated the value of domestic labour. Some of them drew upon the Los Angeles activist Mary Inman, whose work the Communist Party USA had rejected in the 1940s as unorthodox on "the woman question." Casting housework, like factory work, as productive labour, Inman prefigured much of the later domestic labour debate by claiming that "widespread denigration of housework and child rearing" was what led to women's

---

[54] Federici, *Caliban and the Witch*, p. 25.
[55] For the best concise summary, see Lise Vogel, "Domestic-Labour Debate", *Historical Materialism* 16 (2008), pp. 237–243, Lenin quoted from p. 238. See also, Rohini Hensman, "Revisiting the Domestic Labour Debate: An Indian Perspective", *Historical Materialism* 19 (2011), pp. 3–28.
[56] Charlotte Perkins Gilman, *The Home, Its Work and Influence* (New York, 1903); Angela Davis, The Approaching Obsolescence of Housework: A Working-Class Perspective", in *Women, Race, and Class* (New York, 1981), pp. 222–244.
[57] Daskalova and Zimmermann, "Women's and Gender", emphasize the differential impact among women. Alena Heitlinger, *Women and State Socialism. Sex Inequality in the Soviet Union and Czechoslovakia* (London, 1979), pp. 8–9; Kristen Ghodsee, *The Left Side of History. World War II and the Unfulfilled Promise of Communism in Eastern Europe* (Durham, NC, 2015).
[58] Susan Strasser, *Never Done. A History of American Housework* (New York, 1982), pp. 300–312; Renate Bridenthal, "The Dialectics of Production and Reproduction in History", *Radical History Review*, 10 (1976), pp. 3–11.

subordination, not the economic function of the work itself that produced future and present labour power. Housewives engaged in "necessary social labour;" the work of all the separate households was "the pivot of the system."[59] Three decades later, feminists in the US, Britain, and Western Europe argued whether household labour produced exchange or use value and whether it was the source of women's oppression and exploitation. Italian writers Mariarosa Dalla Costa, Leopoldina Fortunati and Silvia Federici advanced the discussion by underscoring the production of labour power. Fortunati stressed that the housewife (and the prostitute) both work for capital in reproducing the labour power of the male worker. With American Selma James, Della Costa pushed for wages for housework, though she also called for the refusal of work.[60] Others argued that the housewife produced no surplus value; her labour was for household consumption. Rather than indirectly working for the capitalist, she worked for her husband. The struggle, as French feminist theoretician Christine Delphy contended, was against men as a sex class. In subsequent decades, feminists revived reproductive labour as the key term to describe a central, if unrecognized, component of economic life.[61]

These discussions occurred amid an overall decline of the family wage, earnings that from the mid-19th century in different times and places throughout the industrialized West had allowed organized craftsmen and then unionists in mass productive industries to earn enough to support an unwaged wife and children.[62] From 19th century Netherlands to 1950s Argentina and Italy, the housewife became the consumer of ready-made goods and later new technologies, indirectly sustaining capitalist production.[63] Lack of labour saving devices, as much as social services, led to double exploitation of working-class women's labour power, as in socialist China and capitalist United States.[64] In India, professionals as well as the wealthy also substituted the labour of wives, who entered paid work, with the work of migrants, the lower-caste, and even children "at a heavy cost to the reproduction of labour-power in

---

59 Mary Inman, *In Women's Defense* (Los Angeles, 1940), pp. 137, 145.
60 Mariarosa Dalla Costa and Selma James, *The Power of Women and the Subversion of the Community* (Bristol, 1972); Silvia Federici, *Revolution at Point Zero. Housework, Reproduction, and Feminist Struggle* (Oakland, 2012), pp. 15–40; Leopoldina Fortunati, *Arcane of Reproduction* (New York, 1989).
61 See articles in, "Social Reproduction", *Viewpoint Magazine* (2015) at https://viewpointmag.com/2015/11/02/issue-5-social-reproduction/
62 Jane Lewis, "The Decline of the Male Breadwiner Model: The Implications for Work and Care", *Social Politics*, 8 (2001), pp. 152–170.
63 De Vries, *Industrious Revolution*; Luisa Tasca, "The 'Average Housewife' in Post-World War II Italy", *Journal of Women's History*, 16 (2004), pp. 92–115; Inés Pérez, "Modern Kitchens in the Pampas: Home Mechanization and Domestic Work in Argentina, 1940–1970", *Journal of Women's History*, 27 (2015), pp. 88–109.
64 Jean C. Robinson, "Of Women and Washing Machines: Employment, Housework, and the Reproduction of Motherhood in Socialist China", *The China Quarterly*, 101 (1985), pp. 32–57; Lynn Weiner, *From Working Girl to Working Mother. The Female Labor Force in the United States, 1820–1980* (Chapel Hill, 1986).

the households of the workers who take up the burden", according to Indian scholar Rohini Hensman.⁶⁵ Household labour long had depended on slaves, servants, and other insourced workers who undertook the dirtiest and more tasking jobs, whether hauling wood for fires or washing upper windows. The resulting mistress-maid relationship generated conflict, whether in the form of employer violence or worker malingering and sabotage.⁶⁶ These tensions reemerged in the late 20th century when shifts in the global economy and structural adjustment policies helped to generate both the dual-career family and the migrant domestic worker in Singapore and Dubai, no less than New York City and Rome.⁶⁷ Simultaneously, the financialization that characterizes post-Fordism, as Australian gender researchers Lisa Adkins and Maryanne Dever explain, "suggests that the social energy implicated in the unpaid work of social reproduction […] is now connected to flows of value creation [through stocks, credit, and mortgages] which are not necessarily hardwired to the extraction of surplus from (paid) human labour."⁶⁸

Beyond women and development

In the mid 1970s, Meillassoux underscored the uneven and unequal global reach of subsistence and household production, asserting that "capitalism … depends both on the domestic communities of the colonized countries and on its modern transformation, the family, which still maintains its reproductive functions although deprived of its productive ones."⁶⁹ This observation paralleled feminist observations on the significance of the domestic economy, but without a profound understanding of male dominance. In the late 1970s, Maria Mies with collaborators Veronika Bennholdt-Thomsen and Claudia von Werlhof conceptualized "the subsistence perspective" out of heady debates over modes of production; their own research on India, Mexico, and other "underdeveloped" places; and a feminist sensibility that valued

---

65 Hensman, "Revisiting the Domestic-Labour Debate", p. 17.
66 Thavolia Glymph, *Out of the House of Bondage. The Transformation of the Plantation Household* (New York, 2008); Andrew Urban, *Brokering Servitude. Migration and Political Economies of Domesticity in the United States, 1850–1924* (New York, 2017); Judith Rollins, *Between Women. Domestics and their Employers* (Philadelphia, 1985); Victoria Haskins and Claire Lowrie (eds), *Colonization and Domestic Service. Historical and Contemporary Perspectives* (New York, 2015).
67 Zahra Meghani (ed.), *Women Migrant Workers. Ethical, Political and Legal Problems* (New York, 2016); S. Huang, B.S.A. Yeoh and N. Abdul Rahman (eds), *Asian Women as Transnational Domestic Workers in Asia* (Singapore, 2005); Pierrette Hondagneu-Sotelo, *Domestica: Immigrant Workers Cleaning and Caring in the Shadows of Affluence* (Berkeley, CA, 2007); Helma Lutz, *The New Maids. Transnational Women and the Care Economy* (London, 2011).
68 Lisa Adkins and Maryanne Dever, "Housework, Wages and Money: The Category of the Female Principal Breadwinner in Financial Capitalism", *Australian Feminist Studies*, 29 (2014), pp. 50–66, quote at 59.
69 Meillassoux, *Maidens, Meal and Money*, p. xiii.

the making of life and rejected the devaluing of housework.[70] "Nature, women, and the exploited countries of the Third World" became "'the colonies of the White Man'", subject to forceful expropriation. A continuing process generated capital accumulation.[71]

This fundamental insight contrasted with the main thrust of feminist writing on development. "Women in Development" (WID) informed United Nations actions during the late 1960s and 1970s, propelled by the foreign assistance work of Washington DC feminists like Irene Tinker and UN researchers like Ester Boserup. The Danish Boserup postulated a female farming system that had led to equality between the sexes that development targeted to men was undermining. Adhering to conceptions of meritocracy and the market, WID proponents argued for policies that treated peasant women in the global South as workers and not merely mothers, calling for integrating women into production through training and/or directing resources to women agriculturalists to enhance overall development programs and thus improve overall economic outcomes. Peasants were not to become housewives with rising GNP, but gender inequality would subside from women's market based income generating activities in food production, crafts, and services. There was some success where women had engaged in subsistence provisioning, as in sub-Saharan Africa. But, as small scale projects, these efforts may have had greater impact in undermining subsistence relations of production than alleviating poverty. By the late 1970s, scholars recognized the need to think in terms of social relations, forging the more critical "Gender and Development" (GAD).[72] Advanced by the UN, ILO, and World Bank, such a perspective became part of development beyond subsistence.

By the early twenty-first century, household production represented an alternative to corporate capital that, nonetheless, was made possible by the very inequalities generated by globalization. Ecofeminists, like Mies, and other advocates of sustainability argued for a return to subsistence practices. In contrast, urban homesteaders, do-it-yourself-culture, farmer's markets, local exchange trading systems, and other "think globally, act locally" movements attracted a range of participants from various political persuasions, most of whom had enough resources or social capital to participate in such ventures. Community gardens aside, most poor and working-class people lacked time and money to engage in household production, even if they still had to stretch wages through foraging, "thrifting", stretching, remak-

---

[70] Maria Mies, "Housewifisation–Globalization–Subsistence-Perspective", in: Marcel van der Linden and Karl Heinz Roth with Max Henninger (eds), *Beyond Marx. Theorising the Global Labour Relations of the Twenty-First Century*, (Leiden and Boston, 2014), pp. 220–221.
[71] Bennholdt-Thomsen and Mies, *Subsistence Perspective*, p. 12.
[72] Shahrashoub Razavi and Carol Miller, "From WID to GAD: Conceptual Shifts in the Women and Development Discourse", United Nations Research Institute for Social Development, United Nations Development Programme, *Occasional Paper* 1 (Geneva, February 1995).

ing, and doing without.⁷³ In the new gendered international division of labour, household production in the global North stood apart from subsistence relations as a new arena for commodification, while households of all sorts struggled for subsistence.

---

73 I am indebted here to exchanges with Leigh Dodson, PhD student in Feminist Studies, University of California, Santa Barbara.

Suggested reading

Benería, Lourdes (ed.). *Women and Development. The Sexual Division of Labor in Rural Societies* (New York: Praeger, 1982).
Bennholdt-Thomsen, Veronika and Maria Mies. *The Subsistence Perspective. Beyond the Globalized Economy* (London: Zed Books, 1999).
Bennholdt-Thomsen, Veronika. "Subsistence Production and Extended Reproduction", *Journal of Peasant Studies*, 9, 4 (1982), pp. 241–254.
Berlin, Ira and Philip D. Morgan. *The Slaves' Economy: Independent Production by Slaves in the Americas* (London: Psychology Press, 1991).
Boserup, Ester. *Women's Role in Economic Development* (New York: George Allen & Unwin, 1970).
Chayanov, A.V. *The Theory of Peasant Economy* (Homewood, IL: American Economic Association, 1966).
Collins, Jane L. and Martha Gimenez (eds). *Work Without Wages. Domestic Labor and Self-Employment within Capitalism* (Albany, NY: SUNY Press, 1990).
De Vries, Jan. *The Industrious Revolution. Consumer Behavior and the Household Economy, 1650 to the Present* (New York: Cambridge University Press, 2008).
Elwert, Georg and Diana Wong. "Subsistence Production and Commodity Production in the Third World", *Review* (Fernand Braudel Center), 3 (1980), pp. 501–522.
Haskins, Victoria K. and Claire Lowrie (eds). *Colonization and Domestic Service. Historical and Contemporary Perspectives* (New York: Routledge, 2015).
Heitlinger, Alena. *Women and State Socialism. Sex Inequality in the Soviet Union and Czechoslovakia* (London: Macmillan, 1979).
Lutz, Helma. *The New Maids. Transnational Women and the Care Economy* (London: Zed Books, 2011).
Mariarosa Dalla Costa and Giovanna F. Dalla Costa (eds). *Women, Development and Labor of Reproduction. Struggles and Movements* (Trenton, NJ: Africa World Press, 1999).
Medick, Hans. "The Proto-Industrial Family Economy: The Structural Function of Household and Family during the Transition from Peasant Society to Industrial Capitalism", *Social History*, 1, 3 (October 1976), pp. 291–315.
Meillassoux, Claude. *Maidens, Meal and Money. Capitalism and the Domestic Community* (New York: Cambridge University Press, 1981).
Mies, Maria, *Patriarchy and Accumulation on a World Scale* (London: Zed Books, 1986).
Parreñas, Rhacel. *Servants of Globalization. Migration and Domestic Work*, second edition (Stanford, 2015).
Schlegel, Alice and Herbert Barry III. "The Cultural Consequences of the Female Contribution to Subsistence", *American Anthropologist*, New Series, 88, 1 (March 1986), pp. 142–150.
Stolcke, Verena. "The Labors of Coffee in Latin America: The Hidden Charm of Family Labor and Self-Provisioning", in: William Roseberry, Lowell Gudmundson, and Mario Samper Kutschbach (eds), *Coffee, Society, and Power in Latin America*, (Baltimore, MD: The Johns Hopkins University Press, 1995), pp. 65–93.
Strasser, Susan. *Never Done. A History of American Housework* (New York: Macmillan, 1982).
Waters, Tony. *The Persistence of Subsistence Agriculture: Life Beneath the Level of the Marketplace* (Lanham: Lexington Books, 2007).

Christian G. De Vito
4.3. Convict Labour

Convict labour is "the work performed by individuals under penal and/or administrative control".[1] It is the work of prisoners and deportees, individuals impressed into the army and the navy, prisoners of war, and military convicts. Arguably a ubiquitous phenomenon in human history, it stretches from Antiquity to the present, appears in virtually all parts of the world, and cuts across multiple punitive institutions and labour contexts: from the Roman mines to contemporary concentration camps, through the early modern Mediterranean and Oceanic galleys, penal transportation, workhouses, and penitentiaries. This chapter addresses convict labour from three distinct perspectives. In the first section, I discuss its definition by pointing to the ways by which an individual becomes a convict labourer. I contend that some historical processes are especially likely to produce such transformation: war; empire and state building; the search for labour flexibility; conceptualizations of the function of punishment; and ideas on ethnicity, class, and gender. The second section highlights the new trends in both labour history and the history of punishment that have been, and still are, transforming the study of convict labour. I argue that three approaches have been especially relevant: the reconceptualization of the "working class" beyond wage labour, to include other labour relations imbricated in the process of labour commodification; the attention paid to the multiplicity of forms that punishment has taken historically, rather than to single punitive institutions; and the focus on the spatiality of punishment, i.e. on the fact that punishing has often involved not only the immobilization of convicts, but also their relocation across space. The concluding section reflects on how these new insights might provide the basis for a new theory of the relationships between punishment and labour, both in the past and in the present.

Defining and locating convict labour

Convict labour emerges at the crossroads of two dynamic social processes: the enforced social definition of the "convict" and the commodification of labour. In other words, in order to become a convicted labourer, an individual has to undergo a double process: he or she has to be constructed as a convict, through the social and cultural dynamics of the legal and administrative systems (laws, rules, orders, and trials); subsequently, this convict has to be turned into a forced labourer, by

---

[1] Christian G. De Vito and Alex Lichtenstein, "Writing a Global History of Convict Labour", *International Review of Social History*, 58, 2 (2013), pp. 285–325, at 291. For examples of contexts where convict labour has emerged across history, see *idem* (eds), *Global Convict Labour* (Leiden and Boston, 2015).

means of both discourses that legitimize his or her labour coercion and organizational instruments that make it possible. The complex making of convict labour has significant implications. Individuals held under distinct legal regimes and with different statuses belong to the category of "convict". They are military, common-law, and political prisoners, together with prisoners of war, vagrants, and those who are subjected to legal control both while awaiting sentence and after its completion. They depend on multiple formal and informal administrative agencies (including police, overseers, and religious chiefs) and are sentenced by various types of courts (lower and higher, military, and religious courts for example). At the same time, not all convicts become forced labourers. Across history, for example, elite convicts have typically been excluded from the obligation to perform coerced labour. Under certain circumstances, the same has been the case for political prisoners. Moreover, not all convict labour is connected to labour commodification, as I will discuss later in this section. Finally, in many contemporary Western prison regimes work is not compulsory, nor is it available to all those who voluntarily apply for it.

Some social processes appear especially conducive to the emergence of convict labour, even though their actual impact largely varies through time and space, and combines differently in distinct contexts. Here I will address a selected group of them in order to provide an idea of the broad variety of economic, political, social, and cultural aspects that have been imbricated in the making of convict labour.

War inevitably plays a major role in the emergence of convict labour.[2] Accompanied by cultural processes of production and dehumanization of the "enemy", military conflicts typically create "states of exception" that legitimize the recourse to multiple repressive measures and a broader array of punitive regimes. At the same time, war produces labour needs that across history have been frequently met through the multifaceted mobilization of convict labour: in the early modern period and up to the early twentieth century, it has facilitated large-scale impressment into the army and the navy; it has required convicted workforce for military-related labour at the frontline and, particularly during modern armed conflicts, at the home front; and it has fostered the employment of convicts in public works and reconstruction during and after the conflicts.

Partially connected with war, empire and state building has been another historical process typically associated with the production of convict labour. Especially the need to claim sovereignty over and colonize new territories and the borderlands, and the scarce availability of voluntary settlers to perform these tasks, has made convict transportation one of the most long-term features in the history of punishment and convict labour, as I will explain in more detail in the next section.

---

[2] For a more detailed analysis of this aspect, see Christian G. De Vito, Ralf Futselaar, and Helen Grevers (eds), *Incarceration and Regime Change. European Prisons during and after the Second World War* (New York and Oxford, 2016). For the reference to the "states of exception", see Giorgio Agamben, *State of Exception* (Chicago, 2005).

The need for convict labour has additionally stemmed from the search by employers and policymakers for labour flexibility, that is, their "quest to synchronise the availability of what they perceive as the most appropriate workforce, with their productive and political needs".³ From this perspective, the coerced labour of the convicts has usually been appreciated for its relative cheapness and high spatial mobility, although the productivity of convicts has often been deemed insufficient. Moreover, a dialectics has frequently developed between state and private actors, with convicts leased to private employers being an option in many and diverse historical contexts.

Whereas focusing on labour flexibility foregrounds the connection of convict labour with the process of labour commodification, one has to keep in mind that the production of convict labour equally depended on broader conceptualizations of the social functions of punishment that were not necessarily or solely designed to serve economic purposes. In this context, not only did certain forms of punishment not imply the exploitation of the work of prisoners, they could also privilege non-commodification-related functions of convict labour. One example of this can be found in those daily occupations performed by convicts in modern prisons that merely serve the purpose of the penal institutions themselves: the cleaning of the cells and corridors, the preparation of food, and administrative work. More extreme, but not infrequent, historical cases of non-commodified convict labour are associated with the merely punitive work political prisoners have been assigned to under multiple penal regimes across the world: one only has to think of the African National Congress (ANC) activists forced to uselessly break stones with hammers in the courtyard of the prison on Robben Island; or the Ecuadorian political convicts carrying huge stones in order to build the "Wall of Tears" (*Muro de las Lágrimas*) in the penal colony of Isabela, in the Galapagos islands (1940s-1950s).⁴ Often related to conceptions of punishment allegedly meant to "redeem" the convicts, those dramatic human experiences remind us of the multifaceted nature of "rehabilitation" through punishment, and of its frequent disentanglement from the progressive idea that we tend to associate with it. After all, draconian regimes of human exploitation have been legitimized under self-defined "enlightened" eighteenth-century imperial schemes to "redeem" the vagrants, Lombrosian distinctions between "born-crimi-

---

3 Christian G. De Vito, "Precarious Pasts: Labour Flexibility and Labour Precariousness as Conceptual Tools for the Historical Study of the Interaction Between Labour Relations", in: Karl Heinz Roth (ed.), *On the Road to Global Labour History. A Festschrift for Marcel van der Linden* (forthcoming).
4 On the ANC prisoners, see Padraic Kenney, "'A Parade of Trick Horses': Work and Physical Experience in the Political Prison", in: De Vito and Lichtenstein, *Global Convict Labour*, pp. 380–399. See especially the picture on p. 380. On the *Muro de las lágrimas*, see Antonio Constante Ortega, *Basalto. Etapa de terror y lágrimas durante la colonia penal en Isabela (Memorias de un colono de Galápagos)* (Guayaquil, 2006). A picture of the twenty-five-metre-high wall can be found on p. 36.

nals" and "occasional criminals", and Stalinist attempts to create the "socialist man".[5]

Broader conceptualizations of society, not directly related to punishment, have also played a key function in the production of convict labour. Ideas around ethnicity, class, and gender are a case in point, and have additionally contributed to differentiate the experiences of convicts vis-à-vis coerced labour. In many colonial contexts, for example, identifying someone as "black" or as "native" led to supplementary punishments being administered that were typically associated with corporal punishment and the exploitation of labour. Moreover, while for thousands of transported and imprisoned convicts whiteness proved no guarantee of not being subjected to involuntary labour, it did create dialectics of power within the convicted population and beyond, as in the standard colonial discussion regarding the undesirability of having black or native overseers guarding white prisoners. When associated with elite status, whiteness, but also other ethnic definitions, effectively exempted convicts from the harshest employment, and often from coerced labour at all. The geography of punishment of elite convicts sometimes overlapped with the political ones, and presented distinct features vis-à-vis those of their subaltern (and common-law) counterparts. A similar distinction in the spatiality of punishment characterized the experiences of male and female convicts well before strict gender separation was introduced in the penitentiary.[6] Indeed, the imbalance of gender – that is, the absence or lack of women – in sites of deportation was a constant worry for early modern and modern colonial authorities alike, and not infrequently triggered schemes for that peculiar form of coerced labour migration that was the deportation of prostitutes.[7] At the same time, the conceptualization of gender was a key source for the differentiation in the employment of male and female convicts, with military and construction work being a typical task for the former, while cleaning, sewing, and assisting in hospitals and monasteries were deemed appropriate "women's work".

All in all, the awareness of the constructed nature of convict labour and the analysis of the historical processes more likely to facilitate its emergence contribute greatly to shifting from a static definition of convict labour to the study of its functions among other labour relations and across punitive regimes. In turn, this step from asking ourselves "what is convict labour?" to investigating "why convict labour?" is of

---

[5] See, for example, Rosa María Pérez Estévez, *El problema de los vagos en la España del siglo XVIII* (Madrid, 1976); *Criminal Man: Cesare Lombroso*, trans. Mary Gibson and Nicole Hahn Rafter (Durham, 2006); Sanne Deckwitz, "Gulag and Laogai: Ideology, Economics and the Dynamics of Space and Scale", *Workers of the World*, 1, 3 (2013), pp. 175–191.

[6] For the importance of gender analysis in the history of convict labour, see Mary Gibson, "Gender and Convict Labour: The Italian Case in Global Context", in: De Vito and Lichtenstein, *Global Convict Labour*, pp. 313–332.

[7] See, for example, John Scott, "Penal Colonies", in *Encyclopedia of Prostitution and Sex Work* (Westport, CT, 2006), pp. 355–356.

fundamental importance in order to write convict labour back into the history of labour and punishment. As I argue in the next section, this is a goal that recent developments in scholarship have made considerably more feasible.

Punitive pluralism, geographies of punishment, and convict labour

The history of convict labour lies at the crossroads of labour history and the history of punishment. This provides a privileged perspective for doing innovative research, but such potential has remained largely unexplored so far. Indeed, in both sub-disciplines convict labour has been traditionally marginalized because of a double teleology: first, the focus on "free" wage labour has dominated labour (and migration) history, conflating wage labour with capitalism and modernity, and, by contrast, coerced labour with pre-capitalism and pre-modernity; second, in the history of punishment the quest for the "birth of the prison" has played a similar role, sketching an alleged one-way shift to the "modernity" of the penitentiary. The two discourses have also reinforced each other, producing a deterministic narrative of the penitentiary as an instrument for the formation of wage labourers and for factory discipline.[8]

New trends have emerged in the last few decades within the scholarly literature that disclose the opportunity to reverse this situation. On the one hand, as this volume shows, global labour historians have recentred the field of labour history around the issue of labour commodification, and reconceptualized the "working class" beyond the traditional exclusive focus on wage labourers.[9] In this way they have been able to include slaves, coolies, tributary labourers, and other groups of subaltern workers that participated in the process of labour commodification. Convict labour has consequently found a place in the taxonomy of the Global Collaboratory on the History of Labour Relations, albeit one that almost exclusively foregrounds its participation among non-commodified forms of labour.[10] Conversely, Marcel van der Linden's identification of the "coerced commodification of labour

---

[8] Especially in Dario Melossi and Massimo Pavarini, *The Prison and the Factory: Origins of the Penitentiary System* (London, 1981) [first edition in Italian: *Carcere e fabbrica. Alle origini del Sistema penitenziario (XVI–XIX secolo)* (Bologna, 1977)]. See the concluding section for further comments on this approach.
[9] The main contributions include Jan Lucassen (ed.), *Global Labour History. A State of the Art* (Bern, 2008); Marcel van der Linden, *Workers of the World: Essays Toward a Global Labor History* (Leiden and Boston, 2008); Marcel van der Linden and Eva Himmelstoss (eds), *Labour History Beyond Borders. Concepts and Explorations* (Vienna, 2009). For an overview of the formation of the GLH programme and network, see Christian G. De Vito, "New Perspectives on Global Labour History. Introduction", *Workers of the World*, 1, 3 (2013), pp. 7–31.
[10] For the taxonomy of the Global Collaboratory, see Karin Hofmeester's introduction to part 4 of this handbook, or https://collab.iisg.nl/web/labourrelations, last accessed 5 February 2017.

power" as a key aspect of the making of a global working class has provided implicitly a broader way to integrate convict labour with other forms of free and unfree labour.¹¹ The dialectic between the two classifications offers the advantage of raising the important issue of convict labour being both commodified or non-commodified labour, depending on the historical circumstances and especially on the conceptualization of punishment, as I noted earlier in this piece.

The evolution in the field of global labour history provides the backbone against which a renovated approach to the history of convict labour is possible. Indeed, it is from within that area of research that the first attempt at a comprehensive understanding of the topic has emerged. The volume *Global Convict Labour* especially provides an overview and theoretical definition of the field and points to three directions for its study: long-term genealogies; the entanglements of convict labour with coloniality, ethnicity, and racialism; and the key role that polities, and therefore governmentality, have played in the production of the coerced work of convicts.¹²

The scholarship on the history of punishment has hitherto offered more contradictory inputs to the history of convict labour, possibly as a consequence of its persisting fragmentation in multiple sub-fields and because of its unwillingness to engage in broader theorization. I will return to this point in the concluding section of this chapter. Significant areas of exception to this rule exist though, particularly within research on the following topics: colonial prisons; concentration camps and the penal system under National Socialism; the Soviet gulags; and, more systematically, in the studies on early modern and modern convict transportation. It is to these fields that I will now turn in order to foreground their specific contributions to the study of convict labour so far. More generally, I contend that, for all their differences, they share a tendency to question the standard conflation of punishment and imprisonment and the related view of punishment as immobilization in isolated institutional contexts. In other words, in addressing punishment these scholars also look beyond the prison and are fully aware that punishing frequently meant relocating convicts across empires and nation states. Consequently, their approaches provide a vantage point to reflect on the relationships between punishment, spatiality, and labour, that is, on the entanglements between multiple punitive geographies and convict labour.¹³ At the same time, they are better positioned to appreciate the entan-

---

11 Van der Linden, *Workers of the World*, p. 34.
12 De Vito and Lichtenstein, *Global Convict Labour*. See also Nigel Penn, "Towards a History of Convict Labour in the Nineteenth Century Cape", *Workers of the World*, 1, 3 (2013), pp. 118–138; Kelvin Santiago-Valles, "Forced Labor in Colonial Penal Institutions across the Spanish, U.S., British, French Atlantic, 1860s-1920s", in: Marcel van der Linden and Magaly Rodríguez García (eds), *On Coerced Labor. Work and Compulsion after Chattel Slavery* (Leiden and Boston, 2016), pp. 73–97; Justin F. Jackson, "'A Military Necessity which Must be Pressed': The U.S. Army and Forced Road Labour in the Early American Colonial Philippines", in: van der Linden and Rodríguez García, *On Coerced Labor*, pp. 127–158.
13 The multidisciplinary field of "carceral geography" has similarly insisted on the importance of addressing the spatiality of punishment. However, this area of study has hitherto taken a presentist

glements among the multiple types of punishment that have characterized the long-term, global experience.[14]

Taylor Sherman has noted that the new generation of studies on colonial justice has created "much scope for examining colonial coercive institutions and practices in a single frame, and as a function of larger political, administrative, economic, social and cultural processes".[15] Accordingly, she has proposed thinking about "coercive networks", including capital and corporal punishments, incarceration, and penal transportation. Beyond the colonial experience, my suggestion is that the adoption of the concept of "punitive pluralism" might be an even more appropriate and broader conceptual frame to address the simultaneity of multiple punitive regimes. Building on the multidisciplinary concept of "legal pluralism", it retains three key ideas of that field of studies. First, the simultaneity of multiple legal systems within the same society as the standard in history. Second, the plurality of state law, constituted of distinct types of jurisdictions, courts, and authorities. Third, the plurality of imperial legal orders, or the fact that different ideas and practices of justice existed within the same empire. To these features, the concept of "punitive pluralism" adds three extra dimensions, as it: expands the focus beyond the legal system, to include administrative enforcement and military justice; foregrounds punishment, whereas the literature on legal pluralism is mainly concerned with sentencing; and highlights the tensions produced by those forms of punishment that implied relocation across imperial spaces.

In her insightful review essay on "global perspectives on the birth of the prison", Mary Gibson has pointed to the contribution of five recent studies on the colonial prison to the field of prison history.[16] Addressing respectively the nineteenth- and

---

stand and has almost exclusively focused on contemporary prisons and detention centres for undocumented migrants. Moreover, it has paid no attention to the question of labour. In the text, I use the expression "punitive geographies" in order to indicate the need for a trans-punitive perspective, i. e. an approach that relates not only to incarceration. For the main publications on "carceral geography", see Dominique Moran, Nick Gill, and Deirdre Conlon (eds), *Carceral Spaces: Mobility and Agency in Imprisonment and Migrant Detention* (Farnham, 2013); Dominique Moran, *Carceral Geography: Spaces and Practices of Incarceration* (Farnham, 2015). For an attempt to build a dialogue between "carceral geography" and historical studies, see Clare Anderson et al., "Locating Penal Transportation: Punishment, Space, and Place c.1750 to 1900", in: Karen M. Morin and Dominique Moran (eds), *Historical Geographies of Prisons. Unlocking the Usable Carceral Past* (London and New York, 2015), pp. 147–167.
14 On "legal pluralism", see Sally Engle Merry, "Legal Pluralism", *Law and Society Review*, 22, 5 (1988), pp. 869–896; Brian Z. Tamanaha, "Understanding Legal Pluralism: Past to Present, Local to Global", *Sydney Law Review*, 30:3 (2008), pp. 375–411; Lauren Benton and Richard J. Ross (eds), *Legal Pluralism and Empires, 1500–1850* (New York, 2013).
15 Taylor C. Sherman, "Tensions of Colonial Punishment: Perspectives on Recent Developments in the Study of Coercive Networks in Asia, Africa and the Caribbean", *History Compass*, 7, 3 (1999), pp. 659–677, at 671.
16 Mary Gibson, "Global Perspectives on the Birth of the Prison", *American Historical Review*, 116, 4 (2011), pp. 1040–1063. The volumes reviewed are: Peter Zinoman, *The Colonial Bastille. A History of*

twentieth-century history of the prison in Vietnam, various African countries, China, Japan, and Peru, this new scholarship fundamentally questions Foucault's idea of a linear shift from corporal punishment to penitentiary discipline taking place between the late eighteenth and the early twentieth centuries. In all those contexts, especially the perceived insufficient punitiveness of the standard penitentiary model for colonial subjects led to regimes of corporal punishment and forced labour being maintained or introduced within and beyond the prison systems. Other studies reached similar conclusions regarding an even broader range of colonial settings: the persisting importance of convict labour both within and outside the prisons (i.e. "intramural" and "extramural" labour) as a means of labour commodification and/or mere torment has been demonstrated, for example, for the colonial Middle East and Asia and for colonial and post-independence Latin America.[17] However, I contend that this significant expansion of the geographical scope has not always been accompanied by a truly global historical perspective that allows for the overcoming of Eurocentric and methodologically nationalist approaches. Indeed, a tendency exists in this literature – possibly in the one on Latin America particularly – to conflate the "birth of the prison" with modernity, and therefore to prioritize the penitentiary, marginalize coexisting punitive regimes, and interpret the gap between the penitentiary model and its concrete realization as a sign of the "backwardness" or incompleteness of colonial and post-colonial contexts vis-à-vis supposedly "modern" Western experiences. Yet, Foucault himself warned in *Discipline & Punish* about the failure of the (Western) prison to accomplish its ideal goals of modernity and rehabilitation,[18] and recent historical works have largely substantiated this claim. This is most notably the case in the scholarship on the history of the US penal system, which has foregrounded the persisting role of convict labour – i.e. convict lease, the chain gangs, and intramural work in the penitentiary – in marking ethnic and

---

Imprisonment in Vietnam, 1862–1940 (Berkeley, 2001); Florence Bernault (ed.), *A History of Prison and Confinement in Africa* (Portsmouth, 2003) [first edition in French: *Enfermement, prison et châtiments en Afrique du 19ᵉ siècle à nos jours* (Paris, 1999)]; Frank Dikötter, *Crime, Punishment and the Prison in Modern China* (New York, 2002); Daniel V. Botsman, *Punishment and Power in the Making of Modern Japan* (Princeton, 2005); Carlos Aguirre, *The Criminals of Lima and Their Worlds. The Prison Experience, 1850–1935* (Durham, 2005).

17 See, especially, Ricardo D. Salvatore and Carlos Aguirre (eds), *The Birth of the Penitentiary in Latin America. Essays on Criminology, Prison Reform, and Social Control, 1830–1940* (Austin, 1996); Frank Dikötter and Ian Brown (eds), *Cultures of Confinement. A History of the Prison in Africa, Asia, and Latin America* (London, 2007). For an important overview, see Sherman, "Tensions of Colonial Punishment". The author especially mentions the following three works: Clare Anderson, *The Indian Uprising of 1857–8. Prisons, Prisoners and Rebellion* (London, 2007); Diana Paton, *No Bond but the Law. Punishment, Race, and Gender in Jamaican State Formation, 1780–1870* (Durham, 2004); David Anderson, *Histories of the Hanged. The Dirty War in Kenya and the End of Empire* (London, 2005).
18 Michel Foucault, *Discipline and Punish. The Birth of the Prison* (New York, 1977) [first edition in French: *Surveiller et punir. Naissance de la prison* (Paris, 1975)], especially pp. 293–308.

social boundaries within the process of "modernization".[19] In Europe, new publications on the nineteenth- and twentieth-century Italian prison system, for example, have similarly highlighted the long-term gap between the theory and practice of the prison system. Combined with a refreshing focus on penal and administrative confinement in liberal and Fascist Italy, and with new studies on the spatiality of punishment in Italy and the Italian empire, this approach promises to provide an articulated picture of the ways by which extramural and intramural convict labour has worked as a "pillar" of the punitive system as a whole.[20]

Until recently, a striking feature in the discussion on the birth of the prison in Europe was its separation from the extensive scholarly field of the history of the concentration camp. Indeed, the twentieth century has been viewed alternatively as the age of the full hegemony of the penitentiary or as "the century of the camps", with insufficient attempts to move from such contradictory assumptions to a more comprehensive reflection on the implications of the entanglements and co-existence of the two punitive regimes for the history of punishment.[21] However, Nikolaus Wachsmann's *Hitler's Prisons* has broken this taboo:[22] this major work on "legal terror in Nazi Germany" has addressed the role that the criminal justice system and state prisons played in the broader punitive practices of the Third Reich. Inevitably, the author repeatedly dealt with multiple forms of convict labour, most notably in connection with prisons becoming "penal factories", the policy of "annihilation through labour", and the experience of the over 10,000 prisoners impressed in the "Probation

---

19 See, especially, Alex Lichtenstein, *Twice the Work of Free Labor. The Political Economy of Convict Labor in the New South* (London, 1996); David M. Oshinsky, *"Worse than Slavery": Parchman Farm and the Ordeal of Jim Crow Justice* (New York, 1996); Matthew J. Mancini, *One Dies, Get Another. Convict Leasing in the American South, 1866–1928* (Columbia, 1996).
20 See, especially, Simona Trombetta, *Punizione e carità. Carceri femminili nell'Italia dell'Ottocento* (Bologna, 2004); Roberto Giulianelli, *L'industria carceraria in Italia. Lavoro e produzione nelle prigioni da Giolitti a Mussolini* (Rome, 2008); Christian G. De Vito, *Camosci e girachiavi. Storia del carcere in Italia* (Bari and Rome, 2009); Eleanor Canright Chiari, *Undoing Time. The Cultural Memory of an Italian Prison* (Bern, 2012); Gibson, "Gender and Convict Labour"; Ilaria Poerio, *A scuola di dissenso. Storie di resistenza al confino di polizia (1926–1943)* (Rome, 2016); Francesca Di Pasquale, "La colonizzazione penitenziaria nella costruzione nazionale. Madrepatria e oltremare a confronto (1861–1933)", in Gianluca Bascherini and Giovanni Ruocco (eds), *Lontano vicino. Metropoli e colonie nella costruzione dello Stato nazionale italiano* (Rome, 2016), pp. 157–177; Christian G. De Vito, "Paradoxical Outcomes? Incarceration, War and Regime Changes in Italy, 1943–54", in: De Vito et al., *Incarceration and Regime Change*, pp. 33–52.
21 On the nineteenth and twentieth centuries as the "age of the triumphant prison", see Michelle Perrot, "Délinquence et système pénitentiaire en France au 19e siècle", *Annales ESC*, 30 (1975), pp. 67–91, at 81; Rudolph Peters, "Egypt and the Age of the Triumphant Prison: Legal Punishment in Nineteenth Century Egypt", *Annales Islamologiques*, 36 (2002), pp. 253–285. On the "century of camps", see Joël Kotek and Pierre Rigoulot, *Le siècle des camps. Détention, concentration, extermination. Cent ans de mal radical* (Paris, 2000).
22 Nikolaus Wachsmann, *Hitler's Prisons. Legal Terror in Nazi Germany* (New Haven and London, 2004).

Battalion 999" to fight in Africa, the Balkans, and Soviet Union. A more recent edited volume on *Incarceration and Regime Change* has appropriated Wachsmann's approach and sought to expand it in three directions:[23] first, by applying it to a broader range of European countries, including Francoist Spain, Belgium, France, and the Netherlands; second, by addressing a longer periodization that allows one to study the relationship between punishment and regime changes around World War II; and third, by systematically exploring the entanglements among different punitive regimes, including prisons, workhouses, deportation, and camps. As a result, not only have certain groups of forced labourers gained a new visibility, as in the case of the colonial prisoners of war in occupied France and the members of the national socialist movement of the Netherlands Indies; the perspective has also shifted from a single-institution view to larger social processes, including convict labour. Moreover, the broader spatial scope has allowed the editors to propose the hypothesis that the flows of deported convicts to Germany from the countries occupied by the Nazis constituted a "single integrated system", albeit one articulated according to the distinct legal and political relations each of those countries maintained with the Third Reich.[24]

The possibility for writing connected histories of punishment across multiple punitive regimes during World War II owes much to the "new histories" of the Nazi concentration camps that have been published (or made available to English readers) during the last decade.[25] Through extensive empirical studies of individual camps and specific aspects of their organization, these new narratives have offered a more complete picture of the groups of inmates and of those involved in the management of the camps. Moreover, they have fully historicized the development and the experiences in the *lagers* by paying "close attention to differences among the camps and to changes over time".[26] The result has been an immersion in the complexity of the camp system that has greatly improved our understanding of the forced labour within it. In particular, the awareness of the internal spatial and functional differentiations of the system has allowed one to overcome the traditional question of the primacy of ideology or economics as motivations for the exploitation (or the annihilation) of convicts.[27] Indeed, a more dynamic view has emerged by which ideo-

---

23 De Vito *et al.*, *Incarceration and Regime Change*.
24 Christian G. De Vito, Ralf Futselaar, and Helen Grevers, "Introduction: Incarceration and Regime Change", in: *ibid.*, pp. 1–14, 10–11.
25 See, especially, Jane Caplan and Nikolaus Wachsmann (eds), *Concentration Camps in Nazi Germany. The New Histories* (London, 2010); Nikolaus Wachsmann, *KL. A History of the Nazi Concentration Camps* (London, 2015). For an overview of the recent literature, see Marc Buggeln, "Forced Labour in Nazi Concentration Camps", in: De Vito and Lichtenstein, *Global Convict Labour*, pp. 333–360.
26 Jane Caplan and Nikolaus Wachsmann, "Introduction", in: *idem*, *Concentration Camps in Nazi Germany*, pp. 1–16, 7.
27 Jens-Christian Wagner, "Work and Extermination in the Concentration Camps", in: *ibid.*, pp. 127–148, 128. See also Marc Buggeln, *Arbeit und Gewalt. Das Aussenlagersystem des KZ Neuengamme* (Göttingen, 2009) [English edition: *Slave Labour in Nazi Concentration Camps* (Oxford, 2015)].

logical and economic goals played shifting roles in shaping convict labour regimes in different geographical contexts, through the dialectics of main and affiliate camps, and in relation to distinct groups of inmates. At the same time, a more precise periodization has been proposed – usually along the tripartition 1933–1938, 1938–1943, and 1943–1945 – at the crossroads of shifting geographies of the overall system and changing functions of work.[28] Parallel developments have led to new insights into the internal articulation of the Gulag system and its "continual administrative flux", and into the role of convict labour in the hundreds of camps and special settlements that comprised that system.[29] Ongoing research on the continuities between convict transportation during the tsarist regime and Soviet deportation is likely to provide further inputs, especially as far as the connection among colonization, punishment, and convict labour is concerned.[30]

The field of studies on early modern and modern convict transportation has witnessed a profound and rapid transformation during the last three decades, showing a tendency to progressively expand its spatial reach, embrace a refined version of global history, and pay increasing attention to convict labour. Whereas the first generation of studies, in the 1980s-1990s, dealt almost exclusively with convict transportation from Britain to Australia,[31] the late 1990s and especially the 2000s saw the publication of works by Tim Coates on the Portuguese empire, Andrew A. Gentes on the tsarist empire, and Kerry Ward's on banishment and convict transportation in the Dutch East India Company. The latter's focus on the connections between the Cape and Batavia joined Clare Anderson's *Convicts in the Indian Ocean* in pointing to the relevance of inter-colonial routes of penal transportation – a major shift in the understanding of systems of penal transportation that reinforced the findings of the "new imperial histories".[32] In the third, and present, generation of studies, the

---

28 On the spatial dimension, see Anne Kelly Knowles, Tim Cole, and Alberto Giordano (eds), *Geographies of the Holocaust* (Bloomington, 2014). See also the "Holocaust Geographies Collaborative", available at https://web.stanford.edu/group/spatialhistory/cgi-bin/site/project.php?id=1015, last accessed 4 November 2016.

29 For an overview, see Lynne Viola, "Historicising the Gulag", in: De Vito and Lichtenstein, *Global Convict Labour*, pp. 361–379, 362. For other publications with a particular awareness of spatiality, see Lynne Viola, *The Unknown Gulag. The Lost World of Stalin's Special Settlements* (Oxford, 2007); Steven A. Barnes, *Death and Redemption. The Gulag and the Shaping of Soviet Society* (Princeton, 2011); Alan Barenberg, *Gulag Town, Company Town. Forced Labor and Its Legacy in Vorkuta* (New Haven, CT, 2014).

30 See, especially, the ongoing research by Zhanna Popova as part of the team of the "Four Centuries of Labour Camps" project.

31 For an overview of the first generation of studies, see Ian Duffield and James Bradley (eds), *Representing Convicts. New Perspectives on Convict Forced Labour Migration* (London, 1997). However, isolated but outstanding publications did focus on other contexts: Ruth Pike, *Penal Servitude in Early Modern Spain* (Madison, 1983); Joanna Waley-Cohen, *Exile in Mid-Qing China: Banishment to Xinjiang, 1758–1820* (New Haven and London, 1991).

32 Clare Anderson, *Convicts in the Indian Ocean. Transportation from South Asia to Mauritius, 1815–1853* (Basingstoke, 2000); Timothy J. Coates, *Convicts and Orphans. Forced and State-Sponsored Col-*

geographic scope of the field continues to expand, with ongoing research addressing the Japanese, Spanish, French, German, Habsburg, Danish, Swedish, and Italian empires, and introducing new insights into the Australian, Russian, and Dutch contexts.[33] More generally, the long-term chronological scope (typically from the sixteenth to the twentieth century), the focus on the broad geographies of empire, and the spotlight directed on punitive regimes associated with spatial mobility have arguably placed the scholarship on convict transportation at the forefront of new trends in the history of punishment as a whole. Especially within and around the ongoing project "The Carceral Archipelago", the empirical study of convict transportation has fostered broader thoughts on the entanglements between punishment, mobility, empire- and nation-building, and labour.[34] The persistence of penal transportation in what has traditionally been considered the "age of the triumphant prison" has inspired reflections on the essentially pluralist punitive regimes of the early modern and modern periods. Consequently, the need has emerged to reconceptualize the entanglements between the galleys, the penal colonies, military impressment, re-

---

onizers in the Portuguese Empire, 1550–1755 (Stanford, 2001); Clare Anderson, Legible Bodies. Race, Criminality and Colonialism in South Asia (Oxford and New York, 2004); Kerry Ward, Networks of Empire. Forced Migration in the Dutch East India Company (Cambridge, 2008); Andrew A. Gentes, Exile to Siberia, 1590–1822. Corporeal Commodification and Administrative Systematization in Russia (Houndmills, 2008); Clare Anderson, Subaltern Lives. Biographies of Colonialism in the Indian Ocean World, 1790–1920 (Cambridge, 2012); Miranda F. Spieler, Empire and Underworld. Captivity in French Guiana (Cambridge and London, 2012); Jean-Lucien Sanchez, À perpétuité. Relégués au bagne de Guyane (Paris, 2013); Timothy J. Coates, Convict Labor in the Portuguese Empire, 1740–1932. Redefining the Empire with Forced Labor and New Imperialism (Leiden and Boston, 2014); Timothy J. Coates, "The Long View of Convict Labour in the Portuguese Empire, 1415–1932", in: De Vito and Lichtenstein, Global Convict Labour, pp. 144–167; Matthew P. Fitzpatrick, Purging the Empire. Mass Expulsions in Germany, 1871–1914 (Oxford, 2015). On the new imperial histories see, especially, Alan Lester, "Imperial Circuits and Networks: Geographies of the British Empire", History Compass, 4, 1 (2006), pp. 124–141; Stephen Howe (ed.), The New Imperial Histories Reader (London, 2009).
33 Most outcomes of the present generation of studies have not yet been published. The key forthcoming publication, including chapters on early modern and modern convict transportation in many different contexts, is Clare Anderson (ed.), A Global History of Convicts and Penal Colonies, 1415–1960 (forthcoming). The research that has been published includes Clare Anderson and Hamish Maxwell-Stewart, "Convict Labour and the Western Empires, 1415–1954", in: Robert Aldrich and Kirsten McKenzie (eds), The Routledge History of Western Empires (London and New York, 2013), pp. 102–117; Clare Anderson, "A Global History of Exile in Asia, c. 1700–1900", in: Ronit Ricci (ed.), Exile in Colonial Asia. Kings, Convicts, Commemoration (Honolulu, 2016), pp. 20–47; Stephan Steiner, "'An Austrian Cayenne': Convict Labour and Deportation in the Habsburg Empire of the Early Modern Period", in: De Vito and Lichtenstein, Global Convict Labour, pp. 126–143; Matthias van Rossum, "From Contracts to Labour Camps? Desertion and Control in South Asia", in: Matthias van Rossum and Jeanette Kamp (eds), Desertion in the Early Modern World. A Comparative History (London, 2016), pp. 187–202; Christian G. De Vito, "Convict Labor in the Southern Borderlands of Latin America (ca. 1750s-1910s): Comparative Perspectives", in: van der Linden and Rodríguez García, On Coerced Labor, pp. 98–126.
34 See http://www2.le.ac.uk/departments/history/research/grants/CArchipelago and www.convictvoyages.org, last accessed 4 November 2016. Clare Anderson is the project's principal investigator.

gimes of public works and personal service, the workhouses, the prison, and the camps. The observation of the complex logistics of penal transportation across land and sea, short- and long-distance routes, has led to a perception of the centrality of the relationship between punishment and spatiality (or the spatialities and geographies of punishment) and its necessary substitution for the standard narrative of punishment as immobilization in the penitentiary. On this basis, the double relationship between punishment and empire/state building emerges: on the one hand, the extreme flexibility of punishment vis-à-vis the processes of colonization and sovereignty is foregrounded; on the other, convicts appear as agents of those broad societal processes, together with other free and coerced migrants and workers.

Within this picture, convict labour assumes a new centrality, both as a topic and as an epistemological perspective. Rather than being a remnant of a "backward" past, it claims its role in the definition of a contradictory and conflictual "modernity". Moreover, it proves a vantage point from which multiple punitive and political regimes can be studied in conjunction, at the crossroads of their ideological, social, and economic legitimations. The relevance of these findings is confirmed by their convergence with those of another ongoing project – the "Four Centuries of Labour Camps" project.[35] In addressing the question of labour camp formation by asking "why and under which particular social conditions have forced labour and internment converged over the past four centuries", the researchers on this project have reached a similar awareness of the importance of the intersections and fluidity among institutional contexts within complex punitive and labour geographies.

The road ahead

The four main theories of punishment the twentieth century has passed on to us are all, more or less explicitly, connected with the issue of the relationship between punishment and labour. Thorsten Sellin's *Slavery and the Penal System* (1976) foregrounded the influence of the social institution of chattel slavery on the evolution of penal practices in the Western world, thus generalizing the thesis originally proposed by Gustav Radbruch in 1938, according to which "punishments originally reserved for those in bondage were later inflicted for crimes committed by low-class freemen, and ultimately regardless of their social status".[36] In *The Prison and the Factory* (1977) Dario Melossi and Massimo Pavarini pointed to the close relationship between the origin of the penitentiary and industrial capitalism, building on the broader

---

[35] See https://socialhistory.org/sites/default/files/docs/projects/four_centuries_of_labour_camps.pdf, last accessed 4 November 2016.
[36] Thorsten Sellin, *Slavery and the Penal System* (New York, 1976), citation on p. viii. Gustav Radbruch's article that triggered Sellin's interest in the topic is "Der Ursprung des Strafrechts aus dem Stande der Unfreien", in: Gustav Radbruch, *Elegantiae Juris Criminalis. Sieben Studien zur Geschichte des Strafrechts* (Basel, 1938), pp. 1–11.

claim of the connection between punishment and the labour market put forward by Georg Rusche and Otto Kirchheimer in *Punishment and Social Structure* (1939).[37] Michel Foucault's *Discipline and Punish* (1975) saw the shift away from corporal punishment as the "birth" of a new "disciplinary society". Less specifically focused on labour, and more on the "microphysics of power", this theory nonetheless foregrounded the centrality of the prison as a "laboratory" for broader mechanisms of societal "governmentality" that inevitably include the management of labour.[38] Finally, Norbert Elias's theory on the "civilizing process" that gradually transformed post-medieval European cultural and ethical standards (1939)[39] has been the inspiration for unconvincing histories of growing prisoners' rights, but also, and more interestingly, for Pieter Spierenburg's studies on the early modern workhouses.[40] The latter have pre-dated the "birth of the prison" to the early modern period and showed the centrality of work in the "prison experience".

Recent studies have produced numerous, detailed, and pertinent critiques of these theories, and especially Foucault's, without any doubt the one that has had the most impact on the field.[41] Partly repeating what was already reproached to the French philosopher in the late 1970s, in the last decades scholars have radically questioned his periodization and the idea of the shift from corporal punishment towards the "disciplinary society". Appropriately, as I have showed in the previous section, they have also exposed Foucault's deep Eurocentrism – a decisive critique that can be extended to the other three theories as well. And yet, painstaking deconstructions of received theories have not been followed by new comprehensive theoretical visions. The priority assigned to empirical research and a sometimes prejudicial aversion to theory have prevented that further step being taken. However, new proposals for theoretical syntheses appear vital at this stage in the scholarship, not the least in order to instil some order into the ever-growing and increasingly fragmented field, and to substitute the anti-Foucauldian mantra that now features in many academic

---

37 Melossi and Pavarini, *The Prison and the Factory*. Georg Rusche and Otto Kirchheimer, *Punishment and Social Structure* (New York, 1939).
38 Foucault, *Discipline and Punish*.
39 Norbert Elias, *Über den Prozeß der Zivilisation* (Basel, 1939) [English edition: *The Civilizing Process*, 2 vols (Oxford, 1969 and 1982)].
40 See, especially, Herman Franke, *Twee eeuwen gevangenen. Midsdaad en straf in Nederland* (Utrecht, 1990). For two key works by Pieter Spierenburg, see *The Prison Experience. Disciplinary Institutions and their Inmates in Early Modern Europe* (New Brunswick and London, 1991), and "Prison and Convict Labour in Early Modern Europe", in: De Vito and Lichtenstein, *Global Convict Labour*, pp. 108–125. For the suggestion of the need to further predate the birth of the prison to the middle ages, see Guy Geltner, *The Medieval Prison. A Social History* (Princeton, 2008).
41 For an overview of past and present critiques, see Gibson, "Global Perspectives on the Birth of the Prison", especially pp. 1045–1051. For an exemplary critique of Foucault's paradigm, see David Arnold, "The Colonial Prison: Power, Knowledge and Penology in Nineteenth-Century India", in: idem and David Hardiman (eds), *Subaltern Studies VIII. Essays in Honour of Ranajit Guha* (New Delhi, 1994), pp. 148–194. For a critical engagement with Foucault's theory as part of a renovated, broader framework, see Sherman, "Tensions of Colonial Punishment".

texts with truly refreshing questions and hypotheses. This is an urgent but challenging task, especially considering that the four theories established distinct types of dependence between punishment and society (and labour): indeed, whereas Sellin fundamentally wrote about an *internal* evolution of penal practices starting from the institution of slavery, Melossi and Pavarini and Elias/Spierenburg highlighted the impact of societal changes *on* punishment, and Foucault envisaged punishment (i.e. the prison) as *producing* broader techniques of societal power. Will a new theory of the relationship between punishment and labour prioritize the impact of social processes on punishment, or vice versa? Or will such a theory be able to embrace both aspects at once?

From the perspective of this chapter, the question is whether convict labour can become the basis for this new theory. More specifically, the point is whether a new conceptualization of the relationship between punishment, labour, and society can emerge out of the awareness of the centrality of the connections between punishment, labour, and spatiality that I have described so far. At this stage, a full answer appears beyond reach, but the previous pages of this contribution suggest at least four key characteristics for such a future theory: a truly global scope and the explicit refusal of ethnocentric and methodologically nationalist explanations; the capacity to address plural and complex punitive regimes, rather than prioritize single institutions or specific groups of convicts; the importance of the connected spatiality of punishment and labour; and the understanding of punishment and convict labour as social constructions, at the crossroads of economic, political, social, and cultural processes.

The quest for such a theory is not simply an intellectual exercise to understand the past better. It is an equally necessary task in order to address the contemporary relationship between punishment and labour, especially considering the inadequacy of the most influential explanations. In particular, I contend that the conceptual efforts produced in the last twenty years in order to explain the latest phase of mass incarceration in the Western world present typically Eurocentric, presentist, and determinist biases.[42] Their Eurocentrism is striking, since they exclusively focus on North American and Western European cases and dismiss "the rest". In this way, contemporary mass experiences of coerced work by the inmates of the Chinese, North Korean, and Russian labour camps are entirely removed from the picture, preventing any discussion on the role of convict labour in contemporary coerced labour regimes and "new slavery".[43] Moreover, once the world has again been reduced to

---

[42] See, especially, the works of Loïc Wacquant: *Les prisons de la misère* (Paris, 1999); *Simbiosi mortale. Neoliberalismo e politica penale* (Verona, 2002); *Punishing the Poor. The Neoliberal Government of Social Insecurity* (Durham and London, 2009). See also the works of Alessandro De Giorgi: *Zero tolleranza. Strategie e pratiche della società di controllo* (Rome, 2000); *Il governo dell'eccedenza. Postfordismo e controllo della moltitudine* (Verona, 2002).

[43] For a broader discussion on contemporary coerced labour, see van der Linden and Rodríguez García, *On Coerced Labor*.

"the West", the view is proposed in part of this scholarship that a shift has occurred from the Foucauldian "disciplinary society" to a regime of social control designed to manage the "surplus" of population structurally excluded within the allegedly "post-Fordist" society.[44] All transformations are addressed within a chronological scope of no more than four decades, and in this frame recent changes appear detached from the longer history of convict labour. As a consequence, convict labour is marginalized. Apparently, this mirrors the "lack of work" lamented by many prisoners held in Western penal facilities;[45] however, it simultaneously hampers the possibility to address significant phenomena such as the employment of thousands of (mainly black and Latino) inmates in productive intramural work in US prisons. Indeed, this issue is hardly ever mentioned in this literature. The opposite perspective of a "prison-industrial complex" is more useful in this respect, but no less partial: it has the advantage of making long-term connections with slavery and segregation regimes visible, but by focusing only on that part of the US penal system where convict labour is a central feature it fails to embrace the system as a whole.[46] What is typically missing in both approaches is also a reference to the expanding semi-coerced work performed by individuals on probation or anyway subjected to penal control outside the prisons. Determinism is another striking feature of sociological analyses of contemporary punishment. In these studies, social processes like mass incarceration and the lack or excess of work in penal institutions are seemingly set in motion by anonymous mechanisms, with human agency taking no part in them. At most, abstract private capital and business are mentioned. Convict agency especially is completely ignored.

Against this background, there is much scope and need for a truly global, fully historical, and agency-based perspective on punishment and labour. This requires a closer integration between the debates on contemporary punishment and the historiographical approaches and insights presented in this chapter. Some recent historical studies have shown the potential of such an encounter.[47] Although still exclusively

---

44 Especially in De Giorgi, *Il governo dell'eccedenza*.
45 On contemporary prison labour in Western penal institutions, see Dirk van Zyl Smit and Frieder Dünkel (eds), *Prison Labour: Salvation or Slavery?* (London, 1999); Evelyne Shea, *Le travail pènitentiaire, un défi européen. Etude comparée: France, Angleterre, Allemagne* (Paris, 2006).
46 On the prison-industrial complex, see Angela Davis, "Marked Racism: Reflections on the Prison Industrial Complex", *Colorlines*, 10 September 1998, available at http://www.colorlines.com/articles/masked-racism-reflections-prison-industrial-complex, last accessed 4 November 2016; Heather Ann Thompson, "The Prison Industrial Complex: A Growth Industry in a Shrinking Economy", *New Labor Forum*, 21, 3 (2012), pp. 38–47.
47 For some examples, see Robert Perkinson, *Texas Tough. The Rise of America's Prison Empire* (New York, 2010); Heather Ann Thompson, "Rethinking Working Class Struggle through the Lens of the Carceral State: Toward a Labour History of Inmates and Guards", in: De Vito and Lichtenstein, *Global Convict Labour*, pp. 400–437; Christian G. De Vito, "Processes of Radicalization and De-radicalization in Western European Prisons (1965–1986)", in: Lorenzo Bosi, Chares Demetriou, and Stefan Maltha-

focused on "the West" (but not necessarily Eurocentric), this scholarship presents two significant features. First, it recentres the field around convicts' agency, and makes labour a centrepiece in this endeavour. When focusing on the transnational prisoners' movements of the 1960s and 1970s, for example, it interrogates their role into the history of the exploitation and commodification of prison labour. At the same time, these scholars aim to fully historicize contemporary punitive regimes by contextualizing them in longer-term research including, at least, the whole post-World-War-II period, and in some cases going back to the nineteenth century. In the case of the US punitive practices, for example, this allows one to appreciate the specific and shifting connections between the legacy of slavery and criminal justice across the decades, understand recent mass incarceration "as a response to labour unrest and the search for alternatives beyond the waged labour/capital relationship", and address the most recent movement to decarceration accordingly. By bringing the convicts and history back centre stage, these scholars fully participate in the renewed interest in the relationship between labour and punishment – and convict labour more specifically – which this chapter has foregrounded. Hopefully their contributions, and the wealth of historical knowledge produced in the last few decades around convict labour, will also find their ways to impact the debate on contemporary punishment and labour.

---

ner (eds), *Dynamics of Political Violence: A Process-Oriented Perspective on Radicalization and the Escalation of Political Conflict* (London, 2014), pp. 71–90.

Suggested reading

Anderson, Clare and Hamish Maxwell-Stewart. "Convict Labour and the Western Empires, 1415–1954", in: Robert Aldrich and Kirsten McKenzie (eds), *The Routledge History of Western Empires* (London and New York, 2013), pp. 102–117.
Barenberg, Alan. *Gulag Town, Company Town. Forced Labor and Its Legacy in Vorkuta* (New Haven, CT: Yale University Press, 2014).
Buggeln, Marc. *Slave Labor in Nazi Concentration Camps* (Oxford: Oxford University Press, 2015).
Coates, Timothy J. *Convict Labor in the Portuguese Empire, 1740–1932. Redefining the Empire with Forced Labor and New Imperialism* (Leiden and Boston: Brill, 2014).
De Vito, Christian G. and Alex Lichtenstein (eds). *Global Convict Labour* (Leiden and Boston: Brill, 2015).
Duffield, Ian and James Bradley (eds), *Representing Convicts. New Perspectives on Convict Forced Labour Migration* (London: Leicester University Press, 1997).
Gentes, Andrew A. *Exile to Siberia, 1590–1822. Corporeal Commodification and Administrative Systematization in Russia* (Houndmills: Palgrave Macmillan, 2008).
Gibson, Mary. "Global Perspectives on the Birth of the Prison", *American Historical Review*, 116, 4 (2011), pp. 1040–1063.
Lichtenstein, Alex. *Twice the Work of Free Labor. The Political Economy of Convict Labor in the New South* (London: Verso, 1996).
Mancini, Matthew J. *One Dies, Get Another. Convict Leasing in the American South, 1866–1928* (Columbia: University of South Carolina Press, 1996).
Penn, Nigel. "Towards a History of Convict Labour in the Nineteenth Century Cape", *Workers of the World*, 1, 3 (2013), pp. 118–138.
Perkinson, Robert. *Texas Tough. The Rise of America's Prison Empire* (New York: Metropolitan Books, 2010).
Pike, Ruth. *Penal Servitude in Early Modern Spain* (Madison, WI: University of Wisconsin Press, 1983).
Sellin, Thorsten. *Slavery and the Penal System* (New York: Elsevier Scientific Publishing, 1976).
Van der Linden, Marcel and Magaly Rodríguez García (eds). *On Coerced Labor. Work and Compulsion after Chattel Slavery* (Leiden and Boston: Brill, 2016).
Van Zyl Smit, Dirk and Frieder Dünkel (eds). *Prison Labour: Salvation or Slavery? International Perspectives* (Aldershot: Ashgate, 1999).
Waley-Cohen, Joanna. *Exile in Mid-Qing China. Banishment to Xinjiang, 1758–1820* (New Haven, CT: Yale University Press, 1991).

Rosemarijn Hoefte
4.4. Indentured Labour[1]

Introduction

In legal terms, indentured labour describes "a contract committing one party to make a series of payments to or on behalf of the other – settlement of transport debt, subsistence over the (negotiable) contract term, and final payment in kind or, less usually, cash at the conclusion of the term. In exchange the payee agrees to be completely at the disposal of the payor, or the payor's assigns, for performance of work, for the term agreed."[2] The system of indenture curtailed the freedom and mobility of the workers, who could not easily disengage from the contract when criminal laws reinforced it. Refusal or inability to work, misbehaviour, or other transgressions of disciplinary codes were punishable breaches of contract. In those cases the indentured workers were subject to fines, hard labour, or incarceration.

Indentured labour was widespread in (pre)colonial Asia. Indentured labour also existed as 'White Servitude' in seventeenth and eighteenth-century British and French America, where debt servants, political and religious dissenters, petty criminals etc. were put to work.[3] With the expansion of the sugar plantations, enslaved Africans became the preferred labour force. In the nineteenth century the expanding global sugar market and a shortage of cheap, servile labour revived the system. The abolition of the slave trade and slavery and the subsequent actions by the imperial powers, particularly Great Britain, had enormous worldwide consequences. The "new" indentured system relocated millions of Asians to work under contract on sugar plantations in the Caribbean, Peru, Hawai'i, Réunion, and Mauritius. Asian indentured labourers were also often used in the exploitation of natural resources or in other jobs demanding hard physical labour in new economic activities. Examples of such activities were the exploitation of guano in Peru and rubber production in Southeast Asia, underlining the point that Asian indentured labour was also used in Asia itself. In fact, the overwhelming majority of Asian indentured migrants did not travel outside South and Southeast Asia. Increasing colonial intervention and expansion transformed regional economies, pushing people out, but also creating new Western enclaves of labour intensive production.

---

[1] The present entry is largely based on a longer article: Rosemarijn Hoefte, "Indentured Labor", published in Keith Bradley, Paul Cartledge, David Eltis, and Stanley Engerman (eds), *Cambridge History of World Slavery*, Volume IV (Cambridge and New York: Cambridge University Press, 2017). © Cambridge University Press, reproduced with permission.
[2] Christopher Tomlins, "Reconsidering Indentured Servitude: European Migration and the Early American Labor Force, 1600–1775", *Labor History*, 42, 1 (2001), pp. 5–43, at 6–7.
[3] David Galenson, *White Servitude in Colonial America. An Economic Analysis* (Cambridge, 1981).

Indenture is one of many forms of bound labour, including debt bondage, convict labour, or corvée labour. These forms of labour mobilization merit separate coverage. Here I will only use the term indentured labour and not contract labour as this term may be confused with other forms of labour contracts. The indentured labourers were often called "coolies." The origin of the word "coolie" is unclear; it might be from the Hindi and Telugu *kūlī*' meaning "day labourer", and is probably associated with the Urdu word *ḳulī*' or "slave." In the nineteenth century it became a common European term to characterize an unskilled physical labourer of Asian origin. In some areas, such as South Africa, it even could mean anyone of Asian descent. In this chapter the word will not be used, except in official terminology, because of its association with negative and racist stereotypes.

The British were the pioneers in organizing the nineteenth-century intercontinental system of indenture. After pressurizing other European nations to follow their lead in banning the slave trade, in 1806 the British were the first to ship 200 indentured Chinese to Trinidad for a five-year period of what they euphemistically called "industrial residence". The system really took off in the 1830s, when slavery and apprenticeship came to an end in the British Empire, and the British transported thousands of Indian indentured workers to their colonies in Asia and the Caribbean. Planters argued that only massive, regular imports of malleable labour could save their enterprises. Indian indentured migration thus was closely tied to the expansion of the tropical regions and the abolition of slavery in the Empire.

However, it is misleading to regard indentured servitude as an intermediate stage in a linear process from slavery to free labour. Although indenture often came on the heels of abolition and apprenticeship, and thus at various times throughout the world, it did not always follow slavery. Cuba is an example of a mixed labour system where Chinese indentured labourers were imported before the abolition of slavery, while Hawai'i used contracted indentured labourers without ever resorting to slave labour. Nor did indentured labour preclude the hiring of free labour. Thus free, indentured, and slave labour could exist side by side in the same economic setting.

As was the case with slavery, abolition of indenture took place at different times. The Chinese indentured trade was banned as early as 1874. In India indenture was abolished in 1917, while in Indonesia or the Netherlands East Indies the penal sanction was repealed in 1931, thereby also affecting labour relations with Javanese indentured migrants in the Dutch Caribbean colony of Suriname. That last mentioned indentured labour influx from Indonesia is frequently forgotten, encouraging the mistaken assumption that Indian abolition entailed the end of Asian indentured migration to the Americas.

Despite the fact that both slavery and indentured labour are forms of unfree labour and are often associated with back-breaking work on plantations, it is questionable whether the equation between the two is correct. The main differences are that indentured labourers did not become the legal property of their employers (who were often their owner in the case of slavery) and that there was a time limit to the contracts, which also prescribed the rights and duties of labourers and employers, albeit in Western terms. Indenture was a compulsory labour system, which was safeguarded by so-called penal sanctions, which made neglect of duty or refusal to work a criminal offense. Importantly, the enforcement of contracts, their supervision by authorities, the quality of indentured life in general, and labour conditions in particular, varied across time and space.

Origins, destinations, and recruitment

The nineteenth century saw a global movement of commodities and people, and of the capital required to accomplish this. The growing demand for labour in mineral, industrial, infrastructural, and urban projects and on plantations could only be met since an increasing number of individuals were pushed to migrate because of hardship in their home land and were pulled by the lure of opportunities in places of which they had previously probably never heard. The new indentured labour migration was a product of changing socioeconomic and political realities in the countries of origin, the extant patterns of (bound) labour migration, and the imperial nexus providing the legal and logistical basis (including recruitment and transport) for this type of migration. In short, old and new factors fused in this process, and the mix varied in the different areas of the migrants' origin.

The largest supplier was India, where Great Britain oversaw the recruitment, transport, and overseas labour conditions of more than 1.3 million indentured migrants, 900,000 of whom were transported to British colonies in Asia and the Caribbean. Imperial regulation and control checked the number of abuses, without being able totally to eliminate foul play. Indian indentured migration was directly tied to expansion of capitalist enclaves in the British orbit in the nineteenth century. Indian indentured migration was not a new phenomenon in the nineteenth century as traders and labourers had previously traveled to other parts of Asia or East Africa. The new migrants, however, no longer came from coastal areas but from inland communities.

Recruiting efforts took off when planters from the island of Mauritius (which was British from 1810) turned to Indian labour after the abolition of slavery in 1834. Within five years, more than 25,000 Indians had been transported to Mauritius. Local planters were confident that their business would boom with these migrant labourers who were considered cheaper, more productive, and easier to control than the former slaves. But compulsion of labour trumped all other factors in the choice of workers. The optimism of the Mascarene planters inspired Caribbean planters to recruit Indian labour too.

The first group of Indian workers leaving for the Caribbean was not made to sign a contract before departure, or even on arrival, but soon contracts signed in advance were legalized in all colonies. The terms of indenture also changed: in 1849 Mauritius made the minimum length of the labour contract three years; the Caribbean followed this policy. When some colonies provided a free return passage after completing a minimum of five years under contract, the five-year contract became standard in the Caribbean in 1862. As soon as the system was firmly in place, the number of destinations, including non-British colonies, expanded. Indentured Indian immigration was legalized for Natal and Réunion (1860), the French Caribbean (1865), Suriname (1873), Fiji (1879), and East Africa (1895).

The number of intercontinental indentured migrants was less than 10 percent of the total number of indentured and non-indentured departures from Indian shores. Major Asian destinations such as Ceylon, Burma, and Malaysia attracted millions; annual departures climbed to over 425,000 in the last decades of the century. The seemingly endless supply of Indian migrants was the result of demography and overpopulation, political unrest, economic changes, famine and other natural disasters which set millions on the move looking for work and shelter in the cities, where many would be lost and thus a potential prey for recruiters. Infrastructural changes, including the building of railroads, made easier the movement of people to the cities and also to the depots in the ports. Although it is difficult to pinpoint the exact reasons for migration, emigration data suggest that the Indian Rebellion of 1857 caused a peak in overseas departures.

It is hard to gauge individual motives for signing a contract of indenture, but the army of recruiters played a crucial role in this decision. The actual recruiting was done by the so-called *arkatia* or unlicensed recruiter, who looked for candidates in busy places like markets, railways stations, and temples. The *arkatia*, who received a fee for every recruit, often painted a deceptive picture, promising riches and concealing the long voyage across the *kala pani* (the black water, the crossing of which was a taboo in Indian culture) or the penal system. When successful he handed the candidate over to the licensed recruiter, also an Indian, who took care of the administrative process and forwarded the recruit to the ports of Madras or Calcutta.[4]

Like India, China had a long tradition of labour migration, which took on new dimensions in the nineteenth century. And as in India demographic, socioeconomic, political, and ecological pressures explained the growing willingness to leave. Finally, similarly to India, a majority of the migrants originated from specific sending areas. Historically the southern coastal provinces of Guangdong and Fujian were the areas of recruitment. In the nineteenth century, migrants to Southeast Asia came from Fujian, while Guangdonese dominated the labour trade to the Western hemisphere.

---

4 Principal destinations of Indian labour in the period 1838–1924 were in rounded figures: Ceylon 2,321,000; Malaya 1,754,000; Burma 1,164,000; Mauritius 455,000; British Guiana 239,000; Natal 153,000; Trinidad 150,000 (144,000 indentured); French Caribbean 79,000; Réunion 75,000; Fiji 61,000; East Africa 39,500 (32,000 indentured); Jamaica 38,600 (36,500 indentured); Suriname 34,400; other British Caribbean 11,200. Source: David Northrup, *Indentured Labor in the Age of Imperialism, 1834–1922* (Cambridge, 1995). map 6, p. 53. Note that these are figures for labour migration, not indentured migration. The figures for regional migration to Ceylon, Burma, and Malaya are likely to be inflated by the inclusion of re-migrants (Northrup, *Indentured Labor*, p. 64).

Immediately after the banning of the slave trade in 1807 the British showed interest in Chinese workers with their reputation for stamina and endurance. Yet, after the failed experiment in Trinidad in the early nineteenth century, the next transport of indentured Chinese to overseas European colonies took place only in 1843 when the planters' demand for labour was stronger than racial and legal objections as recruitment was technically illegal under Chinese law. In total, some 2 million Chinese traveled beyond Asian shores, but even this estimate represented only a modest part of total Chinese migration. In contrast to the Indian labour trade, which was largely directed to other parts of the British Empire, Chinese migrants left for a larger number of countries and colonies with different historical, political, legal, and socioeconomic backgrounds, as far apart as the Caribbean and Australia.

In 1847, the first Chinese indentured labourers arrived in Havana, and soon after Peruvian entrepreneurs followed the Cuban example. As elsewhere, coercion, abuse, fraud, and deception about the final destination and the contract were oftentimes used to lure men to sign up. Spanish and local officials contended that in the late 1850s, 90 percent of the indentured migrants boarded ship against their will. Scandals about corruption, kidnapping, and other abuses prompted investigations uncovering even more irregularities in la *trata amarilla* or the yellow trade. The subagents, locally despised as "pig brokers", were seen as the major culprits. Chinese contract migration was depicted as a new slave trade.

Indentured migration from Java started later than in India or China and continued longer. There existed various overlapping systems of recruitment in Java: by informal indigenous networks, commercial agencies, and by employers. As in India and China, overpopulation served as a push factor in Java. And as in the other sending territories Java had a long tradition of labour migration though informal networks. Brokers, who organized pilgrimages to Mecca, also employed professional recruiters to arrange for Javanese temporary labour migration to plantations in Malaya and British North Borneo, and later New Caledonia and French Cochin China. After 1900, two commercial firms were additional players on the recruitment market. Recruitment for Suriname too was in these commercial hands. In total almost 32,000 Javanese indentured migrants left for the West in the period 1890–1932. The flow of migrants to Suriname was exceedingly small compared to the tobacco and rubber plantations in East Sumatra (Deli): Deli in its economically most prosperous years imported annually as many Javanese indentured immigrants as Suriname did in a forty-year period. Around 1910 a third system in the recruitment of Javanese labourers came into operation, when employers started organizing their own recruitment system in Java. This so-called *laukeh* (old hand) system, legalized in 1915, focused its activities on the social network of experienced labour migrants with a good track record.

Japan and the Pacific Islands were places of origin of smaller numbers of indentured migrants. In Japan, the Meiji government's opening of the country from 1868 led to an unprecedented international migration of indentured labourers and free migrants. The main destination was Hawai'i, which saw the arrival between 1868 and

1900 of approximately 65,000 indentured Japanese. Although the United States had banned indentured contracts in 1885, Japanese immigrants were still in bondage as they were in debt, often for brokerage and transport services, to the contracting agencies. When in 1908 the United States restricted Japanese immigration, the flow turned to Peru, which received 18,000 Japanese indentured migrants in total.

Recruitment in the Pacific Islands was known as "blackbirding", indicating the use of force and fraud by private agents. From the 1880s the migration process was monitored by the British administration, which cut out major abuses. The majority of the indentured islanders came from Melanesia. More than 80 percent of the migrants were transported to plantations in Queensland (which alone received more than 60,000), to Fiji, and to the nickel mines in New Caledonia. In Fiji, more than 60,000 Indian indentured migrants, *Girmitiyas*, were imported when competition for Melanesians created a labour shortage and drove up recruitment costs. In the end, indentured Indian labourers vastly outnumbered the imported Pacific Islanders in Fiji.

The emergence of plantations in the western Pacific was fueled by the crumbling of the cotton production in the U.S. South during the Civil War and the abolition of slavery there. Cotton turned out to be a transitional crop, and was overtaken by sugar and copra. The indentured labour trade was closely linked to existing trading networks and maritime labour practices. In contrast to other processes of indenture, the Melanesians did not sign a written contract; their recruitment was based on oral agreement. Another difference was that the labour trade in the western Pacific lacked the infrastructure of other source areas and depended on beach-based exchanges between recruiters and potential candidates.

Despite the large number of migrants to destinations far outside their region of origin the overwhelming majority of the skilled and unskilled Chinese, Indian, and Javanese migrants remained in South and Southeast Asia.[5] Their migration was relatively short distance, often preceded by internal migration to urban areas, caused by the transformation of local and regional economies. Transportation improvements facilitated both types of migration flows.

The contract

The contract of indenture, which minimally listed the name of the labourer, regulated the legal relationship between worker and employer, stipulating a number of obligations for both parties. Its content varied over time, area, and economic branch, but

---

[5] Walton Look Lai, "Asian Diasporas and Tropical Migration in the Age of Empire: A Comparative Overview", in: Walton Look Lai and Tan Chee-Beng (eds), *The Chinese in Latin America and the Caribbean* (Leiden, 2010), pp. 35–63, at 38–39, states that 6.5 million of the 7.5 million Chinese and 5 million of the 6.3 million Indian migrants remained in the region. Only a minority was actually indentured.

the main clauses concerned the length of the contract, working days and hours, and wages. The length of contract varied over time and in different areas and corresponded to the costs of recruitment and transportation. Employers recouped their initial expenses by the work of the indentured. The higher the costs, the longer the contract would run. Chinese labour for Cuba and Peru was the most expensive and eight-year contracts were the standard. Intra-Asian recruitment and transportation costs were the lowest, resulting in contracts of three years or less.

Additional stipulations prescribed that the employer had to provide housing and medical care at his own expense. The worker could not leave the premises of the enterprise without consent. The core of the indenture contract was the penal clause, which subjected the worker to criminal jurisdiction in case of a breach of contract by refusing work or other infractions threatening labour discipline.

Actual surveillance of contracts was in the hands of civil servants who were the backbone of the (colonial) state in both the source and receiving areas. They could play an important role in supervising and checking the system, but they were not always united in their philosophy and operations. Required to keep the economic motors behind the systems in mind, some officials had greater cultural affinity with the Western employers, while others also tried to maintain a certain degree of autonomy in relation to the enterprises. Thus besides official rules and regulations, the size and quality of the controlling bureaucracy and the personal efficacy of civil servants determined the level of inspection and the enforcement of the rules. The policy of these monitoring agencies could also shift over time.

Indian immigrants in non-British territories had the right to claim the assistance of the British consul. Communication with this official should have been free and without restrictions. Indentured labourers could request his help to appeal against the decisions of the highest local authorities. The consul could also report on shortcomings in the living and working conditions of Indians under indenture. In Suriname, planters and colonial officials identified the role of the British consul and the right of appeal as one of the major reasons for the perceived lack of submissiveness of the Indian labour force and a reason for promoting immigration from Java. Indonesian scholars later claimed that some Indians felt superior to Javanese because of the protection they enjoyed of the British consulate.

Although the contract stipulated a fixed wage, the wages actually paid out could lead to conflict as "official" and real wages often differed. According to many arrangements the indentured labourers could be paid on the basis of days or hours worked or the number of tasks completed. Generally, employers preferred to pay for each finished task in order to increase labour productivity. Employers thus defined a task as the work an average labourer could perform in one day. The management argued that they were acting according to the contract. Indentured workers, however, frequently complained that the tasks assigned were too heavy to finish in one day, particularly when weather conditions such as heavy rain made their work even harder. Thus employers and indentured labourers, sometimes supported by colonial officials, differed on what a worker could do in one day. The arbitrary definitions of an "average worker" and "average performance" were the main elements in wage conflicts. In practice wages and thus the capacity of indentured workers to accumulate savings varied enormously, depending on their health and stamina, their experience, the type of work they undertook (with overseers, for example, earning more), or opportunities to gain extra income from other activities. Moreover, to obtain a clear measure of any earnings, income needed to be compared to the local cost of living. In many instances, the price of rice was an important indicator of the actual standard of living of the labourers.

After expiration of their contracts labourers had several options: to sign a new contract, to return home, or to find employment elsewhere. The last option could be restricted as former indentured migrants were explicitly prohibited from working in certain industries to protect the non-immigrant population. Gold mining in Suriname is but one example. Many contracts included free return passage to convince those signing up of the, at least in theory, finality of the agreement. Many factors influenced decisions about whether to return or to stay. They included the formation of family and other relations in the host country, the power of the caste system in the case of Indian migrants, a failure of meeting savings goals, or the irregular sailing of return ships which caused time-expired migrants to incur debts. Distance from the homeland could also play a role in the decision to return. In Cuba and Peru, free return was not part of the contract and the high cost of the voyage made it difficult to return. In contrast, the overwhelming majority of Indian migrants in the Mascarene Islands repatriated. In the late nineteenth century, many Caribbean governments offered former indentured workers plots of land to populate the colony and to further develop smallholding agriculture. Repatriation rates varied through time among ethnic groups and destinations, and according to economic opportunities in places of destination and of origin.

Reception in host societies

Governments and employers determined the conditions of the labour contracts, but the migrants themselves also shaped conditions in their new, possibly temporary, homes. Their places of work were often spatial and social enclaves. Upon arrival most newcomers were allocated to their employers, but in some cases, including Cuba and Peru, slavery-style auctions were common. The arrivals had to adjust to a new environment including different diseases, diet, work rhythm, culture, and social stratification.

Needless to say, circumstances varied by territory, time period, and product. In Peru, for example, the mortality rate among Chinese migrants was exceedingly high, but it is unclear whether this was caused by ill treatment and malnutrition or the encounter with a different disease environment. The organization of production and the profitability of the enterprise had a great impact on labour conditions and levels of wellbeing. A common denominator was a clearly defined hierarchical organization demanding unconditional discipline and obedience. Moreover, language differences increased the sense of alienation of contract workers from their employers. Yet management cultures could vary by economic sectors or even among employers. Another important factor was the macro-economic climate. Rapid economic expansion might lead to increased workloads and mounting tensions, lower health standards, and more crowded housing. It is a matter of debate whether material conditions such as housing, medical care, drinking water and food provisions improved over time. Finally, factors such as age, experience, social relations, and the physical state of migrants influenced how well and how quickly they might adjust.

Specific case studies, whether for particular places, ethnic groups, or economic sectors, reveal little about individual experiences, through there are some indirect indicators. Frustration about the circumstances in which indentured labourers found themselves may have prompted a variety of reactions, ranging from gambling and drug taking to suicide or even to rebellion. Heavy workloads and poor wages were often the main reasons for discontent. Desertion, that is leaving the enterprise without consent, was a clear act of dissatisfaction with prevailing conditions relative to opportunities elsewhere.

Other obvious forms of protest, certainly to the outside world, were personal attacks on supervising staff or mass strikes and rioting. In case of open defiance, the army or police might be used to suppress unrest. Particularly in the late colonial period employers used allegations of anti-colonial agitation as an argument to call in the support of the state to curb unrest on their enterprises, sometimes with perverse consequences for their workers. In Indonesia in the 1920s, the fear of agitation by alleged "outsiders", such as nationalists and communists, led to ever more regressive policies, which did not lead to better treatment of the workers. Where resistance was more covert, involving, for example, feigning sickness or not following orders, the penal sanction gave the employers the right to take recalcitrants to court as such breaches of contract were deemed criminal offences. Open confrontations may have been more eye-catching, but the rates of convictions may have been a clearer indication of resentment. Finally, contemporaries had little awareness of cultural strategies of survival, such as escapism, to accommodate to the new life in an unfamiliar setting.

Though often from different cultural backgrounds, indentured workers moving overseas tried to form communities within the new and often alien world in which they found themselves. Adaptation and sociocultural identity formation often went hand in hand, but uneven sex ratios, and in particular a low ratio of females, sometimes made it more difficult to (re)build communities and to generate a sense of wellbeing and stability. This was especially so among Chinese and Pacific Islanders, making it even harder for them to settle in the host society. The British government ordered that specified quotas of women needed to be recruited, while Caribbean planters stated that they wanted women not for their labour power but to tie the men to the plantations. The status of women within the indenture systems remains, however, debatable. Some have argued that women were at the bottom of a race-class-gender hierarchy, subject to double exploitation by employers and by men from their own group, while others have pointed to the opportunities for women in a society with a shortage of females.

The arrival and settlement of different ethnic groups sometimes caused outbreaks of open racism. The migrants were often seen as intruders taking jobs, weakening the bargaining position of local workers, mainly, in the Caribbean, African freedmen, and thus lowering wages. In particular, Chinese were frequently targeted, both during and after the indenture period, not only because of their ethnic distinctiveness, culture, and language, but also because of their perceived economic success. Not surprisingly, in times of economic crisis migrants were often scapegoats accused of taking jobs at cutthroat wages and undercutting local entrepreneurs. Ethnic tensions may even have harmed development in postcolonial countries such as Guyana or Fiji, where rivalry between descendants of indentured labourers and other population groups continues to provoke discussion about social exclusion, which, in turn, is seen deeply to affect the socioeconomic, cultural, and political functioning of the country. Outcomes vary, however, for whereas twenty-first century Mauritius and Suriname provide examples of non-Asian countries where people of Asian descent form today the majority of the population, in other countries, such as Jamaica or the French Caribbean islands, the presence of indentured migrants has basically "vanished."

The end of indenture

Like the abolition of slavery, the end of indenture did not occur simultaneously in all receiving countries. Moreover, as with slavery, the debate surrounding the end of indenture focused on freedom in general and the concept of free labour in particular. Temporal and geographical factors influenced debates over the meaning of free labour. What was lauded as free labour in one place at a particular time was often labeled as slavery by any other name at other places at the same or different times. The system's abuses fueled the debate. This controversy is still visible in current publications. Proponents stressed and continue to stress that indentured migrants signed a contract out of their own free will, while opponents pointed to deceptive recruitment methods, the penal sanction, and the labour and living conditions in new host societies. Sometimes governments acted on critical reports regarding labour conditions and the legal rights of the indentured workers, but calls for reform were often ignored on account of the socially marginal position or the ethnic background of the indentured migrants. Ultimately, politics with a capital P and new socioeconomic realities made the difference. Hawai'i was the first major receiving country where indentured labour was banned when the U.S. anti-Peonage Act (1867) prohibiting the "voluntary or involuntary servitude" was extended to the newly annexed islands (1898). However, it was in the sending countries where the rising nationalist tides signaled the end of the system. China was the first to act when in the 1870s the country adopted a more assertive policy and first regulated and then suspended the system, even though debt and other forms of involuntary migration to Hawai'i, Natal, and Europe continued to exist.

In 1916 the Indian Viceroy, Lord Hardinge, abolished the indentured trade. Indenture was seen, in Hardinge's words, as "a system of forced labour entailing much misery and degradation and differing but little from a form of slavery." Consequently, he urged "the total abolition of the system of indentured labour" in Fiji, Jamaica, British Guiana, Trinidad, and Suriname.[6] This *volte face* by the British authorities was prompted by increasing nationalist pressure in India. Following Mohandas Gandhi's protests in southern Africa over the precarious legal position of Indians there, indentured labour became a vehicle for highlighting wider forms of discrimination against Indians by the British. During the Great War indentured migration was thus abolished by London in order to save the British Raj.

Other developments leading to the international abolition of indentured labour were socioeconomic in nature. The nineteenth century had witnessed two major, distinct streams of migration: from Europe to temperate settlements and from Asia to (sub)tropical lands. At certain places these streams converged, as for example in Australia and southern Africa. Where at first the European settlers regarded indentured labour as an asset, soon they considered the growing number of non-Europeans as a threat to European rule and jobs. Consequently, by the turn of the twentieth century governments in these settler areas restricted entry of non-Europeans by adopting discriminatory legislation and thereby promoting the interests of people of European descent at the expense of the Asian populations.[7]

In the plantation zones, changing economic circumstances sometimes made bound labour unattractive, either because economic downturns and unemployment militated against continuing recruitment or because in some cases offered wages were high enough to attract non-indentured workers. In Java, both political and economic factors prompted abolition of the "contract coolie" system in Indonesia and Suriname in 1931.

Conclusion

The indentured labour system exhibited temporal, regional, and industrial variations depending, among other things, on the prevailing colonial authority that managed it, production regimes in new host societies, the local labour history, laws and customs

---

[6] Quoted in respectively Northrup, *Indentured Labor*, pp. 144–145, and Hugh Tinker, *A New System of Slavery. The Export of Indian Labour Overseas 1830–1920* (London, 1974), p. 339.
[7] Despite its White Australia policy, this country "continued to import indentured Asian labour for the pearl-shell industry until the early 1970s." Julia Martinez and Adrian Vickers, *The Pearl Frontier. Indonesian Labor and Indigenous Encounters in Australia's Northern Trading Network* (Honolulu, 2015), p. 132.

in both source and host areas, the strength of the entrepreneurial class, the state of demand for workers in host areas, and supervisory structures. Many kinds of arrangements were simultaneously at work in both sending and receiving areas. Studies of the different systems in operation reveal a complex picture with different shades of coercion and freedom and that borders between forms of labour were fluid.

In whatever regime one considers, it was evident that the level of coercion involved was determined from the outset by whether an individual was forced to leave or made his or her own decision to leave. In either case, the role of recruiters was crucial. Those recruiters "fished in two pools." First, they pursued mobile labourers in search of work and who were willing to consider the opportunities of new life elsewhere. Second, recruiters targeted more sedentary people living in villages. Chicanery could be a part of the process encouraging people to leave, and might include providing misleading information about work and contract conditions as well as final destinations, especially if they involved traveling long overseas distances. The costs of recruitment and transport were ultimately reflected in the length of initial contract that migrants signed.

Indentured migrants faced onerous conditions on sugar plantations, a major destination for such migrants and one where employers had often previously been slave owners and working conditions had historically taken a heavy toll on the enslaved. But decades after slavery had ended, working conditions for indentured labourers in new and expanding economic enclaves were arduous too. After an initial period of trial and error in the first half of the nineteenth century, the indentured labour system reached both its historic peak numerically and its greatest diversity in the third quarter of the nineteenth century. Thereafter, the number of indentured migrants slowly declined, notably in the wake of the formal abolition of the system in China and India, but it still survived well into the twentieth century. Its final collapse came in the 1930s with repeal of the penal clause in the Dutch East Indies in 1931, and its subsequent ending in Suriname, the last refuge of indentured labour in the Americas.

The categorization of the revived system of indenture has been debated since its early-nineteenth-century beginnings. It was hailed as free labour based on voluntarily signed contracts, but the fact that in many places it was a direct successor to slavery, with the mental legacy of that system as well as the material remnants such as slave barracks, made it suspect then and now. As with slavery, racism was a cornerstone of the indentured migration system, even though its depth varied across colonial settings and depended on global and local economic conditions influencing how employers, civil servants and other population groups treated "foreign" labourers.

Despite these continuums indentured labour was not an intermediate phase in a teleological development from slavery to free labour. Indentured labour existed in places without a history of slavery and in other settings where enslaved, free, and indentured labourers worked side by side. The way the system was implemented showed clear variations in time and locality, calling for a nuanced approach to indentured migration and labour.

Suggested reading

Alderman, Clifford Lindsey. *Colonists for Sale. The Story of Indentured Servants in America* (New York: Macmillan, 1975).
Allen, Richard B. *Slaves, Freedmen, and Indentured Laborers in Colonial Mauritius* (Cambridge: Cambridge University Press, 1999).
Ballagh, James Curtis. *White Servitude in the Colony of Virginia. A Study of the System of Indentured Labor in the American Colonies* (Baltimore: Johns Hopkins Press, 1895; New York, Johnson Reprint Corp., 1973).
Bhana, Surendra. *Indentured Indian Emigrants to Natal, 1860–1902. A Study Based on Ships' Lists* (New Delhi: Promilla & Co., 1991).
Carter, Marina. *Servants, Sirdars, and Settlers. Indians in Mauritius, 1834–1874* (Delhi: Oxford University Press, 1995).
Christopher, Emma, Cassandra Pybus and Marcus Rediker (eds). *Many Middle Passages. Forced Migration and the Making of the Modern World* (Berkeley, CA: University of California Press, 2007).
Clarke, Colin, Ceri Peach and Steven Vertovec (eds). *South Asians Overseas. Migration and Ethnicity* (Cambridge: Cambridge University Press, 2009 [originally 1990]).
Drescher, Seymour. *The Mighty Experiment. Free Labor versus Slavery in British Emancipation* (Oxford: Oxford University Press, 2002).
Eltis, David (ed.). *Coerced and Free Migration. Global Perspectives* (Stanford, CA: Stanford University Press, 2002).
Emmer, P. C. (ed.). *Colonialism and Migration. Indentured Labour before and after Slavery* (Dordrecht: Martinus Nijhoff, 1986).
Galenson, David. *White Servitude in Colonial America. An Economic Analysis* (Cambridge: Cambridge University Press, 1981).
Green, William A. *British Slave Emancipation. The Sugar Colonies and the Great Experiment 1830–1865.* (Oxford: Oxford University Press, 1976).
Hoefte, Rosemarijn, *In Place of Slavery. A Social History of British Indian and Javanese Laborers in Suriname.* (Gainesville: University Press of Florida, 1998).
Houben, Vincent et al. *Coolie Labour in Colonial Indonesia. A Study of Labour Relations in the Outer Islands, c. 1900–1940* (Wiesbaden: Harrassowitz, 1999).
Kale, Madhavi. *Fragments of Empire. Capital, Slavery, and Indian Indentured Labor Migration in the British Caribbean* (Philadelphia: University of Pennsylvania Press, 1998).
Laurence, K. O. *A Question of Labour. Indentured Immigration into Trinidad and British Guiana 1875–1917* (New York: St. Martin's Press and Kingston: Ian Randle Press, 1994).
Laurence, K. O. *Immigration into the West Indies in the 19th century* (Barbados: Caribbean Universities Press, 1971).
Look Lai, Walton. *Indentured Labor, Caribbean Sugar. Chinese and Indian Migrants to the British West Indies, 1838–1918* (Baltimore: Johns Hopkins University Press, 1993).
Look Lai, Walton and Tan Chee-Beng, (eds). *The Chinese in Latin America and the Caribbean* (Leiden and Boston: Brill 2010).
Marks, Shula and Peter Richardson (eds). *International Labour Migration, Historical Perspectives* (Hounslow, Middlesex: M. Temple Smith, 1984).
McNeill, James and Chimman Lal. *Report on the Condition of Indian Immigrants in the Four British Colonies Trinidad, British Guiana or Demerara, Jamaica and Fiji, and in the Dutch Colony of Surinam or Dutch Guiana.* (London: His Majesty's Stationary Office, 1915).
Northrup, David. *Indentured Labor in the Age of Imperialism, 1834–1922* (Cambridge: Cambridge University Press, 1995).

Palmer, Colin A. (eds). *Worlds of Unfree Labour. From Indentured Servitude to Slavery* (Aldershot and Brookfield, VT: Ashgate/Variorum, 1998).

Prasad, Shiu. *Indian Indentured Workers in Fiji* (Suva: South Pacific Social Sciences Association, 1974).

Saunders, Kay. *Workers in Bondage. The Origins and Bases of Unfree Labour in Queensland, 1824–1916* (St. Lucia: University of Queensland Press, 1982).

Schuler, Monica. *"Alas, Alas, Kongo". A Social History of Indentured African Immigration into Jamaica, 1841–1865* (Baltimore: Johns Hopkins University Press, 1980).

Shepherd, Verene. *Transients to Settlers. The Experience of Indians in Jamaica, 1845–1950* (Leeds: Peepal Tree/University of Warwick, 1994).

Shineberg, Dorothy. *People Trade. Pacific Island Laborers and New Caledonia, 1865–1930* (Honolulu: University of Hawai'i Press, 1999).

Steinfeld, Robert J. *Invention of Free Labor. The Employment Relation in English and American Law and Culture, 1350–1870* (Chapel Hill, NC: University of North Carolina Press, 1991).

Tinker, Hugh. *A New System of Slavery. The Export of Indian Labour Overseas 1830–1920* (London: Oxford University Press, 1974).

Patrick Manning
4.5. Slave Labour

This essay reviews the literature on the slave-labour dimension of slavery since 1500. I seek to emphasize slavery as labour history, in an effort to make it directly comparable to wage labour and other dimensions of labour history—rather than consider the full range of the historiography of slavery. Inevitably, however, some broader consideration of slavery as a social institution and historical process will enter the discussion. That is, the literature on the labour history of slavery is encompassed within a larger and more general literature that mixes the labours of the enslaved with studies of the institutional structures of slavery, the recruitment of slaves, the social and cultural history of slaves, and the individual and collective campaigns for emancipation. To clarify the literature on the labour history of slavery in the overall context of slavery studies, this essay begins with an introductory characterization of the literature on slavery and continues with sections discussing the debates over slave labour within four periods of historical writing.

The topics and debates in historical writing on slavery and slave labour differed substantially from period to period, as a result of changes in the global regime of slavery and also in response to more general shifts in the socio-economic order. In each temporal section I begin with comments on the political economy of slavery and labour, then discuss specific contributions and debates in the literature published in that period. Since slavery is based on social conflict and oppression, the interpretation of slavery in each period highlighted differences between those who saw slavery as a natural, minimal, or negligible element of the social order to those who saw slavery as a focus of oppression, exploitation, and social transformation. (1) In the era of imperial slavery, from 1500 to 1800, enslavement expanded steadily and came to be reformulated in increasingly racial terms, but was rarely challenged at the level of literate society. In this era, debates focused especially on who was subject to enslavement; only at the end of this period did objections to slavery itself became prominent. (2) In the era of emancipation within colonialism, from 1800 up to 1950, debates and struggles over slavery became central social issues. Enslavement expanded and spread to new regions, but a great movement of emancipation challenged the institution of slavery and brought its downfall progressively in Europe, the Americas, Asia, and Africa. In this era, the proponents of slavery argued for its profitability and indeed for its social necessity but also for the inferior character and value of those enslaved, while opponents of slavery claimed it to be immoral; in latter parts of this period, voices from enslaved communities began to be heard. (3) In the post-colonial era, from 1950 to 1990, powerful processes of decolonization and anti-racism brought an outpouring of studies on past slavery. In this period, dominated by rejection and critique of the role of slavery in individual societies, some researchers documented slavery and condemned its effects on slaves and society generally; others argued that slavery, while lamentable, had few seriously negative effects. (4) In the years after 1990, slave labour came to be studied in global context, as the increasingly global conceptualization of history brought reinterpretations of slavery as a significant factor in global social transformation. After 1990, some researchers treated slavery as a global system of forced labour, while others preferred to treat slavery region by region; in this period, slave labour began to be integrated into labour history more broadly.

Where does the study of slave labour fit into the larger discourse on labour history? Certainly slave labour must fit as an important dimension of labour in general, but three obstacles tend to restrict the ease of integrating slave labour with wage labour and all the other forms of labour. The three obstacles are the neglect of slavery in studies of labour history, the neglect of labour in the literature on slavery, and the isolated, national frameworks of analysis in both labour history and slavery studies, Thus, the early studies of labour history in the nineteenth century narrated and celebrated the industrial proletariat and its organizations, leaving slavery in the margin except as a metaphorical alternative to wage labour. Only gradually did slave labour enter into the purview of labour history.[1] Scholars still need to clarify the significance of the apparent fact that the number of labourers held in slavery appears to have exceeded the number of wage labourers until slavery itself contracted in the later nineteenth century.[2] Second, within the extensive though widely scattered literature on the history of slavery, labour history forms a relatively small part of the totality. That is, the literature on slavery focuses not so much on the labour of the enslaved as on the institutions and practices of slave control, the social conditions of slave life, the recruitment of slave labour through slave trade, and the escapes and rebellions of the enslaved. While the literature on wage rates for free labour is huge, the equivalent literature on slave prices (and on the wage earnings or rental of slaves) is small by comparison. Occupational structures are described in far greater detail for wage labour than for slave labour. In these ways, the literature on slavery is deficient in its coverage of key issues in labour history. In other ways, the literature on slavery documents important questions in labour history. For instance, workplace, home, and family are considered at once within slavery, while workplace is commonly separated from home and family in studies of wage workers. Thirdly, the narrow, national perspective of both labour history and slavery studies minimized the possibility of tracing the interplay of slave and free labour in the productive system as a whole. Isolated European studies of industrialization, paralleled by isolated studies on Caribbean plantations, led to neglect of the flows of labour, raw materials, finished goods, and capital from place to place. The "methodological nationalism" of both la-

---

[1] Marcel van der Linden, *Workers of the World. Essays Toward a Global Labour History* (Leiden and Boston, 2008).
[2] To my knowledge, there has been no serious effort to compare the relative size of slave-labour and wage-labour work forces at national, continental, or global levels. I assume that the slave-labour work force, especially as it expanded from the 16th into the 19th centuries, greatly exceeded the wage-labour workforce until late in the nineteenth century.

bour history and slavery studies slowed the incorporation of slave labour into the historiography of labour.

For each chronological section of the chapter, a brief opening narrative describes the contemporary social conditions in which the literature on slavery and slave labour was produced. Then follows the literature published in that period, largely in chronological order, but also with regard to several main topics. First of these is the Interpretive approach of works on slavery—whether they express opposition to or support for slavery; whether they see slavery as a significant or marginal factor in economic and social history. Second is the work and labour conditions of people in slave status—the principal objective of this chapter (but as will be seen, this dimension of the literature only becomes prominent in the twentieth century). Third is the other aspects of the social history of slavery, including the recruitment and socialization of slaves, family and community life, institutional structures of slavery, and the individual and collective campaigns for emancipation.

The imperial and colonial era, 1500 to 1800

A great shift in global relations took place in the fifteenth and sixteenth centuries with the European-led expansion in trans-oceanic voyaging: commercial relations and migration became truly global. Within the global economy, Europeans led in spreading enslavement from its Eurasian core to all the shores of the Atlantic and Indian Oceans, accumulating wealth and power as slavery encroached on island and mainland terrains. Some slaves escaped to upward mobility, joining peasant or commodity exchange sectors; more fell under expanding techniques of oppression, and some were forced into industrial-scale production.

Of the debates on enslavement that arose with the European expansion of colonization, the best known is that over the status of Amerindians within the Spanish empire. In a formal debate at Valladolid in Spain, organized by King Charles V in 1550–1551, Bartolomé de las Casas argued that Amerindians were fully capable of reason, were qualified to become full Christians, and should not be enslaved. Juan Gines de Sepulveda argued that Amerindians fit Aristotle's category of barbarians and were natural slaves.[3] In the succeeding years, Amerindians were rarely enslaved; they could be Christians but could not enter the priesthood. Nevertheless, Africans were enslaved throughout the Spanish empire, while both Amerindians and Africans were commonly enslaved in Portuguese Brazil.

When the West Indian system of plantation slavery became fully established in the eighteenth century, supporters and opponents of slavery made their respective

---

[3] Las Casas (1484–1566) wrote his *Historia de las Indias* in the years after the debate; it was published posthumously in 1575. Bartolomé de las Casas, *Historia de las Indias. Selections* (New York, 2012); Juan Ginés de Sepúlveda, *Tratado sobre las Justas Causas de la Guerra contra los Indios* (Mexico: Fondo de Cultura Económica, 1941).

cases. In France, l'abbé Raynal led in preparation of a 4-volume *Philosophical and Political History of the Two Indies* (1770) that was sharply critical of the colonial order and the exploitation of slaves. Four years later, the Jamaican planter Edward Long published a 3-volume *History of Jamaica* (1774) including great detail on slave life and strong support for the subordination of Africans in slave status; Moreau de Saint-Méry wrote a parallel interpretation and defense of slavery for French St. Domingue that appeared just before the Haitian revolution.[4] The Society for Effecting the Abolition of the Slave Trade, founded in London in 1787, immediately commissioned a medallion, produced by ceramicist Josiah Wedgwood, of a black man on bended knee with the caption, "Am I not a Man and a Brother?" This direct challenge to the institution of slavery was succeeded, in 1789, by an image inspired by Thomas Clarkson that showed the placement of some 400 captives in the slave ship *Brookes*. The Society chose to focus on slave trade rather than slavery: its persistent campaign led to British abolition of slave trade in 1807.[5]

Colonialism and emancipation, 1800 to 1950

The nineteenth century brought further industrialization of slavery, especially in Cuba, the United States, and Brazil. At the same time, slavery expanded in Africa and Asia, as new elites sought to build empires and nations, amassing great numbers of slaves. Where slavery was best established, a powerful movement for emancipation arose: in the early stages, fuelled by the self-liberatory efforts of the slaves and by the plan to turn ex-slaves into an industrial wage-labour force. In Africa and Asia at a later stage, the emancipation campaign was directed from Europe against the new elites, to limit their control of labour. Under colonialism, slave labourers worked under two sets of masters: new-elite rulers and colonial overlords. Communities of freed workers carried out impressive campaigns of economic and cultural renewal on every continent, but had to contend with a new oppressive force, explicit racism and social segregation.

Debates over slavery and emancipation raged until Atlantic emancipation had largely succeeded. As the campaign for emancipation moved to Africa and Asia, the writings of David Livingstone, missionary and traveller, came to symbolize the persistence of enslavement in Africa.[6] Near the end of the nineteenth century, one

---

[4] L'Abbé Guillaume-Thomas Raynal, *L'Histoire philosophique et politique des établissements et du commerce des Européens dans les deux Indes*, 4 vols (Amsterdam, 1770); Edward Long, *History of Jamaica*, 3 vols (London, 1774); Médéric Louis Elie Moreau de Saint-Méry, *Déscription topographique et politique de la partie française de Saint-Domingue* (Philadelphia, 1789).
[5] Thomas Clarkson, *An Essay on the Impolicy of the African Slave Trade* (London, 1788).
[6] Thomas Fowell Buxton, *The African Slave Trade and its Remedy* (London, 1840); David Livingstone, *The Last Journals of David Livingstone in Central Africa*, 2 vols. Edited by Horace Waller (London, 1974).

of the first academic studies of slavery appeared, by W. E. B Du Bois on the suppression of slave trade to the United States.[7] Social scientists, often self-trained, began at the same time to write about slavery in region after region. A remarkable such volume was Herman J. Nieboer's *Slavery as an Industrial System* (1900), which described institutions of slavery and their economic role, especially in societies of the Dutch East Indies—though, surprisingly, it made no reference to the history and practice of enslavement by Dutch owners. In Cuba, shortly after its independence from Spain (though under United States hegemony), Fernando Ortiz Fernández wrote the first two of what would be a substantial list of works on black people, slavery, and plantation life in Cuba.[8] In the United States, where Civil War and Reconstruction had been followed by a period of intimidating racism under Jim Crow laws, Ulrich B. Phillips wrote histories of American antebellum slavery (after the abolition of overseas slave trade) that emphasized the paternalism of the owners.[9]

In the interwar years, critical studies of slavery and slave trade appeared in growing numbers. Lowell Ragatz, in the United States, published several volumes on history of the British West Indies, mostly notably on the downfall of the planter class. Gaston Martin's study of the slave trade of Nantes initiated what became a substantial number of studies of European slave-trade ports.[10] Two larger-scale studies brought forth great quantities of documentation on slave trade and enslavement in the United States. Elizabeth Donnan edited four volumes of documents on slave trade, published by the Carnegie Institution of Washington; the Federal Writers' Project, an institution of the Roosevent-era New Deal, conducted and published hundreds of interviews in the 1930s with ex-slaves in which they recalled slavery as they had known it seventy years earlier.[11] Large-scale studies by individual authors included Gilberto Freyre's study of plantations and slave life in Brazil and W. E. B. Du Bois's *Black Reconstruction*, an analysis of the agency of African Americans in the era of the American Civil War and especially of the Reconstruction Era, 1865–1877. In the same period, as the world suffered from a serious economic depression, the Trinida-

---

[7] W.E.B Du Bois, *The Suppression of the African Slave-Trade to the United States of America, 1638–1870* (New York, 1896).

[8] Fernando Ortiz Fernández, *Hampa afro-cubana. Los negros brujos* (Madrid, 1906); *Hampa afro-cubana. Los negros esclavos* (Havana, 1916).

[9] U. B. Phillips, *American Negro Slavery* (New York, 1918); and Phillips, *Life and Labor in the Old South* (Boston, 1929).

[10] Lowell J. Ragatz, *The Fall of the Planter Class in the British Caribbean, 1763–1833* (New York, 1928); Gaston Martin, *Nantes au XVIIIe siècle. L'ère des négriers (1717–1774)* (Paris, 1931).

[11] Elizabeth Donnan, *Documents Illustrative of the History of the Slave Trade to America*, 4 vols (Washington, DC, 1930–1935); Federal Writers' Project, *Slave Narratives. A Folk History of Slavery in the United States, from Interviews with Former Slaves*, 17 vols in 33 parts (Washington, DC, 1936–1938).

dian scholar C. L. R. James published his study of slave rebellion, the overthrow of slavery, and the establishment of an independent state.[12]

New debates on slave society developed as the literature became more sophisticated. E. Franklin Frazier, a leading sociologist, argued that the family and cultural patterns of African Americans in the American South arose entirely from the experience of plantation slavery. In contrast, anthropologist Melville J. Herskovits, whose research extended to West Africa and the Caribbean, argued that African American families maintained many cultural survivals from Africa, even if they had been attenuated by the influence of European-based society. In a work published during World War II, Eric Williams advanced the historical theses that slavery had provided profits essential to the expansion of British industrial production and that the expansion of wage labour in industry encouraged British industrialists to press for the abolition of slavery. Frank Tannenbaum, concisely comparing slavery throughout the Americas, concluded that slavery was most severe in the United States, as indicated especially by the rate of manumission.[13] Each of these theses was to be debated for years.

Critical views in the post-colonial era, 1950–1990

Defeat of the race-based campaigns of the Axis powers in World War II brought a general reaction against racial categorization that fuelled decolonization in Asia, Africa, and the Caribbean, as well as the parallel Civil Rights movement in the United States. Most Asian countries had gained independence by 1950 (Malaya and Vietnam were exceptions). Independence for sub-Saharan Africa began with Sudan in 1955 and Ghana in 1957. Decolonization brought forceful critique of the colonial era, focusing on its heritage of slavery and slave labour. For descendants of slaves under racially white direct hegemony, this was a campaign of democratization. In the new nations, decolonization opened contending social and ideological social movements for democratization by descendants of slaves and peasants, but also efforts by the surviving elites from the nineteenth century to rebound and seek hierarchical control.

The atmosphere of decolonization fuelled the preparation of numerous works on slavery and slave trade. In an extensive study, Charles Verlinden analysed medieval slavery, with particular concentration on the steady extension of slave-produced

---

12 Du Bois's interpretation included treating the response of black communities during the Civil War as a "general strike". Gilberto Freyre, *Casa Grande e Senzala* (Rio de Janeiro, 1933); Du Bois, *Black Reconstruction* (New York, 1935); C. L. R. James, *The Black Jacobins. Toussaint L'Ouverture and the San Domingo Revolution* (New York, 1963).
13 E. Franklin Frazier, *The Negro Family in the United States* (Chicago, 1939); Melville J. Herskovits, *The Myth of the Negro Past* (New York, 1941); Eric Williams, *Capitalism and Slavery* (Chapel Hill, NC, 1944); Frank Tannenbaum, *Slave and Citizen. The Negro in the Americas* (New York, 1946).

sugar on islands of the Mediterranean from Cyprus in the east to the Balearic islands in the west, and to the Atlantic islands and the coast of Morocco. M. I. Finley, a distinguished scholar on the classical Mediterranean, turned to study of ancient slavery, publishing the first of several books in 1960.[14] Mauricio Goulart published a book on African slavery in Brazil and, in the first book on slave trade for a North American audience since that of Du Bois, Daniel Mannix and Malcolm Cowley published *Black Cargoes* in 1962, gaining wide attention in a country where a social movement for civil rights had become powerful.[15] As this movement gained strength, more and more studies of U.S. slavery appeared. Kenneth Stampp's study of "the peculiar institution" challenged the justification of slavery by U. B. Phillips; Stanley Elkins drew on imagery from World War II and concentration camps to describe the character and impact of enslavement; and John Blassingame emphasized the perspective from within the slave community.[16]

The expanding fields of labour history and social history soon brought echoes in the study of slavery. Edward P. Thompson's *The Making of the English Working Class* (1963) – radical working-class history, drawing on Marxism, post-war concern for workers' welfare, and drawing attention to the agency of common people in construction of their own future – inspired a generation of historians to apply this vision of the past. Thompson's eclectic analysis was soon followed by more formal analysis of modes of production, which included attention to slavery. Through both of these approaches to work, parallels in the experience of slavery throughout the Atlantic became increasingly apparent. In cautious response, other scholars sought to explore slavery yet minimize its significance as a factor in modern history. In a mix of outlooks, David Brion Davis reached from North America across the Atlantic to consider slavery as an intellectual problem in Western culture, tracing the evolution of abolitionist thought.[17]

A recurring dimension of the study of slavery was that scholars who took up the study of slavery with an ideological predisposition to minimizing its significance nevertheless launched empirical studies that greatly expanded the understanding of slavery's significance. Philip Curtin, a historian of Africa, drew on secondary literature and demographic analysis to propose in 1969 a new total—roughly 10 million persons—for the number transported across the Atlantic in slavery.[18] Curtin's figure

---

14 Charles Verlinden, *L'Esclavage dans l'Europe médiévale*, 2 vols (Bruges, 1955); M.I. Finley, *Slavery in Classical Antiquity. Views and Controversies* (Cambridge, 1960).
15 Mauricio Goulart, *Escravidão africana no Brasil* (São Paulo, 1950); Daniel P. Mannix and Malcolm Cowley, *Black Cargoes. A History of the Atlantic Slave Trade, 1518–1862* (New York, 1962).
16 Kenneth M. Stampp, *The Peculiar Institution. Slavery in the Ante-bellum South* (New York, 1956); Stanley M. Elkins, *Slavery: A Problem in American Institutional and Intellectual Life* (Chicago, 1968); John W. Blassingame, *The Slave Community. Plantation Life in the Antebellum South* (New York, 1972).
17 David Brion Davis, *The Problem of Slavery in Western Culture* (Ithaca, NY, 1966); Davis, *The Problem of Slavery in the Age of Revolution, 1770–1823* (Ithaca, NY, 1975); and other works.
18 Philip D. Curtin, *The Atlantic Slave Trade: A Census* (Madison, WI, 1969).

was lower than some previous speculations, and it has since been increased by further research. In one sense, this result served to diminish claims of imperial exploitation of Africans, and it brought critical opposition from some scholars. In another sense, it opened the door to a generation of detailed archival research and analysis, with the result that the various national literatures were brought into contact; more slowly, research on Africa and the Americas were brought into contact. John Fage responded immediately to Curtin's estimates by using them to project the effects of slave trade on the population of West Africa, concluding that the loss of slaves may have done "no more than cream-off surplus population" of Africa.[19] Fage's argument established a minimalist orthodoxy that remained little challenged for some time.

Economic theorization, developing on various topics, now entered the analysis of slavery, mostly with minimalist approach, suggesting that the economy was controlled from the top and that the lower social strata were invisible and without agency. Eugene Genovese expanded Marxian analysis into the history of U.S. slavery with his 1967 *Political Economy of Slavery*. Genovese's later works continued his class analysis of slavery, but they also emphasized paternalism in the slave regime in a way that reflected the earlier work of U.B. Phillips.[20] Evsey Domar, proposed a 1970 model explaining the presence and absence of slavery in terms of the relative scarcity of land and labour.[21] In a 1974 follow-up, Henry Gemery and Jan Hogendorn drew on Hla Myint's vent-for-surplus model for agricultural exports to propose a vent-for-surplus model for export of African population. This era of minimization of the significance of slavery and slave trade included reconsideration of the theses of Eric Williams' theses. Stanley Engerman argued that the profits of British West Indian slavery were too small to have financed the expansion of the British textile industry.[22] The greatest debate over slavery came with the publication of *Time on the Cross*, an eco-

---

[19] John D. Fage, "The Effect of the Export Slave Trade on African Populations", in: R. P. Moss and R.J.A. Rathbone (eds), *The Population Factor in African Studies* (London, 1975), p. 20.

[20] Eugene Genovese, *Political Economy of Slavery* (New York, 1965); Genovese, *Roll, Jordan, Roll. The World the Slaves Made* (New York, 1974). Genovese also edited a volume of essays by U. B. Phillips: Genovese (ed.), *The Slave Economy of the Old South* (Baton Rouge, 1968). Ultimately Genovese renounced his radical views and became an ideological conservative.

[21] Domar drew on the Russian historian and analyst of serfdom, Vassilii Kliuchevsky, and paralleled the analysis of Nieboer. Evsey Domar, "The Causes of Slavery or Serfdom: A Hypothesis" *Economic History Review*, 30, 1 (March 1970), pp. 18–32; Henry A. Gemery and Jan S. Hogendorn, "The Atlantic Slave Trade: A Tentative Economic Model" *Journal of African History*, 15 (1974), pp. 223–246.

[22] Stanley L. Engerman, "The Slave Trade and British Capital Formation in the Eighteenth Century: A Comment on the Williams Thesis", *Business History Review*, 46, 4 (Winter 1972), pp. 430–443. This discussion went on for more than another decade, including a critical response to Engerman by Ronald Bailey and a co-edited volume by Barbara Solow and Stanley Engerman in which the criticism of Williams was greatly muted. Ronald W. Bailey, "Africa, the Slave Trade, and the Rise of Industrial Capitalism in Europe and the United States: A Historiographical Review", *American History: A Bibliographical Review*, 2 (1986), pp. 1–91; Barbara L. Solow and Stanley L. Engerman (eds), *British Capitalism and Caribbean Slavery. The Legacy of Eric Williams* (Cambridge, 1987).

nomic-historical analysis of slavery in the American South that emphasized both the profitability and the viability of slavery as a system of production, and also emphasized how the enslaved were able to sustain themselves as a community and grow in population. Among the many critical responses, the best known is that of Herbert G. Gutman, whose *Slavery and the Numbers Game* focused with particular emphasis on estimates of the number of beatings received by slaves.[23]

Research on slavery and slave trade outside the United States continued, largely along a separate track—it was still to be some time before the various segments of the literature on slavery became well connected. Robert Conrad wrote another sort of narrative on anti-slavery, this one on the campaign against Brazilian slavery up to 1888: this work made clear the parallel of two great slave migrations: the movement of U.S. slaves from tobacco along the Atlantic to cotton in the Deep South, and the movement of Brazilian slaves from sugar in the Northeast to coffee in São Paulo. Walter Rodney, a Guyanese historian of Africa trained in Britain, published his critical narrative, *How Europe Underdeveloped Africa*, in 1972, expanding on earlier work arguing that Portuguese enslavement had brought decay to the society of Upper Guinea.[24] In an effective use of official documents, B. W. Higman wrote two books on slave population and economy in the British West Indies. Higman relied on the detailed annual reports on the number and characteristics of slaves, 1808–1834, intended to ensure that no additional people were brought in slavery to British Caribbean colonies.[25]

Anthropological studies of Africa led in contending directions. Claude Meillassoux's edited volume on led Francophone West Africa analysed slavery in terms of political economy and the conflicts among social strata. Suzanne Miers and Igor Kopytoff led a collection which, relying especially on U.S.-based scholars and addressing many regions of Africa, gave a somewhat romanticized image of African slavery by de-emphasizing hierarchy but underscoring the varieties, specificities, and protections within African slavery.[26] Part of the difference in approach between these volumes was in the period targeted. Chapters in the Meillassoux volume focused on the precolonial era in which a brutal slave trade was still active; chapters in the Miers and Kopytoff drew mostly on evidence from early colonial years (generally after 1890)—in these cases, raiding and other forms of enslavement were no longer permit-

---

23 Fogel won the Nobel Memorial Prize in Economic Sciences, especially for this work, in 1993. Robert William Fogel and Stanley L. Engerman, *Time on the Cross. The Economics of American Negro Slavery*, with supplementary volume (Boston, 1974); Herbert G. Gutman, *Slavery and the Numbers Game. A Critique of Time on the Cross* (Urbana, IL, 1975).
24 Robert Conrad, *The Destruction of Brazilian Slavery* (Berkeley, CA, 1972), pp. 47–69; Walter Rodney, *How Europe Underdeveloped Africa* (Kingston, Jamaica, 1972).
25 B. W. Higman, *Slave Population and Economy in Jamaica, 1807–1834* (Cambridge, 1976); Higman, *Slave Population in the British West Indies, 1807–1834* (Baltimore, 1984).
26 Claude Meillassoux, ed., *Esclavage en Afrique précoloniale* (Paris: F. Maspéro, 1975); Suzanne Miers and Igor Kopytoff, (eds), *Slavery in Africa: Historical and Anthropological Perspectives* (Madison: University of Wisconsin Press, 1977).

ted, and the maintenance of slavery required masters to treat slaves, especially women and children, so as to preserve their lives since they could not easily be replaced.

By the late 1970s, the public debate on slavery, civil rights, and decolonization had died down considerably, but the institutional basis for studies of slavery had expanded considerably: university appointments in history of Africa and the Caribbean expanded in the Americas, Europe, and Africa; university programs in Black Studies and Ethnic Studies expanded, especially in North America. The parallels among area-studies disciplines clarified, creating links among African, Latin American, and Asian studies. In this era, Ann Pescatello wrote a substantial essay on Africans in Portuguese India; though the research agenda she proposed in that essay was pursued only after a substantial delay. James Warren launched study of nineteenth-century slavery in the islands of the Indonesian and Philippine archipelagos; James Watson edited a 1980 book that allowed comparison of systems of slavery in Asia and Africa.[27] On African slavery, Frederick Cooper analysed plantation slavery on the east coast of Africa, where nineteenth-century production focused on cloves and grains. Joseph Inikori's study of firearms in West Africa documented the positive correlation between the import of firearms and the export of captives.[28] Substantial studies of African slave prices appeared in the 1970s, though studies of African slave prices declined in quantity thereafter.[29]

From the 1980s, the pace of publication on the history of slavery slowed somewhat, while the studies that appeared offered summations and new perspectives. Patrick Manning's 1981 model of slavery showed relationships among population sizes and sex ratios in a demographic system linking Africa and overseas regions: mostly males in the Americas, mostly females in Africa and Asia, and in each case shifts in marital relations and sexual division of labour. Christian limits on cross-racial marriage meant that distinct black populations persisted in the Americas, while Islamic patterns of intermarriage led to steady incorporation of slaves into host pop-

---

[27] Ann M. Pescatello, "The African Presence in Portuguese India", *Journal of Asian History* 11 (1977), pp. 26–48; Indrani Chatterjee and Richard M. Eaton, (eds), *Slavery and South Asian history* (Bloomington: Indiana University Press, 2006). James F. Warren, "Slave Markets and Exchange in the Malay World: The Sulu Sultanate, 1770–1878", *Journal of Southeast Asian Studies* (1977), pp. 162–175. James L. Watson, ed., *Asian and African Systems of Slavery* (Berkeley: University of California Press, 1980).

[28] Frederick Cooper, *Plantation Slavery on the East African Coast* (New Haven: Yale University Press, 1977); Joseph Inikori, "The Import of Firearms into West Africa, 1750–1897: A Quantitative Analysis", *Journal of African History* 18 (1977), pp. 339–368.

[29] Richard Bean, *The British Trans-Atlantic Slave Trade, 1650–1775* (New York: Arno Press, 1975); Joseph C. Miller, "Slave Prices in the Portuguese Southern Atlantic", in: Paul E. Lovejoy (ed.), *Africans in Bondage* (Madison: University of Wisconsin Press, 1986), pp. 43–77. Other studies of slave prices were published by David Tambo, Emmanuel Terray, Patrick Manning, Robin Law, and Paul Lovejoy.

ulations.³⁰ Richard Hellie documented slavery in Russia from the sixteenth to eighteenth centuries; Michael Craton wrote on resistance of Caribbean slaves; Claire Robertson and Martin Klein edited an important collection on women and slavery in Africa; Jan Hogendorn and Marion Johnson conducted a global study documenting the role of cowrie shells in slave trade; and Sidney Mintz surveyed the expanding role of sugar in the Atlantic economy.³¹ Paul Lovejoy's 1983 survey of slavery in Africa advanced the thesis of slavery's progressive transformation of African societies. ³² Major works of the late 1980s included Abdul Sheriff's study of slavery and society on the Swahili coast; David Eltis's analysis of the role of slave trade in New World economic growth; and Joseph C. Miller's study of the Angolan slave trade in Atlantic context.³³ Nuclear families could and did exist among Caribbean slaves, especially if African values survived and high-status male slaves had garden plots, but in the United States the sale and forced migration of slaves from the tobacco-growing Old South to the cotton-growing New South involved the breakup of many families.³⁴

Neoliberalism and global interpretation, since 1990

The late twentieth century brought three important shifts in academic and political outlook. First was the rise of neoliberalism, which used the ideology of free markets to attack regulation, used the monopoly power of great corporations to expand inequality in domestic and international relations, and expanded the influence and profitability of the financial sector. Second was the development of global social movements, calling for broad unity among workers and professionals, which had periodic significance in political affairs. Third was the expansion of global frameworks

---

30 Patrick Manning, "The Enslavement of Africans: A Demographic Model", *Canadian Journal of African Studies*, 15 (1981), pp. 499–526.
31 *Idem*; Manning, "The Formal Demography of a Global System", *Social Science History*, 14 (1990), pp. 225–279; Richard Hellie, *Slavery in Russia, 1450–1725* (Chicago, 1982); Michael Craton, *Testing the Chains. Resistance to Slavery in the British West Indies* (Ithaca, NY, 1982); Claire C. Robertson and Martin A. Klein (eds), *Women and Slavery in Africa* (Madison, WI, 1983); Jan S. Hogendorn and Marion Johnson, *The Shell Money of the Slave Trade* (Cambridge, 1986); and Sidney Mintz, *Sweetness and Power: The Place of Sugar in Modern History* (New York, 1986).
32 Paul E. Lovejoy, *Transformations in Slavery. A History of Slavery in Africa* (Cambridge, 1983).
33 Stuart Schwartz, *Sugar Plantations in the Formation of Brazilian Society: Bahia, 1550–1835* (Cambridge, 1985); Abdul Sheriff, *Slaves, Spices, and Ivory in Zanzibar* (London, 1987); David Eltis, *Economic Growth and the Ending of the Transatlantic Slave Trade* (Oxford, 1987); Joseph C. Miller, *Way of Death. Merchant Capitalism and the Angolan Slave Trade, 1730–1830* (Madison, WI, 1989). See also the study of Thomas M. Ricks on the work of slaves in the Persian Gulf. Ricks, "Slaves and Slave Traders in the Persian Gulf, 18th and 19th Centuries: An Assessment", *Slavery and Abolition*, 9 (1988), pp. 60–70.
34 Marietta Morrissey, "Women's Work, Family Formation, and Reproduction among Caribbean Slaves", *Review (Fernand Braudel Center)*, 9 (1986), pp. 339–367; Michael Tadman, *Speculators and Slaves. Masters, Traders, and Slaves in the Old South* (Madison, WI, 1989).

of interpretation, supplementing the previously dominant national and binational analyses with more complex understandings of history and current affairs. In this circumstance, both hegemonic and democratic influences sought to recast their visions in global terms. The history of slavery and the experience of slave labour remained significant in these contending interpretations. Perhaps in response to the neoliberal climate and its weakening of the conditions of labourers, but perhaps because of the maturation of studies in slavery, this period brought a substantial increase of attention to the labour of the enslaved.

From 1990, the literature on slavery, itself increasingly wide-ranging and interconnected, found its linkages reaffirmed by a broad shift in historiography toward interest in global patterns. Patrick Manning's *Slavery and African Life* presented an economic and demographic analysis of slavery throughout Africa, tracing the interpenetrating flows of slaves and other commodities to regions across the Atlantic, the Indian Ocean, and the Sahara—confirming that African populations declined because of losses to the slave trade and showing, for instance, that female captives came from coastal regions of Africa while males came from the interior.[35] Janet Ewald expanded the documentation of enslavement in the Nile Valley; W. G. Clarence-Smith edited a volume on Indian Ocean slavery; Gwendolyn Hall traced the rise of Louisiana's slave system through the eighteenth century; Stuart Schwartz analysed the role of black ex-slaves as peasants in Brazil; and John Monteiro published a volume on Amerindian enslavement in Brazil.[36] Paul Lovejoy and Jan Hogendorn traced the last decades of slavery in the Sokoto Caliphate, under British rule: among the distinctive contributions of this volume is the detail of its documentation of concubinage.[37] In contrast, a study of church records in a community in eighteenth- and nineteenth-century São Paulo province showed high levels of marriage among slaves, and a study of slave families based on the African-American slave narratives of the 1930s showed that over half of all respondents had two-parent families.[38]

---

[35] Patrick Manning, *Slavery and African Life. Occidental, Oriental, and African Slave Trades* (Cambridge, 1990).
[36] Janet Ewald, *Soldiers, Traders, and Slaves. State Formation and Economic Transformation in the Greater Nile Valley, 1700–1885* (Madison, WI, 1990); W. G. Clarence-Smith (ed.), *The Economics of the Indian Ocean Slave Trade in the Nineteenth Century* (London, 1989); Gwendolyn M. Hall, *Africans in Colonial Louisiana. The Development of Afro-Creole Culture* (Baton Rouge, 1992); Stuart Schwartz, *Slaves, Peasants, and Rebels. Reconsidering Brazilian Slavery* (Urbana, IL, 1992); John Manuel Monteiro, *Negros da terra. Indios e bandeirantes nas origens de São Paulo* (São Paulo, 1994).
[37] Paul E. Lovejoy and Jan S. Hogendorn, *Slow Death for Slavery. The Course of Abolition in Northern Nigeria, 1897–1936* (Cambridge, 1993).
[38] Alida Metcalf, "Searching for the Slave Family in Colonial Brazil: A Reconstruction from São Paulo", *Journal of Family History*, 16 (1991), pp. 283–297; Stephen Crawford, "The Slave Family: A View from the Slave Narratives", in: Claudia Goldin and Hugh Rockoff (eds), *Strategic Factors in Nineteenth Century American Economic History. A Volume to Honor Robert W. Fogel* (Chicago, 1992), pp. 331–350.

As an important dimension of global thinking, the concept of the African diaspora became widely adopted beginning in the 1990s. This framework emphasized the continuities and connections among people of African origin for the African continent and the diasporas to the north, east, and west. Attention to the diaspora framework encouraged greater attention to comparison of slave systems around the world, showed the evolution of slave communities, confirmed that there were always significant numbers of freed people in slave communities, and documented the complexity of the nineteenth century, in which waves of emancipation and enslavement collided.[39] Work of global scope on bibliography of slavery expanded in parallel. Bibliographic references on slavery and slave trade worldwide appeared in the 1970s, continuing through the end of the century; numerous collective volumes appeared with chapters on slavery and slave trade.[40] Encyclopedias of slavery began appearing in 1997.[41]

The development of the internet meant that data on slavery and slave trade could then be placed online. The largest collection was the compilation of data on the trans-Atlantic slave trade edited by David Eltis and colleagues. This dataset drew on research results submitted by many scholars, and has been updated at various times since it first appeared as a CD-ROM in 1999. Another major online resource of a different sort, directed by Jane Landers of Vanderbilt University, reproduces religious and secular documents on slaves and slave life in the Americas.[42] The expansion of these resources enabled the integration of studies of slave trade into a developing global framework for migration studies.[43]

Additional major contributions to the history of slavery, including the history of slave labour, have continued to appear in the twenty-first century. Sylviane Diouf's collection on anti-slavery campaigns within African societies provided an important

---

39 Joseph E. Harris (ed.), *Global Dimensions of the African Diaspora* (Washington, DC, 1980); Michael Gomez, *Reversing Sail. A History of the African Diaspora* (Cambridge, 2005); Patrick Manning, *The African Diaspora. A History through Culture* (New York, 2009).
40 The most recent bibliography, which cites earlier bibliographies, is Joseph C. Miller (ed.), *Slavery and Slaving in World History. A Bibliography* (Armonk, NY, 1999). For a listing of most collective works on slavery up to 1996, see Patrick Manning, *Slavery. Globalization of Forced Labour* (Aldershot, UK, 1996), pp. xxx–xxxiv.
41 See, for instance, Junius P. Rodriguez (ed.), *The Historical Encyclopedia of World Slavery*, 2 vols. (Santa Barbara, CA, 1997); and Paul Finkelman and Joseph C. Miller (eds), *Macmillan Encyclopedia of World Slavery* (New York, 1999).
42 *Voyages: The Trans-Atlantic Slave Trade Database* (Emory University, 2013), http://slavevoyages.org; *Ecclesiastical and Secular Sources for Slave Societies* (Vanderbilt University Department of History, 2017), http://www.vanderbilt.edu/essss/. See also the work of Henry Lovejoy in *The Liberated Africans Project*, http://www.liberatedafricans.org.
43 Patrick Manning, *Migration in World History* (London, 2004); Jan Lucassen, Leo Lucassen and Patrick Manning (eds), *Migration History in World History. Multidisciplinary Approaches* (Leiden and Boston, 2010); Jan Lucassen and Leo Lucassen (eds), *Globalising Migration History. The Eurasian Experience (16th–21st Centuries)* (Leiden and Boston, 2014).

corrective to an absence in the literature.⁴⁴ Luiz Felipe Alencastro's early-colonial analysis showed the centrality of Angola and slave trade in every dimension of colonial Brazilian history. Drawing on Spanish state and church archives, Alejandro de la Fuente's study of sixteenth-century Havana shows the interplay of slave and free in creating a port and hinterland that became central to Atlantic commerce, while David M. Stark documented the work of Africans on ranch work in Puerto Rico.⁴⁵ James Sweet's study of Afro-Brazilian culture confirmed the value of Inquisition documents in the social history of slavery. For nineteenth-century Brazil, a major collective work shows the interplay of labour systems, free and slave. For Brazil at the same time, additional recent studies show the precarious labour relations of slaves and the manumitted, as contracts could guarantee their work but also extend their term of enslavement.⁴⁶ For coffee porters in early twentieth-century Rio, in contrast, their background as enslaved porters provided the basis for a successful trade union.⁴⁷ On North American slavery, which continued almost as long as that of Brazil, Gavin Wright's review of the literature privileges the issue of economic growth, effectively summarizing the continuing (if still somewhat isolated) work in that field.⁴⁸

The assembly of new research results is clarifying larger historic patterns in enslavement. Thus, Chouki El Hamel's analysis of Moulay Isma'il's late-seventeenth-century enslavement of black Moroccans, to build his army, fit precisely with imposition of the *Code noir* by Louis XIV of France, in that racialization of slavery took place simultaneously on both sides of the continental and religious divides.

This tidal shift in enslavement can be fit into a longer-term narrative of alternations in upward mobility of subaltern blacks, followed by periods of expanded re-

---

44 Sylviane A. Diouf (ed.), *Fighting the Slave Trade: West African Strategies* (Athens, OH and Oxford, 2003).
45 Luiz Felipe de Alencastro, *O Trato dos viventes. Formação do Brasil no Atlántico Sul* (São Paulo, 2000); Alejandro de la Fuente, *Havana and the Atlantic in the Sixteenth Century* (Chapel Hill, NC, 2008); David M. Stark, *Slave Families and the Hato Economy in Puerto Rico* (Gainesville, FL, 2015).
46 James H. Sweet, *Recreating Africa. Culture, Kinship, and Religion in the African-Portuguese World, 1441–1770* (Chapel Hill, NC, 2003); Marcela Goldmacher, Marcelo Badaró Mattos and Paulo Cruz Terra (eds), *Faces do trabalho. Escravizados e livres* (Niterói, 2010); Enrique Espada Lima, "Freedom, Precariousness, and the Law: Freed Persons Contracting out their Labour in Nineteenth-Century Brazil", *International Review of Social History*, 54, 3 (December 2009), pp. 391–416; Sidney Chalhoub, "The Precariousness of Freedom in a Slave Society (Brazil in the Nineteenth Century)", *International Review of Social History*, 56, 3 (December 2011), pp. 405–439; Sidney Chalhoub, "The Politics of Ambiguity: Conditional Manumission, Labor Contracts and Slave Emancipation in Brazil (1850s to 1888)", *International Review of Social History*, 60, 2 (August 2015), pp. 161–191.
47 Maria Cecilia Velasco e Cruz, "Puzzling Out Slave Origins in Rio de Janeiro Port Unionism: The 1906 Strike and the Sociedade de Resistência dos Trabalhadores em Trapiche e Café", *Hispanic American Historical Review*, 86, 2 (2006), pp. 205–245; Marcelo Badaró Mattos, *Laborers and Enslaved Workers. Experiences in Common in the Making of Rio de Janeiro's Working Class, 1850–1920* (Oxford and New York, 2017).
48 Gavin Wright, *Slavery and American Economic Development* (Baton Rouge, 2006).

pression.⁴⁹ In another new approach, Michael Zeuske and Dale Tomich opened discussion on the "second slavery" of the nineteenth-century Atlantic in such a fashion that debate expanded to include contemporaneous enslavement in the Old World as well.⁵⁰ It is clear that innovations in the historical study of slavery continue to unfold. In the present atmosphere, where the work forces of the world are experiencing increasing integration and—perhaps—common consciousness, it is reasonable to expect that studies of slave labour will be pursued in greater depth, giving greater attention to linkages and comparisons with other elements of the human work force.

---

49 Chouki El Hamel, *Black Morocco. A History of Slavery, Race, and Islam* (New York, 2013); Jean-François Niort, *Le Code noir. Idées reçues sur un texte symbolique* (Paris, 2015); Patrick Manning, "Locating Africans on the World Stage: A Problem in World History", *Journal of World History*, 26 (2015), pp. 630–631.
50 Michael Zeuske, *Amistad. A Hidden Network of Slavers and Merchants*, Trans.Steven Rendall (Princeton, NJ, 2015); Dale Tomich and Michael Zeuske, "Introduction, the Second Slavery: Mass Slavery, World-Economy, and Comparative Microhistories", *Review (Fernand Braudel Center)*, 31 (2008), pp. 91–100.

Suggested reading

Chatterjee, Indrani and Richard M. Eaton (eds). *Slavery and South Asian history* (Bloomington, IN: Indiana University Press, 2006).
Clarence-Smith, W. G. (ed.). *The Economics of the Indian Ocean Slave Trade in the Nineteenth Century* (London: Frank Cass, 1989).
Conrad, Robert. *The Destruction of Brazilian Slavery* (Berkeley: University of California Press, 1972).
Cooper, Frederick. *Plantation Slavery on the East African Coast* (New Haven: Yale University Press, 1977).
Craton, Michael. *Testing the Chains. Resistance to Slavery in the British West Indies* (Ithaca, NY: Cornell University Press, 1982).
De las Casas, Bartolomé. *Historia de las Indias. Selections* (New York: Digitalia Inc, 2012).
Domar, Evsey. "The Causes of Slavery or Serfdom: A Hypothesis" *Economic History* Review, 30, 1 (March 1970), pp. 18–32.
Du Bois, W.E.Burghardt. *Black Reconstruction. An Essay toward a History of the Part which Black Folk Played in the Attempt to Reconstruct Democracy in America, 1860–1880* (New York: Russel & Russel, 1935; several reprints).
El Hamel, Chouki. *Black Morocco. A History of Slavery, Race, and Islam* (New York: Cambridge University Press, 2013).
Finkelman, Paul and Joseph C. Miller (eds). *Macmillan Encyclopedia of World Slavery* (New York: Macmillan Reference USA, 1999).
Finley, M.I. *Slavery in Classical Antiquity. Views and Controversies* (Cambridge: W. Heffer, 1960).
Fogel, Robert William and Stanley L. Engerman. *Time on the Cross. The Economics of American Negro Slavery*, with supplementary volume (Boston: Little, Brown, 1974).
Freyre, Gilberto. *The Masters and the Slaves. A Study in the Development of Brazilian Civilization*, Trans. Samuel Putnam (New York: Afred Knopff, 1946).
Genovese, Eugene. *Roll, Jordan, Roll. The World the Slaves Made* (New York: Pantheon, 1974).
Gutman, Herbert G. *Slavery and the Numbers Game. A Critique of Time on the Cross* (Urbana, IL: University of Illinois Press, 1975).
Hellie, Richard. *Slavery in Russia, 1450–1725* (Chicago: University of Chicago Press, 1982).
Heuman, Gad and James Walvin (eds). *The Slavery Reader* (London and New York: Routledge, 2003).
James, C.L.R. *The Black Jacobins. Toussaint L'Ouverture and the San Domingo Revolution* (New York, The Dial Press, 1938; several reprints).
Lovejoy, Paul E. *Transformations in Slavery. A History of Slavery in Africa* (Cambridge: Cambridge University Press, 1983).
Manning, Patrick. *Slavery and African Life. Occidental, Oriental, and African Slave Trades* (Cambridge: Cambridge University Press, 1990).
Mattos, Marcelo Badaró. *Laborers and Enslaved Workers. Experiences in Common in the Making of Rio de Janeiro's Working Class, 1850–1920* (Oxford and New York: Berghahn, 2017).
Miers, Suzanne and Igor Kopytoff (eds.). *Slavery in Africa. Historical and Anthropological Perspectives* (Madison, WI: University of Wisconsin Press, 1977).
Miller, Joseph C. (ed.). *Slavery and Slaving in World History. A Bibliography* (Armonk, NY: M. E. Sharpe, 1999).
Robertson, Claire C. and Martin A. Klein (eds). *Women and Slavery in Africa* (Madison, WI: University of Wisconsin Press, 1983).
Rodriguez, Junius P. (ed.). *The Historical Encyclopedia of World Slavery.* 2 vols. (Santa Barbara: ABC – CLIO, 1997).

Schwartz, Stuart. *Sugar Plantations in the Formation of Brazilian Society. Bahia, 1550–1835* (Cambridge: Cambridge University Press, 1985).

Sheriff, Abdul. *Slaves, Spices, and Ivory in Zanzibar* (London: J. Currey, 1987).

Solow, Barbara L. and Stanley L. Engerman (eds). *British Capitalism and Caribbean Slavery. The Legacy of Eric Williams* (Cambridge: Cambridge University Press, 1987).

Tannenbaum, Frank. *Slave and Citizen. The Negro in the Americas* (New York: A. A. Knopf, 1946).

Watson, James L. (ed.). *Asian and African Systems of Slavery* (Berkeley, CA: University of California Press, 1980).

Williams, Eric. *Capitalism and Slavery* (Chapel Hill, NC: University of North Carolina Press, 1944; several reprints).

Zeuske, Michael. *Amistad. A Hidden Network of Slavers and Merchants*. Trans. Steven Rendall (Princeton, NJ: Markus Wiener, 2015).

Jan Lucassen
4.6. Wage Labour

Definitions of wage labour in the legal and social sciences are useful for historians of work, but they never cover the full human experience. The following definition attempts to include as many aspects as possible: "Wage labour is work, which is performed on the basis of a contract between a worker (or a group of workers) and an employer, and which the employer remunerates in the form of a wage."[1] Wages may consist of money or goods in kind. Cases in which employers remunerate workers arbitrarily (without taking into account a specific amount of work), in which remuneration takes place without a contract (for example, when a housewife feeds and clothes her husband and children), and in which employers coerce workers into employment without a real contract, as in the case of corvée labour in pre-market societies like Ancient Egypt or the Pre-Columbian societies in the Americas, convict labourers, or chattel slaves are therefore excluded. Frequently, the recipient of the wage is free to spend it at will, but not always. Exceptions include child labourers, who have to pass their wages on to their parents or guardians, or workers in a truck system, who are obliged to spend at least a part of their wage in the employer's shop. Sometimes wages are also paid to slaves-for-hire, who have been sent out by their owner to earn money with an employer, and who are usually allowed to keep a part of their remuneration. They perform a kind of wage labour if they themselves, and not their owner, makes an agreement with their employer. In sum, wages are but one type of remuneration for work. In this chapter, we will only use the term wage labour if wages are paid based on a contract.

According to our definition, wage labour is based on market exchange: the workers offer their capacity to work, and the employers offer remuneration in money or kind in return. A major characteristic of wage labour is that it presupposes a contract, implicit or explicit, oral or written. The contract specifies (i) the identity of the contracting parties; (ii) the relationship between performance and remuneration; (iii) the duration of the agreement; and (iv) the conditions under which it may be terminated prematurely by the worker or the employer. In the remainder of this article I will discuss systematically, but briefly, these four elements of the labour contract, thus further clarifying what wage labour is and how it overlaps in multiple ways with other labour relations. Thereafter, I will give a concise historical outline of wage labour from its origins to the present day.

---

[1] General works on which this essay is based are Marcel van der Linden, *Workers of the World. Essays toward a Global labor History* (Leiden and Boston, 2008); Marcel van der Linden and Leo Lucassen (eds), *Working on Labor. Essays in Honor of Jan Lucassen* (Leiden and Boston, 2012); and Jan Lucassen, *Outlines of a History of Labour* (Amsterdam, 2012). The latter publication and this essay adopt the global taxonomy on labour relations as developed over the last decade at the International Institute of Social History (see chapter 4.1).

The labour contract and its elements

Historical evidence shows that it is much more important to know whether a contract is recognized by the contracting partners and by local or broader society than whether parties have entered into it implicitly or explicitly and—in the latter case—whether and how it has been put on paper. Recognition of such an agreement by the polity is, after all, essential for the enforcement of the contract and for solutions in the case that the contract is breached by one of the parties involved. The way that it is documented—in memory, on a piece of paper that is or is not signed, by a notarial deed, etc.—may be very important in a particular case but not for the definition of wage labour. The different forms of entering into a contract relate more closely to the levels of literacy and the juridification of a society.

i. The contracting parties

In labour history, we nearly always talk about the relation between the wage labourer and the employer as if these were two individual people.[2] The reality is often very different. Labourers are often hired as a group and not individually, or individual labourers agree amongst themselves, locally or nationally, to accept work only under certain conditions. Journeymen's guilds, mutual benefit societies and trade unions are examples of more permanent workers organizations that collectively bargain.[3] Another example of groups that collectively take on work are production cooperatives, dating back to the nineteenth century, but this does not pertain to wage labour.[4]

Employers can unite in order to impose conditions on workers who wish to be employed by them. An employer doesn't need to be an individual but can also be the state in a market economy or another corporate body that does not work for profits. In terms of contract enforcement this has major consequences, as we will see below. The Soviet Union and other socialist countries, which existed in the twentieth

---

[2] For collective wage-labour relations see Jan Lucassen, "The Other Proletarians: Seasonal Labourers, Mercenaries and Miners", *International Review of Social History*, Supplement 2 (1994), pp. 171–194; and Piet Lourens and Jan Lucassen, *Arbeitswanderung und berufliche Spezialisierung. Die lippischen Ziegler im 18. und 19. Jahrhundert* (Osnabrück, 1999).
[3] An autonomous division of tasks within a group was historically the rule in printing houses and amongst the porters and heavers at the docks. Jan Materné, "Chapel members in the Workplace: Tension and Teamwork in the Printing Trades in the Seventeenth and Eighteenth Centuries", *International Review of Social History*, Supplement 2 (1994), pp. 53–82; Jan Lucassen, "Work on the Docks: Sailors' Labour Productivity and the Organization of Loading and Unloading", in: Richard W. Unger (ed.), *Shipping and Economic Growth 1350–1800* (Leiden and Boston, 2011), pp. 269–278.
[4] David F. Schloss, *Methods of Industrial Remuneration*. Third edition revised and enlarged (London, 1898), pp. 319–365, 406–419; Van der Linden in this volume Ch. 7.

century, were special cases. There markets, including labour markets, were abolished and replaced by state organized employment that left out labour contracts but maintained remuneration by way of wages. This is another example of work for which wages are paid but which, according to the definition used in this chapter, is not considered wage labour.

Because of the historical importance of collective contracting and its relative obscurity this phenomenon needs some more elucidation. According to David F. Schloss, cooperative work is characterized by the following elements: a) the members of the cooperative are associated by their own free choice, and they determine for themselves how many people and which people are part of the group; b) the associated workers select amongst themselves their own leader; c) they arrange the division of the collective wages between all of the members of the group (including the leader) in such a manner as is mutually agreed upon as being equitable. According to rules made before the work starts, the group determines which members receive which part of the total sum received by the group.[5]

This so-called *cooperative subcontracting* was already documented amongst Mesopotamian brick makers in 484–477 BCE.[6] With the spread of large mono-cultures, cooperative subcontracting became very popular in market economies, as it enabled employers to respond quickly to short term demand and take on many labourers at once. It was first found to be a common practice in Classical Antiquity and again from the late Middle Ages onwards in Western Europe. Outside agriculture, it dominated seasonal work like mining, the public and private construction of dikes, canals, and (rail)roads, and the construction industry.

In the mining industry, the basis of the group was often the household, and men, woman, and children could be part of the group. A particular seam, from which coal or ore was to be extracted, was subcontracted to the group.[7] Breaking ore at the surface was also subcontracted to groups of women. The demise of serfdom in Central and Eastern Europe enhanced this type of organization. In Europe it reached its peak

---

[5] Lucassen, "The Other Proletarians", after Schloss, *Methods of Industrial Remuneration*, pp. 155–165. See also Lourens and Lucassen, *Arbeitswanderung und berufliche Spezialisierung*, and Gijs Kessler and Jan Lucassen, "Labour Relations, Efficiency and the Great Divergence. Comparing Pre-Industrial Brick-Making across Eurasia, 1500–2000", in: Maarten Prak and Jan Luiten van Zanden (eds), *Technology, Skills and the Pre-Modern Economy in the East and West* (Leiden and Boston, 2013), pp. 259–322.
[6] Michael Jursa, *Aspects of the Economic History of Babylonia in the First Millennium BC. Economic Geography, Economic Mentalities, Agriculture, the Use of Money and the Problem of Economic Growth* (Münster, 2010), pp. 261–263, 280.
[7] E.g. J. Taylor, "The Subcontract System in the British Coal Industry", in: L. S. Pressnell (ed.), *Studies in the Industrial Revolution* (London, 1960), pp. 215–235; Tim Wright, "'A Method of Evading Management'. Contract Labor in Chinese Coal Mines before 1937", *Comparative Studies in Society and History*, 23 (1981), pp. 656–678.

before WWI. After the war, mechanization diminished the need for seasonal wage labour, especially in agriculture and construction.⁸

When mechanization spread, workshops were replaced by electrically powered factories with machines. Supervisory challenges were solved by the introduction of piece rates—but collective bargaining, which had already existed in the agricultural sector and in other sectors, as described above, did not take place. Instead, the cotton industry contracted the much sought-after skilled labourers who could work the new machines individually. These *piece-wage foremen*, in turn, engaged unskilled urban workers, amongst which were many children, against time wages—a practice called *sweating*, according to Schloss. The result was one of the horrors of the classical Industrial Revolution: the extreme exploitation of one group of labourers by another, while employers declared themselves free of responsibility.⁹

ii. Performance and remuneration: wage types and modes of wage payment

Any employer, whether of wage labour or slave labour, must make sure that the worker's labour capacity is maintained, at least in the short term. Therefore, he or she must make sure that the worker directly receives or is able to buy the appropriate amount of food, rest, clothing, and shelter. This is the bare and often barren relationship between performance and remuneration. Employers (should) also understand that by adding positive incentives they may get more or better results (see Chapter 7). This may be achieved by the level of the wage and other, secondary, labour conditions, like paid leave, sick leave, a pension, and other perks, but also by linking performance and remuneration directly, as in the case of piece or task-based wages.

When the employer can easily supervise the quantity and quality of the work done by his or her labourers time wages are common. This is true for most small-scale workshops. When supervision is more difficult, because of the distance to the workforce (e.g. in the cottage industry, in mining, public works, and agriculture) or the size of the workforce, indirect supervision is more appropriate. In those cases, not the work process itself but its results must be measured and assessed and expressed in a piece wage. Therefore, time matters less, although minimal and maximal periods may be stipulated.

Collective piece rates are an intrinsic part of cooperative subcontracting. As a rule, they are not distributed simply in equal parts, as experience and responsibility play a certain role. Mixed forms of (individual) time wages and (collective) piece rates appear in the form of *progressive wages* or in the form of *profit sharing*. In

---

8 Jan Lucassen, *Migrant Labour in Europe 1600–1900. The Drift to the North Sea* (London, 1987); Jan Lucassen (ed.), *Global Labour History. A State of the Art* (Bern, 2006); Leo Lucassen and Jan Lucassen, *Winnaars en Verliezers. Een nuchtere balans van vijfhonderd jaar immigratie* (Amsterdam, 2015).
9 Ludwig Bernhard, *Die Akkordarbeit in Deutschland* (Leipzig, 1903), pp. 16–22.

the nineteenth century, both were propagated as an answer to the emerging labour unrests. Progressive wages imply that a fixed minimum wage is supplemented by a premium, related to the efficiency of the performance. One of its appearances was *time-wage piece-work*, in which a fixed time rate was supplemented with a premium per unit of output in excess of a standard quantity.[10] Premium wages were advocated around 1830 by men like Charles Babbage (1791–1871), Robert Owen (1771–1858), and Charles Fourier (1772–1837). Profit-sharing, also sometimes called *industrial partnership*, became popular one generation later.[11]

Product sharing is a related form of remuneration, directly linked to performance. Historically, it was used amongst sailors, bargemen, fishermen, and crews of whaling boats. Sailors and bargemen could be paid a share of the freight, fishermen part of the catch. The oldest and best known example is share cropping in agriculture, documented for the first time in ancient Mesopotamia. Small tenants with few or no means of their own could become tenants. Not only did they receive the land, but they also were given seeds and utensils and—in return for their labour—could keep between one quarter and one half of the crop.[12]

The combination of piece wages for a foreman and time wages for the actual labourers, paid to them by the foreman, who thus becomes an exploiter of his fellow workers—a perversion of cooperative subcontracting described above, started in the cotton industry. This abusive practice encouraged the emergence of the early British trade unions in the 1830s, after the repeal of the Combination Acts in 1824. From then on, with piece-rate foremanship, piece rates as such became anathema for most trade unionists, an issue discussed by theorists like Louis Blanc and, borrowing from him, Karl Marx himself.[13] Nevertheless, around 1900, cooperative subcontracting with piece rates dominated not only wage labour in German agriculture, construction, and brick making, but it also prevailed in the metal industry and made headways in the woodwork and textile industries. At about the same time, in the United Kingdom, according to the Webbs, nearly half of the principal trade unions, representing almost 60% of the aggregate membership, insisted on piece-work. These examples

---

10 Schloss, *Methods of Industrial Remuneration*, pp. 48–49, 87–113. This differs from a task wage in which the workman has to perform a certain task at a fixed time wage, without any premium, and with the risk to receive less if the task has not been finished.
11 Schloss, *Methods of Industrial Remuneration*, pp. 239–248, 254–318, 366–404; Bernhard, *Akkordarbeit in Deutschland*, pp. 30–38.
12 Schloss, *Methods of Industrial Remuneration*, pp. 249–253; Bas van Bavel, *The Invisible Hand. How Market Economies Have Emerged and Declined since AD 500* (Oxford, 2016).
13 Bernhard, *Akkordarbeit in Deutschland*, pp. 51–67: they saw the abolition of piece wages as a precondition for the abolition of *piece-wage foremanship* (French *marchandage*; German *Zwischenmeister-* or *Akkordmeistersystem*) by 'task-masters'.

demonstrate that there is no simple unilineal movement from individual to collective remuneration or the reverse.¹⁴

Individual time wages combined with strict quality assessments in large-scale factories and leaving out intermediate task-masters were greatly enhanced by the introduction of the assembly-line in combination with scientific management. Elaborated in the Taylor-system (named after Frederick W. Taylor, 1856–1915) and in Fordism (named after Henry Ford, 1863–1947), it not only became a favourite in market economies but was also emulated in communist countries.

These organizational innovations in large scale industries implied that it became harder for collective or individual piece work in the labour market at large. Piece rates, individually and collectively paid out, and mixed forms of time and piece wages globally played and still play an important role, although in the North Atlantic their importance was reduced in the twentieth century.

The more direct the supervision, the more likely it was that employers also determined the working time. This became most acute with mechanization and their concern to pay of the machines' purchasing price by keeping them going as long as possible. The abuses in the textile industry provoked the first factory laws in the United Kingdom in 1818, restricting working hours, to be followed by many more.

For the labourers, not only the wage level and the relation between it and performance but also the modalities of wage payment mattered greatly in daily life. They were affected by the frequency of payments of wages and advances to wages, the method of payment, and possible restrictions on the spending of the wages.

Regarding payments, room and board, i.e. payment in kind, is undoubtedly the oldest form of wage payment. Above, the examples of soldiers and share cropping in classical Mesopotamia were discussed. And for soldiers in barracks and sailors on board ships this continued to be an essential part of their remuneration, although soldiers on the move often had to take care of their own food. Other labourers whose remuneration consisted mainly of room and board were live-in servants and apprentices.¹⁵

Since the advent of deep monetization¹⁶ in the Mediterranean, Northern India and China more than 2000 years ago, wages could be paid in coins equalling hourly

---

14 Schloss, *Methods of Industrial Remuneration*, pp. 50–51; Bernhard, *Akkordarbeit in Deutschland*, pp. 176–177; for France see Charles Rist, "Introduction", in: David F. Schloss, *Les modes de rémunération du travail* (Paris, 1902), pp. v-xlviii.
15 Bert De Munck, Steven L. Kaplan and Hugo Soly (eds), *Learning on the Shop Floor. Historical Perspectives on Apprenticeship* (New York and Oxford, 2007).
16 Regarding the production of small change in sufficient amounts, facilitating the payment of daily and hourly sums and their spending at markets and in shops, see Jan Lucassen, "Deep Monetization in Eurasia in the Long Run", in: Bert van der Speck and Bas van Leeuwen (eds), *Money, Currency and Crisis. In Search of Trust 2000 BC to AD 2000* (London, 2017, forthcoming). Deep monetization was equally important for small-scale producers, peasants, share croppers, artisans, and workers in the cottage industries, who depended on advance payments as they were unable to live on credit until

wages or less. This made the emergence of labour markets more feasible, because, with these easy means of exchange, workers could purchase food and other necessaries in market places and shops. This also added to the choice wage labourers had in the way they could spend their earnings. Such a choice could be limited by wages paid out in tokens only accepted in specific shops. This is the *truck system*, in which the employer could make an extra profit (as often he or one of his relatives owned the shop).[17]

In periods of heavy price fluctuations of bread grains employers and workers strategically tried to convert money wages into wages in kind and vice versa. When the price of bread grains rose quickly, workers preferred payment in kind instead of in coins, whereas employers were inclined to prefer the contrary.

The regularity of wage payments as well as the terms under which actual payments take place (after the performance of a task, daily, weekly, bi-weekly, monthly, or even less frequently) determine the need for credit, as wage labourers, as a rule, do not have extensive savings. When small change was rare, like most of the time in early-modern England, credit became very important for wage earners because their employers paid them in long intervals. Credit was available from local shopkeepers, but only to a certain limit. There was extensive legislation for extorting money from debtors, culminating in the imprisonment of many debtors.[18]

The actual level of the wages and their purchasing power in a market economy is not only the end sum of all individual contract negotiations between workers and employers. It depends as much on the collective strategies of both sides and on state interventions stipulating minimum, maximum or average wages. Collective strategies were common amongst cooperative subcontracting groups as well as journeymen associations and similar migratory groups, like traveling brothers.[19]

iii. The length of the contract

In order to discuss to what extent wage labour may be called free or unfree it is not only important to know whether the contract period is limited but also how long the contract period is. The longer the duration of the contract, the fewer the opportunities for a worker to change jobs and thereby improve his position. However, a long-term or lifelong contract doesn't have to be despised by a labourer. To the contrary, as

---

they had harvested or sold a piece of cloth, see Catharina Lis and Hugo Soly, *Een groot bedrijf in een kleine stad. De firma de Heyder en Co. te Lier 1757–1834* (Lier, 1987).
17 George W. Hilton, *The Truck System: Including a History of the British Truck Acts, 1465–1960* (Cambridge, 1960); Karin Lurvink, "Beyond Racism and Poverty. The Truck System on Louisiana Plantations and Dutch Peateries, 1865–1920" (Ph.D. Dissertation, Vrije Universiteit Amsterdam, 2016).
18 Jerry White, *Mansions of Misery. A Biography of the Marshalsea Debtor's Prison* (London, 2016).
19 Robert A. Leeson, *Travelling Brothers. The Six Centuries' Road from Craft Fellowship to Trade* (London, 1979).

long as the remuneration is high enough, it can be seen as very favourable. Higher ranking professional soldiers or workers in the so-called secret cities of the Soviet Union benefitted from long-term contracts and high remuneration. The latter were very well cared for specialists in the weapon industry. During the Cold War, they were forbidden to talk about their work to others, let alone leave their job or the town they lived in, which did not even appear on official maps. Despite the advantages of well-paid, tenured jobs, the liberty for a worker to change his or her employer after giving reasonable notice may be seen as an essential character of a free labour contract.[20]

In labour history, the length of the contract has become an issue of contention when discussing indentured labour and other forms of advances to wage labourers that lead them to incur debts or enter into peonage. To what extent should these forms of labour be seen as free or unfree? Are they forms of slavery?

Wage labourers may be indebted for many reasons, e.g. because of the adversities of life that they could not cope with because they lacked the necessary savings. Another reason is the cost involved in acquiring paid work. The necessary funds can be advanced by so-called jobbers, who take care of work placements and travel costs if the placements are far away. These jobbers are most successful when prospective workers are suffering from dire circumstances. Take the big farmers of the Roman Campagna around 1800 who sent their agents up to the Apennine mountains with grain at the end of the winter season. The starving peasants, turned into debtors, were simply asked to descend in the summer to assist in the harvest and thereby pay back their loan. To this day, the poor in India take advances from jobbers, which they must pay back by doing seasonal work afterwards. If the loans cannot be paid off, the debtors must come back every year until their children inherit the obligation. In this way, families become eternal debt peons, totally at the mercy of the employer.[21]

As a rule, the costs necessary for finding work overseas are prohibitive for wage labourers and that is why intermediaries offer to advance the necessary funds. In return, the future worker, now indebted like in the Italian example, must commit him- or herself to perform work for an overseas employer in order to pay back the loan. The best-known example is that of the *indentured labourers* who left England for the American colonies in the seventeenth to the nineteenth centuries. In the similar French case, they were called *engagés*. Their debt was transferred from the original creditor to the captain who shipped them to their new destination, and after arrival it was transferred to their new employer, who, for a fixed number of years, had his indentured labourers entirely at his disposal. After the abolition of the slave trade, Indians became indentured labourers in the British and Dutch colonies worldwide

---

[20] Robert W. Pringle, *Historical Dictionary of Russian and Soviet Intelligence* (Lanham, MD, 2015), p. 375.
[21] Lucassen, *Migrant Labour in Europe, 1600–1900*, p. 118; Kessler and Lucassen, "Labour Relations, Efficiency and the Great Divergence".

and the same happened to the Chinese, the Japanese, and the inhabitants of the Pacific. (See also chapter 4.4.)

Income insecurity was and still is one of the most threatening characteristics of wage labour, but long contracts with one employer and the accompanying lack of freedom are hardly desirable either. Decent working conditions and inexpensive labour intermediation have always been aspired to by workers. Early forms were the placement bureaus of craft guilds and especially of journeymen associations, which cherished the tramp. After arrival in a new town, their members knew which inn to go to and where to find a "father" and a "mother" who, besides treating them with hospitality, could tell them where jobs were available in their craft. Early trade unions provided the same services. In the twentieth century, together with local and later national authorities, they tried to monopolize labour intermediation in public labour exchanges. This was achieved in several countries, most completely in Germany, where labour mediation was combined with unemployment benefit provisions.[22]

iv. The conditions under which the contract may be terminated prematurely by a worker or an employer

Whatever the length of the contract, many do end earlier than expected or stipulated by the parties involved. Because this is so common, conventions exist for what is considered a normal term of notice. But what is the consequence when one of the parties does not abide by the conventions? What is considered to be a legitimate reason for such a breach of contract by the labourer or the employer and what are the consequences of illegal breaches?

In England, the rules regarding breaches of contracts were very strict from the late Middle Ages onward. Because of labour shortages after the Black Death, employers successfully managed to bridle what they considered to be excessive demands of the workers. The *Ordinance and the Statute of Labourers* (1349–1351), culminating in the *Statute of Artificers* (1562–1563) prohibited departure before voluntary service agreements had been fulfilled and mandated penal sanctions for breaches of contracts. Under these laws no adult was allowed to walk around without a paid job and looking for work was easily defined as "vagrancy" and accordingly punished. A labour contract had to be concluded for a year and wages had to be fixed according

---

[22] Pierre Barret and Jean-Noël Gurgand, *Ils voyageaient la France. Vie et traditions des Compagnons du Tour de France au XIXe siècle* (Paris, 1980); Sigrid Wadauer, Thomas Buchner and Alexander Mejstrik (eds), *The History of Labour Intermediation. Institutions and Finding Employment in the Nineteenth and Twentieth Centuries* (New York and Oxford, 2015).

to governmental rates. The penal sanctions for breaches of contracts were only abolished in the United Kingdom in 1875.[23]

This system was expanded throughout the British colonies, starting in North America (in the USA it was repealed in the early nineteenth century), and later in India and other colonies in Asia, Africa and Oceania. Parts of the Dutch East Indies followed the British example for a short while in the 1860s. On the European continent, however, the situation was different. In general, labour contracts were part of civil law. This meant that indemnities mostly had to be paid to the party that could prove to have been damaged by the breach of contract. Mostly, workers had to pay. More rarely, employers paid.

This is not to say that changing jobs on the European continent was easy. Going as far back as the Ancien Regime, employers blacklisted workers who had been sacked or had left their job against the will of the employer. This happened locally and sector wise.[24] Even more serious was the introduction of the *livret* in France in 1803 (after earlier examples in 1749 and 1781). All factory workers had to carry this personal work passport and hand it in for registration with the employer. When the worker left the job the employer had to return it. Inside the *livret*, the employer wrote remarks about the worker's performance, including bad behaviour or debts not yet settled (because of advances received). From this point on, employers could only hire people carrying such a *livret*. In France, the *livret* was abolished in 1890. In other countries, previously part of the French Empire, it also had a long life. In Luxemburg and the Prussian Rhine provinces it existed until 1860, and in Belgium it was used until 1883, although in the case of Belgium the employers did not use it properly. Besides, in France and Belgium work passports were also used for domestic servants, and many other countries issued such documents for travelling workers and workers in general.[25]

A special type of labour contract enforcement was universal for sailors and soldiers from very early on. Any infringement on discipline, let alone breach of contract, was immediately punished by the ship master or the military officer. Punishments varied from fines to corporal or even capital punishment. Particularly in wartime and for army personnel around the world such laws are still in use. Nevertheless, the ILO convention, in force since 1958, aims at abolishing penal sanctions worldwide.

---

23 Robert J. Steinfeld, *The Invention of Free Labor. The Employment Relation in English and American Law and Culture, 1350–1870* (Chapel Hill, NC and London, 1991).

24 Jan Lucassen, *Jan, Jan Salie en diens kinderen. Vergelijkend onderzoek naar continuïteit en discontinuïteit in de ontwikkeling van arbeidsverhoudingen* (Amsterdam, 1991); Kessler and Lucassen, "Labour Relations, Efficiency and the Great Divergence"; René Leboutte, *Le livret d'ouvrier dans la province de Liège. Une source méconnue en Histoire sociale. Présentation et premiers résultats d'exploitation* (Liège, 1988), pp. 19–20.

25 Leboutte, *Livret d'ouvrier*; Robert J. Steinfeld, *Coercion, Contract and Free Labor in the Nineteenth Century* (Cambridge, 2001).

Historical developments

The earliest examples of wage payments date back to some 5000 years ago, when the first states emerged in Mesopotamia. Like their city-state predecessors and like somewhat later in Egypt, for a very long time these polities organized their subjects according to tributary and redistributive obligations. Nevertheless, in two ways new types of labour relations could emerge there. Because these concentrations of power easily provoked wars, many prisoners were made, and instead of killing them they were reduced to slaves. At the same time, professional soldiers were maintained on a more regular basis, which implied regular payment in kind. Of King Sargon (c. 2,350 BCE) it is said that "5,400 men [= soldiers] eat before him."[26]

Labour markets emerged later, between 2000 and 1000 BCE, when officials organizing work for temples turned into subcontractors. At the same time, commodity markets were needed on a regular basis, where independent producers sold food and other necessaries to labourers.[27] Wages were paid in silver (in the shape of chips) and grain, but it was not until the 'invention' of coins as medium of exchange around 600 BCE that there was a break-through of waged labour.

In Babylon, at about that time, self-employed labour and wage labour were much more prevalent than slave labour, while reciprocal labour had become relatively unimportant.[28] Monetization and wage labour spread quickly from Anatolia into the Mediterranean and the Near-East. Only Egypt was late to adopt it; this did not happen until it was conquered by Alexander the Great. Nevertheless, the last pharaohs, who stuck to their tributary and redistributive state model, occasionally hired Greek soldiers, who had to be paid in coin.[29]

In North-Western India and in China similar developments took place a few centuries later. In the Mauryan Empire in North India (c. 321–185 BCE), small change was abundantly available and the *Arthashastra* distinguished amongst slaves, bond-

---

[26] Gwendolyn Leick, *Mesopotamia. The Invention of the City* (Harmondsworth, 2002), p. 95; Marc Van de Mieroop, *A History of the Ancient Near East, ca. 3000–323 BC*. Second edition (Malden, Oxford, Carlton, 2007), p. 231.
[27] Van de Mieroop, *History of the Ancient Near East*, pp. 93–94; Roger Matthews, *The Archeology of Mesopotamia. Theory and approaches* (London and New York, 2003), pp. 182–188.
[28] Muhammad A. Dandamaev, *Slavery in Babylonia. From Nabopolassar to Alexander the Great (626–331 BC)* (DeKalb, IL, 2009); Jursa, *Aspects of the Economic History of Babylonia*; R.J. van der Spek, "Cuneiform Documents on the Parthian History: The Rahimesu Archive. Materials for the Study of the Standard of Living", in: Josef Wiesehöfer (ed.), *Das Partherreich und seine Zeugnisse* (Stuttgart, 1998), pp. 205–258; R.J. van der Spek, "Feeding Hellenistic Seleucia on the Tigris and Babylon", in: Richard Alston and Otto M. van Nijf (eds), *Feeding the Ancient Greek City* (Leuven, 2008), pp. 33–45; Reinhard Wilfried Pirngruber, "The Impact of Empire on Market Prices in Babylon in the Late Achaemenid and Seleucid Periods, c. 400–140 B.C." (Ph.D. Dissertation, Free University Amsterdam, 2012).
[29] Sitta von Reden, *Money in Ptolemaic Egypt. From the Macedonian Conquest to the End of the Third Century BC* (Cambridge, 2007).

ed labourers, corvée labourers, casual labourers, and permanent labourers working for piece or time wages.[30] In Qin-China (well-known for its "terracotta army") small *banliang* coins were introduced around 350 BCE to replace bigger denominations. It was used both to pay corvée labourers (15–30% of the male productive population), convicts and casual labour. After the collapse of the Qin their Han successors (206 BCE–222 CE) abolished much of the forced work, restored the labour market and enlarged the circulation of small change.[31]

Monetized wage labour was there to stay, although it had its ups and downs. Remarkably, between 400 and 1100 it retreated in Western and Southern Eurasia, whereas at about the same time the opposite happened in the Arab world and China. Roles were reversed after 1100, when markets and wage labour reappeared in Europe and India but retreated for a few centuries in China until they experienced a renaissance under the Ming and first Qing emperors. In North-Western Europe, around 1500 half or more of the population depended on wage labour. Further towards the East, forms of unfreedom re-emerged (the "second serfdom").[32]

All great Pre-Columbian American polities were organized along similar lines as what we have seen in Eurasia before the advent of markets, monetization, and wage labour, although the Aztecs were in the process of developing markets when the Europeans arrived. At home and in their newly-colonized Atlantic islands the first conquerors, the Spaniards and the Portuguese, considered free wage labour to be the norm. However, aside from that they kept a lot of slaves because of their so-called just war with non-Christians.[33] On their newly-won Atlantic islands, slave labour was wide-spread and became the model for the use of slaves in the Americas. In the sixteenth century, the Spaniards applied this model, to the detriment of the indigenous population. The Portuguese, who also conquered important ports on the West African coast, nearly completely depended on slave labour in Brazil.[34]

The Dutch, the French, and the English, who took important parts of the Caribbean from the Spaniards after 1650, did not replicate the labour relations back home but copied the Luso-Brazilian example—including the use of slaving stations on the West African coast. An exception was the emigration of indentured labourers from

---

30 Osmund Bopearachchi, *From Bactria to Taprobane. Selected Works*, 2 Vols (New Delhi, 2015); Kautilya, *The Arthashastra*. Edited, Rearranged, Translated, and Introduced by L.N. Rangarajan (New Delhi, 1992).
31 Yuri Pines et al. (eds), *Birth of an Empire. The State of Qin Revisited* (Berkeley, CA, 2014); Lothar von Falkenhausen, *Chinese Society in the Age of Confucius (1000–250 BC). The Archaeological Evidence* (Los Angeles, 2006); Anthony J. Barbieri-Low, *Artisans in Early Imperial China* (Seattle and London, 2007).
32 Van Bavel, *Invisible Hand*.
33 Jean-Pierre Berthe, "Les formes de travail dépendant en Nouvelle-Espagne XVIe–XVIIIe siècles", in: Annalisa Guarducci (ed.), *Forme ed evoluzione del lavoro in Europa: XIII–XVIII secc.* (Prato, 1991), pp. 93–111.
34 For Latin-America see David J. McCreery, *The Sweat of Their Brow. A History of Work in Latin America* (New York and London, 2000).

England to the Caribbean—a temporary success in the seventeenth century—and to Northern America.[35] However, from the late 1680s African (American) slave labour began to dominate, including in North America. This continued, increasing with time, over the next two centuries.

While the transatlantic slave trade had an adverse effect on the development of wage labour in the Americas and certainly in Sub-Saharan Africa, Eurasia offers a mixed picture in the early modern period. Wage labour and self-employed labour (bearing in mind the proto-industrialization, which included women and children) were the dominant forms of labour in Western Europe, and they were only mixed with slave labour in the Mediterranean. The same held true in most of the other successful polities like the Ottoman Empire, the Safawid Empire, and especially the Moghul Empire as well as the Ming/Qing Empire in China. Nevertheless, slave labour was already present in Asia before the arrival of the Europeans—i.e. imported from Africa to the Middle-East and Western India—and the Europeans rather gave it a boost. The Portuguese—but also private European traders—were instrumental in increasing the use of slave labour.[36]

In the nineteenth century, wage labour underwent several major changes. First, slowly but surely it lost the severe competition from unfree labour after the abolishment of serfdom and slavery—notwithstanding serious drawbacks that occurred regularly (Hitler's Germany, Stalin's Russia, Mao's China, Pol Pot's Cambodia). Second, urbanization and industrialization induced a slow demise of independent producing groups like artisans and peasants. Slow, because for generations factory workers tried to stick to cottage and home industries and certainly to small scale food production on garden plots as much as possible. As a consequence, the proportion of wage labourers in the total working population increased. Laws restricting the (night-time) labour of women and children caused shifts in the gender and age composition of waged labourers. The same was done by welfare state arrangements in both the communist and the capitalist world, including old age care, pension schemes, the increase of general wage levels, the decrease of working hours, and, in many countries, the leaving of the workforce by females who became housewives. This happened in the first decades after the Second World War. Consequently, social equality increased, first inside developed countries and rather recently in countries around the world.

The demise of the Soviet Union and its satellite states and reforms in China initially seemed to reinforce tendencies already visible in the North Atlantic world. As a consequence, the poverty gap between the North Atlantic and countries like China, and to a lesser extent other parts of the so-called Global South have been narrowed. However, inequality within the countries of the so-called Global North and Global

---

[35] David W. Galenson, "Labor Market Behavior in Colonial America: Servitude, Slavery and Free Labor" in: *idem* (ed.), *Markets in History. Economic Studies of the Past* (Cambridge, 1989), pp. 52–96.
[36] Matthias van Rossum, *Kleurrijke tragiek. De geschiedenis van slavernij in Azië onder de VOC* (Hilversum, 2015).

South have increased substantially over the last decades. They have experienced multiple economic crises and repeatedly volatility since the 1970s. In fact, many positive trends have been reversed. The rights of the employees, enshrined in elaborate legislation, collective labour contracts, and public job mediation, have been weakened, and independent production has been propagated, thereby undermining the formal ideal of free wage labour. This has been successful to a certain extent, although at times independent production is merely a form of disguised unemployment. In an attempt to maintain the newly won material welfare, both husbands and wives engaged in wage labour and the working hours per household started to grow again. No wonder the labour movement has continued to become weaker since the 1980s.[37]

---

[37] Lucassen, *Outlines of a History of Labour.*

Suggested reading

Behal, Rana P. and Marcel van der Linden (eds). *Coolies, Capital, and Colonialism. Studies in Indian Labour History* (Cambridge: Cambridge University Press, 2006).
Biernacki, Richard. *The Fabrication of Labor. Germany and Britain, 1640–1914* (Berkeley, CA: University of California Press, 1995).
Botton, Alain de. *The Pleasures and Sorrows of Work* (Harmondsworth: Penguin, 2009).
Deakin, Simon and Frank Wilkinson. *The Law of the labour Market: Industrialization, Employment, and legal Evolution* (Oxford: Oxford University Press, 2005).
Donkin, Richard. *Blood, Sweat and Tears. The Evolution of Work* (New York and London: Texere, 2001).
Ehmer, Josef and Catharina Lis (eds). *The Idea of Work in Europe from Antiquity to Modern Times* (Farnham: Ashgate, 2009).
Gorski, Richard (ed). *Maritime Labour. Contributions to the History of Work at Sea, 1500–2000* (Amsterdam: Amsterdam University Press, 2007).
Hofmeester, Karin and Christine Moll-Murata (eds). *The Joy and Pain of Work. Global Attitudes and Valuations, 1500–1650* (Cambridge: Cambridge University Press, 2011).
Lis, Catharina and Hugo Soly. *Worthy Efforts. Attitudes to Work and Workers in Pre-Industrial Europe* (Leiden and Boston: Brill, 2012).
Lucassen, Jan (ed.). *Global Labour History. A State of the Art* (Bern: Peter Lang, 2006).
Lucassen, Jan. "Labour and Early Modern Economy", in: Karel Davids and Jan Lucassen (eds), *A Miracle Mirrored. The Dutch Republic in European Perspective* (Cambridge: Cambridge University Press, 1995), pp. 367–409.
Lucassen, Jan. *Outlines of a History of Labour* (Amsterdam: IISH, 2012).
Sonenscher, Michael. *Work and Wages. Natural Law, Politics and the Eighteenth-century French Trades* (Cambridge: Cambridge University Press, 1989).
Thomas, Keith (ed.). *The Oxford Book of Work* (Oxford: Oxford University Press, 1999).
Tilly, Chris and Charles Tilly. *Work under Capitalism* (Boulder, CO: Westview, 1998).
Van der Linden, Marcel and Leo Lucassen (eds). *Working on Labor. Essays in Honor of Jan Lucassen* (Leiden and Boston: Brill, 2012).
Van der Linden, Marcel and Richard Price (eds).*The Rise and Development of Collective Labour Law* (Bern: Peter Lang, 2000).
Van der Linden, Marcel. *Workers of the World. Essays toward a Global Labor History* (Leiden and Boston: Brill, 2008.)
Wadauer, Sigrid, Thomas Buchner, and Alexander Mejstrik (eds). *The History of labour Intermediation. Institutions and Finding Employment in the Nineteenth and Early Twentieth Centuries* (New York and Oxford: Berghahn, 2015).
Zürcher, Erik-Jan (ed.). *Fighting for a Living. A Comparative History of Military labour, 1500–2000* (Amsterdam: Amsterdam University Press, 2013).

Karin Hofmeester
5. Attitudes To Work

The importance of research on attitudes to work

Attitudes to work are an important aspect of the history of work. In addition to providing income, in kind or as money, work invests one with status, low or high. For many people work determines their position in society, and not having work – either by choice or involuntarily – in part determines an individual's identity. One important question concerns the grounds on which we categorize work as status-enhancing or status-diminishing, as honourable or dishonourable, or as useful or not useful. Work can provide satisfaction, but it can also be numbing, sickening, and even potentially fatal. If people have a choice, why do they opt for a certain type of work? Do status or background play a role? What about the desire for autonomy? And if people are forced to work, how is that coercion legitimized? In sixteenth-century Brazil, Portuguese slave owners legitimized their owning of slaves and their own "notworking" by reference to the European medieval ranking of "those who pray", "those who fight", and "those who labour". In the colony, the slave owners, who were originally traders, regarded themselves as belonging to the nobler classes who were not expected to work. Jesuit missionaries at the time argued too that it was to save their souls that slaves were being confined and forced to work, comparing the suffering of slaves with that of Christ.[1] Both of those extremely different ideologies were intended to legitimize what is the most extreme form of unfree labour.

Another important question is how different labour ideologies determined how workers viewed their own labour and how the rest of the world viewed it. Negative impressions and lack of respect from others – coupled with dissatisfaction over poor working conditions – might lead some workers to protest, as in the Zanj rebellion of black African slaves and other labourers in and around Basra at the end of the ninth century, or the various Dalit protests in India in the nineteenth and twentieth centuries.[2] Based on a comparison of worldwide attitudes to work from 1500 to 1650, we

---

1 Tarcisio Botelho, "Labour Ideologies and Labour Relations in Colonial Portuguese America, 1500–1700", in: Karin Hofmeester and Christine Moll-Murata (eds), *The Joy and Pain of Work: Global Attitudes and Valuations, 1500–1650* (Cambridge, 2011), pp. 275–296. He also shows clearly that Jesuits discussed the legitimacy of slavery, and that they had differing views of its legitimacy.
2 Ghada Talhami, "The Zanj Rebellion Reconsidered", *The International Journal of African Historical Studies*, 10:3 (1977), pp. 443–461; Maya Shatzmiller, *Labour in the Medieval Islamic World* (Leiden and Boston, 1994), pp. 375–376; Shashi Bhushan Upadhyay, "Dalits and the Ideology of Work in India", in: Marcel van der Linden and Prabhu P. Mohapatra (eds), *Labour Matters: Towards Global Histories* (Delhi, 2009), pp. 152–171; and Shashi Bhushan Upadhyay, "Meaning of Work in Dalit Autobiographies", *Studies in History*, 26, 1 (2010), pp. 31–60.

may conclude that people define themselves and have always been defined by others in terms of their work.³ Some authors claim that the adage "you are what you work" was particularly true for people dependent on wages, but is even more likely to have applied to people working under other forms of labour relations.⁴

Work, workers, and labour relations have changed over the past five centuries. Do those changes – such as the increase or decrease in the extent of wage labour – give cause to think differently about work, workers, and labour? In what follows, we shall first consider the sources and methods that one might use to investigate attitudes to work. Next, we shall provide a survey of the current literature in the field, while the final section is largely a consideration of Catharina Lis and Hugo Soly's *Worthy Efforts: Attitudes to Work and Workers in Pre-Industrial Europe*. The main findings of their study, which focused exclusively on Europe, will be considered in light of whether they too can be tested and substantiated for other parts of the world.

Sources and methods

In seeking answers to the questions just outlined concerning attitudes to work, it is important to distinguish – as Lis and Soly did – between work and workers. People often appreciate work done, or rather, they appreciate the results of work such as the harvest gathered by farmers; but the same people are less likely to appreciate the farmers themselves. The same often applies to trade and merchants.⁵ Important too is the distinction between what others thought and wrote about work and workers – something of which we know a great deal – and how workers saw themselves and their work – something of which we know much less. Often the sources researchers have at their disposal are normative texts: religious works, texts written by theologians or philosophers, enlightened thinkers, world travellers, or they might be legal texts and manuals. They tell us a lot about how influential members of the administrative, religious, and intellectual elite viewed work, though such people often had a certain ideal in mind that did not necessarily correspond to reality. They tell us little or nothing about how workers themselves regarded the work they did. To interpret normative texts properly it is important to contextualize and analyse them carefully. For Europe, Lis and Soly looked at an enormous number of texts and asked themselves, "Who says what to whom, about what, where, when and why?"⁶ We

---

3 Karin Hofmeester and Christine Moll-Murata, "The Joy and Pain of Work: Global Attitudes and Valuations, 1500–1650: Introduction", in *idem*, *Joy and Pain of Work*, pp. 1–23, 18.
4 Catharina Lis and Hugo Soly, *Worthy Efforts. Attitudes to Work and Workers in Pre-Industrial Europe* (Leiden and Boston, 2012), p. 432.
5 *Ibid.*, p. 159.
6 *Ibid.*, p. 5.

might also ask "How and using what words?", because the semantics of the terms and concepts associated with work and workers can be significant.[7]

In his contribution to *The Joy and Pain of Work: Global Attitudes and Valuations, 1500–1650*, Marcel van der Linden urged scholars to look not only at normative texts and their social impact on entrepreneurs, but more importantly to look too at how the labouring poor regarded their work and labour relations.[8] Van der Linden suggested that for the early modern period it is advisable to look at things like the songs people sang while working, at proverbs, and at collective fantasies of another, better, life. Christine Moll-Murata in her essay in the same volume, on work ethics and work valuation in Ming China, offers several good examples of work songs that tell us something about labour relations and how they were experienced. Hired labourers in particular complained about poor working and living conditions and the bad character of their bosses.[9] Regine Mathias's essay on work ethics in Japan, again in that same volume, offers examples that illustrate the same relationship between employer and employee.[10] Shireen Moosvi describes the religious songs of a group of manual labourers in Mughal India which emphasized the dignity of their profession in the eyes of God, while they also, in passing, deprecated both Hinduism and Islam because of their caste-based constraints.[11]

Sources of that type, and particularly collective fantasies of a better life, may be interpreted in multiple ways. Van der Linden, for instance, regards Cockaigne as an imaginary better world where food flies into people's mouths without any effort needing to be expended and where nobody can be forced to work against their will. Lis and Soly on the other hand explain the popularity of that sort of story in terms of comic effect, rather than because a world in which there is no obligation to work was considered a "worthy ideal".[12] In this respect, Henk Looijesteijn's chapter on the writings of Pieter Plockhoy offer a revealing insight into the ideal of a seventeenth-century Dutch artisan, who envisaged a community where everyone could work under reciprocal labour relations while also having enough time to pursue spi-

---

7 Jörn Leonhard and Willibald Steinmetz (eds), *Semantiken von Arbeit: Diachrone und vergleichende Perspektiven* (Cologne, 2016).
8 Marcel van der Linden, "Studying Attitudes to Work Worldwide, 1500–1650: Concepts, Sources, and Problems of Interpretation", in: Hofmeester and Moll-Murata, *Joy and Pain of Work*, pp. 25–43, 26.
9 Christine Moll-Murata, "Work Ethics and Work Valuations in a Period of Commercialization: Ming China, 1500–1644", in: Hofmeester and Moll-Murata, *Joy and Pain of Work*, pp. 165–195, 190–193; Regine Mathias, "Japan in the Seventeenth Century: Labour Relations and Work Ethics", in: *ibid.*, pp. 217–243, 241–242.
10 Mathias, "Japan in the Seventeenth Century", pp. 241–242.
11 Shireen Moosvi, "The World of Labour in Mughal India (c.1500–1750)", in: Hofmeester and Moll-Murata, *Joy and Pain of Work*, pp. 245–261, 256–257.
12 Van der Linden, "Studying Attitudes to Work Worldwide", p. 33; Lis and Soly, *Worthy Efforts*, p. 551.

ritual obligations.[13] For subsequent periods we have workers' autobiographies, although workers seldom wrote explicitly about work and their attitudes to it.[14]

For many parts of the world in the early modern period we have to rely for our sources on visitors from elsewhere who wrote such things as travel accounts and missionary reports. However, many of the descriptions of work and workers – and of those not working – we find in those sources are distorted by the ideas such "visitors" had of the societies they encountered in foreign lands. As van der Linden shows, many of their descriptions tell us more about the ideal of work in their own society than about the actual work practices they found, let alone about how local labourers themselves looked upon their work. We may infer something from their texts, though a degree of caution is required. Official texts, such as reports on the local situation and laws regulating work and labour relations, often show not only what workers were expected to do, but also what they actually did do, or what they failed to do. Finally, different observations drawn from different parts of the world can be used heuristically, for example to infer the almost universal deprecation among elites of manual labour in societies in which slavery was prevalent.[15]

In addition to texts, there are other sources that allow us to infer what workers and others thought about work: Roman tombstones and epitaphs referring proudly to the professions of the deceased; signed pieces from Ancient Greece and the Mediterranean Islamic countries during the Middle Ages, as well as portraits and frescoes in studios and workshops.[16] Besides archaeology and art history, ethnography too can provide useful material from participatory research and interviews. A good example here is the work of Gerd Spittler, who spoke with the Tuareg as they herded their

---

13 Henk Looijesteijn, "Between Sin and Salvation: The Seventeenth-Century Dutch Artisan Pieter Plockhoy and His Ethics of Work", in: Hofmeester and Moll-Murata, *Joy and Pain of Work*, pp. 69–88.
14 See, for example, James S. Amelang, "Lifting the Curse: Or Why Early Modern Worker Autobiographers Did Not Write About Work", in: Josef Ehmer and Catharina Lis (eds), *The Idea of Work in Europe from Antiquity to Modern Times* (Farnham, 2009), pp. 91–100, and the titles to which he refers. For a survey of predominantly European and American worker autobiographies, see https://networks.h-net.org/node/7753/pages/77840/labor-worker-autobiographies. For India, see Upadhyay, "Meaning of Work in Dalit Autobiographies", and Jeevan Prakash (ed.), *Autobiography of An Indian Indentured Labourer: Munshi Rahman Khan (1874–1972)* (Delhi, 2005). A global inventory of workers' autobiographies would be valuable in researching global attitudes among workers to work.
15 Van der Linden, "Studying Attitudes to Work Worldwide", pp. 34–37.
16 For tombs, epitaphs, and signed works by craftsmen in Ancient Greece and Rome, see Lis and Soly, *Worthy Efforts*, pp. 48–51 and 69–71. For signed works in the Islamic world, see Shatzmiller, *Labour in the Medieval Islamic World*, p. 382, and Barbara Finster as cited in Jessica Dijkman, "Worthy Efforts and the Medieval Economy", *TSEG / The Low Countries Journal of Social and Economic History*, 11, 1 (2014), pp. 105–115, 115. For visual images, see Gerhard Jaritz, "The Visual Representation of Late Medieval Work: Patterns of Context, People and Action", in: Ehmer and Lis, *Idea of Work*, pp. 125–148; Ilja M. Veldman, "Representations of Labour in Late Sixteenth-Century Netherlandish Prints: The Secularization of the Work Ethic", in: *ibid.*, pp. 149–175; and Peter Burke, "Representing Women's Work in Early Modern Italy", in: *ibid.*, pp. 177–187. See also Annette de Vries, *Ingelijst werk. De verbeelding van arbeid en beroep in de vroegmoderne Nederlanden* (Zwolle, 2004).

camels and noted the semantics of words associated with work and working. Spittler was interested in identifying any age- or gender-related differences in views regarding certain tasks.[17] Within the anthropology of work there is a focus too on attitudes to work, although much of that research relates to the modern period.[18] For those periods and regions for which we have no easily available first-hand written sources, a combined multidisciplinary approach to different types of source is probably the best way to identify what workers themselves thought about work.

Where written records do exist but are written mainly by visitors from elsewhere, the danger of projection is considerable. Van der Linden in his article gives examples of alleged East Asian "decadence" which, it is claimed, caused the natives to be indisposed to work, and resulted in the lack of economic development. The "myth of the lazy native", the idea among Europeans that most non-Europeans did as little work as they could, is perhaps the most widespread form of projection, and we shall say more about it later.[19] The researcher should therefore be aware of this matter of projection, and of false generalization. An extremely critical approach to sources, self-reflection, and an acknowledgement of one's own prejudices as well as due consideration of contextual explanations of observations found in sources – all those will certainly help scholars to make fruitful use of those sources.[20] The "Who says what to whom, about what, where, when, and why?" questions posed by Lis and Soly will serve as a useful guide here, supplemented by the question, "How and in what words?"

In their volume *The Joy and Pain of Work*, editors Hofmeester and Moll-Murata raise a number of other questions that might give an insight into attitudes to work, workers, and labour relations. Have there been hierarchies of professions in different societies? If so, on what were they based? Who was permitted to do what sort of work? What was the division of labour relating to gender and age, to ethnic and religious affiliation, or to belonging to particular families or lineages. What

---

[17] Gerd Spittler, "Arbeit zur Sprache bringen – ethnographische Annäherungen", in: Leonhard and Steinmetz, *Semantiken von Arbeit*, pp. 158–166.
[18] Hélène d'Almeida-Topor, Monique Lakroum, and Gerd Spitter (eds), *Le travail en Afrique noir. Représentations et pratiques à l'époque contemporaine* (Paris, 2003), including Mamadou Diawara, "Ce que travailler veut dire dans le monde mandé", pp. 67–80. For a survey of the recent literature see http://www.ethnologie.uni-bayreuth.de/de/Wichtige-Publikationen/Anthropologie_der_Arbeit/index.html.
[19] For the secondary literature on the lazy native in South-east Asia, see Syed Hussein Alatas, *The Myth of the Lazy Native: A Study of the Image of the Malays, Filipinos and Javanese from the 16th to the 20th Century and its Function in the Ideology of Colonial Capitalism* (London, 1977), and Norani Othman, "Auffassung, Wahrnehmung und Kultur der Arbeit in der malaiischen Gesellschaft", in: Jürgen Kocka and Claus Offe (eds), *Geschichte und Zukunft der Arbeit* (Frankfurt, 2000), pp. 148–162. For Africa see Klas Rönnbäck, "The Idle and the Industrious – European Ideas about the African Work Ethic in Precolonial West Africa", *History in Africa*, 41 (2014), pp. 117–145; idem, *Labour and Living Standards in Pre-Colonial West Africa. The Case of the Gold Coast* (London etc., 2015), ch. 4.
[20] Van der Linden, "Studying Attitudes to Work Worldwide", p. 39.

were the roles of voluntary associations, such as guilds? How was free labour valued, and unfree labour legitimized?

Historiography

We have already discussed a number of studies on attitudes to work, but a systematic, albeit non-exhaustive survey is useful as a "pre-history" of the work by Lis and Soly. Their work, although admittedly only about Europe, offers a research agenda that is valuable to a global approach too. Influential studies on the concept of work in European history can be traced to Herbert Applebaum's impressively pioneering work *The Concept of Work*, which described and analysed trends and tendencies from antiquity to the industrial age.[21] In an earlier study, the same author had already addressed the subject of work from an anthropological perspective. The volume he edited entitled *Work in Non-Market and Transitional Societies* comprises collected essays on work organization among hunters and gatherers in pastoralist societies, among cultivators and gardeners in villages, and in cultures and societies where non-market and market-oriented work values underwent change and adaptation. The studies discuss mostly contemporary non-European cases. In his categorizations of work in non-market societies Applebaum defines work as being embedded in the total cultural fabric, with strong communal aspects that involve mutuality and reciprocal exchange. Work is intended mostly for subsistence, is not very specialized, and is task-oriented rather than time-oriented.[22] While Applebaum treated Europe and many non-European regions and communities separately, other historians have focused on both.

The volume edited by Michel Cartier, *Le travail et ses représentations*, follows in the tradition of Maurice Godelier[23] and has a strong anthropological and linguistic focus. The case studies there discuss extra-European communities in Oceania, Africa, and South America from the eighteenth century to the present, and the book includes an essay by the editor himself on work in ancient China.[24] Of particular interest in this collection are the contemporary articles on rituals and work, but also the discourse analysis of eighteenth-century texts from Madagascar that focus on the various forms of labour relations, including reciprocal, tributary, and commodified

---

21 Herbert Applebaum, *The Concept of Work: Ancient, Medieval, and Modern* (New York, 1992).
22 Idem, "Theoretical Introduction", in: idem (ed.), *Work in Non-Market and Transitional Societies* (Buffalo, 1984), p. 2.
23 Lis and Ehmer, "Introduction", in: Ehmer and Lis, *Idea of Work*, p. 6, give an outline of Godelier's initiative.
24 Michel Cartier, "Travail et idéologie dans la Chine antique", in: idem (ed.), *Le travail et ses représentations* (Paris, 1984), pp. 275–304.

labour relations.²⁵ Similarly based on texts, but mainly literary ones, is the work of Keith Thomas, who in *The Oxford Book of Work* provides a thematically structured anthology of mainly European and especially British poetry and literature on work. In his interesting introduction Thomas describes how for a long time work was not a popular theme in poetry and literature, and how that fact relates to attitudes to work among the writing elite.²⁶

More recently Jürgen Kocka and Manfred Bierwisch have separately edited collected volumes of articles on the history of work.²⁷ Both share a concern about contemporary changes in work, the decrease in the extent of wage labour and long-term commitment on the part of employers. They both link to periods when dependent wage labour was not the norm, and they look to extra-European regions too for patterns of work organization that diverged from the West European case. They do so for reasons of contrast in a situation where the West is in crisis rather than on the rise. As for the European historical experience, both still offer the standard narrative. In their introduction, Kocka and Offe stress the impact on the rise of capitalism of Christianity, the discipline imposed on urban citizens, the Protestant work ethic, and the philosophy of the Enlightenment.²⁸ The non-European cases they present are from India, Japan, Malaya, Africa, and the Islamic world and mostly refer to the present. They can be understood as providing a contrast with the European, to be more precise the German, case. The intention of these volumes is to explain the current occupational crisis in Europe and to offer suggestions for "therapy",²⁹ or to propose a new orientation for the relationship between work and life.³⁰ Bierwisch's collection intends not to offer new details but to provide overviews. He looks at work from the time of European antiquity, work organization in twentieth-century industrial Russia with its rural roots, conceptual aspects of work in China from antiquity to the present, work in Islam, and offers a case study of concepts of work in a present-day African rural community.

The recent study by Jörn Leonhard and Willibald Steinmetz, *Semantiken von Arbeit*, is in line with that tradition.³¹ The prevailing history of the concept of work is no longer adequate now that so many new forms of work and non-work have emerged. Instead of taking that history as a given, Leonhard and Steinmetz follow the historical and semantic development of how work has been conceived, linking it to socio-

---

25 Françoise Raison-Jourde, "Le travail et l'échange dans les discours d'Adianampoin Imerina (Madagascar – XVIIIe siècle", in: Cartier, *Le travail et ses représentations*, pp. 223–274.
26 Keith Thomas (ed.), *The Oxford Book of Work* (Oxford, 1999).
27 Kocka and Offe, *Geschichte und Zukunft der Arbeit*; Manfred Bierwisch (ed.), *Die Rolle der Arbeit in verschiedenen Epochen und Kulturen* (Berlin, 2003).
28 Jürgen Kocka and Claus Offe, "Einleitung", in: *idem, Geschichte und Zukunft der Arbeit*, p. 20.
29 Kocka and Offe, *Geschichte und Zukunft der Arbeit*, section "Beschäftigungskrise in Europa: Konkurrierende Erklärungen und Therapieangebote", pp. 195–261.
30 Manfred Bierwisch, "Arbeit in verschiedenen Epochen und Kulturen – Einleitende Bemerkungen", in: *idem, Die Rolle der Arbeit*, p. 16.
31 Leonhard and Steinmetz, *Semantiken von Arbeit*.

historical developments and to ethnographic insights specific to a particular period and place. Their collection contains a number of articles on Europe in the pre-industrial, industrial, and post-industrial periods, as well as one about Europe in the Middle Ages and another on the early modern period. It also includes five articles on regions outside Europe: the Iberian empires and their colonies; Africa; the Arab world; and Japan. The historical-semantic approach taken shows how many different terms for work – and thus forms of work and opinions about it – circulated, not only in post-industrial Europe and Asia where its pluriformity was growing but also in earlier periods than that as well as elsewhere in the world. That polyphony can be found in non-European regions too as sooner or later most of them came into contact with European colonizers and the attitudes to work they brought with them and to which they obliged their subjects to relate.[32] Alongside the dynamics of how work was discussed, the authors identify continuity, and repeated reversion to more traditional "interpretations" of work.[33]

It was in their *The Idea of Work in Europe from Antiquity to Modern Times* that Josef Ehmer and Catharina Lis as editors first presented their view that the standard narrative – which borrows heavily from Max Weber – of linear development from a work ethic based on sixteenth-century Christian values to one rooted in capitalist culture and directed towards success remains largely unchallenged in the current literature.[34] That perspective not only neglects variant views on work in earlier periods, it lacks differentiation in the linear narrative, which moreover remains excessively focused on the perspective of the "Rise of the West".[35] An important feature of the volume by Ehmer and Lis, in addition to the critical analysis of the standard narrative, is the long period it covers and the wide variety of sources used, especially to determine the attitudes of workers. Those sources include merchants' handbooks, workers' autobiographies, and court documents. The merchants' handbooks reveal a strong sense of professional ethics and a professional mentality, both of which helped craft the social identity of merchants. Artisans have left us autobiographies, from which it is clear that they were often organized into guilds, each with its own rituals and regalia to demonstrate their professional pride and self-esteem. For example, from court documents relating to porters working in Milan in the seventeenth and eighteenth centuries we discern a strong group identity and sense of pride based on a shared immigrant background and support from the political representatives of their native country, from which they had emigrated, but temporarily, in order to carry out their demanding and dirty work in Milan.[36]

---

[32] *Idem*, "Von der Begriffsgeschichte zur historischen Semantik von 'Arbeit'", in: *ibid.*, pp. 9–59, 48–49.
[33] *Ibid.*, p. 42.
[34] Lis and Ehmer, "Introduction", in: Ehmer and Lis, *Idea of Work*, pp. 1–30, 5–6, 8–9.
[35] *Ibid.*, p. 16.
[36] Jaume Aurell, "Reading Renaissance Merchants' Handbooks: Confronting Professional Ethics and Social Identity", in: Ehmer and Lis, *Idea of Work*, pp. 71–90; Luca Mocarelli, "The Attitude of Mila-

Some of the criticism voiced by Ehmer and Lis and by Lis and Soly regarding the standard narrative on the discontinuity between ideas about work in antiquity and in the Middle Ages can be found too in Birgit van den Hoven's study, *Work in Ancient and Medieval Thought*, where the ideas of ancient philosophers, medieval monks, and theologians and their concept of work, occupations, and technology are given a central role. Van den Hoven shows that there was not necessarily any real discontinuity in ideas about work such as those cherished in ancient times and those described in the Middle Ages, while the Christian appreciation of work initially applied chiefly to spiritual work.[37] A fine addition to the studies by Ehmer and Lis and by van den Hoven is the collection of essays edited by Verena Postel, *Arbeit im Mittelalter: Vorstellungen und Wirklichkeiten*. The contributions to that volume are based on the history of the concept of work and on the semantics of Latin and Middle High German, and on legal historical and art historical approaches.[38] Like Lis, Johannes Engels refers to the writings of a number of Greek philosophers not necessarily all of whom always viewed manual work with disdain. Kay Peter Jankrift details how the work of physicians was described by members of the profession itself and by others, with the physicians themselves emphasizing largely the human, more empathetic aspect of their profession while the outside world tended to regard what they did as the work of God, with the physicians serving merely as intermediaries.[39]

As part of the project "A Global Collaboratory on the History of Labour Relations 1500–2000" (see chapter 4.0 of the present volume), Karin Hofmeester and Christine Moll-Murata edited a collection of essays – *The Joy and Pain of Work: Global Attitudes and Valuations, 1500–1650*. For the earliest years in the sample, 1500 and 1650, quantitative data on work were based mainly on rough estimates. A qualitative approach is needed to interpret the data properly, and an inventory of attitudes to work can help in that. In addition to the essays already mentioned, the collection includes contributions examining labour ideologies and women in the Northern Netherlands, attitudes to work and fair wages in Italy, and religious aspects of labour ethics in Russia. Though some of the case studies relate to Europe, others are drawn from other parts of the world, namely the Arab-Islamic world, Ming China, Tokugawa Japan, Mughal India, Portuguese America, and the Colonial Andes.

---

nese Society to Work and Commercial Activities: The Case of the Porters and the Case of the Elites", in: Ehmer and Lis, *Idea of Work*, pp. 101–121; Amelang, "Lifting the Curse".

37 Birgit van den Hoven, *Work in Ancient and Medieval Thought: Ancient Philosophers, Medieval Monks and Theologians and their Concept of Work, Occupations and Technology* (Leiden, 1996). See also Wilfried Nippel, "Erwerbsarbeit in der Antike", in: Kocka and Offe, *Geschichte und Zukunft der Arbeit*, pp. 54–66.

38 Verena Postel (ed.), *Arbeit im Mittelalter: Vorstellungen und Wirklichkeiten* (Berlin, 2006).

39 Johannes Engels, "Merces auctoramentum servitutis – Die Wertschätzung bestimmter Arbeiten und Tätigkeiten durch antike heidnische Philosophen", in: *ibid.*, pp. 57–78; Kay Peter Jankrift, "Arbeit zwischen Handwerk und Kunst: Selbst- und Fremdwahrnehmung ärtzlicher Tätigkeit", in: *ibid.*, pp. 203–210.

In almost all the regions described, for the period 1500 to 1650 we can see the effects of an expanding global market economy and as a consequence shifts towards commodified labour. In some areas wage labour became more extensive, in others reciprocal labour was transformed into slave labour. In all cases the changes led to debates and action. To the extent the sources allow, one may conclude that – if at all possible – workers themselves made choices. Tributary workers in Potosí performed heavy and burdensome work in the silver mines as "free" wage labour in order to buy off their tribute.[40] Normative texts, both religious and "secular", have been found for all regions, and usually such texts, many of them written in response to socio-economic and political changes, depict an ideal rather than the actual situation. Almost everywhere one can find texts that say something about labour – and wage labour – done by women. Many of those texts are worded disapprovingly but, as the articles by Ariadne Schmidt and Karin Hofmeester show, the paid work performed by women was valued, as long as it was neither too publicly visible nor carried out in a public space frequented by men.[41] That kind of text reveals to us that women did actually perform paid work – in addition to all the unpaid work they were obliged to do. Moreover, almost every society had a hierarchy of occupations which, although in practice it could be interpreted in various ways and was constantly changing, nonetheless determined attitudes to work.

The idea of work in Europe

The most remarkable recent study in the field of attitudes to work is undoubtedly that by Catharina Lis and Hugo Soly, *Worthy Efforts: Attitudes to Work and Workers in Pre-Industrial Europe*, to which we have already made many references. The main question in their book is "which population groups in pre-industrial Europe defined which efforts as work, and which they did not, how these activities were valorized, and in what measure those performing them were appreciated".[42] Lis and Soly's work is based on an impressive list of primary and secondary sources meticulously analysed and above all contextualized, on the basis of "Who says what to whom, about what, where, when and why?" As a result of their robust and critical approach

---

[40] Raquel Gil Montero, "Free and Unfree Labour in the Colonial Andes in the Sixteenth and Seventeenth Centuries", in: Hofmeester and Moll-Murata, *Joy and Pain of Work*, pp. 297–318, 313–317.
[41] Karin Hofmeester, "Jewish Ethics and Women's Work in the Late Medieval and Early Modern Arab-Islamic World", in: *ibid.*, pp. 141–164; Ariadne Schmidt, "Labour Ideologies and Women in the Northern Netherlands, c.1500–1800", in: *ibid.*, pp. 45–67. For ideologies of women's work in the Netherlands and Netherlands Indies in later periods, see Elise van Nederveen Meerkerk, "Grammar of Difference? The Dutch Colonial State, Labour Policies, and Social Norms on Work and Gender, c. 1800–1940", *International Review of Social History*, 61 (S24) (2016), pp. 137–164. On the Netherlands, see Corinne Boter, "Ideal versus Reality? The Domesticity Ideal and Household Labour Relations in Dutch Industrializing Regions, circa 1890", *The History of the Family*, 22, 1 (2017), pp. 82–102.
[42] Lis and Soly, *Worthy Efforts*, p. 2.

the standard narrative concerning the development of a work ethic in Europe has had to be rejected once and for all. Their study shows that there is no major difference between the work ethic of Ancient Greece, the Roman Empire, and the early Middle Ages; the prevailing norm of work as important and necessary was ubiquitous. However, for a philosopher-scientist like Aristotle and other members of the elite the possibility of a broader-based democracy with the threat that it would undermine their position was cause to express their disdain of workers who were dependent for their income on others. Because of their dependence, workers lost their moral integrity and were therefore unsuitable for citizenship and political influence.[43] For both the Roman Empire and the Middle Ages Lis and Soly argue that similar expressions of disdain for work did not reflect a generally accepted view of work but rather informed the defensive mechanisms of members of the elite towards the nascent middle groups. Moreover, within Western Christianity no single continuous linear development can be observed of a work ethic that would have enabled the emergence of a prosperous, capitalist Western Europe through monasticism, urban expansion, humanism, the Reformation, and the Enlightenment. Lis and Soly show in minute detail how many different views concerning the nature of work coexisted within Christianity. At the same time, they also show that there was in fact nothing new in the ideas of Luther and Calvin, paralleling this polyphony, that work is a calling from God and that everyone must work in their God-given vocations.[44] It is important to scrutinize the Weber narrative critically because it was projected not only onto modern Europe but onto earlier periods too, as Lis and Soly demonstrate with reference to the work of Moses Finley.[45] Moreover, Finley's characterization of the ancient economy again plays a role in the interpretation of economic developments in the Islamic world in the Middle Ages.[46] In assessing work ethics in India too Weber's thesis plays a role, as the work of Shashi Bhushan Upadhay shows.[47]

Lis and Soly's approach is highly effective and worth adopting, as evidenced by the various review articles in a special debates section devoted to *Worthy Efforts*.[48] Their premise is that "changes in social positions and sets of relations brought on recurrent debates and polemics about work and workers".[49] It was the aforesaid defensive mechanisms to counter the emergence of social middle groups (artisans, merchants, but also intellectuals) "demanding permanent space to manoeuvre, intending to distinguish themselves, and having every interest in basing status on achievement or merit" that gave rise to debates about what value should be ascribed

---

[43] *Ibid.*, pp. 33–34.
[44] *Ibid.*, pp. 148–152.
[45] *Ibid.*, pp. 55–56.
[46] Shatzmiller, *Labour in the Medieval Islamic World*, p. 401.
[47] Upadhyay, "Dalits and the Ideology of Work in India", pp. 153–156.
[48] *TSEG / The Low Countries Journal of Social and Economic History*, 11, 1 (2014), pp. 61–174.
[49] Lis and Soly, *Worthy Efforts*, p. 6.

to work and workers.⁵⁰ From the late Middle Ages the increase in the number of individuals wholly or partly dependent on wage labour and the corresponding geographic and social mobility of workers, both upwards and downwards, confused both the elite and some of the middle groups.⁵¹ For the medieval and early modern periods Lis and Soly focus on three occupational groups: farmers, merchants, and artisans. They examine both the attitudes of others to those workers and their work, and – as far as possible – the attitudes of the workers themselves. For farmers, that is much more difficult than for merchants and craftsmen, who, as we saw earlier, expressed pride in their profession in a number of different ways. Further, Lis and Soly devote by far the longest chapter of their book to a single type of labour relation, namely wage work. Wage workers could, of course, be found among peasants and artisans, so there is some overlap in their chapters; but their view is that it was wage labour that led to such major debates about work, and so their approach can be justified. From the perspective of a global history of work it is unfortunate that they ignore other forms of labour relations, but one cannot hope to cover everything in a single book.⁵² They also put forward two important propositions, both of which say something about the rest of the world. The first is that the imperative to work hard can be found not only in pre-industrial Europe; it can be found in religions, philosophies, and cultural traditions all over the world. It was only pre-industrial Europe that saw the polyphony of "co-existence of different criteria for qualifying activities as worthy efforts".⁵³ Their second proposition is that "the process of proletarianization in many parts of Europe between the eleventh-twelfth centuries and the mid-nineteenth century influenced attitudes towards work and workers more deeply than any other social change, also more deeply than the rise of new religious doctrines, the introduction of new ideas about knowledge/science, or the emergence of new schools of thought". It was this proletarianization, a "gradual but continuous and ultimately massive process that distinguished late-medieval and early-modern Europe both from Classical Antiquity and from other parts of the world".⁵⁴ We might hold reservations about both propositions. We see, or rather hear, similar polyphony in other parts of the world too, even if the voices are not always as audible nor distinct. However, just as in Europe "the power of the messenger set the volume of the megaphone",⁵⁵ so it did elsewhere in the world. Furthermore,

---

50 Ibid., p. 561.
51 Ibid., p. 568.
52 On slavery, see, for example, Jan Lucassen, "Worthy and Unworthy Efforts: Europe as a Comparative Unit", *TSEG / The Low Countries Journal of Social and Economic History*, 11:1 (2014), pp. 117–126.
53 Lis and Soly, *Worthy Efforts*, pp. 553–555. On the valuation of work in other religions and cultures, see F.S. Niles, "Towards a Cross-Cultural Understanding of Work-Related Beliefs", *Human Relations*, 52, 7 (1999), pp. 855–867, at 865–866, quoted in: Upadhyay, "Dalits and the Ideology of Work in India", p. 155.
54 Lis and Soly, *Worthy Efforts*, p. 567.
55 Ibid., p. 556.

from very early on several parts of Asia were characterized by large population groups active in commercialized agriculture and manufacturing, as we shall see below. The interesting question, then, is whether in those regions too the growing prevalence of wage labour led to increased debate on attitudes to work. Moreover, do we see defensive mechanisms being used there too by elites and middle groups attempting to contain the mobility of new groups, for example by drawing up labour laws? The elites wanted to maintain social order while at the same time ensuring that labour was cheap. In order to force workers to perform wage labour the elites were prompted to categorize as "idle" those who combined different forms of labour in an effort to keep their heads above water.[56] In regions where instead of wage labour other, more unfree forms of labour were the result of the transition to commodified production, the question arises as to whether that transition too stimulated debate. In both cases, the question of what workers thought about their work and labour relations is highly relevant. In what follows we shall look in more detail at attitudes to work in the Islamic world, then briefly discuss developments in several parts of Asia and Africa. Not all the questions set out above can be addressed in this brief discussion, but the research agenda will perhaps be broadened slightly as a result.

The idea of work in the Islamic world, Asia and Africa

Like Christianity, Islam ascribes no abstract social significance to work. How work is valued depends on the tasks fulfilled by an individual or group for the community of believers.[57] At several points in the Koran, prayer and work are said to be equally important. Individuals have an obligation to use the tools and talents given them by God to support themselves and, where possible, further the well-being of the Muslim community. Those able to work should work; begging is reprehensible if there is no immediate need.[58] Alongside strictly religious texts there are also the medieval Islamic writings on the subject of work by religious and social thinkers, men of letters, and philosophers.[59] Even in a "limited region" such as the Islamic lands of the Mediterranean and a "limited period" such as the Middle Ages, one finds differences in opinions, and especially shifts in them. In her *Labour in the Medieval Islamic World*, Maya Shatzmiller includes a chapter on concepts of work that can serve as a useful introduction to the polyphony of the Islamic world, but that can also be qualified on

---

56 *Ibid.*, p. 440.
57 Rudiger Klein, "Arbeit und Arbeiteridentitäten in Islamischen Gesellschaften", in: Kocka and Offe, *Geschichte und Zukunft der Arbeit*, pp. 163–174, 165.
58 Ulrich Haarmann, "Arbeit im Islam", in: Bierwisch, *Die Rolle der Arbeit*, pp. 137–152, 138–140.
59 Reinhard Schulze, "Arbeit als Problem der arabischen Sozialgeschichte", in: Leonhard and Steinmetz, *Semantiken von Arbeit*, pp. 191–208, makes an impassioned plea for the contextualization of the concept of "work" in socio-historical processes within Islamic societies.

the basis of subsequent literature and in particular in light of the questions posed by Lis and Soly.[60] Shatzmiller describes various texts written by urban intellectuals from the eighth century onwards in which are expressed respect for commerce and contempt for manual labour.[61] In the literature, one reason given for the high status attributed to trade is that Muhammad was originally a merchant, and that his wife enjoyed a highly successful mercantile career herself. It was also partly a reflection of the context within which Islam emerged: the region prospered owing to international trade.[62] The aversion to manual labour is more difficult to explain, and can probably be attributed to the pre-Islamic beliefs of Arab Bedouin and other, sedentary, populations.[63] Influenced by the Islamic conquests of the seventh, eighth, and ninth centuries, a link was then established between manual labour and the ethnic background of workers, since it was often non-Arabs who did the work. Moreover, black slaves from Africa were recruited for lower manual occupations, while white slaves, later manumitted, were conscripted into the army.[64] All this did nothing to raise the status of manual labour in the eyes of the Arabs.

With the economy growing and both agriculture and manufacturing becoming increasingly commercialized, commerce flourished in the ninth century, and therefore so too did cities such as Baghdad and Basra. These developments led to debates concerning the position of manual labour, and the debates also found their way into the literature. Al-Jāḥiẓ was an eighth-century writer, philosopher, and theologian who wrote on diverse subjects and was the first to enrich the literature with humour. One element of this new genre was "compositions about tradesmen", in which representatives of various professions played a specific role, as if in a kind of play. More works in the same genre appeared, and they continued to be popular for centuries.[65] Shatzmiller argues that this new genre ridiculed the lives of manual workers and depicted their behaviour as offensive, ridiculous, and repulsive.[66] If we apply the questions posed by Lis and Soly to al-Jāḥiẓ and his work – "Who says what to whom, about what, where, when and why?" – it becomes apparent that the reality was more complex. Although we have little information about al-Jāḥiẓ's background, we do know that he was of humble origin and spent his childhood among Basra's craftsmen and market traders, so presumably he earned a living from that type of work. Moreover – as one of his biographers claims – during his studies in philosophy

---

60 Shatzmiller, *Labour in the Medieval Islamic World*, pp. 369–398.
61 *Ibid.*, p. 365.
62 Haarmann, "Arbeit in Islam", p. 141.
63 There is some debate on this in the literature. See Shatzmiller, *Labour in the Medieval Islamic World*, pp. 371 and 374; Joseph Sadan, "Kings and Craftsmen, a Pattern of Contrasts: On the History of a Medieval Arabic Humoristic Form. Part II", *Studia Islamica*, 62 (1985), pp. 89–120, 90; Ahmad Ghabin, *Ḥisba, Arts and Craft in Islam* (Wiesbaden, 2009), p. 226.
64 Shatzmiller, *Labour in the Medieval Islamic World*, p. 327.
65 Sadan, "Kings and Craftsmen II", p. 93, note 142, gives a summary of this literature.
66 Shatzmiller, *Labour in the Medieval Islamic World*, p. 372.

and theology al-Jāḥiẓ had learned that he should no longer "despise those who appear lowly".⁶⁷ His writings show that he assumed each individual is automatically "biased in favour of his own type of work and role in society". At the same time, his acceptance of the differences in professions and their corresponding status was consistent with his desire to preserve the existing social order.⁶⁸

In his "On the Crafts of the Masters" (*Risāla fī ṣināt al-quwwād*) al-Jāḥiẓ humorously juxtaposed the world and language of educated upper-class Arabs with the world and language of tradesmen. The latter are instructed to draw up an account, in their own way, for the caliph and his entourage of a battle between two parties. This leads to hilarious monologues, in which each representative of a profession (a physician, tailor, farmer, baker, schoolmaster, keeper of a Turkish bath, sweeper, wine merchant, cook, and manservant) is required to describe in terms that would be used by their own profession the place where the battle had been fought, the time-frame, and the weapons employed.⁶⁹ Charles Pellat claims that the document should be interpreted as a warning against too one-sided an education, and a plea for a general education. The parody ends as follows: (Caliph) al-Mu'tasim "laughed heartily; then he sent for his children's tutor and instructed him to teach them all branches of knowledge".⁷⁰ But there is more. After describing the battle, the representatives of each profession were required to recite a poem in which two lovers part.⁷¹ To express the pain of separation, some tradesmen used very colourful words: the doctor refers to diarrhoea, the keeper of the Turkish bath to depilatory paste.⁷² It is not just who says what to whom, about what, where, and why that are important questions, "how and in what words" also yields some interesting insights. The words used to express love are terms derived from classical Arabic, while the "occupation-related words" used to express pain are often vulgar and non-Arabic in origin.⁷³ The non-Arabic background of the tradesmen in the work of al-Jāḥiẓ, as expressed in their language, is consistent to some extent with the reality described above. The ninth century was not only the century of urbanization but also of incorporation, and especially of the integration of large groups of non-Arabs into Islamic-controlled territories.⁷⁴ Was this description a way to maintain the existing social order? Or to confront elite readers with their own preconceptions?

---

67 Sadan, "Kings and Craftsmen II", p. 92.
68 Thomas Hefter, *The Reader in al-Jāḥiẓ: The Epistolary Rhetoric of an Arabic Prose Master* (Edinburgh, 2014), pp. 98–99.
69 Charles Pellat, *The Life and Works of Jāḥiẓ: Translations of Selected Texts* (London, 1969), pp. 115–116.
70 *Ibid.*, p. 116.
71 Pellat does not reproduce this part of the text in his book. For the text, see Joseph Sadan, "Kings and Craftsmen, a Pattern of Contrasts: On the History of a Medieval Arabic Humoristic Form (Part I)", *Studia Islamica*, 56 (1982), pp. 5–49, at 13, note 7.
72 *Ibid.*, p. 12.
73 Sadan, "Kings and Craftsmen II", p. 101.
74 Shatzmiller, *Labour in the Medieval Islamic World*, p. 373.

Real debates about work and non-work emerged after groups within Sufi circles began to reject all worldly possessions and all activities that would lead to economic gain. We know of this Zuhd movement mainly from the writings of those opposed to it, including the Ḥanbalites, a school of Sunni law which was of especially traditionalist orientation during the period.[75] Abū Bakr al-Khallal was a leading Ḥanbalite scholar, and in the tenth century he wrote a "Call to engage in commerce, in production, in labour, and to reject those who call for indifference in forsaking of labour".[76] It states *inter alia* that there is no difference between commerce and manual labour. Other religious and intellectual circles too began to re-evaluate manual labour. In a late tenth- or eleventh-century "encyclopaedia" written by an ascetic religious and political community called the "Brethren of Purity" (Eḵwān al-Ṣafā) there is an entry on craftsmanship and a hierarchy of occupations based, in part, on their "usefulness" to society. Weaving, agriculture, and building are at the top. The text also examines the various work processes.[77] Finally, reference should be made to *Muqadimma*, the work of the historian and philosopher Ibn Khaldūn, written in 1377 in the Maghreb. He also compiled different occupational hierarchies based on social utility, and they closely resemble that of the Brethren of Purity. New, however, is Khaldūn's Adam Smith-like appreciation of wage work. "But human labour is necessary for every profit and capital accumulation ... the capital a person earns and acquires, if resulting from a craft is the value realized from his labour".[78] Moreover, from the terms used by Ibn Khaldūn we can discern his appreciation of "creative work", which was greater than his appreciation of "practical work": for "creative work" a plan, a design, was required and knowledge was necessary; that was not the case for practical work.[79]

This brief overview of Islamic views on work in the Middle Ages shows a clear polyphony, which could be extended to the early modern and modern periods in which "guilds" (*asnāf*)[80] played an important role. Perhaps too we could say more about how workers saw their work – apart from the fact that we know that even in the early Middle Ages craftsmen signed their work[81] – up to and including the nineteenth century when efforts were made to develop a new "Islamic work ethic" in the Ottoman Empire.[82] Let us now turn our gaze to Asia.

---

75 http://www.iranicaonline.org/articles/hanbalite-madhab.
76 Quoted in Shatzmiller, *Labour in the Medieval Islamic World*, p. 377.
77 Bernard Lewis, "An Epistle on Manual Crafts", *Islamic Culture*, 17 (1943), pp. 142–152, and Dijkman, "Worthy Efforts and the Medieval Economy", p. 111.
78 Quoted in Shatzmiller, *Labour in the Medieval Islamic World*, p. 395.
79 For the wording used by Ibn Khaldūn, see Schulze, "Arbeit als Problem", pp. 199 and 202–203.
80 For the debates on the role of guilds, see Klein, "Arbeit und Arbeiteridentitäten", pp. 166–168; Schulze, "Arbeit als Problem", pp. 203–204.
81 Dijkman, "Worthy Efforts in the Medieval Economy", p. 111.
82 Melis Hafez, "The Lazy, the Idle, the Industrious: Discourse and Practice of Work and Productivity in Late Ottoman Society" (Ph.D. dissertation, University of California, 2012).

In late Ming China agriculture and manufacturing were being commercialized on a considerable scale. In the cities, where wage labour had been a feature since 1000, wage labour continued to expand while a process of urbanization took place at the expense of rural areas in which reciprocal and tributary labour was transformed into commodified labour.[83] This led to defensive texts by members of the Confucian elite, who emphasized the traditional subdivision into scholar/officials and farmers (the roots of society) on the one hand and merchants and artisans (the branches) on the other. However, several other sixteenth- and seventeenth-century Confucian thinkers took the view that the occupational groups were all equally fundamental and important. In some Confucian writings we can even detect a slight irony in relation to the traditional hierarchy, probably because by then this ideal situation had long succumbed to reality.[84] One particular case study on the attitudes of the late Ming elite compared with those of courtesans shows even more clearly that the subject of work as "worthy efforts" was debated in Confucian circles during this period, and that attitudes were changing owing to a blurring of social strata. The courtesans operated within elite circles and were often indistinguishable from women from the upper or gentry class. Courtesans' skills in music, poetry, and painting became so valued that even the upper classes came to regard them as a cultural ideal.[85]

In Tokugawa Japan (1600–1868) the feudal system was abolished, leaving agriculture restructured and commercialized based on labour-intensive cultivation methods in which the entire household, including women, played a role.[86] Cities grew, and they too saw an increase in commercialized labour. The traditional labour relations – serfdom, lifelong service, and corvée labour – disappeared to some extent as a result, a development the shogunate would have preferred to stifle. A wide range of measures designed to constrain the mobility of wage labourers were put into effect, but in practice they failed. Some neo-Confucian scholars approved of the new developments; others did not.[87] In Japan, just as in early modern Europe, there was significant fear of vagrants – de facto migrant wage labourers on short-term contracts. The shogunate therefore switched to actively disseminating among workers a specific work ethic based on the neo-Confucian concept of *shokubun*: "one's occupation or

---

83 Moll-Murata, "Work Ethics and Work Valuations in a Period of Commercialization", pp. 165–166 and 182–183. For a survey of early concepts of work in China, see *idem*, "Non-Western Perspectives: The Chinese Dimension", *TSEG / The Low Countries Journal of Social and Economic History*, 11, 1 (2014), pp. 141–152. For a survey of later interpretations of the concept of work in China, see Rudolf G. Wagner, "The Concept of Work/Labor/Arbeit in the Chinese World. First Explorations", in: Bierwisch, *Die Rolle der Arbeit*, pp. 103–135.
84 Moll-Murata, "Work Ethics and Work Valuations in a Period of Commercialization", pp. 170–171.
85 Harriet T. Zurndorfer, "Prostitutes and Courtesans in the Confucian Moral Universe of Late Ming China (1550–1644)", in: Hofmeester and Moll-Murata, *Joy and Pain of Work*, pp. 197–216.
86 See also Gareth Austin and Kaoru Sugihara (eds), *Labour-Intensive Industrialization in Global History* (London, 2013), and the role of work discipline.
87 Mathias, "Japan in the Seventeenth Century", pp. 236–237.

trade (*shoku*), fulfilling an allotted part (*bun*) in society". Self-cultivation was encouraged, but everyone had their own role in society and there had to be mutual respect among the different status groups.[88] The doctrine was widely disseminated by the authorities, but was it also internalized? Satirical literature of the period ridicules unreliable, lazy, gossiping servants. But was it amusing because it ran counter to Confucian ideals? Or was it just what you see when workers are on short-term contracts, and bonds to their masters become looser?[89]

In India in the seventeenth century wage labour developed on a large scale as a result of the commercialization of agriculture and manufacturing. In analysing attitudes to that type of labour relation, the specific situation of the caste system must be considered. Since ancient times India had developed a hereditary hierarchical system in which one's origin in a particular community, or *jati*, was linked to a certain occupation, and ritual degradation of certain kinds of work and contempt for manual work in general played a role.[90] Work deemed impure was performed by untouchables, or Dalits.[91] In rural communities, members of the *jatis* were required to render services to the dominant castes, with a plot of land, a share of the grain harvest, or sometimes cash being given in exchange for those services.[92] In practice, not every caste was strictly bound by the occupation assigned to it, and vertical social mobility did occur. For some groups, the early development of wage labour brought an end to labour relations based strictly on the community or village. There was even a term for the wage labourer: "coolie". Under subsequent colonial rule the word came to mean an unfree labourer, but in eighteenth-century Madras it was applied to a free wage labourer. As such, the position of "coolie" and the term associated with it were valued, as is suggested by the statement "he was a coolie, and no one's servant".[93] In the literature we find no early modern debates about the caste system in relation to wage labour.

Colonialism did cause major shifts in the role of the caste system and its relationship with wage labour, and the coupling of caste to occupation became much more inflexible than had hitherto been the case. Moreover, the British master and servant law was implemented, which, as in England, greatly limited the mobility of wage labour and endeavoured to ensure a stable supply of cheap labour.[94] In rural areas the

---

88 *Ibid.*, pp. 238–239.
89 *Ibid.*, p. 241.
90 Upadhyay, "Dalits and the Ideology of Work in India", pp. 156–157.
91 *Ibid.*, pp. 159–160. While in theory Muslims were not part of the caste system, they too adopted the idea of a hierarchical framework which related occupation to birth. Moosvi, "The World of Labour in Mughal India", p. 253.
92 Ravi Ahuja, "Geschichte der Arbeit jenseits des kulturalistischen Paradigmas", in: Kocka and Offe, *Geschichte und Zukunft der Arbeit*, pp. 121–134, 124; Moosvi, "The World of Labour in Mughal India", p. 249.
93 Ahuja, "Geschichte der Arbeit", p. 125.
94 *Ibid.*, p. 126, and Douglas Hay and Paul Craven (eds), *Masters, Servants, and Magistrates in Britain and the Empire, 1562–1955* (Chapel Hill, NC, 2004).

colonial administration allied itself with the dominant class, causing the Dalits there to resume their servant-like roles, while in the cities they could become wage labourers.[95] Untouchables too found work, in the mining industry; it was hard and dangerous but it was wage labour nonetheless. They glorified their new role in their work songs, and described it in their stories as a form of liberation.[96]

Labour laws were one way to limit the mobility of wage labour. Another was to label those workers who had a multiform subsistence base as "idle", and then "force" them to work. This consciously or unconsciously ignoring of work is reflected in the myth of the lazy native. As Norani Othman for Malaysia and S.H. Alatas for Malaysia, the Philippines, and Java have shown, various traders, travellers, and colonial administrators from the sixteenth to the twentieth centuries regarded Malays, Filipinos, and Javanese as lazy.[97] Especially for the nineteenth century, Alatas explains that designation with reference to the colonial context. Malays were not wage labourers and therefore did not fit into the strict colonial definition of work. That they fished, grew rice, sold fruit, and made mats was not registered as work. Moreover, they refused to grow cash crops and to work on plantations. This demonstrates therefore not only the colonial attitude to the work done by the local population, but also the attitude of the population to the work the colonial ruler tried to impose on them.[98]

For West Africa, Klas Rönnbäck has analysed a large number of travel accounts to explore the context of the "myth of the lazy native".[99] Like many of the scholars from whose work he quotes he takes the view that this myth was used to justify slavery and other forms of unfree labour.[100] He shows on what the stereotype was based: ideas about idleness that were imported from Europe, the idea that Africans were satisfied with very little, and that they could easily live off the land. Such claims failed to perceive the seasonality of certain types of work and the difficult and demanding agricultural work performed by women.[101] However, Rönnbäck also found references to industriousness. Curiously, any such reference was always to a designation more specific than "the African", and was more likely to be to "the Banhu" or "Balanta" and often – though not always – to men with a specific occupation. The first people to really attack the stereotype were convinced abolitionists, who believed laziness was "a fate of slaves".[102] Rönnbäck claims that the persistence of the stereotype

---

95 On the dual labour market that emerged as a result, see Upadhyay, "Dalits and the Ideology of Work in India", p. 163.
96 Janaki Nair, *Miners and Millhands. Work, Culture and Politics in Princely Mysore* (New Delhi, 1998), quoted in Ahuja, "Geschichte der Arbeit", p. 130.
97 Othman, "Auffassung, Wahrnehmung und Kultur der Arbeit in der malaiischen Gesellschaft"; Alatas, *Myth of the Lazy Native*.
98 Alatas, *Myth of the Lazy Native*, pp. 70–82.
99 Rönnbäck, "The Idle and the Industrious"; *idem, Labour and Living Standards in Pre-Colonial West Africa*, pp. 73–92.
100 *Idem*, "The Idle and the Industrious", p. 121.
101 *Ibid.*, pp. 125–126; 136 and 139.
102 *Ibid.*, pp. 129 and 133.

can be explained partly by the fact that it served the interests of the colonizers: in the nineteenth century it became increasingly popular in order to justify various forms of coerced labour, to encourage Africans to work as wage labourers – something they were often reluctant to do since wages were low and they could earn more doing other types of work – and to make them work longer.[103]

What Nguni workers in Natal in the nineteenth century and the Kazi in Congo in the twentieth century thought about work, including wage work, is nicely reflected in studies by Keletso T. Atkins and Julia Seibert.[104]

Concluding remarks

In recent years, a number of important steps have been made in research on attitudes to work and workers. The research field has expanded in terms of both periodization – with the classic split between antiquity and the Middle Ages effectively eliminated – and geography, with a number of studies discussing non-European regions. Moreover, we are seeing the deployment of new methods and disciplines, such as semantics, a development that is certain to prove valuable given the progress being made in text-mining techniques. If this expansion in time and place continues, expansion in terms of labour relations too will have to be considered, and scholars will need to explore all possible types of work and labour relations, and the relationship between the two.

---

[103] Rönnbäck, *Labour and Living Standards in Pre-Colonial West Africa*, pp. 80–82 and 88.
[104] Keletso E. Atkins, *The Moon is Dead! Give us our Money! The Cultural Origins of an African Work Ethic, Natal, South Africa, 1843–1900* (Portsmouth, 1993); Julia Seibert, "Kazi. Konzepte, Praktiken und Semantiken von Lohnarbeit im Kolonialen Kongo", in: Leonhard and Steinmetz, *Semantiken von Arbeit*, pp. 209–223.

Suggested Reading

Alatas, Syed Hussein. *The Myth of the Lazy Native: A Study of the Image of the Malays, Filipinos and Javanese from the 16th to the 20th Century and its Function in the Ideology of Colonial Capitalism* (London: Frank Cass, 1977).
Applebaum, Herbert. *The Concept of Work: Ancient, Medieval, and Modern* (New York: State University of New York Press, 1992).
Atkins, Keletso E. *The Moon is Dead! Give us our Money! The Cultural Origins of an African Work Ethic, Natal, South Africa, 1843–1900* (Portsmouth: Heinemann, 1993).
Bierwisch, Manfred (ed.). *Die Rolle der Arbeit in verschiedenen Epochen und Kulturen* (Berlin: Akademie Verlag, 2003).
Cartier, Michel (ed.). *Le travail et ses représentations* (Paris: Éditions des archives contemporaines 1984).
D'Almeida-Topor, Hélène, Monique Lakroum, and Gerd Spitter (eds). *Le travail en Afrique noir. Représentations et pratiques à l'époque contemporaine* (Paris: Éditions Karthala, 2003).
Ehmer, Josef and Catharina Lis (eds). *The Idea of Work in Europe from Antiquity to Modern Times* (Farnham: Ashgate, 2009).
Hofmeester, Karin and Christine Moll-Murata (eds). *The Joy and Pain of Work: Global Attitudes and Valuations, 1500–1650* (Cambridge: Cambridge University Press, 2011).
Kocka, Jürgen and Claus Offe (eds). *Geschichte und Zukunft der Arbeit* (Frankfurt: Campus, 2000).
Leonhard, Jörn and Willibald Steinmetz (eds). *Semantiken von Arbeit: Diachrone und vergleichende Perspektiven* (Cologne: Böhlau, 2016).
Lis, Catharina and Hugo Soly. *Worthy Efforts. Attitudes to Work and Workers in Pre-Industrial Europe* (Leiden etc.: Brill, 2012).
Postel, Verena (ed.). *Arbeit im Mittelalter: Vorstellungen und Wirklichkeiten* (Berlin: Akademie Verlag, 2006).
Rönnbäck, Klas "The Idle and the Industrious – European Ideas about the African Work Ethic in Precolonial West Africa", *History in Africa*, 41 (2014), pp. 117–145.
Shatzmiller, Maya. *Labour in the Medieval Islamic World* (Leiden: Brill, 1994).
Thomas, Keith (ed.). *The Oxford Book of Work* (Oxford: Oxford University Press, 1999).
Upadhyay, Shashi Bhushan. "Dalits and the Ideology of Work in India", in: Marcel van der Linden and Prabhu P. Mohapatra (eds), *Labour Matters: Towards Global Histories* (Delhi: Tulia Books, 2009), pp. 152–171.
Van den Hoven, Birgit. *Work in Ancient and Medieval Thought: Ancient Philosophers, Medieval Monks and Theologians and their Concept of Work, Occupations and Technology* (Leiden: Brill, 1996)

Marlou Schrover
6. Labour Migration

There are excellent studies—including Dirk Hoerder's *Cultures in Contact*—on the subject of labour migration, chain migration, and related concepts, which provide overviews of the literature and try to take stock of the number of people on the move.[1] There is so much literature on this subject that it is impossible and useless to list all the publications that have appeared. Rather than repeat what has been written, this chapter looks at recent publications, paying special attention to gender and class. There are biases in the literature. In the first place, the literature on labour migration is still inspired by the rather outdated push-pull paradigm, tends to focus on free movement and ignores forced labour migration. Secondly, there is much more literature on labour migration from and to Western countries than on labour migration from and to China, Latin America, the (former) Soviet Union, and Africa.[2] In the nineteenth century, Finns, for example, rushed west to the goldfields in Alaska, as well as east to golden opportunities in the oilfields in Azerbaijan. The eastward labour migration only became visible after Russian archives recently opened. Also, attention to Chinese labour migration is rather recent and tends to be discussed separately from other migration. Between 1840 and 1940 20 million Chinese emigrated overseas, in order to work in the gold fields of California and Australia and on plantations in Latin America and the Caribbean.[3] Despite calls to remedy these biases, studies about migration to and from Europe or the US outnumber those regarding other areas, and migration within, for instance, Asia and Africa continues to be seen or presented as the results of what Europeans did or did not do.[4] Thirdly, the literature about labour migration of women is discussed in different terms than

---

[1] Dirk Hoerder, *Cultures in Contact. World Migrations in the Second Millennium* (Durham, NC, 2002); For references also see: Jan Lucassen and Leo Lucassen (eds.), *Migration, Migration History, History: Old Paradigms and New Perspectives* (Bern, 1997); Jan Lucassen and Leo Lucassen, "The Mobility Transition Revisited, 1500–1900: What the Case of Europe Can Offer to Global History", *Journal of Global History*, 4, 3 (2009), pp. 347–377; Jan Lucassen and Leo Lucassen, *The Mobility Transition in Europe Revisited, 1500–1900. Sources and Methods*, IISH Research Paper (Amsterdam, 2010) (socialhistory.org/sites/default/files/docs/publications/respap46.pdf); Leo Lucassen et al., *Cross-Cultural Migration in Western Europe 1901–2000: A Preliminary Estimate*, IISH-Research Paper 52 (Amsterdam, 2014) https://socialhistory.org/sites/default/files/docs/publications/researchpaper-52-lucassen-lucassen-et.al-versie_voor_web140801.pdf
[2] For a favourable exception see: Lewis H. Siegelbaum and Leslie Page Moch, *Broad is My Native Land. Repertoires and Regimes of Migration in Russia's Twentieth Century* (Ithaca, NY, 2014).
[3] Adam McKeown, "Chinese Emigration in Global Context, 185 0–1940", *Journal of Global History*, 5, 1 (2010), pp. 95–124.
[4] Adam McKeown "Global Migration, 184 6–1940", *Journal of World History*, 15, 2 (2004), pp. 15 5–189; Prabhu P. Mohapatra, "Eurocentrism, Forced Labour, and Global Migration: A Critical Assessment", *International Review of Social History*, 52, 1 (2007), pp. 110–115.

that of men.⁵ Stories about domestic servants dominate the literature on the labour migration of women, suggesting that all or most migrant women were working in that sector.⁶ This literature is characterized by discussions about restricted rights, poor labour conditions, abuse, and exploitation. Lastly, there is much more literature about current or recent (nineteenth and twentieth century) migration, than about migration in earlier periods. There is some justification for this last bias. Human mobility did reach unprecedented levels in the nineteenth and twentieth centuries. In the period of 1840 to 1940, 60 million people left Europe, 21 to 23 million left South China, 30 to 33 million moved from China to Manchuria, 43 to 50 million moved within or left India, 20 to 40 million moved within China, 9 to 13 million left from the Eastern Mediterranean and Western Asia, 74 million moved within Europa and 35 million within the America's.⁷ These numbers were higher than the numbers of migrants in earlier periods.

This chapter starts with remarks about categorization and continues with a discussion of chain migration and the ever-expanding range of related concepts.

Categorization

In the nineteenth century, authorities needed statistics for their attempts to control migration. Counting people came with categorization, which, in itself, is the key element of governmentality in the Foucauldian sense. Categorization does not describe social order but rather shapes and reshapes power relations, according to Foucault.⁸ States have the authority to decide who is who and differentiate rights accordingly.⁹ Categorization is used to legitimize differences within policies and between groups of people. Categorizations are constantly renewed with the intention to exclude or deny

---

5 Marlou Schrover and Deirdre Moloney, "Introduction. Making a difference", in: Schrover and Moloney (eds), *Gender, Migration and Categorisation: Making Distinctions Between Migrants in Western Countries (1900) 1945–2010* (Amsterdam, 2013), pp. 7–54.
6 Janet Henshall Momsen (ed.), *Gender, Migration and Domestic Service* (London, 1999); Bridget Anderson, *Doing the Dirty Work? The Global Politics of Domestic Labour* (London, 2000); Rhacel Salazar Parreñas, *Servants of Globalization. Women, Migration, and Domestic work* (Stanford, CA, 2001); Barbara Ehrenreich and Arlie Russell Hochschild (eds.), *Global Woman: Nannies, Maids and Sex Workers in the New Economy* (New York, 2002); José M. Moya, "Domestic Service in a Global Perspective: Gender, Migration and Ethnic Niches", *Journal of Ethnic and Migration Studies*, 33, 4 (2007), pp. 559–579; Marta Kindler, *A "Risky" Business? Ukrainian Migrant Women in Warsaw's Domestic Work Sector* (Amsterdam, 2011).
7 José C. Moya and Adam McKeown, "World Migration in the Long Twentieth Century", in: Michael Adas (ed.), *Essays on Twentieth-Century History* (Philadelphia, 2010), pp. 9–52; McKeown "Global Migration, 1846–1940".
8 Michel Foucault, Power/Knowledge. Selected Interviews and Other Writings, 1972–1977 (New York, 1980).
9 Pierre Bourdieu, "Rethinking the State: Genesis and Structure of the Bureaucratic Field", *Sociological Theory* 12: 1 (1994), pp. 1–18.

rights (mostly) or to include and grant rights (rarely).[10] As a rule, authorities group migrants into four major categories: labour migrants, refugees, (post-) colonial migrants, and family migrants. Scholars tend to follow the categorizations that policymakers use, partly because sources are organized according to these categorizations.[11]

Formalized categorization is, however, largely artificial.[12] For instance, when possibilities for labour migration to North-Western Europe became fewer after the mid-1970s, refugee migration and family migration became more important, numerically. Whether migrants can switch between categories depends on the migrants (their gender, ethnicity, class, and religion) and the number of migrants. Categories of migrants are like communicating vessels: migrants can change categories, or bureaucrats, who decide on entry or residence, can allocate them to different categories.[13] Policy makers and bureaucrats seek to interpret categories narrowly and to exclude people who do not fit their definitions. In contrast, support groups tend to stretch categories and create sympathy for those who seemed to be inhumanly harmed by the government's rigour.[14]

Over time, scholars and policy makers introduced numerous sub-categorizations. The stretching and blurring of categories and the introduction of neologisms reflect that categories were inadequate in describing realities. In line with Castles's ideas, this chapter claims that debates frequently led to a conceptional closure paradox: debates about definitions and categorizations became the enemy of the effective study of migration.[15] Debates became more about definitions than about the explanatory and predictive value of categorizations and concepts. Categorizations and typologies were meant and introduced to create a common language which would enable comparisons over time and between countries. In reality—and despite large debates—this hardly happened.

Researchers tend to over-stabilize the categories they study and start out with the categorizations they seek to explain. McCall, in response to this criticism, identified three approaches: *anti-categorical*, *intra-categorical*, and *inter-categorical*.[16] The anti-

---

[10] Schrover and Moloney, *Gender, Migration and Categorisation*.
[11] Marlou Schrover et al., "Editorial", *Journal of Migration History*, 1, 1 (2015), pp. 1–6.
[12] Rogers Brubaker, Mara Loveman and Peter Stamatov, "Ethnicity as Cognition", *Theory and Society*, 33, 1 (2004), pp. 31–64.
[13] Tycho Walaardt, "New Refugees? Portuguese War Resisters and one American Deserter in the Netherlands in the late 1960s and early 1970s", in: Schrover and Moloney, *Gender, Migration and Categorisation*, pp. 75–104.
[14] Schrover and Moloney, Gender, Migration and Categorisation.
[15] Stephen Castles, *Ethnicity and Globalisation: from Migrant Worker to Transnational Citizen* (London, 2000), pp. 15–25.
[16] Leslie McCall, "The Complexity of Intersectionality", *Signs. Journal of Women in Culture and Society*, 30, 3 (2005), pp. 1771–1800, at 1773–1774; Marlou Schrover, "Integration and Gender", in: Marco Martiniello and Jan Rath (eds), *An Introduction to Immigrant Incorporation Studies. European Perspectives* (Amsterdam, 2014), pp. 117–138.

categorical approach deconstructs analytical categories and moves away from essentializing the categories that are the subject of analysis. It questions the existence of social categories and sees them as linguistic constructions. The approach starts by breaking down categories and deconstructing the idea that clear divisions exist, since this ignores the complexities of relationships. In practice, the *anti-categorical* approach makes analyses difficult or impossible. The *intra-categorical* approach focuses on social groups at neglected points of intersection. It challenges the use of broad categories and seeks to refine them. Its disadvantage is that it shifts the focus away from larger social processes and structures that might be causing inequalities. Lastly, the *inter-categorical* approach provisionally adopts existing categories. It starts from the idea that categories may be (linguistic) constructions, but that they are widely used, especially by policy makers and other stakeholders, and, as a result, do have actual societal consequences. It is more interesting and more useful to analyse the categorizations which are used rather than introduce or refine categories: how and why do authoritative bodies define and redefine categories? Rather than attempting to avoid categorizations or introduce endless sub-categorization, the way forward is to identify how authorities implicitly or explicitly use categorizations, how academics reproduce them, and how and why this changes over time.

The observations regarding the categorization of migrants also apply partly to migration typologies. In order to distinguish migration typologies, Lucassen and Lucassen used the term *cross-cultural migration*, based on Mannings concept of cross community migration.[17] Manning looks at language differences while Lucassen and Lucassen define cross cultural as a different cultural outlook, which includes language, family systems, religion or worldviews, technologies, the nature of civil society organization, the structuring of the public sphere, and labour relations. However, cultural differences are in the eye of the beholder; they are constructed and emphasized with specific aims in mind. Van Schendel and Abraham have pointed out that mobility of groups is of interest (to authorities) when they move between units that count.[18] In the West and from the nineteenth century onwards, the borders that counted were usually state borders. Before the nineteenth century and outside the West other borders were more important. Several authors have therefore suggested to move away from the concept of migration and use mobility instead. Mobility

---

[17] Lucassen and Lucassen, "Mobility Transition Revisited", pp. 347–377; Patrick Manning, *Migration in World History* (New York and London, 2005); Patrick Manning, "Homo Sapiens Populates the Earth: A Provisional Synthesis, Privileging Linguistic Evidence", *Journal of World History* ,17, 2 (2006), pp. 115–158.

[18] Willem van Schendel and Itty Abraham, "Introduction", in: Willem van Schendel and Itty Abraham (eds), *Illicit Flows and Criminal Things. States, Borders and the Other Side of Globalization* (Bloomington, IN, 2005), pp. 1–37, at 11.

underlines the need to make clear which boundaries matter to whom, when, and why.[19]

The observations about categorization, presented above, are relevant to the discussion about chain migration and related concepts that follow in the next sections. This chapter is about labour migration, but since people can and do move in and out of this category, labour migration cannot be discussed without including other categories of migration. Labour migration is the most important form of migration—this applies both today and when looking at the past. Currently, the International Labour Organization (ILO) estimates that 150 million of the world's approximately 244 million international migrants are migrant workers (about 60 per cent).[20] Although it is not completely clear which definition the ILO uses, and, keeping in mind the observations regarding categorization made above, the estimate that roughly 60 per cent of international migrants are labour migrants is probably the nearest we get to reality, both now and in the past. In 2007, the UNHCR explicitly expressed the idea that most migration should be labelled mixed migration.[21] A distinction can be made between primary and secondary motives—for instance, safety as a first motive and work as a second—but migrants with different priorities do use the same paths and networks. In recent literature, the idea of mixed migration has only partly caught on.[22] In September 2016, the UN Summit for Refugees and Migrants, which tried to find a solution for dealing with the increasing numbers of refugee migrants, made mixed migration the key concept of its New York Declaration, which was accepted by the 193 member states. Refugee migration cannot and should not be separated from other forms of migration, according to the declaration.[23]

The sections below describe the concept of chain migration and related concepts, such as migration networks, systems and infrastructures.

---

19 John Urry, "Connections", *Environment and Planning D: Society and Space*, 22, 1 (2004), pp. 27–37; Tim Cresswell, "Towards a Politics of Mobility', *Environment and Planning D: Society and Space*, 28, 1 (2010), pp. 17–31.
20 http://www.ilo.org/global/topics/labour-migration/lang–en/index.htm.
21 UNHCR, Refugee Protection and Mixed Migration: a 10-Point Plan of Action, January 2007, available at: http://www.unhcr.org/protection/migration/4742a30b4/refugee-protection-mixed-migration-10-point-planaction.html.
22 Martin Geiger and Antoine Pécoud, "International Organisations and the Politics of Migration", *Journal of Ethnic and Migration Studies*, 40, 6 (2016), pp. 865–887.
23 http://refugeesmigrants.un.org/declaration.

Chain migration

The plant metaphors of Handlin (*The Uprooted*, 1951) and Bodnar (*The transplanted*, 1987) emphasize the severing of ties.[24] Most of the migration literature is, however, about the maintenance of ties. In 1964, MacDonald and MacDonald coined chain migration as a concept.[25] Chain migration does not apply to labour migration only. Refugees, family migrants, and (post-) colonial migrants can be part of chains as well. At one end of the scale, the definition of chain migration is clear: it is the stereotypical man who migrates first, while his wife and children join him later. At the other end of the scale, chain migration blurs and breaks down into concepts such as network migration, serial migration, migration systems, and migration cultures, which will be discussed below.

Chain migration means that individuals move from one place to another via a set of social arrangements, in which people at the destination provide aid, information, and encouragement to new or potential immigrants. Behavioural scientists use the word serial migration to describe a very similar situation, in which (one of) the parents migrate(s) first and children follow later.[26] Chain migration is incremental, works via personal ties, and differs from incidentally organized group migration. Group migration can lead to chain migration; it does not have to be one single migrant who starts a chain.

It is difficult to say how many people migrate inside or outside chains.[27] People who migrate as part of chains are more visible and have attracted more interest from authorities and academics than those who do not. Driven by the interest of policy makers, researchers tried to calculate the so-called multiplier effect: how many relatives and friends does each primary migrant bring?[28] Each new migrant can start a

---

[24] Oscar Handlin, *The Uprooted. The Epic Story of the Great Migrations that Made the American People* (Boston, 1951); John Bodnar, *The Transplanted. A History of Immigration in Urban America* (Bloomington, IN, 1987).
[25] John S. MacDonald and Leatrice D. MacDonald, "Chain migration, Ethnic Neighborhood Formation and Social Networks", *Milbank Memorial Fund Quarterly*, 42, 1 (1964), pp. 82–97; Marlou Schrover, "Chain Migration (Network Migration)", in: John Stone *et al.* (eds), *The Wiley Blackwell Encyclopedia of Race, Ethnicity, and Nationalism* (Chichester 2016), pp. 1–5, http://onlinelibrary.wiley.com/doi/10.1002/9781118663202.wberen592/references.
[26] Dana Ruscha and Karina Reyes, "Examining the Effects of Mexican Serial Migration and Family Separations on Acculturative Stress, Depression, and Family Functioning", *Hispanic Journal of Behavioral Sciences*, 35, 2 (2013), pp. 139–158.
[27] Clé Lesger, Leo Lucassen and Marlou Schrover, "Is There Life Outside the Migrant Network? German Immigrants in 19th century Netherlands and the Need for a More Balanced Migration Typology", *Annales de démographie historique,* 104 (2002), pp. 29–45.
[28] Fred Arnold, Benjamin V. Cariño, James T. Fawcett and Insook Han Park, "Estimating the Immigration Multiplier: An Analysis of Recent Korean and Filipino Immigration to the United States", *International Migration Review*, 23, 4 (1989), pp. 813–838; Stacie Carr and Marta Tienda, "Family Spon-

new chain and can bring a new cluster of relatives and friends into the country. Comparisons over time or between countries are difficult because some researchers only include primary relationships, while others also include secondary relationships or non-family relationships. Some migrants say that they received help from people who were like family. That complicates matters: must people have actual family ties or can they also be just like family?

Researchers found that each migrant brings one to three additional people into a country. There are differences according to countries of origin: in countries where nuclear families are large, the potential number of people that can join the primary mover is also large. The multiplier also differs according to the country of settlement. The US allows migrants to bring siblings and parents, while European countries, as a rule, do not. The later only recognize nuclear family members as family.[29]

There are differences according to gender. The differences in men's and women's migration patterns have been explained using the concept of perceived profitability; it is a concept that is relevant to debates about chain migration. The key idea—used both in the neo-classical, or push-pull, model as well as in the family strategy model—is that people move if a cost-benefit analysis points to positive gains.[30] The assumption is that, as a rule, men can earn more than women, and it is therefore more advantageous for men to migrate. When women migrate in equal or greater numbers to men it is explained from a remittance perspective; women may earn less than men, but, if they send more money home, it may be more profitable for the families left behind if women migrate, rather than men.[31] The problem with these models is that it is difficult to assess profitability, because men and women do not have the same (access to) resources, the labour market, power, agency, interests, knowledge, or networks. As yet, it is not clear what difference perceived profitability makes to the gendered nature of migration chains. In her 2015 article, Fidler showed that the person important for starting a chain is not the stereotypical single man. In the case that she studied, the British wives of South Asian seafarers in the UK were instrumental in fostering ties with the country of origin of their husbands

---

sorship and Late-Age Immigration in Aging America: Revised and Expanded Estimates of Chained Migration", *Population Research and Policy Review*, 32, 6 (2013), pp. 825–849.

29 Haime Croes and Pieter Hooimeijer, "Gender and Chain Migration: The Case of Aruba", *Popul. Space Place*, 16 (2010), pp. 121–134; Constance Lever-Tracy and Robert Holton, "Social Exchange, Reciprocity and Amoral Familism: Aspects of Italian Chain Migration to Australia", *Journal of Ethnic and Migration Studies*, 27, 1 (2001), pp. 81–99.

30 Oded Stark, *The Migration of Labour* (Oxford, 1991); Larry A. Sjaastad, "The Costs and Returns of Human Migration", *Journal of Political Economy*, 70, 5 (1962), pp. 80–93; Caroline B. Brettell, *Men Who Migrate, Women Who Wait. Population and History in a Portuguese Parish* (Princeton, NJ, 1986).

31 Gordon De Jong, Kerry Richter and Pimonpan Isarabhakdi, "Gender, Values, and Intentions to Move in Rural Thailand", *International Migration Review*, 30, 3 (1995), pp. 748–770; Benjamin Davis and Paul C. Winters, "Gender, Networks and Mexico-US Migration", *Journal of Development Studies*, 28, 2 (2001), pp. 1–26.

and in facilitating additional migration—thus creating and maintaining migration chains.[32]

If travel is difficult, dangerous, or expensive, migrants are more likely to start a chain, since they can less easily travel to and from friends and relatives without these support structures. Migrants who are in a country longer are more likely to stand at the beginning of a chain: they know the country, the routes, the labour market and the language. Some migrants help friends and relatives migrate and expect nothing in return. Others, however, expect that the newly arrived will help out on the farm or in the shop, in order to repay the assistance they received.[33] Those who arrived first may profit from the cheap labour of relatives or acquaintances who arrive later. This type of help can slip into semi-professional brokerage and smuggling. Employers can benefit from recruiting new migrants via chains. They delegate the recruitment to the workers who have been in their employment for a while, whom they trust and whom they expect to help the new immigrants. By doing so, employers enforce chain migration.

Network migration, migration system, and migration culture

Network migration is frequently used as a synonym for chain migration, although some authors reserve the term *chain migration* for situations in which only close relatives are helped to migrate and use *network migration* for situations in which friends, people from the same village, region or country, co-religionists, or people working in the same job receive assistance.[34] In 2005, Krissman highlighted that the network approach underplays the influence of employers and labour recruiters, and thus, in his view, is unable to adequately explain migration.[35]

The concept *cumulative causation*, introduced by Douglas Massey *et al.* in the 1980s, has been used to explain migration via networks.[36] Cumulative causation is the process whereby the propensity to migrate grows with each additional migrant. Networks and accumulated migrant experience demonstrate benefits, diminish familial resistance, and increase security by providing information about and access to

---

32 Ceri-Anne Fidler, "The Impact of Migration upon Family Life and Gender Relations: the case of South Asian seafarers, c.1900–50", *Women's History Review*, 24, 3 (2015), pp. 410–428.
33 H. Ø. Haugen and Jørgen Carling, "On the Edge of the Chinese Diaspora: The Surge of Baihuo Business in an African City", *Ethnic and Racial Studies*, 28, 4 (2005), pp. 639–662.
34 John M. Liu, Paul M. Ong and Carolyn Rosenstein, "Dual Chain Migration: Post-1965 Filipino Immigration to the United States", *International Migration Review*, 25, 3 (1991), pp. 487–513.
35 Fred Krissman, "'Sin Coyote Ni Patron': Why the "Migrant Network" Fails to Explain International Migration", *International Migration Review*, 39, 1 (2005), pp. 4–44.
36 Douglas S. Massey, "Social Structure, Household Strategies, and the Cumulative Causation of Migration", *Population Index*, 56, 1 (1990), pp. 3–26.

labour market opportunities. Networks make migration less risky for individuals by circulating information among potential migrants. As a result, the nature of migration changes over time. The initial high risk, resulting from a lack of information, declines when more family and friends migrate. Denser networks of migrants provide potential migrants with more and increasingly reliable information.[37] Tight knit networks, arising from physical and social proximity, make it easier to enforce trust and support.[38] Networks are assumed to play a crucial role in reducing perceived vulnerability and that explains why migrant women use older networks.[39] Networks of women tend to be less formalized and less visible than those of men.

The concept *migration system*—originally introduced by geographers—is like that of network migration related to chain migration.[40] The migration system approach sees migration as part of the global flow of goods, services and information. In 1984, Jan Lucassen proved the usefulness of the approach for the history of labour migration in Europe.[41] Migration systems show continuity over time. They can exist long after the original factors—including labour demand—that led to their creation have disappeared. At one point the migrant community which sprang from the system, rather than the system itself, becomes the reason to migrate.[42] Migrants follow well-trodden paths, and authorities influence the creation and continuation of

---

[37] Alejandro Portes and Robert Bach, *Latin Journey. Cuban and Mexican Immigrants in the United States* (Berkeley, CA, 1985); Julie DaVanzo, "Does Unemployment Affect Migration? Evidence from Micro Data", *Review of Economics and Statistics*, 60, 4 (1978), pp. 504–514; Charles Tilly, "Migration in Modern European History", in: William H. McNeill (ed.), *Human Migration. Patterns and Policies* (Bloomington, IN, 1978), pp. 48–72.

[38] Alejandro Portes and Julia Sensenbrenner, "Embeddedness and Immigration: Notes on the Social Determinants of Economic Action", *American Journal of Sociology*, 98, 6 (1993), pp. 1320–1350.

[39] Mark S. Granovetter, "The Strength of Weak Ties", *American Journal of Sociology*, 78, 6 (1973), pp. 1360–1380; Leslie Page Moch and Rachel G. Fuchs, "Getting Along: Poor Women's Networks in Nineteenth-Century Paris", *French Historical Studies*, 18, 1 (Spring 1993), pp. 34–49; Sara R. Curran and Abigail C. Saguy, "Migration and Cultural Change: A Role for Gender and Social Networks?", *Journal of International Women's Studies*, 2, 3 (2001), pp. 54–77; Monica Boyd, "Family and Personal Networks in International Migration: Recent Developments and New Agendas", *International Migration Review*, 23, 3 (1989), pp. 638–670.

[40] Marcelo J. Borges, "Migration Systems in Southern Portugal: Regional and Transnational Circuits of Labor Migration in the Algarve (Eighteenth-Twentieth Centuries)", *International Review of Social History*, 45, 2 (2000), pp. 171–208.

[41] Jan Lucassen, *Naar de Kusten van de Noordzee. Trekarbeid in Europees Perspektief, 1600–1900* (Gouda, 1984); Also published as: Jan Lucassen, *Migrant Labour in Europe, 160 0–1900. The Drift to the North Sea* (London, 1987). Several authors have followed up on this. See: Leslie Page Moch, *Moving Europeans. Migration in Western Europe since 1650* (Bloomington, IN, 1992); Hoerder, *Cultures in Contact*. And for early publications by non-historians: Akin L. Mabogunje, "Systems Approach to a Theory of Rural Urban Migration", *Geographical Analysis*, 2, 1 (1970), pp. 1–18.

[42] Marlou Schrover, *Een Kolonie van Duitsers. Groepsvorming onder Duitse Immigranten in Utrecht in de Negentiende Eeuw* (Amsterdam, 2002).

migration systems, hoping that migrants will benefit from mutual support or exchange of information, reducing the cost of migration for the migrant and others.[43]

Lastly, *migration culture* is also a related concept: people migrate because *everybody* does, often as part of the rites of passage to adulthood for young men.[44] Fostered within communities of young men, this is borne out of a lust for adventure, which is associated with locally entrenched masculine ideals.[45] In Morocco, for instance, there are villages where migration has been so common for men since the 1950s that those who do not migrate are ridiculed and equated with children, women, or the elderly.[46]

Migration industry

Light, in a 2013 article, pointed out that the *migration industry* is an important facilitator, next to migration networks.[47] Migration itself is not an industry, but the facilitation of migration is. The migration industry differs from the migration networks because personal ties, kinship and friendship are not important, while businesses are. As such, the term more or less overlaps with *career migration* or *organizational migration*. The migration industry includes travel agents, lawyers, bankers, labour recruiters, brokers, interpreters and housing agents. These agents have an interest in the continuation of migration and work, in an organized manner, against government restrictions. The migration industry, furthermore, not only profits from travel but also from facilitating integration or adaptation by providing, for instance, integration courses, publishing foreign language news media, or training people. This section discusses five numerically important and different examples of migration industries: shipping, slavery, trafficking, forced labour and missionary work.

Shipping companies are an example of a migration industry that was important in the interwar period.[48] In its 41-volume report from 1911, the US Dillingham Commission concluded that the prospect of (better paying) work attracted migrants to

---

[43] Dirk Hoerder and Jorg Nagler (eds), *People in Transit. German Migrations in Comparative Perspective, 1820–1930* (Cambridge, 1995); Ewa Morawska, *Insecure Prosperity. Small-Town Jews in Industrial America, 1890–1940* (Princeton, 1996).
[44] Hein de Haas and Aleida van Rooij, "Migration as Emancipation? The Impact of Internal and International Migration on the Position of Women Left Behind in Rural Morocco", *Oxford Development Studies*, 38, 1 (2010), pp. 43–62.
[45] Ali Nobil Ahmad, *Masculinity, Sexuality and Illegal Migration. Human Smuggling from Pakistan to Europe* (Aldershot, 2011); Nobil Ahmad, "The Romantic Appeal of Illegal Migration: Gender Masculinity and Human Smuggling from Pakistan", in: Marlou Schrover et al. (eds), *Illegal Migration and Gender in a Global and Historical Perspective* (Amsterdam, 2008), pp. 127–150.
[46] De Haas and Van Rooij "Migration as emancipation?", pp. 43–62.
[47] Ivan Light, "The Migration Industry in the United States, 188 2–1924", *Migration Studies*, 1, 3 (2013), pp. 25 8–275.
[48] Idem.

the US. However, the propaganda by steamship ticket agents was an additional and important driving force. Shipping companies bought foreign language newspapers in order to gain access to potential migrants. These papers published immigrant letters and, by doing so, they promoted migration. These papers became part of the migration industry. The Dillingham Commission sought to forbid shipping companies to promise work in the US. The shipping companies, whose activities have been described in detail by authors such as Feys and Brinkmann, not only transported passengers across the water but also organized overland transport by train across Europe.[49] Migrants were transported, frequently in sealed train carriages, from Central and Eastern Europe to port cities such as Antwerp, Rotterdam and Hamburg. Along the routes, shipping companies selected migrants, making sure that only migrants who were likely to get into the countries of destination would make the trip. For their selection, the shipping companies set up and ran selection stations along the routes. Private shipping companies, rather than state authorities, were given the task of exercising control over the people who left Europe.[50] In addition to the large companies crossing the Atlantic, there were smaller companies, which sometimes had different aims. In 1907, Norway, for instance, sponsored its own transatlantic shipping line—the Norway Mexico Gulf Line—and hired a successful writer to describe first ship's maiden voyage. The idea, however, was not to increase migration, but rather trade.[51]

Slavery, trafficking of women, and forced labour are generally excluded from studies on labour migration. Three factors may explain that. In the first place, as pointed out by Adam McKeown in a 2012 publication, before the twentieth century, attention from lawmakers, journalists, and reformers focused on brokers and migration infrastructure. In the late nineteenth century, brokers and middlemen were, however, increasingly seen as the source of evil when it came to migration and as the remnants of a pre-modern culture that undermined the benefits of migration. New immigration laws, introduced in the early twentieth century, focused on regulat-

---

[49] Torsten Feys, "The Visible Hand of Shipping Interests in American Migration Policies 1815–1914", *Tijdschrift voor Sociale en Economische Geschiedenis*, 7, 1 (2010), pp. 38–62; Tobias Brinkmann, "Traveling with Ballin: The Impact of American Immigration Policies on Jewish Transmigration within Central Europe, 1880–1914", *International Review of Social History*, 53, 3 (2008), pp. 459–484.
[50] Tobias Brinkmann, "Strangers in the City: Transmigration from Eastern Europe and its Impact on Berlin and Hamburg 1880–1914", *Journal of Migration History*, 2, 2 (2016), pp. 223–246; Torsten Feys, "Steamshipping Companies and Transmigration Patterns: The Use of European Cities as Hubs during the Era of Mass Migration to the US", *Journal of Migration History*, 2, 2 (2016), pp. 247–274; Allison Schmidt, "The Long March through Leipzig': Train Terminal Chaos and the Transmigrant Registration Station, 1904–1914", *Journal of Migration History*, 2, 2 (2016), pp. 307–329.
[51] Mieke Neyens, "The Good, the Bad and the Rationale. Desirable and Undesirable Migration to Cuba and Mexico (1907–1909)", in: Steinar A. Sæther (ed.), *Expectations Unfulfilled. Norwegian Migrants in Latin America, 1820–1940* (Leiden and Boston, 2016), pp. 102–126.

ing entry at the border and made brokers invisible.⁵² Slavery, trafficking, and forced labour are excluded from studies on labour migration because of the implicit assumption that labour migration means choice. The dominance of the traditional push-and-pull paradigm, with its emphasis on choice, obscures the fact that slavery was, in essence, labour migration. Secondly, the rigid categorizations, discussed above, make it difficult to deal with in-between categories. Lastly, claim-makers feel that forms of amoral migration (such as slavery, forced labour, and trafficking) should not be normalized by including them in a standard categorization such as labour migration.

Slavery existed in Ancient Egypt, Ancient China, the Roman Empire, and many other old civilizations. Vikings in Early Modern Europe captured slaves on their raids and sold them on Islamic markets. In the Middle Ages, Arab slavers brought people from Sub-Saharan Africa to Europe. Furthermore, in early medieval Europe there was the system of penal enslavement, enslaving people as a form of compensation for the wrongs they had committed: theft, arson, rape, murder, adultery, or inappropriate conduct harming the family's honour. Penal enslavement was, however, not labour market driven, but rather sprang from the wish to sever ties between the culprit and his or her kin and community.⁵³ Slavery also occurred between the sixteenth and the nineteenth century, when Babarby pirates attacked coastal towns in Italy, Portugal, and Spain, captured the inhabitants and sold them or used them as slaves.⁵⁴ Spain, Portugal, Britain, and the Netherlands built their colonial empires using slave labour.⁵⁵ Slavery was big business: a well-oiled and profitable industry. European slavers moved millions of enslaved people across the Atlantic. There is a large debate about numbers. The website *slavevoyages*⁵⁶, which collected a lot of data, estimates that the number was 12 million (see figure 1), while Matlou Matlotleng estimates that 22 million people were enslaved. There are also authors that set the number as high as 100 million. The most cited number, however, is 12 million.⁵⁷ Although slaves were meant to be workers, the slavers did not see the enslaved people as such, nor did they see them as people at all. Slave-traders insured their 'cargoes' of slaves—of which a third did not survive the Atlantic crossing—against losses at sea, just like they insured cargo. Slaves were considered to be goods.

---

52 Adam McKeown, "How the Box Became Black: Brokers and the Creation of the Free Migrant", *Pacific Affairs*, 85, 1 (2012), pp. 21–45.
53 Alice Rio, "Penal Enslavement in the Early Middle Ages", in: Christian De Vito and Alex Lichtenstein (eds), *Global Convict Labour* (Leiden and Boston, 2015), pp. 79–107.
54 Marlou Schrover, "History of Slavery, Human Smuggling and Trafficking 1860–2010', in: Gerben Bruinsma (ed.), *Histories of Transnational Crime* (Amsterdam, 2015), pp. 41–70.
55 Jennifer Lofkrantz and Olatunji Ojo, "Slavery, Freedom, and Failed Ransom Negotiations in West Africa, 1730–1900", *The Journal of African History*, 53, 1 (2012), pp. 25–44.
56 http://www.slavevoyages.org/assessment/estimates.
57 Matlotleng P. Matlou, "Africa, South of the Sahara, Intra- and Intercontinental Population Movements", in: Immanuel Ness et al. (eds), *The Encyclopedia of Global Human Migration*, Vol. I (Chichester, 2013), pp. 460–467.

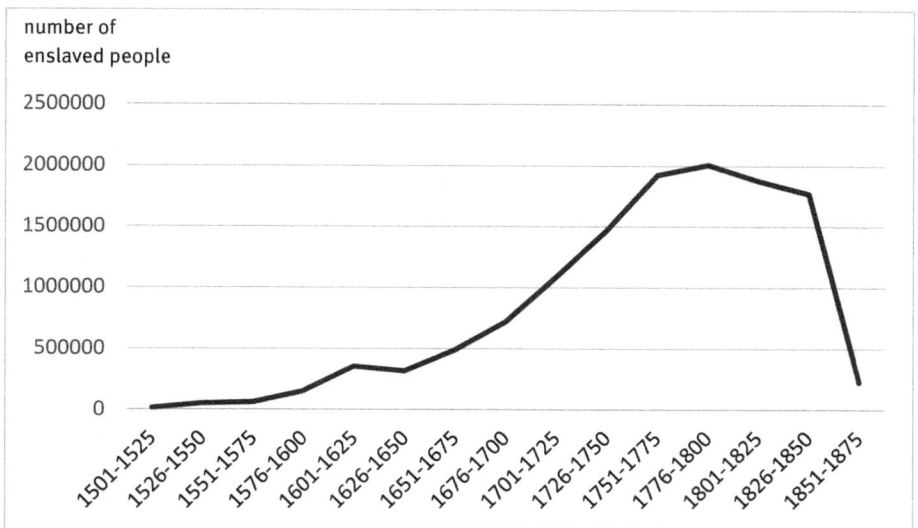

Based on: http://www.slavevoyages.org/assessment/estimates

Figure 1: Number of enslaved people who made the Atlantic crossing

England abolished slavery in 1833, France did so in 1848, and the Netherlands followed in 1863.[58] The abolition of slavery did not mean that slaves were emancipated, nor did it end slavery. Enslaved people continued to work as slaves or under slave-like conditions. In 2017, the ILO estimated that there were 21 million slaves and forced labourers worldwide.[59] The redefinition of slavery and force labour, however, makes it difficult to count people. Slavery is defined as the act of buying and selling people as if they were goods or animals. Recent authors have stretched the definition to include also all sorts of bondage, coerced labour, and restrictions on choice.

After the formal abolition, slavery was partly replaced by indentured labour. In 1852, France, for instance, brought Indians from French India (geographically separated enclaves on the Indian subcontinent) to the West-Indies, as well as a group of workers called *Neg Congo* from their colonial possessions in Africa. About 10,000 Indians arrived in the French West Indies.[60] In 1885, there were 87,000 Indians in Martinique, Guadeloupe and French Guiana. In 1870, the Dutch got permission from the British authorities to contract labourers in the British colonies in Asia. In total 30,304 British Indians were brought to Surinam. This migration continued until 1916, when the British stopped it, under the pressure of British nationalists. Between 1890

---

58 Bonham C. Richardson, "Caribbean Migrations, 1838–1985", in: Franklin W. Knight and Colin A. Palmer (eds), *The Modern Caribbean* (Chapel Hill, NC, 1989), pp. 203–228; Rosemarijn Hoefte, *In Place of Slavery. A History of British Indian and Javanese Laborers in Suriname* (Gainsville, FL, 1998).
59 http://www.ilo.org/global/topics/forced-labour/lang-en/index.htm.
60 Richardson, "Caribbean Migrations, 1838–1985".

and 1939, the Dutch also brought 33,000 workers from Java to Surinam. British contract labourers from neighbouring British Guiana also moved to Surinam. In total, about one million indentured workers were brought from India to the Caribbean (see table 1). In addition, there were indentured workers from other countries.

Table 1: Number of indentured workers brought from India to the Caribbean

Colony	Period of migration	Number of migrants
Mauritius	1834–1900	453,063
British Guiana	1838–1916	238,909
Trinidad	1845–1916	143,939
Jamaica	1845–1915	36,412
Grenada	1856–1885	3,200
St Lucia	1858–1895	4,350
Natal	1860–1911	152,184
St Kitts	1860–1861	337
St Vincents	1860–1880	2,472
Reunion	1861–1883	26,507
Surinam	1873–1916	34,304
Fiji	1879–1916	60,965
East Africa	1895– ?	32,000
Seychelles	? –1916	6,315
total		1,194,957

Source: Brij V. Lal and Chalo Jahaji, *A Journey Through Indenture in Fiji* (Canberra, 2000), p. 75.

When slavery in British India ended in 1860, it was followed by the creation of a system of voluntary indentured labour. Labour brokers paid travel costs, and the migrants had to work off their debts. Within this system, many Indian migrants moved from India to Malaya, under the jurisdiction of the Colonial Office in London. Married men were not allowed to be accompanied by their wives. Chinese traders set up a parallel system of organized migration, which used similar structures. After the 1870s, the Malayan government became the official state agency for organizing Indian labour recruitment and developed a migration infrastructure. British authorities managed emigration procedures at ports, and legislated shipboard conditions. The government stimulated migration by improving transport infrastructures, subsidizing travel, initiating liberal migration regulations, and establishing indentured labour regimes.[61]

After indentured labour migration systems were formally abolished, the bulk of Indian migration in Asia continued to be modelled on the former system of inden-

---

[61] Amarjit Kaur, "Labour Brokers in Migration: Understanding Historical and Contemporary Transnational Migration Regimes in Malaya/Malaysia", *International Review of Social History*, 57, 2 (2012), pp. 225–252.

tured migration. Systems of debt and advances tied labourers to employers through the mediation of the labour contractors.⁶² The analogies between the colonial and independent Malaysian migration policies are remarkable: the provision of assisted passage for workers continued to exist, the repayment of advances through salary deductions was held onto as a practice, and migrants continued to be tied to a specified employer.

In the US, the abolition of slavery was also followed by the introduction and expansion of a system of peonage, which tied workers to their employers and to the land they worked on because they were under the obligation to pay off debts. About 450,000 to 900,000 people—mostly Afro-Americans—lived as unfree labourers in the US in the 1930s and 1940s.⁶³

After the end of formal slavery in Africa, former slaves migrated within European colonial territories hoping to find work. They moved away from the sites at which they had been enslaved. The former slaves became migrant workers. Studies on labour migration in Africa focus on ethnicity, rather than on the mobility that resulted from slavery, and its abolition. Emancipation and labour migration should, however, not be treated separately.⁶⁴ In her 2011 study, Pelckman shows how labour migration in Africa is, to a large extend, shaped by (former) slave status, (former) slave employment, and remnants of slave networks and hierarchies.⁶⁵

Forced labour migration in Nazi Germany has been labelled slavery, but that is stretching or misusing the concept. The forced labourers in Nazi Germany were (unlike slaves) partly worked to death on purpose, and they were not owned or sold by their employers. They did work in slave-like conditions, and they were moved as workers and put to work for profit.

The movement and deployment of foreign workers during wars did not start with the Second World War. During the First World War, Germany deployed 1.5 million Prisoners of War (POWs), and Austria-Hungary put to work more than 1 million Russian POWs. 2.1 million Austrian-Hungarian and 170,000 German POWs worked in Russia, and tens of thousands of German POWs worked in France and Britain. In 1916, the German occupation forces deported 5,000 Polish workers, of which most were Jews, from Lodz and 61,000 Belgian workers to Germany. In the Second World War the scale of these types of forced labour migration increased dramatically. Two Soviet decrees of 1942, for instance, forced 316,000 ethnic Germans living in the Soviet Union into so-called labour armies and moved them to far away sites to cut

---

62 Mohapatra "Eurocentrism, Forced Labour", pp. 11 0–115.
63 Nicola Pizzolato, "'As Much in Bondage as They was Before. Unfree Labor During the New Deal (193 5–1952)", in: Marcel van der Linden and Magaly Rodríguez García (eds), *On Coerced Labor. Work and Compulsion after Chattel Slavery* (Leiden and Boston, 2016), pp 208–224.
64 Rossi Benedetta, "Migration and Emancipation in West Africa's Labour History: The Missing Links", *Slavery and Abolition*, 35, 1 (2014), pp. 23–46.
65 Lotte Pelckmans, *Travelling Hierarchies. Roads in and out of Slave Status in a Central Malian Fulɓe Network.* (Leiden, 2011).

timber, build factories and railroads, work in coal mines, and work in the oil industry.[66] During the Second World War, Japan established a forced labour regime and deported 1 million Korean men and women and 40,000 Chinese to Japan.

In Nazi Germany differences were made between forced labour migrants. The German word for guest worker—*Gastarbeiter*—was coined in Nazi Germany in order to distinguish the more or less voluntary temporary labour migrants form other migrants—*Zwangsarbeiter* and *Ostarbeiter*—who were forced to migrate and work, and who were deemed racially inferior and thereby incapable of carrying out all types of labour.[67] Nazi Germany categorized its foreign workers, allocating them within a hierarchy. Workers from Scandinavia, the Netherlands, and Flanders were placed at the top, and Poles, Soviet citizens, 'Gypsies', and Jews were at the bottom of the hierarchy. Some of the labour migrants who belonged to the top were recruited on a more or less voluntarily basis and were allowed to return to their home countries, sometimes regularly, in the early years of the Second World War. Most of the forced labourers were forced migrants. In 2002, Spoerer and Fleischhacker estimated that the number of foreign forced labourers in Nazi Germany between 1939 and 1945 was 13.5 million, of whom 12 million were coerced to move.[68]

Trafficking, like slavery and forced labour, can be labelled an industry. There is a wide-ranging debate on whether prostitution, which is assumed to result from trafficking, should be discussed in terms of labour migration: is prostitution work? Here, the same idea applies as in the case of slavery and forced labour: the fear exists that grouping prostitution in the category of labour migration normalizes something that is morally wrong. However, although it may not have been a choice, in essence, prostitution is work.

Around 1900, the women's movement started to attract attention to the problem of trafficking in women and claimed that prostitution was a form of slavery. Between 1899 and 1913, conferences were held in several European cities. During the First World War, prostitution increased and in 1919, the League of Nations Covenant declared that it would oversee the international anti-sex trafficking movement.[69] The League of Nation wanted to gather evidence to counterweight distortions in the press. As Julia Laite pointed out in 2017, anti-trafficking activists disconnected de-

---

[66] Irina Mukhina, "Gendered Division of Labor among Special Settlers in the Soviet Union, 1941–1956", *Women's History Review*, 23, 1 (2014), pp. 99–119.
[67] Ulrich Herbert, *Geschichte der Auslanderbeschaftigung in Deutschland 1880 bis 1980. Saisonarbeiter, Zwangsarbeiter, Gastarbeiter* (Berlin, 1986); Friedrich Didier, *Europa arbeitet in Deutschland. Sauckel mobilisiert die Leistungsreserven* (Munich, 1943), p. 63; Rüdiger Hachtmann, "Fordism and Unfree Labour: Aspects of the Work Deployment of Concentration Camp Prisoners in German Industry between 1941 and 1944", *International Review of Social History*, 55, 3 (2010), pp. 485–513.
[68] Mark Spoerer and Jochen Fleischhacker, "Forced Laborers in Nazi Germany: Categories, Numbers, and Survivors", *Journal of Interdisciplinary History*, 33, 2 (2002), pp. 169–204.
[69] Jessica R. Pliley, "Claims to Protection: The Rise and Fall of Feminist Abolitionism in the League of Nations' Committee on the Traffic in Women and Children, 1919–1936", *Journal of Women's History*, 22, 4 (2010), pp. 90–113.

bates about trafficking from those about women's labour migration and the inequalities and exploitation it involved on purpose. Trafficking was seen as a wrong that could be remedied, while claim makers sought to stay away from issues regarding working conditions.[70]

The migration industry metaphor applies to trafficking in three ways. In the first place, there is the trade in women by agents, traffickers, and organized pimps, although, in reality, it was repeatedly found that there were never any business-like organizations.[71] Secondly, there is the very large industry comprised of organizations that try to save women. For the saving industry, trafficking provides leverage because it enabled them to claim moral authority. Lobbyists campaigning against trafficking use the metaphor of the market place and speak about 'trade centres', 'offices', 'trade agents', 'enterprises', 'depots', 'customers', 'stores' and 'orders'.[72] The metaphor is used to highlight the dehumanizing element of trafficking. Lastly, there is the business of newspapers, which found that stories about trafficking increased their sales and readership.[73]

In the 1920s, the concept of trafficking was stretched to include practices in Hong Kong that were called *mui tsai*.[74] This debate is interesting within the context of this chapter because to some *mui tsai* was labour migration, while others redefined it as slavery. *Mui tsai* referred to young girls (5 to 14 year old) who were transferred from their parents' household to another household, where they worked as domestic servants from when they were about 13 until a suitable marriage was arranged for them, or they became a concubine at age of 20. The girls were not at liberty to leave their new household, and the parents were paid a lump sum the moment the girl was transferred.[75] After Hong Kong became a British colony in 1841, lobbyists emphasized that the *mui tsai* system was slavery and since Britain was a nation of civilization and

---

[70] Julia Laite, "Between Scylla and Charybdis: Women's Labour Migration and Sex Trafficking in the Early Twentieth Century", *International Review of Social History*, 62, 1 (2017), pp. 37–65.
[71] Gretchen Soderlund, "Covering Urban Vice: the New York Times, 'White Slavery' and the Construction of Journalistic Knowledge", *Critical Studies in Media Communication*, 19, 4 (2002), pp. 438–460; Petra de Vries, "'White Slaves' in a Colonial Nation: the Dutch Campaign Against the Traffic in Women in the Early Twentieth Century", *Social and Legal Studies*, 14, 1 (2005), pp. 39–60; Frank Bovenkerk et al., *'Loverboys' of Modern Pooierschap in Amsterdam* (Utrecht, 2006); Laura M. Agustin, *Sex at the Margins. Migration, Labour Markets and the Rescue Industry* (London, 2007).
[72] For more references see: Mariëlle Kleijn and Marlou Schrover, "The Dutch State as a Pimp. Policies Regarding a Brothel on Curaçao (1945–1956)", *Tijdschrift voor Sociale en Economische Geschiedenis*, 10, 3 (2013), pp. 33–54. See also: Petra De Vries, *Kuisheid voor Mannen, Vrijheid voor Vrouwen. De reglementering en Bestrijding van Prostitutie in Nederland 1850–1911* (Hilversum, 1997); de Vries, ""White Slaves" in a Colonial Nation".
[73] Schrover, "History of Slavery, Human Smuggling and Trafficking", pp. 41–70.
[74] Susan Pedersen, "The Maternalist Moment in British Colonial Policy: The Controversy over "Child Slavery" in Hong Kong 1917–1941", *Past and Present*, 171 (May 2001), pp. 161–202.
[75] Sarah Paddle, "The Limits of Sympathy: International Feminists and the Chinese 'Slave Girl' Campaigns of the 1920s and 1930s", *Journal of Colonialism and Colonial History*, 4, 3 (2003), pp. 1–22.

Christianity it should not tolerate this evil.⁷⁶ Leading Chinese in the colony pointed out that obtaining girls for domestic work was a longstanding Chinese practice—it was not slavery. The food, clothes, and other necessities the girls were given by their masters could be considered a wage. The British authorities disagreed it was domestic work, and in 1922 declared that the *mui tsai* system was slavery. Even though the *mui tsai* system was not very different from the system under which young domestic servants worked in North-Western European countries,⁷⁷ the British authorities called it slavery because of the criticism by lobbyists.

In the late 1920s, definitions of trafficking and of slavery started to converge. The 1956 *Supplementary Convention on the Abolition of Slavery, the Slave Trade and Institutions and Practices Similar to Slavery* expanded the definition. It marked a turning point, since it stretched the concept of slavery to include all sorts of servitude. In 2000, the *Palermo Protocol* (to *Prevent, Suppress and Punish Trafficking in Persons, Especially Women and Children*, a supplement to the *UN Convention against Transnational Organized Crime*) connected trafficking and slavery even more strongly. The *Palermo Protocol* was the first convention that distinguished between trafficking and smuggling. According to the *Palermo Protocol*, smuggling is the facilitation and (attempted) transportation of persons across borders illegally or the assistance of persons in entering a country using fraudulent documents. Trafficking is the recruitment, transportation, transfer, harbouring, or receipt of persons, by means of threat, use of force, or other forms of coercion, abduction, fraud, deception, or the abuse of power for the purpose of exploitation. Exploitation includes prostitution, forced labour, slavery, practices similar to slavery, servitude, or the removal of organs. The consent of a victim to the (intended) exploitation is regarded as irrelevant. The definition of trafficking emphasizes that people are transferred against their will, while the definition of smuggling stresses movement to which migrants agree and for which they pay. Trafficking is used more often for women, denying them agency, while smuggling is used more for men, denying their role as victims.⁷⁸

In recent years, the topic of trafficking has dominated conferences on (migrant) women.⁷⁹ The literature, discussions and conferences on trafficking of migrant women are so numerous and show such continuity in their choice of topics and focus that they tend to push out other subjects related to women and migration. The assumption that large numbers of women are trafficked has resulted in stronger

---

76 Y.K. Ko, "From 'Slavery' to 'Girlhood'? Age, Gender and Race in Chinese and Western Representations of the Mui Tsai Phenomenon, 1879–1941" (Ph.D. Thesis, University of Hong Kong, 2008).
77 Frans van Poppel, Jona Schellekens and Evelien Walhout, "Oversterfte van Jonge Meisjes in Nederland in de Negentiende en Eerste Helft Twintigste eeuw", *Tijdschrift voor Sociale en Economische Geschiedenis*, 6, 4 (2009), pp. 37–69.
78 Schrover, "History of Slavery, Human Smuggling and Trafficking", pp. 41–70.
79 Gretchen Soderlund, "Running from the Rescuers: New U.S. Crusaders Against Sex Trafficking and the Rhetoric of Abolition", *National Women's Studies Association Journal*, 17, 3 (Fall 2005), pp. 64–87, at 65.

monitoring of migrant women, as opposed to men.[80] It has also led to the generalization that all migrant women are at risk of being raped or being subject to other forms of sexual harassment.[81] The narrative of victimhood and the assumption that women are forced to migrate and work in prostitution has brought about protective measures, which sometimes help women but also restrict their choices, and labour market opportunities.[82]

Lastly, missionary work can also be seen as an example of a migration industry. Missionaries were involved in child rescue operations: saving children from their parents, from heathen influences, from slavery, or from forced marriages. They constructed and led orphanages, in which former slave children, abandoned children, children at risk, orphans, and half-orphans were housed. Their aim was to bring up these children as Christians who as adults would be able to act as intermediaries between the colonizers and the colonized. Thus, one form of migration industry—that of missionaries—led to another form—the forced and institutionalized removal of children from their families. When colonialism came to an end these children were frequently taken to the country of the former colonizers.[83] The mission was, to a certain extent, replaced by *voluntourism:* a combination of tourism and volunteering activities.[84] Voluntourism refers to mostly young people form Western countries who go to so-called underdeveloped countries (in Asia, Africa, Central and South America) to do voluntary work and who are driven by motives such as 'giving back' and 'doing good'. In this type of migration women outnumber men because of the organized and, according to perceptions, rather safe way of travelling and living abroad that is offered. Organizations advertise the trips and residencies as emotional journeys.[85] The voluntourists keep travel blogs which are used by organizations to attract new voluntourists, in a manner very similar to how shipping companies used immi-

---

[80] Umut Erel, "Soziales Kapital und Migration: Die Kraft der Schwachen?", in: Castro Varela, Maria Do Mar and Dimitria Clayton (eds), *Migration, Gender, Arbeitsmarkt. Neue Beitrage zu Frauen und Globalisierung* (Königstein, 2003), pp. 154–185.
[81] Susan Moller Okin, "Is Multiculturalism Bad for Women?", in: Joshua Cohen, Matthew Howard and Martha C. Nussbaum (eds), *Is Multiculturalism Bad for Women?* (Princeton, NJ, 1999), pp. 9–24.
[82] Tarneen Siddiqui, "An Anatomy of Forced and Voluntary Migration from Bangladesh: A Gendered Perspective", in: Mirjana Morokvasic, Umut Erel and Kyoko Shinozaki (eds), *Crossing Borders and Shifting Boundaries, vol. I. Gender on the Move* (Opladen, 2003), pp. 155–176; Annelies Moors and Marina de Regt, "Migrant Domestic Workers in the Middle East", in: Marlou Schrover et al. (eds), *Illegal Migration and Gender in a Global and Historical Perspective* (Amsterdam, 2008), pp. 151–170; Donna Hughes, "The "Natasha" Trade – Transnational Sex Trafficking", *National Institute of Justice Journal* (January 2001), pp. 9–15.
[83] Sarah Heynssens "Practices of Displacement: Forced Migration of Mixed-Race Children from Colonial Ruanda-Urundi to Belgium", *Journal of Migration History*, 2, 1 (2016), pp. 1–31.
[84] Kate J. Zavitz, "Not That Alternative: Short-Term Volunteer Tourism at an Organic Farming Project in Costa Rica", *ACME: An International Journal for Critical Geographies*, 10, 3 (2011), pp. 412–441, at 413.
[85] Jennie Germann Molz, "Giving Back, Doing Good, Feeling Global: The Affective Flows of Family", *Journal of Contemporary Ethnography*, 44, 1 (2015), pp. 1–27.

grant letters in the newspapers they owned. The young temporary migrants are usually skilled, although often not in the jobs they work in. They give language courses, teach children, and build orphanages mostly without being trained as professional language instructors, teachers, or brick layers. Their stay is short but the organizational infrastructure that is put in place to organize this migration is permanent. Furthermore, their temporary stay leads to new (chain) migration: marriage migration, and student migration from the countries they visit to the countries they come from.

Migration infrastructure

In 2014, Xiang and Lindquist described the changes in recent Indonesian and Chinese labour migration, and introduced the concept of *migration infrastructure*, which they defined as the systematically interlinked technologies, institutions, and actors that facilitate and condition mobility. Migration infrastructure relates to mediation, but the interplay between different dimensions of migration infrastructure make it self-perpetuating and self-serving. Rather than describing how migration becomes self-sustaining through networks, the migration infrastructure approach seeks to examine how networks function as part of the migration infrastructure. Xiang and Lindquist use the concept of migration infrastructure to explain why labour migration has become both more accessible and more cumbersome in many parts of Asia since the late 1990s. Migration is easier, since more people have gained legal access to overseas job opportunities, and journeys are quicker and safer. It is cumbersome, since the process of migration has become more complicated with growing numbers of regulations, which have often led to higher migration costs. Xiang and Lindquist break down migration infrastructure into the commercial (recruitment intermediaries), the regulatory (state apparatus and procedures for documentation, licensing, training, and other purposes), the technological (communication and transport), the humanitarian (non-governmental organizations (NGOs)) and international organizations), and the social (migrant networks). Migration can be fragmented and short-lived, but infrastructure retains stability and coherence. According to Xiang and Lindquist, migration infrastructure differs from yet again another concept: *mobility regime*. Mobility regime or migration regime focuses on how mobility is structured and how it is part of hegemonic power relations. The migration industry approach constructs migration as a form of business and pays less attention to the fact that migration brokers are not simply selling opportunities for migrating, but are also dealing with various components of infrastructure—such as collecting documents, organizing medical tests, or conducting pre-departure training—which have far-reaching regulatory effects. According to Xiang and Lindquist, migration should not be imagined as a line between two places, but rather as a multi-faceted space of mediation occupied by commercial recruitment intermediaries, bureaucrats, NGOs, migrants, and technologies.[86] Siegelbaum and Page Moch added that it is not only state projects that move people—as the migration regime concept stipulates—but also the migrants' practices, their relationships and networks. They labelled this *repertoires of migration*.[87]

In the field of labour migration, the mediation by NGOs and intergovernmental organizations (IGOs) has not been studied enough, given the fact that both types of organizations are important to the migration infrastructure. The ILO, which is a relevant organization when it comes to organized labour migration, was part of the migration infrastructure. After the First World War, the ILO tried to create standards for the recruitment and treatment of foreign workers. In the 1920s and 1930s, attempts were made to take stock of how many people moved in order to find work. It resulted in important publications by Ferenczi and Willcox.[88] As of 1920, Imre Ferenczi was the Technical Adviser on Migration and Population Questions at the International Labour Office in Geneva and was acting chef of its Migration Section. In 1921 and 1924, the US installed quota measures, which severely restricted migration from Eastern and Southern Europe. In 1924, the CIOPPM (Comité International des Organisations Privées pour la Protection des Migrants) was created in response, supported by the ILO. In the first months of 1924, 60 NGOs joined the CIOPPM. It campaigned for transportation costs to be fixed before departure, for a reduction of waiting times at stations, and for help with visa applications: these were all issues the shipping companies also tried to address. In the interwar years, the ILO sought to harmonize workers' rights at the international level, but they failed in the midst of the Depression. Increased workers' rights also led to the (perceived) need to restrict the entry of migrants, who might compete for labour.[89] Non-migrant workers urged for the protection of the labour market from foreign workers. The extension of voting rights made politicians sensitive to these demands. But preferential treatment of non-migrant workers was only possible if they could be distinguished from foreigners. As a result, workers and their unions started to press for more registration.[90] The ILO's task did not become easier. During the Second World War, the ILO created a Permanent Migration Committee to organize the selection of (labour) migrants after the war.[91] Recently, the ILO increasingly has been working together with the International Organization for Migration (IOM), although both also compete with each other. The ILO and

---

[86] Biao Xiang and Johan Lindquist, "Migration Infrastructure", *International Migration Review*, 48, 1 (Fall 2014), pp. 12 2–148.
[87] Siegelbaum and Page Moch, *Broad is My Native Land*.
[88] Imre Ferenczi and Walter F. Willcox, *International Migrations*, 2 vols (New York, 1929–1931).
[89] Leo Lucassen, "The Great War and the Origins of Migration Control in Western Europe and the United States (1880–1920)", in: Anita Böcker *et al.* (eds), *Regulation of Migration. International Experiences* (Amsterdam, 1998), pp. 45–72.
[90] Clifford Rosenberg, *Policing Paris. The Origins of Modern Immigration Control Between the Wars* (Ithaca, NY, 2006), pp. 17–44, at 46–49.
[91] Johannes-Dieter Steinert, *Migration und Politik. Westdeutschland–Europa-Übersee 1945–1961* (Osnabrück, 1995).

the IOM have sought more cooperation with NGOs. The IOM—which has recently become a UN organization—is now involved in the pre-migration training of labour migrants. In 2010, it presented a training manual for labour migration, which is used to train government officials, members of local NGOs and potential migrants.[92]

The concept migration infrastructure can be used to explain or describe the migration within empires, and the large-scale migration organized by state authorities in conjunction with others. Migration to and within empires was frequently the result of a joint or concurrent effort of more than one actor. Authorities tried to encourage migration to the colonies (especially from the end of the nineteenth century onwards) and so did so-called migration societies (civil society organizations that were partly driven by the aim to reduce poverty in their home countries).[93] Migration within, for instance, the Habsburg, Chinese, Russian, or Ottoman Empires was long distance migration, as was migration within colonial Empires such as the French, the Dutch, the Portuguese, Spanish, and British empires. People moved to the colonies as sailors, soldiers, merchants, and missionaries. They used the same routes and the same information networks.[94]

Career migration, care drain and care chain, brain drain, and brawn drain

In 1976, Charles Tilly defined *career migrants* as a sub-category of labour migrants.[95] A career migrant is, according to Tilly, a person who moves (with or without a household) in response to opportunities within large structures: organized trade, firms, governments, mercantile networks, and armies, for instance. The career migrant differs from the chain migrant because social bonds (for instance with kin and kind) are less important than the large structures they move in. Help is provided by colleagues and not by (former) neighbours, kinsmen, or co-religionists. In 2015, Lucassen and Smit sub-categorized the concept of career migration and distinguished *organizational migrants* as people (plus their dependents) whose migratory behaviour is primarily determined by the interests of the organization they have joined (voluntary or

---

[92] Frank Georgi and Susanne Schatral, "Towards a Critical Theory of Migration Control: The Case of the International Organization for Migration (IOM)", in: Martin Geiger and Antoine Pécoud (eds), *The New Politics of International Mobility. Migration Management and its Discontents. IMIS Beiträge*, 40 (2012), pp. 193–221.
[93] C. van Drimmelen, "Kolonisatie van het Blanke Ras in de Tropen", *Nieuwe West-Indische Gids*, 4, 1 (1923), pp. 193–204.
[94] Jessica Vance Roitman, "Portuguese Jews, Amerindians, and the Frontiers of Encounter in Colonial Suriname", *New West Indian Guide*, 88 (2014), pp. 18–52; Hoefte, *In Place of Slavery*.
[95] Charles Tilly, CRSO Working Paper #145 Migration in Modern European History (Michigan, 1976).

forced).⁹⁶ Also, the *expat* is a sub-category of the career migrant. Originally, the term was used for communities of creative and political bohemians, such as the Russians and Americans in interwar Paris. In recent decades, the term has been adopted by labour migrants, the organizations they work for, and the states who court them, to emphasize that expats are high-skilled, and upper-class. The expats are currently mostly young white Western men, who are moved by firms across the globe and do not seek to settle or adjust to their new surroundings. There is a difference between high-skilled workers who move outside organizational networks and migrants who move inside networks. Those who move outside these networks frequently find it difficult to have their diploma's recognized. Those who move across national borders within firms (Unilever or Shell, for instance) will have their diplomas validated within the firm and do not have to go through procedures in the country of destination.

Class and gender are important to the definitions of career migrants and related concepts, although that is frequently not made explicit. Career migration and related phenomena are usually discussed separately from the migration of skilled workers. The migration of skilled workers has always been an important part of labour migration. Migrant workers were recruited by organizations and governments because of their special skills. Samis from Northern Finland—to name a little-known example—were brought to Alaska by US authorities to teach the Inuit—who were, at that time, mainly living from fishing—how to herd reindeer. In a similar vein, linen and jute spinners were brought from Scotland and England to France and the Netherlands,⁹⁷ and porcelain painters were moved from the UK to the Netherlands.⁹⁸ Butter makers were sent to other parts of the world to learn or teach butter making techniques.⁹⁹ In the 1930s, the Volkswagen plant in Fallersleben in Germany, modelled on Ford Motor Company's River Rouge plant in Dearborne, imported engineers from the US.¹⁰⁰ This list can be extended endlessly. The migration was usually meant to be temporary. The migration of these specialized workers was not discussed in terms of *brain drain*. In the literature, the concept brain drain was mostly used to describe the migration of specialists from underdeveloped countries—for instance doctors and IT specialists—to developed countries. It was less about opportunities and careers and much more about how the countries they left would be negatively affected by the departure of these high-skilled workers, stereotypically portrayed as men.

---

96 Leo Lucassen and Aniek X. Smit, "The Repugnant Other: Soldiers, Missionaries, and Aid Workers as Organizational Migrants", *Journal of World History*, 26, 1 (2015), pp. 1–39.
97 Fabrice Bensimon and Christopher A. Whatley, "The Thread of Migration: A Scottish-French Linen and Jute Works and its Workers in France, c. 1845–c. 1870", *Journal of Migration History*, 2, 1 (2016), pp. 120–147.
98 Gertjan de Groot, "Foreign Technology and the Gender Division of Labour in a Dutch Cotton Spinning Mill", in: Gertjan de Groot and Marlou Schrover (eds), *Women Workers and Technological Change*, pp. 52–66.
99 Marlou Schrover, "Cooking up Women's Work: Women Workers in the Dutch Food Industries 1889–1960", in: de Groot and Schrover, *Women Workers and Technological Change*, pp. 170–192.
100 Hachtmann, "Fordism and Unfree Labour", pp. 485–513.

Singers and theatre performers are career migrants as well, although they are also frequently not recognized as such.[101] In the nineteenth and twentieth centuries, these performers travelled the globe, usually with a director or manager, who decided where they would go. Athletes form a similar group of highly visible mobile people, who are seldom described as career migrants. An example are rugby players from Fiji. Their highly-organized migration, and that of other athletes, has been labelled *brawn drain* and *muscle trade*. Fijian authorities and organizations have actively developed networks and structures to pave the way for future Fijian migrants. In Fiji, rugby has been developed as part of the countries national identity and Fijian rugby players are playing in all major teams of the world. In a similar manner, West Indian cricket players, Dominican baseball players, and Kenyan middle and long distance runners are, and have been for decades, part of highly organized labour migration networks.[102] In 2013, Darby described the migration of Ghanaian football players, whom he regards both as labour migrants and as commodities that are traded in international markets. By 2010, 350 Ghanaian football players were playing as professionals or semi-professionals for mostly European teams. European football clubs—such as the Dutch teams Ajax, Feyenoord, and FC Utrecht—have set up youth academies in Ghana to train young players, aged 10 to 14. The boys are to play for the European teams who run the academies, or they are sold to other teams when they are 18.[103]

Care workers are career migrants, despite the fact that they are not discussed in those terms. From the 1960s onwards, nurses were recruited by hospitals or via government programmes by countries such as the UK, Canada, and the Netherlands, from countries such as Suriname, South Africa and, most importantly, the Philippines. In the Philippines, the government organized the 'export' of nurses to other countries, hoping that remittances would stimulate the Philippine economy. The migration of nurses was followed by and led to the migration of domestic servants and other care-givers from the Philippines.[104] Currently, there are domestic servants and other care workers from the Philippines in almost all countries of the world. The total

---

[101] Ute Sonnleitner, "Moving German-Speaking Theatre: Artists and Movement 185 0–1950", *Journal of Migration History*, 2, 1 (2016), pp. 93–119.

[102] Yoko Kanemasu and Gyozo Molnar, "Pride of the People: Fijian Rugby Labour Migration and Collective Identity", *International Review for the Sociology of Sport*, 48, 6 (2012), pp. 72 0–735.

[103] Paul Darby, "Moving Players, Traversing Perspectives: Global Value Chains, Production Networks and Ghanaian Football Labour Migration", *Geoforum*, 50 (2013), pp. 4 3–53.

[104] B.S.A. Yeoh, S. Huang and J. Gonzalez, "Migrant Female Domestic Workers: Debating the Economic, Social and Political Impacts in Singapore", *International Migration Review*, 33, 1 (1999), pp. 114–136; P. I. Panayiotopoulos, "The Globalisation of Care: Filipina Domestic Workers and Care for the Elderly in Cyprus", *Capital and Class*, 29 (2005), pp. 99–134; Ryan Urbano, "Global Justice and the Plight of Filipino Domestic Migrant Workers", *Journal of Asian and African Studies*, 47 (2012), pp. 605–619; H.E.S. Nesadurai, "Malaysia's Conflict with the Philippines and Indonesia over Labour Migration: Economic Security, Interdependence and Conflict Trajectories", *The Pacific Review*, 26, 1 (2013), pp. 89–113.

number of overseas workers from the Philippines is 10 million, of which 3.5 million are in the US and 1 million in Saudi Arabia. The Overseas Contract Workers—an official Philippine policy category—are expected to return. They are responsible for a large part of the remittances, which constitute 30 to 40 per cent of the Philippines's BSP. Regarding gender, the Philippine immigrant population is skewed in most countries, with women outnumbering men at four or five to one. The migration of domestic servants and other care workers from the Philippines is not discussed in the same context as that of the about 255,000 Filipino seafarers, who work as deck hands, engine room oilers, cabin cleaners, and cooks aboard container ships, oil tankers, and luxury cruise liners.[105] Since they are aboard ships most of the time, they are less visible, also in migration statistics, than the women who migrated from the Philippines.

Over centuries, domestic service has been an important sector of employment for immigrant and non-immigrant women alike. Many immigrant women worked as domestic servants, although—as said above—the sector is not as important as the number of publications on migrant domestic servants suggests. The sector was important to migrant women from some countries, but not from all.[106] Domestic work was important to labour migration in the nineteenth century, but the number of domestic servants sharply declined in the second half of the twentieth century. The sector is now on the rebound and offers new opportunities to migrant women.[107] Migrant women currently manage to dominate certain sub-sectors of the labour market for domestic services, such as live-in child-care or care of the elderly, especially in countries where this care has not been institutionalized.

The concept *care drain* was introduced to describe how women migrate and care for the children or elders of others in foreign countries, leaving behind dependents in the care of others.[108] Care drain is combined with the concept *care chain*, which labels women as mothers, rather than as workers. The care chains are believed to sustain gender inequality: women in rich countries hire women from poor countries to do what is stereotypically seen as women's work (caring), rather than contesting the separation of work between the private and the public sphere. Part of this literature about *missing mothers* has strong moral undertones: *we* are depriving children elsewhere of care. This claim is made without proving if the women who migrate were indeed caregivers before migration. Furthermore, debates about *transnational moth-*

---

[105] S.C. McKay, "Filipino Sea Men: Constructing Masculinities in an Ethnic Labour Niche", *Journal of Ethnic and Migration Studies*, 33, 4 (2007), pp. 617–633.
[106] Moya, "Domestic Service in a Global Perspective", pp. 559–579.
[107] B. Gratton, "Ecuadorians in the United States and Spain: History, Gender and Niche Formation", *Journal of Ethnic and Migration Studies*, , 33, 4 (2007), pp. 581–600.
[108] Roda Madziva and Elisabetta Zontini, "Transnational Mothering and Forced Migration: Understanding the Experiences of Zimbabwean Mothers in the UK', *European Journal of Women's Studies*, 19, 4 (2012), pp. 428–443; Helma Lutz and Ewa Palenga-Möllenbeck, "Care Workers, Care Drain, and Care Chains: Reflections on Care, Migration, and Citizenship", *Social Politics*, 19, 1 (2012), pp. 15–37.

ering are not matched by debates about men who leave their children behind or about the use of the term *transnational fathering*.[109]

Hochschild introduced the concept *global care chain*. It refers to a series of "personal links between people across the globe based on the paid or unpaid work of caring".[110] The global care chain focuses on social interactions between various actors in networks and their structural outcomes.[111] At first, the care chain literature only included women. However, in recent years, Filipino men, trained as foreign care workers, and male doctors from the Philippines, retrained as nurses to gain access to the US and Europe, have been included as well. After gender, authors also started to pay attention to how the chain was shaped by religion: Saudi Arabia prefers Muslim nurses and recruits them from the Islamic Southern Philippines and Indonesia.[112] The use of terms like the *Filipino–US nanny trade* and the *global healthcare market* suggests that this is a migration industry.[113] The concept global care chain drew on the Wallersteinian *global commodity chain* approach in the *world system* analysis. The global commodity chain approach, recently relabelled the *global value chain*, has been criticized because it oversimplifies relationships, adopts a static view of governance and relations of power, overemphasizes the role of firms in the global North, and allocates a subordinate role to those in the South. As a result, it is seen as having little explanatory power.[114]

Circular migration and return migration

The concepts of *circular migration* and *return migration* are both frequently connected to (government) recruitment programmes: governments recruited workers, or sanctioned programmes to recruit workers, with the idea that their migration would be temporary and that the migrants would return to their country of origin. Frequently, the idea was that this migration would take the form of circular migration: either the same migrant would travel back and forth between countries, or different migrants would move within the same circuit.

---

109 Albert Kraler et al. (eds), *Gender, Generations and the Family in International Migration* (Amsterdam, 2011).
110 Arlie R. Hochschild, "Global Care Chains and Emotional Surplus Value", in: Will Hutton and Anthony Giddens (eds) *On the Edge. Living with Global Capitalism* (London, 2000), pp. 130–146, at 131.
111 Nicola Yeates, "A Dialogue with 'Global Care Chain' Analysis: Nurse Migration in the Irish Context", *Feminist Review*, 77, 1 (2004), pp. 79–95.
112 Nicola Yeates, "Global Care Chains: A State-of-the-Art Review and Future Directions in Care Transnationalization Research", *Global Networks*, 12, 2 (2012), pp. 135–154.
113 Silvia Wojczewski et al., "African Female Physicians and Nurses in the Global Care Chain: Qualitative Explorations from Five Destination Countries", *PLoS One* (June 12, 2015), pp. 1–20.
114 Peter Dicken et al., "Chains and Networks, Territories and Scales: Towards a Relational Framework for Analysing the Global Economy", *Global Networks*, 1, 2 (2001), pp. 89–112.

As may be clear by now, in the cases of circular migration and return migration there is also an intersection with other concepts. Career migrants show circular migration patterns, and chain migration was partly circular. Migrants with circular migration patterns moved within migration systems. Vagrants were involved in circular migration.[115] They were of concern to policy-makers long before modern states started to establish migration controls at a national level.[116] Circular migration also occurred in the case of colonial migration.[117] This migration continues in a semi-post-colonial setting. The population of the Caribbean parts of Britain, France and the Netherlands—called British Overseas Territories, French Overseas Departments (départements d'outre-mer (DOMs)), and Dutch special municipalities—, for instance, travels across the Atlantic frequently, while staying within one state.

There is no consensus about the definition of circular migration. Some authors consider one move enough to speak of circular migration, while they exclude seasonal migration because stays are short (6–9 months) and migrants maintain ties with their country of origin. In 2004, Duval defined circular migration as "the actual physical movement of migrants back and forth between multiple localities". He labelled returns a *transnational exercises:* migrants are travelling back and forth while they are deciding on where to settle; a process that was sometimes terminated by death before they could make a choice.[118]

Circular migration was originally conceptualized as temporary migration, with migrants making repeated moves between two or more countries. The seasonal migrants of nineteenth-century Western Europe—such as brick makers and agricultural workers, to name only a few—came at Easter and left at Michaelmas.[119] In a similar fashion, about half a million agricultural labourers travelled to Southern Russia in the 1880s, were they hired themselves out at labour fairs for the season.[120] Some seasonal workers—joint by traders and others following the same routes—made these international trips for years on end, while others participated in the systems for a

---

115 Charles Tilly, "Migration in Modern European History", in: William H. Mc Neill and Ruth Adams (eds), *Human Migration. Patterns and Policies* (Bloomington, IN, 1978), pp. 48–73, at 49.
116 Rosenberg, *Policing Paris.*
117 Stephanie A. Condon and Philip E. Ogden, "Afro-Caribbean Migrants in France: Employment, State Policy and the Migration Process", *Transactions of the Institute of British Geographers,* 16, 4 (1991), pp. 440–457.
118 David Timothy Duval, "Linking Return Visits and Return Migration among Commonwealth Eastern Caribbean Migrants in Toronto", *Global Networks,* 4, 1 (2004), pp. 51–67.
119 Lucassen, *Naar de kusten van de Noordzee.*
120 Timothy Mixter, "The Hiring Market as Workers' Turf: Migrant Agricultural Laborers and the Mobilization of Collective Action in the Steppe Grainbelt of European Russia, 1853–1913", in: Esther Kingston-Mann and Timothy Mixter (eds), *Peasant Economy, Culture, and Politics of European Russia, 1800–1921* (Princeton, 1991), pp. 294–340.

few years only.¹²¹ Earlier tramping systems within guild regulations showed comparable forms of circularity. The temporality of the migration was gendered; in the nineteenth century, many authorities did not allow young men to leave permanently until they had fulfilled their military duties. Sailors, who went back and forth between destinations, were also circular migrants, unless their (rather common) death en route broke the planned circle. Miners, who moved between mines in one region—the Rhine-Meuse coal basin for instance—were circular migrants moving between three countries, from the perspective of states, but they moved within one labour market, as seen from the perspective of unions, and employers, and workers.¹²²

Labour market changes led to new migration. The discovery of oil in the 1920s and 1930s, for instance, led to large scale migration into the Gulf region. The migrants were senior staff of the oil companies from the US and UK, high-skilled workers from India, and low skilled migrants form countries in the region. The early development of the oil industry in the 1930s became the driving force behind the first organized introduction of foreign workers to the oil-producing countries of the Arab Gulf States (AGSs). The migration policy in this period was driven by the necessity to favour the migration of skilled and semi-skilled workers from British India and to hire the local workforce.¹²³ After the discovery of oil, and the oil shock of the mid-1950s, migration from Asia to the member states of the Gulf Cooperation Council (GCC) increased sharply.¹²⁴ Large numbers of construction workers moved to the Middle East during the oil boom of the 1970s and 1980s. The migrants, which were recruited, were called Contractual Temporary Labour. In 2010, there were 15 million of these workers; 29 percent of them were women.¹²⁵

Contractual Temporary Labour was one of the many circular labour migration projects put in place. The migration projects most widely discussed in the literature are guest worker migration in North Western Europe from the 1960s until 1975, and the Bracero Program between the US and Mexico between 1942 and 1960s.¹²⁶ From the 1960s onwards, Canada had a similar programme for the recruitment of tempo-

---

121 Marlou Schrover, "Immigrant Business and Niche Formation in a Historical Perspective. The Netherlands in the Nineteenth Century", *Journal of Ethnic and Migration Studies*, 27, 2 (2001), pp. 295–311.
122 Ad Knotter, "Changing Border Regimes, Mining, and Cross-border Labor in the Dutch-Belgian-German Borderlands, 1900–1973", *Journal of Borderlands Studies*, 29, 3 (2014), pp. 375–384.
123 Gennaro Errichiello, "Foreign Workforce in the Arab Gulf States (1930–1950): Migration Patterns and Nationality Clause", *International Migration Review*, 46, 2 (2012), pp. 389–413.
124 GCC: United Arab Emirates, the State of Bahrain, The Kingdom of Saudi Arabia, The Sultanate of Oman, the State of Qatar, the State of Kuwait; for Kuwait see: Nasra M. Shah and Indu Menon, "Chain Migration Through the Social Network: Experience of Labour Migrants in Kuwait", *International Migration*, 37, 2 (1999), pp. 361–381.
125 Mohammed Dito, "Arab Gulf Cooperation Council in Southwest Asia Migration", in: Ness et al., *Encyclopedia of Global Human Migration*, pp. 535–538.
126 Nathan R. Blank, "Bilateral Labor Agreements", in: Ness et al., *Encyclopedia of Global Human Migration*, pp. 706–711.

rary workers, mainly from the Caribbean. The Bracero Program was originally established in 1942 as a temporary wartime measure. It was extended by US Congress and expanded in the latter half of the 1950s. The Bracero Program was phased out between 1965 and 1967. The lion's share of the migration was temporary, and the migration was meant to be circular. During the period 1955–1959, about half a million Mexicans were entering the USA each year. In total, the programme brought 4 to 5 million people into the US, 89 per cent from Mexico and about 4 per cent from the British West Indies or Jamaica.[127] The end of the Bracero Program did not mean the end of migration from Mexico. After the end of the Bracero Program, migration became less circular, and migrants increasingly travelled without authorization. To a large extent, labour migration from Mexico became illegal migration. Those who did gain legal entry became US citizens more often than they had in the past.[128]

The guest worker migration programme in North Western Europe—which ran from the 1950s until the mid-1970s—was rather similar. Already before the guest worker migration regime was put into place there were systems in which employers and states collectively recruited migrant workers. In France, for instance, the employers cooperated in a Société Générale d'Immigration, which, between 1920 and 1930, recruited 490,000 Polish migrants to work as miners.[129] The first post-war guest workers were recruited in a similar manner by employers or via agencies. About 8 million work permits were issued to guest workers to work in Belgium, France, Italy, Luxembourg, the Netherlands, and West Germany in the period of 1958 to 1972. Originally, they were mainly recruited to fill vacancies in mining and the steel industry. This explains why 80 per cent of the guest workers were men. It led to a masculinization of migration. In the UK, which was outside the European Coal and Steel Community (established in 1951) and the European Economic Community (established in 1957), workers from the (former) colonies were used to fill vacancies. People used the possibilities to migrate within the guest worker migration regime to flee Franco's fascist regime in Spain, the Colonels regime in Greece, Salazar's repressive regime in Portugal, and Portugal's colonial wars in Mozambique and Angola. Not all guest workers came with a work permit. Especially in the later period of the guest worker migration regime, migrants came via chain migration structures. Employers delegated recruitment to the workers who had been in their employment for a while, whom they trusted and whom they expected to help the new immigrants. By doing so, they saved money that they would have spent on mediation. In the early years, guest

---

[127] Luis F.B. Plascencia, "State-Sanctioned Coercion and Agricultural Contract Labor: Jamaican and Mexican Workers in Canada and the United States, 190 9–2014", in: van der Linden and Rodríguez García, *On Coerced Labor*, pp. 225–266.
[128] Douglas S. Massey and Karen A. Pren, "Unintended Consequences of US Immigration Policy: Explaining the Post-1965 Surge from Latin America", *Population and Development Review*, 38, 1 (2012), pp. 1–29.
[129] Ad Knotter, "Migration and Ethnicity in Coalfield History: Global Perspectives", *International Review of Social History*, Special issue, 60 (2015), pp. 13–39.

workers were circular migrants. Labour migrants from Spain, Portugal, and Italy repeatedly moved between their countries of origin and recruiting countries such as Germany, Belgium, and the Netherlands.[130] Authorities emphasized the circular nature of the guest worker migration in order to pacify the labour unions which feared that the guest workers would stay and compete with local workers when economic growth decreased. The emphasis on the temporariness and circular nature of guest worker migration was a way to make this migration acceptable, so shortly after hundreds of thousands of people had been motivated to migrate from Europe to Australia, Canada, and the US. When the guest worker migration system came to an end in the mid-1970s, guest workers reduced the number of trips back and forth, fearing (correctly) that they would not be able to re-enter the recruiting countries once they had left. The economic crisis, which was the reason for stopping the recruitment of guest workers, also hit the countries of origin. Migrants did not want to return to their home countries in the midst of an economic crisis. Furthermore, some of the countries of origin were simultaneously affected by political instability, such as the political coups of the 1970s in Turkey and the *Years of Lead* in Morocco. Years of Lead refers to the 1960s until the 1980s, when the regime of King Hassan II repressed dissidents, and hundreds of people died and disappeared. Many more were driven across the borders, including to France, Belgium, and the Netherlands, making use of the possibilities within the guest worker migration regime.[131]

The German Democratic Republic (GDR) also had a guest worker migration regime, albeit with smaller numbers of labour migrants than West Germany. Labour migrants were called *ausländische Werktätige* and *Vertragsarbeiter*. In addition, there were *Facharbeiter*, who were to learn skills in the GDR and bring these to their countries of origin. Until German reunification, there were 69,000 Vietnamese, 50,000 Poles, 40,000 Hungarians, 25,000 Cubans, 22,000 migrants from Mozambique, 8000 from Algeria, 2000 from Angola, and several hundred from China and North Korea. About 70 per cent of them were men. Bilateral treaties were concluded between the countries of origin of the labour migrants and the GDR. Workers received a five-year contract and did not have a right to family housing. Permission by the state was required (and seldom granted) for marriages with a German partner. Migrant women who got pregnant were offered a choice between abortion and return.[132] After reunification, 40,000 Vietnamese returned to Vietnam, of whom 10,000 were contract labourers whose contracts had expired. Both in 1995 and 1996, Vietnam received 100 million Deutsche Mark to help facilitate the resettlement of the retur-

---

130 Amelie F. Constant and Klaus F. Zimmermann, "The Dynamics of Repeat Migration: A Markov Chain Analysis", *International Migration Review,* 46, 2 (2012), pp. 362–388.
131 Laetitia Grotti and Eric Goldstein, *Morocco's Truth Commission. Honoring Past Victims During an Uncertain Period.* Human Rights Watch 17: 1 E, New York, November 2005.
132 Ann-Judith Rabenschlag, *Völkerfreundschaft nach Bedarf Ausländische Arbeitskräfte in der Wahrnehmung von Staat und Bevölkerung der DDR* (Stockholm, 2014).

nees.¹³³ In the 1980s, there were a total of 300,000 mostly unskilled workers who were sent abroad to work in Communist Bloc countries, including the Soviet Union, Bulgaria, Czechoslovakia, and East Germany. The collapse of the Soviet Union brought this migration to an abrupt halt.

Labour migration from Vietnam to Germany was replaced by labour migration to other countries. In recent decades, Vietnamese workers have migrated to East and Southeast Asia, Australia, Europe, and North America. Between 2001 and 2005, 295,000 workers travelled abroad on labour contracts. After stories about fraud, breeches of contract, and violations of rights the Vietnamese National Assembly approved its first Law on Vietnamese Overseas Contract Workers.¹³⁴

Before the sharp increase in the number of asylum seekers in Europe in the Autumn of 2015, several European countries were talking about reintroducing new systems of circular and temporary labour migration. The reason for this was the so-called demographic suicide in Western Europe: when the baby boomers start receiving their pensions there will not be sufficient workers to finance these. Schemes were put in place (especially in Germany) to recruit labour from outside Europe and increase mobility within Europe. Authorities highlighted the circular nature of this migration. Foreign domestic servants in Germany, for instance, must leave for three years after they have been employed for three years in Germany.¹³⁵ In a similar fashion, Canada has started new temporary migration recruitment programmes, targeting the regions from which temporary migrants came in earlier decades. In 2013, however, Leach showed that potential migrants from the Caribbean shy away from these programmes, with their emphasis on temporary and unskilled labour, and prefer to move to Canada via (family) migration networks, which came about because of the earlier migration.¹³⁶

From the 1960s onwards, the concept of circular migration was used to emphasize the double benefit circular migration would generate: migrants would learn skills—nursing skills, for instance—which would be of use to the them, when they returned to their countries of origin. This idea was used to counter criticism regarding the brain drain. This migration-development nexus was one of the justifications for migrant recruiting policies. Within the guest worker migration system, however, migrants were recruited specifically as unskilled workers or acquired skills which were of little use when they returned (they, for instance, were trained as miners, while they aspired to work as farmers upon return). Circular migration is also advocated as a

---

133 Patrick R. Ireland, "Socialism, Unification Policy and the Rise of Racism in Eastern Germany", *International Migration Review*, 31, 3 (Autumn, 1997), pp. 541–568.
134 Christina Schwenkel, "Rethinking Asian Mobilities", *Critical Asian Studies*, 46, 2 (2014), pp. 235–258.
135 Jan Schneider and Bernd Parusel, "Circular Migration between Fact and Fiction. Evidence from Germany", *European Journal of Migration and Law*, 17, 2–3 (2015), pp. 184–209.
136 Belinda Leach, "Canada's Migrants Without History: Neoliberal Immigration Regimes and Trinidadian Transnationalism", *International Migration*, 51, 2 (2013), pp. 32–45.

means to reduce illegal migration: the idea is that if sufficient people can legally migrate, illegal and uncontrolled migration can be reduced. This idea is a key element of the above mentioned UN Summit for Refugees and Migrants that took place in September 2016. At this summit, it was discussed that a possible solution to the recent refugee migration and a way to reduce the number of applications for refugee status would be to provide more opportunities for legal labour migration.[137]

Return migration is discussed somewhat separate from circular migration. The return of migrants has been labelled a myth. Already in 1974, in one of the first publications on return migration, Bovenkerk wrote that "one will seldom find so much philosophizing about returning to the homeland as among emigrants who will never return."[138] At the same time, there is the myth of non-return.[139] In 2000, King observed that the assumption was made that many migrants would never return, while in fact they did. A quarter to a third of the Europeans who crossed the Atlantic in the late nineteenth and early twentieth century returned to Europe. Similarly, about a third of the people who moved from Europe to Australia and Canada in the 1950s returned, even though they left thinking they never would.[140]

The literature on return migration tends to look at the transatlantic return migration or that from Europe in the 1950s. There were, however, numerous other cases of return migration. In 1921, for instance, Lenin called upon the three million Russians who had migrated to America between 1880 and 1920 and urged them to return home to build the new Soviet Union. The First World War, the Civil War, crop failures, and the famine of 1919–1921 had reduced the population by 20 million people. The Soviet Union needed experts to set up and modernize agriculture. Communist parties worldwide were not keen on the idea of return migration, since they feared that the departure of many their party members would decrease the Communist Party's influence in their respective country and thus forestall a possible revolution. The Society for Technical Aid to Soviet Russia, however, set out to organize this migration. Russians, who had not been able to find work in their new countries of settlement, and who had been hit by the repression of communist organizations, planned to return. They were joined by people who had migrated to Canada and the US from other European countries. Overall, 70,000 to 80,000 foreign workers moved to the USSR between 1917 and 1939, half of whom were Germans and Austrians, and a quarter Americans and Canadians.[141] Not all of these migrants were thus real *returnees*, although they were referred to as such. The returnees were to form cooperatives before depar-

---

137 http://refugeesmigrants.un.org/summit
138 Frank Bovenkerk, *The Sociology of Return Migration. A Bibliographic Essay* (The Hague, 1974).
139 Russell King, "Generalizations from the History of Return Migration", in: Bimal Ghosh (ed.), *Return Migration: Journey of Hope or Despair?* (Geneva, 2000), pp. 7–55.
140 Loretta Baldassar and Joanne Pyke, "Intra-Diaspora Knowledge Transfer and 'New' Italian Migration", *International Migration*, 52, 4(2014), pp. 128–143.
141 Andrea Graziosi, "Foreign Workers in Soviet Russia, 1920–40: Their Experience and Their Legacy", *International Labor and Working-Class History*, 33 (1988), pp. 38–59.

ture. The Soviet Government gave them land and provided housing. The returnees had to bring means of production (machinery, tools), food, clothes, and other necessities, that would enable them to survive the first two years. Between 1922 and 1928, 35 agricultural communes were founded in the USSR by these returnees.[142]

Return migration is also related to decolonization. Many of the returnees had never previously been to the country they were said to be returning to. They were labelled returnees, in order to emphasize ties and belonging to their new society.[143] *Pieds noirs*, Anglo Indians, the Indo-Dutch, and *retornados* were given some preferential rights—over other migrants—when they moved from the former colonies to France, the UK, the Netherlands or Portugal. Germany, in a similar fashion, gave preferential rights to the 10 to 12 million ethnic Germans coming from outside of Germany. These so-called *expellees* or *Heimatvertriebene* made use of a pre-war Nazi rule regarding belonging and a post-war clause concerning refugees, deportees, and others of German ancestry. Since they got citizenship upon arrival, they do not show up in naturalization statistics. The expellees were explicitly not labelled refugees (to make sure that they did not fall within the scope of the 1951 Refugee Convention), and they were not labelled labour migrants either. Part of the expellees, however, did, shortly after arrival, acquire the label of labour migrants. Among the expellees were, for instance, the 80,500 Germans who made their way to Australia as labour migrants in the immediate post-war years. The expellees thus shifted from one category to another, within a short period.[144] When they migrated to Australia, they were registered as German labour migrants (and not as expellees) and as a result the percentage of expellees amongst the post-war migrants to Australia is unknown. The same was true for the 200,000 Germans who migrated to Canada between 1951–1957. Their migration was part of Canada's *bulk-labour* programme. During "the 1950s, Germany became a major source of manpower for Canada, supplying more farm hands and domestic servants than any other country as well as a disproportionately high number of skilled workers".[145]

The expellees or *Heimatvertriebene* were later followed by *Aussiedler* and *Spätaussiedler*. Since 1950, 4.5 million people moved to Germany within this frame-

---

142 Mikko Ylikangas, "The Sower Commune: An American-Finnish Agricultural Utopia in the Soviet Union", *Journal of Finnish Studies*, 15, 1–2 (2011), pp. 51–84.
143 Charlotte Laarman, "Dutch Colonization and Settlement", in: Ness et al., *Encyclopedia of Global Human Migration*, pp. 1271–1275; Laarman, "The Dutch Nation as an Imagined Family. Family Metaphor in Political and Public Debates in the Netherlands on Migrants from the (Former) Dutch East Indies 1949–1966", *Ethnic and Racial Studies*, 36, 7 (2013), pp. 1232–1250.
144 Jan Schmortte, "Attitudes towards German Immigration in South Australia in the Post-Second World War Period, 1947–60", *Australian Journal of Politics and History*, 51, 4 (2005), pp. 530–544; Evan Jones, "The Employment of German Scientists in Australia after World War II", *Prometheus. Critical Studies in Innovation*, 20, 4 (2002), pp. 305–321; Marlou Schrover "The Deportation of Germans from the Netherlands 1946–1952", *Immigrants and minorities*, 33, 3 (2015), pp. 264–271.
145 Ronald E. Schmalz, *Former Enemies Come to Canada. Ottawa and the Postwar German Immigration Boom, 1951–57* (Ottawa, 2000), p. 9.

work. About half of them came from the Soviet Union and its successor states. In recent years, new EU member states mirrored these policies of return and gave preferential rights to *returnees*, frequently descendants of people who left generations ago or were deported under Soviet and communist rule. Poland does so for co-ethnic returnees from Kazakhstan, Greece for co-ethnic returnees from the former republics of Georgia, Kazakhstan, Russia and Armenia, and Hungary does so for co-ethnics from Romania, Ukraine and former Yugoslavia. The numbers are not negligible. In 1990, the Finnish president Mauno Kovisto, for instance, called upon the Ingrian Ethnic Finns (Lutheran labour migrants who had moved to the Russian province Ingria in the seventeenth century and who were reallocated to other parts of the Soviet Union around the time of the Second World War) to return. About 32,000 Ingrian Finns have since answered this call, while another 30,000 are on a waiting list to get their migration to Finland approved. Until 2010, the Ingrian Finns received automatic residency. After 2010, they were treated as foreigners and were eligible for citizenship after five years. Kivisto, like other leaders, made his call partly because in some parts of the country population figures were falling and industries could not get sufficient workers.

Conclusion

This chapter sought to map and critically review recent developments in the scholarship on labour migration, chain migration, and related concepts. From the review presented above it becomes clear that there are biases in the literature: there is much more literature about Europe, or the West, and related to Europe and the West. The migration of women is discussed separately from that of men. And the migration of unskilled migrants is discussed separately from that of skilled labour migrants. Forced migration is seldom discussed within the context of labour migration.

Most striking is the endless introduction of new concepts. It is a common thing academics do: by introducing a new concept, they are staking a claim to part of the field. Migration researchers seem, however, to be especially prone to introducing new concepts. In part, this reflects what policymakers and politicians do: they introduce endless subcategories in order to restrict or grant rights. This conceptional diarrhoea, which was mapped out in this chapter, has not moved the field forward. It has not led to more or better diachronic or synchronic comparisons. The use of the rigid categorizations of policy makers by academics denies the mobility of migrants between categories. As presented above, the New York Summit of September 2016 moved away from rigid categorizations and emphasized the mixedness of migration. Migration researchers should and will follow up on this.

Suggested reading

Benedetta, Rossi. "Migration and Emancipation in West Africa's Labour History: The Missing Links", *Slavery and Abolition*, 35, 1 (2014), pp. 23–46.

Borges, Marcelo J. "Migration Systems in Southern Portugal: Regional and Transnational Circuits of Labor Migration in the Algarve (Eighteenth-Twentieth Centuries)", *International Review of Social History*, 45, 2 (2000), pp. 171–208.

Brinkmann, Tobias. "Strangers in the City: Transmigration from Eastern Europe and its Impact on Berlin and Hamburg 1880–1914", *Journal of Migration History*, 2, 2 (2016), pp. 223–246;

Fidler, Ceri-Anne. "The Impact of Migration upon Family Life and Gender Relations: the case of South Asian seafarers, c. 1900–50", *Women's History Review*, 24, 3 (2015), pp. 410–428.

Heynssens, Sarah. "Practices of Displacement: Forced Migration of Mixed-Race Children from Colonial Ruanda-Urundi to Belgium", *Journal of Migration History*, 2, 1 (2016), pp. 1–31.

Hoerder, Dirk. *Cultures in Contact. World Migrations in the Second Millennium* (Durham, NC: Duke University Press, 2002).

Kaur, Amarjit. "Labour Brokers in Migration: Understanding Historical and Contemporary Transnational Migration Regimes in Malaya/Malaysia", *International Review of Social History*, 57, 2 (2012), pp. 22 5–252.

Knotter, Ad. "Changing Border Regimes, Mining, and Cross-border Labor in the Dutch-Belgian-German Borderlands, 1900–1973", *Journal of Borderlands Studies*, 29, 3 (2014), pp. 375–384.

Laite, Julia. "Between Scylla and Charybdis: Women's Labour Migration and Sex Trafficking in the Early Twentieth Century", *International Review of Social History*, 62, 1 (2017), forthcoming.

Lesger, Clé, Leo Lucassen and Marlou Schrover. "Is There Life Outside the Migrant Network? German Immigrants in 19th century Netherlands and the Need for a More Balanced Migration Typology", *Annales de démographie historique*, 104 (2002), pp. 29–45.

Light, Ivan. "The Migration Industry in the United States, 1882–1924", *Migration Studies*, 1, 3 (2013), pp. 258–275.

Lofkrantz, Jennifer, and Olatunji Ojo. "Slavery, Freedom, and Failed Ransom Negotiations in West Africa, 1730–1900", *The Journal of African History*, 53, 1 (2012), pp. 25–44.

Lucassen, Jan, and Leo Lucassen (eds.). *Migration, Migration History, History: Old Paradigms and New Perspectives* (Bern: Peter Lang, 1997).

Lucassen, Jan. *Migrant Labour in Europe, 1600–1900. The Drift to the North Sea* (London: Croom Helm, 1987).

Massey, Douglas S., and Karen A. Pren. "Unintended Consequences of US Immigration Policy: Explaining the Post-1965 Surge from Latin America", *Population and Development Review*, 38, 1 (2012), pp. 1–29.

McKeown, Adam. "Chinese Emigration in Global Context, 1850–1940", *Journal of Global History*, 5, 1 (2010), pp. 95–124.

McKeown, Adam. "How the Box Became Black: Brokers and the Creation of the Free Migrant", *Pacific Affairs*, 85, 1 (2012), pp. 21–45.

Mohapatra, Prabhu P. "Eurocentrism, Forced Labour, and Global Migration: A Critical Assessment", *International Review of Social History*, 52, 1 (2007), pp. 110–115.

Moya, José M. "Domestic Service in a Global Perspective: Gender, Migration and Ethnic Niches", *Journal of Ethnic and Migration Studies*, 33, 4 (2007), pp. 559–579.

Neyens, Mieke. "The Good, the Bad and the Rational. Desirable and Undesirable Migration to Cuba and Mexico (1907–1909)", in: Steinar A. Sæther (ed.), *Expectations Unfulfilled. Norwegian Migrants in Latin America, 1820–1940* (Leiden and Boston, 2016), pp. 102–126.

Nobil Ahmad, Ali. *Masculinity, Sexuality and Illegal Migration. Human Smuggling from Pakistan to Europe*. New edition (London: Routledge, 2011).

Pedersen, Susan. "The Maternalist Moment in British Colonial Policy: The Controversy over 'Child Slavery' in Hong Kong 1917–1941", *Past and Present*, 171 (May 2001), pp. 161–202.

Pelckmans, Lotte. *Travelling Hierarchies. Roads in and out of Slave Status in a Central Malian Fulße Network* (Leiden: African Studies Centre, 2011).

Pizzolato, Nicola. "'As Much in Bondage as They was Before. Unfree Labor During the New Deal (193 5–1952)", in: Marcel van der Linden and Magaly Rodríguez García (eds), *On Coerced Labor. Work and Compulsion after Chattel Slavery* (Leiden and Boston, 2016), pp 208–224.

Pliley, Jessica R. "Claims to Protection: The Rise and Fall of Feminist Abolitionism in the League of Nations' Committee on the Traffic in Women and Children, 1919–1936", *Journal of Women's History*, 22, 4 (2010), pp. 90–113.

Schmortte, Jan. "Attitudes towards German Immigration in South Australia in the Post-Second World War Period, 1947–60", *Australian Journal of Politics and History*, 51, 4 (2005), pp. 530–544.

Schrover, Marlou and Deirdre Moloney (eds). *Gender, Migration and Categorisation: Making Distinctions Between Migrants in Western Countries (1900) 1945–2010* (Amsterdam: Amsterdam University Press, 2013).

Siegelbaum, Lewis H., and Leslie Page Moch, *Broad is My Native Land. Repertoires and Regimes of Migration in Russia's Twentieth Century* (Ithaca, NY: Cornell University Press, 2014).

Spoerer, Mark, and Jochen Fleischhacker. "Forced Laborers in Nazi Germany: Categories, Numbers, and Survivors", *Journal of Interdisciplinary History*, 33, 2 (2002), pp. 169–204.

Marcel van der Linden
7. Work Incentives and Forms of Supervision

People working together cannot do without coordination of their separate activities: "in all labour where many individuals cooperate, the interconnection and unity of the process is necessarily represented in a governing will, and in functions that concern not the detailed work but rather the workplace and its activity as a whole, as with the conductor of an orchestra. This is productive labour that has to be performed in any combined mode of production."[1] There are two possibilities. Either the workers coordinate their activities themselves through mutual consultation (autonomy or self-management), or their activities are co-ordinated by some external agent whom they do not control (heteronomy). From a quantitative point of view, autonomous co-operation probably carries much less weight than heteronomy. Currently, there are about 10 million autonomously cooperating workers on a world-scale, while the total number of heteronomous wage-earners approaches three billion. There is some literature on self-management, but the literature on heteronomous management is much more extensive, although it has two significant weaknesses: it tends to neglect the historical dimension and, insofar as it is interested in the past, it is almost completely Eurocentric. Fundamental books, like Sidney Pollard's *The Genesis of Modern Management*, and all important works which followed on this seminal work, discuss the development of management as a purely European ("industrial") innovation, and do not pay any attention to contemporary of preceding trends in colonial countries or what is now called the Global South. The rise of modern labour-management techniques is, therefore, usually explained through the technological changes caused by the Industrial Revolution as an isolated event. The colonies and unfree labour are blind spots; they are almost never part of the story. This is not to deny, that during the last few decades very important work has been done in the field of management history and that we now understand many aspects of the way in which employers have dealt with their employees much better than we used to.

Mainstream historiographies of labour management usually start by saying that labour management has been around for thousands of years, and that large-scale projects like the Egyptian pyramids or China's Great Wall would not have been possible without the conscious coordination of labour processes. Modern labour management, however, began in the middle of the eighteenth century, with the birth of the factories and their capitalist logic: "unlike the builders of pyramids", the new managers "had not only to show absolute results in terms of certain products of their efforts, but to relate them to costs, and sell them competitively."[2] Modern

---

[1] Karl Marx, *Capital*, vol. III. Trans. David Fernbach (Harmondsworth, 1981), p. 507.
[2] Sidney Pollard, *The Genesis of Modern Management. A Study of the Industrial Revolution in Great Britain* (London, 1965), pp. 6–7.

time discipline, technical training, and other innovations were the outcome. During the second half of the nineteenth century further important changes took place, primarily in the United States, resulting in the invention of Scientific Management, etc.

This narrow historiographical perspective broadened when critical criminologists began to pay attention to parallels between prisons and factories.[3] Building on this trend Michel Foucault and others focused on the rise of disciplinary power in schools, psychiatric institutions, barracks, and factories, and claimed that "the technological mutations of the apparatus of production, the division of labour and the elaboration of the disciplinary techniques sustained an ensemble of very close relations. Each makes the other possible and necessary; each provides a model for the other."[4] An increasing number of studies explored the homologies between monastic, military and industrial discipline.[5]

Despite such revisions and extensions, the approach to the history of labour management continued to be based on two hidden assumptions. On the one hand the model was deeply internalist: the developments in the North Atlantic region were explained through developments in the North Atlantic region; all the big innovations began in Britain, the United States, France or Germany. On the other hand, the emphasis was very much on "free" wage labour. Few historians paid attention to unfree labour. An exception confirming the rule is Alfred Chandler who, in his great book *The Visible Hand*, of over 600 pages, devotes less than three pages to the slave plantation, arguing that, "as the first salaried manager in the country, the plantation overseer was an important person in American economic history", though the plantation followed "a traditional pattern" and "had little impact on the evolution of the management of modern business enterprise."[6]

Contrary to the mainstream Global Labour History suggests that important innovations were born outside the North Atlantic region – especially in the colonies – , in attempts to control *unfree* workers; that some of these innovations date from long before the Industrial Revolution; and that knowledge about such innovations travelled through all parts of the globe. Research on these issues is in its early stages. It is, however, already becoming clear that core elements of the modern factory (huge cap-

---

[3] Pathbreaking was Georg Rusche and Otto Kirchheimer, *Punishment and Social Structure* (New York, 1939).

[4] Michel Foucault, *Discipline and Punish. The Birth of the Prison*. Trans. Alan Sheridan (Harmondsworth, 1977), p. 221.

[5] For example, Didier Deleule and François Guerry, *The Productive Body*. Trans. and introduction Philip Barnard and Stephen Shapiro (London, 2014; French original 1972); Dario Melossi and Massimo Pavarini, *The Prison and the Factory. Origins of the Penitentiary System*. Trans. Glynis Cousin (London and Basingstoke, 1981; Italian original 1977); Hubert Treiber and Heinz Steinert, *Die Fabrikation des zuverlässigen Menschen. Über die "Wahlverwandtschaft" von Kloster- und Fabrikdisziplin* (Münster, 2005; first edition 1980); Lion Murard and Patrick Zylberman (eds), *Le Soldat du travail. Guerre, fascisme et taylorisme* (Paris, 1978).

[6] Alfred D. Chandler, *The Visible Hand. The Managerial Revolution in American Business* (Cambridge, MA and London, 1977), pp. 65–66.

ital investment and alienated work based on the complete non-possession of means of production) were also typical for other, earlier, productive organizations such as e.g., the seventeenth-century sugar plantations in the Caribbean. These plantations were based on large fixed capital outlays (buildings, sugar mills, etc.), and on the labour of workers (slaves) without any property and even without any legal rights.[7]

It is quite well possible (though not yet sufficiently proven), that managers during the 18th-19th centuries in Britain and other industrializing countries have learned lessons from the colonies. According to Robin Blackburn, the notion of the "plant" (i.e. the industrial complex) is derived from the older notion of the "plantation": "By gathering the workers under one roof, and subordinating them to one discipline, the new industrial employers were able to garner the profits of industrial co-operation and invigilation – as it were adapting the plantation model (which is why people came to speak of steel 'plants')."[8]

It is not entirely certain that Blackburn is right. Chronologically, his hypothesis makes sense. "Plantation" in the sense of a large estate where cotton, tobacco, or other cash crops are grown, was first recorded in 1706 in Phillips' *Dictionary*.[9] "Plant" – in the sense of productive complex – was mentioned for the first time in 1789. But not all etymologists agree. Many of them seem to believe, that "plant" is not derived from "plantation", but that both "plant" *and* "plantation" are derived from the verb "planting", the activity of putting something in a place. Whether this is testimony of a Eurocentric bias or not, needs to be investigated. In any case, it seems worthwhile to explore the affinities between "unfree" and colonial labour-management techniques on the one hand and "free" labour-management techniques on the other hand. Some slave holders, for instance, anticipated aspects of Scientific Management methods (Taylorism) developed in US industry during the 1880s and '90s. In the 1830s, the former slave John Brown told in an interview: "My old master [...] would pick out two or more of the strongest [hands], and excite them to race at hoeing or picking. [...] He would stand with his watch in his hand, observing their movements, whilst they hoed or picked [...]. Whatever [the winner] did, within a given time, would be multiplied by a certain rule, for the day's work, and every

---

[7] This insight has grown by leaps and bounds. R. Keith Aufhauser, "Slavery and Scientific Management", *Journal of Economic History*, 33 (1973), pp. 811–824, at 823 had already argued convincingly – though exclusively on the basis of US material –, that "the master-slave relationship is quite similar to the capitalist-wage-labor relationship in scientifically managed enterprises." A second major step was made by Bill Cooke, "The Denial of Slavery in Management Studies", *Journal of Management Studies*, 40, 8 (December 2003), pp. 1895–1918, though he also mainly focused on slave management in the United States. His line of research was pursued further in Elizabeth Esch and David Roediger, *The Production of Difference. Race and the Management of Labor in U.S. History* (New York, 2012). Probably the first attempt to broaden the approach to the Global South was Marcel van der Linden, "Re-constructing the Origins of Modern Labor Management", *Labor History*, 51, 4 (November 2010), pp. 509–522.
[8] Robin Blackburn, *The Making of New World Slavery* (London and New York, 1997), p. 565.
[9] *The Barnhart Dictionary of Etymology* (n.p., 1988), p. 802.

man's task would be staked out accordingly."[10] Knowledge of new management methods circulated globally, through the migration of managers, engineers and skilled workers, and through expert committees traveled back and forth between colonies, studying planting methods, workers' housing, etc.[11]

The crucial question for labour management is always: how to maximize labour productivity, that is the cost of the employed workforce in relation to the value of the produced output. Labour productivity may be influenced by a number of factors, such as the level of applied technology (energy and machinery); skills (education and training of the workforce); the workers' standard of living (food, housing, working hours, etc.); social technology (division and organization of labour); and work motivation. Here we will concentrate on the last two factors.

Division of labour

The notion of a "division of labour" can have several meanings. It can be seen as social differentiation and co-operation between people performing distinct forms of labour, resulting in different final goods or services. The oldest and most persistent form of this kind of division of labour is the one between the sexes. Already among hunter-gatherers it was (and is) usual that women devote themselves to child care and food gathering, while men focus on hunting. At a later stage further divisions of labour of the same type developed, for example, between peasants and merchants, and between agriculture, manufacturing and services. The division of labour may, however, also refer to separate activities within one labour process resulting in *one* final product. Within the latter sense the notion can be further divided into different firms undertaking complementary steps of the process (e.g. the growing of coffee in Brazil, the shipping of the beans, and the roasting of the beans in the United States), and the division of labour between workers in one particular farm, factory, mine or office.[12]

The various divisions of labour are not only influenced by technical and economic requirements, but also by cultural distinctions; almost everywhere employers and managers assume semiconsciously or unconsciouslessly that specific jobs should be

---

10 John Brown, *Slave Life in Georgia: A Narrative of the Life, Sufferings and Escape of John Brown, a Fugitive Slave*. Edited by F.N. Boney (Savannah, 1972; first published London 1855), pp. 145, 160. Quoted in Mark M. Smith, "Time, Slavery and Plantation Capitalism in the Ante-bellum American South", *Past and Present*, No. 150 (February 1996), pp. 142–168, at 156.
11 See, e.g., for an interesting case study: Richard A. Lobdell, "'Repression is not a Policy': Sydney Olivier on the West Indies and Africa", in: Roderick A. McDonald (ed.), *West Indies Accounts. Essays on the History of the British Caribbean and the Atlantic Economy in Honour of Richard Sheridan* (Kingston, 1996), pp. 343–354.
12 For the history of the concept, see Lisa Hill, "Adam Smith, Adam Ferguson and Karl Marx on the Division of Labour", *Journal of Classical Sociology*, 7 (2007), pp. 339–366.

done (or should not be done) by people with a certain gender, ethnicity, education, or physique. A frequent (but not universal) classification of people by gender looks like this:[13]

Female	Male
Requiring delicacy	Requiring strength
Safe	Dangerous
Day work	Night work
Fixed locations, especially near home	Involves traveling
Refined	Coarse, vulgar
Respectable	Sexually approachable
Managing interpersonal relations	Managing money
Subordinate	Authoritative
Nurturant	Impersonal
Peaceable	Violent
Segregation of work from care of the person	No segregation of toilets and sleep from work
Work in mixed or female group	Work in solidary male group
Work with soft goods	Work in shaping metal
High culture consumers	High culture producers

The division of labour within manufacturing developed early in China. "If a factory is defined by its systemic properties, such as organization of the workforce, division of labour, quality control, serial production, and standardization, then it is possible to speak of bronze, silk, and possibly jade factories as early as the Shang period (about 1650 – about 1050 B.C.)."[14] These factories used modular production methods, that is, they prefabricated parts in great quantity and put them together in many different combinations, thus constructing a wide variety of products from a relative small numbers of components. Work was therefore compartmentalized and split up into a number of separate steps. The performance of workers became more regimented, and a separate layer of managers devising, organizing and controling production was created.[15] Modular production does not necessarily have to take place in factories. In the so-called proto-industry workers often also make part products at home which are later combined under the supervision of a 'manager' (the merchant or *Verleger*) who ordered these part products.

---

[13] Arthur Stinchcombe, "Work Institutions and the Sociology of Everyday Life", in: Kai Erikson and Steven Peter Vallas (eds), *The Nature of Work. Sociological Perspectives* (New Haven and London, 1990), pp. 99–116, at 107.
[14] Lothar Ledderose, *Ten Thousand Things. Module and Mass Production in Chinese Art* (Princeton, NJ, 2000), p. 4.
[15] *Ibid.*, p. 5.

Managers frequently delegated some of their tasks to outsiders. For the recruitment of workers they often used (and use) intermediaries, known as crimps, jobbers, *sirdars*, temping agencies, etc. Middlemen reduced the transaction costs involved in labour recruitment. They always performed at least one of the following three services: recruiting potential labourers in places outside the potential employers' information sphere (if labourers were to be found in a huge urban labour pool or in remote villages); pre-selecting potential labourers and thus reducing the employer's risk of hiring a man or woman inappropriate for the job; and acting as interpreters in case of communication problems due to language or other reasons.[16] It was not unusual, that middlemen worked for the employer together with the labourers they had recruited, thus overseeing their "recruits" for the central management – a phenomenon called "inside contracting" or "subcontracting".[17]

The question which functions managers fulfil has led to much debate. In the 1970s the economist Stephen Marglin argued that managers' historical success was not caused by their capacity to increase the efficiency of labour processes, but was due to their hierarchical position which gave them the possibility to break the workers' power on the shopfloor. The centralized factory and its management were therefore not the result of technological progress, but of a class struggle from above. Meantime it has become clear, that this hypothesis in its pure form cannot be defended, but the debate Marglin set going has nevertheless elucidated that class antagonisms strongly influenced the making of modern capitalist methods of production.[18]

---

[16] The literature is most extensive on South Asian intermediaries. See e.g., Morris D. Morris, *The Emergence of an Industrial Labour Force in India. A Study of the Bombay Cotton Mills, 1854–1947* (Berkeley, CA, 1965), pp. 129–153; Dick Kooiman, "Jobbers and the Emergence of trade Unions in Bombay City", *International Review of Social History*, 22 (1977), pp. 313–328; Rajnarayan Chandavarkar, "The Decline and Fall of the Jobber System in the Bombay Cotton Textile Industry, 1870–1955", *Modern Asian Studies*, 42, 1 (January 2008), pp. 117–210; Tirthankar Roy, "Sardars, Jobbers, Kanganies: The Labour Contractor and Indian Economic History", *Modern Asian Studies*, 42, 5 (September 2008), pp. 971–998; Samita Sen, "Commercial Recruiting and Informal Intermediation: Debate over the Sardari System in Assam Tea Plantations", *Modern Asian Studies*, 44, 1 (January 2010), pp. 3–28; Crispin Bates and Marina Carter, "*Sirdars* as Intermediaries in Nineteenth Century Indian Ocean Indentured Labour Migration", *Modern Asian Studies*, forthcoming. A Chinese case study is Tim Wright, "'A Method of Evading Management:' Contract Labor in Chinese Coal Mines before 1937", *Comparative Studies in Society and History*, 23 (1981), pp. 656–678.

[17] John Buttrick. "The Inside Contract System", *Journal of Economic History*, 12, 3 (Summer 1952), pp. 205–221; J. Taylor, "The Sub-Contract System in the British Coal Industry", in: L.S. Pressnell (ed.), *Studies in the Industrial Revolution. Presented to T.S. Ashton* (London, 1960), pp. 215–235.

[18] Stephen Marglin, "What Do Bosses Do? The Origins and Functions of Hierarchy in Capitalist Production", *Review of Radical Political Economy*, 6 (1974), pp. 60–112. Important contributions to this predominantly Anglophone debate were: Kenneth L. Sokoloff, "Was the Transition from the Artisanal Shop to the Nonmechanized Factory Associated with Gains in Efficiency? Evidence from the U.S. Manufacturing Censuses of 1820 and 1850", *Explorations in Economic History*, 21 (1984), pp. 351–382; David S. Landes, "What Do Bosses Really Do?", *Journal of Economic History*, 46 (1986), pp. 585–623; S.R.H. Jones, "Technology, Transaction Costs, and the Transition to Factory Production in the British Silk Industry, 1700–1870", *Journal of Economic History*, 47, 1 (March 1987), pp. 71–96; Jens

Over time managers seem to have gained more and more control over their labour force. Even under new forms of teleworking (employees working from home) employers try to check on their employees.

Overseeing

Once the workers are put to work, the entrepreneur or manager must be certain that his inferiors produce enough, that the labour products are of sufficient quality, and that the workers are careful with the means of labour.[19] This supervision consists in i) overseeing and ii) disciplining the workers by fines and rewards.

The less workers are interested in the quantity and quality of the results of their labour, the less intensively and carefully will they normally proceed. Overseeing means in general that the entrepreneur appoints overseers ensuring that workers do their job well. In principle there are two methods to supervise the workers: overseeing the *effort*, or overseeing the *result*. An example of overseeing the result is the so-called task system on early rice plantations in the American South. The normal daily task of a slave involved working 1/4 acre (circa. 1000 m^2). If the task, according to the opinion of the overseer, had been orderly fulfilled, the working day was over.[20] Overseeing results becomes easier, the more different workers work independently from each other. Conversely, the greater the interdependence of the tasks, the more difficult it becomes for the overseers to judge the individual result. In overseeing the effort, the overseer makes sure that the worker works hard enough. This type of overseeing presupposes permanent control, and is all the easier the simpler the

---

Christiansen und Peter Philips, "The Transition from Outwork to Factory Production in the Boot and Shoe Industry, 1830–1880", in: Sanford M. Jacoby (ed.), *Masters to Managers: Historical and Comparative Perspectives on American Employers* (New York, 1991), pp. 21–42; William Lazonick, "What Happened to the Theory of Economic Development?", in: Patrice Higonnet, David S. Landes, and Henry Rosovsky (eds), *Favorites of Fortune. Technology, Growth, and Economic Development since the Industrial Revolution* (Cambridge, MA, and London, 1991), pp. 267–296, esp. 291–295; Peter Temin, "Entrepreneurs and Managers", in: Patrice Higonnet, David S. Landes, and Henry Rosovsky (eds), *Favorites of Fortune. Technology, Growth, and Economic Development since the Industrial Revolution* (Cambridge, MA, and London, 1991), pp. 339–355; Maxine Berg, "On the Origins of Capitalist Hierarchy", in: Bo Gustaffson (ed.), *Power and Economic Institutions. Reinterpretations in Economic History* (Aldershot, 1991), pp. 173–194; Lars Magnusson, "From *Verlag* to Factory: The Contest for Efficient Property Rights", in: ibid., pp. 195–222; Stephen A. Marglin, "Understanding Capitalism: Control versus Efficiency", in: ibid., pp. 225–252.
19 The parallels between "free" wage labour and slavery are greater here than is commonly assumed. Aufhauser, "Slavery and Scientific Management", has already pointed to essential agreements with management methods. Blackburn, *Overthrow of Colonial Slavery*, p. 335 has demonstrated that the slave plantations in the new world, "denying the individual producer control over much of the labour process, anticipated some of the features of capitalist industrialism."
20 Albert V. House, "Labor Management Problems on Georgia Rice Plantations, 1840–1860", *Agricultural History*, 28 (1954), pp. 149–155, at 152–153.

tasks to be fulfilled are. If additional qualifications and skills are necessary, it becomes more difficult for the overseer to estimate the intensity of labour.[21]

There are also cases in which it is hardly possible – or even not at all – to oversee the workers. In these cases, the entrepreneur will normally try to compel the workers to work well with persuasion and rewards. An example is that of herdsmen who cover large distances with their herds; their employment of labour can hardly be measured, while, however, their task demands attentiveness and a sense of responsibility. The entrepreneur is in these circumstances reliant on the good will of the herdsmen, and this good will is often created by making the herdsman into a type of junior partner of the master by means of a *peculium* (earnest-money).[22] More generally, Arthur Stinchcombe showed that an optimal labour contract (in the eyes of the entrepreneur) without overseeing consists in labourers handing over a fixed sum to the entrepreneur, and being able to keep the variable remainder.[23] This is in fact the construction we encounter with the slaves-for-hire in Brazil in the nineteenth century.[24]

---

21 Michael Burawoy and and Erik Olin Wright. "Coercion and Consent in Contested Exchange", in: Wright, *Interrogating Inequality. Essays on Class Analysis, Socialism and Marxism* (London and New York, 1994), pp. 72–87, at 81–82. Yoram Barzel, *Economic Analysis of Property Rights* (Cambridge, 1989), p. 80 says that both forms of overseeing inevitably allow the slaves some room for their own business: "Assuming that the supervision of effort is subject to diminishing marginal productivity, owners would, in their supervision effort, have stopped short of extracting the maximum output of which slaves were capable. The difference between slaves' maximum output and their actual output became, in practice, the slaves' property." On the other hand: "Slaves' output supervision also required output quotas, since, left to their own devices, they would have produced as little as they could. Moreover, quotas could not have been set simply by observing past performance, since slaves' incentive to produce little during the demonstration period would have been strong indeed. Since quotas were subject to error, and since too high a quota would have resulted in the destruction of slaves, the quotas owners would have selected to maximize their own wealth were expected to leave their slaves with the difference between the quota and the maximum they could produce, a difference they could take advantage of. Since owners' confiscation of slaves' accumulation would have been equivalent to raising the quota, confiscation would have defeated the purpose for which the quota was set to begin with. In pursuit of their self-interest, owners permitted slaves to own and to accumulate."
22 Stefano Fenoaltea, "Slavery and Supervision in Comparative Perspective: A Model", *Journal of Economic History*, 44 (1984), pp. 635–668, at 656.
23 Arthur Stinchcombe, *Sugar Island Slavery in the Age of Enlightenment* (Princeton, NJ, 1995), p. 147.
24 "They could keep any amount in excess of the stipulated payment." (Maria Cecilia Velasco e Cruz, "Puzzling Out Slave Origins in Rio de Janeiro Port Unionism: The 1906 Strike and the Sociedade de Resistência dos Trabalhadores em Trapiche e Café", *Hispanic American Historical Review*, 86, 2 (2006), 205–245, at 218.) A somewhat different variant was found at the gold mining frontier in Barbacoas (Colombia) in the seventeenth century, where the enslaved Afro-indigenous mine workers "lived in widely scattered riparian camps, virtually independent of their independent of their owners. Fearful of disease, many slave owners preferred to live with their families in the cool highlands. Production quotas were regularly set or negotiated with these absentee masters, with surplus dust (i.e., that exceeding quotas often collected independently in unclaimed areas on Sundays and feast days) used by the slaves to purchase market goods and even freedom." Kris Lane, "Africans and Natives in

One of management's greatest challenges is to motivate workers (including slaves and other unfree labourers) to work hard and with care. Which incentives appeal to workers? What motivates or discourages them in their performance? Work motivation consists of two major components: discipline and creativity.

* Discipline, says Max Weber, "is the probability that by virtue of habituation a command will receive prompt and automatic obedience in stere[o]typed forms, on the part of a given group of persons."[25] This includes, as William Chase observed "a wide variety of production traits and attitudes [such as] punctually arriving at work; conscientiously performing one's job; respecting machinery, materials, and products; obeying the instructions of foremen, and other responsible personnel; and minimizing absence from work."[26]

* Creativity is necessary for every labour process. Harvey Leibenstein was justified in noting, that it is "exceedingly rare for all elements of performance in a labour contract to be spelled out. A good deal is left to custom, authority, and whatever motivational techniques are available to management as well to individual discretion and judgement."[27]

Both factors are essential for the functioning of an industrial enterprise. Total control and domination of human labour is impossible, as has been argued before by many authors, including Wilhelm Baldamus and Christian Brockhaus.[28] Managers always need some voluntary cooperative effort from their workers. The fact that "working to rule" can be an effective form of employee action proves this point: if workers carry out instructions to the letter, then it becomes transparent that these instructions are always incomplete and partly inconsistent; the labour proces breaks down.[29] Absolute control is impossible, even under extreme circumstances.[30]

In heteronomous industrial relations, the two components of work motivation (discipline and creativity) result from a combination of three factors: compensation, coercion, and commitment, which together explain why workers are more or less

---

the Mines of Spanish America", in: Mathew Restall (ed.), *Beyond Black and Red. African-Native Relations in Colonial Latin America* (Albuquerque, NM, 2005), pp. 159–184, at 169.
25 Max Weber, *The Theory of Social and Economic Organization* [*Wirtschaft und Gesellschaft*, Part I]. Trans. A.R. Henderson and Talcott Parsons (London, 1947), p. 139.
26 William Chase, *Workers, Society and the Soviet State: Labor and Life in Moscow, 1918–1929* (Urbana, IL, and Chicago, 1987), p. 35.
27 Harvey Leibenstein, "Allocation Efficiency and 'X-Efficiency'", *American Economic Review*, 56 (1966), pp. 392–415, here 407.
28 W.G. Baldamus, *Efficiency and Effort: An Analysis of Industrial Administration* (London, 1961); Christian Brockhaus, *Lohnarbeit als Existenzgrund von Gewerkschaften* (Frankfurt am Main, 1979).
29 Ulrich Beck and Michael Brater, "Grenzen abstrakter Arbeit", *Leviathan*, 4 (1976), pp. 178–215, at 182.
30 About the Nazi concentration camps Barrington Moore, Jr. observes: "[...] the officials could not control, through fear or other sanctions, absolutely every detail of the prisoner's life. Some areas of autonomy, or at least pseudo-autonomy, have to be left to prisoners in order to get them to do such simple things as march to their eating and sleeping quarters at the appropriate moment." Moore, *Injustice: The Social Bases of Obedience and Revolt* (Armonk, NJ, 1978), p. 70.

motivated to do their jobs according to the employer's standards: (i) compensation, or the offer of contingent rewards like wages and other benefits; (ii) commitment, or the invocation of solidarity; (iii) coercion, or the threat to inflict harm.[31] In this view, the relative weight of these three motives, which varies over time and from job to job, defines the various work-incentive systems.

Compensation can be divided into three categories:

* Direct wages, i.e. money wages. These can be further subdivided in a) compensation for the *time* people work (time rates).[32]; b) compensation for the *results* of people's work (piece rates: payment for each item produced; commission (for salespeople): workers receive a fraction of the value of the items they sell; gainsharing: group-incentives that partially tie gains in group productivity, reductions in cost, increases in product quality, or other measures of group success; profitsharing and bonus plans (relate wages to the enterprise's profits); c) combinations of time and result-based wages (hybrids).

* Indirect wages, like insurance arrangements, pay for holidays and vacations, services, and perquisites. "Inasmuch as these are generally made uniformly available to all employees at a given job level, regardless of performance, they are really not motivating rewards. However, where indirect compensation is controllable by management and is used to reward performance, then it clearly needs to be considered as a motivating reward."[33]

* Invisible wages, i.e. the non-contractual appropriation by employees of enterprise goods and services. This category covers a range of wage-forms, including open and legal perks, semi-legal pilfering and outright theft.[34]

Coercion comprises disciplinary rules and their sanctioning. Coercion can be applied to enforce discipline, but hardly as a punishment for a lack of creativity. Three areas in which coercion may be applied can be distinguished:[35] a) The area of disciplinary liability, i.e. the breaking of rules. Punishment may include reprimand, demotion (transfer to other lower-paid work for a certain period), and dismissal; b) The area of criminal liability, i.e. the breaking of criminal law, with corresponding punishments; c) The area of material liability. Punishment includes restitution in cash or kind to the enterprise for damage to its property resulting from an infringement of labour discipline.

---

[31] Chris Tilly and Charles Tilly, *Work Under Capitalism* (Boulder, Co. and Oxford, 1998).
[32] This is most common in the West: in 1991 86% of US employees were paid either by the hour or by the month. See Ronald G. Ehrenberg and Robert S. Smith, *Modern Labor Economics: Theory and Public Policy* (4th edn, New York, NY, 1991), p. 412.
[33] Stephen P. Robbins, *Organizational Behavior: Concepts, Controversies, Applications* (7th Edn, Englewood Cliffs, NJ, 1996), p. 660.
[34] Jason Ditton, "Perks, Pilferage, and the Fiddle: The Historical Structure of Invisible Wages", *Theory and Society*, 4 (1977), pp. 39–71.
[35] Barker, *Some Problems of Incentives*, pp. 98–99.

Commitment comprizes incentives based on desire for public recognition and approbation; pride in craftsmanship or in record achievements; local or kinship loyalties; and sometimes social or political ideals. These motives are very much linked to the cultural context. Illustrative is what the English observer Barker wrote in the 1950s about the Soviet Union: "The stimuli most widely used in the USSR, for example, would generally prove useless or worse in our conditions. The honours awarded to categories of people regarded as socially valuable in the way of uniforms, medals, decorations and badges would provoke not competition for them, as visible tokens of high status, but embarassment and possibly even contempt. In this respect, the USSR was probably fortunately placed in having (a) a tradition upon which it was easy to build, and (b) in starting from a cultural level which largely reflected pre-capitalist conditions, in which awareness of the 'cash nexus' was not very fully developed – at any rate not so fully developed as to make it very difficult to persuade workers to accept such symbols of status as being equal or of comparable value to higher wages."[36] Examples of commitment-incentives include: the enterprise "Book of Honour", publicity for model-workers ("their pictures and records of their achievements are published in the appropriate newspapers, depending upon the significance of what they have done. They receive the title of 'Hero', and orders, medals or badges which indicate to all who meet them how high is the status they have gained on account of their work."[37]

Compensation, coercion and commitment can be combined in a multitude of ways. The specific mix used by management is the outcome of social experience and complex strategic considerations. Which combination of these incentives happens to be applied, is immediately connected with the type of labour relation. Coercion includes threat with or without the application of force, including incarceration, tormenting, mutilation, sale (of slaves), dismissal (of wage workers) or even death. Such negative sanctions may indeed lead to the workers working hard, but not to them doing their work well. And negative sanctions encourage resistance and sabotage (which, in turn, are more effective the more complicated and skilled the labour process is). Compulsion is therefore most effective for very simple labour processes which are easy to oversee.[38] Heavy physical punishments can, in addition, have the economic disadvantage that workers become temporarily or permanently unable to work.

Formal and informal rules

All employers use a system of rules – both formal and informal – prescribing the behaviour of employees. Behaviour that is considered to be improper may be punished and proper behaviour may be rewarded. These punishments and rewards can be dis-

---

36 *Ibid.*, pp. 113–114.
37 *Idem*, p. 115.
38 Fenoaltea, "Slavery and Supervision", pp. 639–640.

cretionary (i.e. they can be applied at pleasure by the management), or they may be bound by formal and informal rules. The more unfree workers are the stronger management's discretionary power is. Managers on slave plantations, for example, could often workers punish at will. But even their power was not always absolute. Already in 1685, the French *Code Noir* (1685) provided a legal framework for slavery. Among other things it stipulated that slaves should not work on Sundays and holidays, that they should have a day per week to work for their own ends, that their masters should not torture, mutilate or kill them, and that slaves who were "not fed, clothed and supported by the masters" according to the law had the right to notify an "attorney of this and give him their statements".[39] These were, of course, 'offical' statements, and it is doubtful if masters obeyed the law, or if slaves – if they were aware of the *Code* at all – dared to start a formal procedure if their master tresspassed the law. Much later, during the last decades before the Civil War of 1860–65, courts in the South of the United States also began to limit the rights of slave owners, restricting them from brutalizing slaves, and requiring them to provide adequate clothing.[40]

Historically, employees have generally been in favour of restricting management's discretionary power as much as possible, and of expanding the domain of rules and meta-rules (rules about the making of rules).[41] In the case of 'free' wage labour, the sociologist Philip Selznick has spoken about the transition from a so-called "'prerogative' contract – according to which the sale of labour power carries with it few, if any, proscriptions or prescriptions on its consumption by management – to the 'constitutive contract' and to 'creative arbitration,' which does establish procedures and regulations for the utilization of labour."[42] Michael Burawoy adds to this: "Restrictions on managerial discretion and arbitrary rule, on the one hand, and enhanced protection for workers, on the other, reflect not only the ascendency of unions and *internal* government, but also indirect regulation by agencies of *external* government."[43] In the case of a highly developed "constitutive contract" the rule system becomes relatively autonomous, "because it ensures the reproduction of relations in production by protecting management from itself, from its tendency toward arbitrary interventions that would undermine the consent produced at the point of production."[44]

An enterprise is a special type of rule system, which consists of a kind of "grammar" of rules that gives answers to a whole series of questions, like: who is in and who

---

39 *Le Code Noir ou Edit du Roy [...]* (Paris, 1735). https://archive.org/details/lecodenoirouedi00fran.
40 Jenny Bourne Wahl, "Legal Constraints on Slave Masters: The Problem of Social Cost", *The American Journal of Legal History*, 41, 1 (January 1997), pp. 1–24, at 4.
41 Sanford M. Jacoby, *Employing Bureaucracy: Managers, Unions, and the Transformation of Work in American Industry, 1900–1945* (New York, 1985), has argued that trade-union opposition against managerial discretionary power has furthered the bureaucratization of American industrial firms.
42 Philip Selznick, *Law, Society and Industrial Justice* (New York, 1969), p. 154.
43 Michael Burawoy, *Manufacturing Consent. Changes in the Labor Process under Monopoly Capitalism* (Chicago and London, 1979), p. 116.
44 *Ibid.*, p. 117.

is out, i.e. who is a member of the organization, or a specific part of it; which activities, resources, purposes and outcomes are proper and legitimate; when and where do specific activities have to take place?[45] The rules applied in an organization are only in part formal, that is laid down in by-laws and regulations. An import role is always played by informal rules. These rules may reflect the formal rules, but not necessarily so. Formal rules are sometimes difficult to implement fully, and they do not cover all shopfloor practices. The formal structure of an organization is always, to use the expression introduced by John Meyer and Brian Rowan, to some extent a "ceremonial façade" – a "façade" because the formal structure does not fully determine organizational practice. The façade restricts the room for organizational manoeuvring, but nevertheless, the formal and the practical level remain more or less loosely coupled. The attribute "ceremonial" points at a second loose coupling: the formal structure needs to be somewhat congruent with the organization's institutional environment if the organization wants to acquire the legitimacy that is required for its survival.[46]

If the precarious relationship between the formal and the practical levels gets disturbed, two possibilities emerge: either the façade collapses and the organizational practice is left behind "naked". Or the organizational practice collapses and only the façade remains. The latter possibility seems to have become a reality in the case of the Communist Parties in Eastern Europe in the 1970s and '80s; and this example shows that façades may continue to exist for quite a long time. The historical anthropologist Richard Rottenburg speaks in this context about a "mirror façade": "In the case of a mirror façade, the attempt made by the observer to look at the building in front of him, only makes him see himself against his own background."[47]

Rule systems can, of course, be transgressed or changed. In fact, struggles are going on continuously about the interpretation of existing rules and the changing of these rules. Rules are constantly contested, made and remade. "Such *meta-processes* – entailing exchange, conflict and power struggles among the agents involved – are specifically oriented to maintaining or changing particular rules, sub-systems of rules, or entire rule systems."[48]

---

45 Tom R. Burns and Helena Flam, *The Shaping of Social Organization. Social Rule System Theory With Applications* (London, 1987), p. 107.
46 In as much as the institutional environment itself comprizes different societal sectors with separate logics and meaningful orientations, ambivalencies and contradictions may result.
47 Richard Rottenburg, "'We Have to Do Business as Business is Done!' Zur Aneignung formaler Organisation in einem westafrikanischen Unternehmen", *Historische Anthropologie*, 2 (1994), pp. 265–286, at 269.
48 Burns and Flam, *Shaping of Social Organization*, p. 11.

Time rules

The central process of rule-making and rule-transgression concerns time-discipline, that is the extent to which other persons may decide the disposition of a worker's effort within the working year.[49] Time-discipline concerns the beginning, duration, and end of the working day, the timing of breaks, holidays, the number of activities that have to be performed during a certain labour time, and so on. Different societies can have very different time rules. About the Iatmul, for example, a people in Papua New Guinea, it is said that they worked completely autonomously before they became "civilized":

> "whether a task is to be done or not, where it is to be done, how long it may take, how large the group is to be, and whether particular persons are to take part are matters to be decided by the individuals concerned in accordance with the situation at the moment. No one is entitled to dictate the tempo at which a job is done, or when the work must be finished; every working individual determines this himself. Communal decisions of short-term validity are reached in loose cooperation with other members of the group and in direct relation to technical necessities or personal needs. Work may be interrupted by intervals of relaxation, joking, or ritual, as desired."[50]

The starkest contrast with autonomous time-management is the "Scientific Management" developed by the US-engineer Frederick W. Taylor (1856–1915) and his followers.[51] In their struggle against output regulation ("soldiering") by workers – who consistently tried to keep their employers ignorant of how fast work can be done – Taylorists devised time-and-motion studies by sub-dividing specific tasks in elemental

---

[49] I adapt this definition from Chris Tilly and Charles Tilly, *Work under Capitalism*, p. 30.
[50] Milan Stanek, "Social Structure of the Iatmul", in: Nancy Lutkehaus *et al.* (eds), *Sepik Heritage. Tradition and Change in Papua New Guinea* (Bathurst, 1990), pp. 266–273, at 266. For some useful general reflections, see Nancy D. Munn, "The Cultural Anthropology of Time: A Critical Essay", *Annual Review of Anthropology*, 21 (1992), pp. 93–123.
[51] Historical and sociological research on Scientific Management seems to have been most intense in the 1970s. see e.g., Harry Braverman, *Labor and Monopoly Capital: The Degradation of Work in the Twentieth Century* (New York, 1974); Aimée Moutet, "Les origines du système de Taylor en France: le point de vue patronal (1907–1914)", *Le Mouvement Social*, No. 93 (October-December 1975), pp. 15–49; Katherine Stone, "The Origins of Job Structures in the Steel Industry", *Review of Radical Political Economics*, 6, 2 (July 1974), pp. 113–173; David Noble, *America By Design: Science, Technology and the Rise of Corporate Capitalism* (New York, 1977); Heidrun Homburg, "Anfänge des Taylorsystems in Deutschland vor dem Ersten Weltkrieg", *Geschichte und Gesellschaf*, 4 (1978), pp. 170–194; David Gartman, "Origins of the Assembly Line and Capitalist Control of Work at Ford", in: Andrew Zimbalist (ed.), *Case Studies on the Labor Process* (New York and London, 1979), pp. 193–205; Richard Edwards, *Contested Terrain: The Transformation of the Workplace in the Twentieth Century* (London, 1979); Dan Clawson, *Bureaucracy and the Labor Process: The Transformation of US Industry, 1860–1920* (New York, 1980).

motions. A 1960 study of "clerical time standards" specifies, for example, the following motions:[52]

Open and close	Minutes
File drawer, open and close, no selection	.04
Folder, open or close flaps	.04
Desk drawer, open side drawer of standard desk	.014
Open centre drawer	.026
Close side	.015
Close centre	.027
Chair activity	
Get up from chair	.033
Sit down in chair	.033
Turn in swivel chair	.009
Move in chair to adjoining desk or file (4 ft. maximum)	.050

Scientific management became also very popular in the Soviet Union. Lenin admired Taylor, and Trotsky argued that a socialist organization of the economy should be one big conveyor belt.[53] After World War II, state-socialist governments in Eastern Europe strongly promoted Taylorism as well.[54]

Obviously, workers moving from a pre-industrial, more or less autonomous to a heteronomous regulation of working time, can be expected to experience huge adaptation problems. These problems may become larger if the workers are simultaneously small peasants who necessarily have to leave their heteronomous work site during harvest time. These tensions have contributed to the persistent colonialist myth of the "lazy natives". But early industrial workers in other parts of the world knew similar adaptation problems.[55]

---

52 Braverman, *Labor and Monopoly Capital*, p. 321.
53 Robert Linhart, *Lénine, les paysans, Taylor* (Paris, 1976); Leon Trotsky, *Problems of Everyday Life and Other writings on Culture and Science* (New York, 1973), pp. 241–244; Kendall E. Bailes, "Alexei Gastev and the Soviet Controversy over Taylorism, 1918–1924", *Soviet Studies*, 29 (1977), pp. 373–394; Melanie Tatur, *"Wissenschaftliche Arbeitsorganisation". Arbeitswissenschaften und Arbeitsorganisation in der Sowjetunion, 1921–1935* (Berlin, 1979); Zenovia A. Sochor, "Soviet Taylorism Revisited", *Soviet Studies*, 33 (1981), pp. 246–264; Angelika Ebbinghaus, *Arbeiter und Arbeitswissenschaft. Zur Entstehung der "wissenschaftlichen Betriebsführung"* (Opladen, 1983); Reinhart Kössler and Mammo Muchie, "American Dreams and Soviet Realities: Socialism and Taylorism", *Capital and Class*, No. 40 (Spring 1990), pp. 61–88.
54 See e.g., Michael Burawoy and János Lukacs, "Mythologies of Work: A Comparison of Firms in State Socialism and Advanced Capitalism", *American Sociological Review*, 50, 6 (December 1985), pp. 723–737. Miklos Haraszti has described his work experiences at the Red Star Tractor Works in: *A Worker in a Worker's State. Piece-Rates in Hungary*. Trans. Michael Wright (New York, 1975).
55 For an extensive critique see Syed Hussein Alatas, *The Myth of the Lazy Native. A Study of the Image of the Malays, Filipinos and Javanese from the 16th to 20th Century and its Function in the Ideol-*

The first elements of "modern" time discipline were perhaps introduced in the European textile manufactures during the fourteenth century. As a consequence, work bells announcing the beginning and the end of the working day began to proliferate, which in turn inspired revolts of workers aimed at silencing the bells.[56] Sidney Pollard summarized the adaptation problem of new factory workers as follows: "The worker who left the background of his domestic workshop or peasant holding for the factory, entered a new culture as well as a new sense of direction. It was not only that 'the new economic order needed ... part-humans: soulless, depersonalised, disembodied, who could become members, or little wheels rather, of a complex mechanism'. It was also that men [and of course: women! – MvdL] who were non-accumulative, non-acquisitive, accustomed to work for subsistence, not for maximization of income, had to be made obedient to the cash stimulus, and obedient in such a way as to react precisely to the stimuli provided."[57]

Convincing as the contrast between pre-industrial and industrial time-rules may seem, we should however be careful not to generalize too quickly. A fine instance of false generalization is E.P. Thompson's theory of "task-orientation". Drawing on the English situation, Thompson argued that the task-orientation of pre-industrial workers was characterized by three features: their work rhythm was determined by the "observed necessity" of the natural environment; they made no clear distinction between "work" and "life" (i.e. social intercourse); and their attitude to work was, to modern eyes "wasteful and lacking in urgency".[58] That generalization has been con-

---

ogy of Colonial Capitalism (London, 1977). See also Shashi Bhushan Upadhyay, "The Myth of the Indolent Worker: Length of Working Time and Workers' Resistance in Bombay Cotton Mills, 1875–1920", in: Brahma Nand and Inukonda Thirumali (eds), *Repressed Discourses. Essays in honour of Prof. Sabyasachi Bhattacharya* (New Delhi, 2004), pp. 150–178. On adaptation problems, see *inter alia* E.P. Thompson's classical essay, "Time, Work-Discipline and Industrial Capitalism", *Past and Present*, No. 38 (december 1967), pp. 56–97, reprinted in E.P. Thompson, *Customs in Common* (Harmondsworth, 1991), pp. 352–403; Michael French Smith, "'Wild' Villagers and Capitalist virtues: Perceptions of Western Work Habits in a Preindustrial Community", *Anthropological* Quarterly, 57, 4 (1984), pp. 125–138; Alan Pope, "Aboriginal Adaptation to Early Colonial Labour Markets: The South Australian Experience", *Labour History*, No. 54 (May 1988), pp. 1–15; Touraj Atabaki, "From '*Amaleh* (Labor) to *Kargar* (Worker): Recruitment, Work Discipline and Making of the Working Class in the Persian/Iranian Oil Industry", *International Labor and Working Class History*, No. 84 (Fall 2013), pp. 159–175. For a study focusing on managerial methods, see Roger Knight, "The Visible Hand in *Tempo Doeloe*: The Culture of Management and the Organization of Business in Java's Colonial sugar Industry", *Journal of Southeast Asian Studies*, 30, 1 (March 1999), pp. 74–98.

56 Jacques Le Goff, "Labor Time in the 'Crisis' of the Fourteenth Century: From Medieval Time to Modern Time", in: Le Goff, *Time, Work, and Culture in the Middle Ages*. Trans. Arthur Goldhammer (Chicago and London, 1980), pp. 43–52, at 45–46.

57 Sidney Pollard, "Factory Discipline in the Industrial Revolution", *Economic History review*, second series, 16, 2 (1963), pp. 254–271, at 254.

58 Thompson, "Time, Work-Discipline and Industrial Capitalism", p. 60. Henri Lefebvre, *Critique de la vie quotidienne*. 3 vols (Paris, 1958–61), vol. II, pp. 52–6 made a similar distinction between the cyclical (seasonally related) time of pre-industrial labour and the linear time of capitalist accumulation.

vincingly refuted, however, based on studies of agricultural producers in late Tokugawa Japan. Owing in part to the pressure of a growing population density, peasants were forced to plan their crops in advance, to coordinate a variety of activities over longer periods, and to keep records.[59]

Autonomous management

Most self-managed enterprises have existed only briefly. To succeed, they had to meet at least four conditions: capable management, skillful staff with a strong democratic impulse, sufficient capital, and adequate opportunities for selling the product. Here I will only say a few things about the first two points.[60]

Managers need several qualities. They are responsible – possibly assisted by other members – for identifying one or several market outlets for the new enterprise, purchasing the right commodities and labour equipment as inexpensively as possible, coordinating the company's activities, and spreading the risks. Moreover, they should have enough authority to encourage the other cooperative members to satisfy the expectations of them. Such skills require talent and experience, which are not necessarily attributes of producer cooperative members. Even if any members have such skills, they will be inclined – except if their social-moral impetus is strong – either to work for a heteronomous company, or to opt for self-employment. In both cases, their income will probably be higher.[61] Examples abound of producer cooperatives that failed for lack of managerial skills.

In addition to being experts in their trade, producer cooperative members must be able to transcend their authoritarian primary and secondary socialization (in the family, at school, at heteronomous companies) and to adopt a permanent anti-hierarchical view, without thereby obstructing the management. This lesson is often difficult to learn, as "the ability to participate democratically in the work setting is unlikely to be created by schools that function in a strictly hierarchical fashion where rules, regulations and bureaucratic control characterize the learning and social process."[62] The lack of entrepreneurial and anti-hierarchical skills often tempts producer cooperative members to maintain small, simple organizational structures, and to mistrust organizational expansion. Alternatively, a member with strong entrepreneu-

---

59 Thomas C. Smith, "Peasant Time and Factory Time in Japan", *Past and Present*, No. 111 (May 1986), pp. 165–197.
60 I offer a more comprehensive analysis in *Workers of the World. Essays toward a Global Labor History* (Leiden and Boston, 2008), chapter 8.
61 Avner Ben-Ner, "The Life Cycle of Worker-Owned Firms in Market Economies: A Theoretical Analysis", *Journal of Economic Behavior and Organization*, 10 (1988), pp. 287–313, at 290.
62 Henry Levin, "Issues in Assessing the Comparative Productivity of Worker-Managed and Participatory Firms in Capitalist Societies", in: Derek C. Jones and Jan Svejnar (eds), *Participatory and Self-Managed Firms: Evaluating Economic Performance* (Lexington: Lexington Books, 1982), pp. 45–64, at 57.

rial skills may, when fellow members are insufficiently anti-hierarchical, be tempted to "hijack" the organization.

Once producer cooperatives have been established, they will probably operate as efficiently as or even more efficiently than heteronomous companies.[63] First, a producer cooperative requires comparatively less supervision than a conventional enterprise. Producer cooperatives have internalized the contradiction between capital and labour, and therefore have considerably smaller asymmetries of information, mistrust, and the like than heteronomous firms.[64] "In activities in which centralized monitoring is difficult to carry out, mutual monitoring and better incentives for worker-members help overcome shirking and make for superior performance of producer cooperatives."[65] In his study of contemporary plywood manufacturing cooperatives in the American West, Christopher Gunn writes: "The co-ops use significantly fewer supervisors than their conventional counterparts; the average in the co-ops is one or two per shift of 60 to 70 people as opposed to five to seven in conventional firms."[66]

In addition, the stronger work ethic in producer cooperatives enhances general efficiency. Various authors have noted that producer cooperatives often yield superior output, and waste fewer raw materials than in the case of production by heteronomous firms.[67] Moreover, the entrepreneur's non-productive consumption is eliminated. All these factors keep the operating costs of producer cooperatives considerably below those of heteronomous firms.

A final word

Heteronomous work incentives usually begin as external influences: managers from outside try to induce workers to act in certain ways. But over time, workers may internalize at least some of the incentives. If at time t_1 an individual must be stimulated to work by external compensation or coercion and at time t_2 does so on their own

---

[63] "An accumulating body of evidence suggests that producer cooperatives often enjoy higher levels of productivity than do otherwise similar conventional firms." Louis Putterman and Gilbert L. Skillman. "The Role of Exit Costs in the Theory of Cooperative Teams", *Journal of Comparative Economics*, 16 (1992), pp. 596–618, at 596.
[64] Raymond Russell, "Employee Ownership and Internal Governance: An 'Organizational Failures' Analysis of Three Populations of Employee-Owned Firms", *Journal of Economic Behavior and Organization*, 6, 3 (1985), pp. 217–241.
[65] Avner Ben-Ner, "Producer Cooperatives: Why Do They Exist in Capitalist Economies?", in: Walter W. Powell (ed.), *The Nonprofit Sector. A Research Handbook* (New Haven, CT, and London, 1987), pp. 434–449, at 436.
[66] Christopher Gunn, *Workers' Self-Management in the United States* (Ithaca, NY, 1984), p. 111.
[67] Franz Oppenheimer, *Die Siedlungsgenossenschaft. Versuch einer positiven Überwindung des Kommunismus durch Lösung des Genossenschaftsproblems und der Agrarfrage* (Berlin, 1896), p. 55; Sigmund Engländer, *Geschichte der französischen Arbeiter-Associationen* (Hamburg, 1864), 4 vols., IV, pp. 160–161.

initiative, then he or she can be said to have internalized those external incentives. Internalization is thus a psychological process that converts external incentives (coercion, compensation) either entirely or partly into internal incentives (commitment). Consistent with that, David Landes has made a distinction between "time-discipline" and "time-obedience", or punctuality coming "from within" or "from without".[68] In relation to chattel slaves in the antebellum American South, Mark Smith has defined that difference as follows: "time-obedience refers to a respect for mechanical time among workers that, unlike time-discipline, was not internalized, but was rather enforced by time-conscious planters, either with the threat or the use of violence or with the constant repetition of mechanically defined time through sound, as with the chiming of clock-regulated bells."[69]

Frequently workers who had internalized heteronomous work incentives introduced these incentives also in their autonomous activities. John Iliffe has, for example, revealed that the trade union of dockworkers in 1930s Dar es Salaam showed "that intense concern for time and punctuality which is so obsessive for the new industrial worker". The union rules stipulated that "Every member will attend at his work before the prescribed time in order that he may not be late", and "No member should leave his work before the proper time or without his employer's permission."[70] Unions would even copy coercive methods (e.g. fine systems) used by heteronomous management in order to enforce discipline in their own ranks.[71]

---

68 David S. Landes, *Revolution in Time. Clocks and the Making of the Modern World* (Cambridge, MA, 1983), p. 7.
69 Mark M. Smith, "Time, Slavery and Plantation Capitalism in the Ante-bellum American South", *Past and Present*, No. 150 (February 1996), pp. 142–168, at 145.
70 John Iliffe, "The Creation of Group Consciousness Among the Dockworkers of Dar-es-Salaam 1929–50", in: Richard Sandbrook and Robin Cohen (eds), *The Development of an African Working Class. Studies in Class Formation and Action* (London, 1975), 49–72, at 56.
71 See the examples in Rudolf Braun, *Sozialer und kultureller Wandel in einem ländlichen Industriegebiet (Zürcher Oberland) unter Einwirkung des Maschinen- und Fabrikwesens im 19. und 20. Jahrhundert* (Zürich, 1965). Much can be learned from anthropological and ethnographic studies. See e.g., Charles F. Harding III, "The Social Anthropology of American Industry", *American Anthropologist*, New Series, 57, 6 (December 1955), pp. 1218–1231; Sandra Wallman (ed.), *Social Anthropology of Work* (London, 1979); Michael Burawoy, "The Anthropology of Industrial Work", *Annual Review of Anthropology*, 8 (1979), pp. 231–266; James M. Acheson, "Anthropology of Fishing", *Annual Review of Anthropology*, 10 (1981), pp. 275–316; Carol S. Holzberg and Maureen J. Giovannini, "Anthropology and Industry: Reappraisal and New Directions", *Annual Review of Anthropology*, 10 (1981), pp. 317–360; Herbert Applebaum (ed.), *Work in Market and Industrial Societies* (Albany, NY, 1984); Herbert Applebaum (ed.), *Work in Non-Market and Transitional Societies* (Albany, NY, 1984); Eugene Cooper, "Mode of Production and Anthropology of Work", *Journal of Anthropological Research*, 40, 2 (Summer 1984), pp. 257–270; Ricardo A. Godoy, "Mining: Anthropological Perspectives", *Annual Review of Anthropology*, 14 (1985), pp. 199–217; S. Linstead, "The Social Anthropology of Management", *British Journal of Management*, 8 (1997), pp. 85–98; Chris Ballard and Glenn Banks, "Resource Wars: The Anthropology of Mining", *Annual Review of Anthropology*, 32 (2003), pp. 287–313; Sutti Ortiz, "Laboring in the Factories and Fields", *Annual Review of Anthropology*, 31 (2002), pp. 395–417; Gerd Spittler, *Founders of the Anthropology of Work. German Social Scientists of the 19th and Early 20th Centuries and the First Ethnographers* (Berlin, 2008).

Suggested reading

Alatas, Syed Hussein. *The Myth of the Lazy Native. A Study of the Image of the Malays, Filipinos and Javanese from the 16th to 20th Century and its Function in the Ideology of Colonial Capitalism* (London: Frank Cass, 1977).
Applebaum, Herbert (ed.). *Work in Market and Industrial Societies* (Albany: State University of New York Press, 1984).
Applebaum, Herbert (ed.). *Work in Non-Market and Transitional Societies* (Albany: State University of New York Press, 1984).
Braverman, Harry. *Labor and Monopoly Capital: The Degradation of Work in the Twentieth Century* (New York: Monthly Review Press, 1974).
Burawoy, Michael. "The Anthropology of Industrial Work", *Annual Review of Anthropology*, 8 (1979), pp. 231–266.
Burawoy, Michael. *Manufacturing Consent. Changes in the Labor Process under Monopoly Capitalism* (Chicago and London: University of Chicago Press, 1979).
Chandavarkar, Rajnarayan. "The Decline and Fall of the Jobber System in the Bombay Cotton Textile Industry, 1870–1955", *Modern Asian Studies*, 42, 1 (January 2008), pp. 117–210.
Chandler, Alfred D. *The Visible Hand. The Managerial Revolution in American Business* (Cambridge, MA and London: The Belknap Press of Harvard University Press, 1977).
Cooke, Bill. "The Denial of Slavery in Management Studies", *Journal of Management Studies*, 40, 8 (December 2003), pp. 1895–1918.
Ditton, Jason. "Perks, Pilferage, and the Fiddle: The Historical Structure of Invisible Wages", *Theory and Society*, 4 (1977), pp. 39–71.
Esch, Elizabeth and David Roediger. *The Production of Difference. Race and the Management of Labor in U.S. History* (New York: Oxford University Press, 2012).
Fenoaltea, Stefano. "Slavery and Supervision in Comparative Perspective: A Model", *Journal of Economic History*, 44, 3 (September 1984), pp. 635–668.
Holzberg, Carol S. and Maureen J. Giovannini. "Anthropology and Industry: Reappraisal and New Directions", *Annual Review of Anthropology*, 10 (1981), pp. 317–360.
House, Albert V. "Labor Management Problems on Georgia Rice Plantations, 1840–1860", *Agricultural History*, 28 (1954), pp. 149–155.
Jacoby, Sanford M. *Employing Bureaucracy: Managers, Unions, and the Transformation of Work in American Industry, 1900–1945* (New York: Columbia University Press, 1985).
Landes, David S. "What Do Bosses Really Do?", *Journal of Economic History*, 46 (1986), pp. 585–623.
Ledderose, Lothar. *Ten Thousand Things. Module and Mass Production in Chinese Art* (Princeton: Princeton University Press, 2000).
Linstead, S. "The Social Anthropology of Management", *British Journal of Management*, 8 (1997), pp. 85–98.
Marglin, Stephen. "What Do Bosses Do? The Origins and Functions of Hierarchy in Capitalist Production", *Review of Radical Political Economy*, 6 (1974), pp. 60–112.
Melossi, Dario and Massimo Pavarini. *The Prison and the Factory. Origins of the Penitentiary System*. Trans. Glynis Cousin (London and Basingstoke: Macmillan, 1981).
Ortiz, Sutti. "Laboring in the Factories and Fields", *Annual Review of Anthropology*, 31 (2002), pp. 395–417.
Pollard, Sidney. *The Genesis of Modern Management. A Study of the Industrial Revolution in Great Britain* (London: Edward Arnold, 1965).
Smith, Thomas C. "Peasant Time and Fatory Time in Japan", *Past and Present*, No. 111 (May 1986), pp. 165–197.

Spittler, Gerd. *Founders of the Anthropology of Work. German Social Scientists of the 19th and Early 20th Centuries and the First Ethnographers* (Berlin: Lit Verlag, 2008).

Taylor, J. "The Sub-Contract System in the British Coal Industry", in: L.S. Pressnell (ed.), *Studies in the Industrial Revolution. Presented to T.S. Ashton* (London: Athlone Press, 1960), pp. 215–235.

Thompson, E.P. "Time, Work-Discipline and Industrial Capitalism", *Past and Present*, No. 38 (December 1967), pp. 56–97, reprinted in E.P. Thompson, *Customs in Common* (Harmondsworth: Penguin, 1991), pp. 352–403.

Tilly, Chris and Charles Tilly. *Work Under Capitalism* (Boulder, Co. and Oxford: Westview Press, 1998).

Wallman, Sandra (ed.). *Social Anthropology of Work* (London: Academic Press, 1979).

Wright, Tim. "'A Method of Evading Management:' Contract Labor in Chinese Coal Mines before 1937", *Comparative Studies in Society and History*, 23 (1981), pp. 656–678.

Zimbalist, Andrew (ed.). *Case Studies on the Labor Process* (New York and London: Monthly Review Press, 1979).

8. Organization and Resistance

Marcel van der Linden

8.1. Mutualism

"Mutualism" refers to all voluntary arrangements, in which people make contributions to a collective fund, which is given, in whole or in part, to one or more of the contributors according to specific rules of allocation. The concept goes back to the nineteenth century and was probably coined by the French social anarchist Pierre-Joseph Proudhon. The idea behind mutualism is simple: there are things in everyday life people desire but cannot acquire for themselves as individuals. Such things can consist of labour, of goods, or of money. There are two possible reasons for the existence of such items. On the one hand, there are tasks that individuals cannot possibly execute on their own, within a reasonable period of time. For these, they need other people to help them. And on the other hand, there are tasks which an individual could well execute him- or herself, but which would have significant negative effects on the person involved, for example because working to obtain a good on one's own is frightening or stultifying. In both cases, individuals benefit by asking others for help. In compensation for this help, they can perform a similar (reciprocal) task in return, or pay for it. Mutualist activities not only occur among all kinds of workers, but also among other social classes. Mutualism is in this sense not class-specific, although it often is an important component of proletarian survival strategies.

In a great variety of circumstances workers have utilized mutualist arrangements to make their lives more liveable and less risky. Mutualism took a great variety of forms in the past, and still does today. Yet patterns and relations can be discerned. In general there are three kinds of mutualist arrangements, based on (i) scheduled demand and rotating allocation; (ii) scheduled demand and non-rotating allocation; and (iii) contingent demand and non-rotating allocation.

Scheduled demand means that the people involved know in advance that they will have to perform a certain amount of labour, or to pay a certain sum of money or goods at some point in the future. There are two kinds of scheduled demand: one-off and recurring. *Single expenses* may for instance be refunded for ceremonies or parties, on the occasion of rites of passage, such as weddings or funerals. On such occasions, the individuals or households involved are in acute need of a large amount of goods or money which they cannot supply by themselves in a short period of time. Among these single expenses, I include the purchase of durables and investments in capital goods. The second variety of scheduled demand is a matter of *regularly recurring expenses*, such as the periodic strain on household resources at the end of the month. In these cases, mutualist associations can also provide a solution.

Non-scheduled demand is unpredictable and unplanned, and usually comes as an unpleasant surprise (illness, unemployment, etc.).

Rotating allocation means that all participants in a mutualist arrangement will come in for their turn; there is then necessarily always a maximum number of participants (roughly between 10 and 200), because everyone wants to have his or her turn within a reasonable period of time. Non-rotating arrangements imply that only some of the participants will receive money, labour or goods from the common fund. With non-rotation, there is no technical limit to the membership in these cases, and therefore such associations can contain large groups of people.

Scheduled demand and rotating allocation

In some cases mutualism revolves around the provision of labour; the participants in an arrangement can either rotate labour, or use labour for the production of one good, by which all can benefit. In the first case (rotation), one person first "consumes" the labour of the rest of the group, and after that another, etc. Such forms of labour rotation are known around the world.[1] Nicolaas van Meeteren describes such an arrangement on Curaçao, which was popular there until the first decades of the twentieth century: "Whenever one needed to weed, plant or harvest, the custom was implemented that was known as 'saam.' All neighbors then agreed to work for each other once or twice in the week in the evening by moonlight. The beneficiary of the work provided rum and refreshments. As the workers encouraged each other by singing in turns in 'guenee' or 'Macamba,' the work went smoothly and everyone benefitted by it."[2] Van Meeteren thinks that a *saam* had the advantage that the work was done much faster, because workers encouraged each other, which is very important, especially for strenuous labour in the fields.[3] Other writers confirm this conjecture. David Ames offers two explanations: working in a group both stimulates friendly competition among workers, and is more agreeable: "Working with one's companions, joking and singing, is obviously less tedious than solitary labour."[4]

In the second form of labour mutualism, the joint effort results in a *shared* product. The members of the collective gather once or several times to work together, for

---

1 See e.g., T.S. Epstein, *Economic Development and Social Change in South India* (Manchester: Manchester University Press, 1962), p. 73; Alan Dawley, *Class and Community. The Industrial Revolution in Lynn* (Cambridge, MA, and London: Harvard University Press, 1976), p. 57; Diana Wong, *Peasants in the Making. Malaysia's Green Revolution* (Singapore: Institute of Southeast Asian Studies, 1987), p. 120.
2 Nicolaas van Meeteren, *Volkskunde van Curaçao* (Willemstad: no publisher, 1947), p. 35.
3 *Ibid.*
4 David W. Ames, "Wolof Co-operative Work Groups", in: William R. Bascom and Melville J. Herskovits (eds), *Continuity and Change in African Cultures* (Chicago [etc.]: Chicago University Press, 1959), pp. 224–237, at 231.

the production of a good from which they all hope to benefit when it is finished. Collectively building a community centre or a church are good examples.

Labour mutualism often becomes less important when the role of money increases in the local economy. The tendency to buy labour tasks individually with money then usually grows. On Curaçao, the *saam* seems to have disappeared from the 1920s or 1930s onwards. Similar trends are visible in many places.[5] But there are also exceptions to this rule. In the case of the Maka in Southeastern Cameroon, the rise of the cash crop cultivation instead stimulated labour rotation, because the Maka refused to perform wage labour for the other villagers.[6]

It is a small step from labour mutuals to mutualist institutions, where the fund consists partly or wholly of goods or money. Labour rotation corresponds exactly to the simplest kind of the so—called *rotating and credit savings association* (ROSCA), in which, however, the labour input is replaced by a contribution in kind or in money. For example, an anthropological study in the early 1960s recorded that Indian migrants on the island of Mauritius operated a ROSCA called a *cycle* or *cheet:* "A man or a woman calls together a group of friends and neighbours. Suppose there are ten of them, and each puts in Rs. 10. They then draw lots and the winner takes the Rs. 100. (Sometimes the organizer automatically takes the first 'pool'.) The following month each again puts in Rs. 10, and another member takes the resulting Rs. 100; and so it continues for ten months until each member has had his Rs. 100."[7] In other words, sums of money were deposited in the *cheet*, but for the rest the logic was the same as in labour rotation. It is therefore not surprising that some scientists believe ROSCAs originated in rotating labour pools.[8] Whether this explanation is correct has yet to be established by empirical research.

But ROSCAs can also be much more complex than in the simple case outlined above. The allocation of the order of rotation is central to ROSCAs. It can be determined by a common arrangement among participants; an allocation by the organizer; by auction; or by drawing lots. In an auction, participants can of course exert a strong influence on the order of allocation, and this method can therefore lead to complex relations of debt and credit within the arrangement. In the case of Mauri-

---

[5] Charles J. Erasmus, "Culture, Structure and Process: The Occurrence and Disappearance of Reciprocal Farm Labor", *Southwestern Journal of Anthropology*, 12 (1956), pp. 444–469; Paul F. Brown, "Population Growth and the Disappearance of Reciprocal Labor in a Highland Peruvian Community", *Research in Economic Anthropology*, 8 (1987), pp. 225–245.
[6] Peter Geschiere, "Working Groups or Wage Labour? Cash-crops, Reciprocity and Money among the Maka of Southeastern Cameroon", *Development and Change*, 26 (1995), pp. 503–523.
[7] Burton Benedict, "Capital, Saving and Credit among Mauritian Indians", in: Raymond Firth and B.S. Yamey (eds), *Capital, Saving and Credit in Peasant Societies* (London: George Allen and Unwin, 1964), pp. 330–346, at 341.
[8] Anthony I. Nwabughuogu, "The *Isusu:* An Institution for Capital Formation among the Ngwa Igbo; its Origin and Development to 1951", *Africa*, 54, 4 (1984), pp. 46–58, at 47; Mark W. Delancey, "Credit for the Common Man in Cameroon", *Journal of Modern African Studies*, 15, 3 (1977), pp. 316–322, at 319.

tius, we find that, like the Indian immigrants on the island, the Chinese also had ROS-CAS. But these functioned in a different way:

> "The Chinese on the island – as elsewhere – operate a variant of the cycle in which the 'lenders' (late drawers) in effect receive interest payments from the 'borrowers' (early drawers). The participants bid for turns; a man in need of quick cash may bid to take Rs. 90 instead of Rs. 100, if permitted to draw first, or he may agree to put in a total of Rs. 110 over the cycle if he can have Rs. 100 immediately. Thus the other members of the cycle receive in due course more than their contributions; the difference is a form of interest paid to them by those with more urgent need of money. If the second and third drawings are bid for as well, the total interest payments to the more patient members increase."[9]

The number of varieties of allocation through ROSCAs that have been invented is astounding, and the arrangements could become very complex. Why some ROSCAs are more complex than others is still largely unknown.

The sum that has to be deposited in every "meeting" in a ROSCA can vary considerably. Large sums of money must for example have circulated in the rotating manumission funds with which Brazilian slaves-for-hire bought their freedom in the nineteenth century.[10] There are obviously goods too expensive to pay for with ordinary ROSCAS. Houses are a clear example. In general, they cost so much that households have to save many years for them (if indeed they can save this amount of money at all). In such cases, a ROSCA can be employed in which the members do not receive a payment in *every* round, but after *several* rounds. If, for instance, ten families each want a house worth 10,000 and if these families deposit 1,000 every year in a shared fund, then one family can buy a house after one year and after ten years all families have a house. Such 'extended' ROSCAs were established in the United States in the first half of the nineteenth century. Later they were introduced in many other countries. ROSCAs of this type were also referred to as "terminating societies", discontinued when all the founders had had their turn.

Scheduled demand and non-rotating allocation

As the ROSCAS are in a sense homologous to forms of rotating labour, the second form of labour allocation has a counterpart in the domain of goods and money. In

---

9 Benedict "Capital, Saving and Credit", p. 341; see also Maurice Freedman, "The Handling of Money: A Note on the Background to the Economic Sophistication of Overseas Chinese", (1959) in: Freedman, *The Study of Chinese Society: Essays*. Selected and Introduced by G. William Skinner (Stanford, CA: Stanford University Press, 1979), pp. 22–26.
10 Maria Cecilia Velasco e Cruz, "Puzzling Out Slave Origins in Rio de Janeiro Port Unionism: The 1906 Strike and the Sociedade de Resistência dos Trabalhadores em Trapiche e Café", *Hispanic American Historical Review*, 86, 2 (2006), pp. 205–245, at 223, observes, that "the model of the manumission funds "seems to have been the *esusu* [ROSCA], a Yoruba institution [...] that the African diaspora introduced in several parts of the Americas."

this variety, a group saves a certain amount of money by means of a periodic contribution. They can subsequently do one of three things with this sum. They can buy a common good that remains a collective possession (a joint good), they can distribute the saved sum again among the participants (individual allocation of money), or they can buy goods that will subsequently be distributed among the participants (individual allocation of goods).

A *joint good* can be anything. The Ethiopian *mahaber* is an example: "It usually has the purpose of providing assistance to those who are still in the countryside, not having migrated to an urban area. Thus, the residents of a principal city will meet periodically, and provide funds to support some project back in the home village or in the countryside, such as building a school, hospital, road, community hall, or furnishing one of these facilities, or some other needy purpose."[11]

A fund created to be allocated simultaneously can, in the meantime, also be used as a credit facility. In that case, all members of a group regularly deposit money in the fund, but they can also temporarily take money from it, promising to repay later. Usually, a member who takes out a loan will have to pay interest. Such an arrangement is also referred to as an Accumulating Savings and Credit Association (ASCRA).[12] Migrant workers in Cameroon have an institution which they call a *family meeting* or *country meeting*. These are associations of people from the same region, or from an area, where the same language is spoken. Delancey describes the arrangement:

> "The get-together frequently opens with some business transactions. Members contribute money to be held as savings by the associations until the end of the year, and the treasurer deposits these funds in a bank and/or may make interest-payable loans to members – and, occasionally, to non-members. All savings and accumulated interest are returned to the members in November or December, and this enables them to pay their heavy Christmas expenses. But many immediately return a large proportion of the accrued funds to the savings programme for the next year, which opens at the same meeting."[13]

When a group of people establishes a collective fund to buy means of production (instruments etc.) and starts a business on own account, this is actually a combined buying, production and selling cooperative employing its members. Such arrange-

---

11 Victor Gerdes, "Precursors of Modern Social Security in Indigenous African Institutions", *Journal of Modern African Studies*, 13 (1975), pp. 209–228, at 219.
12 F.J.A. Bouman, "ROSCA and ASCRA: Beyond the Financial Landscape", in: F.J.A. Bouman and O. Hospes (eds), *Financial Landscapes Reconstructed: The Fine Art of Mapping Development* (Boulder, CO: Westview Press, 1994), pp. 375–394, at 376–377.
13 Delancey, "Credit for the Common Man", p. 320. See also the case of the *pork societies* in Hong Kong's New Territories in the 1950s (Marjorie Topley, "Capital, Saving and Credit among indigenous Rice Farmers and Immigrant Vegetable Farmers in Hong Kong's New Territories", in: Raymond Firth and B.S. Yamey (eds), *Capital, Saving and Credit in Peasant Societies* (London: George Allen and Unwin, 1964), 157–86Topley, "Capital, Saving and Credit", p. 178).

ments have a long history. The association which fourteen unemployed piano makers set up in Paris, one and a half century ago, offers an illustration:

> "They began [...] by collecting contributions of a few pennies from each member. Since they worked from home, most owned some of the necessary material for their trade: they contributed to the society in kind. On 10 March 1849 they established the society with 2,000 francs worth of inventory and 229.50 francs in cash. Following this major accomplishment, the society was ready for clients. None came for two months. Of course, the members obtained neither profit nor salary; they survived by pawning their personal belongings. The fourth month they found a bit of repair work and earned some money. Dividing it amongst themselves, they obtained 6.60 francs apiece. Each member kept 5 francs from this modest dividend. The surplus (i.e. 1.60 francs per person) was used for a fraternal banquet with their wives and children to celebrate the association's auspicious beginning. [...] In June, a few weeks later, they had a windfall, an order for an entire piano costing 480 francs!"[14]

Contingent demand and non-rotating allocation

It is also possible that a collective fund is set up on the basis of periodic contributions, paid out in part or as a whole only when a calamity occurs. The savings fund is then used as an insurance scheme. Again, there are two varieties: the money is used to cover either individual risks or collective risks.

There is a *collective coverage of risks* when the group is threatened by a common danger – a danger that can only be averted by a joint good. Daniel Defoe provided an example, when he wrote about farmers in Essex, Kent, and the Isle of Ely, who were jointly maintaining walls against floods: they all contributed to the keeping up of those walls: "and if I have a piece of land in any level or marsh, though it bonds nowhere on the sea or river, yet I pay my proportion to the maintenance of the said wall or bank; and if at any time the sea breaks in, the damage is not laid upon the man in whose land the breach happened, unless it was by his neglect, but it lies on the whole land, and is called a level lot."[15]

There is an *individual coverage of risks* when members of an association are individually threatened by a danger, such as for instance illness, death, or disabilities caused by labour. In that case, all members may periodically contribute to a mutual insurance society, but only those members who need compensation for a specific reason receive a benefit from the fund. Mutual insurance societies are based on a variety of social categories. Workers have organized mutual insurance according to

---

[14] Charles Gide, *Les obstacles au développement des Coopératives de production* (Paris: Association pour l'enseignement de la Coopération, 1923), pp. 19–20. An account of an eyewitness can be found in: V.A. Huber, "Skizzen aus dem französischen Genossenschaftsleben", in: *V.A. Hubers Ausgewählte Schriften über Socialreform und Genossenschaftswesen*. Edited by K. Munding (Berlin, s.a. [c. 1895]), pp. 889–957, at 923–933.

[15] Daniel Defoe, *An Essay Upon Projects* (London: Tho. Cockerill, 1697), section "Of Friendly Societies".

their occupation, place of residence, neighborhood, ethnicity, religion, temperance, or a combination of these categories. They often excluded women and aged people. John Iliffe reports about such an insurance arrangement organized by immigrant casual labourers in the port of Dar-es-Salaam in 1937:

> "The subscription was Shs. 1.50 a month for committee members and Shs. 1.00 for ordinary members, relatively high figures because the union planned to provide benefits for its members. 'They say their union is for the purpose of helping one another when sick and for burial purposes,' it was reported, and the rules promised that 'the union will assist any member in distress.' [...] Besides their desire for security, the members also sought advancement. 'Every member should learn to read and write', the rules stated, for which purpose 'the Union will employ a teacher to instruct members in reading and writing'."[16]

It is not uncommon that mutualist associations are linked to each other directly or indirectly. People are sometimes members of several associations of the same type at once. A mutualist arrangement can also be transformed into a commercial enterprise, or a game of chance. And other forms of organization (guilds, for instance) can be transformed into mutualist associations. A special kind of transformation occurs when mutualist associations become permanent, or are formally institutionalized. If the rotation principle is from rotating associations, they can become institutionalized in this way. Institutionalized forms of non-rotating arrangements, such as ASCRAS, are well-known, for instance in the case of Credit Unions. Like many ASCRAs, their members share certain features, such as their religion or profession. They have a corporate structure, and their function is mainly to provide short-term cash credits to members at nominal rates of interest. In the course of the twentieth century, credit unions have spread from North America over large parts of the world.[17]

Men and women take part in all forms, but it seems that rotating associations are often made up mainly of women, whereas men comprise a relatively large part of contingent associations. A satisfactory explanation of this difference in gender composition has not yet been given.[18]

---

16 John Iliffe, "The Creation of Group Consciousness Among the Dockworkers of Dar-es-Salaam 1929–50", in: Richard Sandbrook and Robin Cohen (eds), *The Development of an African Working Class. Studies in Class Formation and Action* (London: Longman, 1975), pp. 49–72, at 55–56.
17 E. g., Eli Shapiro, *Credit Union Development in Wisconsin* (New York: Columbia University Press, 1947; reprint New York: AMS Press, 1968); Neil Runcie (ed.), *Credit Unions in the South Pacific: Australia, Fiji, New Zealand, Papua and New Guinea* (London: University of London Press, 1969).
18 See also Shirley Ardener and Sandra Burman (eds). *Money-Go-Rounds. The Importance of Rotating Savings and Credit Associations for Women* (Oxford and Washington, DC: Berg, 1995).

Threats and securities

Like any other collective activity, mutualist associations can also fail in many ways. In order to assess the specific nature of these threats, it is useful to remind ourselves of the essence of mutualist funds. In *all* cases, members contribute money, goods or labour to a shared fund, from which subsequently payments are made to some or to all members. In *some* cases, especially in scheduled non-rotating associations, members can also borrow money or goods from the fund for a certain period of time.

We can now distinguish between two fundamentally different kinds of threats. Firstly, there are *external* threats, i.e. threats against which participants in the arrangement can do very little on their own. These threats can take the following forms.[19]

- Members may no longer be able to deposit money or goods or pay off a loan, because of changed circumstances. Take for instance mutuals in a working-class area, where families are almost completely dependent on one employer for their income. In that case, the bankruptcy of the employer will also endanger the mutual arrangements in that working-class neighborhood.
- The fund of mutuals is threatened by violence, inflation, and so on. In China at the end of the nineteenth century, "the T'ai-píng rebellion, with its long train of sorrows, and the continual famines and floods of later years in Northern China, have tended to bring loan societies into discredit, because experience has shown that thousands of persons have put into them what could never be recovered."[20]
- Especially in contingent associations, the danger exists that a natural disaster or economic downturn can affect an entire population, so that many or all members of a mutual demand payment at the same time, and the fund is quickly exhausted. A friendly society whose members work in the building trade will get into great difficulty, for example, if a recession occurs in the building industry causing widespread unemployment among many members of the association at the same time, and makes them apply for a benefit.
- Apart from these external threats, there are also *internal* threats caused by individual imperfections.
- Individual members do not pay the deposit agreed upon. The severity of such defaults varies considerably. In rotating societies, it makes a big difference whether a participant failed to pay her contribution before she received her payment, or afterwards. In the first case, the damage is limited; in the second case, the other participants suffer a great loss.

---

19 Compare Shirley Ardener, "Women Making Money Go Round: ROSCAS Revisited", in: Ardener and Burman, *Money-Go-Rounds*, pp. 1–19, at 5–7.
20 Arthur H. Smith, *Village Life in China. A Study in Sociology* (New York [etc.]: Fleming H. Revell Company, 1899), p. 157.

- The administrator appropriates money illicitly from the fund, or manages it badly. The person who has the kitty in his home is continually tempted to borrow money from it "just for a short while." Hotze Lont noted that this is not uncommon in Java, where administrators "usually try to repay the loan before the association needs the money." In this way, their actions remain hidden and they continue to have personal access to a convenient source for financial emergencies. Sometimes, however, they lose control, and the fund suffers.[21]
- Especially in contingent organizations, members may claim a payment on false grounds by simulating illness, unemployment etc.
- Members may claim and receive a loan on false pretenses, or not repay a loan in time, or only partly, or not at all.

Mutuals cannot do much against *external* threats (like wars, crises etc.) as such. At best, they can in some cases try to make themselves less vulnerable by spreading the risk. Friendly societies, for example, reduced the likelihood that all members would suffer the same adversity at the same time by means of supra-regional amalgamation, which ensured that members came from different regions and trades. And some ROSCAs deliberately tried to recruit members with different economic backgrounds.[22]

Mutuals have many more ways of combatting *internal* threats. Mutuals that are part of a very close community will suffer relatively little fraud and default. Shirley Ardener already pointed out how much people in such circumstances were prepared to do to save face.[23] There are known cases of fathers who preferred that their daughters became prostitutes, rather than fail in their obligations to the local mutuals. Sometimes, 'technical' factors make fraud more dificult. It is, for instance, no coincidence that many mutual insurance associations initially focused on funerals, because it is very difficult to simulate death. Verification becomes more difficult if the social bonds between members of a mutual are not so strong or, in an even more extreme case, if members of a group do not even know each other personally. The last case is relatively unusual, although there are several known examples of this variant.[24] In case of asymmetrical information (when the founder of a mutual has insufficient information about the reliability of a candidate member), precautions become crucial.

---

[21] Hotze Lont, "Juggling Money in Yogyakarta. Financial Self-Help Organizations and the Quest for Security"' (Ph.D. thesis, Universiteit van Amsterdam, 2002), p. 188.
[22] Anon. "Partners: An Informal Savings Institution in Jamaica", *Social and Economic Studies*, 8 (1959), pp. 436–440, at 437.
[23] Shirley Ardener, "The Comparative Study of Rotating Credit Associations", *The Journal of the Royal Anthropological Institute*, 94 (1964), pp. 201–229.
[24] Abdoulaye Kane, "Les caméleons de la finance populaire au Sénégal et dans la diaspora" (Ph.D. thesis, Universiteit van Amsterdam, 2000), pp. 23 f.; Aspha Bijnaar, "Kasmoni. Spaarzame levensgenieters in Suriname en Nederland" (PhD thesis, Universiteit van Amsterdam, 2002).

In principle, there are three kinds of security measures available. Firstly, there are *rules for selection:* the threat to the arrangement can be reduced by only allowing persons to join who are likely to meet their obligations. Here are some examples.

- Entry is permitted only for persons with whom members have not just a financial relationship – for instance relatives, or people with the same ethnic background, or people who went to the same school.[25]
- Entry is permitted only for persons who are not likely to "disappear" suddenly without trace. If the mutual has a kitty which is more or less permanent, it is especially important to find an administrator who is firmly tied to a place in one way or another. In ROSCAs in Jamaica, for instance, it was a rule that the administrator should be a person "with real property, such as a home", and "with a permanent address where he can always be found."[26] Similarly, mutual benefit societies often entrusted their kitty to publicans or clergymen – persons who would risk a great deal, if they were found guilty of fraud.
- Entry of new, unknown members passes through a trial period or (in the case of rotating arrangements) puts them at the end of a cycle, so that potential deceit does little harm.
- New members are selected on the basis of their reputation or their good name, i.e. the probabilistic beliefs the others hold about the potential member's preferences or feasible actions.[27]
- Existing members act as guarantor for dubious members. In the Ethiopian *ekub* (a ROSCA), each member was obliged to supply one or more guarantors, who would pay in case of default, regardless of the reason why a member had failed to meet his obligations.[28]
- New members are required to pay an entrance fee or bond to encourage their loyalty, and/or are required to provide a security or collateral for the loan.

Monitoring provides a second means of security. This practice is especially important in mutual insurances. In his study of mutual aid societies in early nineteenth-century Paris, Michael Sibalis shows how closely members kept an eye on each other. On the one hand, *visiteurs* were appointed, who were supposed to visit those who received sick benefits – both in order to check them out, and as an act of charity. In this context, the articles of association state that "The obligations of the visitors consist of surveillance, benevolence and humanity. The interests of the Society are entrusted to them; they should not make an exception for anyone." Sometimes, the member of the board responsible for the selection of *visiteurs* was "not allowed to select them either from among his friends, or from among the neighbours who were too

---

25 Compare Gerdes, "Precursors of Modern Social Security", p. 215.
26 Anon., ""Partners"", p. 436.
27 Christopher J. Ellis, "Reputation", *The New Palgrave Dictionary of Money and Finance* (London: Macmillan, 1992), pp. 331–332.
28 Gerdes, "Precursors of Modern Social Security", p. 214.

close to the sick person."[29] On the other hand, ordinary members often spontaneously scrutinized each other as well, as happened in 1823 when "a society of engravers cancelled the sick benefits of a member named Vialard when someone spotted him drunk in a wineshop."[30]

Sanctions are a third precaution. We can distinguish between external and internal sanctions. In the case of internal sanctions, members of the mutual meet out punishments themselves. It is important to know in this case in whose direct interest it is that the rules of the mutual are adhered to. If all the members have to pay for a loss together, they all benefit by punishing the offender. But if for example it was agreed that the coordinator of a ROSCA personally would act as guarantor for default or fraud[31] only that person has an immediate interest in the punishment. In the case of external sanctions, either officials (the state authorities) can administer punishment, or the larger community (such as the entire village). Such sanctions sometimes have a formal character, but they are often informal as well: in that case, the defaulter quite simply loses his reputation, and is therefore unable to join a mutual again. In the case of the Ethiopian mutual insurance *idir*, "any members in arrears for two or more consecutive periods may be expelled – this news quickly spreads, and an ex-member may be barred from joining another *idir*."[32]

Conclusion

Mutualist arrangements were and are operated around the world. However, the frequency of their occurrence varies considerably, depending on the social context. Associations with scheduled demand seem to be especially common in poor countries, and among migrants in poor *and* rich countries. Associations with contingent demand seem to be universal, but in advanced capitalist countries they lost their small-scale and non-bureaucratic character, insofar they had not been replaced altogether by government provisions. What is the explanation for the popularity of mutualism, or the lack of it, in given social and historical circumstances?

There have of course always been alternatives for mutualism.[33] Indeed, anyone with a certain degree of autonomy who regularly needs money, goods or labour can usually borrow these on an individual, private basis, from other people in his or her direct social environment. In the case of fairly small sums of money, one

---

29 Michael David Sibalis, "The Mutual Aid Societies of Paris, 1789–1848", *French History*, 3, 1 (March 1989), pp. 1–30, at 17.
30 Ibid., pp. 16–7.
31 As in the *cundina*. See Donald V. Kurtz, "The Rotating Credit Association: An Adaptation to Poverty", *Human Organization*, 32 (1973), pp. 49–58.
32 Gerdes, "Precursors of Modern Social Security", pp. 215–6.
33 See e.g., Peer Smets, "Housing Finance and the Urban Poor: Building and Financing Low-Income Housing in Hyderabad, India" (Ph.D. thesis, Vrije Universiteit Amsterdam, 2002), Chapter 4.

can often appeal to relatives or acquaintances. In the case of larger amounts of money, approaching a superior and asking for credit would be the obvious thing to do. In all these cases, a relationship of dependence is formed, which can impede personal freedom and, in the case of patronage by a superior, could even result in debt bondage. It is therefore likely that, normally, one would only resort to this kind of solution if, for some reason, other solutions were not possible.

These other solutions fall, broadly speaking, into two categories: mutualism and formal institutions, such as banks and insurance companies. What factors play a part in the choice between these alternatives? No doubt, an important aspect of this choice is that mutualism is usually more than just a form of "micro-finance". Apart from their manifest function of redistribution, mutualist associations usually have a latent function as well: they satisfy a need for company, and a sense of community solidarity. There is, especially among new immigrants, a great need for "clubs" and similar organizations, because they help the newcomers to adjust.[34]

The sociable character of mutualist arrangements and their roots in communities differs from banks and insurance companies in important respects. In the first place, mutualism offers a solution to people who lack the will to save a certain amount of money or goods on their own. By means of mutualism, an individual may reach what Jon Elster called "imperfect rationality": an individual recognizes his or her own weakness, and voluntarily appeals to external compulsion to realize what he or she would not achieve by him or herself.[35]

A second difference is that mutualist associations are often psychologically and/ or practically more accessible than banks: official institutions are sometimes located at a great distance, and one has to be prepared to make a long journey to visit them; banks ask for a surety or guarantors for a loan, while mutualist arrangements need not do so in most cases because the participants know each other personally; official institutions are impersonal and formal, whereas mutualist associations are personal

---

[34] ROSCAS are very common among migrants. In Papua New Guinea in the 1970s, ROSCAS were known among migrants in the towns as "sundaying" or "fortnighting." One author comments: "it is a characteristic of the labouring and lower income groups from all parts of Papua New Guinea; it is not typical of public servants or other white collar workers." In a sample of 28 working families in Lae, 22 heads of family engaged in "sundaying" and in a sample of 89 migrant workers around Goroka, 59 "sundayed", percentages 66 and 79 respectively. Skeldon regards this as a process of adaptation: "The system appears to recreate in a modified form the cycles of debt and credit, of exchange and reciprocity in the traditional society. It helps to integrate the migrant into a network of social responsibility in the urban environment." Ronald Skeldon, "Regional Associations among Urban Migrants in Papua New Guinea", *Oceania*, 50 (1979–1980), pp. 248–272, at 252–253.

[35] Jon Elster, *Ulysses and the Sirens. Studies in Rationality and Irrationality* (Cambridge [etc.]: Cambridge University Press, and Paris: Editions de la Maison des Sciences de l'Homme, 1979), Chapter 2; see also Abram de Swaan, *In Care of the State. Health Care, Education, and Welfare in Europe and the USA in the Modern Era* (Cambridge: Polity Press, 1988), pp. 144–145.

and informal;³⁶ official institutions sometimes operate considerable financial or legal barriers.³⁷

---

36 F.J.A. Bouman and K. Harteveld. "The Djanggi, A Traditional Form of Saving and Credit in West Cameroon", *Sociologia Ruralis*, 16 (1976), pp. 103–118, at 115–116.
37 In Papua New Guinea, for instance, the colonial authorities had, for a long time, laid down restrictions on the access of Chinese migrants to banks. "According to Chinese informants, the first bank loan was not granted to a Chinese until the 1950s." David Y.H. Wu, "To Kill Three Birds With One Stone: The Rotating Credit Associations of the Papua New Guinea Chinese", *American Ethnologist*, 1 (1974), pp. 565–583, at 570–571.

Suggested reading

Ardener, Shirley and Sandra Burman (eds). *Money-Go-Rounds. The Importance of Rotating Savings and Credit Associations for Women* (Oxford and Washington, DC: Berg, 1995).
Ardener, Shirley. "The Comparative Study of Rotating Credit Associations", *The Journal of the Royal Anthropological Institute*, 94 (1964), pp. 201–229.
Bouman, F.J.A. and K. Harteveld. "The Djanggi, A Traditional Form of Saving and Credit in West Cameroon", *Sociologia Ruralis*, 16 (1976), pp. 103–118.
Brown, Paul F. "Population Growth and the Disappearance of Reciprocal Labor in a Highland Peruvian Community", *Research in Economic Anthropology*, 8 (1987), pp. 225–245.
De Swaan, Abram and Marcel van der Linden (eds). *Mutualist Microfinance. Informal Saving Funds from the Global Periphery to the Core?* (Amsterdam: Aksant, 2006).
Erasmus, Charles J. "Culture, Structure and Process: The Occurrence and Disappearance of Reciprocal Farm Labor", *Southwestern Journal of Anthropology*, 12 (1956), pp. 444–469.
Geschiere, Peter. "Working Groups or Wage Labour? Cash-crops, Reciprocity and Money among the Maka of Southeastern Cameroon", *Development and Change*, 26 (1995), pp. 503–523.
Kurtz, Donald V. "The Rotating Credit Association: An Adaptation to Poverty", *Human Organization*, 32 (1973), pp. 49–58.
Raymond Firth and B.S. Yamey (eds), *Capital, Saving and Credit in Peasant Societies* (London: George Allen and Unwin, 1964).
Sibalis, Michael David. "The Mutual Aid Societies of Paris, 1789–1848", *French History*, 3, 1 (March 1989), pp. 1–30.
Van der Linden, Marcel (ed.). *Social Security Mutualism.The Comparative History of Mutual Benefit Societies* (Bern: Peter Lang, 1996).
Wu, David Y.H. "To Kill Three Birds With One Stone: The Rotating Credit Associations of the Papua New Guinea Chinese", *American Ethnologist*, 1 (1974), pp. 565–583.

Matthias van Rossum
8.2. Desertion

From conscripts and coolies, to housemaids and peasants, most workers in history were not entirely free to leave their work at their own choosing. In response to this, to walk away, despite restrictions and punishments, has been perhaps the most important form of resistance to injustice, inequality, or exploitation. Although the strategy of running away has received limited attention, from academic scholars and from political and labour activists alike, its persistent and widespread character seems to indicate that it might have been one of the most accessible and effective ways to gain (or regain) some degree of control over one's life.[1]

It is therefore no wonder that the theme of people escaping injustice and hardship keeps recurring, from the workers building the pyramids to the workers building the Qatar World Championship football stadiums, or servants working in embassies in a city like The Hague, in the Netherlands.[2] For historians, therefore, the act of running away is significant in multiple ways. Whether it concerns desertion, absconding, or some other form of criminalized absence, the act itself simultaneously reveals the bonds and the agency of labour. This chapter aims to give an overview of historical patterns of desertion across the globe and to provide insight into the continuous battle between actors aiming to control workers and workers striving for autonomy or betterment through strategies of running.

Some views on runaways

The act of running away has been perceived in contrasting ways. First, it has been discarded as a "prepolitical" or even "apolitical" form of resistance.[3] Second, it has been interpreted as a form of "everyday resistance". Studying peasants in postcolonial Malaysia, James Scott associated desertion with "Brechtian – or Schweikian

---

[1] The text builds upon the collective efforts made during the session "Leaving Work across the World" at the conference of the European Network for International Universal and Global History (ENIUGH) in Paris in 2014 (co-organized with Jeannette Kamp) and the international workshops on "Runaways: Desertion and Mobility in Global Labor History, c. 1650–1850" in Amsterdam in 2015 and Pittsburgh in 2016 (co-organized with Titas Chakraborty, Leo Lucassen, and Marcus Rediker). I am grateful to all the contributors, and especially to Titas Chakraborty and Jeannette Kamp, who have greatly contributed to the insights on this topic.
[2] Reports on exploitation in Qatar: Peter Walker, "Dutch Union Suing Fifa over 'Modern Slavery' at Qatar 2022 World Cup Sites in Landmark Case", *The Independent*, 11 October 2016. Reports on maltreatment in embassies in the Netherlands: Marjon Bolwijn, "Bedienden van diplomaten melden uitbuiting op ambassades in Nederland", *De Volkskrant*, 14 July 2016.
[3] Eugene Genovese, *Roll, Jordan, Roll. The World the Slaves Made* (New York, 1974), p. 598.

– forms of class struggle".[4] A third perspective might be found in the notion that "desertion and exodus are a powerful form of class struggle".[5] Desertion, therefore, has been categorized as a form of non-, passive, or active resistance.

There is a distinct difference between the two last perspectives. In their study of new forms of power, Michael Hardt and Antonio Negri deal with desertion as part of "the refusal of exploitation", pointing out that "whereas in the disciplinary era sabotage was the fundamental notion of resistance, in the era of imperial control it may be desertion".[6] Their examples, in which "the desertion of productive cadres disorganized and struck at the heart of the disciplinary system", seem to indicate, however, that desertion was an important form of resistance in earlier times too.[7]

Although seemingly very similar, this perspective is notably different from a perspective in which desertion is part of a repertoire of everyday resistance. This can be seen in the work of Scott. He described everyday forms of resistance as having "certain features in common. They require little or no coordination or planning; they make use of implicit understandings and informal networks; they often represent a form of individual self-help; they typically avoid any direct, symbolic confrontation with authority."[8] Marc Bloch referred to the "patient, silent struggles stubbornly carried on by rural communities".[9] For both, these strategies were something that set the peasantry apart from other workers – namely the workers studied in an earlier phase that focused on histories from below, those working for wages, finding their place in early industries and susceptible to growing class consciousness. Scott dealt with desertion from this perspective as one of the "forms of reluctant compliance" – often going hand in hand with "intrusion [...] of 'offstage' attitudes into the performance [of compliance] itself, an intrusion sufficient to convey its meanings to the directors but not so egregious as to risk a confrontation".[10]

A new wave of studies on desertion considers running away (deserting, absconding, being absent) as a significant workers' strategy that can be studied as an independent historical phenomenon.[11] This leads to a different perspective in several ways. Firstly, partly following new approaches in global labour history, the everyday act of running away appears as a phenomenon that cuts through, and binds across, the dividing lines of different kinds of workers, rather than being located in one specific sector, mode of production, or labour relation. Secondly, the notion that deser-

---

4 James C. Scott, *Weapons of the Weak. Everyday Forms of Peasant Resistance* (New Haven, CT, 1985), p. xvi.
5 Michael Hardt and Antonio Negri, *Empire* (Cambridge, MA, 2000), pp. 208, 213.
6 *Ibid.*, p. 212.
7 *Ibid.*, p. 214.
8 Scott, *Weapons*, p. xvi.
9 Marc Bloch, *French Rural History* (Berkeley, CA, 1970), p. 170.
10 Scott, *Weapons*, p. 26.
11 Forthcoming from various meetings on this topic (see footnote 1); Matthias van Rossum and Jeannette Kamp (eds), *Desertion in the Early Modern World: A Comparative History* (London, 2016).

tion was a form of resistance within the spectrum of compliant behaviour is contested. Running away might often have been – although this was clearly not always the case – a form of passive resistance (evading a direct stand-off); it was simultaneously an active form of conscious non-compliance. It entailed people walking away, against orders or restrictions. Thirdly, studying desertion in such a way confronts the pervasive idea that forms of running away were merely a negative act. Running away appears as an attempt to gain or regain some control over one's living and working conditions. And, as such, desertion was very clearly marked by ideas of justice and by aspirations of creating a better life.

It is crucial to note that the effects of desertion stretched further than the runaways' lives. Social and labour historians might be inclined to think about "the nature of resistance" as being "greatly influenced by the existing forms of labor control and by beliefs about the probability and severity of retaliation".[12] The global histories of runaways and their impact show, however, that the reverse was also true. The nature of labour control is greatly influenced by existing forms of resistance. The impact of everyday forms of resistance extended much further than undermining policies, positive reform, or the deployment of "more coercion" by the state.[13] Employers and states responded directly to acts of desertion – and not only by cruel punishments or more lenient policies, but by a seemingly limitless inventiveness in their endeavours to confine and control their workers.

Especially during the last five centuries, developments in the fields of globalization and control appear to have deeply impacted patterns of and opportunities for the autonomous mobility of workers. The struggle for control over mobility and labour has, in turn, thoroughly changed social, economic, and political relations around the world. Affecting millions of lives across the globe, the expanding world economy mobilized vast numbers of workers through intensely controlled and coerced forms of labour and mobility. From roughly 1500 onwards, the worldwide mobilization of labour needed for the production, processing, and transport of global commodities was directly linked to the spread and intensification of arrangements ranging from slavery to contract labour, and from corvée to convict labour. The most common response of these workers was to run away, run back home, or go into hiding. Such forms of autonomous mobility became the main driving force behind a global transformative process of shifting forms of exploitation and increasingly advanced modes of control over society.

---

12 Scott, *Weapons*, p. 34.
13 *Ibid*, pp. 35–36.

Defining desertion

Authorities and employers defined various forms of unpermitted absence from work as breaches of law or labour obligations, creating different concepts of desertion. The largest multinational of the seventeenth century, the Dutch East India Company (Vereenigde Oost-Indische Compagnie), for example, distinguished between the connected notions of *desertie* (desertion), *absentie* (absence), and *fugie* (fleeing).[14] Seeing the commonalities in these kinds of running away leads to an inclusive or broad definition of desertion that includes all cases in which workers decided to remain absent or walk away despite informal or formal restrictions placed on their mobility or their exiting the labour relationship. Such a history of desertion is highly relevant, especially if we take into account the fact that in many places in the world withdrawing oneself from the work process was a punishable offence well into the twentieth century.

Such an open definition includes, of course, labour relations in which the coercive and binding elements are outspoken (slave labour, corvée labour, convict labour), but also includes labour relations in which the mobility of workers was constrained in other ways, such as through binding labour contracts (military, maritime, and colonial labour), domestic regimes and laws (servants in households), and apprenticeship systems.[15] This means there was a large variety not only in the different groups of workers, but also in the regimes and actors involved (corporations, heads of households, urban and state governments). It is therefore important to look at the refined mechanisms of the formal and informal regulatory regimes affecting people in both working and living environments.

Definitions were not always as clear-cut as one might expect. The lines between temporary absence and more permanent forms of desertion were often fuzzy. Especially for contract workers, some degree of absence was tolerated.[16] Absence could lead to desertion if a worker remained absent too long.[17] For slaves, similar distinctions were employed, such as *petit marronage* (temporary absenteeism) and the permanent *grand marronage*.[18] Under the VOC, temporary absence by slaves was dealt

---

[14] Matthias van Rossum, "'Working for the Devil': Desertion in the Eurasian Empire of the VOC", in: idem and Kamp, *Desertion*, pp. 127–160.
[15] See, for example, Alessandro Stanziani, *Bondage. Labor and Rights in Eurasia from the Sixteenth to the Early Twentieth Centuries* (New York and Oxford, 2014). Idem, "Runaways: A Global History", in: van Rossum and Kamp, *Desertion*, pp. 15–30.
[16] Karwan Fatah-Black, "Desertion by Sailors, Slaves and Soldiers in the Dutch Atlantic, c. 1600–1800", in: van Rossum and Kamp, *Desertion*, pp. 97–126; Pepijn Brandon, "'The Privilege of Using Their Legs': Leaving the Dutch Army in the Eighteenth Century", in: van Rossum and Kamp, *Desertion*, pp. 73–96; van Rossum, "'Working for the Devil'".
[17] Jeannette Kamp, "Between Agency and Force: The Dynamics of Desertion in a Military Labour Market, Frankfurt am Main 1650–1800", in: van Rossum and Kamp, *Desertion*, pp. 49–72.
[18] Fatah-Black, "Desertion".

with under domestic law and desertion by the criminal courts.[19] The authorities actively struggled in employing definitions and legal distinctions.[20]

Labour, resistance, and running

The act of desertion has always been closely connected to other strategies of resistance. It was often just one of the options available to workers. To understand its role and functioning, it is therefore important to locate it in the wider landscape of workers' strategies. Besides desertion – understood as temporary or permanent exit – there were the options of voice and loyalty (Hirschman) or acquiescence (in later reformulations of the trilogy).[21] These strategies could be employed individually or collectively. This results in a whole range of opposing, overlapping and interrelated possible strategies (as indicated in Figure 1).

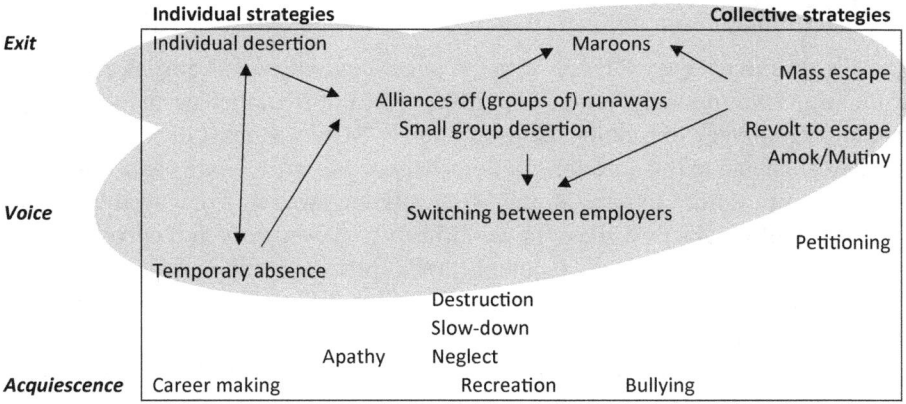

Figure 1. Forms of desertion (grey) and the range of strategies of individual and collective workers

Within this range of workers' strategies, desertion served not only as a negative act (passive resistance) in which workers, either individually or collectively, merely

---

19 Kate J. Ekama, "Just Deserters: Runaway Slaves from the VOC Cape, c. 1700–1800", in: van Rossum and Kamp, *Desertion*, pp. 161–186.
20 This passage stems from Jeannette Kamp and Matthias van Rossum, "Introduction: Leaving Work Across the World", in: van Rossum and Kamp, *Desertion*, pp. 3–14, at 8. For the difficulties faced by the authorities in employing definitions and legal distinctions, see van Rossum, "'Working for the Devil'", pp. 135–137.
21 Marcel van der Linden, "Mass Exits: Who, Why, How?", in: van Rossum and Kamp, *Desertion*, pp. 31–48.

rejected working conditions and power relations. It was simultaneously a strategic act, varyingly aimed at negotiation, at an improvement in collective or individual circumstances, at finding better jobs, or even at social mobility.[22] Desertion, therefore, must be studied both as running from as well as running towards.[23] One common pattern among soldiers in early modern Europe, for example, was to collect the advances promised at recruitment and to disappear before they had sworn their oath. In the context of competing trading companies and armies, contract workers would desert in order to enlist with competing employers offering higher wages, better treatment, or career opportunities. Throughout history, skilled workers especially, such as sailors, artisans, and even administrators, or merchants, have gained by playing out employers against each other, despite legal restrictions.[24] Some of these acts of desertion sometimes seem closer to the strategy of voice than that of exit. At the same time, some forms of temporary absence could be closer to the strategies of acquiescence.

Typical runaways

The act of running away fitted in with the larger landscape of strategies available to workers and was not limited to one specific group. But who, then, were most likely to employ the strategy of running? This question – "Who was most likely to run?" – is intimately related to the question "Under what circumstances were people more likely to attempt to run?" In general, the act of running away was practiced by most of the dominant groups of workers in world history: slaves, serfs and corvée workers, conscripted workers, convict labourers (POWs, prisoners), apprentices and household workers, contract workers, indentured workers, and wage workers on jobs in closed environments.

A range of factors in two domains seems to have deeply impacted the occurrence of desertion: factors related to the experience of working life, and to that of the alternative options available. The motives of runaways were closely related to these factors pushing and pulling people into mobility. Throughout history, and even for much of that part of history that could be associated with capitalism, the incentives to work leaned more to the elements of coercion and compensation than that of

---

22 This point has also been raised in Kamp and van Rossum, "Introduction". On markets in the early modern world: Jan Lucassen, "Deep Monetization, Commercialization and Proletarianization: Possible Links, India 1200–1900", in: Sabyasachi Bhattacharya (ed.), *Towards a New History of Work* (New Delhi, 2014), pp. 17–55; Jan Lucassen, *Een geschiedenis van de arbeid in grote lijnen* (Amsterdam, 2012).
23 See the introduction and other contributions in van Rossum and Kamp, *Desertion*.
24 Kamp, "Between Agency and Force"; *idem* and van Rossum, "Introduction".

commitment.²⁵ The act of desertion or running away testifies to this, as it occurred in situations entailing constraints of some kind on the workers' mobility, resulting from the ties created through coercion or payment. These constraints expressed themselves through institutions (labour relations), laws (and punishment), or physical measures (being confined to worksites, pass systems). The labour relations involved were not necessarily completely coerced (slavery, corvée labour); they could also entail labour relations that are generally perceived as more "free", but that were marked by specific measures of control forced upon the worker (for instance, all kinds of wage labour where exit or movement were restricted – as was the case with sailors, contract workers, and migrants, for example).

Working life

The experience of being coerced and controlled was therefore one of the main motives for desertion. This could be caused by involuntary entry into labour relations caused by physical or legal coercion, as in the case of convicted, enslaved, drafted, or pressganged workers. It could also be caused by deceit, as was often the case with contract workers in labour markets relying on mediated forms of recruitment – focused, for centuries, on public places such as drinking houses and lodges. The experience of coercion was not limited to recruitment, but could be at the core of the labour relation. Once employed, or under the control of a state, employer, or one's physical owner, workers could be forced into unwanted mobility – being taken away to work in remote and unfamiliar places was at the core of the experience of contract workers, such as soldiers and sailors, but also of that of slaves and convicts. Workers could also be forced to work, through hard forms of discipline and even outright forms of physical violence.

Related to the constrained and coercive working situations, issues around criminalized behaviour and the threat of punishment could be an important motive to desert. Punishments could be dealt out for physical crimes (violence on the work floor), property crime (destruction, theft), or various forms of criminalized behaviour (such as temporary absence from the worksite, deviant social or sexual behaviour, but also forms of workers' negotiation or resistance). All this was heavily affected by the process of increasing criminalization of behaviour on the work floor and in other aspects of social life – through the increased regulation of mobility, labour conflicts, and forms of behaviour.

Working conditions – and the failure to pursue or negotiate their improvement – could provide another range of motives to run away. Motives related to working conditions point to the importance of workers' rights and their violation (actual or per-

---

25 For the incentives offered by work, see Chris Tilly and Charles Tilly, *Work under Capitalism* (Oxford, 1998).

ceived) in enticing workers to vote with their feet. These workers' rights could be part of broader sets of sociocultural expectations and conventions, but they were also part of the implicit or explicit "deals" engrained in specific labour relations. Typically, these entailed complaints about the supply or quality of food and drink – as often, for most of the labour relations involved, these were part of a worker's compensation for work. Other circumstances at work could be important as well. Safety risks and disease were reason to respond, especially for contract and corvée workers. Being made to perform kinds of work other than what had been agreed upon – or agreed through contract or custom – could be a reason to run, not only for contract and corvée workers, but even for enslaved workers.

Issues concerning payment were very specific to labour relations in which compensation was an important part of the set of workers' incentives. Contract workers especially might desert if employers paid them irregularly or seemed to be unable to pay them at all. Low wages were another important motive to leave an employer, despite all kinds of obligations, regulations, or measures to prevent wage workers from leaving. Discontent related to forms of compensation as a motive for running away was not exclusive to waged contract labourers however; it was also common to other kinds of workers receiving compensation in non-monetary form, such as slaves and corvée workers. Manto, the slave of an eighteenth-century Batavia bookkeeper, declared that he "had decided to run away [*drossen*] because his master did not want to give him money to buy *pinang*" – a stimulant.[26]

Alternative options

The possibility of improving one's working conditions – a pull factor – was directly related to the issues of poor working conditions and insufficient or irregular compensation. Workers could run away in order to seek better compensation (wages or otherwise), better circumstances, or better treatment. These motives were, again, not limited to wage labourers, but extended to slaves and corvée workers as well. A crucial factor motivating workers to run away could be the aim of achieving more autonomy. Freeing themselves from bonds, runaways could end up in different labour relations (from enslaved or corvée worker to wage labour for example) or in alternative ways of living (from living as a wage or enslaved worker to living in forms of maroon societies, i.e. societies of runaway slaves).

---

26 Nationaal Archief (NA), VOC archive, inv. no. 9510, case H and K, cited in Matthias van Rossum, *Kleurrijke Tragiek. De geschiedenis van slavernij in Azië onder de VOC* (Hilversum, 2015), p. 66.

Ambiguous factors

Several factors complicated this deserters' landscape of incentives to run away or towards a different situation. These factors were ambiguous in the sense that they could be both incentives as well as deterrents for workers to leave their current situation. One obvious factor were the social ties that might bind workers, or entice them to run away from, or back to, specific living and working environments. Even among those workers often perceived to have been completely proletarianized (sailors, soldiers) or socially dead (slaves), this social dimension of workers' lives was crucial in attempts to forge geographical mobility. Social mobility could be another important ambiguous factor.

In specific situations, strategies of loyalty could pay out for workers, leading to advancement in rank or payment in return for cooperation with employers, masters, or superiors. These dynamics are clear, of course, for the hierarchical world of wage labourers, but similar dynamics could also be at play for other kinds of workers, such as corvée labour, slaves, and even convicts. This would reduce desertion in every situation in which more experienced and loyal workers might receive more benefits, more influence on the work process, or be raised to the rank of "overseer". The opposite effect of these dynamics would be – in contrast to those "strategies of loyalty" aimed at making a career under one's current master – the potential for opportunistic strategies in which deserters aimed to find higher-ranked jobs or better career opportunities elsewhere.

One of the most crucial ambiguous factors was indebtedness. Especially among wage labourers, this could be a mechanism binding workers to their jobs. Indebtedness could, however, also be used to lure workers into new jobs and away from their old ones. From the perspective of the range of decisions available to workers, it could be worthwhile to stay around in order to make use of the credit opportunities offered by employers; alternatively, it could be risky, but profitable, to leave one's debts behind by deserting.

Some universal patterns of desertion

Although running away was a strategy common to almost all workers, across the boundaries of different labour relations, the specific forms through which these strategies were employed could be very different. Just as the strategy of running away was not limited to specific groups of workers, nor was it limited to specific environments. Workers ran towards, or away from, urban centres, rural regions, maritime spaces, and frontier territories. The different characteristics of the environments from which runaways fled, or ran towards, were therefore important in shaping the patterns of desertion. The dynamics at work were, as we will see, not only geographical, but also economic, political, and social.

Urban centres were places of recruitment and mobility. Some cities were crucial in the recruitment of contract migrant workers such as sailors and soldiers. Cities often harboured opportunities to find casual wage labour. Like villages, smaller towns could be close-knit communities with high degrees of social control. Larger cities, however, provided a certain degree of anonymity, and these places especially could be interesting places to flee to, with runaways hiding in the urban sprawl. Cities therefore became places highly invested with ways of keeping populations manageable, developing mechanisms of control and spatial segregation.[27] Rural regions were places of production, and for most of history therefore also places with high (although possibly seasonal) demand for labour. Here, the less densely populated rural terrains could provide opportunities for runaways, either by making use of possibilities for mobility and casual labour, or by finding spaces that provided opportunities to move into independent agriculture. Cities and rural environments were complemented by two sectors that created their own environment for mobility, labour, and opportunities for runaways – the maritime and military. Especially in the early modern world, the ongoing mobility ingrained in maritime and military work – and the often uncontrolled international recruitment – made these sectors highly susceptible to desertion, but also made them places of refuge for runaways from other environments.

Throughout history, life and work in cities and agricultural production areas, connected through maritime or overland connections, were surrounded by clear frontiers or borderlands. These could be zones between different empires or political entities, zones between regions that had already been incorporated into the dynamics of the early global economy and regions that had not, or zones between more densely populated areas and their natural frontiers. In all these cases, the frontier zones were marked by economic opportunities for workers – higher demand often led to higher wages and better bargaining positions – as well as detrimental effects – higher levels of coercion, less control, or poorer working conditions. The options for running away were often more strongly influenced by the context in which workers operated. Frontier situations could mean that control over workers became near "totalized" or – the opposite – almost absent. Simultaneously, geographical conditions could be harsh, limiting opportunities to run, or very favourable, opening up the possibility of running away with the aim of establishing or joining communities with independent or self-sustaining ways of living.

Each of these four environments (cities, rural areas, maritime and military spaces, and borderlands) could support runaway workers. In terms of mobility, four options were available to these runaways: they could move away, move back, move through, or remain (in hiding). Looking at the strategy of running away from

---

[27] Jeannette M. Kamp, "Controlling Strangers – Identifying Migrants in Early Modern Frankfurt am Main", in: Hilde Greefs and Anne Winter (eds), *Migration Policies and the Materiality of Identification in European Cities, 1500–2000* (forthcoming); Jeannette Kamp, "Female Crime and Household Control in Early Modern Frankfurt am Main", *The History of the Family*, 21, 4 (2016), pp. 531–550.

this perspective, several patterns can be discerned, often strongly related to the dynamics of specific types of labour. The fact that these were recurring and deeply engrained patterns seems to indicate that they were transmitted through the continuous sharing of experiences and perhaps even conscious traditions.

The first pattern we encounter is a very pragmatic use of running away as a means of representing one's interests or of employing bargaining power by deserting in order to profit from switching employers. This was done mainly by workers in some kind of commodified labour relation, mainly sailors, soldiers, artisans, and servants. Examples of "jumping ship", "enlisting somewhere else", or going to a "different master" point at the use of mobility by workers in relation to the process of recruitment. It indicates that workers in commodified settings designed repertoires through which they exploited opportunities of competition between employers (and authorities), while actively contesting the increasing regulations put in place to control labour, markets, and mobility. Examples of such traditions can be found for large parts of the world.[28]

A very specific variation on this pattern existed among soldiers, who developed a strategy that could best be described as "taking your advance (and run)". Throughout the early modern period, officers and intermediaries seeking soldiers for their armies often competed in or around the same recruitment centres, paying or promising advances to new recruits to lure them in. It could be attractive for soldiers to sign up, take the advance, and run. This seems to have happened in regions where multiple recruiting actors and authorities were in close proximity, making mechanisms of control relying on passes and policing more complex and difficult to impose. Soldiers seem to have actively shared their knowledge of places of recruitment and the landscape of control.[29]

Strategies of running away could also be part of forms of negotiation or resistance on the job. One major example of this existed in the form of taking time off. Both in the individual and collective form, this was basically a way to actively extend or defend the rights of workers in practice within the context of their current working situation. Examples, again, can be found for situations all over the globe and throughout history. Sailors were known for "taking shore time", getting drunk and remaining absent for longer than allowed in port cities before returning to their vessels. Drinking might also mean that sailors could be physically unable to work while on board their ship. Artisans, mainly in Europe, were known to have (more or less collective) traditions such as Blue Monday. For workers in the position of servant, these strategies are likely to have been more individual. Slaves in both the Atlantic and in Asia engaged in *petit marronage* – being absent for a few days. Patterns of taking time off would mostly be characterized by short periods of time and short dis-

---

28 Van Rossum and Kamp, *Desertion*; Devleena Ghosh, "Under the Radar of Empire: Unregulated Travel in the Indian Ocean", *Journal of Social History*, 45, 2 (2011), pp. 497–514.
29 Kamp, "Between Agency and Force".

tances. Knowledge of the policies of punishment by employers (and cooperating authorities), as well as their level of dependence on the labour of the absconding workers, were crucial for assessing both the scope for manoeuvre and the limitations on these kinds of action.

Collective walking away from the job could also be part of explicit bargaining strategies concerning working conditions, such as payment, time off, treatment, or other aspects.[30] Soldiers – often organized in regiments or entire armies – were known to employ the threat of leaving to negotiate higher or actual payment of wages. Communities with specific labour rights or (the opposite) specific duties would at times use collective forms of exit to communicate grievances or dissent to employers and authorities. Guilds in the Low Countries organized *uytganghen* – collective walkouts, with guild members leaving the city as part of their negotiating strategy. The cinnamon peelers of early modern Sri Lanka were known to use collective temporary exit in a similar way. This seems consistent with other examples of walkouts as part of negotiating strategies, such as those of corvée workers. Sailors would sometimes leave the ship and row ashore as part of their strike. Here, mobility became part of a negotiating strategy, often with strong and explicit appeals to labour rights as part of existing perceptions of moral economies. The collective withdrawal – and mobility – of workers often drew the attention of the authorities as well as of a wider audience, creating a public spectacle that enlarged the space in which the workers could manoeuvre, while establishing a form of security for them during their action. However, this also raised the stakes considerably, and increased the likelihood of more severe punitive retaliation by employers or authorities.

The collective walking away aimed at returning was, therefore, closely linked to forms of collective walking away without returning. In the case of soldiers, negotiation could lead to them leaving and switching to other employers. The longer and more difficult the negotiations were, the less likely it was that the soldiers would return. For workers in more mobile or footloose occupations, such as sailors and soldiers, it seemed easier to accept the consequences and to opt to exit if negotiations failed than it was for groups of workers who were either more deeply rooted (guild members) or less likely to be able to find new sources of livelihood (especially isolated workers, workers in challenging frontier situations).

The collective exit could also be intended as a way out from the start. This was the case especially with workers in more extreme and coercive situations, such as slaves and convicts. The aim would then be to put oneself beyond the reach of their former masters, employers, or the authorities. Especially in cases of collective exit, the aim might be to settle elsewhere, de facto creating new settlements or societies (maroons, pirates, and borderland communities). The collective aspect often went hand in hand with heavy ritualized forms of creating plans and shaping

---

30 On this, see also the chapter on strikes by Sjaak van der Velden in the present volume.

bonds, ranging from telling stories, taking blood oaths, to asking for the support of counterforces, such as "the devil". In the case of more individual or small group exits, the forms and aims were often much more diverse in terms of planning, strategies, alliances, and aims. Knowledge, skills, and personal trust between runaways themselves, but also between runaways and helpers or intermediaries, were crucial in making running away work. On many occasions, such individual desertions were so successful that they collectively swelled to assume massive proportions, presenting a major challenge to employers and authorities.

Desertions' afterlife

As Chris and Charles Tilly have noted, "The chief constraint on a worker is the range of jobs available to him or her".[31] Besides the "range of jobs", resulting in running away as a strategy within the existing economic system, this consideration could be widened to include the possibility of opting out of the system entirely (or perhaps moving into different political-economic systems). Especially in the period of early global expansion, this was a relevant consideration for workers, as the centres of trade and production in the early world economy often bordered closely on sometimes quite habitable, but not always clearly controlled, regions that provided spaces for deserters and runaway communities to carve out new lives. This changed completely when the reach of states and empires was extended, and production for global markets intensified. Imperialism created hierarchical and increasingly effective entanglements between authorities across the globe, effectively narrowing the space left to evade control. Global economic expansion further strengthened this process by transforming large areas of the world into areas for economic exploitation through plantations, mines, transport, and factories. This is not to claim that this was a uniform and linear process – in contrast, reshaping global trade, industry, and the countryside must have been a highly disordered and messy process – but it does show that the need of the part of authorities and entrepreneurs to control land, capital, and labour more systematically both intensified and extended globally over the course of the nineteenth and twentieth centuries.

Attempts to find increasingly effective ways to control workers resulted from the responses to the continuous willingness of workers to take matters into their own hands by running away, just as much as from the expansionist desires of economic and political elites. In response to the high levels of desertion that marked the early modern period, especially during that of early modern global expansion, mechanisms of control were tested, refined, and implemented in urban, rural, and frontier environments. These mechanisms were used across the boundaries of labour categories. Pass systems were employed for slaves, to check whether they had permission to

---

31 Tilly and Tilly, *Work under Capitalism*, p. 116.

leave the plantation or to work in the city, but they could also be employed for workers who were perceived to be free. In the city of Batavia, for example, Asian workers discharged from the VOC needed passes to prove their freedom. Other methods ranged from crude hunting systems for runaways, as employed by imperial authorities along the eighteenth-century Malabar Coast, and later in nineteenth-century Sumatra and Andaman Islands, to increasingly refined administrative forms of restriction, as developed for convicts in Australia or for the massive waves of contract migrant workers of the nineteenth and twentieth centuries.

The implications of this can be touched upon only very briefly here, but it would be fruitful ground for further analysis. For example, the maritime sector witnessed increasing physical and bureaucratic control over recruitment, crews, and their movements onshore. Due to the extreme mobility that characterized the sector, however, it retained its character as a place of refuge for a long time. The effects of increasing national regulation of the maritime sector from the nineteenth century onwards would, in turn, be undermined from the mid-twentieth century by the growing attempts on the part of shipping companies to make themselves footloose by using flags of convenience. In the military sector, the professionalization and nationalization of armies, as well as the introduction of conscription, changed the dynamics in even more powerful ways, slowly diminishing the role of the army as a place of refuge, except perhaps for the remaining (but exoticized) "foreign" regiments. Military desertion generally lost its economic and pragmatic character and became tied to more political dynamics, centred on the contestation of nation-building and/or emancipatory, regionalist, pacifist, or socialist ideals.[32]

For national, international, and even global contexts, it has been observed that methods of control over mobility and work shifted from discipline to surveillance.[33] The history of desertion reminds us that some of the roots of disciplinary techniques should be sought outside the world of prisons and punitive institutions, and located in the early modern workplaces and localities where workers were to be contained. The changes this initiated transformed the world of work. For the more recent history of desertion, therefore, it is crucial to note that the criminalization of withdrawal from the work process was slowly transformed into criminalization of the act of not working, or the state of not being employed. In increasingly disciplined and controlled societies, the withdrawal from the world of work became penalized more and more. With the gradual disappearance of open and alternative spaces that remained beyond the reach of this surveillance and of global regulation, running away (like many other forms of resistance) became increasingly both more difficult and more politicized. Although the actual act of running away became more difficult, this did not mean resistance disappeared. For example, the second half of the twentieth

---

32 See, for example, Charles Glass, *The Deserters. A Hidden History of World War II* (New York, 2013); John Hagan, *Northern Passage. American Vietnam War Resisters in Canada* (Cambridge, MA, 2001).
33 Michel Foucault, *Discipline and Punish. The Birth of the Prison* (New York, 1975).

century witnessed protests against societal pressure to work, as in the protests organized by the Dutch "union of workshy thugs" (Bond Werkschuw Tuig) in the early 1980s.[34] More recently, we have seen protests opposing the enforcement of work in exchange for receiving social benefits, such as those for which the Actiecomité Dwangarbeid Nee were responsible.[35]

---

[34] Examples from the collection of the International Institute of Social History, Amsterdam, include posters and publications of the Bond Werkschuw Tuig, such as "Diskussie werketiek" (Utrecht, 1980).
[35] See, for example, http://stopdwangarbeid.nl/, http://dwangarbeidnee.blogspot.nl/.

Suggested reading

Adas, Michael. "From Footdragging to Flight: The Evasive History of Peasant Avoidance Protest in South and South-East Asia", *Journal of Peasant Studies*, 13, 2 (1986), pp. 64–86.

Agostini, Thomas. "'Deserted His Majesty's Service': Military Runaways, the British-American Press, and the Problem of Desertion during the Seven Years' War", *Journal of Social History*, 40, 4 (2007), pp. 957–985.

Anderson, Robert N. "The *Quilombo* of Palmares: A New Overview of a Maroon State in Seventeenth-Century Brazil", *Journal of Latin American Studies*, 28, 3 (1996), pp. 545–566.

Clee, Charles R. "Desertion and the Freedom of the Seaman", *International Labour Review*, 13, 5 (1926), pp. 649–672, 808–849.

Diouf, Sylviane A. *Slavery's Exiles. The Story of the American Maroons* (New York: New York University Press, 2014).

Forrest, Alan. *Conscripts and Deserters. The Army and French Society during the Revolution and Empire* (Oxford: Oxford University Press, 1989).

Glass, Charles. *The Deserters. A Hidden History of World War II* (New York: The Penguin Press, 2013).

Hagan, John. *Northern Passage. American Vietnam War Resisters in Canada* (Cambridge, MA: Harvard University Press, 2001).

Lonn, Ella. *Desertion during the Civil War* (New York: The Century Co., 1928; reprint Lincoln: University of Nebraska Press, 1998).

Penn, Nigel. "Great Escapes: Deserting Soldiers during Noodt's Cape Governorship, 1727–1729", *South African Historical Journal*, 59, 1 (2007), pp. 171–203.

Rashke, Richard. *Escape from Sobibor* (Urbana, IL: University of Illinois Press, 1983).

Roberts, Richard and Martin A. Klein. "The Banamba Slave Exodus of 1905 and the Decline of Slavery in the Western Sudan", *Journal of African History*, 21, 3 (1980), pp. 375–394.

Rossum, Matthias van and Jeannette Kamp (eds). *Desertion in the Early Modern World: A Comparative History* (London: Bloomsbury Academic, 2016).

Sanborn, J.A. *Drafting the Russian Nation. Military Conscription, Total War, and Mass Politics, 1905–1925* (DeKalb: Northern Illinois University Press, 2003).

Scott, James C. *Weapons of the Weak. Everyday Forms of Peasant Resistance* (New Haven, CT: Yale University Press, 1985).

Thompson, Alvin O. *Flight to Freedom. African Runaways and Maroons in the Americas* (Kingston: University of the West Indies Press, 2006).

Van der Linden, Marcel. "The Okanisi: A Surinamese Maroon Community, c. 1712–2010", *International Review of Social History*, 60, 3 (December 2015), pp. 463–490.

Sjaak van der Velden
8.3. Strikes, Lockouts, and Informal Resistance*

If rebellious workers set themselves to obtain a larger share of the national product or start a revolution to overthrow capitalism, they need some means – and perhaps weapons – to achieve their goal. The best known and most studied of those means is most probably strike action, and this chapter will present an insight into the withdrawal of work as a weapon in the hands of workers struggling for a better life. I shall give a glimpse into the logic of the strike and its history from classical times until the present. To strike is not always either permitted nor is it always even an intelligent thing to do in view of what employers or the state might do to counteract it. I shall therefore describe alternative options open to employees to see that their demands are met. The end of this chapter offers a brief insight into strike statistics, together with a view of international waves of strike action. But let us begin with the simple question, "What is a strike?"

What is a strike?[1]

Ever since politicians, economists, and social scientists began to study strikes, they have been trying to define what a strike is. Most of the earliest definitions include the idea that strikers stop work with the intention of restarting it once their demands have been met. So a "strike" means that workers voluntarily and temporarily stop work because there are certain requirements they wish to have fulfilled. While it is true that that is a rather sterile definition, certainly during the nineteenth and early twentieth centuries the concept of industry as a battleground was clearly understood by students of strike action as a social phenomenon. In an 1889 overview of strikes and lockouts in the United Kingdom one author wrote: "It is certain that all such industrial struggles represent the conflict of employers and workmen upon mat-

---

* In writing this chapter, I owe a debt to Marcel van der Linden, *Workers of the World: Essays Toward a Global Labor History* (Leiden and Boston, 2008), especially ch. 9.
1 The English word *strike* was probably used for the first time during a conflict in 1768, although it only gradually replaced the term *turnout* during the late nineteenth century. Sailors in Sutherland struck the sails to stress their demands to the sailing company, and from that day onwards the word strike was used with regard to labour conflicts. See *A New English Dictionary on Historical Principles* (Oxford, 1919). The English word, which is derived from the Indo-European *streig* (= stroke), found its way into other languages, including German (*Streik*) and Swedish (*strejk*), but some languages used their own word for this relatively new event. It is probably related to the French *tric*, a word used before *grève* came in use.

ters which one or both consider to be vital to their interests, and, while engaged in them, the parties concerned are really in a state of moral if not actual warfare."[2]

The author of the overview clearly understood that there is an element of struggle or "warfare" in a workers' strike. He also separated strikes from lockouts, which are in fact the opposite of a strike, for during a lockout an employer temporarily prevents workers from working. However, both those opinions, widely supported at that time, have been slowly eroded. Labour activists saw strikes from the perspective of class struggle in which, according to Friedrich Engels, striking workers "endanger social order" and can end the "whole Political Economy of today".[3] According to that view striking workers would eventually bring capitalism to its knees, while in the meantime going on strike over points of contention.[4] However, mainstream social scientists and statistical investigators developed more neutral views on strikes. In 1994 the *Bulletin of Comparative Labour Relations* (*BCLR*) defined the strike as "a collective and concerted withholding of labour in pursuit of specific occupational demands exercised peacefully".[5] The strike thus moved from conflict – even perhaps the prelude to revolution – to become a peaceful undertaking intended for occupational ends. However, while a peaceful character might be intrinsic to most present-day strikes in industrialized countries, it is most certainly not so for many strikes in developing countries, and, indeed, we need not go a long way into the past to encounter violence in many strike movements in Western countries.[6]

Because strike statistics collected by the International Labour Organization (ILO) are most generally used in comparative strike research, we shall restrict ourselves to their rather neutral definition: "A *strike* is a temporary work stoppage carried out by one or more groups of workers with a view to enforcing or resisting demands or ex-

---

2 *Report on the Strikes and Lock-Outs of 1888* by the Labour Correspondent to the Board of Trade, presented to both Houses of Parliament by Command of Her Majesty (London, 1889), p. 3.
3 ["And precisely because the Unions direct themselves against the vital nerve of the present social order, however one-sidedly, in however narrow a way, are they so dangerous to this social order. [...] The moment the workers resolve to be bought and sold no longer, when, in the determination of the value of labour, they take the part of men possessed of a will as well as of working-power, at that moment the whole Political Economy of today is at an end."] Frederick Engels, *The Condition of the Working-Class in England: From Personal Observation and Authentic Sources*, in: Marx and Engels, *Collected Works*, vol. 4 (Moscow, 1975), p. 507. Note that the Soviet translator changed the original "Reich des Besitzes" (Empire of Property) into "the whole Political Economy of today". See Friedrich Engels, *Die Lage der arbeitenden Klasse in England. Nach eigner Anschauung und authentischen Quellen* (1845), reprinted in: Marx and Engels, *Werke*, vol. 2 (Berlin, 1974), p. 436.
4 Eduard Bernstein, *Der Streik. Sein Wesen und sein Wirken* (Frankfurt am Main, 1906), p. 7.
5 Roger Blanpain and R. Ben-Israel (eds), *Strikes and Lock-Outs in Industrialized Market Economies* (Deventer and Boston, 1994), p. 10.
6 Peter Hain wrote, "Violence is a normal part of the history of strikes in Britain" (*Political Strikes. The State and Trade Unionism in Britain* (Harmondsworth, 1986), p. 13), and the title of the 1931 study by Louis Adamic speaks for itself: *Dynamite. The Story of Class Violence in America* (New York, 1931).

pressing grievances, or supporting other workers in their demands or grievances".[7] Aspects of conflict and violence have been removed from that definition, but it is good to keep in mind that both might play a role. Besides that, compared with the *BCLR* definition, in the view of the ILO solidarity with other workers is an integral part of the goals pursued by striking workers. That is true of all demands that transcend the sphere of "occupational demands", such as political, judicial, and other general aims striven for by strikers.

What is not incorporated into most definitions, including that of the ILO, is the diversity of strikes. A strike might last two minutes or several years. The longest strike in history was probably the lost struggle by 130 employees of the Congress Hotel in Chicago (USA) who between 2003 and 2013 fought management's decision to cut wages and hire subcontracted workers. Strikes differ in scale too. A single company or a whole country might be affected by a conflict between labour and capital. There might be two workers on strike, or two million. Does an entire workforce join the struggle, or only part of it? And does partial participation occur on purpose because the unions want to fight at minimal cost, or does a large proportion of the workers oppose the strike and refuse to join the action? Questions like those arise when looking at bare statistics that indicate only the number of conflicts.

Paid workers are not the only ones who might resort to going on strike, for slaves, indentured workers, and even convicts can do so too. Here, however, I shall focus on strikes organized by wage earners.

Taxonomy of labour conflicts

Although the strike is probably the best known form of resistance by workers in the modern capitalist system, other forms of resistance are available to wage earners. However, despite the ILO's still valid recommendation in 1993 to "also cover other action due to labour disputes", statistical bureaus hardly ever do.[8] In fact all forms of wage-labour conflict can be summarized in a single taxonomy.[9]

---

7 http://www.ilo.org/ilostat-files/Documents/description_IR_EN.pdf. The ILO also defines the lockout: "A *lockout* is a total or partial temporary closure of one or more places of employment, or the hindering of the normal work activities of employees, by one or more employers with a view to enforcing or resisting demands or expressing grievances, or supporting other employers in their demands or grievances."
8 Fifteenth International Conference of Labour Statisticians, Geneva, 19–28 January 1993.
9 The taxonomy is taken from the project Global Hub Labour Conflicts initiated in 2014 and supported by the International Institute of Social History in Amsterdam. See https://datasets.socialhistory.org/dataverse/National.

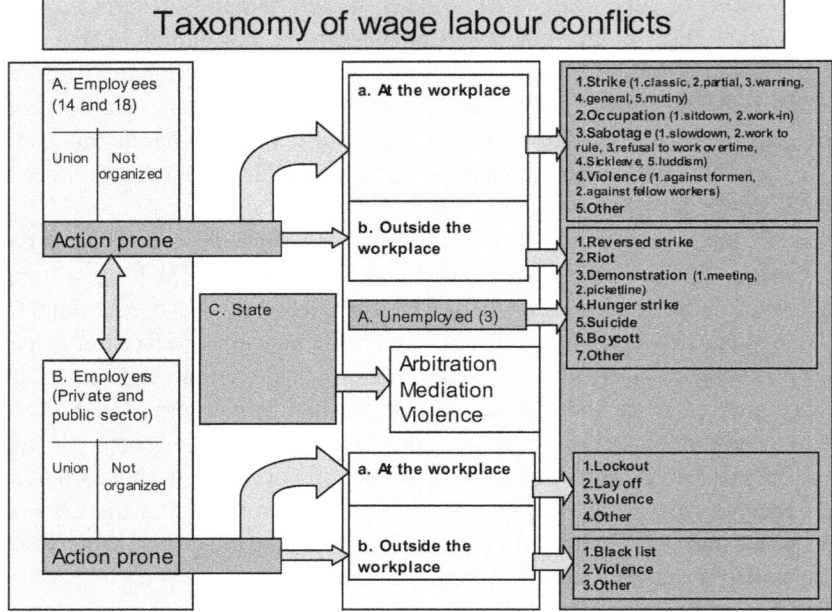

That taxonomy shows how labour (employees) and capital (employers) are able to embark on a number of types of conflict depending on the chosen arena, inside or outside the workplace. Note that both parties might try to strengthen their positions by building or joining more permanent organizations such as trade unions and employers' associations, but that is not a necessary precept for involvement in labour conflicts.

In many labour conflicts some third party might become involved, especially when such conflicts are regarded as threatening normal labour relations or even public order. Then the state can interfere, and sometimes does so, perhaps by mediating to help the two parties end the conflict. In many cases, the state effectively takes sides by using violence to try to force workers to end their action and resume work. Much less often does the state take the side of striking workers.[10] In many cases the state is itself an employer, and in that guise might be expected to act like other employers in reaction to strike action.

Before we consider forms of collective action that are alternatives to the strike and lockout, let us look more closely at what strikes are.

---

[10] During his first term (1916–1922), Argentine President Hipólito Yrigoyen prevented the police from intervening if the workers concerned were potential voters for his own Radical Party: "Yrigoyen supported strikers not because of his ideals but in hope of winning votes". Joel Horowitz, "Argentina's Failed General Strike of 1921: A Critical Moment in the Radicals' Relations with Unions", *Hispanic American Historical Review*, 75, 1 (1995), pp. 57–79, at 60.

A short historical and thematic overview of strikes

Because of a lack of source material it is hard to be certain when wage earners stopped working for the first time because they had grievances, nor do we really know where they did so, although it is commonly agreed that the first strikes occurred in ancient Egypt. The best-known example is the strike of tomb builders in Deir el Medina in 1155 BCE on the 21st day of the 29th year in the reign of Ramses III.[11] Unrest actually began a year earlier when the workers' pay was late and a representative, one Amennakht, persuaded local officials to hand over forty-six sacks of corn to restore peace. But the problems were not over yet.[12] The strike proper commenced when the craftsmen "downed tools", complaining: "We are hungry, for 18 days have already elapsed in this month". Two days later the strikers stated: "The prospect of hunger and thirst has driven us to this; there is no clothing, there is no ointment, there is no fish, there are no vegetables. Send to Pharaoh, our good lord, about it, and send to the vizier, our superior, that we may be supplied with provisions."

That strike was of course a very early one and might seem difficult to compare with strikes that take place nowadays. The idea of the Pharaoh as an omnipotent deity is strange to most modern people, and those workers' relationship with their superiors is practically unknown to us, as are such things as the fact that the positions of craftsmen were hereditary. But otherwise the comparison is striking. People in a subordinate position took their fate into their own hands and resisted existing circumstances. That may well be a common reaction of the subordinate, or as Michel Foucault remarked: "Where there is power, there is resistance."[13] We might therefore conclude that although both the duration of that ancient strike and the number of participants are unclear and the outcome foggy, the fact that the workmen resisted makes the Deir el Medina strike comparable to modern labour conflicts and it can therefore justly be described as the first strike in history.

Other events, too, have been labelled strikes, such as the *secessio plebis*, or withdrawal from society of ordinary people in the Roman Empire, which probably occurred five times between 494 BC and 287 BC. Because a *secessio* was performed by an entire stratum (the *plebs*), including soldiers many of whom owned land, that action, impressive as it might have been to contemporaries, can hardly be termed a strike in the modern sense. However, in Ancient Rome there were strikes that resembled modern work stoppages.[14]

---

11 Paul J. Frandsen, "Editing Reality: The Turin Strike Papyrus", in: Sarah Israelit-Groll (ed.), *Studies in Egyptology*, vol. 1 (Jerusalem, 1990), pp. 166–199.
12 Toby Wilkinson, *The Rise and Fall of Ancient Egypt: The History of a Civilisation from 3000 BC to Cleopatra* (London, 2010), p. 358. This author dates the actual strike to 1558 BCE.
13 Michel Foucault, *Histoire de la sexualité*, vol. 1. *La volonté de savoir* (Paris, 1976), p. 125.
14 Bernstein, *Streik*, p. 9; Ramsay MacMullen, "A Note on Roman Strikes", *The Classical Journal*, 58, 6 (1963), pp. 269–271.

Only during the early stages of modern capitalism did strikes become a regular feature of society. First as rare interruptions of normal relations, such as in strikes by textile workers in late-medieval Italy, Flanders, and Holland,[15] and in a few other early cases like the 1539 strike by typographers[16] in Lyon in France. There was, too, an uprising by Genovese silk workers in 1675, while occasionally during the fourteenth and fifteenth centuries Dutch textile workers in Leiden organized illegal *uutgangen* (walkouts). The textile workers then left Leiden and moved to another city because they found their labour relations unacceptable. Their exit was essentially performed, done in order to renegotiate from a safer place because sometimes a royal decree or in many cases the local authorities forbade the leaving of a city precisely to forestall the interruption of normal production.[17] Because guild regulations in the period meant workers were not free in the modern sense, *uutgangen* lie somewhere between exoduses by plantation slaves and strikes as carried out by free labour. Both sorts of action show that subordinate workers could find ways to resist in their everyday working lives. The same was true for sailors who undertook many mutinies to escape from the strict regimes under which they worked, regimes that might include corporal punishment and the death penalty. Perhaps the best-known mutiny is the one that took place on the British HMS Bounty in 1789.

Both the leaving of plantations by slaves and mutinies at sea were manifestations of resistance by workers who had few rights. Another example is the strike in America by Polish craftsmen demanding greater civil liberties. That action occurred in 1619 and is considered the first strike in American history.[18] However, it was not until the late eighteenth and early nineteenth centuries that strikes by truly legally free labourers became regular events in Europe. Strikes became more frequent in the colonies, too, but until now they have been too little studied. Early examples include the cessation of work by silver miners in Chihuahua in Mexico. As early as the 1730s, they protested against the termination of their work contracts by the owners of the mine where they worked, while in India there were strikes at a huge gunpowder factory in about 1800 and by brickmakers on the Ganges Canal in 1848–1849.[19]

---

15 See, for example, Samuel Kline Cohn, Jr., *The Laboring Classes in Renaissance Florence* (New York, 1980); Marc Boone and Hanno Brand, "Vollersoproeren en collectieve actie in Gent en Leiden in de 14de-15de eeuw", *Tijdschrift voor sociale geschiedenis*, 19, 2 (1993), pp. 168–192.
16 Known as "le grand Tric". Georges Dangon, "Orages sur l'imprimerie: le grand tric de Lyon (1539–1544)", *Le Courrier graphique*, 84 (February-March 1956), p. 7, and 85 (April-May 1956), p. 17.
17 Rudolf Dekker, "Labour Conflicts and Working-Class Culture in Early Modern Holland", *International Review of Social History*, 35, 3 (1990), pp. 377–420, at 387–391.
18 James S. Pula, "Fact vs. Fiction: What Do We Really Know about the Polish Presence in Early Jamestown?", *The Polish Review*, 53, 4 (2008), pp. 477–493.
19 Cheryl English Martin, *Governance and Society in Colonial Mexico: Chihuahua in the Eighteenth Century* (Stanford, CA, 1996), p. 51; Jan Lucassen, "Working at the Ichapur Gunpowder Factory in the 1790s", *Indian Historical Review*, 39, 1 (2012), pp. 19–56, and 39, 2 (2012), pp. 251–271; Jan Lucassen, "The Brickmakers' Strikes on the Ganges Canal in 1848–1849", *International Review of Social History*, 51 (2006), Supplement, pp. 47–83.

Regarding Europe it is important to note that strike action was forbidden in most countries, although almost everywhere the number of strikes increased. Only slowly did national parliaments repeal laws prohibiting free association by workers demanding higher wages, fewer working hours, or less work. It was only then that a more specific word for such stoppages came into existence. People then began to refer to *strikes*, already mentioned, and in French *la grève*, a word loaned to Portuguese and Turkish too. The Spanish used their word *huelga*. Large-scale strikes that affected an entire industry or region occurred for the first time in the nineteenth century, examples being the general strike of 1842 in the North and Midlands of the UK and the Pullman strike of 1894 in the USA. In August 1842 a general strike commenced in protest at wage reductions and it "spread like wildfire".[20] The strike soon assumed a political flavour when the Chartist movement intervened and received support for its campaign for general suffrage. The 1842 strike is sometimes called "The Plug Plot" after strikers who roamed the country bringing mills to a standstill by removing the plugs from their boilers. Despite political support the strike failed and hundreds were arrested. Another famous strike took place in 1894 in Chicago, Illinois, when the workers of the Pullman Palace Car Company faced wage cuts and protested. When three members of the workers' committee were laid off, the local unions issued a strike call. The strike began on 11 May, and although there was no violence nor destruction of property soldiers were sent to the factory. From 26 June railroad workers went on strike in sympathy and boycotted Pullman cars.[21] But it was all in vain. The thousands of soldiers who were sent in drenched the strike in blood, leaving thirty strikers dead and fifty-seven wounded.

The beginning of the twentieth century saw strikes as a regular response by workers spread from the core countries of capitalism in Europe and America to other regions. Of course resistance was already known to people like slaves and contract workers who were forced into coerced labour. Some of the revolts by slaves have become iconic. Although we know of only a few slave revolts in Greek and Roman antiquity, one of the best-known examples in history occurred in that era. The "Spartacus" revolt by tens of thousands of Roman slaves in 74–71 BC has been the subject of commercial films and lent its name to a number of left-wing groups such as the German *Spartakusbund* (Spartacus League) founded by Karl Liebknecht and Rosa Luxemburg. Because slavery in Europe had ceased to be regarded as acceptably normal, the status of people forcibly transported from Africa to the Americas required a race-based justification. Despite the idea that it was for the good of the world that supposedly superior white Europeans should govern "black" people, many enslaved Africans nonetheless fought against their situation so that the newly established slave societies on the American continent were under constant and real threat of

---

[20] G.D.H. Cole, *A Short History of the British Working-Class Movement, 1789–1947* (London, 1947), p. 113.
[21] United States Strike Commission, *Report on the Chicago Strike of June-July 1894* (Washington, DC, 1895), pp. xxxvii–xl.

slave revolt. Revolts sometimes erupted so violently that the concept of a slave society was seriously endangered. In 1526 slaves rebelled in San Miguel de Guadalupe, part of what is now Florida in the United States. That was perhaps the first slave revolt in the Americas, but a long list followed it. Among instances of revolt was the rebellion on Saint-Domingue (1791–1804), which was a success and led to the departure of the planters. However, I prefer here to limit consideration to "free" wage earners, so I shall say no more about slave revolts, even though in certain important respects they do resemble strikes.

As I have stated, from about 1900 large-scale strike action by free labourers spread all over the world, including general strikes in Argentina in 1902, 1904, and 1907,[22] and a spectacular general strike in St Petersburg in Russia on 22 January 1905 when a demonstration by 200,000 Russians in support of political reforms ended in a massacre that left at least 200 demonstrators dead. In response the strike movement that had been gathering pace since December 1904 exploded, culminating in January 1905 in general strikes in Russian Poland and other parts of the Russian Empire. Unrest continued after that wave of strikes ended, and a new general strike was called in October over the eight-hour working day in St Petersburg. The succession of general strikes and the Russian Revolution of 1905 ended with a third general strike, this time in Moscow, but the strikes of 1905 had an international impact. Similar things have happened in more recent times too. For example, in India strikes became numerous in the 1920s and 1930s.[23] In Ceylon (now called Sri Lanka) on 12 August 1953 a so-called *hartal* was organized. It took the form of a nationwide demonstration of civil disobedience and strike action against the government, and resulted in the resignation of the prime minister.[24] In Egypt, "From 1998 to 2010, well over two million workers participated in at least 3,400 strikes and other collective actions – the largest social movement in the Arab world in six decades, except for the Algerian War of Independence (1954–1962)".[25] In the People' s Republic of China the turn to capitalism has led to a huge number of mostly illegal strikes since the 1990s.[26]

In many countries socialists and anarchists discussed the use of the general strike as the ultimate means to overthrow capitalism with a single push. Of course most so-called general strikes have not been truly general because, despite the

---

22 Agustín Santella, *Labor Conflict and Capitalist Hegemony in Argentina: The Case of the Automobile Industry, 1990–2007* (Leiden and Boston, 2016).
23 Susan Wolcott, "Strikes in Colonial India, 1921–1938", *Industrial and Labor Relations Review*, 61, 4 (2008), pp. 460–484.
24 Wesley S. Muthiah and Sydney Wanasinghe, *We Were Making History: The Hartal of 1953* (Colombo, 2002).
25 Joel Beinin, "Workers and Egypt's January 25 Revolution", *International Labor and Working-Class History*, No. 80 (2011), pp. 189–196, at 191.
26 Ching Kwan Lee, *Against the Law. Labor Protests in China's Rustbelt and Sunbelt* (Berkeley, CA, 2007); Chris King-Chi Chan, *The Challenge of Labour in China: Strikes and the Changing Labour Regime in Global Factories* (Abingdon, 2010).

mass participation of many strikers, many companies, and sometimes many regions, they have rarely involved the whole of the working class. Socialist authors in those days often therefore preferred the term "mass strike".[27] We can define a general strike as one in which a substantial portion of the employees of a given country, industry, region, or city participate. More recent history has seen general strikes in Nigeria in 1964, France in 1968, Senegal in 1968, Spain in 2010, and Argentina in 2014. In India, on 2 September 2016 between 150 and 180 million public-sector workers went on strike for twenty-four hours in protest at plans to increase privatization and other economic policies. Ramen Pandey of the Indian National Trade Union Congress spoke of "the world's largest ever" strike.[28]

Apart from small one-off strikes and general or mass strikes, workers on strike can use different forms of strike action.[29] During a classical strike all employees, or the majority of them, stop work with the intention of going back to work only once their demands have been met. Workers and their unions can, however, decide to use other ways to show their strength, without recourse to a classical strike. To spare costs to the unions they might institute a partial strike, in which a limited number of workers walk out. Another option is the selective strike, another partial action but one in which the section chosen to strike is vital to the entire production process, so that the employer comes under pressure at the most vulnerable point. It can also be decided to start a rotating strike. In such an action there will be a plan for several or perhaps even all departments to stop work one after the other and then in turn resume work. The final type of strike to mention here is the symbolic strike, a mere show of force to make clear to an opponent that the workers are ready and willing to join battle. It really amounts to a warning (*Warnstreik* in German) and might be carried on for just a very limited time, perhaps only an hour or so – even as little as fifteen minutes.

A strike has thus been defined here as a cessation of work; but there is a specific form of strike action in labour conflict whereby workers instead of stopping all work do actually continue production. This is a special case called a "sit-down strike". During a sit-down strike – sometimes called a sit-in, a stay-in, or an occupation – the strikers refuse to leave the plant and sometimes even prevent the owner from entering the premises. There are a few early examples of this rather revolutionary action, such as the case in 1873 of a group of Polish miners who were removed by the police with the help of the army.[30] Sit-ins or occupations were a weapon in the

---

27 Rosa Luxemburg, *Massenstreik, Partei und Gewerkschaften* (Hamburg, 1906); Leon Trotsky, *1905* (Harmondsworth, 1971; originally published in 1922); Gerald D. Surh, "Petersburg's First Mass Labor Organization: The Assembly of Russian Workers and Father Gapon" (Part I), *The Russian Review*, 40, 3 (1981), pp. 241–262.
28 www.aljazeera.com/news/2016/09/millions-indian-workers-strike-wages-160902131706206.html, last accessed 13 October 2016.
29 Gérard Dion, *Dictionnaire canadien des relations du travail* (Quebec, 1986).
30 J.C. Visser, *Bedrijfsbezetting. Het verleden van een nieuw actiemiddel* (Amsterdam, 1986), p. 33.

hands of both Russian and German workers during their early twentieth-century revolutions. Workers in revolt occupied factories, pushed their bosses around in wheelbarrows, and formed committees that attempted to take over management.[31] Real "work-ins" or the continuation of production under workers' control occurred similarly in the *Bienno Rossi* strikes during the "two red years" in Italy from 1919–1920. The 1930s, too, witnessed waves of factory occupations notably in France and the USA. The best-known examples of this kind of action are the Flint strikes at General Motors in 1937[32] and the actions in France in 1936. They were mainly defensive moves because the workers involved were resisting cutbacks and layoffs, and so were in a position where a normal strike would by definition have been in vain. In the first few years after World War II more work-ins followed, for example at the Japanese newspaper *Yomiuri Shinbun* in October 1945.[33]

The late 1960s and early 1970s, too, witnessed a wave of factory occupations, once again during an economic downturn when workers were forced to resist layoffs or face unemployment. In Argentina, factory sit-ins occurred during protest waves in Córdoba in 1969 and in Villa Constitución in 1975 among a good number of other cases.[34] Then, during the 1990s and the first decade of the twenty-first century, thousands of Argentinian workers took over bankrupt factories and put them back to work.[35]

A few factory sit-ins became headline news, like the work-in at the Upper Clyde shipyard in Glasgow, Scotland. That action lasted fourteen months, ending in 1972, and was led by a group of young communist shop stewards who received support from all over the country. During a demonstration 80,000 marched and the workers even received a financial donation from Beatle John Lennon, together with a telegram from "John and Yoko". The work-in was intended to prove that the workers were not "work-shy" but were in fact standing up for the "right to work".[36]

---

31 Uwe Brügmann, *Die russischen Gewerkschaften in Revolution und Bürgerkrieg 1917–1919* (Frankfurt am Main, 1972).
32 Sidney Fine, *Sit-Down. The General Motors Strike of 1936–1937* (Ann Arbor, MI, 1969).
33 Joe Moore, *Japanese Workers and the Struggle for Power, 1945–1947* (Madison, WI, 1983).
34 James P. Brennan, *The Labor Wars in Córdoba, 1955–1976. Ideology, Work, and Labor Politics in an Argentine Industrial City* (Cambridge, MA, 1994); Agustín Santella, "Workers' Mobilization and Political Violence: Conflict in Villa Constitución, Argentina, 1970–1975", *Latin American Perspectives*, 35, 5 (2008), pp. 146–157.
35 Graciela Monteagudo, "The Clean Walls of a Recovered Factory: New Subjectivities in Argentina's Recovered Factories", *Urban Anthropology and Studies of Cultural Systems and World Economic Development*, 37, 2 (2008), pp. 175–210; Alice Rose Bryer, "The Politics of the Social Economy: A Case Study of the Argentinean *Empresas Recuperadas*", *Dialectical Anthropology*, 36, 1 (2012), pp. 21–49; Natalia Vanesa Hirtz and Marta Susana Giacone, "The Recovered Companies Workers' Struggle in Argentina: Between Autonomy and New Forms of Control", *Latin American Perspectives*, 40, 4 (2013), pp. 88–100.
36 Alasdair Buchan, *The Right to Work. The Story of the Upper Clyde Confrontation* (London, 1972).

The occupation at the works of watchmaker Lip in Besançon, France, is another iconic example of a work-in from the same period. The workers in action continued production for ten months between June 1973 and April 1974, selling the watches themselves to sympathizers and organizing a constant flow of propaganda to point out the importance and justice of their struggle. The occupation ended successfully with an assurance that most jobs would be retained.[37]

One key element of factory occupations is that they are illegal. In a way they endanger existing property relations and therefore there has always been a certain tension between the activists and labour unions, which by their nature perform within the boundaries of any legal system of proprietary rights, which rights during numerous occupations police have tried to defend by force. A good example of that is the "Battle of the Running Bulls" in 1937, when workers at the General Motors plant in Flint, Michigan (USA), were able to rout police who tried to take over the occupied factory. At the cost of fourteen colleagues wounded by police gunfire, workers were able to gain union recognition from their employer.

We have now seen that the "strike" is not a simple monolithic category but might take many forms, from simple demonstrative action to near-revolutionary attacks on the "political economy of today". In the next section we shall consider the general course of strikes.

The course of strikes

Strikes have been of many forms with as many histories. But to understand the phenomenon it is nevertheless desirable to describe a general pattern along which most strikes develop, so I hope it will be illuminating to offer such a schedule here. First, before a strike breaks out there will probably have been a whole development of causes and triggers. In most cases there are underlying causes perhaps not mentioned by the strikers as explicit demands but which are detectable by observers. These might include poor social conditions, fatigue, frustration at work, and the inferiority of the workers' position.[38] Such underlying causes are of a very general character and refer to the essence of labour in subordinate conditions or capitalism in general. Here we are reminded that strike action has often been regarded as a temporary escape from every day conditions; indeed the Spanish word *huelga*, used to mean "a strike", can also mean rest or recreation. There are similar analogies in other languages and countries.

Immediate causes of strikes might occur within the framework of the sort of underlying causes mentioned above. Immediate causes might be about wages, working

---

[37] François-Henri de Virieu, *Lip: 100.000 montres sans patron* (Paris, 1973); René Lourau, *L'analyseur Lip* (Paris, 1974).
[38] K.G.J.C. Knowles, *Strikes: A Study in Industrial Conflict, With Special Reference to British Experience Between 1911 and 1947* (Oxford, 1952), pp. 212–219.

hours, disciplinary regulations, or an employer's reluctance to recognize a union. There might be some event that triggers an existing willingness to go on strike, such as an announcement of reduced pay, dismissal of a colleague, or whatever might arouse feelings strong enough for action. Such triggers can cause workers to stop work immediately, or they might ask their union to take action. Immediate causes are of the type to be translated into demands made during collective negotiations between unions and employers. In the case of refusal to negotiate with a union official, workers might take their demands directly to their employer. If a union is involved, a negative response might then lead to the suggestion of strike action. It is common practice, especially in countries where labour relations are highly institutionalized, to ballot union members, something that is actually required by law in the UK. If a ballot then confirms that workers wish to go on strike under the leadership of the union, then the union will issue an ultimatum and set a date for action.

Of course, there is a whole range of possible ways for strikes to develop. As van der Linden has noted, "willingness to stage a strike depends on an intricate complex of factors, including whether or not a grievance procedure exists, the ease of forming a group identity, and the general political and economic circumstances".[39] Once a strike starts it is important for the strikers that they continue to support each other while ostracizing strike-breakers, and find sources of financial support such as is available in a number of countries from union strike funds. Public support is sometimes sought by requesting a boycott of the company involved, and strikers will want to try to negotiate with their employer to find a solution. If a strike has consequences for public life the state may be expected to take a hand in matters, perhaps in mediation or arbitration; in fact, arbitration has been compulsory in Australia since 1906. More familiar state interference has been the use of force, seen in many cases. An upsetting recent example of state violence was the Marikana massacre of 16 August 2012, when South African police opened fire on striking miners, injuring 112 workers, thirty-four of them fatally.[40] The shooting might seem reminiscent of police violence during the Apartheid era, but now it was black government agents against black workers, a fact that caused much disbelief. However, the state is not the only player that can intervene with violence, and both workers and employers can use violence – examples of which we have seen before.

Violent or not, with or without outside arbitration or meditation all strikes come to an end. The employer can decide to institute a lockout or can dismiss all the strikers if legally possible. In most cases, however, a strike ends with an agreement, which might be complete victory or defeat for either party, or anything in between. In any event, the workers go back to work.

As it is, a sort of format for strike action has come to exist and seems to be used by many strikers when initiating a conflict, but we should not forget that real life

---

39 Van der Linden, *Workers of the World*, p. 188.
40 Peter Alexander *et al.*, *Marikana: Voices from South Africa's Mining Massacre* (Athens, OH, 2013).

often has surprises in store. Strikes might come out of the blue without prior negotiation, nor any preparations to come out; there might have been no firm indications that workers had had any grievances. Despite many studies of strike behaviour and of reasons why strikes occasionally erupt among seemingly docile employees, it is still impossible to predict strikes. No model nor any statistical calculations have enabled management to prevent social outbursts, and even in periods of social peace managers ought to be aware of that. Apart from their wish to gain support for their own position, employers often resort to conspiracy thinking in which "communist agitators" induce workers to go on strike – workers whom managers had supposed to be satisfied employees. In 1948 retail workers in New York went on strike against Oppenheim Collins. "In perhaps the most controversial strike in retail workers' history, workers stayed out on the picket line for weeks on end without result, and the mainstream press responded with vicious attacks that were largely false: the strike, the *Daily News* reported, was the work of outside communist agitators rather than retail workers themselves, and all the supporters of the strike were communists."[41] During earlier times under colonialism that attitude to strikers might well have had a racist connotation, such as became clear during the 1939 strike in Kenya. There, casual labourers went on strike in July in Dar es Salaam, Mombasa, Kilindini, and Tanga, although, for example, the port manager of Kilindini was convinced that labour was "contended [sic] and had no desire to strike". The strike was not peaceful everywhere and in Tanga especially riots, as well as shots fired by police, caused six deaths. In general the strike was regarded as caused by political interference from outside. When managers were interviewed after the strike, Mr Norton of the railways was sure of his ground. "I do not think the boy is ready for a trade union, he is still in a very primitive form." If unions were to be set up, it must be under the guidance of a "white Chairman".[42]

The frequent accusation by employers and the mainstream press that striking workers had been provoked by outsiders obliges historians to look more closely at who were the leaders and who the followers in labour conflicts. That is especially so when many union officials themselves, perhaps feeling let down by wildcat strikers, blame agitators, agents provocateurs, communists, and the like.[43]

Leaders and followers

Most strikes do not begin overnight, as it were, but are prepared systematically by unions that use them as a show of force or as a real weapon to bring about changes

---

[41] Aaron Brenner, Benjamin Day, and Immanuel Ness, *The Encyclopedia of Strikes in American History* (Armonk, NY, 2009), p. 628.
[42] Anthony Clayton and Donald C. Savage, *Government and Labour in Kenya 1895–1963* (London, 1974), pp. 222–225.
[43] Knowles, *Strikes*, p. 39.

in labour conditions. It may even be said that in many countries the history of the trade union movement is closely connected to the history of strikes. Indeed, it is not easy to say which came first, strikes or unions. In general, however, we might say that workers went on strike before they had unions, especially if we take into account the very early strikes referred to at the beginning of this chapter. Nevertheless, it is true that under modern capitalism the formation of unions in certain industries has sometimes preceded the occurrence of strikes. Even then the histories of both are closely related, which is not to say that all strikes are initiated and led by unions. There have been quite a number of spontaneous or "wildcat" strikes, especially when the union movement has been under siege or even forbidden. In such situations workers sometimes walk out despite there being no real organizing body to lead them and offer financial support. Strikes have occurred under authoritarian regimes, too, although on a limited scale because there striking workers have often faced severe punishment. According to the regime's own records[44] there were wildcat strikes in Nazi Germany between 1936–1937 and in the German-occupied Netherlands between 1940 and 1945. For example, in 1941 a strike of tens of thousands in the Amsterdam area was called to oppose the maltreatment of the Jewish population, while hundreds of thousands went on strike in 1943 to resist the conscription of former prisoners of war. Not long after the war, in 1953, strikers in Berlin protested against the communist regime in the GDR, and more recently mainland China has seen hundreds of strikes. None of those strikes was either called or led by unions, so they may be described as wildcat strikes.

Conflicts of that type developed in countries where there was no freedom of speech nor an independent union movement, although spontaneous strikes happen in democratic countries, too, where unions are an integral and sometimes even thoroughly appreciated part of the system of industrial relations. Strikes might occur in resistance to some collective agreement endorsed by a union but not approved by the rank and file, in most cases because they had been demanding higher wages. A wave of such strikes hit many Western countries in the 1960s, for example during the German *Septemberstreiks* of 1969 and the *autunno caldo* in Italy. The French general strike of 1968 belongs under this heading because the divided union movement had been unable to lead workers. The French action began spontaneously, sparked off by the student movement, and almost resulted in the resignation of President de Gaulle, with the unions only later gaining any grip on events. During the well-known *mouvement de mai* many factories were occupied by workers, so that it was effectively a repetition of the 1936 occupations and the precursor of the Lip occupa-

---

44 Doris Kachulle, "'Arbeitsniederlegungen in Betrieben'. Ein Bericht des DAF-Geheimdienstes über eine Streikbewegung im Jahre 1936", *1999. Zeitschrift für Sozialgeschichte des 20. und 21. Jahrhunderts*, 6, 4 (1991), pp. 85–109; Tim Mason, "The Workers' Opposition in Nazi Germany", *History Workshop Journal*, 11, 1 (1981), pp. 120–137.

tion.⁴⁵ To a lesser extent the same happened in the US, too, where wildcat strikes were a feature of the 1960s and 1970s. One good example from America is the Dodge Trucks strike of June 1974 that followed wildcat action and factory occupations that took place during the summer of 1973.⁴⁶

Most of those movements eventually faded away without making any dramatic change to labour relations nor state policy. However, things went quite differently in South Africa, where the end of the Apartheid regime was signalled by a wildcat strike in Durban in 1973 that surprised the country and indeed the world. There is no indication that any of the existing unions played a decisive role in the outbreak of those strikes, and South Africa had seen no such labour trouble for decades. But the unrest in combination with many other forms of revolt continued until the end of Apartheid in 1990.⁴⁷

Striking electrical and oil workers in Iran (October and November 1978) are another good example of workers who were able to change the political landscape by force. After "months of paralyzing nationwide strikes" they "hammered the final nail into the coffin of the Pahlavis". And just as during the constitutional crisis of 1905, the strikers were supported by the merchants in the bazaar and shopkeepers.⁴⁸

Another noteworthy example of a large strike movement that eventually led to regime change is to be found in Poland. There spontaneous strike movements in 1970, 1976, and 1980 led to the formation of the independent union "Solidarity", which was finally recognized by the Polish government in August 1980.⁴⁹ In Brazil in the late 1970s extensive strikes by metal workers of the so-called ABC region around São Paulo led to the birth of a strong new union movement that ultimately resulted in the founding of the Workers Party (Partido dos Trabalhadores) in 1980.⁵⁰

Of course, it is not always a straightforward task to categorize a strike with reference to its leaders. Clearly, a strike declared by a union official and under the guidance of the union until it ends is unquestionably a union-led strike, but with spontaneous strikes matters tend to be more complicated. It seems that in August 1766 the miners in Real Del Monte in Mexico downed tools without any leaders, or as Noblet

---

45 Jacques Pesquet, *Soviets at Saclay? The First Assessment of an Experiment in Setting up Workers' Councils at the Atomic Energy Commission Centre for Nuclear Research, Saclay* (London, 1976).
46 Millard Berry et al., *Wildcat: Dodge Truck, June 1974* (Detroit, 1974).
47 Gerald Kraak, *Breaking the Chains. Labour in South Africa in the 1970s and 1980s* (London, 1993); Gay W. Seidman, *Manufacturing Militance. Workers' Movements in Brazil and South Africa, 1970 – 1985* (Berkeley, CA, 1994).
48 Mohsen M. Milani, *The Making of Iran's Islamic Revolution* (Boulder and London, 1988), p. 204.
49 *The Birth of Solidarity: The Gdańsk Negotiations, 1980*, translated and introduced by A. Kemp-Welch (New York, 1983); Agnieszka Dębska (ed.), *A Carnival under Sentence: Solidarność 1980 – 81* (Warsaw, 2006).
50 John D. French, *The Brazilian Workers' ABC. Class Conflict and Alliances in Modern São Paulo* (Chapel Hill, NC, 1992); Margaret E. Keck, *The Workers' Party and Democratization in Brazil* (New Haven, CT, 1992).

Barry Danks puts it, it was "a clear example of the spontaneous leaderless revolt".[51] The same could be true of the great labour uprising of 1877 in the United States, but in most cases there is probably no real spontaneity involved. Small groups of radical workers or even an individual will often impose his or her leadership at the beginning of the conflict, and as it continues. In South Asia, for example, men from the upper castes were strike leaders for decades,[52] while in other situations workers who were members of left-wing groups took the same role. Strikers need spokesmen and negotiators, and in many cases people, too, who are able to speak to the group to sustain their willingness to go on with the struggle and encourage their endurance.

It is therefore better to speak of wildcat strikes instead of spontaneous strikes if we wish to refer to the absence of a labour union involvement. Even that distinction might hide what really happened in a given instance, such as when a Dutch judge forbade the metalworkers' union from going on strike in 1972. Almost 30,000 shipbuilders walked out for three weeks in a strike action that seemed to have been spontaneous. However, many commentators discerned the influence of shop stewards. In Vietnam, after its initial years of transition from a state-driven to a market economy, a typical wildcat strike there developed as follows. The strike

> [...] would start with the dissemination of strike calls. A few days before the strike, the call for strike can be found on toilet walls, in leaflets scattered around the company, or simply a spread of word. Workers would suddenly stop working and gather outside the enterprise facility. Strike leaders do not show up. Informed by the employer concerned, the district labour authority official, often accompanied by the district union, rushes to the enterprise. They talk to workers on strike to gather workers' grievances and demands. The police often appear at the strike scene but take no suppressive action. The labour and union officials (or the strike taskforce) would negotiate with the management on the demands. Once the management accepts a part or all of the "legitimate" demands of workers presented by local labour official (on behalf of workers on strike), workers would go back to work – often being paid for their time off during the strike – and the strike situation would end.[53]

In the Vietnamese situation the unions were still operating under the leadership of the Communist Party, so although not independent they did act as negotiators in wildcat strikes. But an important question remains, "Who posted the leaflets?"

In many countries workers taking part in wildcat strikes do not enjoy the same legal protection as they might have had during official strikes. All the same, from time to time workers decide they have no option but to walk out without the support of unions. A wildcat strike is therefore a clear manifestation of unrest among workers

---

51 Noblet Barry Danks, "The Labor Revolt of 1766 in the Mining Community of Real Del Monte", *The Americas*, 44, 2 (1987), pp. 143–165, at 155.
52 Dilip Simeon, *The Politics of Labour under Late Colonialism. Workers, Unions and the State in Chota Nagpur 1928–1939* (New Delhi, 1995), p. 73.
53 Quynh Chi Do, "The Challenge From Below: Wildcat Strikes and the Pressure for Union Reform in Vietnam", available at https://web.warwick.ac.uk/russia/ngpa/ChallengefromBelow.doc, last accessed 28 October 2016.

and, just as with union-led strikes, shows that workers wish to show their power and that they dare to do so. Such shows of force are directed towards one or more goals, so we should now be wondering "For what reasons do workers walk out, and what are the results of their actions?"

Demands and outcome

Workers go on strike when they wish to emphasize their demands but intend to resume work once their employer has met those demands. In the cases of political strikes, the workers' opponent is the state, which is expected to meet their demands. However, in many cases there are really multiple demands from which one is selected as the most important, perhaps even only the most eye-catching one. During the conflict the relative importance of different aspects might change so that in the cases of many strikes it can be difficult to put them under one heading. The main matter might be wages, but it could perhaps turn out that respect – or more probably disrespect – shown by employers or foremen is equally important to the individual strikers. In general we may, however, state that most strikes are over questions of wages, benefits, and working conditions.

The outcomes of strikes are similarly difficult to classify. The three categories – victory, defeat, and compromise – very often remain a part of the struggle. What one party calls a victory might, from the perspective of the other party, too, be hailed as a victory for the sake of immediate interests. Unions tend to call a strike victorious to make it clear to their members that they, the union, have done a good job. Independent observers on the other hand might regard the same outcome as a compromise. At the same time, it is possible that what seemed to be a lost strike might in the end turn out to be a compromise. It is very difficult to classify labour conflicts by their outcomes, and that is why since 1943 British statistics have provided no information on strike outcomes – annoying, of course, to researchers who need then to refer to the sources in particular cases.

While it is difficult then to classify strikes by reference to demands and outcomes, it is even harder to do so when we look at other forms of labour conflict, to consider the invisible or informal signs of unrest that are hardly ever collected in official statistics.

Informal resistance

Although the strike is probably the best-known manifestation of labour conflict, as we can see from the ILO definition the designation "strike" does not cover all conflicts. First of all the initiative might be in the hands of an employer, as it is in the case of a lockout. In such cases, too, employees clearly stop working for a limited period of time – obviously not of their own volition, but because of "employer militancy". Many lockouts are in fact instituted in reaction to a strike, but the lockout can be used as a weapon against union power. Infamous examples of that are the Homestead lockout of 1892 in the USA and the Dublin lockout of 1913–1914.[54]

A more recent example is the Nigerian lockout of April 2016. In Abuja workers were locked out by the Transmission Company of Nigeria over a disagreement with the management and the Federal Ministry of Power. When the workers turned up for work they were denied entry to the TCN's headquarters. Armed mobile police had taken over the premises to prevent a strike called in protest against the sacking of 400 workers from the plant.[55] The lockout is in fact still an important aspect of labour relations in countries like Canada, Denmark, Germany, and India, to mention only a few.[56] Strikes and lockouts are of different characters because the initiative comes from opposites in class relations, but in practice they often tend to cross-fertilize each other. A strike might provoke an employer to lock other, non-striking workers out of the same plant. A single strike might provoke other employers in the same branch to send their workers home as a clear sign of employers' power. Conversely lockouts might be answered by other workers choosing to take voluntary strike action. In such cases it is never easy to see what exactly has occurred and identify who really started things. The nineteenth-century writer F.S. Hall[57] regarded it as unfair to even consider that point because workers would be blamed for most labour conflicts even if in effect they had been forced by their employers into going on strike. According to Hall the lockout was developed among employers as an act of solidarity earlier than the sympathetic strike was. That, he argued, was a demonstration of the disparity of resources between labour and capital, a disparity reflected in the legislation of industrialized countries, where the lockout is rarely mentioned while the right to strike has clearly needed a legal basis.[58]

There are circumstances in which the desire to strike is there among most workers but the power of their opponent is so overwhelming that they refrain from doing so openly. Then they can resort to other weapons or manifestations of discontent. In his 1952 study on strikes Knowles wrote "in industry, as not in politics, a cold war may sometimes be more damaging than a hot one. Even if men could be successfully inhibited from taking strike action, lost confidence in their Trade Unions, and resorted to ca'canny and absenteeism on a big scale, the price would be greater than the

---

[54] Paul Krause, *The Battle for Homestead, 1880–1892: Politics, Culture, and Steel* (Pittsburgh, 1992); David P. Demarest, *The "River Ran Red": Homestead 1892* (Pittsburgh, 1992); Pádraig Yeates, *Lockout: Dublin 1913* (New York, 2000); Francis Devine (ed.), *A Capital in Conflict: Dublin City and the 1913 Lockout* (Dublin, 2013).
[55] Okechukwu Nnodim, "Nationwide Blackout Looms as TCN Locks Out workers", *Punch*, 20 April 2016, available at http://punchng.com/nationwide-blackout-looms-as-tcn-locks-out-workers/.
[56] See, for example, K.R. Shyam Sundar, "Lockouts in India, 1961–2001", *Economic & Political Weekly*, 39, 39 (25 September 2004), pp. 4377–4385; Ruddar Datt, *Lockouts in India* (New Delhi, 2003).
[57] F.S. Hall, *Sympathetic Strikes and Sympathetic Lockouts* (New York, 1898).
[58] Blanpain and Ben-Israel, *Strikes and Lock-Outs*.

benefit bought".⁵⁹ On page 210 of the same study, and in a later contribution to the subject, he added a number of other signs of industrial unrest to the list. They included a high rate of labour turnover, absenteeism, sickness, and accidents, sabotage, and addiction to drink or the cinema. Intensive political activity and habitual pilfering, too, were regarded as signs of "unrest among industrial workers".⁶⁰ Expressions of unrest of that type come to the fore when, because of lack of social cohesion and tradition, strike action is hardly an option. Then, workers resort to more individual expressions of unrest or dissatisfaction. To the modern Western reader it might appear rather an exaggeration to regard industrial accidents as signs of unrest, but studies have shown that there is a negative correlation between accidents and sick leave on the one hand and open forms of unrest or strike action on the other. In the late 1950s German dockworkers whose attitude to their work was negative proved more liable to accidents than their more positive colleagues.⁶¹ In fact, in the absence of strike action most worker reactions of this type to the inconvenience of wage labour are by their very nature individual manifestations of unrest. Knowles showed, for example, that voluntary absenteeism among miners was higher when there were fewer strikes,⁶² and the fact speaks for itself that in Germany the word *Krankfeiern* ("enjoying poor health") exists and some even promote it.⁶³ Other forms of what may be labelled informal resistance are likewise individual, although a certain amount of solidarity between the "offenders" and their colleagues is essential, especially so when we consider the matter of theft. One manager of a German shipyard once remarked about his employees: "they steal everything; they would even have taken the ships had they not been too tall and too heavy".⁶⁴ It is noteworthy that some of the signs of industrial unrest mentioned here were also seen in labour relations in classical times. In Roman antiquity slaves only rarely went into open revolt, but flight, theft, sabotage, inefficiency, and even killings of owners were common reactions to their everyday lives.⁶⁵

There exists an abundance of literature on what Knowles called the other signs of unrest, but their relation to individual circumstances makes it less important to go

---

59 Knowles, *Strikes*, p. xii.
60 K.G.J.C Knowles, "'Strike-Proneness' and its Determinants", in: Walter Galenson and Seymour Martin Lipset (eds), *Labor and Trade Unionism: An Interdisciplinary Reader* (New York and London, 1960), pp. 301–318, at 301.
61 Horst Jürgen Helle, *Die unstetig beschäftigten Hafenarbeiter in den nordwesteuropäischen Häfen* (Stuttgart, 1960), p. 61.
62 Knowles, *Strikes*, p. 225.
63 http://www.krankheit-simulieren.de/wie-krank-feiern/, last accessed 25 October 2016.
64 Karl Heinz Roth, *Die "andere" Arbeiterbewegung und die Entwicklung der kapitalistischen Repression von 1880 bis zur Gegenwart. Ein Beitrag zum Neuverständnis der Klassengeschichte in Deutschland* (Munich, 1974), p. 222.
65 M.I. Finley, "Slavery", *International Encyclopedia of the Social Sciences*, vol. 14 (1968), p. 311; E.M. Staerman, *Die Blütezeit der Sklavenwirtschaft in der Römischen Republik* (Wiesbaden, 1969), pp. 238–242.

deeper into those in a chapter on strike action, so from now on the focus will be on collective informal resistance instead of individual signs of labour unrest. Some resemble strikes, but others differ enormously from the simple strike. At the beginning of the nineteenth century when strikes became more common in Great Britain, Luddism, or machine-breaking, was violently repressed. Luddites resisted modern developments by smashing up the machines that were seen as the root of all evil. Luddism has often been judged a "blind, unorganized, reactionary, limited and ineffective upheaval",[66] but it can also be seen as an appropriate reaction given the circumstances. In fact, so much of it went on that in 1812 machine-breaking was made a capital offence and troops were called in to put a stop to the movement's activities. Workers in other European countries like Germany, Bohemia, Austria, and France used machine-breaking as a means to express grievances, but it occurred in China, the Ottoman Empire, and Brazil too.[67]

In the United Kingdom almost sixty years after the Luddite movement a type of what might be called "Luddism-lite" appeared in the form of sabotage as a weapon used by a labour union. Of course forms of sabotage have been used by subordinate workers since time immemorial,[68] but now a labour union made it official policy. After the Glasgow dock strike of 1889 workers were forced back to work because a large number of strike-breakers had taken over their jobs. Their employer stated that they could have managed without the men who had gone on strike because the strike-breakers had worked as well as the original dockers, so the dockers decided to go "ca'canny"[69] or "go slowly".[70] The idea was that they would work according to the productivity of the strike-breakers, and a few days later the original strike demand of a wage raise was fulfilled after all. That union tactic became popular among the more radical syndicalist unions in France and the US. It was in fact a form of sabotage and was promoted in a pamphlet written by Emile Pouget in 1909. He wrote "Sabotage is in the social war what guerrilla is in national wars: it flows from the same feelings, responds to the same necessities and has identical consequences in workers' minds."[71] The act of sabotage was even heralded in a song by Joe Hill published in a songbook by one of the few US unions in favour of sabotage, the Industrial Workers of the World: "Ta-ra-ra-boom-de-ay! It made a noise that way, And wheels and bolts and hay, Went flying every way."[72]

---

66 John Zerzan, *Elements of Refusal* (Seattle, 1988), p. 91.
67 Van der Linden, *Workers of the World*, p. 174.
68 According to the Roman writer Columella, slaves needed constant overseeing and, as noted before, M.I. Finley mentioned sabotage as one of the weapons used by slaves in antiquity. Lucius Junius Moderatus Columella, *Rei Rusticae* [On Agriculture], Book I, ch. 7, 6.
69 Ca'canny is a compound word comprising "call" (drive, arrive) and "canny" (gentle).
70 Geoff Brown, *Sabotage: A Study in Industrial Conflict* (Nottingham, 1977).
71 Translation by Brown, *Sabotage*, p. 386.
72 Joyce L. Kornbluh, *Rebel Voices: An IWW Anthology* (Ann Arbor, MI, 1972), p. 144.

In more recent times ca'canny has been used in many places as a less confrontational way to express grievances than striking, such as in Nigeria in 1946. Miners in Enugu launched a "ca'canny" under their leader Isaiah Okwudili Ojiyi, who "indigenized the term by calling it '*welu nwayo*' in Igbo".[73] In 2011 a very specific form of go-slow was played out by Australian engineers at Quantas, when right-handed engineers vowed to use only their left hands for screwdrivers and spanners as a form of industrial action by the Aircraft Engineers Association in order to gain a wage increase.[74]

Another thing workers can resort to when they have grievances but are unwilling to go on strike is demonstration, to make clear that they have reached the limits of their patience. Sometimes they adopt that tactic in the hope of gathering support from the wider public. In southern Europe, Greece, Portugal, and Spain witnessed such demonstrations during the anti-austerity campaigns of 2011–2013 when millions of workers and others took to the streets. In the history of the labour movement May Day has since 1890 been a day to demonstrate for all kinds of demands, originally the eight-hour working day. A demonstration is thus not only a show of grievance but also a show of strength. If a demonstration is not accompanied by a riot it is a rather gentle show of force, but one that can serve as the first step towards actions that could affect employers or the state more severely. An even softer form of protest is the petition, although there are circumstances when even that kind of action might endanger job security. European workers often therefore resorted to the "round robin", a written demand for improvements with signatures presented in a circular form. The circular layout is intended to prevent the employer from knowing who was the first to put his name on the list. The habit probably comes from the *ruban rond* (round ribbon) in seventeenth-century France. There, government officials signed their petitions on ribbons attached to the documents in a circular form so that it was unclear who had signed first and should therefore be sent to the executioner. In English the *ruban rond* became "round robin" and the first of the British to use it were sailors of the Royal Navy. Examples from elsewhere show that employees in other countries, too, used it as a safe way of petitioning.

Why do workers strike?

Striking workers often have demands over wages, working hours, and so on, but as Bentley and Hughes stated, "Strikeable issues, however, do not always ignite

---

[73] Carolyn A. Brown, *"We Were All Slaves". African Miners, Culture, and Resistance at the Enugu Government Colliery* (Oxford, 2003), p. 295.
[74] Gabriella Costa, "Qantas Engineers Pledge Whacky, Wrong-Handed Strike Action", *Traveller*, 13 July 2011, available at www.traveller.com.au/qantas-engineers-pledge-whacky-wronghanded-strike-action-1hcxy#ixzz4ONgcn3px, last accessed 25 October 2016.

strikes".[75] So the question remains: "under what circumstances will workers translate their demands into strike action?"

Since the beginning of academic research into strikes an impressive number of studies of strikes have been written. One of the first was the institutional theory by Ross and Hartman, who constructed typologies based on the institutional settings in different countries.[76] They looked at variables such as the organizational stability of unions, the presence of a worker's party, and the involvement of the state in labour relations. Their conclusions were that there are patterns of strike behaviour in different countries, such as the Mediterranean-Asian pattern of large numbers of union members involved in short-duration strikes. In reaction to Ross and Hartman's classification and especially their prediction that strike action will wither away, other researchers similarly developed their own categorizations.[77] The models others developed became ever more complicated and therefore harder to execute, while the result was still open to a great deal of criticism. In his 1995 study Roberto Franzosi mentioned five theoretical approaches.[78] First came the business-cycle approach suggesting that the state of the labour market changes the bargaining position of employees. Then came the economic hardship approach, which suggested that workers are likely to strike when hardship becomes unbearable for them. Third was a political-exchange theory positing that welfare policies of social democratic governments reduce the incidence of strikes. Fourth were institutional theories supposing that institutionalization of collective bargaining causes a specific duration of strikes, which itself depends on the duration of contracts. Franzosi's fifth theory concerned resource mobilization, which suggests that workers organized into unions are more likely to go on strike. All Franzosi's approaches can explain some part of the development of strike activity, as can the Marxist class-struggle approach, which sees strikes as an integral part of capitalist labour relations. Nevertheless they all have their limitations because they can set in place only one piece in the puzzle of strikes. To overcome their limitations Franzosi added a new approach in which strike action is more than a dependent variable but becomes an independent variable explaining itself.

So far, the development of theories was almost exclusively based on post-World War II data from Western countries; one can imagine that in developing countries other mechanisms are at work.[79] Another problem that cannot be solved by all

---

[75] Philip Bentley and Barry Hughes, "Cyclical Influences on Strike Activity: The Australian Record 1952–68", *Australian Economic Papers*, 9, 15 (1970), p. 154.

[76] A.M. Ross and P.T. Hartman, *Changing Patterns of Industrial Conflict* (New York, 1960).

[77] Douglas A. Hibbs, "On the Political Economy of Long-Run Trends in Strike Activity", *British Journal of Political Science*, 8, 2 (1978), pp. 153–175; Walter Korpi and Michael Shalev, "Strikes, Industrial Relations and Class Conflict in Capitalist Societies", *British Journal of Sociology*, 30, 2 (1979), pp. 164–187.

[78] Roberto Franzosi, *The Puzzle of Strikes. Class and State Strategies in Postwar Italy* (Cambridge, 1995), pp. 10–12.

[79] The first explorations in this field include Y.R.K. Reddy, "Strikes in India: Verification of Ross and Hartman's Conclusion", *Indian Journal of Industrial Relations*, 17, 2 (1981), pp. 239–248; R. Bean and

these theoretical approaches is that, partly as a consequence of the availability of data, measures of the motivation of workers to go on strike are based on highly aggregated datasets.

Strikes under modern capitalism have been the subject of study since the impact of them was first felt as the sign of industrial conflict. Because in several countries, including Germany, going on strike was considered illegal, the police were actually the first to collect data on strikes. Strikes also being a clear expression of the "social question", economists, historians, politicians, and national statistical bureaus soon followed suit. Labour unions and socialist parties regarded strikes as a means to achieve power for the working classes and their organizations. They, too, therefore published data and reports of strikes.[80] Since 1927 the ILO has been compiling international data on strikes and lockouts, which data, aggregated on a yearly basis per nation state and economic sector, have been published in the *Yearbook of Labour Statistics*. For each country that collects data on labour conflicts the ILO charts per economic sector the yearly totals of the number of labour disputes, the number of workers involved, and the number of working days lost as a result of disputes. These data are available online for 1969 onwards at www.ilo.org/ilostat/.

In January 1993 the Fifteenth International Conference of Labour Statisticians adopted guidelines for the collection and publication of data on labour disputes, but the guidelines have not been adopted by all statistical bureaus, hence the difficulty of using ILO data for proper comparative research.[81] The main problem facing the ILO in compiling and publishing data on strikes and lockouts is the availability and comparability of national data. For example, postwar German statistics have never supplied the number of conflicts, despite repeated requests from the ILO. A second problem is that because of the high level of data aggregation cross-tabulation is impossible between time series. In the past, national bureaus published data at the micro level, but for various reasons – not least cost – they have stopped doing so. In the recent past, privacy regulations, too, have made it almost impossible to publish such labour conflict information.

Alongside the official publications by the ILO and the national statistical bureaus, historians and social scientists have compiled, analysed, and published data on strikes and lockouts. A good example of such datasets is the publication by Bevan, who as long ago as 1880 used paper clippings to tabulate strikes in the

---

K. Holden, "Determinants of Strikes in India: A Quantitative Analysis", *Indian Journal of Industrial Relations*, 28, 2 (1992), pp. 161–168; and James W. McGuire, "Strikes in Argentina: Data Sources and Recent Trends", *Latin American Research Review*, 31, 3 (1996), pp. 127–150.
80 Franzosi, *Puzzle of Strikes*.
81 Igor Chernyshev, "Decent Work Statistical Indicators: Strikes and Lockouts Statistics in the International Context", available at http://www.ilo.org/public/english/bureau/stat/download/articles/2003-3.pdf.

UK.[82] Data published annually by the ILO therefore forms only a small proportion of the data collected and published by national bureaus. Moreover, there have been many inconsistencies in the data because bureaus very often refuse to collect information in accordance with ILO recommendations. An infamous example is the change in the USA when it was decided to publish information only on strikes with more than 1,000 participants. Problematic, too, is that a single number appearing in the data might refer to a combination of strikes and lockouts. Despite ILO recommendations most countries deliver a set of data which is no more than an aggregate figure for both forms of labour conflicts in which employees are the instigators of strikes and employers order lockouts. Of course it is often true that both are intertwined, but there are a great many conflicts in which they are not. Aggregate data for the USA show that the development of the numbers of strikers and locked-out workers do not always go in the same direction.[83]

Consistency of the time series is altogether a problem.[84] Intensive strike research cannot rely on data published by the ILO because of collection differences and gaps in the statistics. Extraction of information from digitized newspapers is one possibility that might be expected to increase in the near future as new techniques are developed. Software can identify terms in digitized newspapers and other digital sources, and can then connect what it finds to create a structured dataset that will transcend the simple search term now so familiar to all. A few efforts have been made, with promising results, so we must continue the approach of searching for micro data to improve out insight into why workers go on strike.[85]

Strike waves

Ever since the collection of strike statistics began, researchers have looked for patterns. The first extensive statistical study of strikes was published in 1939 by John I. Griffin. He relied exclusively on data from the USA, but his findings are still worth reading. He made calculations and drew a graph showing the growth in the number of workers involved in strikes from 1880 – 1937.[86] Griffin's graph shows yearly

---

[82] G. Phillips Bevan, "The Strikes of the Past Ten Years", *Journal of the Statistical Society of London*, 43, 1 (1880), pp. 35 – 64. Another useful dataset is Charles Tilly and David K. Jordan, "Strikes and Labor Activity in France, 1830 – 1960", ICPSR08421-v2. Ann Arbor, MI: Inter-University Consortium for Political and Social Research [distributor], 2012 – 08 – 15.
[83] John I. Griffin, *Strikes: A Study in Quantitative Economics* (New York, 1939), p. 207.
[84] Dave Lyddon, "Strike Statistics and the Problems of International Comparison", in: Sjaak van der Velden et al. (eds), *Strikes Around the World, 1968 – 2005: Case-Studies of 15 Countries* (Amsterdam, 2007), pp. 24 – 39.
[85] Kalliopi Zervanou et al., "Documenting Social Unrest: Detecting Strikes in Historical Daily Newspapers", in: A. Nadamoto, A. Jatowt, and A. Wierzbicki (eds), *Social Informatics*, vol. 8359 (Berlin, 2014), pp. 120 – 133.
[86] Griffin, *Strikes*, p. 45.

fluctuations, overall growth, and peaks especially in the period just after World War I and at the end of the 1930s. Data from other countries show similar developments. What we can now with hindsight see was in fact a minor peak around 1890 for England, France, and Germany,[87] and although the union movements involved in those strike movements differed in character Friedhelm Boll concluded that they were similar in scope and strengthened collective interest organizations. State intervention meant that social conflicts became more politically controllable, and politics in general became more open to the public.[88]

The second and bigger strike wave occurred at the end of World War I, and another upsurge took place at the end of World War II. Although at the end of the 1950s there was a feeling among researchers that the strike as a phenomenon was on the wane,[89] experience proved that belief to have been mistaken. The late 1960s and the 1970s witnessed strike movements, such as Paris 1968, the *autunno caldo* in Italy in 1969, and the *Cordobazo* in Argentina. There was a general strike in Senegal,[90] and the so-called "Winter of Discontent" of 1978–1979 in the United Kingdom. Researchers were keen to understand those new and unexpected developments,[91] but again history took another course. Strike activity in the West promptly went into a decline from which it has not recovered, so that again we might well wonder if there will be another reversal in the future or if we are now really seeing the final withering away of the strike. On a global scale certainly, the almost disappearance of strike activity in the West might be countered by a rise in developing countries. ILO data indeed show a rise in workers' participation in labour conflicts, and recent unofficial data for China have indicated that workers there are still going on strike.[92] However, there is simply too little data to make a sound judgement on the question. The Chinese data also include informal forms of labour conflict, while the ILO data is formed purely from the sum of strikes and lockouts.

The bigger question is whether or not related movements of class conflicts exist globally or regionally. Can we predict strike waves from existing data for the past 150 years? In the past researchers primarily used Western data to look for strike

---

[87] Friedhelm Boll, *Arbeitskämpfe und Gewerkschaften in Deutschland, England und Frankreich* (Bonn, 1992).
[88] Ibid., pp. 17, 628.
[89] Ross and Hartman, *Changing Patterns*. Their idea has been widely cited, but their relativization that the strike would not wither away in the US as it had done in Northern Europe (p. 181) was mostly neglected.
[90] Françoise Blum, "Sénégal 1968: révolte étudiante et grève générale", *Revue d'histoire moderne et contemporaine*, 59, 2 (2012), pp. 144–177.
[91] Solomon Barkin (ed.), *Worker Militancy and its Consequences, 1965–1975: New Directions in Western Industrial Relations* (New York, 1975); Colin Crouch and Alessandro Pizzorno (eds), *The Resurgence of Class Conflict in Western Europe since 1968*, 2 vols (London, 1978).
[92] http://maps.clb.org.hk/strikes/en.

waves[93] and identified three big international strike waves over the long twentieth century, those being in the early 1870s, then from 1910–1920, and finally from 1968–1974.[94] Can we find those waves in the available data? To investigate that question I have used an index that connects the three labour conflict indicators – the number of conflicts, the number of workers involved, and the number of days lost – to the size of the labour force.[95]

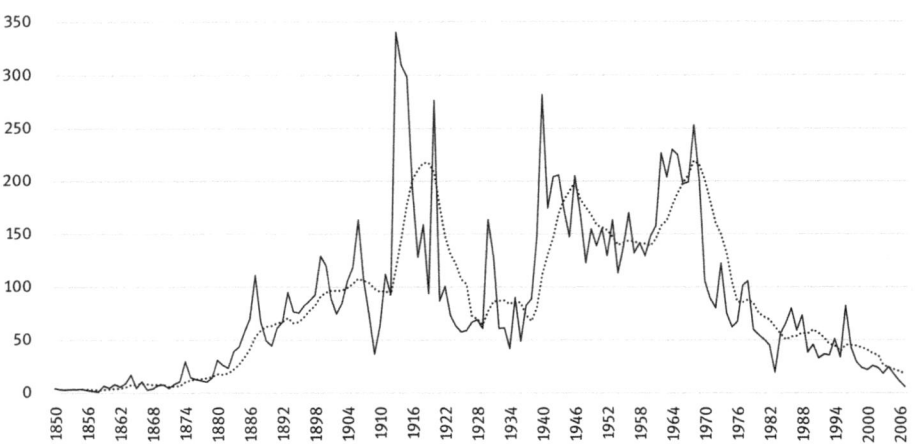

Source: https://datasets.socialhistory.org/dataverse/labourconflicts

Figure 1. Strike index for sixteen countries, and seven-year moving average (dotted line), 1856 to 2012

We can indeed see minor peaks in 1886 and 1893, but the real peaks were in 1912, 1920, 1936, 1946, and 1974. The seven-year moving average indicated by the dotted line indicates three real peaks, in the mid-1920s, the mid-1950s, and the late 1970s and early 1980s. Minor peaks then indicate lesser strike activity around 1910 and 1940, after which strike activity really plummeted from the peak of the 1970s back to the level of the 1870s, a development not unnoticed in many studies. Unlike the "withering away" of the strike mentioned by Ross and Hartman in 1960, which

---

93 Ernesto Screpanti, "Long Cycles in Strike Activity: An Empirical Investigation", *British Journal of Industrial Relations*, 25, 1 (1987), pp. 99–124; Beverly Silver, *Forces of Labor. Workers' Movements and Globalization since 1870* (Cambridge, 2003); Sjaak van der Velden, "Strikes in Global Labor History: The Dutch Case", *Review Fernand Braudel Center*, 26, 4 (2003), pp. 381–405.
94 John Kelly, *Rethinking Industrial Relations: Mobilization, Collectivism and Long Waves* (London and New York, 1998), p. 87.
95 The index has been calculated for sixteen countries: USA, Canada, Australia, New Zealand, Belgium, Germany, Denmark, France, UK, Italy, Norway, Austria, Spain, Sweden, Switzerland, and Japan. Sjaak van der Velden (ed.), *Striking Numbers: New Approaches to Quantitative Strike Research* (Amsterdam, 2012), p. 168.

was immediately followed by impressive growth, the current downward trend has continued for more than thirty years.

Looking at Figure 1 we come to the seemingly unavoidable conclusion that in the developed countries strike activity reached fluctuating heights after rapid growth, with rapid decline completing the picture. But what about other regions? Did developing countries take over the lead in strike activity, or is the decline there the same? Again, those who would calculate a comparable index are hampered by lack of data. The ILO has tried to collect for all other parts of the world data similar to the data they have for Western countries, but that has proved difficult. There is a Dutch saying that "if you cannot turn the wind, you must turn the sails of the windmill", so I have calculated an index for twenty-seven non-Western countries for a shorter period of time, with the number of countries involved fluctuating between twelve and twenty-seven.

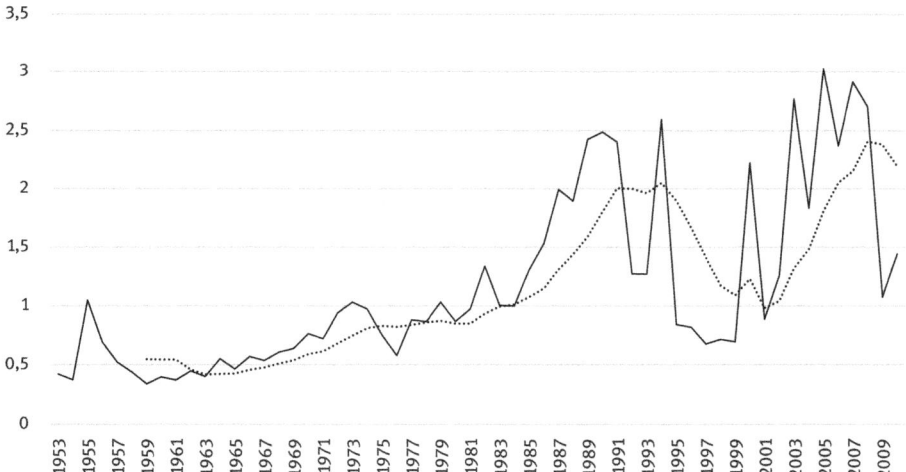

Source: https://datasets.socialhistory.org/dataverse

Figure 2. Strike index for twenty-seven countries from Africa, Asia, Central America, and South America, and seven-year moving average (dotted line), 1953–2010[96]

This index shows a different pattern from that in the Western index. While an initial downward movement since the mid-1970s is discernible, strike development recovered from the early 1980s until 1990. Then the index fell again, to recover after

---

[96] From the ILO data only those years were used for which information for more than ten countries was available. The countries are in alphabetical order: Algeria, Burkina Faso, Burundi, Cameroon, Chile, Egypt, Ghana, Hong Kong, India, Indonesia, Iraq, Malawi, Mali, Mexico, Morocco, Nigeria, Pakistan, Peru, Singapore, South Africa, Thailand, Tunisia, Turkey, Uganda, Venezuela, Zambia, and Zimbabwe. For only a few of these countries are the time series complete.

2001. In short, strike development in those twenty-seven countries differs from what happened in the West. And then there is the observation that in the biggest country on earth strikes have become an increasingly prominent feature of society since the 1990s.[97] Unfortunately no reliable data are available for China, despite the efforts of independent researchers.[98]

The question of whether or not there will be a future resurgence of strikes in Western countries like the ones before is one for future historians to try to answer. But given the history of the strike, which dates back thousands of years, we may expect that as long as subordinate labour exists people will look for ways to improve their circumstances in regard to it. If the strike does indeed go right out of fashion workers will no doubt look for other ways to assert themselves, perhaps ways we cannot even imagine now, at the beginning of the twenty-first century. It is possible that in the meantime there will be a growth of strike activity in developing countries, although there the rebellious attitude might also find expression in informal resistance too.

---

[97] John Pomfret, "China Reports Big Surge in Labor Unrest during 1999", *San Francisco Chronicle*, 24 April 2000, available at http://www.sfgate.com/news/article/China-Reports-Big-Surge-in-Labor-Unrest-During-2763108.php.
[98] http://maps.clb.org.hk/strikes/en.

Suggested reading

Adamic, Louis. *Dynamite: The Story of Class Violence in America* (New York: The Viking Press, 1931).
Alexander, Peter et al. *Marikana: Voices from South Africa's Mining Massacre* (Athens, OH: Ohio University Press, 2013).
Barkin, Solomon (ed.). *Worker Militancy and its Consequences, 1965–1975: New Directions in Western Industrial Relations* (New York: Praeger, 1975).
Brenner, Aaron, Benjamin Day, and Immanuel Ness. *The Encyclopedia of Strikes in American History* (Armonk, NY: M. E. Sharpe, 2009).
Brown, Carolyn A. *"We Were All Slaves". African Miners, Culture, and Resistance at the Enugu Government Colliery* (Oxford: James Currey, 2003).
Brown, Geoff. *Sabotage: A Study in Industrial Conflict* (Nottingham: Bertrand Russell Peace Foundation for Spokesman Books, 1977).
Burns, Joe. *Reviving the Strike. How Working People Can Regain Power and Transform America* (Brooklyn, NY: Ig Publishing, 2011).
Chan, Chris King-Chi. *The Challenge of Labour in China: Strikes and the Changing Labour Regime in Global Factories* (London and New York: Routledge, 2010).
Crouch, Colin and Alessandro Pizzorno (eds). *The Resurgence of Class Conflict in Western Europe since 1968*, 2 vols (London: Macmillan, 1978).
Dobson, C.R. *Masters and Journeymen: A Prehistory of Industrial Relations, 1717–1800* (London: Croom Helm, 1980).
Edwards, P.K. *Strikes in the United States, 1881–1974* (New York: St. Martin's Press, 1981).
Franzosi, Roberto. *The Puzzle of Strikes: Class and State Strategies in Postwar Italy* (Cambridge: Cambridge University Press, 1995).
Godard, John. "What Has Happened to Strikes?", *British Journal of Industrial Relations*, 49, 2 (2011), pp. 282–305.
Griffin, John I. *Strikes: A Study in Quantitative Economics* (New York: Columbia University Press, 1939).
Hyman, Richard. *Strikes* (London: Fontana, 1972).
Jackson, Michael P. *Strikes* (New York: St. Martin's Press, 1987).
Kelly, John E. *Rethinking Industrial Relations. Mobilization, Collectivism and Long Waves* (London and New York: Routledge, 1998).
Kerr, Clarke and Abraham Siegel. "The Interindustry Propensity to Strike: An International Comparison", in: Arthur Kornhauser, Robert Dubin and Arthur M. Ross (eds), *Industrial Conflict* (New York: McGraw-Hill, 1954), pp. 190–212.
Knowles, K.G.J.C. *Strikes. A Study in Industrial Conflict, With Special Reference to British Experience Between 1911 and 1947* (New York: Philosophical Library, 1952).
Korpi, Walter and Michael Shalev. "Strikes, Industrial Relations and Class Conflict in Capitalist Societies", *British Journal of Sociology*, 30, 2 (1979), pp. 164–187.
Lee, Ching Kwan. *Against the Law: Labor Protests in China's Rustbelt and Sunbelt* (Berkeley, CA: University of California Press, 2007).
Muthiah, Wesley S. and Sydney Wanasinghe. *We Were Making History. The Hartal of 1953* (Colombo: A Young Socialist Publication, 2002).
Ross, A.M. and P.T. Hartman. *Changing Patterns of Industrial Conflict* (New York: Wiley, 1960).
Santella, Agustín. *Labor Conflict and Capitalist Hegemony in Argentina: The Case of the Automobile Industry, 1990–2007* (Leiden and Boston: Brill, 2016).
Screpanti, Ernesto. "Long Cycles in Strike Activity: An Empirical Investigation", *British Journal of Industrial Relations*, 25, 1 (1987), pp. 99–124.

Shorter, Edward and Charles Tilly. *Strikes in France, 1830–1968* (London: Cambridge University Press, 1974).
Van den Hoven, Martha, Antal van den Bosch, and Kalliopi Zervanou. *Beyond Reported History: Strikes That Never Happened* (2010), available at https://ilk.uvt.nl/downloads/pub/papers/Amicus10-vdh-vdb-z.pdf.
Van der Velden, Sjaak *et al.* (eds). *Strikes Around the World, 1968–2005: Case-Studies of 15 Countries* (Amsterdam: Aksant, 2007).

Marcel van der Linden
8.4. Trade Unions

About what trade unions are exactly, opinions vary greatly.[1] The literature provides dozens – and possibly even hundreds – of definitions which sometimes highlight very different aspects. The common thread is that trade unions are organizations that enable employees to protect their interests. The employees concerned may include regular wage-earners, but also self-employed workers who are formally independent entrepreneurs, but who in fact work for only one or two employers, or who are agricultural share-croppers, bonded wage labourers, or slaves-for-hire.

Employees who join a union have two main kinds of interests to defend. These concern the exchange of labour power for money (the implicit or explicit labour contract) and the actual "consumption" of the labour power bought by the employer, during the labour process. Trade unions therefore deal both with wage negotiations, sick pay arrangements, etc., and with working conditions, labour intensity, and the like. A strike, or the threat of a strike, is the ultimate weapon a trade union has to enforce these interests. Although strikes are not the only weapon available to unions, a union that never calls a strike, or seriously threatens a strike, is not a trade union.

Trade unions have a long history. On 24 May 1345, the Captain of the Italian City of Florence arrested the wool-carder Ciuto Brandini and his two sons "because he said Ciuto wished to form a company at Santa Croce and make a sect and assembly with the other workmen in Florence." The specific charge of the authorities was as follows:

> "Ciuto had deliberated together with many others seduced by his words to form with the largest membership possible a brotherhood between the wool-carders and wool-combers and the other workers of the *Arte della Lana*, and to nominate from such new corporations, *Consoli* and Heads, and to this end had on different occasions and places assembled very many workmen of the worst reputation, and had in such assemblies proposed that each should contribute a certain sum (a matriculation tax) in order that thus it would more surely succeed."

Despite the massive strike and riots that Ciuto's companions staged in protest, Ciuto was hanged by the authorities.[2]

Ciuto appears to have been trying to organize a union, complete with a dues system and elected leaders. From that time, there have been countless attempts across the whole world to form unions. Although Ciuto's experiment seems to have been a spontaneous, isolated initiative – we cannot be entirely sure – unions arose in many

---

[1] This chapter includes material published in Marcel van der Linden, *Workers of the World. Essays toward a Global Labor History* (Leiden and Boston, 2008), chapters 11 and 12.
[2] Niccolò Rodolico, "The Struggle for the Right of Association in Fourteenth-Century Florence", *History*, 7 (1922–23), pp. 178–190, at 184.

other ways as well, through imitation and transformation of already existing organizations.

Trade unions and strikes

Unions exist primarily to enable collective bargaining over wages, rights and conditions, with the capacity to call a strike as their ultimate bargaining weapon. But they use other means of action as well, such as restriction of output, violence, etc. (see Chapter 8.3) and there is no *necessary* transition from strike action to industrial organization, even though trade unions have often experienced spectacular membership growth during and after strike waves.[3]

Trade unions come in many shapes and sizes. Classified according to their frequency of resorting to strikes, we can distinguish broadly between unions that exist exclusively, or almost exclusively, to organize strikes; unions that organize strikes, but serve other purposes as well; and unions intended to prevent strikes where possible. Given that, apart from autonomous trade unions where the members have a direct or indirect say, there are also heteronomous trade unions ultimately controlled by employers or third parties, we obtain the following typology:

Table 1: A general typology of trade unions

	Autonomy	Heteronomy
Union is intended primarily to organize strikes	Revolutionary Syndicalism, "mushroom" unions	—
Union is not intended primarily to organize strikes	Craft societies Bargaining unions	Autocratic unions Rackets
Union is not intended to organize strikes	—	Yellow unions

Let us elaborate these categories.

i) *Autonomous unions intended primarily to organize strikes* comprise two subtypes. On the one hand, some trade unions are formed at the start of, or during a strike, and disband quickly afterwards (regardless of whether the strike ends in victory, defeat, or compromise). These kinds of unions are often called "mushroom organizations." A great many "mushroom unions" existed. In the early twentieth century, for example, John Commons wrote that newly proletarianized Jewish workers in the United States were zealous, enthusiastic and resolute in labour conflicts, but that

---

[3] Eric Hobsbawm has even noted that all "'explosions' of labour unionism with which I am familiar" were "the *result* of worker mobilization and not its cause." Eric J. Hobsbawm, *Worlds of Labour. Further Studies in the History of Labour* (London, 1984), p. 291. Even if this is true, many cases of worker mobilization did *not* cause an explosion of labour unionism.

"once the strike was settled, either in favor or against the cause [...] that ends the union."[4] The same trend is visible across the world. In Nigeria in the 1950s, many workers "would feel obliged to support the union financially, and otherwise, only when there is a wages agitation, or to make a contribution to its coffers after a new award has been won."[5] Dipesh Chakrabarty has noted about the Calcutta jute workers: "Each outburst of labour protest, especially from the 1920s, resulted in some kind of organization. Once the outburst spent itself, however, the organization as a rule disintegrated."[6] About Argentina, Ruth Thompson writes: "Before the 1900s, most of the unions that existed were short-lived, formed to fight a particular campaign but not durable thereafter."[7]

The second type consists of the trade unions that outlast a single labour conflict, and organize a series of strikes. Best known among such "serial strike organizations" are the revolutionary syndicalist trade unions, which operated on all continents between 1890 and 1940. These organizations regarded the conflict between workers and employers as a "class war", to be won through ongoing guerrilla efforts.[8]

ii) *Autonomous trade unions that do not exist solely to organize strikes,* but develop other activities as well, include three types. Firstly, there are organizations that do *not* negotiate with employers, but instead practice unilateral control. Such organizations were common in early nineteenth-century Britain, where union members frequently refused to work for employers who did not observe the traditional rules of the trade and the rates of pay.[9] Secondly, there are trade unions willing to negotiate about some issues, but not others. Thirdly, many organizations are willing to negotiate with the employers. These organizations are now typical of the "modern" trade union movement everywhere in the world.

iii) *Heteronomous trade unions not intended exclusively to organize strikes* but with other responsibilities as well include two sub-types. In autocratic unions, officials have accumulated so much power that they cannot, or can no longer, be deposed by the members. Secondly, there are "rackets", set up by organized crime to benefit from industrial relations and regulated by violence. This type of "hold-up unionism" (Robert F. Hoxie) disciplines employers by threatening "labour trouble", and exacts tribute from workers. This will often give rise to "a double-sided monopoly", because the union bargains with favored employers "not only for the sale of its labor

---

[4] John R. Commons, quoted in Will Herberg, "Jewish Labor Movement in the United States: Early Years to World War I", *Industrial and Labor Relations Review*, 5, 4 (July 1952), pp. 501–523, at 503.
[5] T.M. Yesufu, *An Introduction to Industrial Relations in Nigeria* (Oxford, 1962), p. 68.
[6] Dipesh Chakrabarty, *Rethinking Working-Class History: Bengal 1890–1940* (Princeton, NJ, 1989), p. 124.
[7] Ruth Thompson, "Trade Union Organisation: Some Forgotten Aspects", in: Jeremy Adelman (ed.), *Essays in Argentine Labour History, 1870–1930* (Basingstoke and London, 1992), pp. 160–176, at 160.
[8] Marcel van der Linden and Wayne Thorpe (eds). *Revolutionary Syndicalism: An International Perspective* (Aldershot, 1990).
[9] Richard Hyman, *Industrial Relations. A Marxist Introduction* (London and Basingstoke, 1975), p. 44.

but for the destruction of the business of rival employers", while "the exclusion of rival workmen from the craft or industry" is achieved.[10]

iv) *Heteronomous trade unions that never or rarely organize strikes* should I think include all unions established by employers, or by institutions working with employers, to keep "industrial peace" and prevent autonomous trade unions. Such organizations are also known as "yellow unions." Examples include the "national" trade unions in Germany and France before and shortly after World War I, the many "company unions" in the United States in the 1920s and 30s, and similar organizations at American multinationals in developing countries.[11]

I am not aware of any heteronomous trade unions intended primarily to stage strikes, or of autonomous trade unions *never* willing to strike. Nor are the distinctions between the different types always clear. In some borderline cases, trade unions cannot be assigned to one specific category. Take for example, the so-called Japanese "second unions" or "unions by appointment" (*goyō-kumiai*), that sometimes arose when a radical trade union organized a strike which caused dissent among the strikers, and management seized the opportunity to encourage the establishment of a second union willing to reach a compromise, and resume work.[12] Such organizations appear midway between yellow unions and bargaining unions.

Some trade unions mutate. Sections of the Italian revolutionary-syndicalist trade union movement turned fascist in the early 1920s, for example, while some radical unions in Shanghai became rackets or yellow unions during the 1920s and 30s.

Domain of control

Labour markets are subdivided into all kinds of more or less permeable segments, and workers intending to establish a trade union will need a domain of control. This means that they must be in a position to close off a segment of the labour market, account for a substantial share of that labour-market segment, and coordinate their operations. The segment could be defined by skill, economic sector, employer, religion, ethnicity, caste, locality, etc. Every union type moreover has its own idiosyncrasies. Craft-based unions for example tend to have a clear gender-bias. The "craft" concept is frequently loaded with masculine connotations which mean the exclusion

---

10 Daniel Bell, "The Racket-Ridden Longshoremen", in: Bell, *The End of Ideology*. Revised Edition (New York: The Free Press, 1962), pp. 175–209; Paul A. Weinstein, "Racketeering and Labor: An Economic Analysis", *Industrial and Labor Relations Review*, 19 (1965–1966), pp. 402–413.
11 George L. Mosse, "The French Right and the Working Classes: Les Jaunes", *Journal of Contemporary History*, 7 (1972), pp. 185–208; Klaus Mattheier, *Die Gelben. Nationale Arbeiter zwischen Wirtschaftsfrieden und Streik* (Düsseldorf, 1973); Jingying Rao, "The Shanghai Postal Workers' Union: Sample of a Yellow Union", *Chinese Studies in History*, 27, 1–2 (1993), pp. 148–161.
12 Ronald Dore, *British Factory – Japanese Factory. The Origins of National Diversity in Industrial Relations* (Berkeley and Los Angeles, 1973), pp. 327–328.

of women.[13] Enterprise-based unions for their part usually serve tenured workers, and are inclined to identify with their "own" enterprise.

Opportunity to close off the labour-market segment. The success of a group of workers depends primarily on the opportunity to separate "insiders" from "outsiders" effectively. "Any convenient and visible characteristic, such as race, language, social origin, religion, or lack of particular school diplomas, can be used to declare competitors as outsiders."[14] If a group of employees lacks the means to establish a threshold, forming an effective organization will become virtually impossible. Benjamin Marquez studied one such case, that of the Mexican-American garment workers in El Paso, Texas, during the early 1990s. He concluded that the would-be trade union La Mujer Obrera faced "virtually insurmountable barriers" to mobilization efforts, as the major manufacturers could easily transfer their operations elsewhere or even abroad.[15]

Relative size. It is difficult to fix a minimum group size relative to the size of the labour-market segment it aims to control. But the numerical ratio of the employees willing to join the trade union to those refusing to join should be sufficient to prevent non-members from taking over members' work. Partial unemployment among the labour segment will make organizations harder to establish.

Coordination. Potential trade union members need to coordinate their operations. To this end, they must at least be aware of each other's existence, and be in a position to communicate with each other. Coordination of members within the chosen domain may be direct-democratic, indirect-democratic or autocratic, but these distinctions may in practice be vague. Direct-democratic coordination proceeds through joint plenary consultation, or elected delegates. Indirect-democratic coordination occurs via controlled union officials, or other "specialized" strike coordinators. Autocratic coordination involves unsupervised managers, such as sub-contractors.

Effective coordination depends mainly on the physical aspects of communicating with members (location and distance, etc.) and the quality of the formal or informal leaders.[16]

Strikes are the ultimate test of the ability to control a domain. If the domain withstands a confrontation with the employer or employers, it is solid enough to establish a permanent organization. That is the deeper reason why strikes have so often resulted in trade unions. Conversely, a group of employees *technically* able to stage a strike

---

[13] Anne Phillips and Barbara Taylor, "Sex and Skill: Notes Towards a Feminist Economics", *Feminist Review*, 6 (1980), pp. 79–88.
[14] Raymond Murphy, "The Structure of Closure: A Critique and Development of the Theories of Weber, Collins, and Parkin", *British Journal of Sociology*, 35 (1984), pp. 547–567, at 548.
[15] Benjamin Marquez, "Organizing Mexican-American Women in the Garment Industry: La Mujer Obrera", *Women and Politics*, 15, 1 (1995), pp. 65–87, at 67.
[16] Marshall Ganz, "Resources and Resourcefulness: Strategic Capacity in the Unionization of California Agriculture", *American Journal of Sociology*, 105 (1999–2000), pp. 1003–1062.

may nevertheless decide against this option, for example because a strike would displease, or harm, the general public. One example is that of nurses, who were typically very difficult to organize in the past, because nurses assumed that unionization would inevitably lead to hospital strikes. Moreover, the idea "that a hospital worker might desert her 'calling' and leave a patient on the operating table to join a picket line was a frightening prospect to both patients and the community at large."[17]

Threats to the domain of control

A union's success in stabilizing control over its domain depends partly on its own ability to organize and partly on external influences over which the organization has little or no control. I will first explore the *internal* risks that trade unions face. To serve as effective coordinator of the domain, the trade union needs to cultivate loyalty and cooperation from its members. Factors influencing such cooperation can be many. They include:
- The relative *burden of membership*. The "costs" can include not just entrance fees and dues, but also a required investment in time (depending on the frequency of meetings, the rotation of delegate duties, and the availability of paid officials) plus other possible costs (the danger of losing one's job, ending up in prison, etc.).
- The relative *burden of non-membership*. Potential members who refuse to join may face certain risks as well. For instance, they may lose their job if the company becomes a closed shop, i.e. an arrangement where the employer makes union membership a condition for employment.
- The presence or absence of *selective benefits*. Goods and services available to members have included travel money (*viaticum*) for artisans and journeymen unable to find work in one city and therefore forced to move to another city; labour mediation for members looking for work; insurance plans (sickness and other funds for members); legal council in the event of individual labour conflicts; and additional opportunities, like access to holiday homes, discounts on household appliances, services etc.

How effective such means can be depends on the rate of labour turnover. If members work at a certain establishment or in a certain occupation only briefly, their union loyalty is much more difficult to cultivate or maintain than if the rank and file is stable and sedentary. Workers with strong rural links were often difficult to organize permanently, because they were frequently short-term migrants, who performed wage

---

[17] Susan Reverby, "Hospital Organizing in the 1950s: An Interview with Lillian Roberts", *Signs*, 1 (1976), pp. 1053–1063, at 1054.

labour to reach a certain financial "target"; as soon as they had accumulated that amount, they returned to their villages of origin.

Excepting "mushroom" organizations, financial stability is a second important internal aspect. Regular payment of membership dues is of course crucial, but for the members trade union dues are always a somewhat risky investment, since their return is never fixed in advance. Whether members pay their dues regularly, depends on the amount and "permanence" of their income, and on their self-discipline. The first factor complicates organizing among seasonal workers, casual labourers, and the like. The second factor is also closely related to seasonal influences. On Java in the 1910s, the managers of the railway and tram workers' union regularly complained of "the difficulty of squeezing dues out of [the members] on a regular month to month basis" – because members "could see little tangible benefit."[18] In Manila in the 1920s, many cigar makers considered themselves union members, although they paid no dues. They argued "that there was no need for that because they would readily contribute to a strike fund if there were a strike. In the meantime, they needed their money for family expenses."[19] In early twentieth-century Argentina, many union members defaulted on their dues. "The union and left-wing press carried frequent appeals to *morosos* ('shirkers') throughout the period to regularize their position with their respective union."[20]

Organizational discipline is of critical importance. Effective organization depends on whether officials do their duty, and on whether members attend meetings. Many organizations have tried to encourage such discipline through a vast system of penalties, a remarkable imitation of sanctions imposed by employers on their staff.

External threats can be both economic and non-economic. *Economic influences* may include many different factors, such as business cycles, concentration trends in corporate industry, or shifts on the world market. *Non-economic influences* may include resistance by the authorities, and entrepreneurs or third parties preventing unions from maintaining control over their domain. Until today, legal measures may outlaw unions, or make it extremely difficult for them to continue their activities with any effect.[21] Unions have been violently repressed, their funds confiscated and their leaders arrested.

If trade unions are legalized, entrepreneurs may nevertheless try to prevent or discourage their employees from joining. One strategy is to intimidate workers, for example by threatening to sack them if they join. As a formalized method of employer intimidation, the so-called *yellow dog contract* is "a promise, made by workers as a condition of employment, not to belong to a union during the period of employment, or not to engage in certain specified activities, such as collective bargaining or strik-

---

18 John Ingleson, *In Search of Justice: Workers and Unions in Colonial Java, 1908–1926* (Singapore, 1986), p. 81.
19 Melinda Tria Kerkvliet, *Manila Workers' Unions, 1900–1950* (Quezon City, 1992), p. 56.
20 Thompson, "Trade Union Organisation", p. 165.
21 See the reports of the International Labour Organization in Geneva.

ing, without which the formal right to belong to a union is wholly valueless."[22] Overt or covert violence occurs as well. In the 1960s, some entrepreneurs in Japan made arrangements so that employees who tried to set up a trade union were physicaly attacked. "Workers reported being kicked, having lit cigarettes put to their skin, and being threatened with worse violence."[23] In contemporary India, employers still beat their "insubordinate" agricultural workers to death sometimes.[24] Entrepreneurs have also mobilized militias and gangs of thugs to break strikes and suppress other forms of resistance. Sometimes they block trade unions by refusing to negotiate and at the same time improve working conditions and the standard of living of employees. In several cases, large companies took the next step by establishing company unions (yellow unions) to reduce support for autonomous trade unions. In addition, employers wage propaganda campaigns against the unions, and try to turn the general public against them, for example by referring to "the red menace". They have also tried to block employee actions through espionage.

Precarious democracy

In an ever-expanding capitalist economy, maintaining union power requires expanding its domain gradually, either horizontally (through endogenous expansion, collaboration with other unions, or setting up new unions with the same domain elsewhere) or vertically (through endogenous expansion, collaboration with other unions, or setting up new unions with adjacent domains in the same region). If the union exists only locally, the need will arise (i) to work with other local unions, (ii) to establish sister organizations in other places, or (iii) to join an established, larger trade union. Unions organized nationally may benefit from international cooperation.

Establishing a stable union that stays effective as its domain expands, invariably affects its internal balance of power. The initial domain of a new trade union is nearly always relatively small, with a rank and file concentrated in one place and/or with one employer. Really small unions nearly always have either a direct-democratic or autocratic structure. The smaller a union, the more homogeneous its membership, the more transparent the interests of members and officials, and the greater the direct-democratic influence of the rank-and-file will tend to be. Autocratic unions, however, usually arise when the founder is one person who aims to retain full control over "his" or "her" initiative. Stephen Large describes how the Japanese trade union

---

[22] Joel I. Seidman, "The Yellow Dog Contract", *Quarterly Journal of Economics*, 46 (1931–1932), pp. 348–361, at 348.
[23] Christena L. Turner, *Japanese Workers in Protest. An Ethnography of Consciousness and Experience* (Berkeley, CA, 1995), p. 35.
[24] Jan Breman, "Silencing the Voice of Agricultural Labourers", *Modern Asian Studies*, 33 (1999), pp. 1–22.

Yūaikai, established in 1912 and camouflaged as a mutual insurance society, was run by its founder Suzuki Bunji: "From his offices [...] Suzuki Bunji maintained a firm personal control over the movement during its initial growth in the 1912–16 period. He had conceived the Yūaikai, named it, selected its leaders, recruited the services of distinguished sympathizers, dominated the formulation of Yūaikai goals and programs, delegated authority in the movement, represented the Yūaikai in dealing with business and political leaders, and even personally designed the Yūaikai emblem."[25] In nearly all cases, the indirect-democratic form arose only derivatively, either when the further growth of a union's domain precluded a functioning direct democracy, or when an autocratic union became more democratic.

Even in relatively small unions, a heterogeneous membership quickly leads to differences in power. Women members, for example, are often less influential than male ones. Women often had more difficulty paying their dues on time, because they ordinarily earnt far less than men, and because their dependent status (usually as wives or daughters) meant they lacked full control over the expenditure of their earnings. Sometimes ethno-cultural influences were relevant as well. In some communities, a woman could not attend an evening meeting without being escorted by a man, while in other communities women had important economic responsibilities, and were considered to be responsible for their own affairs. Factors unrelated to gender can promote power differences within unions as well, such as religion, race, political beliefs, age, education, or region. Wherever they enter the picture, complex interlocking hierarchies can result.

Structural shifts in the internal relationships

The growing union domain eventually creates three interrelated, structural organizational consequences. Firstly, the inevitable increase in the scale of organizing necessitates greater coordination of the activities of more and more branches and work sites. Secondly, as controlling the domain becomes more difficult, full-time union officials ("professionals") are needed to support the organization as a whole. Professionalization may already occur in relatively small unions. In an organization with two hundred members, if each member contributes 0.5 percent of his earnings, enough funds exist to appoint one full-time official. At least four factors can promote professionalization as the union domain expands.
- The number of work sites within the domain, affecting the number of contacts that must be maintained and the caseload of organizers.
- The communicational distance between the work sites, i.e. the amount of time and energy required to maintain contact among workers in the domain.

---

[25] Stephen S. Large, *The Rise of Labor in Japan. The Yūaikai, 1912–19* (Tokyo, 1972), p. 29.

- The nature of work sites, i.e. whether the work sites are relatively permanent (e.g. factories) or move constantly (e.g. construction sites).
- The relative mobility of the workers, i.e. the frequency with which employees change work sites and/or employer.

Third, professionalization leads to anonymization of relationships within the union. Early, small-scale unions often already had elaborate regulations. But professionalization leads to a depersonalized system of rules, i.e. a bureaucracy. The official is transformed from a "commercial traveller in the class struggle" into an "employee equipped with technical knowledge."[26]

Professionalization promotes the transition to centralized structures, because the transaction costs of a unitary organization are proportionately lower. After all, the principal communications are between the branches and the central office, rather than among the local chapters.[27] Centralization coincides with the disappearance of the internal direct democracy, provided that such a system actually exists. A growing membership, dispersed across ever more work sites with large communication distances from each other, virtually precludes regular decision-making by all members on all matters of importance. Inevitably, a system of representation will emerge, in which the rank and file cedes areas of authority, temporarily or permanently, to elected representatives. The measure of indirect influence that the members retain depends in part on the extent to which the professionals are elected democratically.

Collective bargaining, centralization and opposition

Collective bargaining is in fact the opposite of individual bargaining. While the latter term refers to negotiations conducted by *individual* employees with their employer, the former refers to negotiations involving a *group* of employees. Very broadly speaking, *every* workers' collective action involving negotiations with the employer is a form of collective bargaining. Ordinarily, however, the scope of collective bargaining is restricted to negotiations by a group of employees with one or more employers, which culminate in a collective agreement – a written or an unwritten contract that both parties agree to observe for a specific period (e.g., a year), regardless of whether this contract is, or is not, legally enforceable.

Collective labour agreements are reached only under certain conditions. Firstly, neither the employers nor the unions may prevail. Consider the case of a single large union negotiating with several employers, without the employers having formed a combination. Such a situation is conceivable, if the employers expect the costs of

---

26 Robert Michels, *Political Parties. A Sociological Study of the Oligarchical Tendencies of Modern Democracy* (New York, 1959), p. 301.
27 Oliver E. Williamson, *Markets and Hierarchies: Analysis and Antitrust Implications. A Study in the Economics of Internal Organization* (New York, 1975).

forming a coalition to exceed the benefits. In such a case, the union may unilaterally stipulate the conditions. Conversely, an employer who thinks he can easily withstand any union pressure to negotiate will rarely be inclined to negotiate. In other words, unions must be in a position to threaten to industrial action; they must have a "recognized *potential* of power", as a consequence of which "concessions are likely to be made not because members have struck, but in order to avoid a strike."[28] Generally, therefore, a certain power balance is assumed between the two parties. Secondly, employers should be willing to surrender part of their sovereignty in the firm. Thirdly, unions do not expect a radical change of the balance of power in the short term. Fourthly, the negotiating union typically has professional negotiators. Although collective agreements can be reached by direct-democratic unions in theory, they are much more likely to be achieved by unions with full-time officials. After all, negotiations for collective agreements ordinarily require union negotiators who are available for weeks, and possibly even months, and who have sufficient expertise. Fifthly, negotiators for both sides need to be firmly in control of their rank and file, to ensure that each will keep to their side of the bargain when the contract is signed. Finally, the legal and political institutions should allow the unions sufficient freedom to operate.[29]

Overall, few cases where employers and trade unions are pitched against each other meet all these criteria. This is part of the reason why only a minor fraction of the world labour force works according to collective agreements.

As an organization grows and becomes more centralized, bureaucratized and anonymized, members lose influence in how it is run. Under a collective agreement, for example, the union leadership has a moral, and in some cases a legal, obligation to ensure that workers do not go on strike, so long as the employer complies with agreements made. In some cases, however, the rank and file becomes dissatisfied with the agreement, and wants to reopen negotiations, even though the term of the agreement has not yet expired. This may lead to a genuine *wildcat strike*, a strike "in which the formal union leaders have actually lost control and the strike is led by individuals whose position in the formal structure does not prescribe such a role for them."[30] Eventually, new unions may be organized which claim to have closer ties with the rank-and-file members. Thus, despite the constant drive toward centralization, countercurrents may emerge which reverse part of the trend at certain critical moments.

---

[28] Claus Offe and Helmut Wiesenthal. "Two Logics of Collective Action (1980)", in: Offe, *Disorganized Capitalism: Contemporary Transformations of Work and Politics* (Cambridge, 1985), pp. 170–220, at 216.
[29] Adolf Sturmthal, "Industrial Relations Strategies", in: Sturmthal and James G. Scoville (eds), *The International Labor Movement in Transition* (Urbana, IL, and London, 1973), pp. 1–33, at 9–10.
[30] Alvin W. Gouldner, *Wildcat Strike: A Study in Worker-Management Relationships* (New York, 1954), p. 93.

Internationalization

Often, trade unions develop solidarity across national borders. The first significant expressions of organized internationalism stemmed from London, the main centre of world capitalism during the lengthy period of economic growth from the late 1840s to the early 1870s. The establishment of the International Working Men's Association (IWMA, also known as the First International) in 1864 was an expression of this development. It was primarily based on the cooperation of English and Continental European workers; its first piece of activism concerned an attempt at strike-breaking in 1866. In April of that year, the London tailors organized themselves, demanding a wage increase of a penny an hour. The employers responded with a lock-out, and tried to recruit strike-breakers in Germany, which they had done on other occasions. The IWMA helped to block their efforts in Hamburg and Berlin, thus contributing to the successful outcome of the tailors' action.[31] It is important to note that such cross-border solidarity was sub-national. As no national trade unions as yet existed, international contacts were always between local organizations. It was in fact a "sub-national internationalism".

The IWMA collapsed in the early 1870s. Around the turn of the twentieth century, when national consolidation of trade unions in the North Atlantic region was already far advanced, a new stage, that of nation-based internationalism, entered the picture. There seem to have been at least three areas in which international cooperation grew more or less as a matter of course out of practical activities.

Firstly, there was the area of highly skilled (artisan) occupational groups with international mobility. Amongst printers, for example, there were long-standing cross-national relationships, especially in certain regions sharing a common language (e.g. the French region comprising France, parts of Belgium and Switzerland); they had attended the conferences of fraternal trade organizations in other countries as early as the 1860s. Issues like the *viaticum* (travel money) loomed large in those years.[32]

International migration constituted a second area of international activity. Countries with fast-growing economies attracted hundreds of thousands of immigrants from less developed parts of the world. Chinese and Japanese migrated to California, Poles and Italians to Germany, etc. Trade unions in the recipient countries tried either to organize the new arrivals, or to exclude them from the national labour market. The

---

31 Iorwerth Prothero, *Radical Artisans in England and France, 1830–1870* (Cambridge, 1997), p. 116.
32 Paul Chauvet, *Les Ouvriers du livre en France de 1789 à la constitution de la Fédération du Livre* (Paris, 1956), pp., 632–634; idem, *Les Ouvriers du livre et du journal: La Fédération Française des Travailleurs du Livre* (Paris, 1971), p. 245; A.E. Musson, *The Typographical Association* (London, 1954), pp. 305–308.

German federation of construction workers sought to organize Italian immigrants, sometimes successfully.[33]

A third area was international transport. Here the labour market and the labour process were inherently international, which facilitated collaboration. The tendency towards internationalism was particularly marked in this section of the working class, as evidenced by the large-scale international transport strike of 1911, and by the fact that branches of the British seamen's union (NAS&FU) existed briefly in the early 1890s in Norway, Sweden, Denmark, Germany and the Netherlands.[34]

The first organizations set up were international trade secretariats, federations of national trade unions representing different occupational groups. A substantial impetus was given by the founding of the Second International in 1889 as a cooperative mechanism for socialists (and anarchists until 1896). The congresses held by the International were important meeting points for trade unionists. With the establishment of the international trade secretariats well under way, cooperation between national trade union confederations gathered pace as well. In 1903, the ISNTUC (International Secretariat of National Trade Union Confederations) came into being. At the urging of the AFL, it became the International Federation of Trade Unions (IFTU) in 1913. The ISNTUC and the IFTU remained primarily focused on the North Atlantic region well into the twentieth century.[35]

The brief period between 1889 and 1903 was of exceptional importance for the subsequent rise of the international trade union movement. The structures devised during those years persisted, largely unchanged, throughout the twentieth century. The course of events a century ago endowed the international trade union movement with the dual structure of international trade secretariats on the one hand, and international confederations (with changing names) on the other. But it is not altogether the most logical structure. The international trade secretariats could have formed an international federation of their own. Had they done so, only one international umbrella organization would exist today, an arrangement that would probably have been more effective.

While the structure consolidated at the beginning of the twentieth century remained unchanged for many decades, several significant shifts *within* the structure did take place over the years. Prior to the First World War, Germany occupied the dominant position. In 1913, the headquarters of at least seventeen of the twenty-

---

[33] Hermann Schäfer, "Italienische 'Gastarbeiter' im deutschen Kaiserreich, 1890–1914", *Zeitschrift für Unternehmensgeschichte*, 27 (1982), pp. 192–214, at 208–210; Ulrich Herbert, *Geschichte der Ausländerbeschäftigung in Deutschland 1880 bis 1980* (Berlin and Bonn, 1986), pp. 68–70; René del Fabbro, *Transalpini: Italienische Arbeitswanderung nach Süddeutschland im Kaiserreich 1870–1918* (Osnabrück, 1996).
[34] Arthur Marsh and Victoria Ryan, *The Seamen: A History of the National Union of Seamen, 1887–1987* (Oxford, 1989), pp. 51–52.
[35] Geert Van Goethem, *The Amsterdam International. The World of the International Federation of Trade Unions (IFTU), 1913–1945* (Aldershot, 2006).

eight trade secretariats were in that country. The major exceptions to the rule were the miners and textile workers, whose headquarters were in Manchester.[36] After 1918, Great Britain and the USA assumed the leading role. Whereas the German trade union movement had stood more or less "outside" its own state, in the postwar years the TUC and AFL(-CIO) entered into close collaboration with their respective states. For a while, collaboration between the labour federation and the US government and big business was so close, that it was likened by some to a corporative structure, a *blocco storico* à la Antonio Gramsci.[37] During the Second World War, the British TUC moved towards "a close relationship with the government in developing labour policy in the colonies", often emulating the enlightened extension of a colonial power in Africa, Asia and the Caribbean.[38]

In the course of the "national" phase of internationalism, the number of international trade secretariats both swelled through the advent of additional umbrella organizations, and dwindled as the result of amalgamation. The social-reformist mainstream of the IFTU and its successor after 1949, the International Confederation of Free Trade Unions (ICFTU), was in time confronted with a number of rivals. They included not only the syndicalist international calling itself, like the First International, the IWMA (since 1922) but also the communist Red International of Labour Unions (RILU, 1921–37) and the International Federation of Christian Trade Unions (IFCTU, since 1920).[39] In 1945, The IFTU joined forces with the communist trade unions in the WFTU, but their alliance ended with the onset of the Cold War. The ICFTU was founded in 1949, while the WFTU fell under communist domination.[40]

In the inter-war years, interest in trade unionism increased in the peripheral and semi-peripheral countries. The RILU sought to put down roots in those regions almost from the moment of its inception in 1921. It was followed a few years later, from about 1928, by the IFTU, partly to counter the rival communist organization, which was intent on gaining greater influence in the colonial and semi-colonial

---

36 Michel Dreyfus, "The Emergence of an International Trade Union Organization (1902–1919)", in: Marcel van der Linden (ed.), *The International Confederation of Free Trade Unions* (Bern, 2000), pp. 25–71, at 36–9.
37 Robert W. Cox, "Labor and Hegemony: A Reply", *International Organization*, 34 (1980), 159–176.
38 D.I. Davies, "The Politics of the TUC's Colonial Policy", *The Political Quarterly*, 35 (1964), pp. 23–34, at 24.
39 Wayne Thorpe, *"The Workers Themselves": Revolutionary Syndicalism and International Labour, 1913–1923* (Dordrecht, 1989); idem, "Syndicalist Internationalism before World War II", in: van der Linden and Thorpe, *Revolutionary Syndicalism*, pp. 237–260; Patrick Pasture, *Histoire du syndicalisme chrétien international: La difficile recherche d'une troisième voie* (Paris, 1999); Reiner Tosstorff, *Profintern*. The IFCTU became the World Confederation of Labor (WCL) in 1968, and merged with the ICFTU in 2006, out of which the International Trade Union Confederation (ITUC) emerged.
40 Anthony Carew, "The World Federation of Trade Unions, 1945–1949", in: van der Linden, *International Confederation of Free Trade Unions*, pp. 165–184; Carew, "Towards a Free Trade Union Centre", *ibid.*, pp. 187–339.

countries.⁴¹ Another factor was the concurrent growth of the labour movement in the Third World, making the question of what course it would pursue all the more urgent. The IFCTU followed the same path somewhat later. Up to the Second World War, it was solely oriented toward Europe, but this changed of necessity after 1945, in part because several of its former member organizations had disbanded or amalgamated with trade unions encompassing all ideologies (e.g. in Germany and Austria). The IFCTU set up a reasonably successful regional organization in Latin America (1954), and recruited support in Vietnam and Africa as well.⁴²

The IFTU and ICFTU were both dominated by the British TUC and the American AFL(-CIO), investing them in the Third World with the reputation of allies of colonialism and neo-colonialism. Such suspicions were not entirely unfounded. The ICFTU tried for years to propagate a certain "model" of "proper unionism." One of the aims formulated at the time of its founding in 1949 was "to provide assistance in the establishment, maintenance and development of trade union organizations, particularly in economically and socially under-developed countries."⁴³ It was assumed that "proper" trade unions would remain fully independent of political parties and states; concentrate on collective bargaining and lobbying for social security legislation; defend and promote parliamentary democracy. These principles often proved difficult to apply in the so-called Third World.⁴⁴ Much later, Adolf Sturmthal observed that especially in the Anglo-American countries (whose trade unions dominated the ICFTU) there had been "a naïve belief in the universal applicability of some form of collective bargaining."⁴⁵ He listed a series of conditions for "a genuine collective bargaining system", including "a legal and political system permitting the existence and functioning of reasonably *free* labour organizations" (a condition that was fully compatible with the early ICFTU views) and the requirement that "unions be more or less stable, reasonably well organized, and fairly evenly matched with the employers in bargaining strength."⁴⁶

---

41 Ken Post, *Revolution's Other World: Communism and the Periphery, 1917–39* (Houndmills, [etc.]: Macmillan, 1997), p. 49.
42 Gerhard Wahlers, *CLAT: Geschichte einer lateinamerikanischen Gewerkschaftsinternationale* (Witterschlick/Bonn, 1990); Patrick Pasture, *Histoire du syndicalisme chrétien international: La difficile recherche d'une troisième voie* (Paris, 1999).
43 *Official Report of the Free World Labour Conference and of the First Congress of the International Confederation of Free Trade Unions, London, November-December, 1949*, p. 226.
44 Sometimes they also seemed insincere. Regarding the emphasis placed by the British TUC in the 1950s on the non-political nature of "proper" trade unionism, Davies has correctly observed: "Some of these sentiments sound odd in the context of the history of the British trade union movement, which had supported a general strike, maintained a close association with the Labour Party, and in its annual congresses regularly debated resolutions on a large number of issues outside the field of industrial relations" Davies, "Politics of the TUC's Colonial Policy", p. 26.
45 Sturmthal, "Industrial Relations Strategies", p. 5.
46 *Ibid.*, p. 9.

"Effective unions have rarely if ever been organized by 'non-committed' workers, i.e. casual workers who change jobs frequently, return periodically to their native village, and have no specific industrial skill, even of a very simple kind. Yet even fully committed industrial workers with little or no skill are capable of engaging in effective collective bargaining only under certain conditions which are rarely found. In most (though by no means all) newly industrializing countries, large excess supplies of common labour are available for nonagricultural work. Not only are unskilled workers rarely capable of forming unions of their own under such conditions; if they succeed in doing so, their unions have little or no bargaining power."[47]

Since the 1960s, the international trade union movement has been confronted with a substantial number of new challenges that together progressively undermined the old model of "national internationalism." Significant changes include the decolonization process; the new transnational division of labour; the emergence of regionalism and trading blocs, such as the European Union, NAFTA, ASEAN and Mercosur; the collapse of communist governments in the Soviet Union and Eastern Europe; the rise of feminist movements; the spread of wage labour in the periphery and semi-periphery, both expanding the so-called "informal sector" with breathtaking speed and increasing the influence of women; and the digital revolution.

The following major challenges currently facing international trade unionism are worth noting:

- The impressive growth of *foreign direct investment* in the core countries and the semi-periphery of the world economy, and of *transnational corporations*. In response to this development, World Corporation Councils were set up in the mid-1960s, notably in the chemical and automobile industries. Although many trade union militants had high expectations of these new bodies, their effectiveness has been rather less than anticipated, owing to the conflicting interests of employees in different countries.[48]
- The formation of *trading blocs*. They led to a certain equalization of legal and political parameters, so that the building of transnational trade union structures within each bloc was an obvious step. In NAFTA, this collaboration is not evolving primarily at the top level of national trade union confederations, but at the sub-national or branch level. In many cases, institutions other than trade unions (such as religious and human rights organizations) are also partners in projects of this kind. Examples include the 1980s Coalition for Justice in the Maquiladores, the Comité Frontizero de Obreras, and La Mujer Obrera.[49] Equally worthy

---

47 Ibid., p. 10.
48 Burton Bendiner, *International Labour Affairs: The World Trade Unions and the Multinational Companies* (Oxford, 1987); Werner Olle and Wolfgang Schoeller, "World Market Competition and Restrictions upon International Trade Union Policies", in: Rosalind E. Boyd, Robin Cohen and Peter C.W. Gutkind (eds), *International Labour and the Third World* (Aldershot, 1987), pp. 26–47; Kurt P. Tudyka, "Die Weltkonzernräte in der Krise", *WSI-Mitteilungen*, 39 (1986), pp. 324–329.
49 Ralph Armbruster, "Cross-National Labor Organizing Strategies", *Critical Sociology*, 21, 2 (1995), pp. 75–89, at 77–8, 80–2.

of note in this context is the Council of Ford Workers, founded by the United Auto Workers.
- The formation of *new supranational institutions* to regulate the dynamics of the "new"capitalism. The foremost example is the World Trade Organization established in 1995.
- *Social and economic changes in the periphery and semi-periphery* of the world economy, facilitating the emergence of new, often militant, workers' movements (social movement unions) in countries such as Brazil, South Africa, the Philippines, Taiwan and South Korea.
- *New forms of rank-and-file trade unionism* outside the established channels appearing since the 1970s, with international connections at the shop-floor level "bypassing altogether the secretariats, which they see as too often beholden to the bureaucracies of their various national affiliates."[50] A well-known example is the Transnationals Information Exchange (TIE), a centre in which a substantial number of research and activist labour groups exchange information on TNCs. Another example is the "counter foreign policy" existing since the early 1980s in the AFL-CIO.[51]
- *Joint actions against TNCs* conducted over the past decade by trade unions representing particular occupations in different countries (e.g. coal miners, electrical workers).[52] When the French car-maker Renault announced the closure of its Belgian factory in February 1997, solidarity strikes and demonstrations were organized in France, Spain, Portugal and Slovenia, giving birth to the new term "Euro-strike."
- Spurred on by the uneven development of trade unions in core and periphery countries, a growing tendency on the part of international trade secretariats to engage in the *direct recruitment of members in the periphery*. (See the activities of the secretariat for the service sector Union Network International relating to IT specialists in India).
- The increasing number of activities carried out by non-governmental organizations (NGOs) that should in theory be the responsibility of the international trade union movement, such as the struggle to regulate and abolish child labour.

All these challenges compel the international trade union movement to review its aims and activities. The need for such a review is further underscored by the fact that the changing composition of the world working class highlights the relative weakness of the movement. On a global scale union density is almost insignificant.

---

50 Andrew Herod, "Labor as an Agent of Globalization and as a Global Agent", in: Kevin R. Cox (ed.), *Spaces of Globalization: Reasserting the Power of the Local* (New York, 1997), pp. 167–200, at 184.
51 Hobart A. Spalding, "Two Latin American Foreign Policies".
52 Herod, "The Two Latin American Foreign Policies of the U.S. Labor Movement: The AFL-CIO Top Brass vs. Rank-and-File", *Science and Society*, 56 (1992), pp. 421–439, at 342; Armbruster, "Cross Border Labor Organizing."

Independent trade unions organize only a small percentage of their target group worldwide, and the majority of them live in the relatively wealthy North Atlantic region. By far the most important global umbrella organization is the International Trade Union Confederation (ITUC), founded in 2006 as a merger of two older organizations, the secular reform-oriented International Confederation of Free Trade Unions (ICFTU) and the Christian World Confederation of Labour (WCL). In 2014 the ITUC estimated that about 200 million workers worldwide belong to trade unions (excluding those of China's), and that 176 million of these are organized in the ITUC.[53] The ITUC also estimates that the total number of workers is roughly 2.9 billion (of whom 1.2 billion in the informal economy). Therefore, global union density currently amounts to no more than seven percent (200 million as a percentage of 2.9 billion).[54]

---

[53] This calculation is probably misleading. A significant, but unknown, part of the union membership consists of pensioners. It is therefore likely that the number of employed or employable members is lower.
[54] *Building Workers' Power. Congress Statement* (Berlin: International Trade Union Confederation 2014), p. 8.

Suggested reading

Addison, John T. and Claus Schnabel (eds). *International Handbook of Trade Unions* (Cheltenham, UK: Edward Elgar, 2003).
Allen, V.L. *The History of Black Mineworkers in South Africa*. Vol. 1: *The Techniques of Resistance, 1871–1948* (Keighley: Moor Press, 1992); Vol. 2: *Apartheid, Repression and Dissent in the Mines, 1948–1982* (London: Merlin, 2005); Vol. 3: *Organise or Die, 1982–94* (London: Merlin, 2005).
Chesneaux, Jean. *The Chinese Labor Movement, 1919–1927* (Stanford, CA: Stanford University Press, 1968).
Forrest, Kally. *Metal That Will Not Bend. National Union of Metalworkers of South Africa, 1980–1995* (Johannesburg : Witwatersrand University Press, 2011).
Frank, Dana. *Bananeras. Women Transforming the Banana Unions of Latin America* (Cambridge, MA: South End, 2005).
French, John D. *The Brazilian Workers' ABC. Class Conflict and Alliances in Modern São Paulo* (Chapel Hill, NC: University of North Carolina Press, 1992).
Gamba, Charles. *The Origins of Trade Unionism in Malaysia. A Study in Colonial Labour Unrest* (Singapore: Eastern Universities Press, 1962).
Ganguli, Debkumar. *History of the World Federation of Trade Unions (WFTU). Yesterday-Today-Tomorrow 1945–2000* (New Delhi: WFTU, 2000).
Gerteis, Christopher. *Gender Struggles. Wage-earning Women and Male-dominated Unions in Postwar Japan* (Cambridge, MA: Harvard University Press, 2009).
Gordon, Andrew. *The Evolution of Labor Relations in Japan. Heavy Industry, 1853–1955* (Cambridge, MA: Harvard University Press, 1985).
Hensman, Rohini. *Workers, Unions, and Global capitalism. Lessons from India* (New York: Columbia University Press, 2011).
Ingleson, John. *In Search of Justice. Workers and Unions in Colonial Java, 1908–1926* (Singapore: Oxford University Press, 1986).
Kerkvliet, Melinda Tria. *Manila Workers' Unions, 1900–1950* (Quezon City: New Day, 1992).
Large, Stephen S. *The Rise of Labor in Japan. The Yūaikai, 1912–19* (Tokyo: Sophia University, 1972).
Montgomery, David. *The Fall of the House of Labor. The Workplace, the State, and American Labor Activism, 1865–1925* (Cambridge: Cambridge University Press, 1987).
Munck, Ronaldo, Ricardo Falcón and Bernardo Galitelli. *Argentina from Anarchism to Peronism. Workers, Unions and Politics, 1855–1985* (London: Zed Books, 1987).
Phelan, Craig. *Trade Unions in West Africa. Historical and Contemporary Perspectives* (Bern: Peter Lang, 2011).
Phelan, Craig (ed.). *Trade Unionism since 1945. Towards a Global History*. 2 volumes (Bern: Peter Lang, 2009).
Posusney, Marsha Pripstein. *Labor and the State in Egypt. Workers, Unions, and Economic Restructuring* (New York: Columbia University Press, 1997).
Pringle, Tim. *Trade Unions in China. The Challenge of Labour Unrest* (London: Routledge, 2011).
Rodriguez García, Magaly. *Liberal Workers of the World, Unite? The ICFTU and the Defence of Labour Liberalism in Europe and Latin America (1949–1969)* (Bern: Peter Lang, 2010).
Roxborough, Ian. *Unions and Politics in Mexico. The Case of the Automobile Industry* (Cambridge: Cambridge University Press, 1984).
Seidman, Gay W. *Manufacturing Militance. Workers' Movements in Brazil and South Africa, 1970–1985* (Berkeley, CA: University of California Press, 1994).

Tosstorff, Reiner. *The Red International of Labour Unions (RILU), 1920–1937* (Leiden and Boston: Brill, 2016).
Van der Linden, Marcel (ed.). *The International Confederation of Free Trade Unions* (Berne [etc.]: Peter Lang Academic, 2000).
Van der Linden, Marcel and Richard Price (eds). *The Rise and Development of Collective Labour Law* (Bern: Peter Lang, 2000).
Van der Linden, Marcel and Wayne Thorpe (eds). *Revolutionary Syndicalism. An International Perspective* (Aldershot: Scolar, 1990).
Van Goethem, Geert. *The Amsterdam International. The World of the International Federation of Trade Unions (IFTU), 1913–1945* (Aldershot: Ashgate, 2006).
Webb, Sidney and Beatrice Webb. *The History of Trade Unionism* (London: Longmans, Green, 1911).

Acknowledgments

This handbook presents the interim findings of the long-term Global Labour History research programme at the International Institute of Social History (IISH) in Amsterdam, the Netherlands, and of our collaboration with many scholars from around the world. Our thanks go primarily therefore to all those colleagues with whom we have conducted global research, shared data and insights, debated issues, and published in recent years. More especially, we should like to thank those colleagues who agreed to write chapters for this ambitious collection of essays – a commitment that sometimes involved them in venturing far beyond the realm of their core expertise. In preparing this volume we benefited from the unconditional support of Henk Wals, General Director at the IISH, and Leo Lucassen, its Research Director. Rabea Rittgerodt at De Gruyter, our publisher, helped us wherever possible. Chris Gordon, our trusted and perceptive partner in the field of translation and language editing, prepared English versions of the chapters originally written in Dutch and edited most of the English-language contributions of non-native speakers. As the deadline approached, Jessica Eitelberg helped by editing some of the later contributions. Annelieke Vries (Cartographic Studio) produced the maps with her usual efficiency.

Karin Hofmeester and Marcel van der Linden
Amsterdam, April 2017

Notes on Contributors

Touraj Atabaki is Honorary Fellow at the International Institute of Social History in Amsterdam, and Emeritus Professor in the Social History of the Middle East and Central Asia at the School of the Middle East Studies of Leiden University. His books in English include *Azerbaijan. Ethnicity and Autonomy in Twentieth-Century Iran* (London, 1993; revised edition 2000), *The State and the Subaltern. Modernization, Society and the State in Turkey and Iran* (London, 2007) and *Social History of Labour in the Iranian Oil Industry 1908–1951* (forthcoming). He served as president of the European Society for Central Asian Studies and president of the International Society of Iranian Studies.

Özgür Balkılıç is a visiting researcher in the Department of History at the Middle East Technical University, Ankara, Turkey. He is conducting a research on the penetration of scientific management into the private industry in Turkey after WWII and its effects on the contentious labour-capital relations between 1960 and 1980. He obtained his Ph. D. degree from the Wilfrid Laurier University in 2015 with a dissertation entitled *For the Union Makes Us Strong: The Istanbul Metal Workers and Their Struggle for Unionization in Turkey, 1947–1970*.

Rossana Barragán is Senior Researcher at the International Institute of Social History in Amsterdam. Earlier she was Professor of History at the Universidad Mayor de San Andrés (La Paz) and at the Post Graduate School in Social Sciences of CIDES-La Paz. Until 2010 she also was Director of the Historical Archive of the department and city of La Paz. She is the author or co-author of thirteen books in Spanish, and of numerous articles and book chapters in Spanish and English. Her research focuses on social and political processes, identity, and state formation in 19th and 20th century Bolivia.

Rana P. Behal is Associate Professor, Department of History, Deshbandhu College, University of Delhi, and co-founder (1996) and board member of the Association of Indian Labour Historians. His publications include *India's Labouring Poor. Historical Studies, c. 1600 – c. 2000* (New Delhi, 2007), co-edited with Marcel van der Linden; *Rethinking Work. Global Historical and Sociological Perspectives* (New Delhi, 2011), co-edited with Alice Mah and Babacar Fall, and *One Hundred Years of Servitude. Political Economy of Tea Plantations in Colonial Assam* (New Delhi, 2014).

Eileen Boris is Hull Professor in the Department of Feminist Studies and an Affiliate Professor of History, Black Studies, and Global Studies at the University of California Santa Barbara. Her publications include *Home to Work. Motherhood and The Politics of Industrial Homework in the United States* (Cambridge, 1994), winner of the 1995 Philip Taft Prize in Labor History, and, with Jennifer Klein, *Caring for America. Home Health Workers in the Shadow of the Welfare State* (New York, 2012), winner of the 2013 Sara A. Whaley Prize for best book on women and labour, National Women's Studies Association. She is the president of the International Federation for Research in Women's History.

Gavin D. Brockett is Associate Professor of Middle East and Islamic History, and of Religion and Culture at Wilfrid Laurier University, Canada. His publications include *Ottoman and Republican Turkish Labour History* (Cambridge, 2009), co-edited with Touraj Atabaki; *Towards a Social History of Modern Turkey. Essays in Theory and Practice* (Istanbul, 2011); and *How Happy to Call Oneself a Turk. Provincial Newspapers and the Negotiation of a Muslim National Identity* (Austin, TX, 2011).

Peter Cole is Professor of History at Western Illinois University, Macomb. He is the editor of *Ben Fletcher: The Life and Times of a Black Wobbly, including Fellow Worker Fletcher's Writings & Speeches* (Chicago, 2007), and author of *Wobblies on the Waterfront. Interracial Unionism in Progressive Era Philadelphia* (Urbana, IL, 2007). He is a co-editor of *Wobblies of the World. A Global History of the IWW* (London, 2017) and currently writing *Dockworker Power: Race, Technology and Unions in Durban and the San Francisco Bay Area*.

Christian G. De Vito is Research Associate on the ERC project "The Carceral Archipelago", University of Leicester, and Lecturer at Utrecht University. Co-chair of the Labour Network of the European Social Science History Conference (ESSHC) and co-coordinator of the "Free and Unfree Labour" working group of the European Labour History Network (ELHN), he has published extensively on punishment and labour and, together with Alex Lichtenstein, he has edited the volume *Global Convict Labour* (London and Boston, 2014).

Bill Freund is the author of *The African Worker* (Cambridge, 1988) amongst other books and has very recently published at Palgrave Macmillan/Lynne Rienner a revised 3rd edition of *The Making of Contemporary Africa*. He is at present working on a book that will assess pre-1990 South Africa as a developmental state. He is Professor Emeritus at the University of KwaZulu/Natal and Visiting Professor at the University of the Witwatersrand, both in South Africa.

Therese Garstenauer is Senior Research Fellow at the Department of Economic and Social History, University of Vienna. She is currently working on her habilitation on government employees and their conduct of life in interwar Austria. Her publications include *Arbeit im Lebenslauf: Verhandlungen von (erwerbs-)biographischer Normalität* [Work in the Life Course: Negotiations of (Employment-)Biographical Normality)] co-edited with Klara Löffler and Thomas Hübel (Bielefeld 2016), and *Teaching Subjects In Between: Feminist Politics, Disciplines, Generations* (York 2006), co-authored with Josefina Bueno Alonso and others.

Jennifer Hart is an Assistant Professor of African History at Wayne State University, Detroit, Michigan. She is the author of *Ghana on the Go. African Mobility in the Age of Motor Transportation* (Bloomington, IN), 2016), and she writes regularly on the blog <www.ghanaonthego.com>.

Rosemarijn Hoefte is a Senior Researcher at KITLV / Royal Netherlands Institute of Southeast Asian and Caribbean Studies in Leiden, the Netherlands. Her main research interests are the history of post-abolition Suriname, migration and unfree labour, and Caribbean contemporary history. Her most recent monograph is *Suriname in the Long Twentieth Century. Domination, Contestation, Globalization* (New York, 2014). With Matthew L. Bishop and Peter Clegg she edited *Post-Colonial Trajectories in the Caribbean. The Three Guianas* (London, 2017). She is the managing editor of the *New West Indian Guide* and currently serves as president of the Association of Caribbean Historians.

Karin Hofmeester is Senior Researcher and Deputy Director of Research at the International Institute of Social History in Amsterdam and Professor of Jewish Culture at the University of Antwerp. Her publications include *The Joy and Pain of Work. Global Attitudes and Valuations, 1500–1650* (Cambridge, 2012), co-edited with Christine Moll-Murata; *Luxury in Global Perspective. Objects and Practices, 1600–2000* (Cambridge, 2016), co-edited with Bernd-Stefan Grewe; and *Conquerors, Employers, and Arbiters: States and Shifts in Labour Relations, 1500–2000* (Cambridge, 2016), co-edited with Gijs Kessler and Christine Moll-Murata.

Ad Knotter is a Professor of Comparative Regional History and Director of the Sociaal Historisch Centrum voor Limburg [Centre for the Social History of Limburg] at Maastricht University. He published extensively on Dutch and transnational labour history. In 2012 he became a member of the Editorial Committee of the *International Review of Social History*. In 2015 he edited a special issue of this Review on *Migration and Ethnicity in Coalfield History: Global Perspectives* (together with David Mayer).

Andrea Komlosy is Professor at the Institute for Economic and Social History, University of Vienna, Austria, where she is coordinating the Global History and Global Studies programs. She has published on labour, migration, borders and uneven development on a regional, a European and a global scale, recently: "Work and Labour Relations", in: Jürgen Kocka and Marcel van der Linden Marcel (eds), *Capitalism: The Re-Emergence of a Historical Concept* (London, 2016); and *Work: The Last 1000 Years* (London, 2017).

Jan Lucassen is an Honorary Fellow of the International Institute of Social History in Amsterdam, where he previously served as Research Director, and as Senior Researcher. From 1990 until his mandatory retirement in 2012 he was also Professor of International and Comparative Social History at the Free University in Amsterdam. He is the author of inter alia, *Migrant Labour in Europe 1600–1900. The Drift to the North Sea* (London, 1987), and editor of e. g., *Global Labour History. A State of the Art* (Bern, 2006); *Wages and Currency. Global Comparisons from Antiquity to the Twentieth Century* (Bern, 2007); and, with Leo Lucassen, *Globalizing Migration History. The Eurasian Experience 16th-21st centuries* (Leiden and Boston, 2014).

Patrick Manning is Andrew W. Mellon Professor of World History, Emeritus, at the University of Pittsburgh and is Past President of the American Historical Association. He is author of *Navigating World History. Historians Create a Global Past* (New York, 2003), *The African Diaspora. A History Through Culture* (New York, 2010), *Big Data in History* (New York, 2013), *Migration in World History* (New York, 2013), and other works. He continues his research on slavery, migration, and African population since 1650.

David Mayer is Honorary Fellow at the International Institute of Social History in Amsterdam and serves as the Vice-President of the ITH – International conference of Labour and Social History. He is a historian specialized in Latin American social and intellectual history. 2014–2016 he has acted as executive editor of the *International Review of Social History*. His publications in English include *Migration and Ethnicity in Coalfield History: Global Perspectives* (2015, Special Issue 23 of the *International Review of Social History* [*IRSH*]), co-edited with Ad Knotter, and *Brazilian Labour History – New Perspectives in Global Context* (2017, Special Issue 25 of *IRSH*), co-edited with Paulo Fontes and Alexandre Fortes.

Christine Moll-Murata is Associate Professor of Chinese History at Ruhr-Universität Bochum, and Honorary Fellow at the International Institute of Social History in Amsterdam. She specializes in the socioeconomic and technical history of China of the second millennium as well as Chinese local historiography. As a member of the Global Collaboratory on the History of Labour Relations, she co-edited two Special Issues of the *International Review on Social History: The Joy and Pain of Work* (2012) and *Conquerors, Employers, Arbiters. States and Shifts in Labour Relations 1500–2000* (2016).

Bryan D. Palmer is editor of *Labour/Le Travail* and Professor of Canadian Studies at Trent University, Peterborough, Ontario, Canada. He is the author of many books, among them the recently-published *Revolutionary Teamsters. The Minneapolis Teamsters' Strikes of 1934* (Chicago, 2014) and (with Gaetan Heroux) *Toronto's Poor: A Rebellious History* (Toronto, 2016).

Prasannan Parthasarathi is Professor of South Asian History at Boston College. He is the author of *The Transition to a Colonial Economy: Weavers, Merchants and Kings in South India, 1720–1800* (Cambridge, 2001), *The Spinning World. A Global History of Cotton Textiles* (Oxford, 2009), and *Why Europe Grew Rich and Asia Did Not: Global Economic Divergence 1600–1850* (Cambridge, 2011), which received the Jerry Bentley Book Prize of the World History Association. He is a Senior Editor of *International Labor and Working Class History*.

Marlou Schrover is Professor of Economic and Social History at Leiden University, with a special interest in migration history. She is editor in chief of the *Journal of Migration History*. She co-edited, with Deirdre Moloney, *Gender, Migration and Categorisation. Making Distinctions between Migrants in Western Countries, 1945–2010* (Amsterdam, 2013); with Immanuel Ness and others, *The Encyclopedia of Global Human Migration*, five volumes (Chichester, 2013), and with Eileen Janes Yeo, *Gender, Migration and the Public Sphere 1850–2005* (New York, 2010). She co-authored *Illegal Migration and Gender in a Global and Historical Perspective* (Amsterdam, 2008).

Marcel van der Linden is Senior Researcher of the International Institute of Social History, where he previously served for fourteen years as Research Director. He is also a Professor of Social Movement History at the University of Amsterdam, President of the International Social History Association, and co-founder of the Association of Indian Labour Historians (1996), the European Labour History Network (2013), and the Global Labour History Network (2015). He is the author, editor or co-editor of some fifty books, including *Workers of the World. Essays toward a Global Labor History* (Leiden and Boston, 2008; Chicago 2010) which received the René Kuczynski Prize 2009.

Sjaak van der Velden is in charge of the Global Hub Labour Conflicts project of the International Institute of Social History in Amsterdam. He also is an independent historian writing mainly for and about Dutch labour unions and labour in general. He is co-founder of the International Association for the Study of Strikes and Social Conflicts. In English he co-edited *Strikes Around the World, 1968–2005. Case-studies of 15 Countries* (Amsterdam, 2007), *Striking Numbers. New Approaches to Strike Research* (ed.) (Amsterdam, 2012), and *Historical Dictionary of Organized Labor* (Lanham, MD, 2012).

Matthias van Rossum is Senior Researcher at the International Institute of Social History in Amsterdam. He works on global labour history with special interest in maritime labour history, coercion in labour relations and the dynamics of labour conflicts and social relations. He was awarded a NWO Veni Grant for research on the history of slavery and slave trade in early modern Dutch Asia (2016–2019). A recent publication is *Desertion in the Early Modern World: A Comparative History* (London, 2016), co-edited with Jeannette Kamp.

Erik Vanhaute is Professor of Economic History and World History at Ghent University. His publications include *Rural Economy and Society in North-Western Europe, 500–2000. Making a Living: Family, Income and Labour* (Turnhout, 2012), co-edited with Isabelle Devos and Thijs Lambrecht; *World History. An Introduction* (Oxford, 2012) and *Peasants in World History* (Oxford, forthcoming).

Susan Zimmermann is University Professor at the Central European University, and President of the ITH – International Conference of Labour and Social History. Her ongoing research focuses on the politics of class, gender and race of the International Labour Organization in the interwar period, and the history of workplace related gender politics in state-socialist Hungary. Her publications include *GrenzÜberschreitungen. Internationale Netzwerke, Organisationen, Bewegungen und die Politik der globalen Ungleichheit vom 17. bis zum 21. Jahrhundert* (Vienna, 2010), and *Divide, Provide and Rule. An Integrative History of Poverty Policy, Social Policy and Social Reform in Hungary under the Habsburg Monarchy* (Budapest and New York, 2011).

Subject Index

Abadan 191, 195
Abolition of unfree labour relations 9, 67, 85, 89, 91, 93, 142 f., 148, 240, 249, 326, 363–365, 368, 372–374, 380–383, 399, 445, 447
absence from work 477, 508
Accra 79, 280, 282, 285
Accumulating Savings and Credit Association (ASCRA) 495
activism 28, 54, 56, 189, 192, 194, 196, 208, 339, 562, 567
administrative staff 297 f., 300, 302–310, 313 f.
African National Congress (ANC) 71, 347
Afro-Americans 89, 91, 94, 96, 119, 245, 249, 381 f., 388, 447
Afro-Caribbeans 93, 96, 280, 459
Agency 18, 19, 22, 26, 44, 58, 68, 70, 79, 111, 122, 126, 134, 146, 152 f., 169, 187, 190, 194 f., 212, 230 f., 240, 245, 300, 360 f., 381, 383 f., 439, 450, 505
agrarian capitalism 228 f.
agrarian population 137 f.
agrarian reform 98, 148
agrarian society 55, 223, 229
agricultural labour 26, 97, 121, 137 f., 141–144, 146 f., 150 f., 171, 185, 188, 210, 219, 222, 232, 459
agricultural production 100, 152, 217, 224, 514
agriculture 19, 26, 36, 45 f., 48, 52, 63, 65 f., 73, 76, 90, 100, 121, 134, 137–139, 141, 143 f., 146, 148, 151 f., 159, 164 f., 171, 181 f., 185, 210, 217–235, 239, 242–244, 264 f., 283, 326, 333, 370, 384, 397–399, 423 f., 426–429, 459, 464, 472, 485, 514, 551, 558
Ahmedabad 35, 40
Alabama 245, 249
Alaska 433, 455
Algeria 168, 245, 462
All-China Federation of Trade Unions (ACFTU) 28 f.
All India Trade Union Congress 35
allocation, non-rotating 491, 494, 496
allocation, rotating 491 f.
American Civil War 116, 124, 381 f.
American Social History Project 125
Amerindians 379, 388

anarchism 70, 101, 122, 127, 491
Anatolia 200, 202, 204, 206, 337, 405
Ancient Egypt 395, 444, 525
Ancient Greece 414, 421
Andes 88, 419
Anglo-American Corporation of South Africa 242
Anglo-Boer War 69
Angola 77, 284, 390, 461, 462
animals 203, 227, 265, 281, 333, 445
Ankara 214
anthropology 100, 159, 170, 172 f., 220, 243, 318, 329, 335 f., 385, 329, 382, 385, 415 f., 481, 487, 493
antiquity 416 f., 419, 430, 527, 539 f.
Antwerp 443
Anyuan 23 f., 257
apartheid 75 f.
Arab Spring 207, 260, 273
Arabs 170, 204, 207, 260, 273, 406, 418–420, 424 f., 444, 460, 528
archaeology 414
Argentina 9, 96, 97, 100, 101, 102, 103, 104, 105, 264, 272. 273, 340, 524, 528, 529, 530, 543, 545, 553, 557
aristocracy 66, 194, 209, 309
Arkansas 291
arkatia 366
Armenia 147, 466
army 21, 49, 67, 70, 73, 93, 218, 303, 312, 345 f., 366, 371, 390, 404, 406, 424, 447, 454, 510, 515 f., 518, 529
artisans 34, 267, 413, 562
Association of Indian Labour Historians (AILH) 47 f., 322
asylum seekers 463
attitudes to work 11, 411–431, 477, 484, 539
Australasia 6, 283
Australia 1 f., 245, 256, 355, 367, 373, 433, 439, 462–465, 497, 518, 532, 546
Austria 132, 141, 145, 149, 152, 158, 165, 171, 176, 264, 447, 540, 546, 565
Austria-Hungary 132, 145, 165, 447
autobiography 414, 418
autocratic union 553, 559
autonomy 4, 74, 103, 125, 162, 187, 217, 223, 228, 233, 262, 269, 318, 336, 338, 369,

396, 411, 469, 477, 480, 482 f., 487, 501, 505, 507, 512, 552, 554, 558
aviation 288
Awami League 55 f.
Aymara 335
Azerbaijan 146, 433
Aztecs 85, 89

Babylon 405
Baghdad 1, 470, 424
Bahia 90, 387
Balkans 136, 144 f., 165, 169, 202, 204, 353
Bangalore 41
Bangladesh 1, 32 f., 55 – 59, 272
Bantustans 75
Barbacoas 90, 476
bargaining 6, 27, 29, 36, 50, 372, 398, 514 – 516, 542, 552, 554, 557, 560, 565 f.
Basra 411, 424
Batavia (Jakarta) 355, 512, 518
Belgian Congo 73, 74, 76
Belgium 25, 73 f., 76, 239, 242, 245, 250, 252, 354, 404, 447, 451, 460 f., 546, 562, 567
Bengal 35, 38, 41, 43, 45, 48, 247, 263
Berlin 165, 176, 443, 562
Besançon 531
black market 293
black people 64, 71, 73, 75, 249, 280 f., 284, 293, 338 f., 348, 360, 366, 380 – 382, 386, 388, 390, 411, 424, 527, 532
black workers 284, 532
Bolivia 84, 86, 98, 106 f., 241, 243, 256
Bombay (Mumbai) 6, 35 – 37, 39 – 41, 44 – 46, 263, 266, 269 f., 474, 484
bondservants 20
borders 5, 9, 102, 123, 136, 145 – 147, 171, 244, 272, 444, 460, 562
borderlands 516
Bracero Program 460
Brazil 83 – 85, 88 – 94, 96 – 98, 100 f., 103 – 106, 242, 284, 337, 379 – 381, 383, 388, 390, 406, 411, 472, 476, 535, 540, 567
Britain 6, 93, 160, 163, 172, 182, 197, 239, 243, 244, 252, 254, 256, 263, 265, 272, 287, 312, 340, 355, 363, 365, 385, 444, 447, 449, 459, 470 f., 540, 553, 560
British Colonial Office 312
British Guiana 366, 373, 446
British Empire 244, 356, 364, 367
British India 247, 263, 445 f., 460

Brotherhood of Sleeping Car Porters (BSCP) 284
Buenos Aires 90, 94, 97 – 99, 101 f., 104, 106
bureaucracy 22, 46, 211, 297 – 300, 302, 304, 307 – 312, 314, 369, 435, 452, 480, 485, 501, 518, 560 f., 567
Bursa 214, 266
Burma (Myanmar) 366

Cacao 91, 96
Calcutta (Kolkata) 34 f., 37 – 41, 45, 52, 267, 272, 366, 553
California 1, 30, 70, 119, 245, 335, 343, 386, 426, 433, 555, 562
Cambodia 407
Canada 33, 111 – 113, 116 – 123, 120 f., 124, 126, 127, 283, 456, 460 – 465, 518, 538, 546
canoe men 280
Cape Verde Islands 284
capital 3, 5, 21, 48, 51 f., 69, 93 f., 123, 125, 139, 143, 162 f., 175, 223, 227, 229, 232 f., 238, 244, 292, 302, 308, 321, 329, 338, 340, 342, 351, 360 f., 365, 372, 378, 404, 426, 471, 485 f., 491, 517, 523 f., 538, 540
capital owners 223
capitalism 15 f., 33 f., 46 f., 79, 92 – 94, 112, 117, 122 – 126, 133, 137, 142, 144, 152, 157, 159, 161 f., 164, 166, 175, 177, 181 – 183, 187 f., 190, 210, 219, 222 – 225, 227 f., 230, 232 f., 246, 257, 261 f., 277, 279, 283, 289 f., 293, 318, 330 f., 333, 337, 339 – 341, 349, 357, 365, 407, 417 f., 421, 469, 471, 474 f., 484, 501, 510, 521 – 523, 526 – 528, 531, 534, 542 f., 558, 562, 567
capitalist enterprise 72, 79, 87
caravans 66, 68 f., 281
cardenismo 104
care chain 171, 177, 454, 457 f.
care drain 169, 454, 457
care workers 456, 458
Caribbean 9, 54, 83 – 107, 163, 218, 280, 326, 336 f., 363 – 367, 370 – 372, 378, 382, 385 – 387, 406, 433, 445 f., 459, 461, 463, 471, 564
caste 37 – 39, 54, 269, 340, 370, 413, 428, 554
Catalonia 158
Caucasus 146, 182, 186, 202
Central African Republic 79

Central America 1, 85, 106, 158, 547
Central Europe 164 f., 169, 171, 237, 443
Cerro de Pasco Corporation 243, 247
Ceylon (Sri Lanka) 33, 51–54, 366, 516, 528
chain migration 434, 437–441, 459, 461, 466
cheet 493
chibaro 69, 246
Chicago 24, 116, 122, 523, 527
Chihuahua 526
child labour 17–19, 49, 161, 195, 395, 567
children 1, 4, 18, 64, 88, 161, 218, 241 f., 251–253, 260, 264 f., 318, 320, 324 f., 330, 335 f., 338, 339, 340, 386, 395, 398, 397 f., 402, 407, 425, 438, 442, 450, 451, 452, 457, 458, 496
Chile 1, 84, 88 f., 97 f., 100–102, 105 f., 243 f., 250, 256 f., 547
China 6 f., 14–32, 78, 125, 146, 158, 162, 168, 177, 180, 218, 233, 257, 260, 263 f., 267, 272, 280, 282, 292, 298, 300 f., 325 f., 336, 340, 352, 359, 364, 366–372, 374, 397, 400, 403, 405–407, 413, 416 f., 419, 427, 433, 440, 444, 446, 448–450, 452, 454, 462, 469, 473 f., 494, 498, 503, 528, 534, 540, 545, 548, 568
Chinese Communist Party (CCP) 19, 23
Chittagong 55
Christianity 65, 120, 417, 421, 423, 450
circular migration 232, 244, 249, 458 f., 463 f.
cities 34, 39–41, 44, 48, 50, 66, 74 f., 77 f., 86, 88–90, 96, 98 f., 105, 117, 139, 145 f., 181, 188, 191, 195, 202, 205, 241, 260, 263, 272, 285, 287, 289, 366, 402, 405, 424, 427, 429, 443, 448, 495, 505, 514–516, 518, 526, 529, 556
civil administration 303
civil disobedience 49, 528
civil rights 119, 196, 284, 383, 386
civil servants 297, 301 f., 304, 307 f., 310 f., 313 f., 369, 374
Civil Service Reform Act 310
class consciousness 26, 37 f., 51, 193, 268, 506
class distinction 121
class identity 38, 113, 209, 238
class society 318
class struggle 26, 112, 118 f., 174, 187, 474, 506, 522, 560
cloth 1, 26, 72, 87, 259–264, 268–273, 332, 335, 398, 401, 480, 525

cloves 67, 368
coal 3, 22, 34, 41, 69, 73, 183, 194, 205, 237, 239, 242, 244 f., 248 f., 251–254, 256 f., 397, 448, 460, 567
coal industry 239
coal mining 22, 34, 69, 73, 205, 244 f., 248 f., 251–254, 256 f., 448, 567
coalfield 246, 255
Code Noir 480
coerced labour 67–69, 83, 85, 88, 141–143, 159, 161, 165, 171, 204, 207, 219, 237, 241, 248 f., 325, 334, 338, 345–349, 352, 354, 357, 359, 365, 373, 378, 430, 442 f., 445, 447 f., 450, 527
coffee 1, 34, 51–53, 72, 76, 91–93, 95 f., 233, 337, 385, 390, 472
Cold War 76, 101, 133, 168, 206, 402, 538, 564
collective agreements 534, 560 f.
collieries 239 f., 245, 247, 252, 255
Colombia 91, 93, 101, 102, 476
colonato 337
colonial rule 34, 40 f., 48, 50–52, 67 f., 85, 231, 280, 283 f., 312, 369, 428 f.
colonialism 2, 25, 34, 36, 40–43, 46, 48, 50–54, 57, 64, 67–69, 72 f., 75–77, 79, 84 f., 87–90, 93 f., 97 f., 100, 107, 121, 133, 143, 161, 163–165, 182 f., 204, 231–233, 240, 242, 244, 279–281, 283 f., 286–288, 293, 298, 311–313, 323, 330, 334, 348, 350 f., 354 f., 363, 369, 371, 373 f., 377, 379 f., 382, 385, 390, 428 f., 435, 438, 444 f., 447, 451, 454, 459, 461, 469, 471, 503, 508, 533, 564 f.
coltan 1
Combination Acts 399
COMECON 157, 164, 168
Comintern 187–189
commerce 9, 76, 143, 173, 259 f., 280, 380, 390, 424, 426
commercialization 15, 20, 65, 182, 261, 423 f., 427 f.
commitment 36, 49, 74, 205, 210, 213, 231, 279, 313, 357, 417, 444, 477, 479, 487, 511, 566
commodification 20 f., 124, 149, 159, 167, 175, 221, 224, 226 f., 229, 232 f., 290, 321 f., 324 f., 330, 334, 339, 343, 345, 347, 349, 352, 361, 416, 420, 423, 427, 515

commodity   5, 9, 64, 66, 78, 86, 89, 92, 96 f., 100, 103, 106, 124, 142, 157, 163, 177, 181, 183, 219, 221, 224 f., 228, 232 f., 260, 279, 283, 299, 326, 330, 332, 334, 365, 379, 388, 405, 456, 458, 485, 507
commodity production   96, 100, 103, 142, 219, 221, 224, 228, 232, 330
communism   41, 51, 103, 113, 122, 149 f., 165 f., 177, 188–190, 197, 206, 255 f., 400, 407, 464, 466, 530, 533 f., 564, 566
Communist Party of Iran   187–189
Communist Party of Pakistan (CPP)   50 f.
community   38 f., 68, 86, 88, 93, 102, 116, 123, 142, 161, 163, 168, 172 f., 176, 201, 217, 220 f., 224, 234, 245, 250–252, 255 f., 268 f., 286 f., 289, 303, 319–324, 330, 332, 334 f., 337 f., 341, 365, 371, 377, 379, 382 f., 385, 388 f., 413, 416 f., 423, 426, 428, 436, 441 f., 444, 455, 493, 495, 499, 501 f., 506, 514, 516 f., 556, 559
compensation   57, 165, 325 f., 329, 444, 477 f., 486, 491, 496, 510, 512
concentration camps   325, 345, 350, 353 f., 383, 477
conflict   36, 79, 87, 118, 127, 187, 194, 206, 223, 261, 341, 369, 377, 481, 521–524, 529, 532, 536 f., 543, 545 f., 553
Confucianism   20, 301, 427
Congo   79, 242, 243, 430
constitutionalism   183, 187
consumers   1, 9, 75, 78, 103, 124, 168, 185, 340
consumption   3, 9, 18, 182, 194, 221, 227, 232, 270, 272, 330, 333 f., 336, 338, 340, 480, 486, 551
convict labour   141, 171, 210, 237, 248 f., 345–350, 352 f., 355, 357, 359, 361, 364, 395, 507 f., 510
coolies   24, 35, 36, 42, 93, 95, 96, 102, 126, 243, 247, 282, 283, 349, 364, 373, 428, 505
cooperation   89, 167 f., 170, 172 f., 192, 325, 335, 454, 469, 471 f., 482, 513, 556, 558, 562 f.
cooperative subcontracting   397–399, 401
copper   1, 29, 237 f., 242 f., 249, 257
copper mining   29, 243, 249
Córdobazo   105
Cornwall   238 f.
corporal punishment   348, 351 f., 358, 526

corruption   300, 304, 308, 310, 367
Costa Rica   96, 124, 337, 451
Cotton   1, 5, 9, 64, 72, 120, 124, 125, 126, 153, 171, 175, 181, 210, 232, 233, 268, 271, 338, 368, 385, 387, 455, 471, 474
cotton industry   17, 36, 41, 56, 266, 270, 272, 336, 398 f.
coverage of risks   496
craft work   65, 66, 90, 159, 162, 164, 182, 194, 220, 263, 334, 342, 403, 424, 426, 554
craftsman   36, 146, 159, 184, 237, 271, 289, 325, 340, 414, 422, 424, 426, 525 f.
creativity   477 f.
credit   88, 217, 219, 221, 232, 341, 400 f., 493, 495, 497, 502, 513
crime   79, 100, 248, 318, 348, 353, 361, 363, 365, 369, 371, 478, 509, 553
criminalization   363, 505, 511, 518
cross-cultural migration   436
Cuba   89, 91 f., 94–96, 168, 337, 364, 369 f., 380 f., 443
Cuban Revolution   98, 105
Cultural Revolution   23, 26, 257
cultural turn   102, 135, 158, 170, 177
culturalism   38, 112, 116, 119
cumulative causation   440
Curaçao   449, 492 f.
Czechoslovakia   9, 139, 149, 152 f., 168, 339, 463

Dar-es-Salaam   78, 79, 487, 497, 533
de-agrarianization   224, 232
De Beers Consolidated Mines Company   242
de-peasantization   223, 225, 232 f.
debts   46, 52, 83, 88, 97, 232, 237, 247 f., 325 f., 333, 363 f., 368, 373, 402, 447, 493, 502, 513, 521
debt bondage   46, 237, 247, 364, 502
decolonization   2, 163 f., 284, 377, 382, 386, 465, 566
deep monetization   400
deindustrialization   36, 106, 267, 272
Deir el Medina   525
Delhi   33, 37, 39, 41 f., 44–47, 52, 150, 246, 280, 358, 406, 411, 414, 429, 484, 510, 536, 538
Deli   367
democracy   74, 122, 127, 187, 256, 285, 388, 421, 485, 534, 542, 555, 558, 560 f., 565
Democrat Party of Iran   187

democratization   78, 106, 196, 382
demography   86, 89, 223, 226, 320, 366, 383, 386, 388, 463
demonstrations   56f., 476, 528, 530, 541
Denmark   538, 563
dependency theory   83, 94
desertion   505–520
developed countries   218, 407, 455, 547, 565
developing countries   47, 219, 522, 542, 545, 547f., 554
Dhaka   55, 57, 58
dialectics   221, 347f., 355
diamonds   42, 70, 74, 91, 237, 242
diamond mining   62, 70, 74, 77, 242
diaspora   24, 42, 69, 77, 239, 244, 368, 389, 440, 464, 494, 499
Dillingham Commission   442
discipline at work   19, 36, 38, 53, 125, 192f., 211, 250, 262, 265, 299, 306, 349, 352, 369, 371, 404, 427, 470f., 477f., 482, 487, 511, 518, 557
discrimination   28, 54, 59, 139f., 147, 149, 249, 373
division of labour   1, 10, 17, 21, 59, 63, 65, 94, 134, 137, 139, 144, 147, 159, 163, 169, 181, 209, 233, 251f., 259, 264f., 273, 288, 291, 331, 333, 335f., 339, 343, 386, 415, 470, 472f., 566
domain of control   554, 556
domestic labour   99, 150, 195, 251, 326, 329, 332, 339
domestic work   34, 98, 164, 265, 341, 450, 484
domesticity   43f., 330
driving work   288
dulang washers   247
Dubai   341
Dublin   538
Durban   68, 72, 290, 535
Durham   52, 67, 79, 88, 98, 102, 104, 121, 124, 141, 190, 234, 239, 240, 242f., 248f., 293, 329, 334, 339, 348, 352, 359, 433
Dutch East Indies   248

East Africa   1, 63f., 66, 68, 73, 165, 282, 365f., 386, 446
East Central Europe   131, 136, 139, 144f., 165, 169f., 335
East Germany   136, 137f., 333, 463
East India Company (Dutch)   43, 355, 508

East India Company (English)   269, 280, 311
East Indies   364, 374, 381, 404, 465
Eastern Europe   96, 131–155, 157f., 163, 165–167, 169–171, 177, 339, 397, 443, 481, 483, 566
École des Hautes Etudes (EHESS)   159f.
economic boom   28, 106
economic crisis   124, 372, 462
economic development   36, 134, 137, 147–149, 152, 183, 224, 283, 288, 415, 421
economic growth   36, 48, 78, 142f., 230f., 387, 390, 462, 562
economic history   76, 84, 159, 168, 172, 174f., 205, 271, 470
economic reform   15, 26, 28
economic sector   10, 217, 371, 543, 554
economic system   21, 63, 163, 222, 272, 277, 517
Ecuador   84, 87, 93, 106
education   73, 76, 78, 105, 158, 169, 173, 176, 192, 301f., 305, 425, 472f., 559
Egypt   66, 125, 193, 203, 205, 207, 260, 273, 353, 405, 525, 528, 547
El Paso   555
El Salvador   337
El Teniente Copper Mine   102, 243, 250
emigration   78, 144f., 148, 366, 406, 446
employees   301, 413, 477, 558, 560
employers   262, 324, 326, 331, 341, 368f., 395f., 398, 401–404, 413, 447, 474–476, 478, 486f., 498, 511f., 522, 524, 529, 531f., 536–538, 540f., 551, 554–558, 560f.
encomienda   85
energy   190, 222, 239, 244, 257, 341, 472, 559
engagés   402
enganche system   247
England   9, 163, 230, 239f., 252, 255, 259, 267–269, 304, 401–403, 407, 428, 445, 455
enslavement   68, 85, 338, 377, 379–381, 383, 385, 388–390, 444
entertainment sector   79
epistemic community   172, 174f.
Essex   496
Ethiopia   63, 66, 79
ethnicity   49f., 53f., 113, 152, 160, 174, 184, 192, 201f., 205–207, 244f., 249, 284, 345, 348, 350, 352, 370–372, 415, 424, 435, 447, 465f., 473, 497, 500, 554

ethnography 414
Eurocentrism 5f., 47, 63, 159, 162, 175, 183, 213, 226, 257, 278, 298, 352, 358f., 361, 469, 471
European Union (EU) 165–167, 313, 466, 566
Exploitation (of labour) 24, 64, 85, 88, 90, 92, 96f., 106, 122, 126, 137, 152, 166, 171, 225, 228, 271, 332, 340, 347f., 354, 361, 372, 377, 380, 384, 398f., 434, 449f., 505–507
export 55–58, 74, 76f., 83, 86, 89, 92, 94, 96f., 100, 103, 106, 161f., 182, 232f., 270–272, 287, 332, 384, 386, 456

factors of production 3, 36
factories 35–37, 41, 43, 46, 48, 55, 57–59, 76, 83, 92, 102, 105, 117, 139, 150, 162, 168, 171–175, 189, 194f., 197, 203, 206, 208–212, 259, 262f., 265–267, 269, 272f., 289, 330, 339, 349, 353, 398, 400, 404, 407, 448, 469f., 472–474, 484, 517, 526f., 530f., 534, 560, 567
factory labour 36, 46, 83, 105, 150, 194, 265, 404, 407, 484
factory occupation 530f., 535
family 17–19, 26, 44, 114, 151, 217–220, 224, 228f., 232, 246–253, 284, 290–292, 317, 319, 324, 326, 329–331, 333–341, 370, 378f., 382, 435f., 438f., 441, 444, 462f., 485, 496, 502, 557
family labour 218, 224, 253, 290, 330, 335, 337
farm labourers 1, 220
farmers 63, 65, 139, 163, 217f., 220, 224, 226, 228, 232, 248, 290, 302, 322, 335, 342, 425
Federal Writers' Project 381
female employment 58
female miners 253
female workers 140, 205, 252f., 285, 290
feminism 2, 127, 174, 318, 329, 331, 338–342, 566
feminization 106, 219, 291, 310
Fernand Braudel Center 92, 97, 160, 191, 225, 330, 387, 391, 546
feudalism 15, 142, 220, 298, 331
Fiji 366, 368, 372f., 446, 456, 497
Florence 352, 526, 551
food 1f., 70, 90, 100, 218, 232, 248, 250, 259, 265, 291, 293, 324, 336f., 342, 347, 371, 398, 400f., 405, 407, 413, 450, 465, 472, 512
foot-binding 18f.
forced labour, see coerced labour
foreman 398f., 477, 537
France 7, 9, 25, 62, 84, 160, 162f., 197, 245, 250, 252, 254, 291, 302–304, 354, 372, 390, 400, 404, 445, 447, 457, 459, 461f., 465, 470, 480, 518, 521–523, 540f., 545f., 554, 562, 567
free labour 54, 142, 159, 219, 336, 364, 372, 374, 378, 402, 416, 526, 528, 565
free market 95, 387
French Guiana 356, 445
frontier 116f., 165, 225, 228, 231, 334, 337, 476, 513f., 516f.
Fujian 366
fund 151, 213, 217, 312, 491–496, 498f., 557

Galicia 145, 166, 169–171
Gambia 69, 79
garment industry 55–59
Gastarbeiter 448, 563
gender 17, 21, 28, 43, 49, 54, 56, 58f., 64, 99, 102, 113f., 118–121, 134, 151, 160, 174, 176, 184, 192, 195f., 207, 209, 212, 214, 221, 231, 233, 237, 251, 265, 290f., 319, 325, 339, 341f., 345, 348, 372, 407, 415, 435, 439, 455, 457f., 473, 497, 554, 559
genealogy 102, 226
General Motors 530f.
Georgia 147, 466
Georgia (US) 249, 472, 475
German Democratic Republic (GDR) 157, 166, 462, 534
Germany 27, 29, 62, 130, 133, 145, 160, 163–168, 197, 238, 245, 249, 252, 254–256, 304, 318, 329, 331, 334f., 353, 356, 399, 403, 407, 417, 419, 438, 447f., 455f., 460, 462f., 465, 470, 521, 527, 529f., 534, 538–540, 543, 545f., 554, 562f., 565
Ghana 29f., 62, 64, 66, 75, 77, 286–288, 290, 293, 382, 456, 547
Glasgow 530, 540
global capitalism 144, 164, 225, 227, 232f., 277f., 283f., 292, 294, 335
Global Collaboratory 8, 11, 20, 161, 204, 213, 217, 317, 322, 349, 419
Global Economic History Network (GEHN) 160

global economy   1, 141, 159, 170, 174, 289, 331, 341, 379, 514
global expansion   238, 244, 517
global history   1, 4, 7 f., 10 f., 47, 87, 147, 152, 157, 159, 162, 164 f., 170, 172, 175 f., 237, 259, 270, 277, 297 f., 355, 422
global history of work   1, 4, 8, 10 f., 162, 176, 422
global market   51, 94, 148, 243, 271, 420, 517
Global North   164, 184, 278, 407
Global South   2, 94, 133, 149, 153, 157, 160 f., 184, 219, 278, 282, 292 f., 332, 407, 469, 471
globalization   2, 29, 47, 78, 123 f., 131, 153, 157 f., 166, 173, 177, 201, 223 f., 226, 232, 234, 244, 278 f., 298, 314, 330, 342, 507
gold   66, 86, 162, 181, 237
gold mining   24, 29, 34, 39, 40, 41, 66, 69 f., 75, 76, 90 f., 242, 245, 370, 433, 476
goods   3, 64, 72 f., 75, 77 f., 83, 88, 103, 162, 168, 221, 259, 261 f., 264, 270 f., 277–281, 287–289, 292 f., 318, 320, 325 f., 334–336, 338, 340, 378, 395, 441, 444 f., 472 f., 476, 478, 491–494, 498, 501 f.
government   22, 28, 41, 44, 48–51, 55–57, 67, 69, 71 f., 74–77, 98 f., 106, 148, 152, 167, 169, 193, 196, 206, 210, 221, 232 f., 259, 280, 284, 288, 290, 299–305, 307–310, 319, 367, 370–373, 435, 442, 446, 454–456, 458, 480, 483, 501, 508, 528, 532, 535, 541 f., 564, 566
Great Britain   160, 163, 171 f., 244, 254, 266, 287, 363, 365, 469, 540, 564 See also England; Scotland; Wales
Great Depression   73, 97, 103, 263, 310
Great Divergence   7, 16, 18, 30, 162, 239, 271, 397, 402, 404
Great Frontier   225, 231
Great Transformation   183, 331
Greece   149, 214, 461, 466, 541
Guadeloupe   445
Guangdong   24, 366
Guangxi   24
guano   96, 363
Guatemala   84, 97, 337
guest workers, see migrants
guilds   132, 184, 185, 202, 203, 260, 262, 396, 403, 416, 418, 426, 460, 497, 516, 526
Guinea   65, 74 f., 284, 385, 497, 502 f.

Gulag system   141, 348, 350, 355
Gulf region   183, 207, 387, 443, 460

Habsburg Empire   140, 145, 149, 151 f., 163, 165 f., 170, 356
Haiti   90, 92, 96, 338
Hamadan   181
Hamburg   443, 562
handicraft production   15, 18, 19, 72, 145, 172, 333
Havana   24, 98, 367, 390
Hawai'I   363
Heimatvertriebene   465
heteronomy   469, 477, 483, 485–487, 552, 554
histoire croisée   7
Hispaniola   89, 90, 91
historical materialism   15, 184, 186
historical research   5, 8, 84, 132 f., 158, 161, 176, 260, 320
historiography   2, 5, 7 f., 33, 38 f., 44, 47, 51, 58, 74, 83, 101, 115, 117, 121, 124, 131–133, 135, 137, 139, 144, 149, 152 f., 169, 177, 184, 186 f., 189 f., 193, 195, 197, 202, 207, 209, 220, 278, 302, 377, 379, 388
Hong Kong   25, 27 f., 77, 449 f., 495, 547
household   15, 17–19, 30, 44, 63 f., 72 f., 99, 174, 184, 217, 219–221, 223, 237, 249, 251, 267, 273, 299, 319–321, 323–325, 329, 331–336, 338–342, 397, 408, 427, 449, 454, 491, 510, 556
household labour   217, 329, 332, 334, 338–340
housewifes   1 f., 159, 250, 329–332, 339 f., 342, 395, 407
Hungary   9, 132, 134, 136–142, 145 f., 148, 151 f., 157, 165, 167, 169 f., 237, 447, 466, 483
hunger   73, 149, 525

Iatmul   482
ideology   19, 25, 40 f., 43, 56, 73, 91, 97, 101, 103, 106, 113, 134, 140, 168 f., 206, 208, 210, 252, 291, 330, 354, 357, 382–384, 387, 411, 419 f., 565
idir   501
imperialism   133, 163 f., 190, 225, 240, 280, 283
impoverishment   16, 48, 148, 158, 242

incentives 11, 58, 174, 211, 398, 477–479, 486f., 510–513 See also compension; coercion; commitment
income 18, 145, 173, 176, 217, 221, 223, 225, 233, 241, 252, 267, 292, 300, 304, 319, 324, 329, 342, 370, 411, 421, 484f., 498, 502, 557
indentured labour 24, 42, 46, 67, 126, 159, 163, 237, 247, 326, 333, 363–376, 402, 406, 445f., 510, 523
indentured migration 363–368, 370, 372–374, 447
independence (of states) 36, 48–51, 55–57, 74–76, 91, 98, 203, 221, 240f., 245, 284, 313, 338, 381f.
India 6, 32–48, 50–53, 67, 73, 95, 125, 162f., 176, 180, 182, 185, 194, 218, 232f., 242, 246f., 253, 260, 262–272, 280–282, 286, 292f., 311f., 317, 322, 324–326, 336f., 340f., 364–370, 373f., 386, 400, 402, 404–407, 411, 414, 417, 421f., 428f., 434, 445f., 460, 501, 510, 526, 528f., 538, 542, 547, 558, 567
Indian Civil Service (ICS) 311f.
indigenous labour 85f., 89, 337
indigenous people 67, 85f., 89f., 95, 97f., 121, 161f., 233, 334, 337
Indonesia 1, 9, 243, 248f., 364, 371, 373, 456, 458, 547
Industrial and Commercial Workers' Union 71
industrial development 26, 37, 48, 55, 87, 99f., 151
industrial region 157, 172f.
Industrial Revolution 34, 76, 93, 162, 175, 181, 244, 270, 398, 469f., 484
industrial workers 22, 26, 75, 83f., 99, 103, 106, 134, 159, 172, 185f., 210, 272, 483f., 487, 539, 566
industrialism 36, 289, 475
industrialization 15, 17, 22, 26, 36, 44f., 48–50, 53, 55, 75f., 87, 104, 139, 147, 150f., 174f., 177, 181–183, 185f., 192, 211f., 228, 231, 239, 255, 260–265, 280f., 283, 288, 290, 329f., 332, 340, 378, 380, 407, 471, 522, 538, 566
industrialized countries 231, 522, 538
industrious revolution 17
inequality 106, 124, 170, 176f., 259, 342, 387, 407, 457, 505
informal labour 33, 95, 107, 140, 159, 252, 277

informal sector 44f., 47, 76, 78, 100, 106, 293, 566
informal economy 168, 222, 233, 285, 293, 568
informalization 45, 47, 158
infrastructure 51, 76, 96, 135, 158, 204, 277, 286f., 313, 368, 452f.
innovation 16, 79, 469
insecurity 71, 291, 293, 403
insurance 49, 265, 478, 496, 499, 501f., 556, 559
intelligentsia 35, 51, 54, 190
inter-war period 39, 101, 132, 134, 139, 174, 188, 206, 243, 255f., 269, 272, 305, 381, 442, 453, 455, 564
internalization 36, 486
International Confederation of Free Trade Unions (ICFTU) 564f., 568
International Conference of Labour and Social History (ITH) 133, 174, 176
International Federation of Trade Unions (IFTU) 563–565
International Institute of Social History (IISH) 8, 135, 160, 174, 176, 192, 194, 201, 204f., 207f., 213, 317f., 322, 395, 433, 519, 523
International Labour Organization (ILO) 9, 106, 218, 342, 404, 437, 445, 453, 522f., 537, 543–545, 547, 557
International Monetary Fund (IMF) 58, 313
International Organization for Migration (IOM) 453f.
international trade 58, 64, 424, 563f., 566f.
International Trade Union Confederation (ITUC) 564, 568
International Working Men's Association (IWMA) 562, 564
invention 63, 169, 221, 227, 271, 300, 405, 470
investment 51, 69, 75, 92, 103, 157, 163, 167–169, 471, 556f.
involution 16
Iran 147, 181–199, 201, 535
Iranian Revolution 185, 194–196
Iraq 64, 185, 196, 282
Iron Curtain 114, 133, 168
iron ore 34, 74, 237, 239
Ironbridge Gorge Museum Trust 172
İskeçe 208
Islam 181, 391, 413, 417, 423f.
Isle of Ely 496

isolated mass hypothesis   254 f.
Israel   207
Istanbul   202 f., 205 f., 208 – 213
ivory   65, 66, 387
Ivory Coast   66, 72, 77
Italy   1, 29, 96, 136, 162, 285, 340, 353, 414, 419, 444, 461, 526, 530, 534, 542, 545 f.

Jamaica   96, 336 – 338, 366, 372 f., 380, 385, 446, 461, 499 f.
Jamshedpur   35
Japan   16, 33, 228, 230, 245, 248 f., 253, 260, 266, 272 f., 300, 303, 308, 321, 325, 352, 367, 413, 417 – 419, 427, 448, 485, 546, 558 f.
jati   428
Java   311, 367, 369, 373, 429, 446, 484, 499, 557
Jharia   46, 253
Jim Crow   85, 119, 353, 381
jobbers   40, 49, 402, 474
jute   34, 37, 38, 40, 41, 43, 45, 55, 56, 267, 272, 455, 553

kangani   52, 54
Kanpur   35, 39 f., 46
Karachi   48 – 50
karkhanas   262
Katanga   73, 242
Kavala   208
Kennecott Copper Corporation   243, 250
Kenya   63, 73, 75, 79, 280, 352, 533
Kerr-Siegel hypothesis   254
Kilindini   533
Kimberley   70, 242
kinship   36, 220 f., 335, 442, 479
Koran   423
Korea   228, 245, 462, 567

labour action   34, 194
labour contracting   22 f., 152, 247 – 249, 364 f., 370, 395 – 404, 408, 447, 463, 476 f., 508, 551
labour force   24, 28, 34, 36, 42 f., 51 – 53, 70, 76, 86, 137, 139, 141, 149 f., 192, 211, 219, 237, 239, 245, 247 – 250, 272 f., 306, 331, 363, 369, 475, 546, 561
labour history   1, 15, 23, 30, 33, 38 – 43, 47, 49 – 54, 63, 83 f., 91, 99 – 103, 107, 112 – 119, 122 – 124, 126 f., 131 – 133, 135, 141, 144, 147, 149 f., 152 f., 157, 159 – 162, 164, 166, 174 – 177, 184, 186, 189 – 192, 197, 201 – 210, 213, 239 f., 243, 245, 250, 257, 259, 273, 277, 288 – 291, 345, 349 f., 373, 377 f., 383, 396, 402, 506 f.
labour law   42, 46, 48, 50, 57, 423
labour markets   17, 40, 42, 47, 58, 100, 139 f., 177, 218, 240, 251, 293, 333, 358, 397, 400 f., 406, 429, 439 – 441, 444, 451, 453, 457, 460, 511, 542, 554, 562 f.
labour migration   52, 69, 72, 76, 106, 133, 147 – 149, 171, 186, 192, 207, 348, 365 – 367, 433 – 468
labour mobilization   50, 52, 103, 165, 257, 280, 284, 364
labour movement   23, 37, 41, 49, 51, 53, 56, 105 f., 113, 115, 132 f., 136 f., 140, 145, 153, 159, 164, 177, 189 f., 201, 204, 206, 208 f., 293, 408, 541, 565
labour network   292
labour politics   41, 47 – 49, 54, 196, 564
labour relations   2, 4 f., 8 – 11, 15 – 17, 20 – 22, 29 f., 34, 42, 46, 48 – 50, 52, 54, 56, 74, 83, 86 f., 95, 97 f., 102 f., 119, 135, 137, 142, 144, 148, 152, 159, 161, 164, 168, 170, 174, 176, 192, 204, 209, 211, 237 f., 244, 257, 317 – 324, 345, 348, 364, 390, 395, 405 f., 412 – 416, 422, 427 f., 430, 436, 508, 511 – 513, 524, 526, 532, 535, 538 f., 542
labour resistance, see resistance
labour rights   28, 219, 231, 233, 516
labouring poor   45, 185, 192 f., 196, 219, 233, 413
Lancashire   158, 253, 266 – 268
land   36, 51, 63 f., 66 f., 70, 76, 87 f., 97 f., 137, 148, 151, 185, 203, 217 – 222, 225, 227, 230 f., 234, 246 f., 281, 314, 322, 324, 329, 331, 333, 335, 337 f., 357, 365, 370, 384, 399, 428 f., 447, 465, 496, 517, 525
landholder   65
lascars   42
law   28, 47, 49, 76, 114, 118, 125, 165, 182, 187, 252 f., 302, 304, 311, 346, 348, 351, 367, 404, 426, 428, 478, 480, 508 f., 532
leadership   36 f., 40 f., 50 f., 54, 56, 73, 86, 103, 161, 165, 174, 188, 319, 532, 536, 561
League of Nations   313, 448
legislation   28, 50, 57, 67, 139, 158, 190, 192, 373, 401, 408, 538, 565
Leiden   297, 526

Leninism   137, 187
liberalization   15, 28, 55, 58, 152
Liberia   68, 79
Lima   24, 90, 98, 352
Lisbon   24
livret   404
loans   402, 495, 498–500, 502 f.
lockouts   522–524, 532, 537 f.
Lodz   447
London   9, 160, 271, 311, 373, 383, 446, 562
Los Angeles   119, 121, 287, 289, 310, 339 f., 406, 554
loyalty   192, 309, 311, 313, 479, 500, 509, 513, 556
Luddism   259, 268, 540
Lyons   269

machines   263, 265, 267 f., 272, 540
Madagascar   65, 66, 417
Madras   34, 366, 428
mahaber   495
Malaya   243, 366 f., 382, 417, 446
Malaysia   52, 243, 282, 366, 429, 446, 456, 492, 505
male worker   249, 265, 285, 290 f., 340
Mali   336
management   22, 24, 41, 43, 53, 64, 102, 118, 133, 194, 211, 237 f., 240, 289 f., 292, 298, 306, 310, 313, 338, 354, 358, 369, 373, 400, 456, 469–480, 482–487, 523, 530, 533, 536, 538 f., 554 f., 557
Manchuria   434
Manila   557
manufacturing   1, 3, 18, 36–38, 40, 44 f., 48 f., 55–59, 63, 74 f., 78 f., 87, 90, 92, 105, 107, 125, 134, 146 f., 156–158, 161 f., 164, 172 f., 175, 177, 183, 186, 191–194, 205, 209, 259–275, 283, 287 f., 292, 322, 382, 384, 397–400, 402, 423 f., 427 f., 448, 460 f., 471–473, 486, 498, 517, 521, 527, 529, 538, 554, 557
Maoism   23, 26
maritime labour   34, 42, 278, 280, 368
market production   96, 217, 321
Martinique   455
Marxism   16, 23, 26, 34, 36–40, 44 f., 51, 53, 101, 113 f., 127, 133, 137, 142, 169, 184, 187–191, 246, 289, 329, 334, 339, 383, 476, 542, 553
mass production   37, 157, 177

Mauritius   24, 67, 355, 363, 365 f., 372, 446, 493 f.
May Day   121, 541
mechanization   15, 18 f., 21 f., 26, 253, 259, 262 f., 267 f., 271, 281, 398, 400
Mediterranean   163, 171, 202, 345, 383, 400, 405, 407, 414, 423, 434, 542
Melanesia   368
membership   48, 399, 492, 551 f., 556–560, 568
merchants   43, 162 f., 175, 260, 262, 268, 289, 338, 424 f., 473
meritocracy   342
Mesopotamia   399 f., 405
metal   74, 105, 210, 212, 399, 473, 535
Mexico   9, 82, 84, 86–88, 90, 96, 98–101, 104, 106, 236, 260, 264, 272, 286, 335, 341, 460 f., 526, 535, 547
micro-history   7, 159
Middle Ages   163, 170, 226, 229 f., 237–239, 268, 303, 358, 382, 397, 403, 411, 414, 418 f., 421–423, 426, 430, 444, 484, 526
middle class   54, 79, 190, 288, 330
Middle East   187, 201 f., 204, 206 f., 261, 264, 324, 354, 460
migrants   27, 45, 51–53, 69, 102, 116, 149, 167, 186, 192, 194, 197, 206, 208, 210 f., 245, 247, 253, 341, 365, 427, 434, 437–441, 447, 450, 452–454, 457 f., 461, 463, 502, 514, 518
– career migrants   454 f.
– family migrants   435, 438
– organizational migrants   454
migration   5, 11, 24, 29, 52, 66, 96, 107, 134, 138, 144–149, 163, 168, 171, 176, 185, 194, 207, 211, 218, 224, 237, 244–246, 248 f., 257, 279, 330, 333, 349, 364–368, 373, 379, 387, 389, 401, 433–468, 472, 562
migration industry   442, 449, 451 f., 458
migration infrastructure   443, 446, 452–454
migration system   245, 438, 440 f., 446, 459, 462 f.
migratory labour   11, 138, 218, 244–246, 249
Milan   418, 482
militancy   35, 39, 101, 105, 107, 280, 283, 291, 538
military   49–51, 56 f., 75, 105, 165, 177, 181–183, 206, 282, 302, 307, 311, 345 f., 348, 351, 356, 404, 460, 470, 508, 514, 518

millet 63
Minas Gerais 91, 242
mines 3, 72, 117, 237, 239, 242–244, 247 f., 250, 257, 308, 472, 476, 526
mine owners 247 f., 250
miners 3, 237–258
minerals 75, 237, 240, 242
Ming dynasty 16, 19–21, 30, 300 f., 336, 406 f., 413, 419, 427
mingas 86
mining 20, 22 f., 25, 30, 34, 66, 68 f., 71–74, 76 f., 85–87, 94, 100, 140, 158, 165, 186, 237–258, 317, 370, 397 f., 429 f., 461
mining industry 240 f., 244 f., 249, 251 f., 397, 429
missionaries 35, 73, 380, 411, 414, 442, 451, 454
mita system 86, 241 f.
mobile work 158, 277 f.
mobility 42, 47, 52, 54, 58, 65, 76, 78, 123, 144–147, 166, 192, 194, 237, 277 f., 282, 285 f., 292, 307, 347, 356, 363, 379, 390, 422, 427–429, 434, 436, 447, 452, 463, 466, 507 f., 510 f., 513–516, 518, 560, 562
mobility regimes 452
mobilization 23, 34, 42, 50–52, 54, 89, 140, 147 f., 165, 167, 230, 244 f., 249, 346, 507, 542, 552, 555
modernity 94, 220, 263, 349, 352, 357
modernization 6, 36, 38, 45, 53, 169, 183, 192, 204, 213, 220, 222, 298, 331, 334, 353
Moghul Empire 407
Moldavia 147
Mombasa 74, 280, 533
monetization 339, 400, 406
money 40, 69 f., 72, 77, 181, 237 f., 248, 261, 318, 330, 342, 395, 401, 411, 439, 461, 473, 476, 478, 491–496, 498 f., 501 f., 512, 551, 556 f., 562
monitoring 369, 451, 486
monopoly 70, 88, 91, 94, 242, 260, 302, 387, 553
Morocco 201, 245, 283, 391, 442, 462
Moscow 139, 197, 477, 528
motivation 472, 477, 543
motor transport 286–288
Mozambique 69, 70, 77, 78, 168, 245, 461, 462
Mughal India 262, 280, 413, 419, 428

mui tsai 449
Mundos do trabalho 83
Murid 77
museums 172 f.
mushroom organizations 552
Muslims 49, 51, 77, 171, 197, 208, 423, 458
Muslim League 49, 51
mutualism 7, 100, 159, 222, 319, 396, 428, 442, 469, 486, 491–504, 559
Mysore 39, 41, 429

Namibia 63
Natal 67, 76, 365, 366, 373, 430, 446
nation states 5, 7, 33, 201, 206, 213, 228, 245, 279, 294, 298, 350, 543
national market 181
National Socialism 136, 141, 165, 305, 350
nationalism 5, 34–36, 53, 75, 103, 124, 166, 188, 201, 204, 206 f., 233, 352, 359, 372 f., 378
nationalization 306, 518
Nazi Germany 165, 249, 353 f., 447 f., 465, 477, 534
negotiations 231, 234, 278, 510 f., 515 f., 532 f., 536, 553, 558, 561
neo-Marxism 184, 191, 329
neoliberalism 77, 106, 113, 157 f., 177, 224, 233, 278, 292, 387
Netherlands 9, 90, 160, 163, 264, 317, 330, 340, 354, 364, 419 f., 435, 438, 444 f., 448, 455 f., 459–461, 465, 505, 534, 563
network migration 438, 440 f.
New Caledonia 367, 368
New Deal 113, 120 f., 310, 381, 447
new institutionalism 114
new labour history 124, 136, 184, 192 f., 202, 213
New Orleans 290
New Public Management 306, 313
new unionism 105
New York 24, 77, 116, 160, 289, 341, 466, 533
New York Declaration (2016) 437
Nigeria 65–67, 69, 72, 74, 77–79, 243, 255, 284–286, 293, 333, 388, 529, 538, 541, 547, 553
nobility 262, 307, 325 f.
Non-Governmental Organization (NGO) 29, 77
non-working 217, 320–323
Normandy 158
Norway 443, 563

North America 2, 6, 10, 64, 84, 95, 111, 120, 123, 126, 157, 163, 228, 242, 250 f., 264, 330, 334, 337, 359, 383, 386, 390, 404, 407, 463, 497
North Atlantic 6, 84, 99, 160, 400, 407, 470, 562 f., 568
North India 39, 405
North Korea 462
Northumberland 4, 239

obrajes 87, 90
offices 298–300, 302, 304 f., 308–310, 472, 560
official 28, 34 f., 67, 92, 95, 166, 168, 205 f., 312, 364, 369, 385, 402, 446, 457, 502, 532, 535–537, 540, 543, 559 f.
oil 67, 96, 146, 161, 183, 185 f., 191–195, 233, 282, 287 f., 448, 457, 460, 535
oil industry 146, 183, 191–194, 448, 460
oil workers 193 f., 535
Oppenheim Collins 533
Organization of African Unity 313
organized labour 75, 140, 188–190, 194, 202, 453, 456
orientalism 164
Ottoman Empire 145, 162 f., 165, 171, 181, 183, 185, 187, 192, 201–214, 260–262, 267, 272, 284, 289, 298, 302 f., 407, 426, 454, 540
overseeing 474–476, 540
ownership 67, 98, 225, 232, 250, 286 f., 290, 317, 321, 326, 337, 364, 395, 511, 529

Pacific Islands 367 f.
Pakistan 1, 33, 48–51, 55–57, 272, 442, 547
Palermo Protocol 450
Palestine 207
palm oil 67, 233, 282, 288
Pan-African Congress 313
Papua New Guinea 482, 502 f.
Paris 24, 69, 120, 160, 455, 496, 500, 545
participation 28 f., 58, 73, 161, 174, 194 f., 219, 277, 305, 309, 335, 349, 523, 529, 545
paternalism 79, 250, 381, 384
patriarchy 18, 28, 30, 54, 58, 64, 78, 87, 181, 228
patrimonialism 298–300, 302, 307 f., 311
payment 4, 217, 273, 318, 363, 400 f., 405, 476, 478, 494, 498 f., 511–513, 516, 557

peasants 38, 57, 132, 137–139, 145, 150 f., 172, 217–229, 230 f., 233, 244, 246, 248, 261, 329, 331, 333, 336 f., 342, 379, 484
peasant labour 217, 229, 232
peasant movements 38, 97
peasant work 172, 220 f., 247
peasantization 217, 223, 225, 232
Pendleton Act 310
penitentiary 348 f., 352 f., 357
Pernambuco 90
Peronism 104
Persia, see Iran
personal freedom 19, 502
Peru 84 f., 87 f., 90, 96, 101, 243, 247, 335, 337, 352, 363, 368–370, 547
petitions 541
Philippines 350, 429, 438, 440, 456–458, 567
Pidgiguiti 284
piece rates 326 f., 398–400, 406, 478
piece wages, see piece rates
plantations 35, 42, 51–54, 67, 89–91, 93, 126, 143, 163, 247, 326, 373, 379, 381 f., 386, 470 f., 518, 526
Poland 135, 139, 140–142, 145, 147–149, 151, 153, 157, 165, 167–169, 171, 245, 249, 447, 461, 466, 526, 528 f., 535
police 73, 76, 122, 212, 288, 304, 312, 346, 371, 524, 529, 531–533, 536, 538, 543
policy makers 435 f., 438, 466
polygamy 63
populism 103, 105, 196, 223
ports 48, 96, 98, 281 f., 284, 289, 390, 443, 497, 515, 533
Portugal 65, 70, 74, 84 f., 88, 90, 93, 163 f., 245, 281, 317, 355 f., 379, 385 f., 390, 406 f., 411, 419, 435, 439, 441, 444, 454, 461, 465, 527, 541, 567
post-colonial era 97, 100, 107, 201, 336, 352, 377, 382
post-independence era 49–51, 55–58, 352
post-revolutionary period 185, 195 f.
post-war period 41, 73, 101, 196, 256, 272, 383, 461, 465, 543, 564
Potosí 86, 94, 241 f., 244, 420
poverty 45, 49, 55, 78, 104, 106, 120 f., 169, 185, 188, 192 f., 196, 218 f., 229, 233 f., 267, 282, 342, 402, 413
pre-industrial period 38, 184, 260, 262, 264, 269, 272, 289, 418, 420, 422, 483 f.

Subject Index — 591

precariousness   76, 78, 83, 95, 100, 106, 158, 166, 169, 177, 224, 233, 277 f., 287, 290, 293 f., 390
prejudice   6, 318
private property   227
privatization   29, 56 f., 157, 314, 529
pro-market reforms   56 f.
producer cooperative   485 f.
product chain   9
production processes   9, 225, 242, 261, 264, 529
professionalization   304, 518, 559 f.
profitability   94, 291, 370, 377, 385, 387, 439, 444
profits   64, 68, 76 f., 79, 126, 181, 238, 241, 262, 264, 286 – 288, 334, 382, 384, 396, 401, 426, 440, 447, 471, 478, 496
profit maximization   92, 230, 278, 311
profit rate, see profitability
profit sharing   398 f., 478
proletarian   37, 51, 113, 174, 219, 232, 237, 257, 491
proletarianization   22, 30, 37, 125, 137, 219, 232, 238, 244, 246, 257, 422, 513, 552
proletariat   53, 58, 76, 101, 150, 244, 279, 318, 378
property rights   125, 232
prostitution   2, 20, 99, 195, 340, 448, 450 f.
protest   1, 22, 38, 50, 189, 195, 273, 338, 371, 411, 527, 529 f., 538, 541, 551, 553
– See also resistance
proto-industry   15 – 17, 87, 246, 260 f., 334, 339, 407, 473
public administration   297 f., 303, 306 f., 309 f.
Puerto Rico   89, 91, 92, 337, 390
Pullman boycott   283
Pullman Palace Car Company   527
punishment   325, 345 – 354, 356 f., 359 f., 404, 478, 501, 511, 516, 534
punitive pluralism   351
push-and-pull paradigm   444

Qajar dynasty   182
Quazvin   181
Qin dynasty   300, 406
Qing dynasty   16, 20 f., 261, 264, 300 f., 325, 336, 355, 406 f.

race   53 f., 75, 99, 116, 119 – 121, 160, 184, 249, 284, 290, 372, 382, 527, 555, 559
racism   42, 74, 279, 305, 364, 372, 374, 377, 380 f., 533
radicalism   137, 254, 267, 279 f.
radicalization   255, 360
railways   23, 48, 68, 74, 132, 283 f., 286 f., 527, 557
railway workers   23, 74, 283 f., 527
Raniganj   253
rank   41, 98, 246, 299 f., 307 f., 513, 534, 556, 558, 560 f., 567
Rasht   181
rationalization   53, 132, 158, 172 f., 253
raw materials   68, 171, 259, 262, 312, 330, 378, 486
Real del Monte   87, 535, 536
rebellion   21, 137, 371, 382, 411, 498, 521, 528, 548
reciprocal labour   321 f., 405, 413, 420
recruitment   24 f., 37, 49, 86, 88, 95 f., 120, 123, 125, 138, 192 – 194, 219, 243 – 249, 253, 268, 300, 302, 309 – 311, 313, 365 – 369, 371 – 374, 377 – 379, 424, 440, 442, 446, 448, 450, 452 f., 455 f., 458, 460 – 463, 474, 484, 510 f., 514 f., 518, 562
Red International of Labour Unions (RILU)   564
reforms   56, 75, 98, 148, 250, 302, 308, 310, 337, 372, 507, 568
refugees   435, 437, 464
regulation school   227
religion   6 f., 37 – 39, 41, 50, 79, 120, 181, 184, 194 f., 202 f., 206, 209, 214, 217, 279, 291, 302, 325, 346, 363, 389 f., 412 f., 415, 419 f., 422 f., 426, 435 f., 458, 497, 554 f., 559, 566
remuneration   1, 4, 21, 304, 318, 321, 324, 326 f., 395, 397 – 400, 402
repartimiento   86 f.
resistance   11, 42 f., 46, 53, 56 f., 71, 74, 90, 93, 111, 121 f., 125 f., 151, 192, 196, 205 f., 208, 223, 225, 233, 241, 259, 267 – 269, 312, 332, 337 f., 371, 387, 440, 479, 505 – 570
retail workers   99, 290, 292 f., 533
return migration   145, 458 f., 464
Réunion   363, 446
revolts   64, 71, 91, 92, 97, 105, 132, 194, 196, 204, 238, 311, 477, 484, 527, 528, 530, 535 f., 539

revolutions 91, 92, 93, 98, 105, 137, 138, 146, 147, 162, 181–185, 187, 194f., 233, 256, 280, 284, 301, 380, 382, 383, 464, 521f., 566 See also Russian Revolution
rewards 300, 307, 478
Rhodesia 69, 242
rickshaws 3, 282
rights 24, 27, 29, 50, 57, 64, 75, 149, 196, 208, 210, 279, 292, 305, 333, 337f., 358, 364, 372, 408, 434, 453, 463, 465f., 471, 480, 511, 515f., 526, 531, 552, 566
Rio de Janeiro 90, 98f., 282, 382, 390, 476, 494
Rochester 43, 65, 75, 232, 289f., 324
Roman Empire 163, 304, 421, 444, 525
Romania 132, 141, 148, 157, 466
Rome 77, 341, 414, 525
Roorki 34
ROSCA 493–495, 500f.
rotation 241, 302, 309, 491–494, 497–500, 529, 556
Rotterdam 443
rubber 34, 51, 96, 282, 363, 367
rules 4, 42, 168, 225, 227, 298–300, 302, 307, 310, 318f., 334, 345, 369, 397, 403, 478–482, 484f., 487, 491, 497, 500f., 553, 560
runaways, see desertion
rural regions 19, 225, 231, 513
rural society 225, 232
rural ties 44, 53
Russia 25, 133–137, 139–144, 146f., 151, 153, 160, 166, 169, 182f., 185–187, 229, 239, 247, 249, 298, 307f., 318, 322, 325, 356, 387, 407, 417, 419, 433, 447, 459, 464, 466, 528
Russian Revolution 186f., 192, 308, 528

saam 492f.
Safavid Empire 181, 184
Sahara 63, 65, 77, 281, 388, 444
Salaries, see wages
Samsun 208
San Francisco 24, 548
sanctions 364, 371f.
São Paulo 93, 104–106, 337, 383, 385, 388, 390, 535
scheduled demand 491, 501
scientific management 310, 400

Scotland 239f., 245, 256, 267, 272, 335, 455, 530
secessio plebis 525
second serfdom 141f., 169, 171, 406
second slavery 92f., 171, 391
security 27, 65, 79, 167, 176, 287, 293, 302, 304f., 313, 336, 440, 497, 500, 516, 541, 565
self-employment 45, 83, 95, 99f., 107, 159, 217f., 224, 233, 237f., 241, 288, 317, 322, 325, 329, 338, 405, 407, 485, 551
self-exploitation 334, 337
Senegal 9, 67, 69, 73, 77, 79, 499, 529, 544
serfdom 87, 142f., 145f., 148, 159, 171, 239f., 333, 384, 397, 407, 427
servant 47, 317, 428, 515
service labour 289
service sector 3, 158, 339, 567
services 3, 49, 76, 78f., 85, 88, 90, 100, 107, 150, 220f., 250, 277f., 282, 286, 289, 292–294, 304, 306, 312f., 318, 320, 324–327, 331, 334, 340, 342, 368, 403, 428, 441, 457, 472, 474, 478, 556, 559
settlement 74, 146, 148, 224, 230, 363, 372, 439, 464
sexes 57, 72, 259, 264f., 273, 331, 333, 335f., 339, 342, 386, 451, 472, 511
Shandong 22
Shanghai 9, 22, 28, 140, 146, 282f., 554
Shanglin 29
ships 5, 9f., 75, 90, 279, 364, 367, 380, 404, 443, 515f.
shipping company 42, 443, 451, 453, 518
Shiraz 181
Sholapur Assam 35
shokubun 427
Siberia 141, 146, 148, 228, 356
sick leave 398, 539
Sierra Leone 74, 77
Silver 86, 87, 162, 181, 237, 270, 405
silver mining 86, 90, 241f., 420, 526
Singapore 282f., 341, 456, 492, 547, 557
sit-down strikes 529
Six Companies 24
skilled labour 3, 71, 73, 75, 134, 139, 141, 147, 157, 169, 208, 244, 263, 265, 283, 288f., 368, 398, 452, 455, 460, 465f., 472, 479, 510, 562

skills   68, 73, 79, 161, 163, 167, 192, 213, 238, 244, 250, 291, 300, 302, 307, 319, 336, 427, 455, 462f., 472, 476, 485, 517
slaves   9f., 24, 64, 66f., 89–93, 95f., 99, 126, 161, 163f., 171, 202f., 290, 317, 324, 331, 338, 363f., 367, 374, 377–382, 384–389, 391, 398, 402, 405–407, 411, 420, 444f., 447, 451, 470f., 475f., 480, 508, 512, 527
slave labour   9f., 90f., 95f., 126, 171, 202f., 364, 377–380, 382, 388f., 391, 398, 405–407, 420, 444, 508
slave markets   290
slave revolution   91
slave trade   9, 24, 35, 65, 89, 91, 93, 99, 161, 163, 331, 363f., 367, 378, 380–385, 387–390, 402, 407, 444, 450
Slovenia 145, 567
small business   290, 293
smallholding   95, 97, 138, 370
social democracy   190
social history   17, 37f., 41, 49, 87, 111, 133–135, 137, 191–194, 201–204, 290, 379, 383, 390
social identity   193, 418
social movement   47, 98, 105f., 123, 161, 176, 230, 257, 280, 382f., 387, 528, 567
social question   170, 543
social reform   35, 193
social reproduction   149–153, 341
socialism   15, 22, 24, 27f., 30, 56, 98, 101, 104, 113, 115, 132–135, 140, 147–151, 157f., 166, 168f., 187, 190, 197, 210, 225, 229, 231, 339f., 348, 354, 396, 483, 518, 543
Society for Effecting the Abolition of the Slave Trade   380
sociology   104, 122, 213, 222
solidarity   29, 39, 50, 53, 57, 158, 193, 209, 211, 223, 269, 283, 339, 478, 502, 523, 538f., 562, 567
Somalia   79
South Africa   1, 24f., 30, 62f., 67, 69–71, 73–76, 79, 163, 242, 245f., 286, 290, 293, 337, 364, 456, 532, 535, 547, 567
South America   97, 311, 322, 416, 451, 547
South Asia   9, 33–61, 261, 272f., 280, 325, 439, 474, 536
South-eastern Europe   131f., 135f., 139, 163, 165

South India   39, 42, 51f., 264f., 268f.
South Korea   228, 567
South Sudan   63
Southern Rhodesia   69, 73f., 242, 246
Soviet Union (USSR)   113f., 130, 133–136, 139, 147f., 150f., 166, 188, 192, 233, 308, 350, 354f., 396, 402, 407, 433, 447, 463–466, 479, 483, 568 See also Russia
Spain   62, 96, 149, 163f., 305, 332, 346, 379, 381, 446, 461f., 529, 541, 546, 567
Spanish Empire   87, 90f., 95, 311
specialization   4, 310, 333
spinners   9, 261, 264, 266, 272, 455
sprouts of capitalism   15
Sri Lanka, see Ceylon
St. Kilda   335
Stalinism   135, 151, 186, 188f., 348
state industry   177
state servants   303f.
state socialism   132f., 135, 137, 139–141, 147–153, 157, 168, 170, 177, 483
status   19, 39, 45, 50, 64, 87, 98, 133, 140, 150, 159, 166, 168, 176, 181f., 188, 195, 223, 228, 243, 245, 268, 284, 287, 348, 357, 371, 379f., 387, 411, 421, 424f., 428, 447, 464, 479, 527, 559
steel industry   41, 75, 126, 461, 471, 482, 538
strikes   9, 23, 27, 34, 35, 40, 41, 45, 49, 56, 57, 70, 71, 74, 75, 87, 90, 105, 116, 118, 119, 120, 140, 151, 153, 176, 184, 192, 195, 206, 207, 230, 237, 242, 254, 255, 256, 259, 269, 270, 273, 283–285, 288, 289, 371, 382, 390, 476, 494, 516, 521–530, 531f., 534–538, 540–548, 551–558, 561–563, 565, 567
Subaltern Studies group   38
subaltern workers   219, 349
subcontracting   224, 238, 241, 248, 257, 326, 397, 399, 474, 555
subsistence   44, 83, 87, 95, 97, 149–151, 159, 168, 176, 217–219, 221–224, 229, 232f., 246f., 261, 305, 324, 329–339, 341f., 363, 416, 429, 484
subsistence agriculture   95, 97, 151, 218, 246f.
subsistence labour   149–151, 329f.
subsistence production   217, 219, 232, 329–344
Sufi   426

sugar   9, 24, 55, 64, 67, 89–92, 95f., 126, 161, 171, 233, 338, 363, 368, 374, 383, 385, 387, 471, 476, 484
sugar market   363
sugar plantations   24, 67, 89, 91, 338, 363, 374, 471
summás   138, 152
supervision   11, 365, 398, 400, 473, 475f., 486
supranational institutions   567
Suriname   364, 366, 367, 368, 369, 370, 372, 373, 374, 445, 446, 454, 456, 499
surplus   121, 217, 219, 221f., 331, 334, 336, 338, 340f., 360, 384, 476, 496
Sweden   172, 207, 239, 356, 521, 546, 563
Switzerland   302, 562
Sydney   24

Tahuantinsuyu   299
Taiwan   22, 325, 567
Tamils   54
Tanga   533
Tanzania   63, 74f., 287, 333
task-orientation   484
tax farming   299
taxation   68f., 158, 217, 219, 232, 297, 299, 303, 307, 311, 551
taxonomy of labour relation   8, 11, 176, 217, 317, 319, 320, 321, 349
taxonomy of labour conflicts   523, 524
tea   34, 35, 37, 42, 46, 48, 51, 56, 233, 474
technology   22, 53, 79, 92, 94, 104, 161, 172f., 183, 226, 230, 272, 277f., 281f., 285–287, 306, 310, 338, 340, 419, 436, 452, 472
teleconnections   9
teleology   37, 39f., 184, 197, 223, 229f., 261, 374
Tenessee   249
territory   2, 6f., 41, 69, 84, 86, 97, 125, 131, 135f., 139, 145, 158, 182, 189, 204, 228, 234, 249, 303, 334, 346, 367, 369f., 425, 447, 513
textile industry   18, 36, 40, 45, 49, 147, 194, 250f., 384, 400
textile manufacturing   259–264, 267, 270, 272f., 484
textile workers   10, 39, 100, 259–%%%275, 526, 564
Thailand   5, 439, 547
Thessalonika   208, 214

Third Front   26
Third World   329, 331f., 342, 565
threats   498f., 557
time discipline   470, 484
time-management   482
time-obedience   487
time-wages   244, 322, 398–400, 406
tin mining   69, 72, 237, 238, 243, 247f., 256
tobacco   203, 208, 209, 282, 337, 367, 385, 387, 471
Tokugawa   419, 427, 485
Tokyo   24, 285
tools   3, 9, 138, 176, 192, 220, 237, 423, 465, 525, 535
trade   7, 10, 58, 63–%%%66, 77, 86f., 93, 146, 161–164, 167f., 170f., 181f., 189, 233, 241f., 259–%%%261, 270, 272f., 277–%%%295, 325, 365–368, 373, 411f., 424f., 428f., 443, 446, 449, 454, 456, 458f., 517
   See also slave trade
trade routes   281
trade unions   6, 28, 30, 35, 37, 40f., 47–51, 53f., 56f., 59, 74, 103, 105f., 116, 123, 140, 164, 189f., 193, 212, 238, 254, 269, 272, 390, 396, 399, 403, 487, 524, 533f., 551–558, 561–570
trading blocs   566
transnational history   7
transnational turn   123
transport   34, 64, 68, 70, 72, 90, 92, 96, 116, 145, 237, 239, 244, 253, 277–282, 284–289, 293f., 363, 365, 367f., 374, 443, 446, 452, 507, 517, 563
transport workers   34, 281, 285f.
transportation   125, 204, 239, 277f., 281, 285–287, 289, 345f., 350f., 355f., 369, 450, 453
tributary labour   321f., 325, 349, 427
Trinidad   364, 366f., 373, 446
truck system   395, 401
Tsarism   141, 148, 151, 182f., 185–187, 192, 355
Tuareg   414
Tudeh Party   188f.
Turkey   32, 130, 158, 180, 183, 185, 187f., 200–215, 272, 317, 462, 527, 547

Ukraine   130, 138, 148, 165f., 246, 248f., 466
unemployment   28, 76, 106f., 121, 158, 169, 252, 263, 268, 323, 326, 373, 403, 408, 492, 496, 498f., 530, 555
unfree labour   2, 19, 33, 46, 65, 83, 87, 116f., 141, 143f., 203, 221, 242, 247, 257, 282, 321, 325f., 333, 350, 364, 407, 411, 416, 428f., 447, 469f., 477
United Kingdom (UK), see Britain
United Nations   79, 218, 313, 342
United States of America (USA)   6, 16, 41, 91f., 101, 106, 119–129, 160, 163f., 185, 190, 197, 244, 248, 250, 266, 272f., 283, 285–289, 291, 298, 309–310, 339f., 368, 380–382, 385, 387, 404, 461, 470, 472, 480, 494, 523, 527f., 530f., 536, 538, 544, 546, 552, 554, 564
university system   213
unrest   105, 137, 204, 361, 366, 371, 535–537, 539
unskilled workers   79, 134, 463, 566
unwaged workers   331, 339, 340
urban working class   95, 99, 100, 188, 204
urbanization   30, 76, 78, 97, 181, 183, 192, 407, 425, 427
uutgangen   526

Valladolid   379
Vancouver   24, 121
Venezuela   91, 101, 106, 337
Veracruz   90, 98
Vietnam   1, 168, 352, 382, 462, 463, 518, 536, 565
villages   7, 44, 138, 146, 150, 152, 172, 188, 193, 217, 220–224, 232, 248, 308, 428, 440, 495, 501, 566
Virginia   245
violence   66, 85, 94, 279, 341, 487, 498, 511, 522–524, 527, 532, 552f., 558
voluntourism   451

wages   1, 27–29, 34, 49, 57–59, 69, 85, 87f., 96, 106, 139, 145, 147–149, 151, 161, 190, 192, 204, 219, 245, 247–251, 266, 271, 273, 282, 286–293, 329f., 332f., 340, 342, 369–372, 378, 395–409, 412, 419, 430, 450, 478f., 506, 512, 514, 523, 527, 531, 534, 537, 540f., 552f., 562
wage labour   2, 8, 10, 15–17, 30, 33, 44–45, 48, 68, 83, 87, 90, 98f., 107, 122, 125, 136, 138, 142f., 150, 152, 217–219, 223f., 228f., 233, 237f., 241f., 244–246, 257, 278, 280, 282, 284, 286, 288–291, 293f., 318, 321–323, 326f., 331, 333–335, 337–339, 345, 349, 361, 377f., 380, 382, 395–409, 412, 417, 420, 422f., 426–430, 469–471, 475, 479f., 493, 510–514, 516, 523, 525, 528, 539, 551, 564–566
waitresses   3
Wal-Mart   288f., 291f.
Wales   4, 158, 255f.
war   19, 65, 69f., 85, 101, 133, 165, 196, 249, 272, 301, 330, 345f., 354, 398, 406, 453, 465, 522, 534, 538, 540, 553
weavers   9, 261, 264, 267–269, 271
weaving   5, 19, 26, 259, 263f., 266f., 271
welfare   24, 26, 35, 50, 57, 70, 74, 76, 149, 157, 221, 224, 250, 306, 383, 407f., 542
welfare state   157, 306, 407
West Africa   63–66, 73f., 165, 271, 280, 283f., 336, 382, 384–386, 406, 429
West Germany   136, 166f., 461f.
West Indies, see Caribbean
Western Europe   157–178, 224, 255, 262, 283, 298, 301, 303–307, 340, 359, 397, 406f., 421, 435, 450, 453, 459–461, 463
white-collar worker   76, 284, 301
wildcat strike   533–536, 561
withdrawal of work   521
Witwatersrand Native Labour Association (WNLA)   245
women farmer   219
Women in Development (WID)   342
women worker   55, 58f., 133, 140, 151, 251, 266
women's labour   28, 139, 291, 320, 407
work places   209, 211f., 402
work processes   1, 4, 8, 59, 398, 426, 508, 513, 518
work songs   413, 429
workforce   22, 28f., 44, 56, 67f., 78, 86, 89, 100, 134, 139, 146, 211, 217, 239, 247f., 250, 266, 268, 291–293, 337, 346f., 378, 391, 398, 407, 460, 472f., 523
working class   6, 23, 33, 35–41, 43–45, 48–51, 53, 56f., 66, 68, 99, 101, 103, 105f., 111–115, 119f., 122–126, 132–135, 141, 145, 184, 186–189, 191–193, 195–197, 201, 208f., 211–213, 251, 267, 269f.,

278, 287, 291, 340, 342, 345, 349, 383, 498, 529, 543, 563, 567
working-class history   38, 111, 115, 125 f., 191, 278, 383
working conditions   9, 27, 57, 177, 186, 194, 219, 278, 288, 369, 374, 403, 411, 449, 507, 510–512, 514, 516, 537, 551, 558
working hours   4, 151, 190, 290, 318, 400, 407 f., 472, 527, 532, 541
workplace   28, 41, 49, 73–75, 114, 116, 118, 212 f., 254 f., 269, 290 f., 378, 469, 524
workshop   272, 317, 322
World Bank   57 f., 313, 329, 342
world history   7, 159, 202, 277, 510
world market   7, 26, 30, 83, 96, 142, 181 f., 232, 336 f., 557
world system   94, 142, 149, 159, 160, 162, 167, 277, 329 f., 458

World Trade Organization   15, 123
World War I   25, 70, 93, 132, 141, 145, 165, 183, 187 f., 194, 207, 243, 270, 272, 306, 311 f., 447 f., 453, 464, 545, 554, 563
World War II   2, 73, 75, 163, 188–190, 196, 210–212, 249, 272, 354, 382 f., 407, 447 f., 453, 466, 483, 530, 542, 545, 564 f.

Yazd   181
Years of Lead   462
yellow unions   554, 558
Yūaikai   559
Yugoslavia   136, 148, 149, 168, 169, 466

Zambia   29 f., 73, 77 f., 242, 255, 547
Zimbabwe   66, 74 f., 78, 246, 547
Zonguldak   205, 208, 210

Index of Names

Abdullaev, Z.A. 186
Abraham, Itty 436
Abrahamian, Ervand 181, 184f., 190f.
Absar, Syeda Sharmin 58f.
Abu-Lughod, Janet 277
Acemoglu, Daron 94
Adams, Thomas 292, 459
Adkins, Lisa 341
Afacan, Serhan 194
Agha, Amir 196
Ahmad, Kamruddin 56, 424, 442
Ahmadinejad, Mahmoud 196
Ahmed, Mesbahuddin 55f.
Ahuja, Ravi 34, 42, 428f.
Akgöz, Görkem 210, 212
Al-Jāḥiẓ 424
Alatas, S.H. 415, 429, 483
Alencastro, Luiz Felipe 390
Alexander, Robert J. 101, 175, 245, 253, 309, 403, 532
Alexander the Great 405
Ali, Kamran Asdar 48–51, 75, 187f., 210, 442
Allen, Robert 16, 33, 69, 111, 232, 493, 495
Allende, Salvador 105
Althusser, Louis 246
Ames, David 492
Amjad, Ali 50
Anderson, Clare 44, 47, 93, 113, 207, 351f., 355f., 434
Applebaum, Herbert 416, 487
Ardener, Shirley 497–499
Aristotle 379, 421
Arnesen, Eric 284
Arrighi, Giovanni 17, 277
Ashraf, Ahmad 185, 195f.
Astrabadi-Fendereski, Mirza Abulqasem 184
Atabaki, Touraj 187, 189, 191–194, 207, 209, 484
Atatürk, Mustafa Kemal 206, 208, 303
Atkins, Keletso T. 430
Aufhauser, R. Keith 471, 475
Avanesiyan, Ardashes 188f.
Azimi, Fakhreddin 196

Babbage, Charles 399
Babcock, Robert 123
Bachelet, Michelle 106
Baldamus, Wilhelm 477

Balkılıç, Özgür 210, 212
Balsoy, Gülhan 209
Banerji, Sasipada 35
Bao Qiaoni 25
Baptist, Edward E. 126
Barragán, Rossana 86, 241
Barkan, Ömer Lutfi 202
Barker, E.R. 227, 478f.
Barry, Herbert, III 336
Barzel, Yoram 476
Basu, Subho 41
Bayat, Asef 195
Bayly, C.A. 277
Bearnot, Edward 57
Beckert, Sven 9, 115, 124–126, 175, 232f., 270, 336–338
Bedouin, Arab 424
Behal, Rana P. 33f., 42, 44, 46f., 573
Beinin, Joel 207, 273, 528
Bender, Daniel E. 94, 119f.
Bennholdt-Thomsen, Veronika 160, 329–331, 333, 341f.
Benson, Susan Porter 290
Bentley, Philip 279, 541f., 576
Berg, Maxine 76, 243, 262, 264f., 268f., 301, 314, 475, 497
Bergholm, Tapio 285
Bergquist, Charles 101, 123
Berlanstein, Lenard R. 113f.
Bhattacharya, Sabyasachi 33, 41, 45–47, 150, 484, 510
Bierwisch, Manfred 417, 423, 427
Blackburn, Robin 91, 471, 475
Blanc, Louis 399
Blassingame, John 383
Blaut, Jim 6
Bloch, Marc 506
Bodnar, John 438
Boll, Friedhelm 545
Bonacich, Edna 289
Boris, Eileen 330
Boserup, Ester 16, 63, 230, 329, 342
Bossen, Lauren 18f.
Bovenkerk, Frank 449, 464
Bradford, Helen 71
Brandini, Ciuto 551
Braudel, Fernand 92, 97, 159f., 191, 225, 227, 289, 330, 387, 391, 546

Breman, Jan   40, 42, 45 f., 232, 282, 558
Brennan, James   83 f., 101, 105, 107, 530
Bright, Rachel   25
Brinkmann, Tobias   443
Brockett, Gavin   207, 209
Brockhaus, Christian   477
Brook, Timothy   7, 380
Brown, John   68 f., 72, 100, 125, 241, 255, 352, 471 f., 493, 540 f.
Brunnbauer, Ulf   144–146, 148, 171
Bulmer, Martin   87, 96, 250 f.
Bunji, Suzuki   559
Burawoy, Michael   73, 476, 480, 483, 487
Burch, Noël   279

Calvin, John   421
Calvo, Alex   25
Campbell, Alan   33, 65 f., 111, 240, 256
Canbakal, Hülya   204
Candland, Christopher   50
Cantin, Étienne   336
Cárdenas, Lázaro   103 f.
Carlson, Keith Thor   121
Cartier, Michel   416 f.
Castles, Stephen   435
Catherine II   308
Çetinkaya, Y. Doğan   208
Chakrabarty, Dipesh   35, 37–41, 553
Chakraborty, Titas   505
Chan, Anita   27–29, 528
Chandavarkar, Rajnarayan   35, 39–42, 45, 263, 269 f., 272, 474
Chandler, Alfred   311, 470
Chaqueri, Cosroe   197
Charles V   379
Chase, William   217, 219, 477
Chattopadhyaya, Haraprasad   52–54
Chávez, Hugo   106
Chayanov, Alexander V.   220, 223, 229, 318, 334
Chesneaux, Jean   26, 280
Chevaleyre, Claude   19 f.
Church, Roy   120, 254 f., 326
Clarence-Smith, W.G.   388
Clark, Gracia   73, 117, 252, 285, 287, 306
Clarkson, Thomas   380
Coates, Tim   355 f.
Cobble, Dorothy Sue   119, 291
Cobley, Alan Gregor   280
Cole, James   20

Cole, Peter   116
Coleman, D.C.   261
Collins, Jane   329, 533, 555
Columella, Lucius Iunius Moderatus   540
Commons, John   117, 127, 552 f.
Conrad, Robert   165, 385
Cooke, Bill   471
Cooper, Frederick   64, 68, 74, 232 f., 280, 284, 286, 298, 386, 487
Cowie, Jefferson   113, 123
Cowley, Malcolm   383
Craton, Michael   387
Cronin, Stephanie   189, 195
Curtin, Philip   383 f.

Dandamaev, Muhammad A.   405
Danks, Noblet Barry   536
Darby, Paul   456
Dasgupta, Ranajit   37 f.
Davies, Sam   10, 71, 75, 281, 564 f.
Davis, Angela   338 f., 360
Davis, David Brion   94, 383
Debouzy, Marianne   291
Debs, Eugene V.   283
Defoe, Daniel   271, 496
Della Costa, Mariarosa   340
Delphy, Christine   340
Deng, Kent   16
Dennison, T.K.   142 f.
Dever, Maryanne   341
De Vito, Christian   171, 345–350, 353–356, 358, 360, 444
Diouf, Sylviane   389 f.
Dirlik, Arif   22, 26 f.
Domar, Evsey   384
Donnan, Elizabeth   381
Dowlatabadi, Mahmoud   197
Driesen, Ian vanden   52
Drucker, Peter   292
Du Bois, W.E.B.   381–383
Duncan, James   53, 73
Dutt, Rajani Palme   37
Duval, David Timothy   459

Eberstein, Bernd   20
Ebrey, Patricia   300
Ehmer, Josef   175, 414, 416, 418 f.
Ehsani, Kaveh   191, 193 f.
El Hamel, Chouki   390 f.
Eley, Geoff   114

Elias, Norbert   358f.
Elkins, Stanley   383
Elster, Jon   502
Eltis, David   85, 363, 387, 389
Enderle-Burcel, Gertrude   168
Engels, Friedrich   111, 197, 329, 331–333, 339, 522
Engels, Johannes   419
Engerman, Stanley   95, 363, 384f.
Ewald, Janet   388
Eyferth, Jacob   26

Fage, John   384
Fang Zhuofen   16
Faroqhi, Suraiya   202, 302
Faue, Elizabeth   114
Faussette, Risa L.   280
Federici, Silvia   331–333, 339f.
Ferenczi, Imre   453
Feys, Torsten   443
Fidler, Ceri-Anne   439f.
Fink, Leon   115–117, 121, 123f.
Finley, Moses I.   383, 421, 539f.
Floor, Willem   185–187, 190, 192
Fogel, Robert William   385, 388
Ford, Henry   291, 400, 455, 482, 567
Fortunati, Leopoldina   340
Foucault, Michel   226, 262, 352, 358f., 434, 470, 518, 525
Fourier, Charles   399
Fowler, Alan   265f.
Franco, Francisco   256, 290, 461
Frank, Andre Gunder   27, 73, 85, 105, 162, 171, 224, 241, 352, 358, 454
Franzosi, Roberto   542f.
Frazier, E. Franklin   382
Freedman, Alisa   220, 285, 494
French, John   83, 101, 107
Freund, Bill   66, 69, 72, 75, 77, 243, 248
Freyre, Gilberto   381f.
Friedman, Ellen   29, 74
Friesen, Leonard G.   138
Fuente, Alejandro de la   390

Gandhi, Mohandas   373
Ganguly, Dwarkanath   35
Garfield, James A.   310
Gates, Hill   18f., 30, 118
Gaulle, Charles de   534
Gemery, Henry   384

Genovese, Eugene   112, 163, 384, 505, 526
Gentes, Andrew A.   355f.
Germani, Gino   104
Gevorkyan, Aleksandr V.   144, 146
Ghit, Alexandra   131
Gibson, Mary   348, 351, 353, 358
Gimenez, Martha   329
Godelier, Maurice   416
Golestan, Ebrahim   197
Gooptu, Nandini   39, 46
Gordon, George J.   29, 72, 310, 439, 571
Goulart, Mauricio   383
Gramsci, Antonio   27, 564
Gregory, James   25, 111f., 118
Griffin, John I.   544
Gunn, Christopher   486
Gustafsson, Bo   260
Gutman, Herbert G.   111–113, 117, 120, 125, 385

Hakimian, Hassan   147, 186
Hall, F.S.   538
Hall, Gwendolyn   388
Hall, Thomas D.   234
Hall, Valerie   251
Hamilton, Shane   112, 288
Han Dongfang   28
Handlin, Oscar   438
Hansen, Lawrence   24, 73
Hansson, Anders   20
Hardinge, Lord   373
Hardt, Michael   506
Harriss-White, Barbara   46
Hart, Jennifer   286, 288
Hartman, P.T.   542, 545f.
Harvey, Geraint   288f.
Hassan II   462
Hayami Akira   17
Haynes, Douglas   43, 45, 263, 272
Heidemann, Frank   52
Hellie, Richard   146, 387
Hensman, Rohini   46, 339, 341
Herskovits, Melville J.   382, 492
Higman, B.W.   337, 385
Hill, Christopher   191
Hill, Polly   72, 287
Hobsbawm, Eric   191, 220, 224, 230, 266, 269, 552
Hochschild, Arlie R.   434, 458
Hoefte, Rosemarijn   363, 445, 454

Index of Names

Hoerder, Dirk   145, 147, 161, 171, 433, 441 f.
Hofmeester, Karin   21, 242, 317, 322, 349, 411–415, 419 f., 427
Hogendorn, Jan   384, 387 f.
Holmström, Mark   45
Hopkins, Terence K.   160, 282
Hoven, Birgit van den   419
Huang, Philip   16, 341, 456
Hughes, Barry   451, 541 f.
Hunter, Janet   253, 264–266
Huntington, Samuel   6
Hurst, William   27–30
Huxley, Aldous   176

Ibarz, Jordi   281
Iliffe, John   487, 497
İnalcık, Halil   202, 205
Inikori, Joseph   386
Inman, Mary   339 f.
Islamoğlu, Huri   202
Ivanov, Serguey   68, 144

Jackson, Andrew   287, 309, 350
Jafari, Peyman   194, 196
Jaffe, James   240
Jaffer, Aaron   42 f.
James, C.L.R.   392
James, Daniel   101 f., 104, 108
James, Selma   340
Jankrift, Kay Peter   419
Jayaraman, R.   52
Jayawardena, Kumari   52 f.
Jefroudi, Maral   193 f.
John, Angela   251
Johnson, Marion   64 f., 387
Johnson, Paul E.   289 f
Johnson, Simon   94
Johnson, Walter   126, 290
Joshi, Chitra   33, 36, 39 f., 44 f., 278, 282

Kabadayı, Erdem   203, 209, 213 f.
Kabeer, Naila   55, 58
Kamp, Jeannette   356, 505 f., 508–510, 514 f., 576
Katznelson, Ira   114–116
Kautsky, Karl   223, 229
Kazemi, Farhad   185
Keddie, Nikki R.   48 f.
Kenny, Bridget   290, 293
Kerr, Clark   36, 254 f.

Kessler, Gijs   21, 150 f., 317, 322, 397, 402, 404, 574
Kessler-Harris, Alice   111, 113, 115, 119 f.
Keyder, Çağlar   289
Keyvani, Mehdi   184 f.
Khaksar, Nasim   197
Khaldūn, Ibn   426
Khallal, Abū Bakr al-   426
Khan, Ayub   49, 188, 414
Khatami, Mohammad   196
Khodadadeh, Ahmad Ali   188
King, Russell   464
Klein, Martin   64, 387
Knotter, Ad   244–246, 255, 460 f.
Knowles, K.G.J.C.   355, 531, 533, 538 f.
Ko, Dorothy   18, 450
Koçak, Hakan   211
Kocka, Jürgen   162, 168, 175 f., 415, 417, 419, 423, 428, 575
Kolchin, Peter   143
Komlosy, Andrea   149, 152, 157, 163, 170, 175 f.
Kondapi, Chenchal   52
Kopytoff, Igor   385
Kornblith, Gary J.   121, 125
Kovisto, Mauno   466
Kriedte, Peter   147, 246
Krissman, Fred   440
Kuczynski, Jürgen   133 f., 576
Kula, Witold   142
Kumar, Radha   40, 44
Kurian, Rachel   52–55
Kuznetsova, N.A.   185

Lackó, Miklós   134, 152
Ladjevardi, Habib   147, 189
Lahiri-Dutt, Kuntala   243, 251, 253
Laite, Julia   448 f.
Lambton, Ann   185
Landers, Jane   389
Landes, David   474 f., 487
Large, Stephen   28, 229, 238, 381, 460, 494, 514, 527, 558 f.
Larkin, Brian   79, 293
Las Casas, Bartolomé de   379
Latin America   6, 83 f., 86–107, 161–163, 176, 201, 218–220, 223, 230, 232–234, 241–243, 247, 282 f., 286 f., 311, 333, 337 f., 352, 356, 368, 386, 406, 433, 443, 461, 477, 530, 543, 565, 567, 575
Lefebvre, Henri   484

Leibenstein, Harvey   477
Lenin, Wladimir Ilyich   132, 223, 229, 339, 464, 483
Leonhard, Jörn   413, 415, 417, 423, 430
Li Bozhong   16 f.
Li Ju   26
Li Lisan   23
Li Xiang   25
Li Zhixue   25
Lichtenstein, Nelson   76, 126, 249, 291 f., 345, 347 f., 350, 353–356, 358, 360, 444, 574
Liebknecht, Karl   527
Light, Ivan   229, 442
Lindquist, Johan   452 f.
Lindsay, Lisa   284 f.
Linebaugh, Peter   279 f.
Lis, Catharina   20, 175, 220 f., 239, 339, 401, 412–416, 418–422, 424
Liu Mingkui   23
Liu Shaoqi   23
Livingstone, David   380
Lobato, Mirta   99, 102, 104
Lockman, Zachary   193, 195, 207
Lokhande, Narayan Meghaji   35
Long, Edward   380
Lont, Hotze   499
Looijesteijn, Henk   413 f.
Louis XIV   390
Lovejoy, Paul   64, 386–389
Lucassen, Jan   1, 10, 22, 34, 45, 83, 117, 123, 133, 150, 160, 207, 239, 242, 283, 317–319, 322, 349, 389, 395–398, 400, 402, 404, 408, 422, 433, 436, 441, 454, 459, 510, 526
Lucassen, Leo   150, 160, 242, 317, 322, 389, 395, 398, 433, 436, 438, 453, 455, 505
Luther, Martin   119, 421
Luxemburg, Rosa   207, 404, 527, 529

Ma Li   25
Macdonald, Andrew   24 f.
MacDonald, John S.   438
MacDonald, Leatrice D.   438
Macintyre, Martha   243, 251, 253
MacLean, Nancy   119
Macnaughtan, Helen   264–266
Mahmoud, Ahmad   197
Mahmudi, Jalil   189
Malik, Anushay   50 f.
Maljoo, Mohammad   181, 191

Mani, Shokrollah   188
Mann, Michael   5, 18, 65, 137, 151, 449, 459
Manning, Patrick   386–389, 391, 436
Mannix, Daniel   383
Mao Zedong   23
Marglin, Stephen   262, 474 f.
Marquez, Benjamin   555
Marshall, Alfred   3, 307, 555
Martin, Gaston   10, 71 f., 77, 187, 256, 292, 381, 387, 437, 454, 526, 539
Marx, Karl   15, 101, 111, 114, 124, 132, 197, 221, 230, 318, 321, 329 f., 332 f., 342, 399, 469, 472, 522
Massey, Douglas   440, 461
Mathias, Regine   253, 413, 427
Mayer, David   103, 187, 244
McCall, Leslie   435
McCallum, Todd   121
McKeown, Adam   433 f., 443 f.
Medick, Hans   246, 334, 336
Meeteren, Nicolaas van   492
Meillassoux, Claude   64, 331, 335, 341, 385
Melossi, Dario   349, 357–359, 470
Mendels, Franklin   260
Meyer, John   481
Meyer, Stephen   118
Miers, Suzanne   65, 68, 385
Mies, Maria   160, 330–333, 341 f.
Mikhail, Alan   203 f.
Milakovich, Michael E.   310
Miller, Joseph C.   65, 102, 121, 243, 250, 289, 342, 386 f., 389
Mintz, Sidney   9, 91, 387
Mixius, Andreas   20
Moch, Leslie Page   145, 147, 171, 433, 441
Moghadam, Valentine M.   195
Moghissi, Haideh   196
Mohapatra, Prabhu P.   33, 46 f., 150, 411, 433, 447
Moll-Murata, Christine   16, 20 f., 317, 411–415, 419 f., 427
Monteiro, John   87 f., 90, 388
Montgomery, David   111–114, 120
Moore Jr., Barrington   36, 97, 222, 225, 477, 530
Moosvi, Shireen   413, 428
Morales, Evo   106
Morawska, Ewa   145, 171, 442
More, Thomas   176
Moreton, Bethany   291 f.

Morgan, J.P. 243
Morgan, Kenneth 338
Morgan, Philip 337
Morgan, William A. 338
Morris, Morris D. 36
Mosher, Frederick 309 f.
Mudimbe, Valentin 63
Muhammad 424
Muhammad Ali 66
Mundle, Sudipto 46
Murmis, Miguel 104
Myint, Hla 384

Nacar, Can 208–210
Naguleswaran, P. 52
Nair, Janaki 39, 41, 429
Napoleon I 304
Naughton, Barry 26
Negri, Antonio 506
Nieboer, Herman J. 381
Nield, Keith 114
Nisbet, Robert 6
Nuruzzaman, Mohammed 56 f.

O'Brien, Patrick 16, 72, 160
Offe, Claus 175, 415, 417, 419, 423, 428, 433, 561
Ogilvie, Sheilagh 142 f.
Onselen, Charles van 69, 246
Ortiz Fernández, Fernando 381
Orwell, George 2, 252
Osterhammel, Jürgen 164
Othman, Norani 415, 429
Outram, Quentin 254 f.
Owen, Robert 75, 223, 399
Özden, Barış Alp 211
Özveren, Y. Eyüp 289

Pach, Zsigmond Pál 142, 169
Palmer, Bryan D. 111–114, 117, 120–123
Parthasarathi, Prasannan 34, 206, 262, 264 f., 267, 269–272
Patnaik, Utsa 46
Pavarini, Massimo 349, 357–359, 470
Peebles, Patrick 52–54
Pelckmans, Lotte 447
Pellat, Charles 425
Perkins Gilman, Charlotte 339
Perlin, Frank 261
Perón, Juan D. 103

Perry, Elizabeth 23 f., 113, 122 f., 257, 297
Pescatello, Ann 386
Peter I 307
Phillips, Ulrich B. 116 f., 381, 383 f., 471, 544, 555
Plockhoy, Pieter 413 f.
Polanyi, Karl 183, 318
Pollard, Sidney 28, 469, 484
Pomeranz, Kenneth 16, 162, 239
Portantiero, Juan Carlos 104
Postel, Verena 419
Pot, Pol 407
Pouget, Emile 540
Prakash, Gyan 46, 414
Proudhon, Pierre-Joseph 491

Qasemi, Farhang 190
Qin Yucheng 24
Quataert, Donald 204–208, 212, 261, 263, 284, 289

Raadschelders, Jos C.N. 297–299, 303–307, 313 f.
Rafsanjani, Ali Akbar Hashemi 196
Ragatz, Lowell 381
Rahnema, Saeed 196
Randall, Adrian 268
Raynal, Guillaume-Thomas François 380
Raza, Ali 50 f.
Reagan, Ronald 118, 288 f.
Rediker, Marcus 279 f., 505
Rehman, Zia 57
Revel, Jacques 158 f.
Rhodes, Cecil 242 f.
Ripon, Lord 35
Roberts, M.W. 52, 118, 556
Roberts, Richard 68, 265
Robertson, Claire 64, 72, 285, 291, 387
Robinson, James 94, 226, 340
Rockefeller, John D. 243
Rockel, Stephen 66, 282
Rodney, Walter 229, 385
Romero, Luis Alberto 99, 102
Rönnbäck, Klas 415, 429 f.
Rosen, Ellen 292
Rosenthal, Anton 285 f.
Rosenthal, Jean-Laurent 17
Ross, A.M. 119, 124, 254, 287, 351, 542, 545 f.
Rowan, Brian 481
Roy, M.N. 37, 43, 267, 474, 480

Rule, John   239, 268
Rutgers, Mark R.   299, 303–306

Sadeghi-Boroujerdi, Eskandar   181
Sahlins, Marshall   331, 335
Said, Edward   164, 171
Sa'idi, Nasser   189
Saint-Méry, Moreau de   380
Sangster, Joan   113, 118, 120f., 124
Sargon   405
Schattenberg, Susanne   308
Schendel, Willem van   436
Schlegel, Alice   336
Schloss, David F.   396–400
Schlosser, Eric   291
Schmidt, Allison   443
Schmidt, Ariadne   420
Schmidt, Christoph   169
Schrover, Marlou   434f., 438, 441f., 444, 449–451, 455, 460, 465
Schwartz, Stuart   387f.
Scott, James C.   112, 228, 230, 505–507
Scott, Joan   113
Scott, John   348
Scott, Rebecca   92, 95
Seibert, Julia   430
Sekula, Allan   279
Sellin, Thorsten   357, 359
Selznick, Philip   480
Sen, Sukomal   37, 40, 43f., 267, 474
Sewell, William   114
Shah, Reza   188f., 194, 460
Shaheed, Zafar   48f.
Shakespeare, William   4
Shanin, Teodor   151, 220, 334, 336
Shatzmiller, Maya   411, 414, 421, 423–426
Sheriff, Abdul   387
Sherman, Taylor   351f., 358
Shi Qi   16
Shorter, Edward   254
Sibalis, Michael   500f.
Siegel, Abraham   254f.
Siegelbaum, Lewis H.   134f., 147, 433, 453
Silva, Luís Inácio da (Lula)   106
Sio-ieng Hui, Elaine   26f.
Slaten, Kevin   29
Smith, Adam   3, 9, 426
Smith, Mark   487
Smith, Steve   140, 146

Soly, Hugo   20, 220f., 239, 400f., 412–416, 419–422, 424
Sombart, Werner   115, 318
Southcott, Joanna   267
Spalding, Hobart   101, 567
Speranskiy, Mikhail   308
Spierenburg, Pieter   358f.
Spittler, Gerd   414f., 487
Stakhanov, Alexsei Grigoryevich   256
Stalin, Joseph Vissarionovich   132, 140, 355, 407
Stampp, Kenneth   383
Stanziani, Alessandro   19, 142f., 169, 508
Stapel, Rombert   317, 322
Stark, David M.   390, 439
Steinmetz, Willibald   413, 415, 417, 423, 430
Stinchcombe, Arthur   473, 476
Stolcke, Verena   337f.
Stretton, Hugh   8
Stromquist, Shelton   283
Sturmthal, Adolf   561, 565
Sugihara, Kaoru   16, 17, 87, 162, 427
Süleyman the Magnificent   302
Sultanzadeh, A.   187f.
Sweet, James   121, 390
Szabó, István   138

Taghian, Ramin   147
Taghvai, Nasser   197
Tannenbaum, Frank   382
Taştan, Can   210f.
Taylor, Frederick W.   24, 214, 255, 351, 397, 400, 474, 482f., 555
Teh, Limin   22
Teichova, Alice   168
Tenfelde, Klaus   136, 168, 238, 249, 254f.
Thälmann, Ernst   132
Thirsk, Joan   260, 263
Thomas, Keith   417
Thompson, Edward P.   38, 102, 111f., 190–192, 289, 484
Thompson, Ruth   553
Tilly, Charles   21, 221, 254, 318, 441, 454, 459, 478, 482, 511, 517, 544
Tilly, Chris   221, 318, 478, 482, 511, 517
Tinker, Irene   342, 373
Tomich, Dale   92, 391
Torr, Dona   191
Trotsky, Leon   483, 529

Tsing, Anna   289
Turnbull, Peter   288f.

Upadhyay, Shashi Bhushan   41, 411, 414, 421f., 428f., 484
Urry, John   277, 437

Vail, Leroy   69
Van der Linden, Marcel   1, 5, 8, 10, 33f., 42, 44, 47, 90, 99, 123, 150, 160–162, 174–176, 184, 191, 213, 219, 221, 242, 246, 270, 321f., 342, 347, 349f., 356, 359, 378, 395f., 411, 413–415, 447, 461, 469, 471, 491, 509, 521, 532, 540, 551, 553, 564, 571, 573
Van der Velden, Sjaak   516, 544, 546
Van Rossum, Matthias   42f., 356, 407, 505f., 508–510, 512, 515
Vanhaute, Erik   217, 230
Vargas, Getúlio   103
Velasco e Cruz, Maria Cecilia   390, 476, 494
Verlinden, Charles   382f.
Vidyaratna, Ram Kumar   35

Wachsmann, Nikolaus   353f.
Wallerstein, Immanuel   159f., 219, 232, 277
Walsh, Margaret   285
Walton, Sam   96, 291, 368
Ward, Kerry   153, 303, 355f.
Warren, James   282f., 386
Watson, James   386
Way, Peter   123, 126, 387
Weber, Max   298–300, 314, 318, 418, 421, 477, 555
Wedgwood, Josiah   380
Weinhauer, Klaus   281
Weinstein, Barbara   101, 104, 554
Wenzlhuemer, Roland   51f.
Werlhof, Claudia von   341

White, Landeg   69
Wigen, Kären   278f.
Willcox, Walter F.   453
Williams, Eric   4, 20, 93, 256, 382, 384
Wilson, Jake B.   289, 299
Winn, Peter   84, 101, 105
Wolf, Eric   120, 217, 220f., 230
Wolfinger, James   285f.
Wolpe, Harold   246
Wong, Diana   330, 492
Wong, May   29
Wong, Roy Bin   17
Wright, Erik Olin   476
Wright, Gavin   390
Wright, Marcia   65
Wright, Thomas C.   105
Wright, Tim   22, 248, 282f., 397, 474
Wu Chengming   16

Xiang Biao   452
Xie Qingming   25
Xu Dixin   16
Xu Guoqi   25

Yrigoyen, Hipólito   524
Yu Jianrong   24

Zakim, Michael   121, 125
Zarinebaf-Shahr, Fariba   203, 206
Zelnik, Reginald E.   134
Zerker, Sally   123
Zeuske, Michael   92, 95, 391
Zhu Cishou   22
Zijdeman, Richard   317
Zimmermann, Susan   137, 139–141, 150, 166, 170, 335, 339
Zilfi, Madeline   203
Zürcher, Erik-Jan   10, 21, 205, 207
Zurndorfer, Harriet   17, 19f., 427

www.ingramcontent.com/pod-product-compliance
Lightning Source LLC
Chambersburg PA
CBHW060451300426
44113CB00016B/2557